MW01154793

Child's History of Waseca County, Minnesota

Property of Mrs. J. J. Hagner

James E. Child

CHILD'S HISTORY

OF

WASECA COUNTY,

MINNESOTA.

From Its First Settlement in 1854
to the Close of the Year 1904.
A Record of Fifty Years.

THE STORY OF THE PIONEERS

By JAMES E. CHILD.

"Let me speak to the yet unknowing world how these things came about."—Shakespeare.

From the Press of
THE OWATONNA CHRONICLE
Whiting & Luers,
Publishers

PREFACE.

"Why don't you write a history of Waseca county?" asked Rev G. C. Tanner, one day in the year 1890

And as that question often came to me in leisure moments, for several weeks, I finally concluded to invest a dime in cheap paper, and note down, in odd hours, such facts concerning the early settlement of this country as I could recall and as might be of interest to its residents, present and future, and, in connection therewith, to gather together all the historic facts that I might be able to obtain both from persons and from official sources.

In this undertaking I have made no attempt at rhetorical display and effect, but in the plainest language possible, have described the events which make up the history of the county. It may not be possible for one who has been intimately connected with the public and political life of the county to be entirely impartial an unbiased, as its historian, but I have spared no effort to be fair and accurate as regards persons, parties, interests, and localities. I have found many difficulties in this undertaking, for individual tastes and interests differ so widely that what might be of great interest to one would have no attractions for another. I therefore determined, at the commencement, to "spread out a whole bill of fare" and allow my readers to select for themselves. No doubt there are many facts and incidents of note omitted in this work, although I have made every possible effort to include everything of public interest The fact is, dear "Old Settler," you who are left out of the record have not always responded to the invitation to furnish facts within your own recollection for this work, and you should remember this in your criticisms.

I cannot close this preface without expressing my sincere thanks to those who have so materially aided me in this work by furnishing facts and data within their own knowledge

One object of this work, to be frank about it, was to get enough money out of it to pay the printers and paper dealers, and another object, of much greater importance, was to furnish to every person in the county a faithful record of township and county events from the earliest settlement by white men How well I have succeeded I must leave others to judge. I can only hope that this record may be received by the public with the same liberal and charitable spirit in which it has been written.

THE AUTHOR.

CHAPTER I, 1854-5.

PRIMITIVE CONDITION OF COUNTY.

No longer ago than 1854, the present county of Waseca was a portion of that extensive region of country known as Blue Earth county. Not a single white man then had a habitation within its borders. The solitude of nature was broken only occasionally by some hunter and trapper, and by wandering bands of Sioux Indians. The buffalo, the elk, and the deer had, for ages, roamed its wild prairies and woodlands; fishes had basked undisturbed in its lakes and rippling streams; the muskrat, the otter, and the mink had gamboled upon the ice in winter with no white man to molest them. Ducks, geese, and other aquatic fowls, in countless numbers, covered the lakes and streams in summer, and chattered and squawked and frolicked in all their native glory and happiness The prairie wolf howled upon each little hillock, and, coward-like, was always ready to attack and destroy the weak and defenseless Pocket gophers went on with their interminable underground operations, all unconscious of the inroads soon to be made upon their dominions by the husbandman Grouse and prairie chickens cackled, crowed, and strutted in all their pride. Blizzards and cyclones swept unheeded across its vast domains.

The autumnal prairie fires, in all their terrible grandeur and weird beauty, lighted the heavens by night and clouded the sun by day Age after age had added alluvial richness to the soil and prepared it to be one of the most productive fields of the world for the abode of the husbandman and for the uses of civilized man

The enquiring and philosophical mind, at times, finds food for reflection in the fact that an overruling Providence sent the Pilgrim Fathers first to the rock-bound coast of New England to clear the forests and to settle that country, but reserved the rich and productive prairie-lands of the West, ready prepared for the plow and the mower for descendants and followers

It is a pleasure to record the early settlement of a county which, for fifty consecutive years, has never suffered a total failure of crops or even a half failure, and where general thrift and prosperity, for all that time, have attended and rewarded the hand of industry and the spirit of frugality

"Where the glad'ning sunlight nestled,
  Where all Nature's beauty slept
Unrevealed to cultured vision,
  Where the savage wail'd and wept
When his son or sire had given
  To the Spirit World his breath,
Find we here a famous region,
  (Sunny side of 'Minne's' face)
With lovely lakes and richest soil,
  Stately in its quiet grace,—
A healthy home for sons of toil"

CHAPTER II, 1854-5.

FIRST WHITE SETTLEMENT—MR A G SUTLIEF AND FAMILY—JOURNEY FROM DODGE COUNTY, WIS—JUDGE GREEN'S NARRATIVE—JUDGE LOST AND PREPARED FOR DEATH—SUTLIEF'S RETURN—BIG BOOT CREEK—CROSSING THE MISSISSIPPI ON ICE

So far as practicable, the historical events in this volume are recorded in the order in which they came to pass, instead of being grouped under certain headings or classifications This may require a little more space, but the author thinks it will afford an easier comprehension of the various facts presented.

MR AND MRS ASA G SUTLIEF

and Mr Sutlief's three oldest children, Delancy, Rhoda and Delaney, were the first white settlers in this county Taking with them quite a drove of cattle and sheep, they started from the town of Herman, Dodge county Wisconsin, in the month of June, 1854, with ox teams and covered wagons, to seek a new home in the land of "Laughing Waters." They passed over the Mississippi at La Crosse, traveled across the country in a westerly direction, struck the Minnesota river at Traverse, now St Peter, and settled on a claim some five or six miles west of that place

To give an idea of the vicissitudes of such a journey at that time, the following from the pen of Hon G W Green, well known to all the early settlers of this region, will be valuable and interesting. He wrote:

"In the summer of 1854 I left Beaver Dam, Wis., in company with Messrs Hollingsworth, Bradley and Boomer for the purpose of seeing some portion of Southern Minnesota with an idea of settling there Arriving at La Crosse, we purchased material for camping and ferried across the Mississippi river One log house, nearly finished, greeted us on the west side of the river opposite La Crosse That was all there was then of La Crescent The next house, twenty-four miles distant, was occupied by a Thompsonian physician, by name Bently, who had concluded to mix claim-taking and rudimentary farming with his profession Some miles further on, where now is St. Charles, was one more log house kept as a tavern by one Springer. 'There was a newly made wagon track extending about ten miles further on, where a young man and his wife, by the name of Potter, had taken a claim and were building a small house One story of it was finished and the chamber floor laid of loose boards, but without any roof They invited us to stay with them over night We did so During the night it rained hard, and we got thoroughly soaked. After breakfast the next morning we started on without any track and no guide but our pocket compass.

"About noon of this day we came up with Mr A G Sutlief, who was moving with his family from Dodge county, Wisconsin, to a point near Traverse des Sioux (a missionary post near where St Peter now is), so named because it was at this place that the Sioux Indians forded the river Mr Sutlief was a noted pioneer of Wisconsin, but he knew little more than we did as to the most feasible route to his destination Mr Hollingsworth was Sutlief's father-in-law, and we very willingly accepted their kind invitation to keep them company to their new home Mr Sutlief had with him a large herd of cattle and sheep We crossed the Ashland prairie near the head of the Straight and Zumbro rivers, and near the Oak Glen lakes Within one mile of Straight river, we camped for dinner.

LOST ON THE PRAIRIE.

"After dinner Mr Sutlief wanted me to go with him and look for a suitable place to cross the river We went to the river, and, finding no desirable crossing, concluded to cross further up, near what seemed, by the appearance of the timber, to be a very considerable bend in the river, apparently some five or six miles away. It was agreed that Sutlief should go back and guide the teams, while I should cross the river and travel up to the proposed crossing

"Without thinking much about the company, I went slowly on until I came to the place where Dr Kenyon afterwards lived I could see or hear nothing of Sutlief or the company, not even a cow-bell, several of which I knew were in use on the cattle and sheep. I tried as well as I could to find their whereabouts Although but a short distance below the proposed crossing, I could not find any trace of them before it was dark As fate would have it, I had neither coat nor blanket, jack-knife nor matches, ax nor hatchet

"Tired out and hungry, I laid myself under a tree to rest, and was very soon asleep With no breakfast, I renewed my search for the company, going on up the river to a point where a Mr Bennett afterwards settled, but found no signs I then concluded to follow down the river as long as my strength should last, unless I found something more desirable. Before proceeding, however, I pulled off a boot and, with a pin, wrote upon a smooth part of the boot-leg my name, thus: 'G. W Green, Beaver Dam, Wis.,' not knowing but that some one would find my bones and boots, and thereby my friends might hear from me. I had a little matter of $700 in my pockets, which, in case I should be lost, this act might be the means of my family getting. I had no other way of writing." After this preparation for the worst that might befall me, I started down the river, traveling slowly until nearly sun-down, when I found the trail where the company had crossed the river, not over half a mile above where I had left Sutlief With new courage and zeal I started on this trail I followed it a short distance without any trouble, but, darkness coming on, the trail became invisible and I lost it In hunting for it I stumbled and fell, and my weariness and exhaustion were such that I did not feel disposed to rise I unconsciously fell asleep

"When I awoke the sun was high up and shining brightly Reinvigorated by my sound and restful sleep, I soon found the trail, and, following it slowly a short time, I observed two men approaching me. They were of our company Looking up towards the timber, about three miles from where they had crossed the river, I saw the wagons and the remainder of the company. They had camped there early in the afternoon of the day I was lost, expecting I would see and come to them When night came and I did not appear, they built a large fire and kept it going all night, hoping thereby to attract my attention The next day they spent on horseback looking for me without avail

"When I arrived in camp, they represented to me that my eyes were staring, and my lips and tongue swollen. Mrs Sutlief prepared me something to eat, but I had no appetite and could eat nothing of it, instead thereof calling for a cup of sour milk which I drank with relish I took but very little nourishment except sour milk the rest of that day. My appetite slowly returning, the next day I ate sparingly, but it was some three or four days before I could partake of an ordinary meal.

"From that place we proceeded to Beaver lake, just east of New Richland, crossing its outlet where the road now runs Here we saw an Indian and tried to get some idea from him what course to take to reach the Minnesota river, but failed to secure any correct information. Crossing some of the rivulets that unite to form the Le Sueur river and following along down that stream, we forded it near where the village of St Mary was afterwards built We wandered on, we knew not whither, until we struck Minnesota lake Here we stayed two days and looked for signs At last, about three miles west of the lake, we found a freshly-made Indian trail going southwest We concluded that the Indians had gone on a hunting expedition and that they had congregated at the Minnesota river, starting en masse from there Not knowing anything better to do, we took this trail back and struck Mankato July 4th, 1854.

"Mankato then consisted of one family, who kept a log boarding house, and one man, who presided over a saloon made of small poles No other evidence of civilization (?) met our gaze From this point we proceeded to Suthef's claim which he made about six miles west of St Peter, remaining with him one day We then followed the trail down the Minnesota river to St Paul, which was at that time little more than an Indian trading post, not as large as St Anthony then was, and Minneapolis had not yet been spoken of Here we boarded a steamer for La Crosse, from which point we took our way homeward by our own conveyance

"At the time of this trip, the prairies were covered with luxuriant grasses from three and a half to four feet high Deer and elk roved at will, several large herds coming within our view After leaving Potter's house, before mentioned, we saw no other house until our arrival in Mankato

"I made no definite location on this trip, but concluded to return to the vicinity of Straight or Le Sueur river, with my family, and then make my location G W GREEN "

The following August Judge Green returned with his family and settled at Owatonna, as will more fully appear in these annals

Mr Suthef had been staying only a few days on his claim, near St. Peter, when he accepted an offer of $100 for his "right of possession " He then returned to Mankato, where he left his family and stock, and sought a new location "far from the haunts of busy men " After much traveling and a thorough inspection of a large extent of country, he selected a portion of section 32, town of Wilton, as his future home The most of his family still reside there He arrived at this claim with his family and stock early in August, and at once broke about two acres of prairie He then set about building a "shanty" for himself and family, and providing shelter for his cattle and sheep It was a work of some magnitude to prepare for winter, but his energy and industry with the efficient aid of his worthy wife, overcame all obstacles, and, in a few weeks, he was ready to return to Wisconsin with his wife and children to remain during the winter. But before starting for Wisconsin with his family he planned to go to La Crosse to get a supply of provisions for Luther Barrett, a hunter and trapper, who was to stay on the claim and feed and care for the sheep and cattle until Suthef's return the following January.

On his trip to La Crosse he met Judge Green, on Ashland prairie, who, with his family, eleven men, seven ox teams and wagons and eighty head of cattle, mostly cows and young stock left Beaver Dam, Wis, August 12th. Judge Green, having more supplies than he could easily haul, Mr Sutlief concluded to return with him Arriving at Straight river, where Owatonna is now located, they found that stream so swollen with recent copious rains that they could not cross it with their heavy loads Here they found A B Cornell and family, the first settlers of Steele county, and here they pitched their tents and took counsel with each other Judge Green in his reminiscences writes

"As we all desired to locate near together, it was decided to leave the women and children with a couple of men as guards and to watch the stock, while the rest of the company should go on to the Le Sueur river country The next day we crossed Straight river with three wagons, four yoke of oxen and one cow. The men camped on the west side of the river that night, and I went back to the tent and stayed with my family. It rained a large portion of the night. In the morning we started, bearing southwest It rained by spells and there was a well defined stream in every ravine We went on to Beaver lake and struck our old trail made on the first trip In crossing one of the head rivulets of Le Sueur river, then a roaring torrent, one of the men, with boots on as high as his knees, stood upon the back end-board of a wagon box, holding to the top of the wagon cover, and yet got wet, so this was called

BIG BOOT CREEK

"We looked over the prairie and woodlands between Sutlief's claim and what was afterward Wilton We liked the country and concluded to make claims there, which we did, but still it rained, rained! The men got wet and cold and finally homesick or sick of the country They said the country would all overflow in a wet spell, and, should they settle there, no one else would venture so far from civilization for the next 100 years, and for the rest of their natural lives and those of their families they would be there without bridges or other improvements, except such as they should improvise among themselves So we went back to Straight river, reluctantly leaving Mr S and family alone on the Le Sueur On the 20th of September I staked out my claim, at Owatonna, and my men went to work cutting hay In two weeks our hay was cut and stacked, our log house laid up and covered with a "shake-root," with no chinking, no floors, no doors, no windows I could not persuade the men to stay another day They said there would be no other person settling in there for the next fifty years, and that if I managed to live through the winter I would return to Wisconsin in the spring So they started on their return trip, and there I was, left with an invalid wife and three small children, no stables for stock, no house suitable for cold weather, and apparently no help attainable It seemed more than I could do to make things endurable through the winter, but the next day a wagon load of ten men arrived, and I got what help I needed form then on"

Mr. Suthef, having obtained from Judge Green a supply of flour for winter and having made other necessary arrangements, was ready by the latter part of November to convey his wife and children to Wisconsin They made their return trip in a covered ox-wagon. When they reached the Mississippi, opposite La Crosse, the first week in December, 1854, that stream was not yet frozen over, and they were compelled to wait until the ice King formed a bridge On the fourth day after their arrival, although the ice was barely strong enough to bear up a man, Mr. Suthef, in his rash, dare-devil way, crossed the stream by casting the oxen, tying their feet together and sliding them across on the slippery ice by hand The wagon also was taken over by hand, and Mrs Suthef and the children passed over on foot The remainder of their journey was made without any incident worthy of note

CHAPTER III, 1855.

WINTER TRIP TO MINNESOTA WITH OX TEAMS—VENTURESOME CROSSING OF THE MISSISSIPPI ON THE ICE—CLIMBING THE BLUFF—FIRST BLIZZARD AT ZUMBRO FALLS—THE LIQUOR PEDDLER AND HIS GROG—MANTORVILLE THE LAST HOUSE—CAMPING OUT IN MID-WINTER TWO NIGHTS—CATTLE WITH BLEEDING LEGS AND WITHOUT HAY—SAFE ARRIVAL AT THE SUTLIEF SHANTY

Mr Sutlief was thoroughly enamored with Minnesota, as it then was, and lost no opportunity to proclaim her beauty and her merits. He was under agreement with Mr Barrett, whom he had left upon his claim, to return in January, and on the 9th of that month, 1855, he started back to Minnesota with three pair of oxen, a wagon and a sleigh, some household goods, provisions, etc, and a few swine He was accompanied and assisted by the writer whom he had employed for a year to take charge of his Minnesota farming operations At Fox Lake, Wis, they were joined by S. P. Child, of Waupun, Wis, then a boy of nineteen years He was to assist in driving the teams and the swine He owned a few hogs which he drove with Sutlief's herd

Nothing of striking importance occurred on the journey until their arrival at La Crosse At this point, they crossed the river after dark on thin ice that had formed after the January thaw The act of crossing was a dangerous one and a less venturesome man than Mr Sutlief would at least have chosen daylight for the undertaking After crossing the river in safety, they proceeded about two miles, and, at nine o'clock in the evening, stopped at a small house occupied by a Mr Plummer and his wife Here two days were spent while Mr Plummer was getting ready to join the company It took nearly all of one day to haul the loaded vehicles to the top of the river bluff, and the party returned to the Plummer house for the night

All hands turned out early next morning, and the first rays of the rising sun found them on the trail going westward. The day turned to be cloudy and stormy, but the drive was short, and just before dark they stopped at a little frame house, near the road, about five miles southeast of the present village of St. Charles The next morning, an early start was made so as to reach Rochester—then known as Zumbro Falls—that night, if possible The weather that day was pleasant, but the snow was drifted deep in many places, and this made traveling very difficult In some places it was necessary to either shovel out or unhitch the teams from the vehicles and drive them back and forth through the snow drifts, before attempting to pass through with the loads and, although the teams were urged forward as rapidly as shouting and whipping would avail, it was eleven o'clock that night before the travelers reached a stopping place The weather had turned very cold in the afternoon. Mr Sutlief frosted his cheeks, ears, nose, and feet, and Messrs Plummer, Griffin and S. P Child frosted their toes slightly

The log hotel at which they arrived was already filled with travelers The beds were all full, and the floors were nearly covered with sleeping men. There was no sleeping room for these last arrivals, except in a log shanty lean-to, with its Dutch fireplace This shanty afforded about the poorest protection from cold that could well be imagined, even by a western pioneer The roof was made of oak shakes. The crevices between the logs were not yet plastered or daubed. The prairie blizzard whistled through the holes and crevices with a liberality altogether unpleasant that night.

The next morning the wind blew a gale and the thermometer indicated 20 degrees below zero, rendering traveling across the prairie simply impossible. All parties were compelled to remain over during the day There were some forty travelers thus detained, this place being on the stage road from Dubuque to St Paul

Many a good story and some not so good were told that day,

and jokes passed among the hotel guests in a manner peculiar to the West One fellow, a liquor peddler, was quite chagrined at finding his liquor keg bottom end up and his whisky spread out in the snow The crowd insisted that he had been on a spree, and had left the keg in that condition himself; and, as no one pretended to know anything to the contrary, he was obliged to smother his pent-up wrath and make the best of the situation His attempt at the retail business in the morning was, without doubt, the primary cause of his sad bereavement—at least some of the ladies intimated as much to his face.

The wind lulled during the night, and the next morning was bright and pleasant, though still cold Our first settlers tackled up early and started across the prairie for Mantorville That village was then less than a year old and contained only three or four small cabins It was the last settlement on the route of our "first settlers" until they should reach their destination on the Le Sueur

Think of the recklessness not to say foolhardiness, of the trip. Imagine, if you will, good reader, five men and a woman with her babe about to start across a wind-howling prairie, in the midst of winter with the thermometer 10 degrees below zero, without any road, not even a track, and without a tent, to spend three days and two nights, at the least, with no shelter save the starry heavens. The whole company might have perished in a blizzard! Such was the thoughtless undertaking of those men on the morning of the 31st of January, 1855

After loading on what hay they could take along they left Mantorville bearing south of west across the trackless prairie until they struck the southern tier of sections in township 106 They then kept due west, guided by section posts set the fall before by government surveyors A little after noon they ran into one of those deep, narrow creeks which abound along the Zumbro river and nearly lost one yoke of oxen After considerable hard work and some delay, they rescued the "Nucky Steers," as the oxen were called, and finally succeeded in crossing the stream with no serious damage Without further mishap, they traveled until about sunset when they arrived at a small grove of bur oaks, near the source of one branch of the Zumbro river Here they concluded to camp for the night The oxen were soon unyoked

2

and fed, a large campfire was built supper was prepared and consumed, stories were told, and songs were sung The weather was reasonably pleasant, with a slight wind from the west

About nine o'clock, they spread their hay beds upon the snow under the wagons, and laid themselves down for the night covering up head and ears with quilts and blankets All slept soundly until three o'clock the next morning when all hands were aroused by the cry of "fire!" coming from Mr Suthef, who had been warmed out The wind had changed to the south in the night and, blowing briskly, had thrown the fire on Mr Suthef's bed It took some time to extinguish the flames in the bed-clothing and when that had been accomplished and the travelers had about recovered from the excitement caused by the fire, they discovered that the cattle had all left, taking the back track toward the settlement The Child brothers started in pursuit with furious feelings and at a frantic rate of foot-speed The cattle were overtaken at the creek where the difficulty in crossing occurred the day before and were ordered back to camp in the forcible language peculiar to the ox-teamster of the West The two men returned to camp half an hour before sunrise, partook of a hearty breakfast with the rest of the company, and, just as the sun made its appearance all hands started in a due westerly course The day was intensely cold and much activity was required to keep warm There was a hard crust on the snow, which impeded progress and cut the legs of the cattle to such an extent that blood was left in their tracks Several deep snow drifts were encountered within the day These caused some delay and much labor.

That night the emigrants encamped in a thicket of hazel brush and poplar trees, with some bur oaks intermingled This was on the west side of Straight river and several miles south of Owatonna It was an excellent place for a camp in winter, the brush and trees forming a thicket which was an admirable protection for both man and beast The main difficulty of these pioneers was want of food for the cattle No hay was left for them except what was in the beds, and only a small allowance of grain remained That night the company took the precaution to secure the oxen with head ropes

The men clearing away the brush and snow, soon made a cheery campfire, and Mrs. Plummer prepared a warm supper, which was eaten with a relish. No one complained of a lack of appetite

The members of the company were not so much given to song and stories and funny jokes as they had been on the previous evening. The romance of camping out in midwinter had lost to them, after their two days' experience, something of its imaginary charms They piled high the campfire with fuel and retired early to their hay beds, which were spread upon the snow-covered ground. The wind came up from the northwest in the evening, and before morning the weather was intensely cold. Long before daylight, the next morning, they arose, fed the cattle what hay there was in the beds, and ate their own breakfast. As soon as there was light enough to enable them to keep their course, they renewed their journey They crossed the LeSueur river, in the town of New Richland, with some difficulty, the banks of the stream being very steep. Soon after crossing the river, they reached the height of the prairie level They could then see, and took it for their guide, a large bur-oak tree standing alone on section thirty-six, in Wilton about a mile from the Sutlief shanty Never were weary mortals more pleased than were those first settlers when Mr. Sutlief announced that that tree was within a mile of his claim

They reached the Sutlief place at four o'clock p m, rejoiced to find Mr Barrett alive and well To say that every member of the company was thankful for this safe resting place is a very mild way of expressing his feelings on that occasion

The condition and appearance of the country, at that time, however, were neither very pleasing nor inviting to the most of the pioneers, for they had come from a heavy timbered country To the south and west, as far as the eye could reach, there was a vast expanse of bleak prairie, without either tree or shrub, swept by the howling blasts of winter and covered with snow, sleet and ice. The few trees along the river looked to them then to be short and scrubby; the weather was intensely cold, it was thirty-five miles to the nearest postoffice—Mankato; they could get no newspapers and no letters, except at long intervals of time, there were no houses, no barns, no fences, no roads, no bridges, no human beings to be seen in any direction This shanty was then the only human habitation between what was afterwards known as the Winnebago agency and Owatonna—the only one within the present limits of Waseca county.

The writer mentally resolved, within a week after his arrival, to return to Wisconsin as soon as his term of service should expire. But when the month of June came, what a change! The trees had put forth their fresh, green foliage; the prairies were decked with the most gorgeous flowers; feathered songsters held grand jubilee concerts in every grove, and prairie chickens in endless numbers made early morn melodious with their merry love-making. No more enchanting picture of a grand, rich country ever met the eye of man than that presented in the valley of the Le Sueur during the summer of 1855.

MRS. S. P. CHILD.

HON. S. P. CHILD.

CHAPTER IV, 1855.

DRIVE CATTLE TO MANKATO—S P CHILD NEAR UNTO DEATH—CALLENS AND MANSFIELD SHANTY—CHILD CAUGHT ON PRAIRIE AT NIGHT AND FEET BADLY FROZEN—TERRIBLE SUFFERING AND NO PHYSICIAN NEAR—THE WINNEBAGO INDIANS ARRIVE

Shortly after their arrival at Sutlief's place, Messrs Barrett, Sutlief and S P. Child started for Mankato with a portion of Sutlief's cattle in order to get them kept there until spring, as the hay was running short Mr. Sutlief returned within a few days, leaving S P Child at Van Brunt's sawmill to get in logs for lumber Mr Barrett had a claim of his own near South Bend and remained there Van Brunt's mill was on the LeSueur river, about five miles east of Mankato Owing to some misunderstanding S P Child, after remaining at the mill a few days, started to return to Sutlief's claim, intending to stop on the way, over night, at the shanty of Mansfield and Callens, who then resided about four miles south of what was soon after known as Winnebago Agency Mr Child found no one about the home and the door was locked, he therefore concluded to push through to Sutlief's that day This was a most unwise decision, for he had nearly twenty-five miles to travel before he would reach the Sutlief place There was no road, and half the forenoon was already spent. He should have forced open the door and remained over night But he was young, strong, and impetuous, and, thinking he could get through in good time, he started on The snow was deep, especially in low places and in ravines, often taking him in waist deep. It was also covered with crust, strong enough to hold him up in some places, while in other places it would break through. During the middle of the day the weather was mild, and some of the snow that worked into his boots melted, making his socks and boots quite wet. Toward evening the weather became much colder and, despite all his efforts, his feet began to freeze soon after dark. There was no track he could follow, no land mark he could see, and he was enabled to keep his course only by a star which he selected as his guide. One can, perhaps, better imagine than describe the feelings and emotions of one so young thus toiling on with frozen feet, nerved by the hope of reaching shelter and by the prospect of perishing with cold and fatigue on an uninhabited prairie with only prairie wolves to gather at his deathbed. Hour after hour wore away; his feet to his ankles were frozen hard; drowsiness came over him; the prairie wolves howled in the distance; yet no sign of the shanty could be discovered. Though much exhausted and discouraged, he struggled on. He had passed the shanty to the south. Death was certain if he went forward.

Fortunately for him the inmates of the cabin were at work much later than usual that evening; by mere chance he discovered the light, and to the great astonishment of all present came in about eleven o'clock more dead than alive. His boots and socks were frozen tight to his feet and ankles, and some time and much labor were required to remove them.

The suffering he endured for many weeks can not be described. No medical aid could be obtained, and the flesh on his feet literally rotted away, leaving the blackened bones of his toes exposed. Many weeks of pain passed before he could step on his feet and it was months before he could walk without the aid of crutches. Most of the discolored bones of his toes were taken off by his brother who used a razor in the work of amputation. In the latter part of the following April, he was conveyed to Mankato where surgical aid was obtained and the other injured bones were removed. By July following he had so far recovered the use of his feet that he took the position of government cook at the Winnebago Agency among the Winnebago Indians. These Indians had been brought to their reservation during the month of June of that year—Gen. Fletcher being the agent at that time.

CHAPTER V, 1855.

MORE SETTLERS IN MIDWINTER—CHRIS SCOTT AND FAMILY—BUILD A LOG HUT AND COVER IT WITH HAY—SCOTT MAKES TRIP TO LA CROSSE FOR FLOUR THE LAST OF FEBRUARY.

About two weeks after the arrival of Mr. Sutlief and his company, as detailed in chapter three, Mr Christopher Scott and family, accompanied by a man called "Pat," came over from Straight river, where they had been staying since the previous fall They, too, were from Wisconsin, near Fox Lake. This family stayed, or "hung up," in the Sutlief cabin, which, on their arrival, was pretty well filled, at least, it contained twelve persons, although it was only 14x16 feet with no chamber room. But in those days the stranger was welcome so long as there was standing room in the abode of the pioneer.

Mr Scott immediately made a claim about a mile north of Sutlief's. This claim is now owned by Mr John Carmody, Sr Mr. Scott commenced building a cabin, which was constructed of logs notched together at the corners, the building was "shingled" with basswood troughs, the crevices between the logs and troughs were chinked with prairie grass, cut in February, and then daubed, or plastered, with mud the floor was the frozen ground, and the "banking" around the cabin was made of snow. There was no lumber in the country nearer than Mankato, and such a cabin was all that could be constructed with the materials at hand. Mrs Scott having two or three small children, the bottom of a wagon box was brought in and laid upon the ground for them to play on, and for Mrs Scott to use as a sort of sitting room.

Near the close of February Mr Sutlief started for Dodge county, Wis., leaving his business in Minnesota in charge of J E Child Mr Scott, who was going to La Crosse for provisions, accompanied Mr Sutlief They went by way of Owatonna, having learned that several teams had been driven from Owatonna to La Crosse within the month of February Mr Sutlief reached his destination in due time, and Mr Scott, after a long and laborious struggle and much expense, returned with a small supply of flour and pork

CHAPTER VI, 1855.

GREAT THAW IN MARCH FOLLOWED BY A SECOND WINTER—ALONE AND BLIND WITH CATTLE TO CARE FOR—MRS SCOTT'S KINDNESS—TWO MEN FROM IOWA OUT IN ALL THAT STORM AND NEARLY STARVED

The first week in March brought a thaw and a freshet The snow entirely disappeared and the weather was warm and pleasant. So, on a very fine Sunday morning I concluded to take a tour of inspection around Silver Lake In passing around the lake when crossing its outlet on what is now the Pat Madden farm, I broke through the ice and was thoroughly drenched in ice water Very soon after this baptism, the wind sprang up from the northwest and before I reached the cabin that afternoon, a severe snow storm was raging In returning from school section 36, that evening, where I was obliged to go to feed the cattle, I faced the storm for half a mile, and my eyes were injured by the hail and sleet I also contracted a severe cold that day, and the next morning my eyes were so inflamed that I could not open them nor bear the light I was in a "Fletcherian fix" being all alone, with fifty cattle and sheep to feed and water, and I as blind as a bat I tried to raise the only neighbors—those at Scott's claim a mile away—by loading and firing a rifle that was in the cabin, but this availed nothing

However as good luck would have it, the storm ceased about noon, and Mr Plummer from Scott's claim, came over on an errand He fed and watered the stock, brought in some wood and promised to return next morning I could see no better that day than on the previous day, so, when Mr Plummer had cared for the cattle, he proposed that I should go with him to the Scott cabin where Mrs Scott could poultice my eyes and care for them The proposition was gratefully accepted

"Sim" said that as soon as spring should arrive, he could furnish the eyes if "Pat" would the legs, and they would "leg it" back to the scenes of their childhood, etc

After being kindly treated for a week, I so far recovered my sight that I was able to return to the Sutlief cabin and attend to my duties The country was really having a second winter in March The weather was cold, and ice had again formed on all the streams and ponds. A morning or two after I had returned to the Sutlief cabin, and while I was preparing my breakfast, I heard rapping at the door and said "come in." A stranger, looking haggard enough, walked in, and, grasping me by the hand, expressed his joy at finding a cabin and some one living in it He said that he and another man, during the warm spell of weather had left the northernmost settlement, on the Des Moines river, in Iowa, with a horse and "jumper," bound for Mankato On the third day of their journey they had met the heavy snowstorm which had swept over the Northwest, and partly lost their course but struck the headwaters of the LeSueur on the east side, and, supposing it to be the Blue Earth river, had followed along down, expecting to find the Mankato settlement

For three days preceding their arrival here, they had been without anything to eat, except a few ears of corn that they had brought along for horsefeed The horse had subsisted for several days on nothing save dead prairie grass, and the browse from the bushes in the small groves along their route One of the men was nearly blind from exposure to wind, sun, and storm, and both were very much reduced in strength for want of food and rest The horse was nearly starved They had come into the river bend opposite the Sutlief cabin the evening before and had camped over night, almost discouraged and with little hope of ever reaching Mankato or seeing their families again. Within the night they thought they could hear occasionally the sound of a cow bell, and at early dawn they surely heard the roosters crow Hope revived, and as daylight came on the man who could yet see, following the sounds which they had heard, crossed the river and found the shanty They were gladly welcomed, and remained at the cabin several days before they and their horse were strong enough to pursue their journey to Mankato I never saw nor heard of them afterwards.

CHAPTER VII, 1855.

MORE SETTLERS IN MARCH—ROBBINS BROTHERS COME WITH CHRIS SCOTT—"BILL" ROBBINS LOST ON THE PRAIRIE, OUT TWO DAYS AND NIGHTS WITHOUT FOOD—A SHOOTING AFFRAY

The latter part of March after enduring all sorts of hardships Chris Scott returned from his trip to La Crosse for provisions. With him came two brothers George Robbins and Wm Robbins, young and single men from Canada. They made claims on the east side of the river, opposite what was afterwards the village of Wilton, and where once was located a paper town called Waterlynn. Wm Robbins, about this time, had a little experience in being lost on the prairie. He was employed to drive a team and take S. P. Child to Mankato for surgical treatment. That was in April. When they arrived at the Mansfield and Callens' cabin, they learned that the water was so high in the Le Sueur river that they could not cross it to go on to Mankato. So it was arranged that Child and the team should remain with Mansfield and Callens until the waters should subside, and then go to Mankato, and Robbins should at once return to the Sutlief settlement on foot and report the condition of affairs. He left there early in the morning, having with him a rifle and a small supply of ammunition. It seems that he went carelessly along, shooting at birds until well along in the afternoon when it occurred to him that he ought to be near home. He looked in every direction, but could see no object that looked like anything he had ever seen before. But he was on a wagon trail and thought that that would lead him home. He had thoughtlessly expended all his ammunition, and night found him upon the open prairie without food, fuel, or even a blanket He dared not move about much after dark for fear he would lose the wagon track The next morning he was totally at a loss as to which direction to go He finally followed the trail in a southerly direction, and again he spent the night upon the prairie, without food or fire Fortunately on the third day he met some government land surveyors on their way to Mankato who, like good Samaritans, took pity on him, fed and warmed him, and carried him back to the Mansfield and Callens' place It seems that when he left that place he took an old wagon trail leading south, instead of taking the Sutlief track leading east Three days afterwards, he returned to our settlement somewhat wiser than when he left

As soon as the waters subsided so that the Le Sueur could be forded, S P Child proceeded to Mankato, where his feet received the long-needed treatment He then returned to the settlement about two weeks after Robbins' return

RECKLESS SHOOTING

A little matter occurred at this time that shows the recklessness of frontier life Mr Sutlief, while on his trip to Mankato in February, had sold on credit, a pair of young oxen to a man named Wentworth, and had taken as security a chattel mortgage on the team He left the chattel mortgage with me and told me to keep an eye out for the cattle When S P Child returned, he told me that Wentworth was sick of the country and would start for California as soon as the grass should grow Wentworth lived about one and a half miles south of Mansfield and Callens I went out to that place on foot, a few days after my brother's return, and stayed with Mansfield and Callens over night They confirmed the report that Wentworth was selling off his personal effects and making arrangements to leave as soon as possible, and that he was trying to sell the Sutlief oxen So, the next morning, I went to see him, supposing that he would pay for the oxen or, at least, give them up, as he had not paid anything on them He very coolly told me that he should not pay for them nor give them up He said the note was not due till a year from date and he should not pay it till then He admitted that he should leave as soon as he could and take the cattle with him I told him then that the cattle would have to be taken on the mortgage, and tried to convince him that he had no right to hold the cattle, either in law or equity, but talk was of no avail I then went to the yard, put the yoke on the oxen, and started to drive them out through the bars Wentworth stood in the bar-way with a club and drove them back. I then tore down the yard fence on the other side and tried to drive them out there, but Wentworth met them there and drove them back For some time we drove the cattle back and forth, finally we came to a clinch During the struggle, the oxen went out of the yard, and as soon as Wentworth could get loose and regain his feet he ran for the house, I ran for the oxen and started them east as fast as possible I had not gone more than eight rods before Wentworth came out with a shot gun and ordered me to stop or he would shoot Well, matters were getting serious I had no shooting iron I didn't believe, however, that Wentworth would shoot at me, so I said "Shoot and be d—d." And sure enough Wentworth did shoot I was badly scared, but I was satisfied that if I could get hold of Wentworth before the gun could be re-loaded, I could soon put an end to the shooting business so I made a run for the angry man, who ran into his shanty and barred the door before I reached it Then I knew it was time for me to leave if I expected to leave at all, and I accordingly left as fast as my legs could carry me Fortunately for me, the cattle had kept on in the track leading to the Suthief settlement, and I soon overtook them and put them into a trot which was kept up for some distance. I saw Wentworth come out of his shanty with his gun and walk towards me a short distance, then turn back and disappear into his cabin I kept a "weather eye" out for my contestant all that day, and for some days after my return, but I never again saw the man, who soon after left the Territory

MRS ANNIE MCDOUGALL
WILLIAM A HENDERSON
REV O.A. MELBY
ROBERT MC DOUGALL
SEGUND JOHNSON
MRS ELIZA SUTLIEF
ASA G. SUTLIEF
NATHANIEL GARLAND
GOTTLIEB KRASSIN

CHAPTER VIII, 1855.

MARTIN KRASSIN AND JOHN G. GREENING—FIRST SETTLEMENT IN ST MARY—FIRST LOG CABIN TO BURN IN THE SETTLEMENT—JOSEPH AND ABRAHAM BIRD, JOHN WHITE—BERNARD GREGORY AND MR TOWER—JOHN AND DAVID JENKINS LOCATE IN WILTON

Martin Krassin and John G Greening, next to Mr. Sutlief, were the oldest land lookers of the county Martin was a native of Prussia, born in the year 1821, and came to America with his family in July, 1854, stopping temporarily with his brothers, near Princeton, Wisconsin. He left his young wife there in the fall of 1854 and with Greening made an extensive tour of Minnesota, the greater part of the way on foot They passed through this section pushed on to the Minnesota river, thence down that stream and on to St Paul, whence they proceeded to La Crosse by boat. and thence to Krassin's family in Wisconsin As soon as grass started the next spring, Mr Krassin, in company with his father and mother, his wife and one child, his brother, John F, his brother-in-law Gottlieb Prechel, who was accompaned by wife and children, his youngest sister, Justina, now Mrs. J E. Child, Fred Wobschall, Fred Proechel (Big Fred), and John G Greening and family, made preparations to move to Minnesota The journey was a toilsome one, and they did not arrive until about the first of June, 1855

They intended at first to settle about where Steve Krassin has a farm near the southwest corner of St Mary township, but they soon learned that the Winnebago Indians owned the western tier of sections in St Mary, and they were obliged to seek other locations Martin, his father, Gottlieb Sr., and his brother, John F., made claims in sections 34 and 35 Fred Prechel, then a single man, made his claim in section 34, next to Martin's Fred Wobsehall, also a bachelor at that time, made his claim in section 35, where he resided up to the time of his death All of these were in St Mary township Gottlieb Prechel and family first settled in the same township, on section 32, but the next year exchanged with Christian Krassin and settled on section 27, in St Mary, where Mr Prechel resided with his family until his death John G Greening, who came with the Krassins was the first blacksmith to settle in the county, and he decided to make his home in the town of Otisco, on section 7 He constructed the first dugout in the county Late that fall, his log cabin took fire and was consumed It was too late to build another, so he dug out a house in a side-hill covered it with hay and sod, and lived there during the winter very comfortably

Very soon after the arrival of Martin Krassin and his company, two brothers Joseph Bird and Abram Bird, and their brother-in-law, John White, with their families, settled in the vicinity of what has since been known as St Mary Abram Bird settled on section 4, Wilton, Joseph Bird on Section 32 St Mary and John White, on section 33 of the latter town The Bird brothers and their sister, Mrs White, were English by birth, while John White was a native of the Emerald Isle The Birds were industrious and successful farmers Abram died in February, 1869 leaving a widow and several children Joseph about 1870 sold his farm and removed to Oregon John White some years ago removed to Iosco, where he died

Almost simultaneously with the settlement of the Messrs Bird and White, came Bernard Gregory and his brother-in-law named Tower, with their families The Tower family remained long enough to help Mr Gregory build his log house on section 32 St Mary, and then pushed on further west into what was then called the Blue Earth valley Mr Gregory's family consisted of his wife, two daughters women grown and three sons somewhat younger Louise A Gregory the elder daughter, married a Mr Ballard She died August 15, 1878, aged forty-one years five months and twelve days Martha, the younger, became the wife of Mr Robert B Moore, of this county She passed away December 5, 1875, aged thirty-seven years, six months and thirteen days Mr. Gregory died in this county July 12, 1880, aged eighty-one years, five months and thirteen days His wife, Amanda C., died February 28, 1883, aged sixty-seven years, eight months and fourteen days Austin, the oldest son, died in 1888. Mr and Mrs. Gregory were kind hearted, agreeable toward strangers, and, during their first year's residence, kindly entertained many a weary traveler Peace to their ashes.

The latter part of June, the same year, Andrew Scott and wife, parents of Chris Scott, accompanied by their son, Charles D. Scott, with his wife, came on from Wisconsin The old gentleman was a "character," having some peculiar ways. He first made a claim on section 24, in Wilton, which he sold to John Jenkins, and then made one on section 13, in the same town. After much suffering from blood poison, which commenced in his feet, the old gentleman died about 1863 in Wilton C. D Scott made his claim on the town line between Otisco and Wilton, in sections 13 and 18, where he lived for many years, but always in poor health. He finally lost nearly all his property. He died several years ago.

CHAPTER IX, 1855.

LOST MAN ON THE PRAIRIE—HEINRICH F BIERMAN OUT TWO DAYS AND NIGHTS WITHOUT FOOD—MICHAEL ANDERSON IN OTISCO—OTHERS COME IN 1855

About the first day of July that first summer, just after sunrise, while near the cabin door and looking south across the prairie toward the headwaters of Big Boot creek, I saw what appeared to be, at first sight, a lone Indian coming towards me. Living alone, as I did that summer, I always watched the approach of strangers with some curiosity I soon discovered that the man was not an Indian, but an unarmed white man. It was half an hour or more from the time the man was first seen to the time when he arrived at the cabin In the meantime breakfast had been prepared for two As the traveler stepped to the open door, he politely lifted his hat and said, in excellent German, ' Guten morgen,'' and asked me if I could speak German? Finding that he could make himself understood, he went on to say that he left Owatonna two days before, expecting to reach this settlement the first day He lost the trail soon after leaving Owatonna, and wandered off in a southwesterly direction As nearly as could be made out, he must have reached Beaver lake, where the first night overtook him. The next day, he traveled in a westerly direction, and night overtook him on the bank of Big Boot creek, on section 12 town of Byron He had not partaken of any food after leaving Owatonna The mosquitoes and flies had bled him on his face and neck, which were covered with blotches, and he looked as though he had been sick. That morning, about daylight, he had heard the cow and sheep bells, on the Suthef ranch, and, as the morning sun lifted the curtain of night, he was overjoyed to see smoke issuing from the cabin stovepipe, and again to hear the sound of bells in the stock yards. He ate sparingly of bread and new milk for breakfast and then lay down to sleep. At noon he awoke, much refreshed, and during the afternoon helped about the work until evening, when I went with him to the house of Mr Greening, three miles distant He was Mr. Heinrich F Bierman He directly made a claim in sections 13, in Wilton, and 18, in Otisco, where he made his home the remainder of his life. He was a most excellent citizen. His death was accidental, being caused by a fall from a wagon, December 22, 1882

His widow at this writing resides in Waseca, and his children, five in number, are all residents of this state Very soon after Mr Bierman's arrival, one of those odd characters ofttimes found in communities, made his appearance, and with him came his brother and brother's family John Jenkins, the odd genius, was a bachelor from Herkimer county, "Old York State," as any one would learn on the very shortest acquaintance with him David J. Jenkins, his brother, had a fine family "Uncle John," it was given out, had some money, while David was blessed with wife and children, but no money to speak of. "Uncle John" bought a part of the Scott and Plummer claims, on sections 24 and 13, in Wilton. David made no claim at first and lived with his family on John's claim, each having a cabin, although all ate at the same table. More will be said of these people further on, but here suffice it to say that, at the present writing, David J. Jenkins' family are living near Janesville, while "Uncle John" enlisted in the Fifth Minnesota Infantry and died at Iuka, Miss, August 21st, 1862.

In July of the same year, Michael Anderson, a native of Norway, made a claim in sections 28 and 33 of Otisco. He was a first-class man, of native ability, and had the confidence of his countrymen to a marked degree. He accumulated a large farm property in that town, but wishing more land for his children, as they should attain manhood and womanhood, he removed to Norman county, in this state, some years ago, where he shortly afterward died.

Bergoff Oleson settled that fall on section 32, in the same town, where he resided until the time of his death. He was born in Norway, February 28, 1828, and came to America in May, 1851. He first settled in Dodge county, Wisconsin, where he married Julia Anderson, September 16, 1855 Mrs Oleson was born in Norway March 14, 1837. They at once came to this country, thus showing what sensible young people they were. They have been the parents of twelve children, four of whom died in infancy.

Early the same fall, Hugh and Robert McDougall, two brothers from Canada, natives of Scotland, settled on section 6, Otisco. Hugh, after remaining two years, secured his land and returned to Canada, where he still resides at this writing. Robert afterwards married and settled on his land, where he lived until his death, which occurred January 15, 1887 (For particulars of his life, see Biographical Sketches)

G Goetzenberger and family settled on section 21, Otisco, in November of 1855, where they remained until their removal to Waseca Here Mr Goetzenberger died some years ago. His son Edward now resides in Minneapolis

Bernard Bundschu and family, now living on the Pacific coast, settled on section 8, Otisco, late in the fall. Mr Bundschu died in the early part of 1894 in Oregon.

CHAPTER X, 1855.

EARLY SETTLEMENTS IN IOSCO—GREAT HARDSHIPS OF THE FIRST WINTER—PRAIRIE FIRES AND DEEP SNOW

I am under obligations to M S Green, Esq , deceased, for the following

The first permanent settlement in the town of Iosco was made in July 1855 by Luke B Osgood, accompanied by John H Wheeler, Daniel McDaniels, and Buel Welsh Mr Osgood made his claim on section 20, and immediately commenced thereon the erection of a cabin, fourteen by sixteen feet in size, all hands participating in rolling up the logs and putting on a roof of shakes His family moved into it, although at the time it had neither floor, door, nor window. It was late in the fall before these were added to the abode Before the building of the cabin the family had camped out for three months and were glad to get even this humble protection from the weather

Mrs Osgood narrowly escaped death in a prairie fire, as elsewhere detailed in this volume, in the fall of 1855

The residents at this time of this locality, known as the Plum Valley settlement, lost nearly one-half of their cattle within the winter, owing to the poor quality of their hay Many of the settlers did not arrive in time to make their hay before the first frosts

Mr. John Wheeler was also one of the first settlers and became a permanent citizen of Iosco where he lived on his farm until 1886, when he removed to Nebraska. He sold out to Julius Mittelstaedt Buel Welsh went to Faribault where he remained until 1857, working as a carpenter After this he located in the village of Wilton, where he remained until the ancient "burg" became farm lands He then removed to Alma City, where he spent the remainder of his days. Mr Osgood and family, after living on their farm some twelve years, sold out to the Messrs Timlin, and moved back East, where Mr Osgood died about 1883.

Mr. McDaniels, after a few years spent here, removed to Missouri, and there he was living at last accounts Jake Conrad disappeared from the settlement in 1858, and his whereabouts have since been unknown to persons of this section

David Wood settled on section 2, Iosco, the same season, where he resided until his death in May, 1898 He was born in Scotland in 1820, and came to America in 1848 He landed at Quebec and spent the summer as a steamboat employe on Lake Ontario and the St Lawrence river. He then made a trip to New Orleans, but soon returning North, engaged in railroading, first on the Cleveland & Pittsburg, and second on the Pittsburg, Fort Wayne & Chicago He spent several years as sub-contractor and section foreman Later he came to Minnesota and located as above stated He was married in 1853 to Miss Susan Somerville, formerly of Virginia They are, it is said, the parents of the first white child born in the township David W, the child was named, and he still lives at the old home

J. W. Hosmer, Aaron Hanes and Joseph Madrew also came to Iosco in 1855 Mr Hosmer moved to Janesville the next year and was prominently connected with the village until his death, as will fully appear later in these pages Joseph Madrew did not remain long. He sold out and returned to Wisconsin

Mr Hanes settled near Mr. Osgood's place, where he lived until 1859, when he died, leaving a wife and four children, one daughter being married His son James (Jim) served his country during the War of the Rebellion After the war he took up his residence in Waterville, Le Sueur county, where he died July 18 1904. The other son, John, died when a young man, and the younger girl died about 1884

CHRISTIAN REMUND.

CHAPTER XI, 1855.

DEATH OF HENRY HOWELL—FIRST SETTLERS IN BLOOMING GROVE, JANESVILLE, AND BYRON.

Samuel F Wyman, Michael Johnson, Jonathan Howell, and A J. Bell took their claims in Blooming Grove early in the spring of 1855 They were all then single men. They built a little log hut on Bell's claim, and commenced batching At the end of about two years Messrs Wyman and Bell tired of that kind of single blessedness and quit, leaving Johnson and Howell to go it alone. These two bachelors lived together as such about seven years more, when Mr Johnson married and became a permanent resident Mr Howell remained single to the time of his death, which occurred in 1880 Bell afterwards became a resident of Faribault, and Mr. Wyman, who will be noticed more fully in biographical sketches, became a resident of Waseca.

The same season, in the month of June, Christian Remund, with his family, made his claim on sections 8 and 9, where he has since made his home He was born in Switzerland November 21st, 1830, came to America in March, 1850, lived five years in Illinois, and there married, October 21st, 1851, Anna Bumgerdner, who was also a native of Switzerland They arrived at their Minnesota home June 28, 1855, and lived in their covered wagon until October of that fall (See biographical sketch)

Wm M Gray and family settled on section 33, in this township, in June, 1855. Mr. Gray was born in Genesee county, New York in 1806. In 1836 he married Miss Lucina Fuller, who was also a native of the same state They came to this place from

Iowa and resided here the remainder of their lives Mr. Gray died in 1872, and Mrs Gray died a few years later They were very estimable people and highly respected

J M Blivens and family settled on section 32 in this township, in the summer of 1855, where they lived for several years, when they removed to Missouri. The settlement in the early days bore Mr Blivens' name

Mr Curtis Hatch, a blind man, with quite a family, settled in section 15 He sold his claim here after a short time and moved into the western part of the county He afterwards moved to Dakota and died in Moody county in 1884 Mrs H P Chamberlain is his daughter and came with her parents to Blooming Grove

Samuel and Luther Dickenson, of Vermont, settled in the township this year. Luther returned to Vermont during the hard times of 1858, but Samuel remained until 1860, when he sold his farm and removed to Le Sueur county.

M P Ide, son of Col J C Ide, with his young wife, was among the 1855 settlers of Blooming Grove, on section 14 or 15 He afterwards moved to Wilton, enlisted in Company F, Fifth Minnesota regiment, infantry, served during the war, and afterwards lived near Morristown.

Simeon Smith was another of the 1855 settlers. He located on sections 31 and 32 in the month of June. He was an honest, industrious, well-to-do man, who lived to see the wilderness, which he found here, blossom as the rose He died November 6, 1872, aged 78 years, honored and remembered by numerous friends and acquaintances

Alfred C Smith, son of Simeon, with his young wife, accompanied his father, and made a claim on section 5, of Woodville, where he lived until his father's death, when he took charge of his father's estate It might be well to remark in passing that Mr. A C Smith has the honor of being the father of the first white girl born in the county Her name is Lovica She was born October 15, 1855, and is now Mrs. H N. Carlton. Ole Knutson, now of Renville county, also settled in Blooming Grove in 1855

The first death among the old settlers of the township was that of Henry Howell a native of England. He was returning from Faribault with his brother Jonathan and when about half a mile east of Morristown, got out of the sleigh to walk and thus warm himself. His brother, unbeknown to him, stopped in Morristown, and he continued towards home on foot Jonathan, after waiting awhile, supposing Henry had proceeded homeward, drove home, only to find that he had not arrived The next day, after considerable search, his body was found near the Bassett farm, a mile south of Morristown, with life extinct He no doubt became bewildered on the prairie, and, being rather thinly clad and the night a cold one, soon froze to death He left surviving him three daughters

TOWNSHIP OF JANESVILLE

The records of this township for the first ten years of its existence are missing, and the best that can be done is to give what can be picked up here and there from other sources It is among the early traditions that the first white settlers in Janesville were a man named John Douglas and another named Hughes. They did not become permanent settlers, but removed, shortly afterwards, further west The next settlers were two dissolute characters, Alfred Holstein and John Davis Davis claimed a portion of section 28, and Holstein a portion of section 27 Their principal business was trading with the Indians, and, by common reputation, they dealt mostly in whisky and tobacco—Davis, especially, being a great drinker himself Both of them were social, friendly, and kind hearted to all comers, but their ideas of morality and decency were not of high grade. Davis finally went to one of the Carolinas Holstein was sent to state prison by a United States court for stealing horses from the Winnebago Indians A man named John Rowley settled on section 9, the same summer and became a long-time resident

James, Thomas, John and Jerry Hogan, four brothers, came from the state of Kentucky in 1855, and settled in the timber on the west side of Lake Elysian. These were among the hardy pioneers that came here to make homes for themselves and their children, and they became permanent settlers

Mr Patrick Moonan made a settlement in this township the same year Mr. Moonan was born in County Louth, Ireland, March 17, 1825, came to America in 1844, and settled in Janesville Mrs Moonan's maiden name was Mary A. Delaney and they were married in 1853 Mr Moonan was in business at Janesville for several years He came to Waseca in 1882, and built the Sheridan House, now called the Waverly hotel, where he carried on the business until 1887, when he sold out and removed to Minneapolis with his family. He afterwards returned to Waseca, where he died November 22d, 1899. John Moonan, Esq., the well-known attorney of Waseca, is his son

John McCue, who became a wealthy farmer of the county, and his brothers, James and Patrick, also came that summer James remained a bachelor and died in 1885, on the McCue estate. Patrick removed to Parker's Prairie, in this state, while Mr. John McCue removed to Missouri, where he became more wealthy than he was here. He finally went to California, where he died about 1893

George Morrill, now a resident of Alton, settled in Janesville, in 1855 Mr Morrill is a modest, quiet farmer, and has a good home.

John Cunningham was one of those first-class men who settled in Janesville in 1855 He made his claim on section 29, where he resided until his death, August 30, 1870. He was one of the first to respond to the call for men to fight the Indians in 1862, and enlisted October 4th, with ten other men from this county, in Company B, First Minnesota Mounted Rangers, and served until the close of the Indian war. He married Mrs. Mary Crawford, widow of W H Crawford, one of the early settlers of this county. At the breaking out of the war Mr. Crawford was murdered by Texas rebels for the awful crime of being a northern republican

TOWNSHIP OF BYRON

Jeremy Davis and family were among the 1855 settlers and made the first claim in the town of Byron settling on the northwest quarter of section 34 where they lived until the death of Mr Davis, which occurred September 13, 1863

Daniel C Davis, son of Jeremy, came with his father in 1855 Having just reached his majority, he also took a claim and became a permanent resident of the township. He took a homestead on sections 28 and 33 after the homestead law took effect He was married July 18, 1861, to Miss Frances Parvin, daughter of Mr B Parvin, who settled in the county in 1860

(I have thus given the names, as far as I have been able to

remember, or learn, of all those who settled in the county prior to the year 1856. That I have forgotten some names and incidents in fifty years is altogether possible and quite probable.

There were, however, some experiences peculiar to that first year's settlement which will never be forgotten by those who passed the winter of 1855-6 in this county.

In writing this history, I shall endeavor to present the facts, as nearly as possible, in the order of their occurrence, and I know nothing that can be more interesting to future generations of our children, or to the living, than a truthful record of the real dangers and hardships then encountered by the men and women that have made it possible for the present thousands of people in the county to live in the midst of plenty, and with all the advantages of advanced civilization about them

In my next chapter I shall give some sketches of life in Waseca county during the fall of 1855 and the winter of 1855-6.—The Author)

CHAPTER XII, 1855.

THE FIRST ELECTION—FIRST CANDIDATES IN COUNTY—LIST OF VOTERS

THE FIRST ELECTION

The general election in those days was held on the second Tuesday in October, I think, at any rate the election that year fell on the 9th of October. There were two voting precincts The northern half of the county was called "Swavesey," and the southern half "Le Sueur River" There were two polling places—one at the house of J M Bliven in Blooming Grove, the other at the farm of Chris Scott, now owned by Mr Carmody, in Wilton

I was not present at the "Swavesey" precinct but was present at the "Le Sueur" precinct election When the voters came together at Scott s house, there was no ballot box, and one had to be improvised Finally Mrs Scott loaned them a cake box A hole was cut in the cover so as to admit the ballots and the election proceeded The local candidates were as follows

County commissioners—Samuel B Smith, Wm Allen and Melmer P Ide
Register of deeds—Charles Ellison
Sheriff—Wm F Pettit
Treasurer—David Sanborn.
Surveyor—John W Park
Clerk of court—F Wilbur Fisk
District attorney—J M Bliven
Judge of probate—Frank B Davis
Assessors—David Lindesmith, Charles Thompson and Luke B Osgood
Justices of the peace—John Jenkins, of what is now Wilton, and Simeon Smith, of what is now Blooming Grove.

Of the county officers, Mr Ide and Mr Bliven resided in Blooming

Grove. All the other officers were residents of what is now Steele county, except Mr Osgood, who lived in what is now Iosco

It is proper to say here that what is now Waseca county was then a part of Steele county.

The names of those who voted in the Le Sueur precinct, as I remember them, were as follows·

Barney Gregory, Joseph Bird, Abraham Bird, John White, Martin Krassin, Fred Krassin, Gottlieb Krassin, Sr , Fred Prechel, Gottlieb Prechel, Fred Wobschall, David J Jenkins, John Jenkins, John G. Greening Andrew Scott, C D Scott, Chris Scott, James E Child Wm Robbins, George Robbins and H F Bierman—twenty voters in all

The names of those who resided in the "Swavesey" precinct, as near as I can make out from the records, were as follows:

A C Smith, L. B Osgood, Daniel McDaniels, John H. Wheeler, David Wood, Aaron Hanes, J. W Hosmer, Michael Johnson, Jonathan Howell, A J. Bell, S F Wyman, Chris Remund, W. M Gray, J M. Bliven, Ole Knutson, Curtis Hatch M P Ide, Simeon Smith, James, John, Thomas and Jerry Hogan, James and Patrick McCue, Patrick Moonan, George Morrill, John Cunningham and John Rowley.

It is not known to the writer how many of these voted, but there was a "right smart" vote considering the number of people.

The ticket was really non-partisan—Messrs. Pettit and Ellison being non-committal democrats—and all the others abolitionists or republicans Among the voters in the Le Sueur precinct, there were only two democrats, Andrew and C D. Scott

The whole ticket was voted straight, as there was no opposition So you see we started out harmoniously. It was, in fact, the only election the writer ever attended that was entirely harmonious and unanimous. While the fires of sectional and partisan strife were raging in the eastern states, our then territory was comparatively free from such excitement.

CHAPTER XIII, 1855.

PREPARATIONS FOR WINTER—HAULING PROVISIONS FROM IOWA. TRIP MADE TO AUBURN, IOWA, BY THE AUTHOR—DECEMBER 19, 1855 ON THE PRAIRIE ALL NIGHT—ONE MAN FROZEN TO DEATH—A COLD CHRISTMAS

While a few of the earliest settlers in 1855 had raised enough vegetables for their winter supply of food, not one of them had produced a supply of wheat, and every family was compelled to haul flour and other supplies from distant points, the nearest flour mill being over one hundred miles distant Most of the flour was obtained from Auburn, Iowa, a small town on Turkey river.

Among those who were wise enough to prepare for winter before winter commenced were the Krassins Having completed their home preparations for winter, they started with several teams and wagons for Iowa. Justina, afterwards Mrs. Child, accompanied her brothers as cook. They went by way of Owatonna and Austin, and thence southeast to Auburn, where they found an abundant supply of flour and other articles. They returned after an absence of three weeks heavily loaded with provisions As they made the trip in October—the golden month of the year—when Minnesota is clothed in the beauteous garments of Indian summer, they enjoyed a pleasant and profitable journey Their return furnished the settlement with valuable information as to the road to take to reach Auburn, the prices to be paid for flour, pork, groceries, etc.

But most of the settlers had stables to build, cabins to finish up and other fall work to do, so that it was winter before they could get started on the trip to "Egypt for corn"

A journey of one hundred or one thousand miles to-day, in railroad passenger coaches, is a very easy undertaking, but a journey of one hundred miles or more across a country where the streams are unbridged and the sloughs ungraded, where cabins are few and far between, through storms of rain or sleet or snow-blizzards, camping out on the bleak prairie at night, with nothing to charm either the ear or the eye save the howling blasts of winter or the more demoniac howling of prairie wolves as, coward-like, they reconnoiter your position and condition—such a journey may be somewhat romantic to read about, but it is not so very enchanting to those who have made a trial of it The experiences of all those who made the journey that winter were very similar, no doubt, and the writer gives his own and those of the few others he has been able to get as samples

JAMES E CHILD'S STORY.

During the first days of December, 1855, having engaged two pair of oxen and a wagon of the brothers John and David J Jenkins, I made preparations for a journey into Iowa John Jenkins furnished the money (about $150 00), I was to put in my labor and skill, get a load of provisions and groceries, bring them into the settlement and sell them, each of us was to share equally in the profits, if any

I started from the settlement December 5th, and proceeded to Owatonna, where I remained two days to get the oxen shod. Uncle Jo Wilson, the rough, kind-hearted blacksmith, of that place, did the job On the 8th I took the wagon track leading to Austin There were two or three cabins some five or six miles south of Owatonna, a quarter of a mile from the road, and, after passing them, there were no other habitations to be seen until the Vaughn settlement, near the place now called Lansing, was reached Before reaching this settlement, night came on, and the darkness, if it could not be felt like that of Egypt in the days of Pharaoh, was near enough to it to prevent a prudent man from trying to travel in a strange country Camping for the night was the next best thing and I put up in a thicket of red oaks

I built a rousing big fire, warmed up the baked pork and beans, toasted the frozen bread, thawed out the doughnuts, made a cup of tea, ate a hearty supper and smoked the pipe of peace with all the then visible world. I had on the wagon about a quarter of a ton of hay (it was necessary in those days to carry along food for both man and beast), so that the cattle had plenty to eat and the driver had plenty to sleep on under the wagon In such a place, on such a night, under such circumstances even a young man naturally becomes philosophical and looks upon his own life as one of the greatest mysteries of a mysterious and, as yet, incomprehensible universe, the beginning and ending of which is called God, the Father of all

Solitary and alone with the patient oxen, I threw myself upon a pile of hay, wrapped in an Indian blanket, and must have gone to sleep early in the evening In the night I awoke to find that a drizzling rain storm had set in from the northeast I put some more wood on the fire and again went to sleep About an hour before daylight, I was aroused by a prairie wolf concert that was being held in the immediate vicinity and probably for my benefit. Appreciating the compliment of the serenade, I stirred the embers of the camp-fire, put on more wood and soon had a cheerful blaze, notwithstanding the dampness. Those wolves, like some people, seemed to prefer darkness to light, for they left at once

As soon as it was light enough to see the road, travel was again resumed As the day advanced, the storm increased, and, by three o'clock p m, rain and sleet were falling fast. I passed through the village of Austin about noon that day, where I took dinner. Austin then boasted one store, one tavern, one blacksmith shop and several pioneer cabins. After leaving Austin it was found very difficult to keep the right track, owing to the numerous wood roads leading in various directions Unhappily for me, I selected the wrong track, and, about four o clock in the afternoon, found myself a mile off the road but at a comfortable log house, where I stayed over night. About the time I reached here, the rain changed to snow The next morning the ground was covered with three or four inches of snow, and more was still falling

On the morning of the 10th, I was rather late in starting, as I had only twelve miles to make during the day I had traveled a mile or so, when a large drove of elks crossed the road some twenty rods ahead of me, in single file. There must have been fifty or sixty of them They were quite numerous that winter along the two Cedar rivers, but I never heard of any in this

JULIET MARCIA ASHLEY
GEO. E. CHILD
MRS ORRILLA J. GOODSPEED
CAPT. WALTER CHILD
MRS J. E. CHILD
MRS ORRILLA CHILD
MRS DORA. M. ASHLEY
S. M. CHILD
MRS ANNIE E. WOOD

section after that winter. Twelve miles brought me to the western edge of a prairie eighteen miles across, and without a resident person upon it. On the western and southwestern edge of this extensive prairie, there was quite a settlement of Scandinavian Americans, who had located there in 1854-5. I stayed over night with a hospitable Norwegian family. They were young people, with one child. The man could speak only a few words of English, but his comely wife could converse quite fluently in that language. The man, anxious to learn English, made a school teacher of me during the evening, and refused pay the next morning for my entertainment, except for what corn I fed the cattle.

Early on the 11th I started across that beautiful prairie which lies spread out between the two Cedars on the south line of our state. This was a pleasant day, but the soft snow which had fallen made traveling slow and tiresome, and it was already dark when I reached the Brink house, on the east branch of the Cedar.

On the 12th the weather became colder. I passed a tavern and store called Pettibone's, and traveled over a prairie, some ten or twelve miles across, where there were no settlers. That night I put up with a Hoosier family that had come from Indiana the summer before. Here were several other travelers, among them a man living near the Brink house that had been lost on the prairie most of the previous night and had frozen his face, feet, and hands quite severely. During that night the weather moderated and more snow fell.

December 13th, about 10 o'clock in the forenoon, I arrived at Green's creek, a stream then about thirty feet wide, with water three feet deep, which had to be forded. The ice was not strong enough to hold up a team, but yet thick enough to require cutting in pieces before the cattle could be driven through. After much labor in cutting ice and driving the oxen through the stream, everything passed over safely. All along the road that day there were numerous pioneer cabins to be seen, and, in several places, there were indications of several years of settlement. I spent that night with a regular Yankee. He had lived in Iowa for ten years—three years on the farm where I passed the night. I was then only seven miles from Auburn.

On the 14th I drove into Auburn and bought my load, consisting of flour, pork, butter and groceries I returned to the Yankee's to stay over night and to buy some seed corn

The 15th was so stormy and cold that I delayed a day On the 16th I again started Everything went well enough until afternoon, when the forward bolster of the wagon broke and I was compelled to put up with a farmer, unload the wagon and make a new bolster. Fortunately I struck the right house—the home of a carpenter Although the father was not at home, he had some grown up boys from whom I obtained the use of tools to make the necessary repairs It took all the next day to get ready for another start, and most of the day it snowed

On the 18th I started quite early The weather was clear but cold, and the road hard to travel I got as far as the Brink house that day, and as the snow was about a foot deep, and hauling a wagon and breaking the roads were laborious, I accepted a fair offer for a portion of the load that night

It was rather late on the morning of the 19th of December, my twenty-second birthday, when I started from the Brink house to cross that eighteen miles of uninhabited prairie In climbing the hill on the west side of the Cedar, the wagon slid out of the track and the off hind wheel caught in a small tree, which had to be cut down The oxen had become discouraged and I was unable to get them to haul the load to the top of the hill. I was in for a tug I had to unload and carry ten hundred pounds of that flour about two rods to the top of the hill on my shoulders It was noon by the time I had reached the top of the hill and had reloaded, and it was eighteen miles to the house of my Norwegian friends on the west side of the prairie. Not a track had been made since the last fall of snow, across the prairie, and it was a question whether to proceed that day or wait till morning I finally concluded to proceed The snow was drifted in many places and progress was decidedly slow To add to the discomfort of the situation, a storm of wind and fine, hard snow set in from the northwest about the middle of the afternoon; when darkness settled down on the prairie, I was only a little more than half way across it, with little prospect of proceeding much further that night

Very soon after sundown, I could not distinguish the road, the oxen refused to face the storm and turned south; it soon became evident that driver and team must put up on the open prairie for that night

So the oxen were taken from the wagon tongue; one pair hitched to the wagon at the front end; the other pair to the hind end; both on the leeward side. I was somewhat tired, having tugged the flour up the hill in the morning, and walked beside the cattle all day through the deep snow, and that, too, without dinner or supper, or even a drink of water Of course, I could eat snow! The cattle had no hay, but there was some corn on the load and this I fed them, reserving and chewing and swallowing some of it myself. There was also some raw, fresh pork aboard, and I cut off a small piece with an ax and managed to eat a mouthful or two, after a fashion.

The wind increased to a gale in the evening and the air was so filled with snow that no object could be seen fifty feet away. I drew off my boots—overshoes I had none—put on a dry pair of socks, and then put on my boots again Having heard it said that a man might wind himself in a blanket and lie down in the snow and sleep without freezing, I concluded to try the experiment. Accordingly I put my body inside a blanket, and then wound myself with about thirty yards of new cotton cloth, and laid me down to slumber Morpheus came not to my relief, but the Frost King pierced me at every pore of my body. I stuck to my position, however, until I was completely buried in snow, and yet the cold crept through and made such fierce attacks upon me that I was forced to dig out of the snow and protect myself in some other way as best I might After gathering up the cotton cloth and putting it back in the wagon I took the ax which I carried along, cleared away the snow on a patch of ground, and went to pounding it with the ax the same as though I were chopping wood. In a short time I got comfortably warm by this exercise. I was very much fatigued by my exertions through the day, and began to feel the need of husbanding my strength for the morrow I leaned agaınt one of the oxen, the animal heat of which helped to keep me warm. In this position I soon fell into a sleep, when my knees gave out and I partly fell. That awoke me. I tried it again, and again I slept and fell. Then I began to feel chilly and again resorted to the ax for exercise. Then I leaned against the patient old ox once more, slept again, and then took a round with the ax These performances I continued, with a little variation during one of the coldest nights of that cold winter and until the dark shadows of night passed into the gray light of a cloudy, stormy morning

Upon examination in the morning, I found that I had strayed nearly eighty rods from the road. The oxen were soon hitched to the wagon, and the load was finally started with that peculiar screeching noise always made by wagon wheels in snow on a cold morning. About 10 o'clock in the forenoon, I arrived at the house of my Norwegian friends with whom I had stayed on my way down They comprehended at a glance what had been my experience and proceeded to prepare breakfast. In a short time the good woman placed before me warm biscuits, hot coffee, potatoes, meat, etc, and it seems to me yet that no other person in the world ever furnished a better meal

I spent the rest of the day there and enjoyed a night of very refreshing sleep That afternoon, I learned from my hostess of a sad affair of the night before—the night that I camped upon the prairie She said that two of their neighbors had visited Austin on the 19th, and in coming home that night one of them had perished with cold and was found dead, while the other had been found with his hands and feet very badly frozen. The body of the dead man was found within forty rods of his own door, where a patient, loving wife with three children, watched all night for his coming. The other, who was so badly frozen, was found about eighty rods from the dead man unable either to walk or to talk when first found. Empty whisky bottles were found upon them, and there was no doubt as to the real cause of the death of the one and the maiming of the other No wonder Shakespeare said, speaking of intoxicating liquors,

"Let us call thee Devil"

On the night of the 20th, more snow fell On the 21st, I reached Austin The snow had become so deep that I could not well proceed further on wheels and so I purchased an ox-sled at that place The 22d was spent in taking the wagon apart, loading it and its contents upon the sleigh and driving as far as Mr. Vaughn's. That was an intensely cold, stormy night. The Frost Fiend was abroad in all his howling majesty, and many were the expressions of hope that no one was out on the prairie that night to face the merciless blasts that swept the country The storm abated the next morning about ten o'clock, and I made about seven miles on the 23d through the snow drifts, stopping with a kind hearted English family, the last residents on the road home between Vaughn's and Owatonna.

The next morning, I started before sunrise, the weather being clear and very cold The roads had not been traveled since the snow storm and the going was heavy Three times that day I had to shovel through drifts of snow and pry up the sled in order to get through. About two o'clock p m. I met two teams of horses and three or four men going into Iowa for flour After this, traveling was much easier for the oxen In the afternoon the weather grew colder. and before night I began to think my feet would freeze in spite of my efforts to keep warm I finally pulled off my frozen boots and traveled with nothing but socks on my feet At first my feet got very warm, but finally the frost began to work through the socks and I thought I should surely freeze. Suddenly I came upon the remains of a campfire in a thicket of jack oaks, some ten or twelve miles south of Owatonna I at once piled on some more wood and renewed the blaze Here I fed the oxen some corn, overhauled my bundle of clothing and found some dry socks and a pair of new boots, which I put on, I also ate some doughnuts which my hostess of the night before had put into my overcoat pockets, and again started the weary oxen towards Owatonna. Five miles south of Owatonna I struck a pretty fair road, several teams having passed over it since the snow storm The night was bitterly cold and it was a difficult matter to keep from freezing. I finally arrived at Sanford's tavern in Owatonna, about two o'clock Christmas morning. I remained in Owatonna over Christmas and sold a portion of my load at good prices. On the 26th I started for Wilton. Here again the road was unbroken The cattle were already weakened by their long journey, and, just as night came on, in pulling through a deep snow drift, the sled tongue was torn out This made it necessary to leave the load there for the night. This accident happened a little north of what is known as the Vinton farm There was no help for it, I was compelled to unhitch the teams and take my course homeward, guided only by the stars I had along with me a large, white cat that I had bought in Iowa, and that I carried confined in a grain sack on the load It would not do to leave him there for he might perish if anything should happen to prevent my return for a day or two, so I took him out of the sack and called him to follow me. He did so in the most approved manner, keeping close to me all the way. I arrived at the John Jenkins' cabin about 11 o'clock that night, where I found Uncle John sitting by his fireplace eating parched corn He arose in a half dazed way and wondered how I got there such a night as that without any road. He said he had about given up all hopes of my return and thought I must have frozen to death on the prairie

The next morning Uncle John accompanied me and we brought in the load safe and sound.

Very few of the settlers that made trips to Iowa or Wisconsin that winter for supplies fared as well as I Many were badly frosted, some lost their teams; others were obliged to sell their loads on the road at a sacrifice, all suffered more or less severely.

We realized enough out of our load to pay expenses The experience and fifty cents a day was all that I got out of the enterprise But then, I was pretty well satisfied—thankful that I was again at my own bachelor fireside, hale and hearty

CHAPTER XIV, 1855-6.

TOWN SITE BOOMING—WILTON VILLAGE PLATTED BY CORNELL AND ABBOTT OF OWATONNA, AND JOHN AND D. J JENKINS AND CHILD OF WASECA COUNTY—CLAIM-JUMPING—HOUSE BODY TORN DOWN—MANY SETTLERS ARRESTED AND TAKEN TO OWATONNA—LAND SUITS AT WINONA—WAR ON THE LE SUEUR—BUILDINGS TORN DOWN IN WILTON

The first year's settlement did not pass without a town-site boom in this county Speculators were abroad then as now. In October, 1855, A. B. Cornell and John H Abbott, then of Owatonna, came to the settlement and prevailed upon D J and John Jenkins and the writer to join with them in platting a town site Mr Abbott was a surveyor and the parties proceeded to survey and plat the village of Wilton, the first-born city of the county. It soon became evident to John Jenkins and me that A. B Cornell, the moving genius of the firm, intended to get persons to come on from various places and take possession of all the land in the vicinity, and that, too, without regard to the rights of others. D. J Jenkins sided with Cornell and Abbott, and it was quite evident that they proposed to jump claims if they could not get what they wanted in any other way. John Jenkins and I withdrew shortly after the survey was made, and men from Owatonna took our places

D J. Jenkins built, that fall, the first house on the new town plat, or, rather, adjoining it, and it was expected then that, like Jonah's gourd, it would grow to almost a city in a day. But, unfortunately, the prime movers of the enterprise so managed their affairs that the settlers of the surrounding country, even up to the boundary line of the village plat, refused to countenance the building of the new city As evidence of the feeling that existed at the time, a few facts will be given, which, though not very creditable, perhaps, will show the extent to which men will sometimes proceed when thrown together promiscuously beyond the controlling influences of courts and law In the latter part of January, 1856, the Owatonna proprietors of the Wilton plat hired some fellows to jump the claims of four settlers—Robert and Hugh McDougall and George and Bill Robbins—who had settled along the river, just east of the village plat The claim jumpers commenced the erection of houses on these lands, and set up counter claims to them on the ground, as they said, that those young men had claimed more than 160 acres each, that because they were foreign born and had not declared their intentions of becoming citizens prior to their settlement The former of these charges was false, the latter true The men had not declared their intentions to become citizens simply because there was no court nearer than Mankato, and also because they expected to do so as soon as they could get to the land office at Winona.

As soon as it was noised about that claim-jumping had commenced, an impromptu meeting of the boys was held and they concluded to visit the claim-jumpers and inform them that claim-jumping would not be tolerated at all in the settlement. The agents of the "city speculators" were at the time putting up a log house on the claim since known as the O'Brien land It adjoined the village plat, on the east, and lay immediately on the road leading to Owatonna Nearly every man in the settlement was present at the meeting. They all proceeded to the place where the claim-jumpers were at work, and informed them what had been decided upon The claim-jumpers were acting under the legal advice of Mr Cornell and conducted themselves accordingly They evinced none of that blunt, out-spoken honesty so common to western pioneers, but observed a studied purpose to overreach the boys in legal points and yet preserve themselves from physical harm They showed no fight, but quietly stepped aside when told to do so, by the original claimants The latter then proceeded to tear down the building forthwith Cornell's gang quietly withdrew from the premises after witnessing the tearing down process As soon as possible thereafter warrants were sued out before an Owatonna justice (this was then a part of Steele county) for the arrest of five of the men; to-wit John Jenkins, Hugh and Robert McDougall, and George and William Robbins—all but Jenkins having an interest in the claims jumped. The charge was that of maliciously tearing down a building. Nearly all the other settlers on the upper Le Sueur were subpoenaed as witnesses After a trial, which lasted three or four days, three of the five were found guilty and the other two were discharged on motion of the prosecuting attorney. The whole trial was a good deal of a farce If one of the party was guilty of a crime, all were guilty We asked to be allowed to prove that the claim jumpers were committing willful and malicious trespass upon lands belonging to the arrested parties, and that only necessary force was used to expel the trespassers, the request was refused. Those found guilty appealed to the district court and were in due time discharged without costs on account of error in the proceedings before the justice

Immediately after the justice trials, Cornell, through his satellites, commenced suit before the land officers at Winona, and the contesting parties and their witnesses were compelled to make several trips to Winona After about a year of expensive litigation, the matter was compromised and settled, the McDougall brothers giving up one forty and taking another.

During the troubles that grew out of that affair there was actual danger of bloodshed. Some of the men went armed Cornell became so alarmed that he did not show himself in the settlement for a long time. In early spring (1856) several house bodies were erected on the Wilton town-site, but on the night of the 19th of April, 1856, they were all torn down, literally razed to the ground I remember the date, for that was the night of my wedding day, and some of the boys remarked that "They couldn't lay that deviltry onto Pat" As to who did the evil deed, probably no one knows, or ever knew, except those engaged in it This occurrence and the general hostility of all the surrounding settlers to the Wilton speculators, prevented any further growth during the summer following

CHAPTER XV, 1856.

ATTEMPTED DIVISION OF COUNTY—CIRCULATION OF REMONSTRANCE—TRAMP ON FOOT THROUGH MEDFORD, CLINTON FALLS, BLOOMING GROVE AND WOODVILLE

The last chapter necessarily carried this history into the year 1856 There are other matters that took place that winter that belong to both years It is intended to keep the history of each year by itself, as far as possible, but there are some matters that cannot be separated by months without destroying the thread of the narrative Of such matters will this chapter relate.

FIRST ELECTION.

The first election in Steele county, of which the present Waseca county was then the larger part, territorially, was held October 9th, 1855 The LeSueur precinct, as it was called, included the south half of this county and the township of St Mary, the polling place was at the residence of Chris Scott, the farm now belonging to Mr Carmody in Wilton. Twenty votes were cast. The north half of the county, then called Swavesey, also held an election at the same time, but I have been unable to learn how many votes were polled there at that time. Only one hundred seventeen votes were cast at that election in the territory comprising the counties of Steele and Waseca The following officers were elected: County commissioners, S B. Smith, Wm Allen and M. P Ide (Mr. Ide lived then in what is now Blooming Grove), register of deeds, Chas Ellison; sheriff, Wm. F Pettit; treasurer, David Sanborn; surveyor, John W Park; clerk of the court, F. W Fisk, county attorney, John M. Bliven (then a resident of what is now Blooming Grove), judge of probate, F. B. Davis; assessors, David Lindesmith, Chas. Thompson, and Luke B Osgood (Mr. Osgood lived on the line between Janesville and Iosco), justices of the peace, Simeon Smith and Curtis Hatch, of the north part of the county, and John Jenkins, of the south part

Originally the territory of Minnesota was divided into nine counties By act of the territorial legislature, Wabasha county originally occupied all that portion of Southeastern Minnesota east of a line running due south from a point on the Mississippi river, known as Medicine Bottle village at Pine Bend. Dakota county embraced all the territory west of Wabasha county and south of a line beginning at the mouth of Crow river and running up said river and the north branch thereof to its source, and thence west to the Missouri river In 1852, Hennepin county was carved out of Dakota county, and, in 1853, Goodhue, Fillmore, Scott, LeSueur, Rice, Sibley, Blue Earth and Nicollet counties were carved out of Dakota and Wabasha counties Rice county, by that act, included all of what is now Steele county and townships 105, 106, 107 and 108, range 22, of what is now Waseca county Blue Earth county, by the same act, included the townships in ranges 23 and 24, of what is now the larger portion of Waseca county.

By legislative act of February 23, 1854, the counties of Houston, Fillmore, Wabasha and Goodhue were changed, and the county of Winona was organized By act of Feb 20, 1855, the counties of Olmsted, Dodge, Mower, Freeborn, Faribault, and Steele were created and the boundary lines of the old counties changed By that act, Steele county then contained ranges 20, 21, 22, 23 and 24, and townships 105, 106, 107, 108—a territory twenty-four miles north and south and thirty miles east and west The geographical center of the county, as then bounded, was near the western line of the township of Meriden

The county seat of Steele county was not designated, nor the county fully organized by statute until Feb. 29, 1856, although county officers had been elected in the fall of 1855

In the month of December, 1855, I made a trip to Auburn, Iowa, for supplies. In January, 1856, shortly after my return, the settlers in the western part of what was then Steele county learned that Messrs Cornell, Pettit, Abbott & Co, of Owatonna, were endeavoring to get the territorial legislature, then in session, to divide Steele and Dodge counties so as to make three counties of the two—the same as we now have them

The county was then very sparsely settled Probably there were not 1,000 families or voters in all the territory of the three counties The people of Waseca county were nearly all young farmers, just commencing life, and poor in goods, wares, etc. They did not feel able to support a county government while there were so few to pay taxes A meeting of the settlers was held and I was selected to visit the people in all parts of the then county to secure signatures to a remonstrance and forward the same to Hon George A McLeod, then of Sibley county, our representative in the house, the Hon Chas E Flandreau, then of St Peter, our member in the council

We made duplicate remonstrances for the settlers along the LeSueur and had them signed at our meeting The next day I started for Owatonna and the Straight river settlement It was a pretty cold day as I learned when I reached Owatonna, the thermometer registering 22 degrees below zero, at 4 o'clock p m The next day was intensely cold—so cold that the ordinary thermometer failed in its efforts to keep a correct record and I remained in Owatonna all day

I soon learned that the people in Owatonna, with only two exceptions, were in favor of the division of the county. This I learned without divulging my mission, and the next day I started down Straight river, calling upon each settler as I proceeded and explaining our opposition to the division Almost without exception, each farmer signed the remonstrance At Clinton Falls and Medford, I found active co-operation, and obtained the signatures of all I could see In one day's canvass I had good strong lists which I forwarded to Messrs. McLeod and Flandreau, accompanied by a private letter from myself and one from Dr. Finch, of Clinton Falls, explaining to them the situation of affairs and the general condition of the people

I left with the postmaster at Medford a copy of the remonstrance to be signed by those whom I had not seen and to be afterwards forwarded to Mr. Flandreau I then struck across the country on foot, without road or track of any kind, in search of the Remund and Ide settlement, in what is now Blooming Grove I had no guide except the government section posts, many of which were covered with snow drifts It was 12 miles from Clinton Falls to Blooming Grove, then called the Bliven settlement

The trip was a good deal more of a job than I had anticipated. Much of the way I encountered small groves and brush land where the snow was very deep and the crust not strong enough to bear my weight After a hard day's work, I reached the house of a pioneer German, named Reineke, about 4 o'clock p m. Like most of his nationality he did not fall in love with me at first sight, and to my salutation: "It is a wintry day," he replied: "Ich verstehen sie nicht." This was one of the occasions in my experience where the few words of German I could speak served me well, for neither he nor any of his family could, at that time, converse in English As soon as he found that I could speak some German he shook hands with me and became very friendly. He invited me to remain over night, a proposition that I was only too glad to accept He entertained me a portion of the evening with stories of the Fatherland, and then drifted into the difficulties he experienced in not understanding English He seemed much pleased when I offered to write out the names of familiar objects about the house and farm in English opposite the German names

After a good night's rest and a hearty breakfast, having obtained his name to the remonstrance, I bade him "lebewohl" and proceeded to visit the settlers in Blooming Grove, Mr Reineke's farm being in what is now Deerfield, in Steele county.

I proceeded eastward until I struck the settlement known as Swavesey. The first residence I found was that of M P Ide, on what afterwards became known as the Patrick Healy farm. Mel, as he was called, turned out to be a Cornell man and could not be persuaded to sign the remonstrance I put in the whole day going from house to house, and secured the signatures of all the other men in the settlement that I could find It was a laborious job to travel about in the deep snow, and night found me at the hospitable cabin of Wm. M. Gray, on section 33, in what is now Blooming Grove

There was a greeting, a charm, a hospitality, a feeling of fraternity among the pioneer settlers of Wisconsin and Minnesota—especially in the latter territory—entirely unknown at the present day. The stranger was always welcome to such accommodations and fare as the settlers possessed. All gathered around the same table and each served the other. Each told to the other his history, almost without reserve, and in one evening they generally knew more of each other and of each other's affairs than men born and reared in the same town know of each other these days. Not only did they become acquaintances but they took a friendly interest in each other's welfare. There was a sympathy among them which later additions to the population seem not to possess

I spent the night very comfortably and agreeably with Mr. Gray and his family, and the next morning called upon his neighbors, Messrs Simeon Smith, Alfred C Smith and E K Carlton, obtained their signatures to the remonstrance, and proceeded homewards, arriving at the McDougall cabin just as darkness covered the prairie and grove

My only compensation for the laborious tramp was the general satisfaction we all felt in the defeat, for the time being, of the proposition to divide the county Alas! how little man knows of the future

CHAPTER XVI, 1855.

THE FIRST WEDDING—McDOUGALL AND 'SQUIRE JENKINS LOST ON PRAIRIE ALL NIGHT—CEREMONY POSTPONED—MARRIED THE NEXT EVENING

Perhaps it is just as well to start the record of the new year, 1856, with the story of the first wedding among white people in the county. It was appointed for New Year Eve

Mr Ballard, of Mankato, and Miss Louise Gregory, whose father resided near what has since been known as St Mary, had made a contract, through love and affection, to be married on New Year's Eve. The friends had been invited from far and near. John Jenkins, Esq, the only justice of the peace in the precinct, was invited to perform the marriage ceremony.

The 'squire, in order to go ship-shape, secured the services of Mr Hugh McDougall, with his horse and new pung to take him to the place appointed for performing the important ceremony About sundown, the 'squire and his companion left the Jenkins cabin and started for the residence of Mr. Gregory, some six or seven miles distant The weather was intensely cold, the snow deep, and, in many places, badly drifted

The bride and bridegroom were not only ready, but anxious, the bridesmaid and groomsman patiently awaited the arrival of the 'squire, the parents conned over the responsibilities of married life, the evening wore away, and the 'squire came not The younger members of the company peeped out through the frost-covered windows, the young men went out at the door and gazed in vain for the coming of the desired functionary of the law, the night wore wearily on, and yet he came not. All night the company kept watch placing a lighted candle in the window—but where was the squire all this dark, cold night? Lost!

Messrs Jenkins and McDougall, after leaving the Jenkins cabin, got along very well until darkness set in. Then they lost their course and wandered about on the cold, bleak prairie during the whole night, vainly endeavoring to find Mr Gregory's place. About four o'clock the next morning they returned to the cabin, whence they had started the evening before The writer, who had fortunately stayed at home, served up a meal of hot buckwheat cakes, fried pork, gravy and coffee to the chilled and unfortunate night wanderers After breakfast they again started for the place appointed for the celebration of the marriage When they reached Mr Gregory's place, about 11 o'clock a m, it was found that the young men of the company had sallied forth to search for the missing 'squire, and the ceremony must be deferred until their return.

About dark, those who had been out to look for the 'squire returned on his trail, having followed it from his cabin It was necessary to have supper before proceeding to tie the knot, and many were the jokes and laughs about the first marriage ceremony to be performed by our worthy bachelor justice of the peace. A considerable part of the pioneer settlers gathered in during the evening to witness the ceremony which had well nigh caused the freezing of Uncle John, as the 'squire was familiarly called

After all had partaken of a substantial supper, the tables had been cleared off, and the "slab chairs" had been properly arranged, the 'squire stated that he was ready to proceed The ceremony was decidedly short and to the purpose. It was even briefer than the shorter form in Booth's Manual. As near as memory serves me, it was as follows "The parties will join hands Mr Ballard, do you take Miss Gregory to be your wife?" (Answer) "Yes, sir" "Miss Gregory, do you take Mr Ballard as your husband?" (Answer—in a whisper) "Yes, sir." "All right," said Uncle John, "then you're man and wife"

After this short, but characteristic ceremony, the company seemed to be relieved of much former constraint, and the night passed in song, "going to Rome," through the "cedar swamp," playing the "honest miller," etc ; for none of those living at a distance could go home that night, and there were too many present to think of finding beds in a farm house

When morning came, the guests cheered the newly-married couple, bade them a fond adieu, and wended their several ways to bachelor homes.

CHAPTER XVII, 1856.

MANY NEW SETTLERS IN 1856—THOSE WHO SETTLED IN VARIOUS TOWNS THAT YEAR—ST MARY NAMED

There was a perfect flood of immigrants into Minnesota in 1856, and Waseca county received a fair share of new settlers

On the 1st day of January, 1856, Jack Turnacliff, Dr. Ambrose Kellogg and William Young, from Iowa, arrived at the Sutlief plantation on Norwegian snow shoes

Mr Young was a native of Scotland, and claimed one quarter of section 26 in Wilton He was an original thinker, a man of more than ordinary intelligence, a persistent hater, a steadfast friend He was a single man at that time, and divided his time for four or five years between Fillmore county and his farm in Wilton He then married a lady in Fillmore county and afterwards removed to Iowa where, when last heard from, he dwelt with his family

Dr Kellogg made a claim on section 35, in Wilton, which he sold in the spring He prospected around for coal the next spring, but finally went back to Iowa where his brother Silas resided. At the last account of him, he was in Kansas

Jackson Turnacliff made his claim on section 7, town of Otisco, where he made his home until the time of his death Jack was one of the young men who was known as being well-fixed—that is to say his father could and did furnish him with a farm and an outfit And Jack proved himself worthy of it.

A man named Wm Wells, familiarly called Nucky Wells, came with his family in the spring and settled on section 25, in Wilton. His wife, after remaining a year or so, ran off with a "handsomer man" than he Wells kept batch for five or six years afterwards, when he sold his claim and returned to Wisconsin

B F. Weed came up from Iowa, accompanied by Silas Kellogg, and settled on section 23, in Wilton, with his young wife, daughter of Hon Wm Brisbane. At this writing, he is a resident of Montana

Hon Jesse I. Stewart, from Indiana, took up his residence on section 7, in Otisco, in the summer of 1856, and became somewhat prominent as a politician. He served one term as county treasurer, being elected to that office in 1857, and to the legislature in 1859 When last heard of by the writer he was in Oregon

Mr Jacob Brubaker and family, from Pennsylvania, came to the Le Sueur settlement in the fall of 1856, and settled on section 28, Wilton. The family then consisted of himself and wife, the sons Abram and Geo E, and two daughters, the elder now Mrs Whitman, of Iowa, the other Mrs Tom Eldridge, now of Nebraska The old gentleman died at Waseca The older son, Abram, went into the army from Pennsylvania and was never after heard from Geo. E Brubaker is still a resident of the county.

Michael O'Brien, in 1856, made a claim on section 12, Wilton, where he and his sister now reside

Among others who settled in the county in 1856, were Patrick Kenehan, Noah Lincoln, H P Norton and C F Lincoln, of Wilton, Joseph Manthe, Gottlieb Krassin, John Jordan, Anthony Gorman, Michael McGonagle, Sr, Geo H Reibling, and a lawyer, by name McCarthy, of St Mary, J W Hosmer, H P Chamberlain, John F. Allen, Wm Lee, John Minske, Fred Minske, August Minske, Gottlieb Kanne, Fred Kanne, August Kanne Gottlieb Kanne, Wm Marzahn, John Reed, David Hutchinson, Thos Bishop, Thos Gibson, Wm Allen, John G Ward, Silas Ward, John J. Fell, Richard Toner, H W Peck, Geo Leonard, Daniel Tripp, Benj W Gifford A. A Cotton, M S Green, William Long, Seth W Long, Geo. Long, A Wilsey, Jim Chadwick, S. J Willis, Henry Thwing, Nelson Thwing, Jacob Hagadorn and Peter Farrell of Iosco, Hon Lewis McKune, Hon J L. Saufferer, E R. Conner, Geo Dean, John Walker, James Walker, Wm Donaldson, Hon Philo Woodruff, Patrick Healy, Cornelius Hand and his sons, Hon J.N Powers and his father, John Gibson, Daniel Riegle, Andrew Nelson, Patrick Murphy and sons, Jacob Oory, Henry,

Josiah, Joshua Smith, Samuel Smith, Wm. H. Young, Joseph Churchill, B Sharp, Cyrus Ross, Andrew Oleson, Wm. J Wheeler, Gottlieb Petrich, John Remund, Samuel Remund, Rudolph Remund, Albert Remund, Keyes Swift, John Hackett and Gulick Knutsen, of Blooming Grove; H A Mosher, Asa Mosher, E B. Stearns, Z. Holbrook, Hon. J. A. Canfield, Silas Grover and sons, Wm Smith, W S Baker, M D L Flowers, Parselus Young, H G. Mosher, Adam Bishman, Jacob Bishman, Ben G Northrup, Ole Peterson, Charley Johnson, Omer H Sutlief, F L Goetzenberger, Wm Schmidt and B Bundshu, of Otisco, W G Allyn, Paul Wandrie, Charles Wandrie J W Hosmer, Wm. Stanke, Martin Stanke Michael Silkey, W. G Mathews, Thomas McHugo, C De Regan, W H Crawford, Alex Johnston, John Buckhout, "Uncle" Frank Johnson, Patrick Hackett, G Grams, James Henning, Jas Cooledge, David Cooledge, N E. Strong, John Bradish, Esq, George Dreever and Richard Dreever, of Janesville Obadiah Powell, Eri G Wood, Loren C Wood, Henry Watkins, E K. Carlton, Jacob Myers, Wm. Dunn and Austin Vinton, of Woodville, Anthony Sampson, H H Sunde, K. O Rotegard, H T Handgrud, Ole K Hagen, W Anderson, Chris Knudson, E O Strenge, N. C. Koffstad, Martin Anderson, August Miller, K Christenson and Nels Christenson, of New Richland; E. S. Woodruff, B F Haines, E A Clark and Mr Edgerton, of Vivian, Christie McGrath, Wm Bevans, David Bevans, Isaac Lyng and C S Weed, of Byron.

CHAPTER XVIII, 1856.

ASSAULT AND BATTERY—A LAWSUIT—ATTEMPTED CLAIM JUMPING—JOHN GREENING AS CONSTABLE—FIRST STORE AT WATERLYNN.

It is perhaps well enough to say here that the plan of this work is to give the names of all the very early settlers, for a few years, and then, each year, give the events that are deemed of public interest as they transpired

One of those outrages that sometimes stir the indignation of a whole community, whether large or small, occurred early in the summer of 1856 About the first of that loveliest of months in Minnesota, June, two brothers, calling themselves John and William Jaques, came wandering through the county, evidently bent on mischief They said they came from Iowa, and pretended to be in search of government land—something at that time everywhere present in northern Iowa and Southern Minnesota. Upon their first entrance into the county, they camped near A G. Sutlief's farm, in Wilton. They were very inquisitive as to claims They enquired who had pre-empted? Who claimed more land than the law allowed? Who had claims to sell? Who had lived up to the requirements of the law, and who had not?

They seemed anxious, too, to find out who had horses to sell, what kind of horses they were, what kind of men owned horses, etc. They lost no opportunity to ply their inquisitiveness as they passed along through the settlement Going thus from house to house, they became acquainted more or less, with the affairs and condition of each settler, from Otiseo and Byron to St Mary In St Mary they found, what they supposed to be a fine opening for a display of their innate meanness As before stated in this history, several of the Krassins and two of the Prechels had settled in St. Mary, the previous year Gottlieb Prechel had taken a claim on section thirty-two, adjoining the reservation then occupied by the Winnebago Indians In the latter part of the winter of 1855-6, Prechel and the Krassins had proved up and entered their lands, but this was not generally known in the settlement This Prechel land was about three-fourths of a mile down the river from the old townsite of St Mary During the summer of 1855, Prechel had built a comfortable log house, with a thatched roof, and broken about ten acres of prairie At the time he had crops growing upon the plowed land and was engaged in fencing it Owing to the proximity of Indians, and the timidity of his family and himself, he moved into the house with Martin Krassin, after having entered his land Martin's house was on section thirty-four, nearly three miles further up the river Madam Rumor had informed these roving Jaques that Prechel was not living on his land and that his claim could be jumped "Only a Dutchman" claimed it, he could be easily driven off there was a comfortable house ready made, there were breaking and fencing already done, there were fine timber, pure water, rich prairie; there was a glorious chance to take the product of other people's labor without paying for it, and why not improve their opportunity? These men Jaques thought this a fine opening and so moved on to the premises and took possession Prechel soon became aware of the fact, and proceeded at once to see about the matter Accompanied by his brother-in-law, Martin Krassin, he took his team, proceeded to the farm, and commenced cutting and hauling fencing The two Jaques heard the chopping, soon came out where they were at work, and, with much assumed authority, ordered them off the premises Krassin and Prechel could neither speak nor understand much of the English language, but tried to make the Jaques understand that the land belonged to Prechel and that he had paid the government for it But the Messrs. Jaques would not listen, and were peremptory in demanding that the Germans should leave the claim Prechel was somewhat timid, said but little, and desired to retreat, but Martin Krassin, being of a different make and mind, maintained that he had a better right there than the Jaques and ordered them to leave John Jaques at once commenced an assault upon Martin, and pounded him about the face and head in a most brutal manner Martin was badly bruised and, for the time, driven from the land All the German settlers were aroused and justly indignant at this brutal outrage, they concluded to try what virtue there was in law. There was no lawyer at hand, but, after some study, an affidavit of the facts was made before John Jenkins, Esq, who issued a warrant that was plaeed in the hands of John G Greening, then acting constable, for the apprehension of John Jaques Constable Greening summoned a posse and proceeded to perform his official duty

They went to the premises and found Wm. Jaques, but John was not there. He had skipped out, no doubt thinking that

"He who fights, then runs away,
May live to fight another day."

The posse then went to a neighbor's and got sight of him, but he did not purpose to be caught. He ran, the constable and posse pursued, they chased him into the LeSueur river, in water shallow, constable on one side, posse on the other, the constable ordered him to surrender; he refused, the constable drew a pistol, and Jaques a club; Jaques threw his club at the constable, the constable shut his eyes and dodged, Jaques jumped past him, got into the woods and escaped After an unavailing search for John Jaques, the constable arrested Wm Jaques and brought him before the court Of course he was not the man and was discharged They had some property with them and a suit was commenced against them for willful and malicious trespass upon the premises. A lawyer, named McCarthy, who had recently come to St Mary, was employed to prosecute the cause. Wm. Jaques was arrested and required to plead to the charge of trespass. Jaques entered a plea of not guilty and plead his own cause The prosecution made out a clear cause and judgment was rendered against the defendant for treble damages.

John Jaques spent considerable time skulking about the country to avoid arrest; William was being troubled with lawsuits; finally the twain made up their minds that the people of Waseca county did not desire their company any longer In a short time, they packed their personal effects upon their wagons and traveled westward. They settled on the Minnesota river in Brown county, Minnesota, and soon became the terror of that section of country. It was reported more than twenty years ago, that at one time, they were mobbed by the citizens of that section for horse-stealing, and one of them was forced to leave the county for a long time. John Jaques, many years ago, made an incursion into the town of Blooming Grove and stole a span of horses from Patrick McCullough. A warrant was issued for his arrest, but he was never found. His brother, William, was arrested on the same charge and brought to Wilton, where he finally settled with McCullough for the horses.

What finally became of them is not known, but their exit from this county, after so brief a stay, was highly satisfactory to the whole settlement.

Early in the spring of 1856, Messrs. Waters and Chamberlain bought the claims made the year before by George and William Robbins, on the east side of the Le Sueur river over against Wilton. They put in a small country store, and made believe that they would start a village in opposition to Wilton, and even went so far as to name their place Waterlynn. They supplied the settlers with groceries and other goods during the summer, but for want of either money or enterprise, or both, they failed to accomplish anything of importance.

The village of Empire—a more extended notice of which is elsewhere given in this work—was started in the summer of 1856, and a number of its prominent citizens took an active part in the local politics of that year.

St. Mary also received its name that summer, and preparations were made by Chamberlain, Bailey & Co. to start a city the next spring. These men had bought out Patrick McCarthy, the original claimant, who gave the locality its name.

CHAPTER XIX, 1856.

LOCAL POLITICS—COUNTY DIVISION CONTEST—CORNELL DEFEATED—REV THOMAS NO GOOD—THE COUNTY DIVIDED AND WASECA COUNTY ORGANIZED

In 1856 the animosity growing out of claim jumping, which was instigated by Mr Cornell and other Wilton town-site proprietors, and the evident intention of what was then known as the Cornell ring to divide Steele county and make two small counties, together with other rivalries, brought into existence what was known as the Cornell and anti-Cornell parties It was well understood that Mr Cornell and his adherents wanted to elect a legislative ticket favorable to the division of Dodge and Steele counties and the organization of three counties, giving to each of the three twelve townships, as at present, and making Mantorville, Owatonna and Wilton county seats of their respective counties

In order to forestall the opposition of the farming population, Mr Cornell and friends called a people's convention in early autumn, at Owatonna, thereby giving the Cornell party a powerful local advantage. However, a large proportion of the then settlers of Waseca county went to the convention to find themselves outvoted by traveling immigrants who had been hired by the Cornell men, so some of them said, to camp in the vicinity for a few days and vote on that special occasion To say that some of the old settlers were hot that day, expresses the condition of the public mind at that time in very feeble phrase.

The fraud was so outrageous and so self-evident that it was not seriously denied, even by the Cornell men. The anti-Cornell men withdrew in a body from the others and held a convention of their own, calling it a Republican convention, which it really was. Judge Geo W Green, Dr Finch, Elder Towne and others, of Steele county, eloquently denounced the other convention for following the tactics of the Missouri border ruffians in Kansas. The Republicans nominated a county ticket of their own and elected four delegates to attend the Republican legislative convention to be held at Traverse des Sioux, now St Peter, to nominate candidates for the territorial council and house. These delegates were Dr W W Finch and Judge Geo W Green, of what is now Steele county, and Mr Simeon I Ford and James E Child of what is now Waseca county. The Cornell party elected as delegates to the same legislative convention, H M Sheetz, A B Cornell, and a man from Steele county, whose name is forgotten by the writer, and M S Green, then of Empire in Waseca county. The legislative district then comprised all of that portion of Minnesota west and south of Steele and Nicollet counties and included these two counties.

Each of these two sets of delegates claimed to represent the Simon-pure Republican party of the county. Judge Green, a very able man, was principal spokesman on one side, and H M Sheetz, a brilliant young editor, on the other. Both were cool, deliberate and able, and soon convinced the convention that our county possessed men of ability, at least, and that the contention was no trifling affair. The contest was referred to the committee on credentials, and two reports were made by the committee, one in favor of each. This brought the contest before the whole convention and the battle raged fiercely during the whole night. Finally, about daylight in the morning, it was agreed to nominate a candidate for councillor and two for representatives, leaving one candidate for representative to be thereafter agreed upon by Steele county men.

As soon as this understanding had been reached, both factions were admitted to participate in the convention.

It was one of the hardest fought political battles in the history of our local politics, and the Cornell faction was defeated. Both parties returned home with blood in their eyes, as the saying is, resolved to fight it out until the polls closed and the ballots were counted on election night.

Immediately after the return of the delegates from St Peter Mr Cornell was announced as a candidate for the legislature, and those opposed to Cornell and a division of the county very soon afterwards nominated Rev O A Thomas, of Medford, Steele county, as the opposition candidate. Captain Lewis McKune, Mr. Chris Remund and others, in the north part of what is now Waseca county, and Messrs Lincoln, Waters, Chamberlain, Ford, John Jenkins, and others, in the south part, took an active part in favor of Mr Thomas In what is now Steele county, Dr Finch, Judge Green Elder Towne, and others were energetic in their efforts to defeat Mr Cornell Nearly the whole fight turned upon the candidates for the legislature and for register of deeds

The canvass was very thorough throughout this section, every man having been talked with regarding the matter It was the old story of private interests against the public welfare. Mr Cornell represented the town-site speculators, who desired to make three counties out of two with three county seats On the other hand, the farming settlers, few in number, desired larger counties under the belief that a large county would have no more expense than a smaller one, and that the larger the numbr of taxpayers the less tax each would have to pay The campaign was very exciting, considering how few in number were the voters at that time

Election day fell on the 14th of October, 1856, and a majority of twenty-five votes elected Mr Thomas and protested against a division of the county The majority was not large, apparently, but it was in reality, much larger than it appeared to be, for it was well known that a number of transient men cast illegal votes for Mr Cornell at Owatonna

The people that opposed Mr Cornell and his division scheme supposed they had won a victory, and that, for another year, at least, their interests would be safe in the hands of Mr Thomas whom they elected, but they afterwards found out to their sorrow—

> "How vain are all things here below,
> How false and yet how fair "

No sooner was Mr Cornell defeated at the polls than he took an entirely new tack and sailed in an unexpected direction He sent his emissaries to those settlers in the Le Sueur (Wilton) settlement whom he had been trying for a year to plunder, and managed in one way and another, to compromise and settle with them on liberal terms to himself He became so very kind (?) and good that he threw nearly all his old opponents off their guard He succeeded in securing the co-operation of Col J C. Ide, then of Rice county, a very agreeable, obliging and quite an able man, who came to Wilton that fall and built a saw-mill, the first erected in the county This mill was of great value to all the people of the settlement, and furnished lumber for much needed buildings and improvements So successful were Mr Cornell and his associates that they secured a division of the county by the legislature to which the people had elected a man, and a gospel minister at that, especially pledged to prevent just that very legislation It was the worst case of political treason that ever came to my knowledge No wonder the people lose confidence in human nature when even a clergyman will forget his solemn promises and turn traitor to his political friends and his neighbors

The members of the legislature that winter, from this the tenth, district, were P P. Humphrey, in the council, and Joseph R Brown, Francis Baasen, and O A Thomas, in the house.

Just how the Rev Thomas was handled never came to public light but it was quite evident that the "county seat combine" was too shrewd and too powerful for him to cope with. The legislation of those days, as at present, sometimes bore the significant and euphonious name of skul-duggery

The act organizing Waseca county became a law February 27, 1857 At that time there was not a postoffice in Waseca county and the most rapid method of communication was by means of a saddle horse The fact that Steele county had been divided and Waseca county organized did not become generally known in the latter county until two or three weeks after the legislative enactment At first the people of Waseca county could not believe the report, and when the belief was forced upon them, language failed to describe the feelings of those who had contributed to the election of Rev Thomas in the belief that he would protect their interests

The principal fight in the campaign of 1856 was on Mr. Cornell for representative, and on Charles Ellison for register of deeds

Both of them were defeated The Steele county people have preserved a relic of the conflict of that day. Cornell had, at Owatonna the only newspaper printed in the county, and his opponents had no way of publishing their side of the case, except the primitive one of writing and posting in public places. So they wrote out a jingle of verses and posted it on the side of the log house where the election was held. One of the verses is preserved in "An Album of History and Biography," published in 1887, by the Chicago Union Publishing Company, and runs as follows:

"Mr. Ellison, Esquire.
You ought to look higher
Than to think of registering deeds,
The people up here
Feel desperate queer
To know your political creeds"

Mr Ellison, like many another office seeking politician, was all things to all men—hence the verse

Of the officers of Steele county appointed by the governor in 1856, the following resided in what is now Waseca county · John M Bliven, district attorney, Melmer P Ide, county commissioner; Luke B Osgood, assessor, John Jenkins, of the Le Sueur precinct (Wilton), Simeon Smith and Curtis Hatch, of Swavesey (Blooming Grove), and J A Bassett and M S. Green of Empire (Iosco), justices of the peace

CHAPTER XX, 1856.

ANCIENT VILLAGES NOW DESERTED—WILTON BUILT UP—SOME CLAIM JUMPING—ST MARY THRIVES—G R BUCKMAN'S SKETCH

As stated in the last chapter, the Cornell, or old Wilton company, with headquarters at Owatonna had compromised and made financial peace with the men whose claims they had jumped, immediately after election, in the fall of 1856 About that time, Judge Lowell, late an emigrant from New England to Faribault, became interested in Wilton town property, and active operations were commenced in October to build up the town As before stated Col Ide came on, started a steam saw mill and built a house for his family H P Norton, the pioneer blacksmith arrived in Wilton in October, 1856, and erected the first permanent blacksmith shop in the county He was not only the first but one of the best blacksmiths that ever swung a hammer in the county No man could pound a breaking plow lay and make it do better work than he His old shop at this writing, still stands there, but the ring of the anvil is no longer heard by the passersby

Thomas J Kerr, then a young, unmarried man, came to Minnesota in April, 1856, and worked all summer for Col Robinson, who had taken a claim near Wilton He was a prominent actor in one of the stirring incidents of that day. He had staked out a claim, but had made no improvements upon it, neither had he filed on it, when Col John C Ide came to Wilton and wanted that particular claim He offered Mr Kerr $100 00 for his right, and the offer was accepted—Col Ide paying $5 00 to bind the bargain. Col Ide's family was still in Rice county, and thither Col Ide went to settle up his matters and move his family. Scarcely was his back turned before along came our old and esteemed friends, E B Stearns and family, one Saturday afternoon, and camped very close to Ide's claim Tom had a suspicion that the newcomer proposed to take that claim, and he set himself to work to find out. So he strolled along out to the camp of Mr Stearns, and while there learned that one of the Robbins boys was getting Mr Stearns on to that claim

The claim was entirely vacant. No improvements had been made and it had not been filed on. Just what to do Tom did not know, but he consulted Col Robinson and together they concluded to get Uncle Fisk, who had settled on school section 36, in St. Mary, to go over and take the claim So they went over to Fisk's a little late Sunday night and laid the matter before him Fortunately they had no timepiece that night, and when good Mrs. Fisk remonstrated with them for trespassing upon the Lord's day, they assured her that it was after midnight, and therefore Monday. Uncle Fisk entered heartily into the arrangement, and the three went that night and rolled up a shanty of logs, chinked the cracks with hay, made a roof of hay, and when Mr Stearns came to run the lines Monday morning, he found Uncle Fisk in full possession, with a fixed and steadfast purpose to keep and preserve the same from all intruders Mr Stearns, being preeminently a man of peace, hitched his team to his wagon and went south, making a claim in Otisco

But now our friend Kerr found himself in more of a dilemma than when Mr Stearns camped there. Uncle Fisk made up his mind that, instead of holding that claim for Col Ide, he would hold it for himself, and that nothing short of $1,000 00 would induce him to surrender his rights to it However, Fisk continued to live on his school section, and Mr Kerr was not long in finding a man to jump the old man's claim. Mr. Tarrant Putnam happened along just at that time and Mr Kerr laid before him the burden on his mind Putnam soon agreed to take the claim and pre-empt it, and then let Col Ide have it in exchange for another claim nearby, which the colonel was to pre-empt Putnam commenced improvements at once by building a shanty and doing a small amount of breaking As soon as Uncle Fisk heard of Putnam's intrusion, he came over and ordered him off, but the latter was armed and equipped for claim holding, and the old gentleman never returned with his old shotgun, as he threatened to do Mr. Putnam afterwards became prominent as register of deeds for several years, and is, at this writing, a resident of California, while Mr. T. J Kerr and family reside in Waseca

A. J Woodbury and sons built the first hotel in Wilton, the first in the county in fact,—during the winter of 1856-7. It stands there at the present writing, a decaying monument of pioneer enterprise.

During the same winter Messrs Paige and Baker opened a small stock of general merchandise Thomas L Paige was the first clerk of court in this county. He returned East in 1858, as did his partner, Nathan Duane Baker.

McLaurin, who afterwards became somewhat romantically the husband of Miss Ottie Ide, opened a grocery and liquor store the same winter

Hon P C Bailey and H P West, co-partners as Bailey & West, opened the first hardware store in the county, at Wilton, early in 1857

All through the winter of 1856-7, which was tediously cold, stores, shops, residences, and barns were erected, so that in early spring Wilton was a thriving village It soon became the county seat and was the leading village of the county until the building of the Winona & St Peter railroad and the location of the present city of Waseca It then died out as rapidly as it well could, and to-day a stranger would never mistrust, upon visiting the spot, that it was, for a long time, a busy, thriving center of trade for a large extent of country It died on account of a railroad too near and yet too far away

ST MARY

The next spring (1857) St Mary began to expand The plat was laid off in February by Chamberlain, Bailey & Co W. H. Chamberlain had settled there the season before and made arrangements for building and booming the town The following statements are taken from an interview with Mr. G R Buckman of Waseca.

Mr Buckman came to Waseca county from Winona in January,

1857 He arrived at Owatonna about noon, and fell in with George Tremper, who was coming to Wilton with a team They left Owatonna about 2 o'clock p m, and met a regular blizzard before they had proceeded five miles They did not reach Wilton until 9 o'clock in the evening, and Wilton then contained but one "stopping place," kept by Uncle Dave Jenkins The next day Mr Buckman arrived at St Mary, an embryo village just springing into life A Mr Crossman kept a boarding house He died the next April This was the first death in the settlement The village proprietors then residing there were W H. Chamberlain and wife, H B Morrison and wife, John Bailey and Harvey Bailey and wife There were also the original settlers, John White, with his family, and a Mr Clark and wife There was also a character of local note, named McCarthy, who kept a saloon He was his own customer nearly all the time, and frequently "painted the town red," sometimes exposing his person in the most obscene manner He became so objectionable that a little pioneer justice seemed necessary for his instruction. About twenty-five men gathered at McCarthy's shanty, with James Plummer as leader, and after considerable search found two barrels of whisky stowed in a hole under the floor, they emptied out the whisky The next day, armed with a warrant, Sheriff Garland "surrounded" twenty-five of the citizens and marched them to Wilton. That was really the first whisky war in Waseca county It was an amusing sight to see twenty-five sober, quiet, industrious, honorable American citizens put into the criminal dock at the instigation of a bloated, blear-eyed, drunken, obscene vender of rot-gut whisky! Nevertheless they had violated the laws of their country—they had destroyed this man's property unlawfully, and they must take the consequences However, the case was adjourned from time to time, and finally they were all discharged, through the legal efforts of Ike Price, then a resident of Wilton, and the boys got off by paying seventy-five cents each Poor McCarthy afterwards, as a result of his drinking habits, froze his feet severely and was crippled for life At last accounts he was an object of pity and commiseration.

The winter of 1857-8 was one of much social enjoyment in St. Mary The citizens organized a large literary society, held some rousing debates, and read a paper each week entitled the "St

Mary Literary Union," edited by G R Buckman B M Morrill wrote the "machine poetry;" J W Johnson was the Wilton correspondent, John A Wheeler and Mr. Hale, both since deceased, were the principal contributors. The people from all the surrounding country came in to attend the meetings of the society, Its meetings were continued the next winter.

W H Chamberlain built the first frame dwelling house in St Mary. It may be interesting to know that the same house is now a part of Waseca It stands on the corner of Lake avenue and Fifth street and is still in a state of good preservation

The St Mary town proprietors built a steam saw mill in the spring of 1857, which was of great benefit to the early settlers of the vicinity Hon Warren Smith deceased, Capt Geo T. White, who afterwards lost his life in the War of the Rebellion, and many others settled in St. Mary in the spring of 1857, making it an active, busy village St Mary was a lively competitor for the county seat in June, 1857, and reached its largest proportions that season It remained a business center of considerable importance up to the time of the breaking out of the Rebellion in 1861 Its best blood then enlisted in the army, and its business men, one after another, deserted it The saw mill, flouring mill, and shingle factory, while great blessings to the surrounding country did not bring large dividends to their owners When the war broke out they were soon deserted and removed to other places The Catholic church, at St Mary, was one of the first church buildings erected in the county The church society there is no doubt one of the oldest in the county, that in the Remund neighborhood, Blooming Grove, being its only rival in age

CHAPTER XXI, 1857.

FIRST COUNTY OFFICERS—VOTING PRECINCTS ORGANIZED—COUNTY SEAT CONTEST—WILTON, ST MARY AND EMPIRE STRIVE FOR THE COUNTY SEAT—FIRST DISTRICT COURT SESSION—MURDER OF HAGADORN AT EMPIRE—THE FIRST JURORS OF THE COUNTY—THREE INDICTMENTS FOUND—COUNTY FINANCES—INTEREST PAID BY COUNTY 72 PER CENT—COUNTY COMMISSIONERS GAVE PERSONAL NOTES

ORGANIZATION OF COUNTY—COUNTY SEAT, ETC

To the inhabitants of Waseca county in 1857, if not to the present generation, the public developments of the year were very exciting The reader must remember that, up to the beginning of 1857, there was not even a post office in Waseca county, and that the most rapid means of communication was the saddle horse The fact of the organization of the county by legislative enactment was not generally known until two or three weeks after the act had passed and become a law The bill creating the county of Waseca was passed by the territorial legislature, in 1857, and was certified to by John W Furber, speaker of the house, John B Brisbin, president of the senate, and signed and approved by Willis A Gorman, governor, February 27, 1857 That act provided that on the first Monday of June following, the legal voters of said county should hold an especial election in their (to be) established precincts, for the purpose of locating a county seat, and for the proper election of county officers Until that time, and for the purposes of carrying into effect the provisions of the law and setting in motion the machinery of county government, Governor Gorman appointed the following temporary county commissioners to establish election precincts, appoint judges of election, and name such other officers as were provided for by law, viz: John C Ide, John M Bliven and Henry W Peck The governor also appointed Nathaniel Garland, sheriff, and Tarrant Putnam, register of deeds. These were the first officers of the county and they promptly qualified. They were to hold these positions until their successors should be elected and qualified. And thus was the county brought forth. The first meeting of the county commissioners was held at Wilton, on the 16th of March, 1857 Col. John C. Ide was chosen chairman and the board proceeded to business, the register of deeds being ex-officio clerk of the board.

The bond of the register of deeds and also of the sheriff were presented, approved and filed A temporary seal, consisting of a round piece of yellow paper, with the name of the county printed thereon, was adopted. W S Baker of Otisco, who died in Waseca several years ago, was appointed treasurer of the county, and entered upon the duties of his office The labor of the office was not burdensome at that time, as there was not a cent in the treasury At this meeting, the commissioners formed election precincts and appointed the necessary clerks and judges of election.

The first precinct was called Swavesey and contained all of the town of Blooming Grove and the north half of the town of Woodville The election was to be held at the house of Ole Knutsen, and Lewis McKune, Patrick Healy, and Ole Kuntsen were appointed judges to conduct the same. W H Young and Lewis McKune were appointed justices, and Clark Wood and S F. Wyman, constables of that precinct

The next precinct was called Empire, and embraced what is now Iosco and Janesville and the north half of St Mary The election was to be held at the house of John H. Wheeler, in Empire, and N E. Strong, C R. Miller and James Hanes were appointed to serve as judges of election M S Green was appointed justice of the peace and George L Leonard constable for the Empire precinct

The Wilton precinct was composed of the southern halves of St Mary and Woodville and the north two-thirds of both Otisco and Wilton The election was to be held at the hotel of A J Woodbury in Wilton, with Jesse I Stewart, W. H. Chamberlain, and E A Rice as judges of election Geo. W Tremper was appointed constable for the Wilton precinct.

The fourth precinct was called Otisco and consisted of Vivian, Byron, New Richland and the south one-third of the towns of Otisco and Wilton. The election was appointed to be held at the house of Silas Grover, near the southeast corner of the township of Wilton, and E B Stearns, Calvin Chapman and Daniel Grover were chosen to act as judges

At the same meeting the following officers were appointed · for coroner, James Hanes, surveyor, H W. Peck, assessors, N N Norcutt, James E. Child, and E B Stearns Mr Peck resigned as county commissioner to accept the surveyorship and David Smith, of Empire, was appointed to fill the vacancy

A second meeting of the county commissioners was held April 6th, 1857, at which John Bradish, Esq., of Empire, was appointed county attorney, and Henry Thwing, of Empire, and John G. Greening of (Otisco) Wilton precinct, constables Ben. G. Northup and Silas Grover were chosen judges of election in Otisco, in place of Dan Grover and Calvin Chapman, who declined to serve.

A third meeting of the county board was held on the 4th of May, 1857, at which a fifth precinct was carved out of Empire and called Elysian It embraced all the territory in the township of Janesville west of Lake Elysian J C. York, C M. Barnard and Abram Jaqua were appointed judges of the election which was to be held at the house of E H Loomis in said precinct J M. Stoddard was appointed justice of the peace and Abram Jaqua constable for the new precinct.

The commissioners at this meeting also made the following appointments for the precinct of Swavesey: Asa Conner, justice of the peace, and S F Wyman, constable.

These meetings and proceedings were held preparatory to the then great coming struggle for the permanent location of the county seat.

Wilton, St. Mary, Empire—these three—entered the political arena and each strove with all its strength for the ascendency, Although county officers were to be elected, the all-absorbing question was, "How do you stand on the county seat?"

Had the fate of the nation depended upon the result of the

election, there could not have been more intense feeling or excitement than was manifested in these embryo "cities." At first, the St Mary men attempted to work the "boys of '55" against Wilton on account of the claim-jumping troubles, but the "boys of '55" were not disposed to cut off their noses to spite some one else, and voted to suit themselves The contest waxed hot and fierce Strange faces in large numbers mysteriously appeared a few days before election Men from Faribault, Owatonna and other parts of the Territory suddenly became permanent residents of the county Empire St Mary and Wilton grew to large proportions some ten days before the election Their streets without sidewalks literally swarmed with black coats, satin vests and plug hats Promises on the part of town-site speculators were as plentiful as house flies in the month of August There was hurrying to and fro among the speculators in paper cities and corner lots Gray haired usurers and loafing young men played euchre on the prairie green, or lazily lounged upon the corners of imaginary business blocks in these would-be cities. Every artifice of the political party demagogue was resorted to by those interested in the several towns to secure population and win votes

It is said that man soweth, but God giveth the increase In this case there was a very sudden decrease in population immediately after the election The whole number of votes cast was 665 It might have been larger · but was not that a fair-sized election for a farming county of only two years' settlement? At any rate, in 1860, at the presidential election when Mr Lincoln was elected, the county only cast 525 votes—a falling off of over 200 votes in a growing country in three and a half years

Swavesey cast 51 votes for Wilton, 33 for St Mary, and 23 for Empire Elysian cast 29 ballots—23 for Wilton, 4 for St Mary and 2 for Empire Empire cast 11 for Wilton, 49 for St Mary and 100 for Empire Wilton cast 119 for St Mary, 189 for Wilton, and one for Empire The oldest settler has never yet found out who that one lone Empire fellow was He must have had the courage of Ethan Allen Otisco cast 58 votes for Wilton and 2 for St Mary Wilton therefore received 332 votes, St. Mary 207, and Empire 126, making Wilton the county seat

This election, intensely exciting as it was, and presenting as it did the worst phases of our popular form of government, simply showed how deeply rooted in the American mind was the essential and all-important doctrine that the majority must rule and the minority must acquiesce Within three months after that heated contest, the opposing forces met in party convention, and a stranger would not have mistrusted that the men of St Mary, of Empire and of Wilton had ever disagreed on any subject

At that special election E B Stearns of Otisco, L C. Wood of Swavesey (now Woodville), and David Smith of Empire (now Iosco), were elected county commissioners. They held their first session July 6th, 1857. As near as I have been able to learn, the following were the other newly-elected officers to hold until the next general election J W Crawford of Elysian, register of deeds, Nathaniel Garland, of Wilton, sheriff· H W Peck, of Empire, county surveyor, W S. Baker, of Otisco, treasurer, and M S Green, of Empire, county attorney At this meeting of the commissioners, which was the fifth session, David Smith was elected chairman The bonds of the officers-elect were filed and approved by the board Road petitions were presented by Charles L Lowell, Alonzo Heath, J A Canfield, and John S McKune The petitions were signed by other citizens and were acted upon by the board * * *

Notwithstanding our Territorial condition, the great anti-slavery agitation of the day divided the people into distinct political parties Every man was expected to stand to and vote his principles regardless of consequences There was a conscientious courage in those days regarding public questions which amounted to heroism And thus it was that, in the fall of 1857, local jealousies were put to rest, and national politics divided the voters Even at the very time of our county-seat election, the Republicans of the legislative district elected Hon Amos Coggswell, of Steele county, Captain Lewis McKune, of this county, and E Page Davis, of Nicollet county, members of the constitutional convention that framed our present constitution, which was adopted October 13th, 1857.

The contest for county officials that fall was based almost entirely upon national politics, for the voters of the county, at that time, were largely strangers to each other Hon. Lewis McKune, for state senator, headed the local ticket and was elected. Of the county ticket, the Republicans elected E B Stearns, L C Wood, and John Bailey, county commissioners, N Garland, sheriff; A. E. Smith, surveyor, J. I. Stewart, treasurer, James E Child, county attorney, Job A Canfield, probate judge, and W S Baker, assessor. The Democrats elected E A. Rice, register of deeds, and H P Norton, clerk of the court. The vote between the two parties in this county, at that time, was nearly equal, and the personal popularity of the two successful Democrats carried them in.

CHAPTER XXII, 1858.

THE FIRST MURDER

This first general election, October 13, 1857, was the occasion of the first, as well as of the most unprovoked, murder ever committed in this county. Jacob Hagadorn and family and Peter Farrell and family lived neighbors to one another in the town of Iosco, near the village of Empire, where the fall election was held. So far as known, at least, these men were not only neighbors, but friendly toward each other They both attended the election at Empire, and the testimony showed that Hagadorn did not drink much, but that Farrell was crazy drunk The testimony taken before the grand jury the next day or two after the murder showed that there were two rival hotels, or public houses, in the village, and that each kept a bar well stocked with whisky. Whisky was cheap in those good old days, 25 cents a gallon—too cheap to be drugged—and yet men got drunk in those days the same as they do nowadays, and stabbed each other to the heart without any other cause than that they were intoxicated It was at the time charged that one of the hotel men had plied Farrell and one or two others with liquor, during the afternoon, with the intention of getting up a drunken affray in the evening in which the other hotel man was to have been killed by accident. Whether there was any foundation for that theory or not, the fact was that a quarrel took place, and during the row Farrell killed Hagadorn with a large knife

Hon Charles E Flandreau, then associate justice of the Territorial supreme court, was then holding the first term of the district court for this county, and the grand jury, then in session, found indictments against Peter Farrell, as principal, and John H Wheeler and Richard Toner, as accessories Farrell was arrested and taken to Stillwater to be held for trial, but soon after made his escape and has never been brought to trial It is said by some that he and his family are residents of Chicago, living under an assumed name

After the excitement was over and the facts and circumstances were more coolly considered, it was generally admitted that there was no evidence upon which to convict Wheeler or Toner, and after some two years they were discharged

There can be no doubt that that sad and bloody tragedy was the unpremeditated result of insane drunkenness on the part of Farrell and others that were equally drunk

Farrell, with great frankness apparent sincerity, and unaffected sorrow declared that he had no cause for killing Hagadorn, that he never intended to injure him, and that he had not the faintest recollection of committing the crime with which he was charged and which he did actually commit in the presence of many eye-witnesses.

This murder was a sad lesson for Waseca county in more ways than one It kept the district court in session several days, piled up large bills for witnesses, jurors and officers at a time when our people were poor and out of money and when there was not a cent in the county treasury. These bills had to be met with borrowed money bearing interest at a rate of from sixty to seventy-two per cent per annum. It was a long time before the tax-payers had paid off the last of the expenses of that drunk

CHAPTER XXIII.

FIRST DISTRICT COURT

As hereinbefore intimated, the first term of the district court for this county was held at Wilton, commencing October 12, 1857 On the day that court opened, Hon Charles E Flandreau, then a young lawyer of St Peter, not long since deceased, presided The grand jury was impaneled, sworn, and charged in the afternoon, and the court then adjourned until Wednesday morning, the 14th, to give the jurors the privilege of voting on the 13th When the court convened on the morning of the 14th, the sad news of the murder of Hagadorn at Empire on the 13th, had reached Wilton, and the grand jury at once commenced an investigation of the matter which lasted several days. There was little or no other business to be transacted in court, and the judge adjourned from day to day until the grand jury finished its work At this term of court, John Bradish, Esq, was duly admitted to practice law in the courts of the Territory, he being the first resident lawyer of the county admitted to the bar He is, at the present writing, a resident of Janesville, engaged in the real estate and insurance business

COUNTY FINANCES

The financial crash of 1857 had paralyzed the whole country. The state banking system (another name for robbery) had collapsed everywhere throughout the land, and the only persons that were in luck were those who had gold or silver coin Such persons were very few in number Not only were the masses of the people destitute of money, but all departments of government were without funds to pay ordinary expenses Waseca county was especially unfortunate at that time It had not only no money but no credit worth mentioning, as was shown by the records made at that time; and yet it had on hand an expensive murder case growing out of the liquor traffic. This case had to be carried forward at public expense. Hence we find the following entry in the records of the ninth meeting of the board of county commissioners, which was held immediately after the adjournment of the first term of the district court

"At a special meeting, held October 20th, 1857, the board borrowed of Byron Clark the sum of $100 for which a joint note, signed by E B Stearns and L C Wood, was given, payable one year from date thereof, with interest at the rate of six per cent. per month "

But that was only a drop in the bucket. The debts of the county already aggregated more than $1,200, and men were clamorous for their pay. When money was bringing from sixty to seventy-two per cent per annum, every man wanted his money to use, and so another special meeting of the county board was held November 11th, 1857, to devise ways and means to meet the pressing demands of creditors At this meeting George Snyder, living near our county line, in Freeborn county, condescended to loan $200 of his good, hard gold to the county upon a promissory note duly executed and signed by E. B Stearns and L C Wood, who were county commissioners at the time This note bore interest at the rate of five per cent per month—sixty per centum per annum—and was due and payable fifteen months after date. The record also shows the following peculiar transaction: "The treasurer, being absent, the funds in the hands of the commissioners were appropriated by them to pay the most urgent bills against the county " The bills paid were as follows L C. Lowell, $5, E A Rice, $51 85, N Garland, $120 70, J. W Crawford, $29.

From the financial statement made at the close of the year 1857, by Messrs E B. Stearns, L C Wood and John Bailey, county commissioners, we learn that the outstanding indebtedness of the county was $1 258 52 while the assets, if there were any, received no mention

CHAPTER XXIV.

SEVERE HARDSHIPS—DESTRUCTIVE FLOODS—TOWNSHIPS ORGANIZED—ADOPTION OF SUPERVISOR SYSTEM INSTEAD OF COUNTY COMMISSIONERS—COUNTY BONDS ISSUED—BRIDGE APPROPRIATIONS—JURY LISTS—OFFICIAL PROCEEDINGS.

The few that had opened farms so as to plant seeds in the spring of 1857 received bountiful crops in return, with the exception of oats, which lodged, owing to heavy growth of straw Very little wheat was cultivated then, and most of that was of the "club" variety, which never succeeded well here The year 1858 opened with a heavy cloud in the financial sky, and with a general feeling of depression everywhere

The new board of county commissioners, Messrs E B Stearns, L C Wood, and John Bailey, met for the first time January 4th, 1858, and organized by the election of Mr E B Stearns as chairman It was indeed fortunate for the county that at that critical period in our history we had three so honest and capable men at the head of affairs No one was allowed to rob the public, for every bill presented to the board was closely scrutinized and investigated

At the meeting of the county commissioners April 5, 1858, the first separate township organizations were instituted What is now Janesville was then named Okaman and given two polling places; one at the house of A Tuttle, near the north end of Lake Elysian, and the other near the south end of the lake, at the house of Caesar De Regan. Alex Johnston, W N Buckout, and C H Bishop, all since deceased, were appointed judges of election

Iosco then received its name as an organized township, and H

W Peck, Geo L Leonard, and David Smith were appointed judges of the election, which was to be held at the house of Daniel Tripp

Township 108, range 22, was set off and named Blooming Grove, with James Isaac, Patrick Healy, and J M Bliven as judges of the next election, which was appointed at the residence of Patrick Healy

Woodville was the name given to township 107 range 22, and Eri G Wood, J K Meyers and William M Green were chosen judges of the first election which was to be held at the house of E G Wood

St Mary was the name applied to township 107, range 23, the tavern of J W Clark was designated as polling place, and B M Morrill, Warren Smith, and H W Chamberlain were named to serve as judges of election

Township 106, range 23 retained the name of Wilton, the election was appointed at the tavern of A J Woodbury, and I C Price, L Curtis, and J C Ide were appointed as judges

Township 106, range 22 was designated as Otisco election at the house of Owen Salisbury, and H G Mosher, S S Griggs and Owen Salisbury were chosen to serve as judges

Township 105 range 24, was named Vivian, and that township, together with the west half of what is now Byron, was made an election precinct The first election was appointed at the residence of J B Hill, and that gentleman, with S L Daggett and E Woodruff, constituted the board of election judges

At the next meeting of the county board, May 17th, on presentation of a petition therefor, the name of township 108, range 24 was changed from Okaman to Janesville; and now the name of that once busy and beautiful little hamlet of Okaman, at the head of Lake Elysian, remains only in history

The first state legislature after the adoption of our present constitution, substituted the supervisor system of county government for the commissioner system, and the first meeting of the new board was held at Wilton, September 14th, 1858 The members of the new board were E B Stearns, Col W W Robinson, N E Strong, C W Johnston, J W Davis, Philo Woodruff, Obadiah Powell, and J B Hill At this meeting E B Stearns was chosen to preside as chairman of the board for the ensuing year and E A Rice was chosen as clerk of the board. At this session, the matter of ways and means agitated the minds of the local statesmen of the county in no small degree. The last legislature having authorized the borrowing of money by the county, it was ordered after much deliberation "that the county issue its bonds for $3,000, to be made payable March 1, 1862, and to draw interest at the rate of fifteen per cent per annum, payable annually." The bonds were to be issued in denominations of $50 and $100, with a proviso that they should not be sold for less than ninety cents on the dollar

The bonds were to be printed and to be signed by the chairman of the board, and countersigned by the clerk of the board, with the seal of the county attached W W Robinson, afterwards colonel, and E. A Rice afterwards major, were appointed a committee to get the bonds printed and also to negotiate them Afterwards, at the same meeting, the amount of bonds was increased to $3,500 Messrs. Robinson and Rice were required to give a bond of $5,000 each for the proper performance of their duties in the negotiation of the bonds.

At a meeting of the county board, December 20th, 1858, the order passed at the September meeting of the board, regarding the bonds, was so modified that they should be issued in five, ten, twenty, fifty, and one hundred dollar denominations—that two thousand dollars be issued in $50 and $100 denominations, and that the remainder of said amount, $1,500, be issued in equal amounts of five, ten, and twenty dollar denominations These bonds were made payable in 1862, with interest at 15 per cent per annum, payable annually

At the meeting of the board of supervisors, November 1st, 1858, township number 105, range 22, was organized into a town and named Norway The name was shortly after changed to New Richland. Township number 105, range 23, was at this meeting organized and named Byron There is some difference among old settlers as to how this township came by its name. J. B Hill, Esq., one of the first settlers in Vivian, and at the time of that meeting a member of the county board, claims that the town was named in honer of Byron F. Clark, then a resident of Wilton; while it is claimed by Roscoe Philbrook that the town was named for his brother Byron, who now lives in California. It is of no great importance at best, for even if it were named after Lord Byron or Lady Byron it would be just as poetical as it is now. It is getting to be a very beautiful township, and its name is all right, even if Byron F Clark did loan money at that time at six per cent a month—and to Waseca county at that

At the same meeting of the board there was considerable discussion in regard to building a county jail. E. B. Stearns, W. W Robinson, and Philo Woodruff were appointed to select a site for it and also to let the contract for its construction, provided the board could issue bonds to pay for the building. E. A. Rice, clerk of the board, was instructed to get the opinion of the attorney general as to whether the board could issue bonds to build a jail without first submitting the proposition to the people It appears subsequently that there was no legal objection to issuing the bonds and building the jail, as will more fully appear hereafter.

Among the important official acts of this year were the following appropriations for bridges, namely.

For the upper Wilton bridge, over the Le Sueur river, on the Owatonna road, $400 00, for the construction of a bridge over the Le Sueur river, at the village of Otisco, $200 00, for materials and mechanical labor in constructing a bridge over the outlet to Lake Elysian, in the town of Janesville, on the Medford and Mankato road, $200 00, for the construction of three bridges in the town of Vivian, on the St Mary and Vivian road, $100 00; for the construction of a bridge over the inlet to Lake Elysian, town of Iosco, on the Medford and Mankato road, $100 00 These appropriations were made upon condition that the towns in which these bridges were to be built should see that the bridges were completed on or before January 1st, 1859 At the same time one hundred dollars was appropriated toward the construction of a bridge over the Le Sueur river on the Wilton and St. Mary town line road, to be paid in county bonds The county paid all its debts in bonds or orders in those days, for which the needy holder could get seventy-five cents on the dollar in store pay

HARD TIMES.

The year 1858, in more ways than one, was the most disastrous that has ever been experienced since the settlement of the county It will long be remembered by all who then inhabited this section Nearly or quite one-half of the people of the county had settled upon the bottom lands along the Le Sueur river Many of the farmers had no crops except upon these lands adjoining the river. During the early part of the season, the crops grew magnificently, and promised an abundant harvest, but in the latter part of July heavy and oft-repeated storms swept with fury over the whole country. During the first week in August, it seemed as though the windows of heaven were again opened as in the days of Noah. Storm succeeded storm until the whole country was inundated The waters of the rivers and streams were increased to such an extent that all their banks were overflowed. The bottom lands looked like great inland seas Trees were washed out by the roots. Fences were torn down and carried away Hay and grain stacks were raised bodily, torn in pieces by the raging, whirling floods and carried down stream Wheat, oat, potato, corn and garden crops were destroyed in a day

Whole families stood by in helpless astonishment, despair depicted in every feature, and watched the relentless destruction of their only means of subsistence for the coming year. It was indeed a sad time with our people Most of the settlers had spent their generally very limited means in purchasing their lands and improving them, and were entirely dependent upon their growing crops for a supply of food. All the crops on the bottom lands, nearly or quite one-half of the whole in the county, were almost a total loss, while those on the higher lands were also injured

Many settlers gave up in despair and, with what they had remaining, pulled up and left the country for good A general depression like a dark shadow rested upon the whole country, and the succeeding year was really a season of hard times. A whole chapter of incidents might be written of the losses sustained by that flood, and the only thing that could really be said in its favor was that it drowned most of the striped, gray, and pocket gophers that it caught upon the bottom lands For several years afterwards the bottom lands were free from these pests.

This county has never since seen as much deprivation, according to the number of people, as that which our people suffered in consequence of the flood of 1858. Such experience as that tried the souls of both men and women, and those who lived here at that time seldom complain very much of more recent hard times

The real suffering consequent upon the loss of the crops of 1858 came in 1859, of which more anon.

I have never been able to get a full list of the first grand and petit jurors for the fall term of court held in October, 1857, but the following were certainly present at that term, and drew pay, viz W W. Robinson, J B Jackson, James E Child, Robert McFate, A. J Woodbury, S W Long, H G. Mosher, S J Willis, P H Thomas, John Bailey, Caleb Northup, James Chadwick, P. H Young, Buel Welsh, Joseph Clayton, M V. B Morse, E G. Wood, John Forrest, H P. Norton, Francis Green, John Jenkins, Philo Woodruff, Geo. H Bishop, S F. Wyman, E K Carlton, J. K Myers, Z Holbrook, S W Franklin, Noah Lincoln, H P. Chamberlain, and James Roberts

The first complete lists of jurors on record were made by the county board at the November session of 1858 They were composed as follows:

GRAND JURORS

H G Mosher Geo W. Watkins W W Robinson, J B Hill, W M Green, G W Turner, J K. Myers, B. F Haynes Montraville Sias, L C Wood, L S Daggett W H. Young, T R. Chapman, J S Rice, J D Andrews O Powell, James E Child, B G. Northup, B. M Morrill, S W Franklin, J W Clark, W H Wyman, N P Fitzgerald, John C Ide, Geo P Johnson, G W. Ayers, S L Haines, John Bailey C N Hale, Lewis McLelland, George T White (afterwards Capt White), J. J Stewart, David Smith, Lewis McKune, N E Strong, Elias Conner, H D Baldwin, John Bradish, Elias Goodrich, James Isaacs, William Rockwell, Patrick Healy John S McKune, M. S Green, J. C York, A V. Osdale George L. Leonard, W N Buckhout, L. B Osgood, John R Wood

PETIT JURORS

Isaac Hamlin, D J Jenkins, A J Woodbury, David Whipple, Caleb Northup, A Shaffer, E. S Woodruff, Moses Camp, E. G. Wood, Charles Graves, L S Wood, John Sias, John Forrest, Geo Clark, E K Carlton, A S Nelson, Jacob Oorey, John West, Andrew Lynch, John Eldredge, Dow Locke, C Morrill, Duey

McKinster, Peter Lindsay, O Salisbury, C. O. Norton, B F. Clark, James Barrie, J R West, Robert Lanning, Stephen Bailey, Gould Grover, F. A Glover, T J. Kerr, O K. Woodward, Francis Libbey, Thomas Northup, Alvin Wilson, S. S Goodrich, John Pratt, William Byron, Richard Ayares, L. P. Stowell, R H Lowell, J A Wheeler, S S Griggs, William Putnam, Samuel Gleason, C F Cooper, C E Williamson, Richard Dreever, Michael McKenney, Sigur Johnson, J M. Bliven, J. V Hallock, Jeremiah Sullivan, John Cunningham, S T. Isaacs, James Babcock, John McCue, Thomas Cahill, John Wheeler, Ole Knutson, John Douglas, Simeon Smith, A J. Walton, Danel Riegles, James Chadwick, Joseph Churchill, H J Allen, I C. McArthur, J W La Paul.

It is suggested that the jury lists of to-day are not very much better than this list of 1858.

CHAPTER XXV, 1859.

STARVATION PRICES IN 1859—SKETCH BY HON WILLIAM BRISBANE—CASES OF POISONING

The year 1859 opened gloomy enough for the people of Waseca county, as a rule Of course there were exceptions. A few men were fortunate enough to have saved a good crop of corn in 1858, and before the next spring good corn sold at $1 a bushel. A very few men had a little money, and those few gathered in cattle and horses at very low prices, or loaned their money at from forty to seventy-two per cent per annum As is invariably the rule when financial disaster sweeps over the country, the rich became richer and the poor poorer The losses of 1858 made the winter of 1858-9 one of anxiety, and to many a winter of distress Every family had to exercise the greatest economy Many farmers lived for weeks and months upon corn bread, milk, and butter Some lived during the spring months on wild roots, fish, and wild fowls All suffered more or less from deprivations of one kind or another

The haying season of 1858 had been so rainy that there was a scarcity of hay with many and during the early spring time some cattle died of starvation, while the entire lack of grain made both horses and horned cattle look like the lean kine in Joseph's vision.

Hon William Brisbane, who settled in this county in the spring of 1859, though in comfortable circumstances himself, saw the hardships of the earlier settlers, and contributed the following to the "Album" history of the county in 1887

"Speaking of graham bread," said he, "I can assure you that twenty-eight years ago (1859) a loaf of graham bread or a corn dodger, with a very thin sprinkling of molasses, would have been thankfully received and no questions asked. Those were the days that tried men's stomachs as well as their souls, but we lived and hoped for better days, for we had faith in the natural resources of Waseca county Thanks to those resources and the industrious energies of the people, our expectations have been fully realized. As the good book says 'The rain is over and gone, and the time of the singing of birds has come' Yet I never saw nor knew of a tragedy acted but there was always some comical or ludicrous scenes interlarded with it * * * The following is said to be a fact, although it smacks of the improbable A family out in the 'Big Woods' beyond Janesville were sorely pressed, for gaunt Famine was wagging his bony finger in their faces Almost in despair they went into the woods and tried to find some roots, whereby they might satisfy the cravings of hunger They were successful in unearthing the sought-for roots, but were afraid that they might be poisonous Something must be done, they would try an experiment As luck would have it, there was a crazy sort of fellow in the family, so they thought they would try it on him It he should die it would be no great loss, and if he lived why couldn't they? You see they were excellent logicians. Well, the crazy fellow lived, but you can bet that he never fared so well again as he did on the day the life or death experiment was tried on him"

Several persons died that spring from eating poisonous herbs and roots Mr S A Farrington furnishes the following statement

"A sad affliction befell Mr Quiggle's family in the spring of 1859. The children went out to gather cowslips. Two of the girls ate what they supposed to be that herb Both were soon taken very sick One of them, who ate more than the other, vomited and afterwards recovered The other died in a short time in great agony. What they supposed to be cowslip, the doctors called vegetable dog button, a poisonous herb resembling the cowslip. The deceased, who was twelve years old, was buried in a homemade coffin, as there were no undertakers in this section of country at that time"

CHAPTER XXVI, 1859.

NEW BOARD OF SUPERVISORS—COUNTY BONDS ISSUED AT NINETY CENTS ON THE DOLLAR—HIGH RATES OF INTEREST—JESSE I STEWART AND GEO T WHITE REPRESENTATIVES—ABUNDANT CROPS—HAULING WHEAT TO HASTINGS

The last meeting of the county board of supervisors elected in 1858 was held at Wilton. E B. Stearns and E A. Rice were appointed a committee to rent rooms for the use of the county officers for the ensuing year

The board of supervisors elected in the spring of 1859, met for the first time May 24th The following gentlemen constituted the board, viz Philo Woodruff, of Blooming Grove, James Barrie, of St Mary, Obadiah Powell, of Woodville, G W Ayares, of Byron, J W La Paul, of Janesville, John Thompson, of New Richland, H G Mosher, of Otisco, M S. Gove of Wilton, H. D. Baldwin, of Iosco, Ichabod West, of Vivian The Democrats being in the majority, elected Dr M S Gove chairman for the ensuing year He made an able and efficient officer

Messrs H G. Mosher, Philo Woodruff, and James Barrie were appointed a committee on accounts, to whom all bills were referred The first abatement and refunding of taxes occurred at this meeting William Cuddigan (Sn) being unfortunate enough to have suffered from a double assessment, the state tax was ordered to be refunded to him in cash and the other tax in county orders

This session did a good deal of routine business, but nothing of great importance was accomplished

The next, or annual, meeting of the board was held September

13th, 1859, at Wilton The first business transacted was the passage of an order instructing the proper officers to turn over to George C Snyder, at ninety cents on the dollar, enough county bonds, bearing fifteen per cent interest, to pay the two notes held by said Snyder, including the interest thereon at five per cent per month from date of notes until payment in said bonds The bill of Culver, Page & Hoyne, amounting to $487, for books and stationery, was also ordered paid in county bonds at ninety cents on the dollar, with interest thereon at fifteen per cent per annum.

Here are examples of the utter nonsense put forth by money loaners that where there is no law regulating interest, it will be regulated by the security offered Here was a case where the security was most ample, and yet the money loaners wanted to obtain our county bonds at ninety cents on the dollar,—the bonds bearing fifteen per cent interest on their full face

At the meeting of the board October 27, 1859, Dr M S Gove, H G Mosher, and J W La Paul were appointed a committee to purchase the store building of Thomas L. Paige for a court house The building was bought—Mr Paige receiving therefor tax-sale certificates to the face value of $700 This structure served the county as a court house until it was destroyed by fire April 3, 1869, a period of nearly ten years For the $700 in tax certificates, the county saved rent for ten years and then received $600 insurance money for the ashes That $700 was well invested

At the fall election of 1859, the Republicans elected their entire ticket Capt Geo T White and J I Stewart were elected to the lower house of the legislature, S J Willis was elected auditor; J I Stewart, treasurer, David L. Whipple, sheriff, J A Canfield, judge of probate. Hon H. D Baldwin, county attorney J. I Stewart having been elected to the legislature, J S Rice, then of New Richland, was appointed to and accepted the office of county treasurer, which he held for two years

One of the amusing incidents placed on record is the report of Dr M S Gove, who was appointed to "examine the treasurer's account of orders redeemed" His report is recorded as follows:

"To the Honorable Board of Supervisors, Waseca county: Your committee, appointed to examine the treasurer's account of orders redeemed, having performed said duty, beg leave to report Treasurer's register of orders redeemed, to-wit $3,672 52.

The orders redeemed amount to $3,672 80, leaving a default unaccounted for 18 cents.

"(Signed) M. S GOVE, Committee."

Evidently the clerk of the board made a mistake in recording the report or else the good doctor made a default in his own figures amounting to ten cents.

The writer has never been able to find any record showing that this default was ever made good by the defaulting treasurer

For some unexplained reason, no financial statement showing the exact financial standing of the county for the years 1858 and 1859 appears in the records of the county for those years It was about 1859 that people clamored for a change in the court house officials on account of supposed irregularities But if there were any such irregularities in fact, they were never brought to light, and probably did not exist

The most important of all the affairs of 1859 was the abundant harvest of that year It was really our first great wheat year in this county—that being the first general introduction of the Scotch Fife wheat in this section The average yield that year was about twenty bushels per acre, although several fields yielded as high as thirty bushels per acre of the very best quality of wheat A large proportion of that crop weighed sixty-two pounds to the bushel What was true of wheat was true of almost every other crop, although corn was considered a little below the average There were such magnificent crops of all kinds that every resident took hold of the work before him with renewed energy

Of course prices were prostrated Just as the gold syndicate and the trusts and combines, aided by the liquor traffic, in 1892, captured both parties and made cowards of the third, just as the giant monopolies of to-day sway legislatures, influence courts and corrupt the ballot box, even so had the deluded voters in 1859 been hugging the vile harlot of slavery until the political atmosphere was filled with poisonous gases of political corruption The banking system of the politicians of the slaveocratic party was but another name for plundering and robbing the laboring and producing masses The prolonged policy of upholding the great wrong of human bondage had brought upon us, as a nation the inevitable punishment which necessarily follows such wickedness and folly. Strong mechanics were glad to get work then at from seventy-five cents to a dollar a day. Any number of farm hands and common laborers could be hired for fifty cents a day Many suffered for want of even the necessities of life We have not since reached such universal hard times as then prevailed throughout the country although we had fewer tramps then than now

That fall, for the first time, our farmers commenced hauling wheat to Hastings There was no market here, and we were compelled to haul it either to Hastings or some other river town It required a heavy, strong pair of oxen to take through to market forty bushels of wheat at a load, and make the trip from Wilton and return in six days The price of wheat at Hastings averaged about sixty-two cents per bushel Perhaps some of our young farmers can figure out the profits of raising wheat and spending six days on the road in marketing each load of forty bushels! Perhaps, too, some of the young wives of to-day can appreciate the situation of a young, married woman living on the prairie alone, for a week at a time, and being compelled to look after the farm chores, while roving Indians might call at any hour of the day or night! How little do those who have never experienced the labors and vicissitudes of pioneer life know of real hardship!

But the grand crops of 1859 had renewed our courage and inspired our hopes for better times, and every one commenced the year 1860 with the expectation and hope of a "happy new year."

CHAPTER XXVII, 1860.

MILD WINTER—BUILDING OF FIRST JAIL AT WILTON—LIQUOR LICENSES ISSUED—SUPERVISOR SYSTEM ABOLISHED—W T. KITTREDGE, GEO H. BISHOP AND JOHN N POWERS COUNTY COMMISSIONERS,SUCCEEDED BY HAMLIN, HEALY AND LOWELL. —THE OUTLOOK—REBELLION, INDIANS, ETC—ELECTION OF ABRAHAM LINCOLN—LEGISLATIVE ELECTION OF DR. WATSON, WM F PETTIT, JAMES E CHILD—GOOD CROPS—JOHN BROWN RAID—CENSUS BY C O. NORTON—TOTAL POPULATION 2,598

This was not only the most eventful year in the history of this nation, but one of the most eventful in the history of this state. To begin with the winter of 1859-60 was something new in the history of Minnesota The four preceding winters had been of the snow-bound pattern, lined with ice decorated with Pembina frosts and fanned by Manitoba blizzards The four preceding winters had been so uniformly and intensely cold that no one expected anything milder than a 2 40 breeze from Manitoba with the mercury all the way from zero to forty degrees below, in Minnesota. The people of the state were therefore somewhat surprised to have a winter with only one week of sleighing and the thermometer running from zero up to 30 and 40 degrees above I remember the winter very well, for I was interested with my brother, S P Child in furnishing five hundred cords of wood to the St. Mary Mill company We were compelled to haul nearly all of it on wagons

There seemed to be a general feeling that hard times had reached the bottom rung of the financial ladder, and that people must commenee to build anew upon the bed-rock of industry and economy Most of the property of the country had been mortgaged at exorbitant rates of interest and sooner or later fell into the hands of the money loaners who were forced to sell it for what they could get on credit and at a much lower rate of interest The money loaners had killed the geese that had laid the golden eggs, and they were compelled to await the growth of a new brood of goslings before they could again gather in their harvest

As stated in the preceding chapter, a change of county officials was made in the fall of 1859, and about the 1st of January, 1860, S J Willis became county auditor, J S Rice treasurer, and David L Whipple, sheriff On the 11th of January, 1860, the county board of supervisors commenced an important session, and among other matters, decided to build a county jail. As this was the first jail in the county, the proceedings of the board in relation thereto will be of interest The following resolution was adopted by the board

"Resolved by the board of supervisors of the county of Waseca and State of Minnesota, that the sheriff of said county (D L Whipple), be and is hereby empowered, authorized and required to proceed immediately to erect a suitable building for the confinement of criminals or other persons who may be committed or confined therein according to law, and that said building shall be erected immediately in the rear and adjoining to the county building now occupied by the register of deeds, to be built of timber, hewn at least on three sides, (and to be) sixteen by eighteen feet square, one story high, faced on the inside by sheet iron securely nailed to timber That the (said) building shall be in all respects, not herein named, constructed under the immediate supervision and control of said sheriff, in such a manner as he shall think best, in order to accomplish the object sought by this resolution

"And it is hereby ordered that the sum of three hundred dollars be and is hereby appropriated in tax certificates of lands sold and bid off by said county for the taxes for the year 1858, and that said sheriff is hereby authorized to give a receipt for and receive an assignment of said tax certificates equal to one-half the amount herein appropriated when he shall obtain from the commissioners (to be) hereafter elected for the county of Waseca a certificate that one-half of the above amount has been expended by said sheriff in the construction of said building He (the sheriff) is authorized to employ assistance or employ agents to perform the work herein named, in the same manner as he is by this resolution authorized to perform the same, said building to be built in an economical manner, and said sheriff shall not receive tax certificates to a greater amount than what the actual cost of said building amounts to "

"And be it further ordered that the county commissioners hereafter to be elected shall and are hereby appointed a building committee to audit said sheriff's account and authorize the payment of the balance due said sheriff when said building shall have been finished And said commissioners are authorized to accept said building when properly finished in behalf of the said county of Waseca, and make a full settlement with said sheriff for his services, said building not to cost a greater amount than hereinbefore named and as much less an amount as said sheriff can make the cost of the same And said sheriff is hereby authorized to partition off from the first story of the county building in the north end, and contiguous to the contemplated 'shutup,' ten feet for his office And it is further ordered that the sheriff, in acting as agent for the county in the erection of said jail, shall keep a correct account of all labor and material expended, and shall be required to make a certificate of all amounts expended as aforesaid "

At the same meeting, upon the request of B. S Hall and George W Johnson, known as Hall & Johnson, of Wilton, the said county board "being satisfied that they are of good moral character and of sufficient ability to keep a tavern and sell spirituous liquors," and upon receipt of $50 into the county treasury issued a license for the sale of spirituous and other intoxicating liquors to be drunk in the inn, or tavern aforesaid.

On the 26th of April following, Geo. H Woodbury, of the Washington House in Wilton, was also licensed to sell intoxicating liquors for a fee of $50 These were the first legalized dram-shops in the county, although liquors had been sold the same as other merchandise ever since the first establishment of stores and groceries At that time $50 was considered an enormously high tax to pay for the glorious privilege of making a brother man drunk.

By act of the legislature, approved February 28th, 1860, the supervisor system of county government was abolished and substantially the present county commissioner system was adopted Under the provisions of that act, W. T. Kittredge, Geo. H Bishop, and John N Powers were chosen commissioners

Their first meeting was held April 26th, 1860, and a large amount of business was done in a very orderly and systematic manner, showing clearly the lawyer-like hand of Maj Kittredge, who was made chairman of the board Among other orders made and adopted is this one which will make the eyes of modern office-holders green with envy, so magnificent was the salary! It reads as follows:

"Ordered, That, in pursuance of the statute, the sum of $330 is hereby fixed and declared to be the amount allowed to the county auditor as his salary for the eleven months beginning on the 1st day of April, 1860 * * * and the said auditor is hereby authorized to draw from the county treasury at the end of each and every month the sum of thirty dollars in payment of the amount of his said salary due him for that month, depositing a receipt therefor"

This was the salary of Mr. Willis, the first county auditor of the county, for his first year The second year it was raised to $466 66 to be drawn monthly.

At the September session of the board in 1860, John N Powers resigned as commissioner, and M S. Green resigned as county attorney. This was at the meeting of Sept 5, and the two remaining members adjourned till Sept. 11th At this meeting, as the record shows, D. L Whipple and S W Franklin acted with the board, but just how or by what authority does not appear. That was the closing session for the year, and much business was transacted. Among other matters, Seth W. Long was licensed to sell intoxicating liquors at his hotel in Okaman

At the fall election there was an entire change in the county board, the commissioners elected being Isaac Hamlin, Patrick Healy, and B A Lowell. The other officers elected that fall were as follows Member of the lower house of the legislature, James E Child; county auditor, S. J Willis; county attorney, H D.

Baldwin, court commissioner, W. T. Kittredge. The highest vote polled was 508, and the Republicans carried the county by a majority of one hundred and sixty-one for Abraham Lincoln The campaign was quite exciting, Mr Child, Republican, and P. Brink Enos, Democrat, held several joint discussions Both were then rather young men for that kind of business

The year of 1860, like that of 1859, yielded abundant crops, but there was no improvement in market prices, nor had we any better facilities for getting our grain to market There was universal prostration in all kinds of business on account of the general failure of the "wild-cat" banks which had been organized for systematic robbery under state laws. First, interest had ranged for a few years at from fifteen to seventy-two per cent per annum—we had no usury law at that time Unscrupulous men would start banks based on worthless stocks or bonds, and then over-issue for the sake of gathering in the interest on the worthless money loaned.

Second, this, like every other robbery that is permitted by law, soon drew from the farmers and laboring people of the West their hard earnings, reduced all producers to poverty, and reacted upon even the money lenders of small means—many of them being compelled to take the mortgaged property which they could not use and which would not sell for enough to pay back the money loaned upon it. How strange it is that moneyed men never learn from history, which is constantly repeating itself, that they cannot rob and impoverish the people who create all wealth, without finally being ruined themselves by the general crash which necessarily follows an exorbitant rate of interest! But stranger yet is the mental condition of the masses that willingly make serfs of themselves and their families by becoming the slaves of money loaners, thus toiling their lives away for the enrichment of others!

The year closed with dismal forebodings for the future Already the black form of treason had raised its murderous hand at the South and there was so much of party sympathy in the North that brave and hopeful indeed were the men that had no misgivings regarding the immediate future Minnesota occupied a critical position Her people were almost totally without money, both as a state and as individuals The Chippewa Indians occupied the northern portion of the state, the Sioux tribes held all the western border, while the Winnebago Indian reservation occupied the center of southern Minnesota, being located in Waseca and Blue Earth counties It was foreseen by level-headed men that, in case of civil war, the people of this state would be in great danger of an Indian outbreak The writer was ridiculed during the session of the legislature of 1861 for expressing the opinion that, in case the impending civil war could not be avoided, our people would be exposed to Indian outbreaks on the frontier When outbreaks did come those who did the ridiculing were the first to hasten to a place of safety

At the November election in 1860, Abraham Lincoln received 304 votes and Stephen A Douglas 143. For member of congress, William Windom and Cyrus Aldrich, Republicans, received 337 votes each, James George, Democrat, received 188 votes, and John M Gilman, Democrat, 152 votes. The state then elected two congressmen at large

The legislative district of which Waseca county was a part comprised the counties of Freeborn, Steele and Waseca Very little attention was paid to party politics in the choosing of legislators Railroad interests and personal likes and dislikes entered largely into the choice of legislative candidates.

The issue was known as Cornell and anti-Cornell The candidates were: Dr George Watson, of Freeborn county, for senator, and George W Green, of Clinton Falls, Steele county, and James E Child, of Waseca county, for representatives—these three were Republicans and anti-Cornell men, Henry Thornton, democrat, of Freeborn county, for senator, and Wm F. Pettit, democrat, of Steele county, and A E. Smith, republican of Waseca county, for representatives—these three were Cornell men Watson and Child, republicans and Pettit democrat, were elected, each by a small majority.

While the political contentions of the year had been earnest, even fierce, and the black clouds of treason were seen gathering in the Southland, the climatic conditions had been favorable during the year and our people had gathered bounteous crops. The winter of 1859-60 had been very mild, and the spring weather of 1860 was most delightful. Some farmers sowed wheat in the month of February, and he was a slow farmer, indeed, who was not through with seeding small grain on the 15th of March, that year. The weather was fine during the entire season and the harvest all that could be asked for.

It was also a year of intense political activity and discussion throughout the nation. The Kansas-Nebraska struggle which for years had kept alive and increased sectional hatred regarding the institution of human slavery had culminated in the invasion of Virginia, at Harper's Ferry, by John Brown and his followers, Oct. 17th, 1859. Brown, with seventeen white men and five negroes took possession of Harper's Ferry and captured about 100,000 stand of arms in the arsenal. This place was guarded by only three watchmen, who were easily captured. This invasion was made with the avowed intention of freeing the negro slaves of the South. This fanatical and foolhardy enterprise resulted in a number of deaths, the capture, trial, and hanging of John Brown and some of his associates and most intense excitement and indignation throughout the slaveholding states. Brown was hanged on the 2d of December, 1859. While very few people in the North attempted to justify his treason, there were many that admired the courage of the brave old man, who fought, as he believed, for that most sacred of doctrines—the inalienable right of every human being to "life, liberty and the pursuit of happiness."

Brown had been driven from Kansas by the proslavery men, and a prize amounting to $3,250 had been offered for his arrest by the governor of Missouri and the president of the United States.

The greatest political struggle of the ages followed in 1860. Lincoln was nominated by the anti-slavery or republican sentiment of the North, Breckenridge by the pro-slavery men of the South and Douglas by the conservative or commercial democracy of the nation. It was a battle of intellectual and political giants, and resulted in the election of Abraham Lincoln.

The year 1860, so far as county matters were concerned, passed with no occurrence out of the ordinary, except, perhaps, the taking of the United States census. This work was performed by Cole O. Norton, since deceased, a brother of Mr. H. P. Norton, of Waseca. According to his enumeration there were at that time 1,370 males and 1,228 females. There were of men over 20 and under 40 years of age 241, and of females 196; males over 40 and under 50, 118, females of the same ages, 73, males over 50 and under 60, 37, females of the same ages, 36, men over 60 and under 70, 40, females of the same ages, 22, males over 70 and under 80, 9, females of the same ages, 5. The total population of the county was only 2,598.

CHAPTER XXVIII, 1861.

THE STRUGGLE OF 1861—FIRST CALL FOR VOLUNTEERS—CAPT. McKUNE AND WASECA COUNTY VOLUNTEERS—BATTLE OF BULL RUN—ELECTION OF 1861, P C BAILEY REPRESENTATIVE —BIG COMET—MINNESOTA VOLUNTEER REGIMENTS—MEN WHO ENLISTED—THE THIRD, FOURTH AND FIFTH REGIMENTS —LOW PRICES—FIRST NEWSPAPER, "HOME VIEWS" BY JOHNSTON AND WILLIS—TRIBUTE TO CAPT McKUNE.

The year 1861, the most momentous in the history of our nation, opened beneath the storm-clouds of treason which cast their somber and ominous shadows over all the land From every point of view the southern rebellion was the most gigantic political crime of all the ages that had preceded it The hope of liberty, of religious freedom, of manhood sovereignty, of the laboring and producing masses, not only of this country, but of all the world, depended upon the maintenance of the "Union of the States, one and inseparable "

The Minnesota legislature of 1861 authorized an organization of the militia of the state, but the treasury was so destitute of available funds that the organization was nothing more than a make believe The legislature closed its session the first week in March, and on the 12th of April, Ft Sumter was fired upon by the rebel forces of the South Then the first fierce blow was struck, and the states of the South, one after another, in rapid succession, formally seceded from the Union The forts and arsenals of the nation in the South, in contemplation of secession, had been turned over to southern sympathizers by Buchanan's administration and were rapidly surrendered to the rebels.

President Lincoln at once issued a call for seventy-five thousand volunteers to defend the life of the nation. Gov Ramsey, who was in Washington when Fort Sumter was fired upon, was the first governor to tender the president a regiment of volunteers. This he did on the morning of April 13, 1861.

The governor immediately telegraphed Ignatius Donnelly, lieutenant governor, and on the 16th of April, Mr Donnelly as governor ad interim, issued his call for one regiment of volunteer infantry of ten companies, to report at once to Adjutant General Sanborn at St. Paul. Within two weeks the regiment was full, and many that offered to enlist were turned away

Waseca county, considering its population, furnished its full quota The following gallant young men enlisted with Capt Lewis McKune, one of the early settlers in Blooming Grove, but then of Morristown, Rice county, viz · Geo R Buckman, L J. (Jim) Mosher, E E Verplank, John M Churchill, Irvine W Northrup, Michael Hausauer Walter S. Reed, Luman S. Wood, Adam Areman, Omer H Sutlief, Louis E Hanneman, Martin Healy, Neri Reed, C C Davis, George Kline, Philo Hall, John McKinster, Nathaniel Reed, Norman B. Barron, Amos Canfield, Jens T Dahl

These men, without exception, served their country most faithfully and heroically

The regiment was fully organized on April 29th and mustered into the service at Fort Snelling by Capt A D Nelson, of the United States army

The men at once went into training and were drilled every day except Sundays They remained at Fort Snelling until June 22nd when they embarked on steamboats and started for Washington, taking railroad cars at La Crosse and Prairie du Chien. They arrived in Washington June 27th and remained near that city until July 16th when the regiment was ordered to the front. The regiment bore a prominent part in the ill-fated Bull Run battle of July 21st, 1861, during which Capt. Lewis McKune was killed, and E E Verplank, George Kline, and Walter S. and Neri Reed, two brothers, were slightly wounded.

The brave, unselfish, Capt. Lewis McKune was among the numerous immigrants to Minnesota in 1856. He was born in Meriden, Susquehanna county, Pa , on the 22d of July. 1821. He was reared upon a farm and remained in his native state until his twenty-fifth year when he started West, settling in Illinois At the breaking out of the California gold exeitmenet, in 1849, or very soon after, he went to that Eldorado of the West to seek his fortune He was reasonably successful in his mining operations, and returned to Illinois about 1855 He next purchased an emigrant outfit and came to Minnesota by the typical prairie schooner He brought with him some very valuable horses, the breeding of which occupied considerable of his attention He first settled in Blooming Grove and opened a large farm on section one.

The writer's first acquaintance with him was during the political campaign of 1856. Both of them were very earnest, ardent republicans in those days—"Black Abolitionists." He was a born hero, ready to stand by, and fight for, what he believed to be right, regardless of personal ease, safety, or financial sacrifice. He was one of the many grand characters of the great army of American heroes and statesmen of that day How grand it would be were this nation today as patriotic, as unselfish, as devoted to righteousness as were the republican heroes of that day Were it so, the greed and selfishness now concentrated in the hands of corporations, syndicates and money combines, that plunder the masses, would find few defenders.

He participated to quite an extent in the local campaign of 1856, and thus paved the way for his preferment in 1857 In the spring of 1857, the people of Steele and Waseca counties met in convention at Owatonna and elected delegates to attend a district convention to be held at Mankato about the 1st of June, to nominate republican candidates to be elected as members of the constitutional convention Hon Amos Coggswell, an able lawyer, who had settled in Aurora township, Steele county, in 1856, was a candidate and the choice of Steele county, while Waseca county had no aspirants The writer was chosen as one of the delegates to the Mankato convention, and it was soon learned that a delegate would be awarded to Waseca county Capt McKune was not at the convention, nor had he been consulted in regard to the matter; but upon the presentation of his name by the writer he was unanimously nominated Mr McKune had just opened a store in Morristown, though living on his farm, and was unable to devote time to the canvass; but he accepted the nomination and was duly elected. Although not a public speaker, he was a man of sound judgment and made a valuable member of that very able convention.

As a member of the constitutional convention he demonstrated, on more than one occasion, that his "Scotch blood was up" whenever there was a fight on hand. As a result of the election of members to the convention, the political parties were so nearly evenly represented in numbers, that each sought to get party control of the organization The republicans fearing that the Kansas tricks of the pro-slavery men might be repeated in Minnesota, held several private caucuses to devise ways and means to prevent any advantage being taken of them Upon Mr. McKune's suggestion the republican members, in a body, quietly took possession of the hall where the convention was to meet the night before the convention was to assemble and organize. They remained in the hall that night and until 12 o'clock noon, when they proceeded to organize the convention in opposition to the democrat members who appeared at that time in a body and also pretended to organize and then immediately adjourned, leaving the hall to the republicans

It will be remembered, by those familiar with the early history of the state, that our constitution was finally submitted by two conventions which by a committee of conference, agreed upon the constitution under which Minnesota was admitted as a state It was during the session of the conference committee that a brutal assault was made upon Judge Thomas Wilson, then a republican member from Winona by Gen Willis A Gorman, a democratic member from St Paul The assault caused great excitement at the time throughout the country Gorman was a large, powerful man, while Wilson was not only a small man, but in poor health at the time This so incensed Capt. McKune that he sought Gorman and gave him a severe tongue-lashing, giving him to understand that if he desired to whip some black republican, he (Me) was ready to receive and return blows Suffice it to say Gorman gave no blows.

[Gen Gorman afterwards became a strong Union man and was colonel of the First Minnesota at the time of Capt McKune's death]

Upon Mr McKune's return from the constitutional convention, the people were so well satisfied with him that he was chosen our first state senator The session commenced in December, 1857, and continued until the close of March, when it adjourned till the next August. This legislature became notorious for its adoption of the five-million, railroad bond-issue. A lobby of railroad bond-swindlers, accompanied by a large number of trained and genteel prostitutes and bribe givers, debauched a majority of the legislature and secured the passage of the five-million loan amendment Senator McKune honestly fought the proposition from the start, but was in the minority, and the bill passed. He then took the stump against the adoption of the proposition by the people, but, alas! the fools were in the majority, the people were deceived, and they adopted the swindle as their own, repudiating the noble man who fought bravely to protect them from being robbed and plundered It was another striking illustration of the fact that the American public delights in being cheated and humbugged by a set of genteel appearing rascals that make their money by first deceiving and then plundering the people

After this legislative experience Mr McKune abandoned party politics and devoted himself to his own business matters—his farm in Blooming Grove and his sales of merchandise in Morristown. At the close of his senatorial work, he removed his family to Morristown where he resided in 1861 Notwithstanding his retirement from active local politics, he took great interest in the affairs of his country and was among the first to foresee that all compromises would fail, and that the struggle would end, either in the total abolition of African slavery or the destruction of the Union

The writer will never forget the solemnity and earnestness of this man the last time he ever conversed with him I had spent the winter of 1860-1, in St Paul, as a member of the legislature, and was on my return home There were no railroads here then, and on the old stage-coach Morristown was the nearest point to my home, then on a farm in Wilton Capt McKune's kind invitation to become his guest over night was accepted He was even then preparing to arm for the defense of the Union. He went on to explain that war was inevitable The rebel leaders he said, had so long found moneyed and commercial men of the North a set of poltroons and doughfaces that they were infatuated with the idea that all the Northern men were mercenary and cowardly, and would submit to dishonor and disunion rather than sacrifice their money and their lives to maintain the government of their forefathers

We sat up late the night of that 9th day of March, 1861, as he told of the arrangements he had already made to enlist at the first call for volunteers. He said he had a feeling, or premonition, that he should die in the struggle and had arranged matters accordingly Upon retiring he called attention to his two boys and to two swords hanging upon the wall in their sleeping room He said that he had been teaching the boys how to use them, and he expected that, should the struggle be a prolonged one, they would both be called to defend their country It was wonderful how calmly he talked of coming events and possibilities The next morning he accompanied me as far as Chris. Remund's farm, in Blooming Grove, on horseback Upon separating he extended a most affectionate farewell, repeating his conviction that war was inevitable and that he expected to sacrifice his life for his country. Alas! how true were his predictions

The people of all Minnesota watched the opening events of the great struggle with the greatest anxiety Almost every neighborhood had furnished some brave man or boy for the conflict The rebels, on account of the cowardice and imbecility of James Buchanan, had plundered the nation of its money, arms, ammunition, forts and navy, and held the Union people by the throat Delay followed delay, and the slaughter of the Union forces at Bull Run, on that fatal 21st day of July, 1861, cast a terrible gloom over the entire North, and especially over the people of Waseca county, when they learned of the death of Capt Lewis McKune and the other brave men who fell on that occasion, almost at the first fire When the sad news first reached Wilton there were few dry eyes among the men who heard it. All party and personal feeling disappeared for the time, and one universal sentiment of patriotism was aroused

Without disparagement of any other, it is safe to say that no grander sacrifice was ever made for country than that made by Capt Lewis McKune He sacrificed a good business, left a devoted and accomplished wife in poor health, and abandoned his children to all the uncertain vicissitudes of life, while giving his own body as a living sacrifice upon the altar of his country. It is true that his life was spent among the toilers of earth and as one of them He was of the masses—an honest, conscientious, unselfish patriot. Contrast his life and death with some of the so-called great men of to-day, and, if there be justice beyond this life, Lewis McKune will occupy a front seat at the right hand among the noblest souls of this or any other nation.

The proceedings of the county board, consisting of B A. Lowell, Patrick Healy and Isaac Hamline, were of the routine order and nothing of general interest transpired.

The election in the fall of 1861 was almost as exciting as the presidential election of the year before The war excitement was intense Should President Lincoln be sustained and the Union be preserved? Alexander Ramsey, governor, and Ignatius Donnelly, lieutenant governor, were re-elected by large majorities The following legislative and county officers were elected Senator, Hon A B Webber, of Albert Lea, representative, Hon P. C Bailey, of Wilton, treasurer, Hon Geo. T. White of St Mary, register of deeds, Tarrant Putnam, of Wilton, sheriff, D L Whipple; clerk of court H P West, judge of probate and county attorney, Hon H D Baldwin, surveyor, Geo P. Johnson, all of Wilton, court commissioner, Job A Canfield, of Otisco, coroner, Nathaniel Wood, of Woodville, county commissioners John S G. Honor of Iosco, B A Lowell of Otisco, and J B. Jackson, of South Wilton

While there was little doing of local importance, there was much of a general character to interest the people This was the year of the great comet which suddenly appeared on the 30th day of June and created a great sensation To the naked eye, the head of the comet appeared to be larger than a star of the first magnitude. The astronomers "estimated" that on the 2d day of July the breadth of the head of the nucleus was about 150,000 miles and its train of light fifteen million miles in length. It was thought by one astronomer that the earth would pass through the tail of this comet, but it sped onward through trackless space, soon disappeared from view and was forgotten by the multitude

THE FOURTH OF JULY

Independence Day was commemorated with more than usual solemnity that year. A large assembly of people gathered at Wilton, then the county seat, and celebrated the occasion by reading the Declaration of Independence, singing patriotic songs, and listening to short, patriotic speeches by leading citizens.

THE WAR OF THE REBELLION.

The Union forces during the summer met with exasperating delays and some reverses. On the fifth of July, President Lincoln issued a call for 400,000 more men and $400,000,000 to carry on the war for the suppression of the Rebellion The Second Minnesota regiment of infantry was complete as early as August 23. No men from Waseca county enlisted in this regiment

The Third regiment was mustered in at Ft. Snelling Nov 15 Waseca county furnished to this regiment, Hugh Donaldson, C A Peasley, James Broderick, W H H Jackson, Hugh B Withrow, S M Jones, G W Peasley, C W Preston, David Lilly, S F Wyman.

The complete organization of the Fourth regiment followed and on the 23rd of December the regiment was ready for service Waseca county was represented in this regiment by Maj W T Kittredge, Capt E M Broughton, Capt S T Isaac, Capt D L Wellman, Augustus Lintler, Sam Alexander, Orin Coats, James L Connor, N. T. Foster, Silas Hubbell, T B Jackson, Moses Norris, C W Quiggle Jonas Whitcomb, John Teas, Charles Parvin, Myron Sheldon, Loren C Wood, Waldo Lyon, Aaron Bragg, James S Camp, Erastus Fish, James Hanes, Jonathan Isaac, S A Norris, J N Powers, D P. Stowell

THE FIFTH MINNESOTA.

The Fifth regiment was the last to organize under the President's July call for 400,000 men The regiment was mustered in December 19, 1861, but was not complete in numbers until March 20, 1862 This county was represented in the Fifth by the following men:

Capt E. A Rice, M P Ide, Alex Wentworth, Wm. Blaisdell, G F Rice, John Barden, Moses Camp, Edward Guise, Wm Harding, Wm. Hoover, John Jenkins, S M Merrill, Lieut. G W Johnson, G R. Loveland, J W. Pierce, G H Bishop, E. M. Atwood, Patrick Burns, S W. Franklin, W. H. Gray, E. R. Horton, Harvey

Lawrence, John Murphy, E. H Stiles, B. F. Weed, P. Davis, Peter Olson, James E Crook, David Skinner, H H Wallace, Wm. Douglas, Chris. Sampson, Jonathan Hardy Of these Wm Douglas enlisted as a recruit Jan. 4, 1864

While farm products were abundant, prices thereof were not remunerative The local prices were as follows

Wheat, forty to forty-five cents per bushel, corn, twenty cents; beans, forty, oats, eighteen, potatoes, twenty, lard, ten cents per pound, eggs, five cents a dozen, dressed pork, from $3 50 to $4 00 per cwt, brown sugar, ten cents per pound, coffee sugar, a shilling a pound, plug tobacco, thirty to forty cents, smoking tobacco, fifteen cents, coffee, from twenty to twenty-five cents, syrup, and molasses, eighty cents per gallon, salt, per barrel, $4 75; tallow candles, eighteen cents per pound, dried apples, ten cents; calico, from seven to twelve and a half cents per yard; delaines, twenty to twenty-five cents, sheeting, eight to twelve cents, denims, twelve to twenty cents, Kentucky jeans, twenty-five to thirty-five cents, cassimeres, from forty cents to two dollars, cotton flannel, from twelve to eighteen cents, wool flannel, from thirty-five to fifty cents per yard

In closing the history of the year, it is proper to refer to the first newspaper established in the county While it is true that a paper, called "The Home Views," a six column folio, made its appearance in Wilton, then the county seat, March 13, 1860, it was in fact an Owatonna publication, issued by Mr A B Cornell in the name of Mr J W Crawford, of Wilton, as editor Yet the first real newspaper printed, published and edited in the county was

"THE WASECA HOME VIEWS"

This paper made its appearance about the first of March, 1861, and was owned, edited, printed and published by Alexander Johnston and Spencer J Willis at the village of Wilton It was conducted as a neutral in politics, Johnson being a democrat and Willis a republican It was a very good local paper largely devoted to the local interests of the town and county They continued to publish the paper until the ensuing fall, when Mr Johnston became sole proprietor and removed the plant to Faribault. From that town, Mr Johnston continued the publication of the "Home

Views" at Wilton, under the local management of Buel Welch, Esq., until the fall of 1863, as a "Union Democratic" paper. Mr. Johnston sold his interest in the plant in 1863 and went to St. Paul where he became a reporter for the "Pioneer," which afterwards consolidated with the "Press," both papers becoming one and adopting the name of Pioneer Press. He remained in the employ of the daily press in St. Paul until the time of his death, about 1894.

CHAPTER XXIX, 1862.

NEW OFFICIALS—CANFIELD, WARD AND BALDWIN SCHOOL LAND APPRAISERS—SCHOOL EXAMINERS, WOODRUFF, MOSHER, SMITH—HORSETHIEVES, HORSES OF ORRIN PEASE STOLEN—HORSETHIEF DETECTIVES—INDIAN MASSACRE—COMPANY F, 10th REGIMENT, ROSTER THEREOF—THE OUTBREAK AUG 18—TRIP TO MANKATO AND THE AGENCY—PEOPLE PANIC STRICKEN—BRISBANE'S ACCOUNT OF TRIP—MOUNTED RANGERS FROM WASECA COUNTY—INDIANS HANGED AT MANKATO, DEC 26

The new officers of the county, viz.: S J Willis, auditor, Geo. T White, treasurer, Tarrant Putnam, register of deeds, D L. Whipple, sheriff, H D Baldwin, judge of probate and county attorney, Geo P. Johnson, surveyor, J A Canfield, court commissioner, H P West, clerk of court Nathaniel Wood, coroner; and John S G Honor, of Iosco, B A Lowell, of Otisco and J B Jackson, of Wilton, county commissioners, met at the court house in Wilton, Jan 7th 1862, filed the necessary official bonds and duly qualified for their respective duties

The county commissioners were in session but a short time Mr Lowell was elected chairman for the ensuing year. The board of county commissioners at that time, under the statute, fixed the salaries of a number of the county officers

It was ordered that the salary of the county attorney H D Baldwin, be fixed at $180 per annum, the salary of the county auditor, S J Willis (no clerk hire) be fixed at $425 per annum—salaries payable monthly in equal installments Quite a change from that day to this

It was also ordered that $275 be allowed to S. J Willis & Co., proprietors of the "Home Views," for doing the county printing for the year 1862, "said printing to include all printing of tax notices and delinquent tax sales, except only assessors' tax rolls, payment for same to be made quarterly."

The county board met again February 28, but nothing of general interest was transacted The next meeting of the board was held June 26th upon call of the county auditor. At this meeting of the board, John G Ward, of Iosco, J. A. Canfield, of Otisco, and H. D Baldwin, of Wilton, were appointed by the board as land commissioners to appraise the school lands of the county At this session of the board the saloon keepers put in some work on the license question, and, "on motion, B. A Lowell was appointed to receive and accept proposals for liquor licenses, the amount to be paid for the same, where liquors were to be sold by the glass, pint or quart, not to be less than $10 for each license granted."

The next meeting of the county board was held Sept 2d. Besides the usual routine of allowing bills, etc, the following gentlemen were appointed to serve as school examiners (superintendents) in their respective commissioner districts, to-wit Philo Woodruff, of Blooming Grove, H. G Mosher, of Otisco, and Rev E S Smith, of Wilton

The summer of 1862 revealed the fact that we had in our midst a gang of horsethieves In the month of June, Orrin Pease, who had just settled in the town of St. Mary, had a fine pair of horses stolen After considerable search by Sheriff Whipple and others, the horses were found in the possession of men named Eno, Beatty and Anderson, a colored person All three of these were convicted of the larceny, but, pending an appeal to the supreme court, broke jail at Wilton and made good their escape The stealing of these horses, the escape of the thieves, and the expense attending their arrest and trial created a strong feeling of indignation on the part of our people against thieves in general, and against horse thieves in particular and were the primary cause of the organization of the Waseca County Horsethief Detective Society, which still exists and the history of which appears elsewhere in this volume.

The next meeting of the county board was held Oct 4, 1862.

No business of importance was transacted except that Mr Willis, having engaged in the drug business, tendered his resignation as county auditor This was not accepted, at the time, but at a special meeting called Nov 22nd, the resignation of Mr Willis was accepted, and Col. J. C Ide was appointed in his place

THE WAR AND THE INDIAN MASSACRE

On the first day of July President Lincoln called for six hundred thousand more men, volunteers, to more vigorously prosecute the war, and on the 4th of August a draft was ordered of three hundred thousand men to serve nine months The draft order was never enforced in Minnesota But the stirring events of the war, the call of the president for volunteers, and the draft ordered created great activity in enlistments and military organization throughout the whole state

Several public meetings were held at Wilton They were largely attended, and much enthusiasm and real patriotism were manifest among all the people From August 12 to August 18 company F of the Tenth Minnesota infantry, Capt George T White's company, was largely increased by the following men from this county.

Capt George T White, H A Mosher, John A Wheeler, Robert Beith, Nels Bergosen, James Glendenning, Geo Dreever, Knute Hansen, August Krieger, M M Morgan, John Pickett, Benjamin Swan, Barney Vosberg, Wm R. Brisbane, Isaac Lyng, C W Roberts, S A Goodwin, Wm Bliven, Samuel Gleason, A. D Gregory, Thos Eldredge, Christian Hattesaul, John King, Jacob Newkirk, Samuel Preston, S P Satterlee, Lieut Isaac Hamlin, David McDaniels, J R Whitman, G. E Brubaker, Chas Grover, J. A Canfield, Fred Emery, G W. Ives, L A Lafayette, Chas Olebauch, J S Rice, Martin Spankley, G H Woodbury, Hans Hansen, J. B. Hill, M A Francis, Richard Ayres, Edward Brossard, S M Grover, Chas Chadwick, James Gallagher, H A Jones, G. W. Lee, Hans Oleson, M V B. Storer, W W Taylor, P J D Wood, Henry Yarigan, Robert Quiggle, Nathan Satterlee, Ole Johnson, A H. Coddington, Francis Lincoln, M A Robbins

On the 18th day of August 1862 the people on the western frontier of the state were startled by the Sioux Indian massacre of white people at both of the Sioux agencies and in their immediate neighborhoods These massacres were followed each succeeding day for a week by the indiscriminate slaughter of men, women and children all along the frontier, from Glencoe and Hutchinson, on the north, to Spirit Lake, in Iowa, on the south. More than two thousand white settlers were murdered in cold blood, and some two hundred fifty women and children were carried away as captives.

The trouble commenced at Acton, Meeker county, on August 17, 1862, when several settlers were murdered by a few roving Indians, said to have been partially intoxicated Upon receipt of the news of the Acton murders by the Indians at the Upper Agency, on the 18th, the work of death was at once commenced

After the slaughter of the white people at both the Indian agencies, early on the morning of the 18th, a wounded settler with a team drove immediately to Fort Ridgely, thirteen miles below, and gave the alarm Captain Marsh, with eighty-five men, occupied the fort With forty-five men he started for the Lower Agency, having with him a six mule team, hauling supplies and ammunition Upon reaching the river at the agency his little company was surprised and surrounded by Indians in great numbers, who opened a deadly fire About half of his company were instantly killed, and then followed a desperate hand to hand fight, in which the white soldiers fought to the death Only fifteen of the forty-five survived and returned to the fort—Captain Marsh himself being drowned while crossing the river

Before leaving the fort on the 18th, Captain Marsh wisely sent a messenger to Lieutenant Tim J. Sheehan, who was on his way to Fort Ripley with fifty men, to return at once This Sheehan did, arriving at Fort Ridgely on the 19th Indian Agent Galbraith had raised a company of fifty men for the United States service and was on the way to Fort Snelling to be mustered in, having reached St. Peter on the evening of the 18th when news arrived of the massacre at the Upper and Lower Agencies Taking the muskets of the militia company of St Peter he immediately returned with his company to Fort Ridgely, where he arrived on the 19th This increased the number of men at the fort to about one hundred fifty, under command of Lieutenant Sheehan.

A desperate assault was made upon the fort by the Indians on the 20th, which continued from time to time until the 22d. The fort was heroically and successfully defended by Lieutenant Sheehan and his command. Only four men were killed and fifteen wounded in the fort during the siege. At the time of the attack on the fort it contained $72,000 in gold and silver, which had been sent out by the government to make Indian payments.

Then followed the assault upon New Ulm and its defense on the 23d, where the Indians were severely repulsed after burning a part of the town. In one of the battles at New Ulm ten white men were killed and fifty wounded.

The news of the massacre did not reach the settlers of Waseca county until the 23d, about noon, when the stage came into Wilton from the west. A large number of enlisted men of Company F, Tenth regiment, under command of Captain White had left Wilton that morning to join their regiment at Fort Snelling.

What was to be done? was the burning question of the hour. Few of our citizens had anything better than muzzleloading shotguns, in the way of firearms, and very little ammunition of any kind. As usual on such occasions there was great diversity of opinion as to the best course to pursue. While others were deliberating upon and discussing the subject, S. P. Child, Buel Welch, Esq., John Greening, and the writer each obtained a horse, a shotgun, a small amount of ammunition and started for Mankato about 2 o'clock in the afternoon. The roads were slippery and slow progress was made, but we reached the Winnebago Agency about 7 o'clock in the evening. We there found Hon. St. A. D. Balcombe, the agent, and a number of white men residing at the agency, all of them more or less excited in fear of an uprising among the Winnebago Indians. They desired us to remain over night in order to help defend the place should there be an uprising of the Winnebagoes, but S. P. Child, who had spent over a year as a resident among these Indians, concluded from what he could see and hear that there was no danger from the Winnebagoes, so long as they should remain sober. Hence we concluded to push on to Mankato. Shortly after we left the Agency, clouds came up from the west and about dark rain commenced to fall. After we had crossed the LeSueur river and reached the Mankato woods, it became so dark that it was impossible to see the road. In order to keep the road, I pulled off my boots and walked in the road leading my horse, feeling my way as best I could A drizzling rain continued until we reached Mankato, making the latter part of our journey a very slow and tedious one We arrived at the town about 11 o'clock that night Although guards had been placed at different points about the city, we proceeded to the Mankato House without being discovered or challenged by the city guards The Mankato House was able to furnish lunch but no beds. Fred Kittredge then had charge of the hotel and did the very best he could for our comfort Every hotel and house was crowded with people who had come in from the country panic-stricken About daylight the next morning, news was received from the battle at New Ulm and of the repulse of the Indians At the same time there were many rumors of a threatened outbreak by the Winnebagoes who, as was claimed, had made an alliance with the Sioux. The more level-headed gave little credence to these reports regarding the Winnebagos but the masses actually believd that there was great danger of an immediate outbreak by them It was argued by the people of Mankato that inasmuch as the troops from Fort Snelling had reached St Peter there was really no danger from the Sioux, while there was no protection whatever to the people of Blue Earth and Waseca counties from an outbreak by the Winnebagoes. After consultation, those of us who went from Wilton consented to return to the Winnebago Agency and watch for further developments. Upon our arrival there about noon, we found a number of men from Wilton, under the command of Colonel Ide, who had arrived a short time before The excitement at the Agency was still intense owing to fear of an outbreak on the part of the Winnebagoes. After we had discussed the matter with Colonel Ide and others of the Wilton company, it was thought best for me to return to Waseca county to inform the people of the situation and to assure them that there was really no danger of further outrages by the Indians. I immediately returned to Waseca county and traveled the settlement from Janesville to New Richland, assuring the people that there was no real danger, and that it was for their interest to remain at their homes and save their crops; that the Indians had been repulsed at New Ulm and driven west, and that armed men were then guarding the whole frontier.

While most of our people became satisfied with these assurances, still quite a number could not be reasoned with and they determined to leave their homes, crops, and cattle to go to destruction There was a general stampede from the southwestern porton of Waseca county and from the northern portion of Faribault county The people of Wilton and St Mary deemed it best to place a guard at the Wilton bridge to prevent the fleeing people from going further east No doubt this drastic measure saved many families from losing nearly all they possessed and suffering in consequence, for many returned to their homes, saved their crops, and recovered their cattle

The following from the pen of the late Hon Wm Brisbane, of Wilton, who remained at the Agency a day and a night, will be of interest It reads:

"A report had come to the Agency that the Indians had burned Mankato The stage coach being some two hours late, gave color to the report John Greening started on horseback for Mankato to make a reconnoissance and report as quickly as possible John started off in gallant style, an excellent caricature of Don Quixote charging windmills Shortly after, he came galloping back shouting 'Mankato all right, no burn, and stage a comin' ' A few of us promptly seized the stage when it drove up and demanded to be taken back to Wilton This caused considerable flutter One woman said she wouldn't give that —snapping her fingers—for her life if the Waseca county men went away Dyer, head farmer at the Agency, bareheaded and excited, came and told me that Balcombe wanted to see me. I told him to tell Balcombe to go to ——— Col Ide said 'You will be very sorry when you hear that we are all killed' 'Yes,' said I, 'very' * * * You may judge of our surprise when we came to Wilton to find Mrs Balcombe and Mrs Hubbell there waiting for the stage I learned long afterward that they had taken a team at the Agency early in the morning and traveled by what they called the timber road. A day or two after all the Wilton men returned home

"As there were no troops in this section, and our own homes were exposed to danger, a military company was formed at Wilton, called the 'Home Guards' James E Child was elected captain and drilled us in the manual exercises He was assisted by Col Ide, when difficult military maneuvers were to be executed I remember that Warren Smith was one of the lieutenants. I often thought that I would die of laughing when the Colonel was teaching us how to march through a narrow defile We had to march sidewise, which gave us a limping kind of gait, so that a stranger would have thought that we had all been wounded in battle and crippled for life We were dressed in blue-jean jackets and pants. I am sure that if such a military company were to appear on the streets of Waseca today they would be taken for foolish school-boys playing soldier for the fun of the thing"

Aside from Capt. White's company which participated in the Indian war, the following named men served a year in the First Minnesota Mounted Rangers: S P Child, John Cunningham, Gullick Knutesen, Egle Olson, J H Elliston, W. M Fay, Louis W. Krassin, John Murphy, Jordan Smith, L. F Preston, A J Williams. Jonas Whitcomb, Lieutenant T. F. West. They enlisted immediately after the outbreak.

During the winter of 1862-3, most of the enlisted men from Waseca county, in the Fifth and Tenth regiments, were stationed at Mankato and the Winnebago Agency, and had the satisfaction—if it were a satisfaction—of being present in their military capacity at the hanging of the thirty-eight Sioux murderers, at Mankato, Dec 26, 1862.

CHAPTER XXX, 1862.

THE INDIAN MASSACRE AT LAKE SHETEK—THE MURDER OF MRS WM EVERETT AND OTHERS—THE SHOOTING OF VOIGHT—THE TERRIBLE BATTLES OF 1862—CAPTIVITY OF WOMEN AND CHILDREN—MR EVERETT'S WOUNDS AND SUFFERING—RELEASE OF THE CAPTIVES, AMONG THEM LILLY EVERETT

It would be impracticable in a work of this kind to introduce any considerable report of the thrilling and terrible incidents that transpired during the Indian outbreak, but it seems appropriate to give some of the incidents in the experience of Mr. William Everett, so long a useful and respected citizen of this county, who was a suffering participant and an eye-witness of the massacre at Lake Shetek The following account is taken from the Waseca Herald of several years ago

THE INDIAN MASSACRE AT LAKE SHETEK

Intimately connected with the early history of this state and the sad and tragic scenes of the Sioux massacre of 1862, is the name of our townsman Wm Everett He was born near Newton, Sussex county, New Jersey, in 1828 where he lived until about twenty-two years of age In 1850 he settled at Haywarth, Iowa county, Wisconsin, on the Wisconsin river He owned and operated a saw mill, in connection with some logging camps on that river At the age of twenty-four he married Miss Almira Hatch of that place He removed with his family to Minnesota, in May, 1859, coming by way of the Mississippi and Minnesota rivers on Capt. Davidson's packets They stopped at South Bend, near Mankato, during the summer, looked over the country, and in the following

WM. EVERETT.

October located at the south end of Lake Shetek At that time the lands were not yet surveyed—the survey taking place in 1861. Mrs Everett's brother, Chas Hatch, came in the spring of 1861.

There were very few settlers at the lake—some three or four—when Messrs Everett and Wright made their claims Hatch was a single man, Wright had a wife and two children and Mr. Everett and wife had two children, one of them Lilly, now Mrs Curtis

The next season Everett and Wright opened farms, the former breaking thirty acres. He also made arrangements to build a saw mill and had the material all on the ground at the time of the Indian outbreak.

New Ulm, sixty miles away, was their nearest village and trading point They were about one hundred miles from Mankato, the next nearest point There were no settlers west of them nearer than Sioux Falls, and only three families there

The next year a few settlers came in, and in 1861 there was considerable immigration Quite a number settled at the lake, and others settled north and west of them. Occasionally parties of Sioux Indians went through there on hunting expeditions. In the fall of 1861, a party of Sioux, numbering some twenty, old and young, who had been south hunting elk, camped at the lake on their return, and were caught by an early snow storm which detained them there till February The Indians had very little to live on, and were fed by the settlers. In January, provisions began to fail, and Mr Everett and two others started out with ox-teams for New Ulm The snow being deep and crusted, they made only eight miles the first day They pitched their tent, or tepee, on the prairie. During the night a high wind arose which blew down their tent and nearly buried them with drifting snow. They found it impossible to proceed in the morning and returned to the lake They had raised considerable buckwheat, and this they ground in coffee mills, sifted and made it into cakes Thus they lived until February when there came a thaw The Indians then left for their agencies, and Mr Everett and two other men, with two sleighs, went to New Ulm for provisions and groceries for the settlement On their return, while crossing Mound Creek, near where Burns station now is, the water, being high, carried off one sleigh box filled with supplies which they were unable to recover They finally reached the settlement in safety with the other load. Had it not been for the Indians, the settlement would not have run short of provisions. Strange as it may seem some of these same Indians engaged in the massacre of the settlers there.

In May, 1862, Messrs Hurd and Jones, two of the settlers concluded to visit the Bix Sioux river and look over that section of country. Hurd told his wife that if they did not return by a certain time in June she might know that something unusual had happened to them The time came, but Hurd and Jones came not There was considerable anxiety on their account in the settlement, and Messrs. Everett, Wright, Duly, Smith, and Eastlick took two horse teams and started to look for them These men drove as far as Split Rock creek, now called Rock river, and camped for the night The next morning it was decided to leave Duly with the teams in camp, while Everett and Wright should follow down the creek, and Smith and Eastlick should go in the opposite direction to search for the missing men, both parties agreeing to return to camp that night. Everett and Wright soon discovered a buffalo, shot and wounded him They forgot all else in their desire to kill the buffalo, and chased him until late in the afternoon They then began to think of returning, but having given no heed to the directions they had traveled, and night coming on, they soon discovered that they were lost They camped in a slough, covering themselves with grass cut with their knives, the better to protect themselves from the swarms of mosquitoes and the chilly night air They hoped to get their direction by the sun next morning, but when morning came there was a heavy fog, and thick clouds shut out the sun, so that they were compelled to guess as to the proper course to travel. As usual, under such circumstances, they traveled in the wrong direction Not having anything to eat they felt weary, but were encouraged by coming on to the trail leading from Sioux Falls to Shetek. Again they took the wrong direction and traveled until they came in sight of the timber along the Sioux river Then realizing that they were going wrong, they turned about and retraced their steps, reaching the Split Rock camp, near night, to find it deserted They found a piece of paper pinned to a post on which was written "We suppose Everett and Wright have been killed by Indians We have gone home "

As they had had nothing to eat since the day before, and were very much exhausted with traveling on foot, the outlook was discouraging Just at night, however, they had the good fortune to shoot a duck, which they ate raw They camped on the ground, in the shelter of some large rocks, for the night. They were awakened just before midnight by the sound of voices. At first they supposed that Indians were coming upon them They were gladly disappointed, however, to find that the voices proceeded from a squad of soldiers and the mail carrier. The soldiers had with them plenty of provisions. After a bountiful supper, all camped there during the remainder of the night The next day they arrived at the lake just as the settlers were getting ready to send men to the Agency for soldiers to look them up

Hurd and Jones were never heard from afterwards, but at the time of the massacre Mrs Hurd saw one of Hurd's horses, as she believed, ridden by one of the Indian savages.

From that time to the time of the outbreak, nothing occurred at the settlement to arouse any suspicion of danger That settlement was so isolated from others that they seldom heard from the larger towns Everything was quiet and peaceful, and no one had a suspicion of the horrible scenes of bloodshed that were soon to follow.

About the 17th of August, 1862, "Pawn" and five or six other Indians, with squaws and children, came to the lake and camped not far from Mr Everett's place Nothing was thought of this, as roving bands often came that way, and especially as these were the Indians whom the settlers had fed the winter before, and who were supposed to be friendly

Notwithstanding the fact that here and there a slight suspicion existed that the Indians were preparing for war, yet, as a rule, few, if any, believed that there was any real danger.

But on the 20th of August, 1862, the murderous assault commenced all along the line. Men, women, and children, regardless of age or condition, were murdered, mangled, and outraged in the most cold-blooded and barbarous manner.

The people of the little settlement, at Lake Shetek, were industriously pursuing their vocations on the fatal day, and were entirely unprepared for the murderous attack, which commenced near the head of the lake at daybreak.

The first outrage was at the farm of Mr Meyers On account of Mrs Meyers' sickness, Meyers arose at an early hour As he went out of the house, he discovered the Indians, who had torn down his fence and were riding through his corn breaking it down and destroying it. He called to them saying he would whip them if they did not leave, and asked them if he had not always treated them well. They admitted that he had and finally rode away They proceeded at once to the farm of Mrs Hurd, whose husband, with Mr. Jones, had disappeared in the spring A German named Voight was working on the farm When the Indians arrived, Mrs Hurd was milking cows, and on seeing them hastened into the house. The Indians followed her, and, with pretended friendship, asked for some tobacco Voight gave them some, and they commenced to smoke. Mrs Hurd's babe awoke and began to cry, when Voight took it up and walked out into the yard Just as he was turning to go into the house again, one of the Indians stepped to the door, raised his gun and shot him through the breast, killing him almost instantly. They then plundered the house of all its contents, and told Mrs Hurd that if she made any noise they would kill her also, but if she remained quiet they would permit her "to return to her mother" They destroyed nearly everything about the house and then ordered her to leave, telling her which way to go, and informing her that if she should attempt to go to one of the neighbors or make an outcry to warn them they would kill her Mrs. Hurd was compelled to leave by an unfrequented path with her two children, the elder about three years old and the younger less than a year old.

We must now return to the lower, or south, end of the settlement. Early that morning, Mr Everett's brother-in-law, Charles Hatch, started on horseback to go to Hurd's place to get a yoke of oxen to put into a breaking team It was about six miles between the two places When Mr Hatch reached Mr Cook's place, he hitched his horse and went across a marsh, impassable for a horse, to save the time and trouble of going around the marsh, or slough When he reached the Hurd house, a horrid sight presented itself. Voight lay stark dead upon the ground, covered with blood; everything about the house was broken and destroyed, and Mrs Hurd was nowhere to be seen. The tracks at once disclosed the fact that Indians had been there Looking to the east, he saw the Indians making around the marsh He started at once to retrace his steps and warn the settlers; but the Indians arrived at Mr Cook's place ahead of him They found Mrs Cook in the cornfield with her husband's gun, keeping birds from the corn, and Mr Cook at the house They divided, part going to the cornfield and part to the house Those who went to the cornfield asked to see her gun Not suspecting murder, she let them take it. As soon as they got possession of the gun, they told her that she might "go to her mother," for they were going to kill all the white men in the country Those that went to the house asked for a drink of water. As there was none in the house, Cook took the pail to go to the spring He had proceeded but a few steps when one of those cowardly villains, without the least warning shot him in the back, killing him at once Hatch was in sight of the house when Cook was shot. He saw his horse break loose and run off Hatch managed to get past the place unperceived, while the Indians were plundering Cook's home, and went from house to house as fast as he could travel warning the settlers When he reached Mr Eastlick's house he was nearly exhausted Mrs Eastlick, in her account of the massacre, says "My husband and Mr Rhodes had just sat down to breakfast, when my oldest boy, Merton, came to the door saying, 'Charlie Hatch is coming, as fast as he can run ' Hatch was a young man living with his brother-in-law, Mr Everett. Thinking that perhaps some one was sick or hurt, I went to the door As soon as he came near enough to me I saw that he was very pale and out of breath 'Charley, what is the matter?' I asked He shouted—'the Indians are upon us ' 'It cannot be possible,' said I 'It is so,' said Charlie, 'they have already shot Voight.' He then related the other facts he had witnessed, and asked for a horse that he might ride quickly to the lower end of the lake to warn the rest of the settlers. Mr Rhodes let him have one of his horses He asked us for a bridle several times, but we were all so horror-stricken and mute with fear and apprehension that we stood for some time like dumb persons At last I seemed to awake as from a horrible dream and began to realize the necessity of immediate and rapid flight. I sprang into the house and got the bridle for him, urging him to hurry away with all speed He started off, and bade us follow as fast as we could to Mr Smith's house"

Returning to Mrs. Cook, we learn that she remained concealed about the premises until the Indians, tired of plundering the house, departed She then went to the house to find her husband murdered and all her household goods destroyed Notwithstanding the bereavement and the dangers surrounding her, she bravely resolved to warn the other settlers of what had transpired After traveling on foot through brush and timber, and wading in water along the shore of the lake, she reached the lower settlement the same day a little in advance of the murderous savages Mr Hatch had lost no time in notifying every settler of what had taken place Every house was soon deserted Cattle, horses, household goods, and everything were left to be plundered by the merciless savages The settlers all assembled at the house of Mr Wright They were thirty-four in number—men, women and children

"Old Pawn" and his band, who had camped there the Monday before, were at Wright's place and pretended great friendship for the whites They even went so far as to help bring in Mrs Ireland and Mrs Duly and their children, who had been left behind in the flight The men at once prepared Wright's house as well as they could for defensive operations They opened crevices here and there between the logs, as port holes for their guns, and not having entire confidence in "Pawn" and his Indians, told them they could take their stand in the stable. The women were armed with axes, hatchets, and butcher-knives, and sent up stairs with the children These hasty preparations were not fully completed when the murderous savages whooping and yelling like fiends, made their appearance at Mr Smith's house, in full view of Mr. Wright's place, where the settlers were assembled.

At first thought one would suppose that the whites would have remained at the house and defended themselves to the last; but when it is known that the only supply of water was some distance from the house, that they had no provisions for more than a day or two, and that they were surrounded by some two hundred Indians, we can easily understand that any chance of escape, however slim or dangerous, would be eagerly accepted

The murderous Indians had assembled at Smith's house and plundered it From there they sallied forth in squads, mounted on ponies, firing guns and yelling like demons Occasionally they would shoot a cow or an ox, and then ride back to Smith's house. After spending some time in this way, they advanced toward Wright's house Mr Everett noticed about this time one of Pawn's band skulking around to the Indians that were advancing He held a short consultation and sneaked back again Old Pawn who pretended to be friendly, said he would go and see them and find out what they wanted He started out to meet them and had only proceeded a short distance when several of the war party came riding towards him on a gallop He soon halted. As soon as they noticed this, they also stopped and called to him He then went to them and talked for some time, after which he came running back, as though excited, and said there were two hundred warriors coming, and if the whites would quietly go away the "braves" would not harm them, but, if not, they would burn the house and kill them all.

By this time Mr Everett and many of the others were satisfied that Pawn and his band, notwithstanding their pretended friendship, were a part of the conspiracy to murder the settlers

The men had a hurried consultation, and the majority decided to leave the building and take their chances Rhodes and Hatch were sent to Everett's place, half a mile away, to get a wagon for the conveyance of the women and children, and to get some flour, quilts, etc Without waiting for the return of the team, the whole company started across the prairie on foot Rhodes and Hatch overtook them with the wagon by the time they had proceeded half a mile and the women and children, except Mrs Wright and Mrs. Easthck, got into the wagon Mrs Wright bravely shouldered her husband's rifle, he being absent from the settlement at the time of the outbreak They had proceeded a little over a mile when they discovered the Indians following them as fast as they could come, yelling like so many fiends. Old Pawn and his band, who had pretended to be friendly, had joined the others in the work of murder and plunder All was terror and consternation among the settlers They attempted to urge the horses to a run, but the poor creatures were so loaded down that they could not go faster than a walk On came the savages riding at full speed All the fugitives that could run got out of the wagon and hurried on as fast as possible but it was all to no purpose—the savages were soon upon them The men marched at the head of the team, with their guns, in order to protect the women and children who were in advance The men thought at first that perhaps all they wanted was the team, and for that reason sent the women and children ahead As the Indians approached almost to within gunshot, they spread out in a long single line, and came on yelling like demons. When at long range they fired a volley, but no one was hurt Two of the men, Rhodes and Smith, deserted the company, coward-like, and ran for dear life, leaving the others to their fate The two men escaped without a scratch One went to Dutch Charley's and warned his family, and the other went to the Walnut Grove settlement

As soon as the Indians fired the first round, they rushed for the team One of them seized the horses by the bits and turned them around At this juncture, some of the white men fired upon the Indians, and the one having hold of the team fell dead

It was now evident that there was to be a death conflict The men directed the women and children to go to a slough near by and conceal themselves as well as they could in the tall grass the men covering their retreat All started for the slough amid a shower of shot from the Indian guns

Mrs Eastlick received a ball in one heel Mr Ireland's youngest child was shot through one leg Emma Duly received a wound in the arm and Willie Duly received a shot in the shoulder They soon reached the slough, and although the tall grass concealed them from view it afforded little protection There were about two hundred Indians, and only six white men left. For two hours the cowardly savages keeping out of sight as much as possible, poured volley after volley into the slough They would skulk behind the hills, crawl to the top rise and fire, and then drop out of sight It was dangerous for one of the white men to fire his gun, for immediately there would be a volley fired into the grass where he was One after another of the whites was wounded or killed Mr Eastlick, after doing brave work, was killed Mrs Eastlick received a scalp wound and another in the side Mrs Everett received a shot in her neck Mr Everett received a bullet in the thigh which struck the bone, followed around and lodged under the knee Charles Hatch was wounded in the hand and arm, and Bentley in the arm There was little chance for further resistance by the settlers The firing ceased Three of the skulking Indians, one of them old Pawn, then came forward and called upon the women to come out of the slough Mr Everett answered them Pawn, who knew the voice commanded him to come out of the slough. Mr. Everett told him he could not, for he was wounded Pawn said "You lie, you can walk if you want to"

Two of the Indians then fired into the grass where Everett was, one of the bullets striking his arm near the elbow and shattering the bone and a buckshot entering his foot Mrs Everett, forgetting all fear, bravely arose, and in the most piteous manner told them that her husband was dead, they had killed him

Pawn then told her that he would not hurt the rest of them, but that they must come out of the slough, for he wanted her and Mrs Wright for his squaws Mrs Wright could speak the Sioux language, to some extent, and under the advice of Mr Everett, who was now helpless, the two women concluded to go out and confer with the Indians While this hurried conference was going on between Mrs Wright and Mr Everett Uncle Tommy Ireland, a short distance from them arose out of the grass and begged of the Indians to spare the women and children Two of the murderous Indians, only a few rods distant, fired upon him, and he fell to the ground with a groan, saying, "Oh God! I am killed!" He received seven buckshot two of which passed through his left lung one through his left arm and others lodged in various parts of his body

Mrs Wright and Mrs Everett, having been advised by Mr Everett that perhaps by going out to the Indians they might be able afterwards to make their escape, and that refusal would be certain death to all, ventured to go to the Indians After a short talk with the villain, Pawn, they returned and reported that he said he would spare all the women and children if they would come out of the slough After a short consultation the women concluded to go forth with all the children

Ah the sad parting! Mrs Eastlick's husband, was dead. Mrs Ireland bent over the prostrate form of her husband, whom she would never see again, to receive, as she supposed, his dying words and husbands and fathers felt deep anguish as wives and children went forth to death or to a period of suffering worse than death.

Many of the prisoners, as they came forth, were wounded. Mrs Smith, whose husband had fled at the first fire, was wounded in the hip. Next to the youngest of Mrs Ireland's children was shot through the bowels and died in a short time.

Shortly after the surrender the fiendish brutality and devilish cruelty of the Sioux were fully demonstrated. Mrs Eastlick's little five-year-old son while following his mother, who was being led away by an Indian, was attacked by a squaw, beaten over the head with a club and finally ripped open with a knife. Another of her children, Frank, was shot and murdered before her eyes. Mrs Duly's boy Willie was shot in her presence and left in a suffering, dying condition on the prairie. Mrs Ireland and Mrs Smith were murdered in cold blood and left near each other. And near by was the corpse of Mrs Eastlick's third child, Giles.

Shortly after the Indians left the slough with their prisoners, one of the redskins shot Mrs Everett's little boy which so excited her that she broke loose from her captor, and was running back to her boy when she was shot through the body and mortally wounded, dying during the night.

Mrs Eastlick in her account says: "The Indians sent Mrs Wright back to the slough to gather up and bring out the guns. I found that I was quite lame and could hardly walk. * * * The sky soon became overcast with heavy clouds and a furious rain-storm accompanied with thunder and lightning, was coming on. Soon the rain descended in torrents. The Indians caught their ponies, and made all preparations for starting away. We expected to be taken along as prisoners but we were disappointed, as it afterwards proved some were taken while others were put to death, or left in a dying condition. Those of us who afterwards escaped, were, for a long time, in such a plight that death seemed inevitably to stare us in the face."

After giving an account of the death of three of her children, she continues: "Old Pawn came along with Mrs Wright and her children. He brought along a horse which belonged to Charley Hatch, and ordered her to put her children on it, which she did. He then gave her the halter strap and sent her along, telling me to go along with her * * * I asked him what he intended to do with me, and if he meant to kill me? He replied in the negative, then stopped, leaned on his gun, and told me to hurry on * * * I limped along at a rapid pace, but looking back I saw old Pawn standing where I had left him, loading his gun, and I instantly feared that, in spite of all his protestations, he was going to shoot me I had a small slough to cross, and when about half way through it, some one, probably Pawn, shot me again, making four bullets which I had received that day in all The ball struck me in the small of the back, entering at the left side of the spine, and coming out at the right side, just above my hip— also passing through my right arm, between the elbow and the wrist I fell to the ground upon my face, and lay there for some minutes, * * * expecting the Indians would ride over me, as I had fallen in the trail Finding that I could move I crawled about a rod from the trail, and lay down again on my face In a few moments more I heard the step of an Indian, and held my breath, thinking he might pass me, supposing me dead But I was sadly mistaken He came close beside me, stood a moment, then commenced beating me on the head with the butt of a gun He struck me many times so hard that my head bounded up from the sod, and then gave me three severe blows across the right shoulder. I did not lose all presence of mind, although the blows fell heavy and fast. * * * I was so nearly smothered with my face beaten into the grass, that I caught my breath several times. He probably supposed me to be dying, and threw down his gun I thought he was preparing to scalp me I expected every moment to feel his hand in my hair and the keen edge of the scalping-knife cutting around my head But for once I was happily disappointed, for he went away, thinking, no doubt I was dead

I lay here some two or three hours, not daring to stir. * * * The rain had continued to fall all of this time, my clothes were wet through, and I was very cold and chilly. About four o'clock p. m, on trying to get up, I found that I was very weak, and that it required a great deal of painful effort to raise myself to a sitting posture. * * * I then found that the blood had run down from my head and coagulated among my fingers; hence

I knew my head had bled quite freely, or the rain would have washed it away. * * * I was insensible to pain, but by turning my head back and forth, I could plainly hear and feel the bones grate together. I thought my skull must be broken, and this afterwards proved to be true My hair was very thick and long, and this, I think, saved my life by breaking somewhat the force of the blows. Here I sat, wet and cold, not daring to move from the spot I had heard the cry of a child at intervals, during the afternoon, and thought it Johnny (Her son) I thought Merton (an elder son) must have taken him to the wounded men, (in the slough) to stay with them. So I determined to try to go to them, thinking we could, perhaps, keep warm better, for the rain was still falling fast, and the night was setting in, cold and stormy I rose up on my feet, and found that I could walk, but with great difficulty I soon heard Willy Duly, whom I supposed dead long before this, cry out 'Mother! mother!' but a few steps from me * * * Having to pass close by him, as I left the slough, I stopped and thought I would speak to him, but, on reflecting that I could not possibly help the poor boy I passed him without speaking He never moved again from the spot where I last saw him for when the soldiers went there to bury the dead, they found him in the same position, lying on his face, at the edge of the slough "

"I was guided to the place where my children and neighbors were murdered, by the crying of a child, whom I supposed to be Johnny, but on reaching the spot where he lay, he proved to be Mrs Everett's youngest child. Her eldest child Lilly, aged six years, was leaning over him, to shield him from the cold storm. I called her by name, she knew my voice instantly, and said: 'Mrs Eastlick, the Indians haven't killed us yet.' 'No Lilly,' said I, 'not quite, but there are very few of us left Said she, 'Mrs Eastlick, I wish you would take care of Charley ' I told her it was impossible, for my Johnny was somewhere on the prairie, and I feared he would die unless I could find him, and keep him warm She then begged me to give her a drink of water, but it was out of my power to give her even that, or to assist her in any way, and I told her so She raised her eyes, and with a sad, thoughtful, hopeless look, asked, 'Is there any water in Heaven?' 'Lilly,' I replied, 'when you get to Heaven you will never more suffer from thirst or pain ' On hearing this, the poor, little, patient sufferer, only six years old, laid herself down again by her baby brother and seemed reconciled to her fate ''

Mrs. Eastlick then continued her search for her missing children far into the night.

It appears that as soon as the women and children became prisoners they were taken by a portion of the Indians some two miles from the slough where the men were left, toward the Cottonwood river, where the Indians murdered a number of their captives

The other party of Indians returned to Lake Shetek to plunder the houses and gather up the horses and cattle Of the men left in the slough only one was left unwounded, Mr Duly, and he left as soon as the Indians disappeared, making his way to Mankato, leaving the others to care for themselves. Of those left, there were Messrs Everett, Hatch, Bentley and Ireland, and two children of Mrs Eastlick—Merton, about eleven years old, and her youngest child, Johnny, about fifteen months old Mr Ireland was so badly wounded that he did not expect to live, and begged of some of them to kill him outright and end his misery Being shot through the lungs, he breathed with great difficulty, and bloody froth issued from his mouth at every respiration. Mrs Eastlick's children were so young that there was little hope of their being able to go far, and the men left were wounded to such an extent that they could barely get away themselves.

As soon as Messrs Everett, Hatch, and Bentley became satisfied that all the Indians had gone, they left the place as rapidly as their wounds would permit, avoiding the course the Indians had taken, and going in the direction of "Dutch Charley's"—a German settler who lived east of them They left the slough about the middle of the afternoon Along toward night they saw a team and wagon across the prairie, going east, and, knowing that some settler must be making his escape, Mr. Everett told Bentley to go on and overtake the team Bentley, who was only wounded in the arm, started in pursuit, but did not overtake the team till night set in. The team turned out to belong to Mr Meyers, who, with his sick wife, was attempting to escape They reached Dutch Charley's house after dark, to find it vacated. The Meyers family and Bentley staid in the house over night.

Mr Everett was so badly wounded, and so weak from loss of blood that it was with difficulty that he could travel at all, but Charley Hatch staid nobly by him and urged him on with the hope of finding relief at the German's house Late in the night, Hatch and Everett arrived at Dutch Charley's place, but, fearing that there might be Indians in the house, they lay down near the stable Just at daylight, Mr Meyers looked out of the door, and seeing, as he supposed, an Indian peering from behind the stable drew his gun to fire. At the same moment, Charley Hatch looking from behind the stable, thought Meyers was an Indian and aimed his gun at him. Both pulled trigger about the same time Fortunately both guns missed fire By this time Bentley saw Hatch and both parties recognized each other

As soon as possible after the mutual recognition of the parties, the oxen were yoked and hitched to the wagon for a new start Each one felt that his only safety was in getting as far east as Mankato or New Ulm as soon as possible They well knew by what they had seen that the Indians would murder them at sight

They all got into the wagon and soon started, keeping a sharp lookout for Indians The cattle were so exhausted from traveling the day before that they made slow progress The travelers made about fifteen miles that day and camped on Little Creek They had nothing to eat except a little flour, wet with cold water and dried in the sun, for they dared not build a fire, lest the smoke should attract the notice of the savages

By this time Mr Everett's broken arm and wounded leg had become terribly swollen and very painful The jolting of the lumber wagon over the prairie kept up a constant irritation and caused the most intense pain Mrs Meyers, too, was a great sufferer, being very sick, without suitable food or any medicine

We will leave these here at Little Creek, for the present and return to "Uncle Tommy Ireland" As before stated, he was left at the slough, where the attack was made, with two of the Eastlick children. Soon after Mr Everett and the others left, Merton Eastlick told Mr Ireland that he should take Johnny on his back and go to Dutch Charley's Mr. Ireland tried to persuade him not to go, but finding the boy determined on going, he told him he would go with him as far as he could "Uncle Tommy,' as the settlers called Mr. Ireland, followed Merton who carried his baby brother, Johnny on his back After walking about half a mile, Mr. Ireland could go no further and lay down in the grass entirely exhausted

Merton, still carrying Johnny, pursued his course and soon found the trail leading to Dutch Charley's Notwithstanding the heavy rain storm he continued his course and reached Buffalo Lake, Murray county, just before dark. The rain was still falling, and the night was very dark Merton laid his little brother on the ground and bent over him to protect him from the rain During the night the prairie wolves came howling around, but the brave boy shouted at them so lustily that they were frightened away The next morning, at daylight, without food of any kind, he took his little brother and again started on his almost hopeless journey After traveling until about 5 o'clock p m, he overtook Mrs Hurd with her two children, near Dutch Charley's house. They proceeded to the house to find it empty and destitute of provisions They at last found an old cheese, full of skippers, but, having been without food for two days, they were glad to eat of it After eating, they rested till about dark, and then went into the cornfield to remain over night, fearing that Indians might visit the house before morning

It will be remembered that the first man killed by the Indians, at Lake Shetek, was Mr Voight, at Mrs Hurd's house, and that they ordered her to leave with her children at once telling her which way to go and threatening to kill her should she attempt to go to one of her neighbors After traveling for some time with her children, she became bewildered and hardly knew which way to go. The elder child was only three years of age and the younger less than a year old They were on the prairie when the storm came on, without food and no clothing except their every day garments Mrs. Hurd spent the long dreary night watching over, and trying to protect her children from the storm and the mosquitoes. Next day, after wandering around and wading sloughs for some time, she struck the road leading to Dutch Charley's By this time her older child was very sick and unable to walk further—vomiting frequently The poor woman, weak, hungry, and exhausted, was now compelled to carry both children, or leave them to perish alone on the prairie The true mother would never leave her children, under such circumstances, even to save her own life She was so weak that she could carry only one at a time, so she would carry one a short distance and leave it by the roadside, then return for the other—thus traveling three miles to make one In this way she toiled along until she reached Dutch Charley's on the second night, in company with the Eastlick children as herein stated

We now return to Lilly Everett whom we last mentioned as being with her baby brother on the prairie, during the stormy night following the day of the massacre, near where the women and children were murdered, after being taken prisoners It appears that Lilly remained there until the return of the Indians from Lake Shetek, the next day when they again took her prisoner It is not known what was the fate of the poor babe—whether murdered, taken prisoner, or left to perish on the prairie. The Indians, it appears, on the day following the first day of the massacre, collected a drove of cattle and horses from the settlement, and took them and their prisoners into a camp on the Big Cottonwood At this camp were Mrs Wright and her two children, Mrs. Duly and two of her remaining children—a boy and a girl—two of Mr Ireland's girls, Lilly Everett, and others * * *

Mrs Eastlick, after leaving Lilly Everett, as before stated, continued her search for her children She came upon the lifeless forms of Mrs Ireland and Mrs Smith, who had been outraged and murdered She took from the lifeless form of Mrs Smith a heavy apron which she used to protect herself from the storm. She found the young babe of Mrs Ireland sleeping upon the bosom of its dead mother The fate of the babe has never been known, except perhaps to the murderous savages By groping around in the darkness Mrs Eastlick found, not far distant, the corpse of her little boy Giles who had been shot by the Indians and killed almost instantly. Not very far from him her attention was called to the hard breathing of some one, and, upon investigation, she found it to proceed from her son Fred, who had been shot and left there He was unconscious and in a dying condition Who can picture the sorrow of a mother, alone among the dead beside her dying child, with yet other children upon the prairie exposed to the murderous assaults of savages!

"O! that I had found him dead," exclaimed the poor mother, as she reluctantly left the dying to search for the living The poor woman wandered over the prairie in the storm and darkness, thinking at times she heard the crying of her babe, and at intervals calling "Merton," the name of her eldest boy. Thus the night wore on and the dawn appeared without bringing to her the children she sought. At daylight she was unable to know where she was, and could see nothing by which to guide her steps. Being afraid to travel by daylight, lest the Indians should discover her, she hid in a patch of tall weeds

About ten o'clock she heard the report of several guns, and for many hours she could hear the cries and screams of children being tortured At last, about the middle of the afternoon, she heard the discharge of several guns in quick succession, and the wail of the children instantly ceased It is supposed that the Indians, on their return from Lake Shetek, stopped at the scene of the massacre of the day before and tortured and murdered the living infants, taking with them, as prisoner, Lilly Everett

Mrs Eastlick had now passed two days without food or drink She was wounded in four places She then believed that all her children were dead She felt that she had little to live for, and yet the hope of escaping death at the hands of the savages nerved her to renewed efforts During the afternoon she had looked in every direction, and could barely see, in the dim distance, the outline of what appeared to be timber She thought this must be near Buffalo Lake, Murray county, on the road to Dutch Charley's place We continue the narrative in her own language

"As soon as it was dark I started on my weary journey toward the timber I walked some hours and then laid me down to rest on the damp ground I tried to scoop the dew from the grass in my hand to quench my thirst, but it was in vain that I tried it I then took up the bottom of my skirt, and sucked the moisture from it, until I had partially quenched my burning thirst I thought it the sweetest water I had ever drunk I then curled myself upon the ground for a nap, trying to get myself warm by drawing the apron over my head and face, and breathing on my benumbed hands I shook from head to foot I was chilled through, and my teeth chattered Soon sleep and weariness overcame me, and I slept for some time When I awoke, I felt quite refreshed, and started once more on my toilsome journey But by this time, my feet had become very sore, the flesh being worn to the bone, on the top of my toes, by the sharp, coarse prairie grass Indeed, it was quite a hardship for me to walk at all * * * I traveled on in the darkness through sloughs and high tangled grass, and finally came to a slough that was filled with water Here I satisfied my burning thirst, but it was very difficult getting through the marsh, as the grass was as tall as my shoulders, and twisted and matted so that I had to part it before me to get along The water was as much as two and a half feet deep I got so fatigued in wading this wide slough that as soon as I set foot on dry land again, I lay down and rested a long time before starting again

It was now nearly twilight, and I could see timber at a short distance I was so weak that I reeled as I walked, but the sight of the woods revived my strength somewhat, and I dragged myself along, thinking that about five of the sixteen miles to Dutch Charley's were accomplished and vainly hoping that before night I might travel the remaining eleven miles As I neared the timber I heard the crowing of fowls in several directions. It was now broad day and I discovered that this was not Buffalo Lake, but Lake Shetek! I cannot describe my grief and despair at finding myself back there after wandering two long nights, with feet bleeding and torn, and with nothing to eat for three nights and two days My fear of Indians caused me to creep into the first bunch of weeds, where I covered my head and face with the apron to keep off mosquitoes I began to feel sick, and a weak, faint feeling came over me at times There was a house near by which I knew was that of my old neighbor, Thomas Ireland After wavering for a long time between the fear of starvation and the fear of Indians, I chose to risk the danger of being discovered by them, knowing that to remain without food was certain death"

(After giving a description of her difficulty in crossing a slough, with high banks, she continues)

"By pulling myself up by the bushes, I at last reached the top, and found myself within a short distance of a corn field I dragged myself to the field, and plucked the first ear I could reach After many efforts I pulled off the husks, and ate two rows of the green corn They made me very sick at the stomach, but after lying down for some time, I arose, feeling a great deal better and stronger, and soon reached the house * * * I found nothing to eat, but took a cup to the spring, drank some water, and then crawled into a plum-thicket, where I remained until night"

"When it was sufficiently dark, I went back to the house, where I caught and killed a chicken, tore off the skin, and, with my teeth, tore the flesh from the bones This I rendered eatable by dipping it in some brine that was left in a pork barrel I then wrapped the pieces in paper and put them in a tin pail that I found This must be my provision for the next day I also plucked three ears of corn and deposited them with the meat * *. * I put on an old coat to keep me warm, and bound up my raw and painful feet, in old cloths, and started anew on my journey.

"I knew the road to be about two miles due east of this place This night I kept the right direction by the north star, but did not travel far, for I could go but a short distance before I was obliged to lie down and rest Just at daybreak, I reached the road, having made the distance of two miles in the whole night! This I thought was slow traveling, but I was quite encouraged, now that I had found the road and was sure of going right I lay down and slept until after sunrise, then, after eating some green corn, I started again Often did fatigue force me to sit down to rest, and each time after resting, I could scarcely put my foot to the ground My heel, which had been shot through was badly swollen and very sore, but I still pressed onward till I reached Buffalo Lake, at about 11 o'clock a m Here I found that I must cross the outlet of the lake, on a pole When I trusted my weight upon it, over the middle of the stream, it broke, and I fell into the water After laborious and repeated efforts I got out and passed on, but I was soon obliged to stop and repair damages I took off and wrung out some of my clothing and spread them in the sun to dry I also laid the meat in the sun to dry, for it had become so slippery that I could not eat it After this I lay down among the bushes that grew around the lake, and slept very soundly I arose at length, put on my skirt, coat and apron, dressed my feet again, ate some corn and forced down some meat Just as I finished my lonely meal, a flock of ducks flew off the lake and soon a crane followed them This was proof that something had disturbed them, and fearing that Indians were upon my track and close at hand, I hid behind a tree, and watched the road in the direction I had just come

"Presently the head of a horse was seen to rise over the hill near by Indians without doubt, thought I, and shrank down among the bushes, and watched to see a dozen or more savages file along before me!"

"But, oh! what a change from fear to joy! It proved to be the mail-carrier from Sioux Falls to New Ulm I crept out of the brush and addressed him He stopped his horse and staring at me in the utmost astonishment, asked, in the Indian tongue, if I were a squaw I answered yes, not understanding him, and told him the Indians had killed all the white people at the lake 'Why,' said he, 'you look too white to be a squaw'

"'I am no squaw,' I replied, 'I am Mrs Eastlick, you have seen me several times at Mrs Everett's house, I am very badly wounded' He then inquired as to the extent of my wounds, and I showed him my wounded arm and the place where my head was broken He then helped me on to his sulky, and walked along, leading the horse

"About 4 p. m we came in sight of Dutch Charley's when he drove the horse into a ravine away from the road, helped me to the ground, and told me to conceal myself in the grass He said he would go to the house to see if there had been any Indians about He returned presently, saying that there had been none there, that the family had deserted the premises, but that there was an old man there that came from Lake Shetek He helped me to mount the sulky again, and we were soon before the door As soon as I had got to the ground the man made his appearance at the door, and, wonderful to tell, it was poor 'Uncle Tommy Ireland' I hardly knew him, for he looked more like a corpse than a living being His face was deathly pale, his eyes deeply sunk, and his voice reduced to a whisper I hurried to greet him, rejoiced to find, still living, my old friend and neighbor, who had witnessed the same heart-rending sights with myself He clasped his arm around me and we both wept like children at the sight of each other

"He told me that Merton had left the scene of the massacre on the same day, carrying little Johnny, and he thought, perhaps they had reached the house before Dutch Charley's family had left and so gone along with them I was filled with hope and joy to think that perhaps, two of my children were spared."

As before stated, Mr Ireland, after following Mrs Eastlick's sons half a mile from the scene of the first massacre, lay down entirely exhausted, expecting to die He remained stretched upon the ground through all that rainy, stormy night, unable to turn over All the next day and the next night he remained there without food or drink The following morning, Friday, feeling a little better he made his way to Dutch Charley's, where the mail-carrier and Mrs Eastlick found him on Saturday So far he had been unable to get any food or drink The mail-carrier furnished some water, and finally found a cheese which he gave to the wounded man and woman

After feeding the horse and resting a short time the mail-carrier took Mrs Eastlick on the sulky, put some turnips and cheese aboard, and started east again, Mr Ireland accompanying them At first, the wounded man made slow progress but after awhile was able to walk as fast as the horse After following the road about eight miles, they went about half a mile from it and camped for the night, eating turnips and cheese for supper The mail-carrier had a quilt and an oil cloth blanket, and, notwithstanding a heavy rainstorm, during the night, the travelers did not suffer severely.

At early dawn, Sunday morning they again took the road and traveled eastward About noon they espied some persons a long distance ahead of them, and, suspecting they were Indians, the mail-carrier went cautiously ahead to reconnoiter, his two companions slowly following After a while he discovered that the objects they had seen were a woman and two children Upon overtaking them, he found them to be Mrs Hurd and her two children.

Mrs. Hurd and children, and Merton and Johnny Eastlick had left Dutch Charley's place on Friday morning Merton and Johnny were only a short distance ahead of Mrs Hurd, and the mail-carrier and Mrs Eastlick, as may be well imagined, lost no time in overtaking them Merton had then carried his little brother about fifty miles, with very little food or sleep He looked like a skeleton, while the babe was so sick that he did not know his mother His face was a complete scab where the mosquitoes and flies had bitten him

The little company soon arrived at a Mr. Brown's place, found it deserted, and the door of the house fastened The mail-carrier crawled through a window into the house, where he found some bread on the table He brought it out and distributed it among the weary, hungry refugees After feeding his horse, he started for New Ulm alone, advising the others to remain about the premises, and telling them he would send a team and men to bring them to New Ulm

The sufferers being afraid to stay about the house, went to the bank of the Cottonwood, some eighty rods from the house, and secreted themselves in a thicket till night About sunset they returned to the house and crawled in through the window Here they found bedding and clothing, some forty pounds of pork and a crock of lard Mrs Hurd gathered some potatoes and onions from the garden and cooked a meal, which was the first warm meal they had eaten since the Tuesday before Here they remained in constant fear of Indians until Wednesday night, when the mail-carrier returned with sad news of the situation.

He reported that all the settlers on the Cottonwood river were driven away or killed by the Indians; that he had gone in sight of New Ulm, on foot, leaving his horse hidden some miles behind; that he could see the ruins of many burnt houses there, and people, of some kind, walking about the streets, but could not determine whether they were Indians or whites, that, as he was traveling along on foot, he suddenly came upon six Indians, two of whom fired upon and pursued him, that he fled and concealed himself in a slough till his pursuers were tired of hunting for him and gave up the search

All felt that there was no safety in the house, and they again repaired to the thicket—taking with them bedding and clothing. The kind mail carrier then shook hands with them all bidding them good bye, saying that he would return to Sioux Falls and send soldiers to their rescue. When he reached Sioux Falls he found that the settlers had all been killed, and also all the soldiers but two, who managed to escape After many hardships and dangers, he reached Fort Clark in safety

Mr Ireland, the women and children, after great suffering for two days and nights, from mosquitoes and flies, returned to the house, preferring the risk of discovery by Indians to their sufferings in the thicket

We now return to the camp at Little Creek, where we left Mr Everett and his companions The next morning, they started as early as possible Mrs Meyers was no better, and Mr Everett if possible, suffered more than the day before. They drove as far as Leavenworth, that day On every hand there was evidence of the murderous footsteps of the savages The houses were all deserted and the fields laid waste

After looking at several houses they finally went to one a quarter of a mile from the road, just at dusk, and took possession They assisted Mrs Meyers and the children to alight and had just dragged Mr Everett into the house, for by this time he was almost totally helpless—when they heard loud talk not far off Bentley and Hatch crept out through the cornfield, and saw three Indians going past toward a house not far off where the whites first thought of stopping Bentley and Hatch then came back, took Mrs Meyers and children, and hid in the brush some distance from the house Mr Everett could not well be moved so far, so he crawled to a fence and dragged himself through it and out into a buckwheat field He had only just lain down in a hollow when the three Indians came to the house, looked around and finally sat down on the fence, not far from him, and in full view They stayed around the house about three-quarters of an hour, and finally departed without discovering any of the whites It was a very close call, however

All hands remained concealed during the night, Mr Everett staying in the buckwheat patch In the morning they started again, having nothing to eat except flour wet up with water and dried in the sun They crossed the Cottonwood, and drove toward Mankato as rapidly as possible During the forenoon they could hear the booming of cannon at New Ulm This was the day of the battle there

At noon they stopped in a ravine out of sight of the road They were not very far south of New Ulm, but the firing in that direction, and all the indications surrounding them, made them believe that the Indians were in possession of all the country around New Ulm, at least Mr Meyers decided to leave them there and make his way to New Ulm, if possible, hoping to bring a party to their relief He told them that if he did not return or send relief, by the next day at noon, to drive on to Mankato

The situation was indeed critical Bands of murderous Indians were prowling over the country in every direction There was no safety anywhere This little band of settlers was now entirely defenseless The three men were all wounded, Mr Everett so badly injured that he was almost entirely helpless Mrs Meyers was so very sick that there was little hope of her recovery They had no food except a little raw corn and uncooked flour They were worn out with constant watching and anxiety Tormented with an army of flies by day and myriads of mosquitoes by night, they found it almost impossible to sleep A few gopher knolls on a distant hill-side looked like a band of Indians—every rustle of the tall grass brought a startled glance for the cause—every clump of weeds and each little grove might cover the presence of a murderous foe The situation was enough to bring terror to the strongest heart in a robust man, and what must have been the feelings of persons half-starved, wounded, weak, and worn out with constant watching and excitement, as they were compelled to wait and watch for twenty-four hours, with no assurance of relief even then?

After Mr Meyers left for New Ulm, the hours wore slowly away, and at noon the next day he had not returned nor been heard from There was no choice left, the wounded and sick must reach Mankato or perish on the prairie

The oxen were put to the wagon, Mrs Meyers and Mr Everett were lifted into it, and again they started eastward They drove till night and camped near a deserted house Messrs. Bentley and Hatch found some potatoes, which were eaten raw, as the refugees still feared to build a fire lest the Indians should discover them.

At daylight the next morning, they again started east, driving as rapidly as possible When within eight or ten miles of Crystal Lake, they discovered men in the distance, on horseback, whom they supposed to be Indians The horsemen discovered them about the same time and came directly toward them

Bentley and Hatch at once drove to a slough of tall grass, near by, hid Mrs. Meyers, her children, and Mr. Everett in different places, drove the oxen and wagon some distance away; and then secreted themselves in the tall grass Their fear of Indians overpowered every other feeling They had no doubt whatever that the horsemen were Indians, and that if the hidden ones were discovered they would be tortured and murdered.

The horsemen came on rapidly and soon reached the place where the frightened wounded and starved settlers were hiding. They searched the ground thoroughly and soon found one after another of the settlers until all were found except Charley Hatch.

Mr Everett was so sick and weak that he could scarcely speak, but he urged Capt Dane—for he it was with a squad of soldiers—to keep up the search for Hatch. They searched long and called often but could not find him, and were finally compelled to go on to Lake Crystal without him

Poor Charley Hatch heard them plainly enough, but he believed them to be Indians and half-breeds who were calling him, seeking to murder him, so he refused to answer or to stir from his hiding place He remained hidden in the grass all night The next morning Mr Everett prevailed upon the soldiers to renew their search for Hatch. They returned to the slough, and, after much time spent in looking and calling finally rode on to his hiding place His joy at finding them friends instead of murderous savages quite overcame him.

The wounded and nearly famished settlers from Shetek were at once removed to the hospital at Mankato If we are correctly informed, Mrs Meyers died the day after her arrival at Mankato Meyers finally reached Mankato in safety Bentley and Hatch soon recovered from their wounds and suffering but Mr Everett's life hung in the balance for a long time His wounded leg, by constant irritation, was very badly swollen and intensely painful His shattered arm was in an equally bad condition Nothing short of an iron constitution could have brought him from death's door back to life and strength

He remained in the hospital at Mankato until the following February, when he had so far recovered that he could hobble around on crutches, with his arm in a sling, and in that condition he went to Arena, Iowa county, Wisconsin, where he remained for some time

We must now return to follow briefly the history of those made captives at the time of the massacre These were Mrs Wright, her little boy and girl, Mrs Duly and two children, Lilly Everett, two of Mr Ireland's girls, and Mrs Cook The prisoners were first taken from the camp on Cottonwood river to Yellow Medicine, where they remained some time At this place Mrs Wright's son and other captives, including Mrs Cook, were ransomed by Gen. Sibley. About that time Old Pawn took the other Shetek prisoners and started across the country for the Missouri river. The children, especially, were badly treated. An old hag of a squaw seemed to take particular delight in torturing them On two or three occasions Lilly came near being killed by this old squaw, who pounded her with a club most brutally The captives were finally taken into winter quarters, on the Missouri river, some four hundred miles above Ft Randall

Their release was somewhat remarkable Early one morning, Mrs Wright was down at the bank of the Missouri, getting a pail of water, when she discovered two white men in a boat, going down the river She hailed them and told them the story of her capture and of that of the others She said there were two women and six children, and she implored them to rescue the captives. They hesitated some time, but finally concluded that it would be impossible for them to do so They told her, however, that they would make all haste to report the facts to the government officers True to their word, they did so, and the result was published by the Ft. Dodge, Iowa, Times some years ago. We learn from the report that an Indian chief Ma-to To-pa (Four Bear), who was friendly to the whites, was requested to go to the hostile camp and rescue the captives either by force or treaty He called a council of his braves, and it was determined that they would make an effort to rescue the captives He selected ten of his best braves, and with eight good horses started for the hostile camp They took their rifles, bows and arrows, as if going to war, starting in November, 1862, and traveling seven days—snow falling nearly every day. They at last reached the camp of the hostiles, near the mouth of Grand river. The next morning the hostile Indians invited them to a council They tied their eight horses close to the tepee and went in Both parties were armed Four Bear was asked what urgent business had brought him and his braves so far from home at that time of year

He replied that he had heard that they had been on the war path and had taken some prisoners He made quite a speech, and told them that he and his party had come for the captives and would not return without them.

One of the hostiles said "You are all Indians, and belong to the same confederation that we do, and instead of being friendly to the accursed pale face you should unite with us and help slay them as long as there is a Sioux on the face of the earth "

Four Bear replied that he and his braves were friendly to the whites, and always would be—that they would never lift a hand against the women and children of the whites, and that the hostiles must give up the captives

The council was a stormy one, lasting all day; but finally one of the hostiles said they had the captives and they were worth money, and nothing less than $1,000 in ponies would get them Near night they finally agreed that the hostiles should exchange their eight prisoners for the eight horses and saddles The exchange was made that night, and then they smoked the pipe of peace

The hostile band on their retreat from Minnesota, were so afraid of being overtaken by the whites that they took no time to hunt, and in consequence the prisoners were nearly starved to death The first square meal for some time was indulged in that night, and it consisted of venison and coffee Four Bear was of the opinion that the women and children relished his cooking that night.

The prisoners were so destitute of clothing, that their rescuers were compelled to divide their wardrobe with them The weather was intensely cold, but the homeward march began. The six children had to be carried every step of the way, and the two women the greater part of it Some of the Indians would go ahead and kill game, and get the camp ready at night when they arrived. In consequence of the great depth of snow it was a slow, laborious tramp At Swan Lake they met some of their people and traded some ammunition and blankets for sugar and coffee for the captives, and in the morning they all contributed everything they could spare for the use of a big horse to get home with. They made a "travoy," which is two long poles, one end of each fastened to the saddle, extending backward on each side of the horse with crosspieces lashed on The six children were bundled on this vehicle and the party then made fine progress. They arrived at last at their camp, and the next day they took the captives across the river and turned them over to the officer in command, who gave Four Bear the following.

Fort Pierre, D T, Dec 12, 1862

The bearer, Ma-to To-pa, is one of the eleven Indians that recovered Mrs Julia Wright, Mrs Emma Duly and six children from the Ih-Sann-Ta, near the Grand river, in November, 1862. He desires to be kindly treated by all (Signed) John Pattee,

Major First Iowa Cavalry, Expedition in Search of Prisoners

In course of time, the captives were sent down the Missouri river, and across the country to Ft Dodge, Iowa

Mr Everett saw a report in the Chicago papers that the captives would soon be at Cedar Falls, Iowa, He left Arena, Wisconsin on crutches his wounded arm still useless, to meet them at Cedar Falls He was doomed to disappointment. for on his arrival there he learned they had not yet arrived, and that he must go to Ft Dodge to meet them He took the stage for that place, but on his arrival there could hear no news of them. There he was taken sick and confined to his bed for two weeks In the mean time the captives arrived, and among them his daughter, Lilly Mr Wright also met his wife and little daughter at that place

Mr Everett. as soon as he was able to travel, returned again to Wisconsin with Lilly. He remained at Arena until 1867. He lost all his property at Lake Shetek, amounting to $5,000, and received from the government for his loss only $800

He was married to Miss Addison in the spring of 1866, and in the fall of 1867, came to Waseca and built the first store erected in Waseca.

While this substantially closes that portion of the Shetek massacre relating to our townsman, there are other portions yet to be related in order to round out and make complete the history of that awful and tragic event

* * * * * *

It will be remembered by our readers that the mail carrier, after his failure to reach New Ulm, returned to Brown's house where he had left Mrs Hurd and her two children, Mrs Eastlick and two children, and Uncle Tommy Ireland After the mail-carrier left, this party remained at Brown's house for nine days, living upon the vegetables growing on the farm

Mr Ireland gradually recovered from his wounds, while Mrs Eastlick was as yet unable to walk Mr Ireland proposed, at last, to make a trip to New Ulm and get assistance to remove the women and children During their stay there two large dogs had come to them and remained there

On Monday morning, the ninth day they had been there, Mr Ireland, taking two cooked chickens as a supply of food, started for New Ulm, saying that he should try to reach New Ulm that night, and would send relief on Tuesday Mrs Eastlick says

"All the afternoon of Tuesday we looked long and eagerly for some one to come to our relief, until after dark, when I retired and slept some hours About midnight we were awakened by the loud barking of the dogs Mrs Hurd arose and went to the window, but could see nothing The dogs, however, barked more savagely than before, running out a short distance and then back to the door This frightened us very much, as we thought it must be Indians, or the dogs would not act so But, thought I, whether they are friends or enemies, I must arise and dress, though it may be the last time So I began putting on my clothes, still asking Mrs Hurd if she saw anything When I was about dressed, she exclaimed, 'My God! Cook, is that you?' Then I realized that it was some one whom she knew It proved to be a young man named Cook, who lived at Lake Shetek, and some time before the outbreak had gone to Crystal Lake, to work in harvest, and my neighbor, Mr Wright, who was also gone at the time They came into the house and greeted us with tears in their eyes, while Mrs Hurd and I wept aloud for joy They were accompanied by a squad of soldiers, who also came into the house The soldiers stationed guards about the house, to prevent a surprise We now learned that Uncle Tommy had succeeded in getting into New Ulm about noon, on Tuesday, and at once made known our condition to Capt Dane, who ordered fourteen men under Lieut Roberts to prepare to start as soon as possible to our relief It was almost sunset before they were ready to start, when, lo! Messrs Wright and Cook came into town, and learning the facts, volunteered to attend them as guides They reached our place at midnight, and, fearful that the sight of them all at once would frighten us, Wright and Cook came on alone to rouse us. The soldiers brought some tea and crackers, killed some chickens, gathered some vegetables, and prepared a good meal At daylight they placed the feather bed, some quilts and a buffalo robe in a light, two-horse wagon I was then helped in with Mrs Hurd and our children * * * When about five miles on the road, Lieut. Roberts rode back and ordered the driver to turn out of the road, pointing a little distance ahead of us I looked in the direction he pointed, and beheld the body of a gray-haired man, lying in the road. This was the body of Mr Brown, who owned the house where we had stopped We soon crossed a run where stood his wagon with the goods thrown out and scattered upon the ground. There were two feather beds, which the soldiers took along. Near the wagon was the body of Mrs Brown, with her head split open As we started out in the morning, one of the soldiers, Mr Gilfillan, tarried behind, and got lost from the company His remains were found next day, some six miles from New Ulm, shot through the breast and his head severed from his body"

All along the route, the houses had been plundered, and several dead bodies were found

These refugees remained for some time in New Ulm and were kindly nursed and cared for About the 5th of September, they went to Mankato under escort. As soon as Mrs Eastlick was able to travel, she went to friends in Wisconsin

Mrs Cook has given an account of her captivity, from which we condense the following

She was taken with some of the other prisoners from the slough back to the settlement at Lake Shetek, to Mr Ireland's house, where a large number of Indians were camped for the night. They held a big war-dance that night, notwithstanding the storm. The Indian who claimed her told her to stay in the tepee or the other Indians would kill her They kept up the pow-wow nearly all night, and, their chief having been killed during the day, they chose Old Pawn to succeed him

Next morning some of the Indians brought in Lilly Everett, so chilled and wet that she could hardly speak. Mrs Cook and Mrs Duly wrapped her in a shawl and seated her close by the fire. This so enraged the savages that they fired at them, one bullet passing through the skirt of Mrs. Duly's dress, and another piercing the shawl worn by Mrs Cook, just below her shoulders Fortunately neither one of them was hurt.

While returning to the lake, Mrs Cook was leading little Belle Duly, five years old, when the murderous old squaw that killed Fred Eastlick, came along, snatched the child away, whipped her over the face with a raw-hide, raised her as high as she could and threw her upon the ground with all her force, then she tied the child to a bush, stepped back a few paces, and threw knives at her, hitting her in various parts of the body until life was extinct, while the mother was forced to behold the sight with no power to shield her child.

The Indians gathered together quite a drove of cattle, loaded several wagons with plunder, and compelled the women to drive the oxen that drew the wagons, and also the loose cattle. They went to the Cottonwood, and thence across the prairie to the Yellow Medicine country

Mrs Cook was with the savages seven weeks For three or four weeks she had plenty to eat, but was finally sold to an old Indian who was very good to her sometimes, and at other times very cruel One day he told her he was going to another band of Indians, at some distance, and some of the squaws told her that where they were going there was hardly anything to eat He finally started off, compelling her to go with him. She made no resistance, but, after going some five miles, she offered to carry his gun for him. He gave it to her. She soon managed to take the cap and throw it away, then spit in the tube to make sure the gun would not go off She then told him she should go no farther with him He seized his gun from her hands and told her to go on or he would shoot her, at the same time raising the gun She boldly told him to shoot, for she would not go with him, and bared her breast, as if to be instantly killed. He was amazed, and dropped the butt of his gun in astonishment He probably thought her the bravest squaw he ever saw. At least he coucluded to return with her.

That night she intended to escape with a captive squaw that had married a white man, but their plan was defeated by the sickness of the squaw's babe The next morning the child was better and all the Indians left the camp except the one who claimed to own Mrs Cook. This was an opportunity not to be lost. Mrs Cook stole away to the river unperceived, and the squaw rode a pony in the same direction, pretending to be going to water him. She let him go at the river and started with Mrs Cook They traveled as rapidly as possible, crossed the Minnesota river ten times that day in order to hide their trail if followed. They traveled, they thought, about thirty miles, when they came upon "Red Iron's" band of Indians whom they joined After remaining three or four days with this band, they were surrendered, with a great many other captives, to Gen. Sibley's command by Red Iron

The year 1862 was a year of blood for America. We had not only the bloody Sioux Massacre, but many bloody battles occurred between the Union and the Rebel forces.

And thus came to a close the darkest year in the history of the state of Minnesota The frontier had been made desolate, and many familes had lost everything But fortunately the crops had been of the very best, and there was food enough for all The state generously extended aid to the people of the frontier and there was very little suffering.

CHAPTER XXXI, 1863.

EMANCIPATION PROCLAMATION—COUNTY MILITARY DISTRICTS—WAR PRICES—SIBLEY EXPEDITION AGAINST THE SIOUX—BATTLES OF BIG MOUND, DEAD BUFFALO LAKE—DEATH OF LITTLE CROW—GETTYSBURG, SURRENDER OF VICKSBURG AND PORT HUDSON, THE NEW YORK RIOTS—WILTON WEEKLY NEWS—TERRIBLE BLIZZARD DEC 31

In some respects the year 1863 was the most notable in the history of our nation and of the world New Year's day is second only to Christmas as a day of enjoyment throughout the civilized world, even in ordinary times, but this New Year's day was one long to be remembered and held in reverence

> "Ring happy bells across the snow,
> "Ring in the nobler modes of life,
> "Ring out the old, ring in the new "

From the issuing of the Declaration of Independence to this "happy New Year" of 1863, the life of the nation had been a paradox—as some said, a living lie

On this day the paradox was wiped out, for President Abraham Lincoln issued his Emancipation Proclamation forever freeing the black and yellow slaves in the rebel states from the chains of the most odious bondage that the civilized world had ever seen This brave, generous, God-like act—already too long delayed, as many thought—set forever free over four millions of oppressed human beings Not only will the intelligent American citizens of African blood, to the remotest generation revere the name of Abraham Lincoln, but intelligent and Christian American citizens of Caucasian blood will link his name with the greatest of earth for having, as far as possible, emancipated the laborers of the white race from the competition of chattel slavery

There was no change in the board of Waseca county commissioners. Among the proceedings of the board for the year, the following are noted

It was "ordered that the treasurer of the county be directed not to receive soldiers' orders for bounty (taxes) of such persons as were rejected for disability at Fort Snelling, and not now in the service of the United States" At the same meeting the county was divided by the commissioners into seven military districts as follows:

First district, Blooming Grove; Second district, Iosco, Third district, Janesville, Fourth district, St Mary, Fifth district, Wilton and Woodville; Sixth district, Otisco and New Richland; Seventh district, Vivian and Byron Alton and Freedom then belonged to the Winnebago Indians

At a subsequent meeting, June 15th, the board appointed officers for some of the districts In the St Mary district Enoch Plummer was appointed captain, John Byron, now deceased, first lieutenant, and Thomas J Kerr, second lieutenant W H Wyman was appointed captain in the Sixth district, but the record does not show that he had any lieutenant, either first or second In the Second district, Wm. E Allen was appointed captain, J S G. Honnor, first lieutenant, and John G Ward, second lieutenant There is no record of appointments in other districts, nor does it appear that any military organizations were ever perfected under the law

It seems that there was at that time a suspicion that justices of the peace did not pay over promptly all fines collected by them, for in the proceedings of Jan 29, 1863, the following entry appears:

"Ordered that all justices of the peace in the County of Waseca be directed to bring their dockets to the district attorney to be compared with the treasurer's books; and it is further ordered that all fines due the county be paid immediately"

Whether the order received any attention does not appear of record, but it is preserved as one of the many orders made by county commissioners. Such orders were without the authority of law, but serve to show the condition of affairs at the time.

There being at that time two newspapers purporting to be printed in the county, but really printed, one at Owatonna, the other at Faribault, it was "voted that the chairman be authorized to receive bids for the county printing and to contract for the same with the lowest bidder entitled to it" This was the first time our county printing was ever let to the lowest bidder The printing was let to Col J C. Ide, editor of the Courier and also county auditor, for the sum of $130, not including the tax sale list of taxes.

The tax levy for 1863 was as follows: State revenue, four and a half mills, county expenses, three mills, for liquidation of county bonds, four mills, back indebtedness, three mills, one-half cash, school tax, two and one-half mills,—a total of seventeen mills on the dollar This tax levy was made Oct 6, 1863 At the same meeting the county auditor's salary was raised $50, making his total salary $500 per year And it cost more to live then than it does at this writing, 1904

The spring stocks of merchandise brought "war prices" in Waseca county. In consequence of the war, prices of goods which had for some time been gradually advancing, reached pretty high figures as early as March. The first of April, common cotton sheeting was selling for fifty cents per yard; calico, at from thirty-five to forty cotton shirting, at from forty-five to sixty cents, coffee, at from forty to fifty cents per pound, the poorest, cheapest tea, at $1 50 per pound common brown sugar—people do not eat such now-a-days,—from sixteen to twenty-five cents per pound The prices of nearly all merchandise were in proportion

Very many of our people, the majority to say the least, made their table beverages, during the high prices, of barley, carrot, beet, corn, wheat rye, or pea coffee, and pennyroyal or sage tea, and they drank these without much sugar Many people then learned for the first time, that hot water, with a little milk or cream, at meal time, is more conducive to health than the best tea or coffee

The weather was mild during the winter of 1862-3 and the spring months were very favorable to early seeding The sowing of wheat was commenced as early as April 1st, and by the 15th of May, spring crops were all planted There was very little rainfall all through the season, and the hay crop was comparatively light, but the wheat, oat, and barley crops yielded well and were of excellent quality

THE INDIANS AGAIN

A small band of Indians in the month of April, made a raid into the Watonwan river settlement, killed five persons, stole several horses, and made their escape Within the summer, Gen Sibley, with three thousand troops from Minnesota, and General Sully, with about an equal force from Iowa, advanced into the country then occupied by the Indians The battle of Big Mound was fought by the forces under Gen Sibley, July 24th At this battle, Rev Dr Weiser was treacherously shot and killed by the Indians while they were pretending to want peace One white man was killed by lightning during the battle Lieut Freeman, while hunting, was killed by the Indians the morning before the Indians had been discovered by the scouts A large number of the red men were killed and wounded and some of them scalped by the hunters On the 26th of July, at

DEAD BUFFALO LAKE

the Indians, mounted on ponies and led by Grey Eagle, made a dash for the hay cutters and mules, but were promptly met by the Mounted Rangers, who gave them battle. A number of the savages were killed in this engagement, among them their chief, Grey Eagle, who fought bravely but was soon killed.

On July 3, 1863, Little Crow, the chief who had led in the massacre of 1862, was shot and killed near Hutchinson by Nathan Lampson Little Crow also shot Lampson, wounding him in the shoulder The second shot from Lampson's gun proved mortal Little Crow's son, aged 16 years, was with his father at the time of his death, but made his escape He was afterwards taken prisoner and finally sent to the reservation of his people on the Missouri river, where he has since died.

Little Crow died in disgrace, having been deposed by the warriors of his nation shortly after the decisive battle of Wood Lake

BATTLE OF GETTYSBURG.

June 18th, 100,000 rebels entered Pennsylvania, near Chambersburg. On the 1st, 2d and 3d days of July occurred the great battle of Gettysburg, which was one of the greatest of the civil war, and really the turning point in the great struggle It was in this great battle that the First Minnesota regiment conferred imperishable honor and fame upon our state. July 4th, Vicksburg, Miss., surrendered to Grant with her 31,000 rebels, 220 guns and 70,000 small arms July 8th, Port Hudson surrendered to the Union army July 13th, the New York rioting commenced. —the negro orphan asylum was burned, negroes were hanged in the streets, and houses robbed and burned by rebel sympathizers The rioting lasted several days and was finally suppressed by Union troops The last battles of the year occurred at Chattanooga and Lookout Mountain, Nov 23d, in which our Union soldiers were victorious

THE FALL ELECTION

It was a close call for the Republicans in this county at the fall election of 1863 The draft, which had been ordered throughout the country, had been very unpopular The local Republicans that were appointed to conduct it—especially the writer, who was appointed to the very unpleasant position of deputy United States marshal—were accused of many wrongful acts and although nearly all the accusations were false and unjust, as was afterwards admitted, they had their influence upon the voters Waseca county was then in the same legislative district with Freeborn and Steele counties The candidates for state senator were F J Stevens, Republican Amos Coggswell Democrat, and Jacob Mail, independent Stevens received 282 votes, Coggswell 58, and Mail 51

Representatives:—Philo Woodruff, Republican, 262 votes, Wm Brisbane, Democrat, 251 Majority, 11

County treasurer:—P C Bailey Rep., 286 Enoch Plummer, Dem, 234 —Majority, 52

Register of deeds —Tarrant Putnam, Rep, 241, H P. Norton, Dem, 267 —Majority 26

Sheriff —D L Whipple, Rep, 268, N McGrath, Dem, 247 — Majority, 22

Judge of Probate:—H D Baldwin, Rep, 251, P Brink Enos Dem, 258 —Majority, 7

County Attorney —James E Child, Rep, 255 P Brink Enos, Dem, 252 —Majority, 3

Coroner.—W S Baker, Rep, 274, Peter Eckert, Dem, 238.—Majority, 36

Court Commissioner:—James E Child, Rep, 217, John Bradish, Dem, 166, P. Brink Enos, Dem., 20.—Majority over both, 31

Surveyor:—H G Mosher, Dem., (no opposition) 509

County Commissioner, one district.—W G. Kennedy, Rep, 76, Wm Byron, Dem, 69—Majority, 7.

THE FIRST PERMANENT NEWSPAPER

As before mentioned, there were two newspapers, "The Waseca Home Views" and "The Waseca Courier," purporting to be edited and published in Wilton, but they were really side editions of other papers The Courier was printed at Owatonna, Col. Ide, Republican, being the Wilton editor The Home Views was printed at Faribault, Buel Welch, a Democrat, being editor.

The people of Wilton said they wanted a really home paper, so Hon H D Baldwin, who held a chattel mortgage on the press and material of the Home Views plant, at Faribault, arranged to take the plant in satisfaction of the mortgage. He employed a man named James Mowatt, an Englishman by birth, to conduct the mechanical department, and arranged with the writer to edit and take charge of the business management of the paper After some delay in getting the plant in working order, the first number of the

WILTON WEEKLY NEWS

made its appearance It was a six-column folio—Republican in politics. It is said that no paper ever flourished in a country town where the editor and the publisher are separate, neither having entire control And so at the end of the year the writer purchased the plant and took entire control It was three years before the plant paid expenses and four years before the proprietor received any income for his own services, but, then, he enjoyed the excitement of the business and the struggle for success, and has never regretted the hard work that finally brought reasonable success Under the chapter relating to "Journalism," a full account of newspaper enterprises in the county will be given "without hatred or affection"

A TERRIBLE STORM.

The last day of December, 1863, and the first two days of 1864 brought one of the most severe storms that have ever visited the county since its first settlement in August, 1854 The wind blew a gale The air was filled with the tempest-driven snow, and the cold was intense The temperature went as low as 34 degrees, in Wilton, and at St Louis, Mo, and in Kentucky and Ohio, the thermometer registered as low as 24 degrees On the last day of December the air was so filled with fine particles of frost and snow and driven with such force by the wind that objects a dozen feet distant could not be seen It was almost impossible to face the wind for any distance Fortunately the storm arose in the night, and no one in this section was seriously injured

CHAPTER XXXII, 1864.

INTENSE COLD—J B JACKSON, CHAIRMAN OF BOARD—REMOVAL OF THE WINNEBAGOES—SETTLEMENT OF FREEDOM AND ALTON—FINANCES OF COUNTY, ORDERS ISSUED AT NINETY CENTS ON THE DOLLAR—REMOVAL OF JUDGE ENOS—DRAFT FOR 500,000 MEN—BIG SOLDIER BOUNTIES—NEGROES AND THE WAR—EXTENSIVE MAIL ROBBERIES BETWEEN WILTON AND MANKATO—B A LOWELL STATE SENATOR

The year 1864 opened with a terrible storm and most intense cold The remainder of the winter was cold and at times stormy. Winter continued until the latter part of March, and very little seeding was done prior to the middle of April The season as a whole was a dry one, but the state was blessed with abundant crops The harvest weather was all that could be desired, and notwithstanding a scarcity of harvest hands, the crops were all saved in good shape

COUNTY BOARD WORK

At the annual meeting of county commissioners, held Jan 5th, 1864, the board was organized by the election of J B. Jackson, chairman. No business beyond the ordinary was transacted at this session, except that the county auditor's salary was raised from $450 per year to $500 Each commissioner district, at that time, had a school examiner appointed by the county board. The examiners appointed for 1864 were as follows: M S. Green, of Iosco, B A Lowell of Otisco, and Eugene A. Smith, of Wilton. The last refused to serve and Rev. E S Smith was appointed in his place, Jan 27th, 1864 During the legislative session of 1864, the office of county superintendent of schools was created and made appointive by the county board, and on the 9th of March, 1864, Rev E S Smith was appointed county superintendent of schools at the magnificent salary of $100 per year At this March session another $100 was added to the county auditor's salary, making it $600 a year.

THE WINNEBAGO INDIAN RESERVATION

As a result of the Indian outbreak in 1862, the Winnebago Indians were removed from their reservation in this state to a new reservation in Nebraska. In their reservation here there were included the townships now known as Freedom and Alton, and the west tier of sections of the townships of Wilton and St Mary—the larger portion of their reservation being in Blue Earth county adjoining

After the Indians were removed, the lands were sold to white men under sealed bids, the minimum price per acre, as the writer remembers it, being $2 50 The lands were taken very rapidly, and many farms were settled upon and improved in 1864

At the meeting of the county board, March 9, 1864, a petition was received to have the new territory organized as a township with township officers, etc The county board passed an order organizing townships 106 and 107 range 24, which provided that "the first election should be held at the house of Stephen Robinson, situated at the place (then) known as Peddler s Grove, on the same day (April 5) and hour, in this year 1864, which the law provides for the town elections in organized towns and that when so assembled for their town election, the electors shall elect a name by which both townships shall hereafter be known until such time as it shall be found that a sufficient number of inhabitants shall have settled in each or either to entitle them to a separate organization, and that when such separate organization shall take place, town No 106 shall retain the name agreed upon at this, their first election "

There was quite a struggle regarding the name, but "Freedom,' was finally adopted According to the history issued by the Union Publishing Company in 1887 Mr F. D Seaman had the casting vote, which selected the name, he being one of the committee of three to decide on a name At a special meeting of the board in April, Ferdinand Turnacliff, of Wilton, and W W. Cowles, of Janesville, were appointed appraisers of school lands for the county

At a later meeting, April 30, the county board ordered the county attorney to notify all persons who were selling spirituous liquors to take out license or stop selling liquor There was something of a temperance revival at the time, and the board increased the license fee from $25 to $50, except for hotels, which were permitted to deal in liquors by paying a license fee of $15 Fifty dollars was at that time considered a very high license fee

In the month of August, this year, two of the county commissioners resigned John S G Honnor, of Iosco, removed to Redwood Falls, and J B Jackson emigrated to McLeod county, in this state. On the 15th of August, the appointing board, consisting of John C Ide, county auditor, P Brink Enos, judge of probate, and H. P. Norton, register of deeds, met and appointed Fred W Kittredge, then of Okaman, and Hon Warren Smith, of Wilton, to fill the vacancies The new board met on the 22d of the same month and elected Mr Smith chairman of the board.

The financial condition of the county can be judged by the following which was adopted by the board, Sept 23d

"Be it ordered that the county auditor be authorized to settle with the parties holding tax certificates against lands illegally or irregularly issued, or on which taxes may have been paid and the same having been returned delinquent and sold, and to pay such parties in county orders at ninety cents on the dollar"

Early in the fall Judge Enos moved to Nebraska, and at the meeting of the county board, Dec 2, it was "ordered that James E Child be appointed judge of probate to fill the vacancy caused by the removal of P Brink Enos, Esq"

THE WAR OF THE REBELLION

Notwithstanding the victories of the Union forces during the year 1863, the Confederates with great courage and energy maintained their warlike attitude and aggressive movements On the first day of February, the president ordered a draft of 500,000 men, each locality being permitted to furnish its quota of men by enlistment On the 15th of March came an added call for 200,000 more—700,000 in all. Every town became a recruiting station Town bounties for soldiers to fill town quotas ran high—from $100 to $500 in this county. All sections of the country were equally anxious to secure volunteers, and in some towns resort to the draft was unavoidable Scarcely had the first two calls for troops been filled before another half million men were called out This third call was issued July 18th, 1864 And near the close of the year, Dec 19th, another draft was ordered for 300,000 men to fill the depleted ranks of the great Union armies As before noted, large bounties were offered by the several townships and herculean efforts were put forth, especially after the fall election, to fill the ranks and crush the Rebellion, which everyone then realized would soon be accomplished

THE NEGROES AND THE WAR

There was one condition of the public mind or existing prejudice at the time that the writer could never fully understand Up to the very close of the Rebellion, many people at the North protested against the enlistment of negroes in the Union armies While the rebels were using them to build fortifications and roads, to serve as cooks and servants, to raise crops to support the rebels in the field, and while the negro slave was the innocent cause of the rebellion, and his personal liberty and rights depended wholly upon the success of the Union armies, nevertheless many people in the North raised their hands in holy horror at the mere suggestion that the negro should do some of the fighting in defense of those rights. We did not hesitate to use horses, mules, or asses in our military operations, we were willing to sacrifice our best blood, the flower of our youth and the strength of our noblest manhood, in defense of the nation, but the negro slave of the worst rebels that ever attempted the assassination of Liberty and Equal Rights in the world was too sacred to be enlisted to fight for his own personal liberty and those equal rights of all men, which Jefferson taught and the Revolutionary Fathers proclaimed to all nations and all men as the foundation principles upon which was builded our magnificent edifice. It was a fool prejudice that cost the nation rivers of blood and millions of treasure

THE ELECTION OF 1864.

The presidential election was of absorbing interest Union

men of both parties believed that the life of the nation hung in the balance Over a million patriots were upon the battle fields far from their homes They had made great sacrifices Would they be sustained by the men at home at the ballot box? Should the nation live or perish? The struggle was a memorable one and Abraham Lincoln and the "boys in blue" were sustained Waseca county was carried by the Union forces by a good working majority Hon. B A. Lowell was elected state senator—the representatives of the district going to Freeborn and Steele counties W G Kennedy, of St Mary, was re-elected county commissioner, John S. McKune, of Blooming Grove, and Rev C S. Luce, of Wilton township, being the other two members—all Union men Col J C. Ide was again elected county auditor.

The eventful year closed with high hopes among the people of the North that 1865 would bring the end of the Slave-holders' Rebellion, and that before another Christmas the nation would be all free

EXTENSIVE MAIL ROBBERIES.

For several weeks of the late summer and the fall months of 1864, there were frequent complaints that letters along the stage route between Mankato and Owatonna never reached their destination. Little was thought of the matter, however, until by mere accident a large number of letters, stolen from the mail sacks, were discovered at the Globe hotel at Wilton by Mr. Seth W Long, who kept the stage house As soon as he made the discovery, he informed James E Child, who was then deputy United States provost marshal, of the county. Sheriff Whipple was also called in consultation and the letters were hastily examined and listed. Mr Child at once proceeded to the Winnebago agency and, calling upon the Indian agent and the postmaster, instituted a search about the hotel and the stage barn. Nearly two bushels of letters were found in the barn hidden in a partition boarded up on each side, the letters having been dropped in from time to time between the studding Mr Child then went on to Mankato and notified the postmaster there.

The abstracted letters were listed and examined as to their dates and postmarks, and it soon became apparent to the examiners that the letters had all been stolen by one of the Burbank stage drivers Every letter was evidently taken on alternating days by some one between Wilton and the Indian, or Winnebago, agency Only two men drove stage between those points—a youngish man, called "Jimmie" Burns, and an older man known as "Pat" One or the other of these must have stolen the letters

Taking the last letters stolen and tracing the record backward, it was quite evident that Jimmie or an accomplice was the guilty person, but to make sure that "no guilty man escape," the authorities arrested both the men. There was really no evidence against Pat. Yet the popularity of Jimmie Burns was such that for a time suspicion rested heavily upon the other mail carrier At the examination, however, Pat was exonerated and Jimmie was held for trial

As is often the case, a very worthy and influential young lady was in love with the thief, and all her influence and the efforts of her friends were put forth to prevent his conviction Able attorneys were employed and everything that a devoted young woman could say or do was done to save her thief-lover from conviction She succeeded But the stage company having examined into the matter, had no further use for Jimmy

Then it was that the rascal left for parts unknown and deserted the devoted girl that had saved him From worry and disappointment or from some other cause, the young woman soon after fell ill and died—the victim of misplaced affection and confidence

In all, over three bushels of the stolen letters were found, many of them having contained small amounts of money It was estimated that nearly $200 had been stolen from the letters. Many drafts and checks were found and returned to the owners

It was a sad case of miscarriage of justice, and shows that it is sometimes an easy matter to instill into the minds of a jury a "reasonable doubt" of the guilt of the guiltiest rascal on earth.

Jimmie Burns was a complete exemplification of Shakespeare's saying—

"That one may smile and smile, and be a villain "

CAPTER XXXIII, 1865.

COLLAPSE OF SOUTHERN REBELLION—ENO SHACKLES FOUND —LATE SPRING—ASSASSINATION OF LINCOLN—THE INDIANS AGAIN, MURDER OF THE JEWETT FAMILY—JACK CAMPBELL, HALF-BREED HANGED—RETURN OF SOLDIERS—ELECTION OF 1865.

The year 1865 will go down the ages as the most noted in our history. It witnessed the collapse of the Southern Rebellion, the surrender of the Confederate armies, and the restoration of peace throughout the nation And our citizen soldiery might well have said with the poet:

"Now are our brows bound with victorious wreaths,
Our bruised arms hung up for monuments,
Our stern alarms changed to merry meetings,
Our dreadful marches to delightful measures"

Our county commissioners met in annual session Jan. 11th, and organized by the election of W. G. Kennedy chairman On the 12th it was "ordered that the license for retailing liquors in saloons or taverns, for the year 1865, in Waseca county, be $75 for each, and that N E Strong & Co shall pay $10 for a license to retail liquors for medicinal purposes or as druggists" The county auditor's salary was increased to $700 per year at this meeting

At the session of the board, March 31st, five dollars was appropriated to be tendered to Buel Welsh, Esq., who had found and returned the shackles worn by the horsethief, Eno, while in jail Eno had broken jail in 1863 and made his escape by the assistance of outside parties The shackles were found by Mr. Welsh while hunting one day in Otisco

Here is a peculiar entry made by Auditor Ide It is especially so as every member of the board, as well as himself, was a total abstinence man It reads as follows

"October 13th, 1865 Board met pursuant to adjournment. The board being full, proceeded to transact the following business"

The spring of 1865 was much later than usual A very few sowed wheat the last week in March Then the weather turned cold, and it was the middle of April before the majority could seed. In fact, it was a cold, backward spring

VICTORY AND PEACE AT LAST

The first week in April the whole country was made joyous by the glorious announcement that the Union armies had triumphed, and that peace was at hand. No words at the command of the writer could give utterance to the unfeigned emotions of joy and hope and thankfulness which took possession of the loyal millions of the land Even the Copperheads and the Secessionists were glad that brave men would no longer be called upon to sacrifice their lives in the camp and upon the battlefield

THE ASSASSINATION.

But alas! What a sudden transition from the most heartfelt joy to the deepest gloom!

While the loyal people everywhere were expressing the utmost joy—while they were willing to forgive and forget—there flashed to every hamlet in the land the appalling announcement—"PRESIDENT LINCOLN IS ASSASSINATED!!"

The civilized world stood aghast! In the very hour of the final triumph of Liberty over Oppression—of Law and Order over Anarchy—he, the chief actor, the ablest, the most revered and beloved, the purest, the wisest, the best, had fallen by the hand of the dastardly, drunken assassin, J. Wilkes Booth.

The murder of Lincoln by the rebel assassin was the crowning sacrifice of the war It was the final culmination of that demoniac spirit of Slavocracy which sought to destroy the nation by organizing murder everywhere—murder upon land, murder upon the lakes and rivers, piracy and murder upon the high seas murder by burning our cities, murder and highway robbery by organized guerillas, murder by starving thirty thousand helpless prisoners in Southern pens Let us hope that the world may never again be disgraced by the production of another spirit so demoniacal

Probably no man's death, in the history of the world, was ever so universally mourned by all classes of people as was that of Abraham Lincoln

"His faculties so meek hath been
So clear in his great office, that his virtues
Will plead like angels, trumpet-tongued, against
The deep damnation of his taking off—"

THE INDIANS AGAIN

Notwithstanding the defeat of the Indians in 1862-3, the redskins kept up a desultory war upon the western plains, and small bands of them occasionally ventured into sparsely settled neighborhoods for the purpose of murder and robbery Their last raid into Minnesota was made this year. Judge Buck, in his "Indian Outbreaks," says "On the second day of May, 1865, Andrew J Jewett and wife, his father and mother, and a hired man named Charles Tyler, were murdered in the town of Rapidan (Blue Earth county) by Indians and a half-breed, named John Campbell, frequently called Jack Campbell He was a brother of Baptiste Campbell, who was one of the thirty-eight hanged at Mankato, Dec 26, 1862 Jack was at one time in the Union army and did some good service while there But after his brother Baptiste was hanged he swore vengeance, and stated that he would burn Mankato He had a comrade in the army by the name of Marshall Fall, who he knew had sent money to Jewett, and hence he had two objects in view, one the robbery of Jewett, and the other the burning of Mankato With him were several Indians Dr Welcome, then of Garden City, hearing of the murder, visited the place and found Jewett and wife, father and mother and young Tyler dead, and young Jewett, who recovered, badly wounded."

After the murder, Jack left the Indians, the latter going in another direction, and started for Mankato. He was caught on his way by an armed citizen named Dodge, who took him to Mankato, where he was put in jail. It was soon discovered that he had on Mr Jewett's coat and pantaloons and a pair of shoes belonging to the Jewett family The next morning Campbell was tried by a de facto court composed of a jury of twelve men, Lawyer Barney as judge, J H Willard prosecuting attorney, and O O Pitcher as defendant's attorney He was found guilty and summarily hanged by the neck until dead. Before his death he confessed to the priest that he had robbed the Jewett family of $300, which he had put in his jail bed This was found and returned to Marshall Fall, who had sent it to the Jewett family for safe keeping The Indians, though hunted by soldiers and citizens, killed a soldier named James Jolly and a boy named Frank York, and made their way west, where they were finally killed by the patrol scouts under the command of Major Robert H Rose

This was a great year for Waseca county The return of our soldier boys, the large number of immigrants that took homes in the county, the rapid filling up of the towns of Freedom and Alton, all tended to make times prosperous and business good

ELECTION OF 1865

There was no change of county commissioners The following county officers were elected Hiram A Mosher register of deeds Capt E M. Broughton sheriff, Geo R Buckman treasurer, James E Child judge of probate, H D Baldwin county attorney, and O S Canfield county surveyor Broughton, Mosher and Buckman were returned soldiers

CHAPTER XXXIV, 1866.

BIELA'S COMET—DEATH OF COL IDE—APPOINTMENT OF C C COMEE—GREAT STORM, BILLY ADAMS FROZEN—BITTER COLD WEATHER—TERRIFIC STORMS AT HARVEST TIME—EARLY FROST AND EARLY WINTER — BRISBANE REPRESENTATIVE—TOWN OF ALTON ORGANIZED

The year 1866 was ushered in by the masses with the usual cheerful greetings, but the oft-repeated prediction that the world was about to come to an end was solemnly believed by the credulous, simply because some lop-sided Bible students pretended to have discovered in the prophecies that the world would be destroyed in 1866, while other predictions were based upon the supposed effects of the near approach of Biela's comet, supposed to be due in 1866 But the comet, though due, did not appear, and the world is still here doing business as usual.

COUNTY GOVERNMENT

At the annual meeting of the board of county commissioners, Jan 5th, H D. Baldwin resigned the office of county attorney, and his law partner, Major W T Kittredge was appointed in his stead

At the March session of the board, the salary of Rev E. S Smith, county superintendent of schools, was increased from $100 per year to $125,—a trifle less than $11 per month. And yet the "Elder" put in much of his time and all of his ability.

On the 27th of April, 1866, the county board made an order organizing the town of Alton, and appointed the first election to be held at the house of M L Devereaux, May 15, 1866, for the election of town officers This was the last township organization in the county.

At the September meeting of the board, James E. Child, entirely without solicitation on his part, was chosen county superintendent of schools, for the year 1867, at a salary of $300

DEATH OF COLONEL IDE

Col. John C Ide, who had held the office of county auditor since January, 1863 was one of the best known and most popular men in the county and was widely known in the state He was born of New England parents in the state of New York. He was a carpenter and joiner by trade He was a fine singer and an excellent teacher of vocal music For many years he spent his winters teaching music and giving public concerts He was an out-and-out temperance advocate, a strenuous Abolitionist, and consequently, in those days, an ardent republican. He first came West in 1855, and located on East Prairie, Rice county, Minn He was a representative from Rice county in the legislative session of 1856. He came to Wilton, in this county in the summer of 1856, and built the first sawmill erected in the county This mill was of great benefit to all the early settlers of the vicinity. In the fall of 1857 he was the candidate on the republican ticket, with Governor Ramsey, for lieutenant governor, but democracy then held sway in Minnesota, and the whole state ticket was defeated Socially, morally, and religiously he was a worthy and valuable citizen, a kind neighbor, a true friend Few men in this county have died leaving more friends and fewer enemies than he. He had suffered from heart disease for a number of years, and died quite suddenly about Oct 25, 1866.

On the 30th of October, 1866, the county commissioners held a special session and appointed Capt C C Comee, then of Vivian, to succeed Col Ide.

At the meeting of the county board, Nov 14 the salary of the county attorney was increased from $180 to $250 per annum

WEATHER AND CROPS

The winter of 1865-6 was bitterly cold and stormy, and several persons in this county that were exposed were frosted more or less About February 13, 1866, a great snow storm and blizzard prevailed over the whole Northwest, lasting some twenty-four

Mrs SARAH M. NEWELL
JULIA KRASSIN
Mrs JULIA M. WILLIS
COL. W. W. ROBINSON
COL. J. C. IDE.
JOSEPH CLAYTON
S. A. FARRINGTON
ZABINA CHILD
ADAM BISHMAN

hours The wind blew a gale and the cold was intense. Several persons were frozen to death and others badly injured in the state "Billy" Adams, who was driving stage from Wilton to Mankato, at the time, was caught out in the storm, between Wilton and Alma City, and remained out all night. He nearly perished of cold Both hands, his feet, his nose, ears and face were badly frosted. Some of his fingers had to be amputated He had no passengers and was alone with his four horses all that terrible night, suffering most intensely

Deep snow covered the ground during the winter, and the spring was late and cold. Seeding could not be done until late in April The crops were comparatively poor, and the harvest discouraging The month of August brought the most intense heat, accompanied by terrific storms of rain, thunder and lightning. While the more strenuous, industrious, and lucky farmers saved most of their small grain, nevertheless there was considerable loss in this line. To add to the losses already suffered, a heavy frost, followed by cold, prolonged rains, visited the state September 20 Corn, pumpkins, and squashes were badly injured Many of the new settlers found hard times staring them in the face at the close of the season Prices of everything ruled high for the ensuing year, and few there were who had much to sell Winter set in early

> "And now the thickening sky,
> Like a dark ceiling stood, down came the snow impetuous"

At the fall election the following officials were declared elected: County commissioners, James Isaac, democrat, John S. McKune, and Rev C S Luce, county auditor, Capt C C Comee, county attorney, Maj. W. T Kittredge, court commissioner, James E Child, representative, Hon Wm. Brisbane, who was elected over Hon H D Baldwin, by five votes A singular condition was developed by a canvass of the votes for commissioner in the district composed of Blooming Grove, Iosco, St. Mary, and Woodville. The official canvass showed that Eri G. Wood received 75 votes, E G Wood 72 votes, Eri Wood 6 votes, and James Isaac 99 votes The certificate of election was given to Isaac, although Mr Wood received a fair majority of 54 votes The acceptance of Mr Isaac, upon such a vote, was a surprise to many, but Mr Wood, who never sought office, refused to contest for the position, and Mr Isaac served out the term Mr Isaac and Representative Brisbane were the only democrats elected in the county.

CHAPTER XXXV, 1867.

MARKED A NEW ERA—HEAVY FALL OF SNOW, WETTEST YEAR ON RECORD—FIRST RAILROAD BUILT—COUNTY OUT OF DEBT —WEATHER AND CROPS—WASECA SURVEYED AND PLATTED—RAPID CONSTRUCTION OF BUILDINGS—LIST OF STRUCTURES —SHIPPED GOODS VIA CRANE CREEK—LA DOW REPRESENTATIVE—WHEAT BROUGHT FROM $1 60 TO $2 25 PER BUSHEL.

The year 1867 marked a new era in the history of Waseca county. Old villages took a decline and new ones sprang into existence The winter of 1866-7 was remarkable for a very heavy fall of snow. Real winter commenced early in November of 1866, and there was plenty of sleighing until the middle of April, 1867.

The down-pour of rain that spring was unprecedented in the history of the state. All the bottom lands along the Le Sueur river were covered with water, and, at Wilton, the stage coach could not cross the stream for days at a time The early part of the season was remarkable for high prices of grain and provisions, heavy rains and bottomless mud-holes. This year brought the first railroad to the county of Waseca and the depot was established in the town of Woodville where the freight depot of the C. & N.-W. railway now stands It was also notable as the birthday year of the present city of Waseca And it is worthy of note here that goods were shipped by boat from Owatonna, via Straight river, Crane creek and Clear lake, and landed near where the brewery now stands It was a standing joke at Wilton that "Waseca was at the head of navigation" It was the wettest year ever experienced since the first settlement in 1854

There was great scarcity of provisions, especially on the frontier, until after harvest Wheat sold here as high as $2 25 per bushel Oats and potatoes sold for $1 per bushel each Flour sold for $7 per hundred pounds, and pork for 15 to 20 cents. Prices were still higher further west and southwest Potatoes sold in Martin county for $2 50 per bushel, flour for $10 per cwt, and pork for twenty-five cents a pound Such was the distress in some localities that the state was called upon to furnish seed grain and give other aid.

Waseca county suffered less than counties to the south and southwest of it, on account of the building of the W & St P. railway, which furnished work to many of our people that were able to leave their farms for that purpose

COUNTY LEGISLATION

The annual meeting of the county commissioners this year commenced New Year's day On the 3rd day of January, 1867, the board—

"Ordered that drug stores be charged seventy-five dollars for license to sell spirituous liquors during the ensuing year."

This was an "astonisher." It broke all precedent But it was short lived, for on the morrow the "order" was unanimously rescinded—a conversion almost as sudden as that of St. Paul, and certainly not more commendable

Prior to this time there had been held but one term of the district court each year; but the time had come, so the board thought, when two terms instead of one should be held each year So the commissioners petitioned Hon N M Donaldson, then judge of the district court, to hold "an adjourned term of court as near the middle of the current year as possible "

Under the then new law of the legislative session of 1867, county commissioners were required to meet on the second Tuesday of March, each year, and, among other duties devolving upon the board, they were to make and publish a financial statement of receipts and expenditures, fully itemized. This law had become necessary on account of corrupt practices that had scandalized several counties in the state The county commissioners complied with this law and from their report the following summary is taken:

Total amount of orders and certificates issued $4,845 98

Orders redeemed		6,189 24
County bonds redeemed		289 38
Total		$6,478 62
Total receipts	$8,745 38	
Balance in treasury		$2,266.76
Amount due on tax duplicate	$3,908 86	
Estimated amount due on taxes of previous years	$1,600 00	
Total estimated assets		$7,775 62

This was the first time in the history of the county that it had been able to show a balance on the credit side of the ledger The publication of this report showed that the county was substantially out of debt, and everyone felt relieved after eleven years of extortionate interest and heavy discounts on county paper.

At the meeting of the county commissioners, July 17, 1867, Wm H Young, of Woodville, was allowed $100 "for taking Bundt Anderson and returning him to jail" This Anderson was a thief that had escaped from the old wooden jail at Wilton

The county auditor's salary was increased one hundred dollars per year, to commence March 1, 1867

At the September meeting of the board, Mr Jesse Poland was appointed to serve as county superintendent of public schools, and his salary was fixed at $250 a year—about $20.86 per month

At the October meeting of the board of county commissioners, Mr Luce resigned, and Mr Isaac was elected chairman of the board for the unexpired term.

THE WEATHER AND CROPS

These two constitute a never-ending topic of conversation and speculation, and well they may The climate, the soil, the farmer —they are the sources of all prosperity Let these fail, then all business languishes, and misery takes the place of comfort

About the middle of July, 1867, the weather cleared and the harvest weather was as favorable as usual. From that time until the close of the year, with the exception of a light snowstorm in November, the weather was very favorable Plowing and grading upon the streets of Waseca were going on during the latter half of December.

The most important local events of the year were the construction and completion of the W. & St P. railway, now the C

& N.-W. railway, to Waseca, and the platting and rapid building of what is now the city of Waseca.

Early in the year 1867, Mr. I. C. Trowbridge, who had probably received inside information of the location of the railroad depot at this point, bought out Mr. J. K. Meyers, and arranged to lay out a town. The road was definitely located by Engineers W. G. Ward and J. H. Jenkins, early in the summer, and Mr. Trowbridge had the original village surveyed and platted by Surveyor Jenkins, July 22, 1867. In August, as soon as the wheat was harvested and removed, the work of erecting buildings commenced. Mr. Wm. Everett, deceased, was the first man to commence the erection of a business house on the new plat. It was soon completed and occupied on the first floor by Lord, Addison & Co., dealers in general merchandise. The front part, up stairs, was used by Mr. Everett's family as a temporary residence, while the rear end of the building, up stairs, was occupied by the printing office of James E. Child, who came over with the News outfit from Wilton, about the last of October.

In August, also, a Wilton company, in the name of Geo. W. Watkins, surveyed and platted a portion of section 18 and named it Clear Lake City. The survey was made by H. G. Mosher, Esq. The place was started as a rival to Waseca, but in a few years it became a part of this city, and is now embraced in the Third ward.

In September of the same year, Mrs. Judith Trowbridge, H. P. Norton and Baldwin & Kittredge laid out what is known as the First Addition to Waseca, the same being surveyed and platted by H. G. Mosher. Mrs. Justina Child was the first to construct a building on the First Addition.

From the time of the survey and platting of the town until long into the winter, the work of building went rapidly forward. The first week in December, 1867, the "Waseca News," published by the writer, contained the following:

"We have ascertained, as far as possible, the number of new buildings which have been erected at this point since August. On the north side of the W. & St. P. railroad track, there are eighty-two buildings, and on the south side twenty—in all one hundred and two—all built in the short space of three months. Of those north of the big elevator, there are some twenty-five two stories high; one two-and-a-half stories, five one-and-a half stories high, and the others are smaller buildings.

"There are eleven mercantile establishments, eight liquor stores (God save the mark), four hotels, two livery stables, two cabinet and furniture shops and stores, two harness shops, several carpenter and blacksmith shops, two meat markets, and a printing office

"Among the hotels we mention the Trowbridge House, 60x80 feet, two stories high, cost $4,000, which is kept by Mr I C Trowbridge, original proprietor of the village The Vincent Hotel (now known as the Priest Block) is 60 feet on Wood street and 55 on Second street, two stories high and cost $3,500 It is just completed, well furnished and now open to the public * *

"Among the blacksmith shops we can commend that of R. B. Wood, on Lake avenue, near the Devannah & Reynolds livery stable (which then occupied the present court-house grounds)

"The store of Lord, Addison & Co is 22 feet front by 60 feet deep, two stories high, and cost about $1,400. The lower story is filled with No 1 goods of all kinds, while the second story is occupied by Mr Everett's family in front, and our printing office in the back end of the building

"Mills, Follett & Co, bankers, occupy Geo. L Tarbell's building which is 22x45 feet, two stories high Baldwin & Kittredge, bankers and real estate dealers, occupy a temporary building opposite Bailey's hardware store Comee & Young have opened a furniture establishment, 16x20 feet, with a shop in the rear H P Norton's building, wherein he keeps the express office, and where Mr Mollin is prepared to clothe the needy, is 18x30 feet, two stories high, and cost $1,200

"Opposite the Vincent House is the well-known hardware store of Bailey & Watkins It is 22x64 feet, two stories high, and cost $1,800 The next building is owned by Williams & Washburn It is 22x50 feet, two stories high, and is occupied below by H S Swift & Co, dealers in dry goods and clothing (It is now occupied by Preston & Stucky, and belongs to Hon M H Helms)

"The Joe Gatzman building, 20x40 feet, two stories high, is occupied below as a grocery and liquor establishment. The next is McVeigh's store 18x40 feet, two stories high Then comes "Uncle Tom Pierce's establishment—an eating saloon and auction store—16x40 feet, two stories high, with a dwelling in the rear 13x20 feet Then comes the Strong & Wilsey drug store, 22x40 feet, two stories high, and well finished Here are drugs, medicines, toys, etc, and here Dr Young makes his headquarters Next comes a restaurant 18x54 feet, and then A R Foster's grain warehouse, 16x40 feet Moreau & Dulmage have a building near by, 20x40, two stories high

"Near the depot, are the well-known lumber yards of W W. Johnson, Williams & Washburn, and the lumber, coal and salt establishment of Mr Chas Eckenbeck. On the corner of Second and Elm streets is the meat and produce market of A E Dearborn His building is 20x40 feet, two stories high, with a store room back, 16x40 feet, one story (McLoughlin Bros now occupy the site with their large brick store)

"Besides the 102 buildings mentioned to start with, there are others—the large railroad grain-elevator, the depot building, the brick water tank, the engine or round house, all built by the railroad company, and a warehouse built by Geo L Tarbell, Esq

"It is almost incredible that so much work could have been done in so short a time, and still there are many other structures in process of construction, and every man is at work early and late"

In addition to this somewhat lengthy description of the then embryo city, the following appeared in the same paper

"High Wind—A terrible wind storm is raging here to-day Three building frames in Clear Lake City have been blown down The News office is turned into a smokehouse ad interim—a stirring time this"

It also contained accounts of the weddings of the following persons, viz: Mr. Wm. Harding and Mrs. Eliza Reibling, Nov. 20, 1867, in St Mary, Mr F H Harding, son of Hiram Harding, and Miss Mary Green, daughter of M S Green, Esq, of Iosco, Nov 26, 1867, Mr Wm Davidson and Miss Mary E Vars, in the town of Medo, Dec. 1, 1867. All three of these were solemnized by Rev W W Satterlee

The same paper noted that S W Franklin, of New Richland, and Miss Melissa E Freelove, of Manchester, Iowa, were married Nov 19, 1867, by Rev Norton.

The first store of general merchandise opened within the present city limits was that of Mr Wm McVeigh, near where the brewery now stands Tradition says he opened his store in the fall of 1866 During the early part of the season of 1867 he shipped his goods in boats by way of Straight river, Crane creek and the lakes to the boat landing on this side of Clear lake How was that for high water?

THE FALL ELECTION

The election of local officers in 1867 resulted as follows Representative, Geo A La Dow, clerk of court, S J Willis; sheriff, S W Long judge of probate, H. D. Baldwin, county attorney, W. T Kittredge, surveyor, C. E Crane Messrs. Long and La Dow were the only democrats elected Mr La Dow was elected by two votes only

The year 1867 will be remembered as the wettest in the history of the state. The crops were light, with the single exception of grass The level lands could not be cultivated on account of the moisture, and even the high grounds did not produce an average crop But what grain there was brought high prices, and the large immigration made money plentiful and furnished employment for everyone. The price of wheat during the early winter months ranged from $1 60 to $2 25 per bushel, and corn brought from sixty cents to one dollar per bushel The fall weather was very fine, and all in all the year closed hopefully and with favorable prospects.

CHAPTER XXXVI, 1868.

PERSONALS — CONGREGATIONAL CHURCH SOCIETY — COUNTY SEAT—WASECA INCORPORATED — COUNTY MATTERS — GOOD TEMPLARS ORGANIZE—BOILER EXPLOSION — BUSINESS REPORT OF WASECA—G A R ORGANIZED—DEATH OF TARBELL—EPISCOPALIAN CHURCH ORGANIZATION—GRANT CLUB —SCHOOLS AND SCHOOL HOUSES IN WASECA—COUNTY SEAT REMOVAL TALK—FIRST BUSINESS FAILURE IN WASECA—ARREST OF A FORGER—FIRST WORK OF WASECA CITY FATHERS —OTISCO SWEDE CHURCH—THE FIRST WASECA PICNIC—DEATH OF C O NORTON, OF THE FETTERLY CHILD—McINTOSH ATTEMPTS SUICIDE—WASECA A YEAR OLD—THE WHEAT YIELD—PRESBYTERIANS ORGANIZE—LESLIE AND JONES NARROWLY ESCAPE DEATH—FIRST BRASS BAND—RAILROAD DISCRIMINATIONS—FINANCIAL TROUBLES

The new year 1868 opened auspiciously The weather was fine and the "Happy New Year" was generally observed

Wheat was quoted at $1 75 for No 1, and $1.60 for No 2, corn 80 cents, potatoes 75 cents and oats 55 cents

January 7th the county commissioners, two of the three, met at Wilton, and James Isaac was elected chairman, R F. Stevens being the other one present Mr John S McKune the other member was absent during the session The saloon license fee for the year was fixed at $50. Everything else was pretty high, but the privilege of making drunkards was cheap enough No other business of importance was transacted.

We copy the following personals from the "News" of the first week in January

Mr E. P Latham, the genial station agent at this place was married at Norfolk, Conn., the 1st inst . .Messrs Ward and Jenkins, with their fair partners, have returned from their wedding tour They had a host of friends here glad to welcome them back to the head of navigation."

CONGREGATIONAL CHURCH SOCIETY.

On the 15th of Jan., 1868, the Congregational church society of Waseca was organized. We copy the following from the local paper:

In response to the call of a number of Christian disciples, through their committee, Brothers Stevens, Hummiston and E H. Wood, a council convened at the parlor of the Trowbridge hotel for the organization of a Congregational church. Churches from Faribault, Owatonna, Rochester and St Paul were represented by clergy and lay delegates R. Hall served as moderator and L S. Greggs as scribe The articles of faith were read, adopted and signed by the following persons Frederick Stevens, Lyman Hummiston, Wm H Vinton, Gordon Henshaw, Mrs Lucy P Stevens, Mrs Lydia H Vinton, Mrs Eliza Hummiston, Mrs. Anna M Alden, Miss Julia Hummiston, Samuel Hawkes and wife, Wilfred Vinton Edward Bennett and wife, Ezra H Wood and wife, Dr. H. J. Young and wife, Dana McGoun, Miss Matilda Bullis On the 18th of January, 1868, officers were elected as follows Rev E. H. Alden, pastor, E H. Wood and F J Stevens, deacons, Lyman Hummiston, clerk and treasurer, and Ed Bennett, Stevens and Hummiston, trustees"

Jan 21st, 1868, there was quite a large meeting of citizens at Wilton to consider the question of removal of the county seat Mr John C. Hunter called the meeting to order by the nomination of Hon. Wm Brisbane as chairman The subject of the removal of the county seat was discussed by Messrs Brisbane, J A Canfield, A J Woodbury, J C Hunter, Judge Baldwin and others, and, at the close, J C Hunter, Dr M S Gove, and Judge J A Canfield were appointed a committee to draft and circulate remonstrances against any legislation that might be asked for to authorize the removal of the county seat

THE VILLAGE OF WASECA

On the 25th of January, 1868, a large meeting of citizens was held, and it was unanimously decided that a formal application be made to the legislature for an act of incorporation Maj W T Kittredge and Messrs Tarbell and Sam Williams were appointed to draft and forward to our representative a bill to incorporate the village. The act finally passed the legislature and was approved March 2, 1868.

For the purpose of the first election, I. C Trowbridge, H P Norton and P H Swift were named in the act to serve as judges and inspectors of election.

The first election was held on Tuesday, May 5, 1868—the number of votes cast being 125. S B Williams, J Shaw and W G. Ward were the first trustees—Williams and Shaw being elected for two years and Ward for one year P H Swift was elected the first justice These officers were chosen without opposition, the vote being a light one

On Monday, Jan 27, 1868, the Clear Lake House, with most of its contents, was entirely destroyed by fire. The building took fire from a stove pipe, either in the upper ceiling or roof, and, before it was discovered, the flames had so far advanced that the building could not be saved with the means at hand. The building belonged to C A Barr & Co, and was situated on the south side of the C & N.-W R'y. tracks. There was no insurance. Preparations were immediately made to rebuild—the citizens aiding Mr Barr in the matter This was the first fire of any magnitude in what now constitutes the city of Waseca.

At the annual March meeting of the county board, the school district organized of the territory included in the village of Waseca was made an independent district, and recognized as district number seventy-two

The territory then embraced within the village limits was described as "all the north one-half of sections 17 and 18, and the south one-half of sections 7 and 8, in the township of Woodville

At the same meeting of the county board the financial statement was submitted by Auditor Comee, and the summary showed as follows, viz:

Total amount received	$7,854.17
Amount of orders and certificates paid	6,987 76
Balance in treasury Feb 29th	866 41
Outstanding indebtedness	1,596 80
Assets, taxes due and uncollected	8,366 58

April 22nd, the board re-districted and divided the county into five commissioner districts. District No. 1 included Blooming Grove and Woodville, No 2, Iosco and Janesville, No 3, Wilton and Otisco; No 4, St Mary and Alton; No. 5, Freedom, Vivian, Byron and New Richland At the same meeting, Mr Isaac resigned as chairman of the board, and R. F. Stevens was elected his successor. It would appear that shortly afterwards—although the records are silent on the subject—when Mr. Isaac resigned his position upon his removal from this county to Oregon, S. S. Phelps was appointed to fill the vacancy; for on the 23d of June, 1868, we find Mr. Phelps acting as one of the board.

At a special meeting of the board held Dec. 18, 1868, the resignation of W. T. Kittredge, as county attorney, was accepted, and Lewis Brownell, Esq., was appointed to fill the vacancy.

Going back from the commissioners' proceedings and taking up matters in their order, we find that Mr. L. W. Wheeler, father of Whitney L. Wheeler, and one of the early settlers of St. Mary, died Feb. 2, 1868, at Wilton, after a short illness. He was well advanced in years, and highly respected. His descendants are residents of the county.

The first Good Templar lodge organized in Waseca, had its beginning Feb. 24, 1868, and was instituted by Capt. John. The following were its first officers: Rev. W. W. Satterlee, W. C. T., Mrs. L. A. Hicks, W. V. T.; A. E. Dearborn, W. S., Wm. McVeigh, W. F. S., John F. Murphy, W. M.; Etta Taylor, D. M., Mary R. Douglass, I. G., Nathaniel W. Scott, O. G., Mrs. Satterlee, R. H. S., Mrs. E. G. Wood, L. H. S., G. N. Taylor, Chap., E. G. Wood, P. W. C. T. This organization, so long as Mr. Satterlee remained here, exercised a beneficial influence upon the citizens of the plaee.

From the Waseca News of Feb. 21, 1868, the following is taken: "The steam boiler in Mr. Austin's saw mill, situated some five miles north of Alma City, exploded last Friday, doing much damage to the mill, and seriously wounding Oscar Hadley, the fireman. He received a severe cut on the head, had the flesh of his face blown full of sand, his hands badly scalded, and was otherwise bruised and injured. There being no insurance on the building, the loss falls heavily upon Mr. Austin, who will probably not rebuild."

Mr. Hadley afterwards recovered his general health, but his mind was permanently injured.

FIRST BUSINESS REPORT OF WASECA

On March 13, 1868, a report of the amount of business that

had been done during the fall and winter, by merchants, was published, and the summary is here reproduced

Sales of—

Dry goods and groceries	$66,000
Drugs and medicines	2,176
Seeders and drills	10,000
Lumber	30,000
Cattle and hogs, etc	3,750
Hardware (estimated)	5,000
Total sales	$116,926

Waseca was the market town for much of Freeborn county, all of Faribault county and much of Blue Earth county Over half a million bushels of wheat were marketed in Waseca the first winter of its existence

GRAND ARMY OF THE REPUBLIC

The first organization of the Grand Army of the Republic in the county, was perfected March 16, 1868 The first officers were as follows Maj W T Kittredge, post commander, P H. Swift, senior vice, H A Mosher, junior vice, Capt. A H Wellman, post quartermaster, Dr H J Young, post surgeon

The first death noted in the new village was that of Mr Geo L Tarbell, who died of consumption, March 13, 1868 He was a prominent business man and held in high esteem

EPISCOPALIANS ORGANIZE

In the month of March, 1868, the first Episcopal society was organized here Members of the Episcopal faith met at the residence of Mrs Teall, March 7, and proceeded to the organization of a society by adopting by-laws and electing officers The officers elected were: Mrs H S Teall, president: Mrs Knappen vice-president, Mrs E P Latham secretary, Mrs. H D Baldwin, treasurer, Mr and Mrs H J Wadsworth, Mr. Tefft, Miss Hall, Mrs P. C Bailey and Mr P P Smith, committee on entertainment The receipts of the first meeting amounted to $5 85

GEN GRANT CLUB

On March 20, 1868 voters who favored the nomination and

election of Gen. Grant to the presidency, met and organized a Grant club. Its officers were as follows

Judge H D Baldwin, president, Maj Wm C Young, vice-president, Capt P H Swift, secretary, A E. Dearborn, treasurer, Wm. G Ward, James E Child, G W. Comee, D. L Whipple and Capt P H Swift, executive committee

PRICES OF GRAIN

Inasmuch as the prices of grain—especially wheat—show the prosperity or adversity of the people of this section, the prices of wheat are given for the years 1867-8 December wheat, 1867, brought $1 52 for No. 1, and $1 42 for No 2 January 17, 1868 No 1 wheat in Waseca, brought $1 70 The 15th of the next month No 1 wheat was $1.65 per bushel In March it brought $1 55 In May wheat went to $1 85 per bushel, in June it fell to $1.65, and gradually fell during July and into August when the price reached $1 40 In September wheat tumbled to $1 and before the close of the year 1868 the price of wheat had fallen to 78 cents per bushel for No. 1 At the same time wheat was worth, in New York, $1 65 per bushel, showing that the railroad companies got more for transporting a bushel of grain to New York than the farmer received for producing it Is it any wonder that farmers became dissatisfied with that state of affairs and soon after inaugurated what was known as the "Grange" movement?

SCHOOLS AND SCHOOL HOUSES

March 28 1868, a large school-meeting—the first in Waseca—was held, and Hon P C Bailey was elected director, Hon H D Baldwin, treasurer, and G N Taylor, Esq, clerk No action was taken toward building a schoolhouse, although the subject was discussed to some extent.

On the 25th of April, a special school meeting was held to take measures to purchase grounds and raise funds for the building of a schoolhouse The meeting was largely attended and quite exciting, as there was strong opposition to the building of a schoolhouse at that time The majority decided to erect a building, and Eri G. Wood, H P. Norton, and James E Child were chosen a committee to examine, select and report upon a site for a schoolhouse, D L Whipple, Sam B Williams and J Shaw were chosen a committee to make drafts and estimates for cost of building, both committees to report at an adjourned meeting. This was the beginning of a long struggle which finally culminated in the selection of the site where the present high school building now stands, and in the erection of a frame building, one part of which is now owned by the Trowbridge estate and the other by Hon P. C. Bailey, both being situated on the corners of Wood and Sixth streets across from the High School building.

COUNTY SEAT TALK

Of course, at the outset of the life of Waseca, the county seat question was uppermost in the minds of the people The immediate residents of Wilton and Waseca were more deeply interested than others, but all felt an interest As early as the first of the year 1868, discussions were frequent and sometimes animated As showing the condition of matters at that time, the following is quoted from the "News" of April 17, 1868

"We are informed that those who are opposed to the removal of the county seat to Waseca give as a reason that the people are not now able to build new county buildings Upon this question of buildings there can be no issue, at present The old jail at Wilton is now worthless, and, in the opinion of most men, never was good for anything as a jail The courthouse there, so-called, is a very shabby thing at best, and is entirely unfit and unsafe as a repository of the public records Whether the county seat shall be removed or not, the county must, as soon as possible, erect new buildings * * *

"But all this talk about the value of the county buildings at Wilton will only call attention to the worthlessness of those buildings for county purposes and show the fallacy of the Wilton argument It is quite evident to an unbiased mind that the business of the county must center at Waseca, and the majority of the voters of the county, we think, desire a removal of the county seat We call attention to the matter thus early so that it may be thoroughly discussed and fairly decided"

COUNTY SEAT FIGHT POSTPONED

A republican county convention was held at Wilton May 2, 1868 to elect delegates to the state convention to be held at St Paul on the 13th of the same month At this county convention, the county seat question was treated as follows

On motion of Maj W C. Young, of Waseca, the following were adopted

"Whereas, The removal of the county seat, from Wilton to Waseca, has been agitated more or less, therefore,

"Resolved, That the republicans of this county disclaim all intention of making that question a political or party issue this fall"

The delegates elected to attend the state convention were Hon Warren Smith, Hon W G Ward and Capt C C Comee.

BEAUTIFUL TREES

Among other improvements, many shade trees were planted in the spring of 1868, and to this activity on the part of our early settlers, very much of the beauty and present comfort of our city may be attributed While there are some matters of a sanitary character that might be much improved, the numerous beautiful shade trees of the city are a credit to the town and are much admired by all people of good taste

FIRST BUSINESS FAILURE.

The first business failure in Waseca, of much importance, was that of H S Swift & Co, who closed their store May 14 Their liabilities footed up to $5,000—assets $1,500 This was the skirmish line of many failures to follow in many parts of the country—largely on account of the destruction of greenbacks and the issue of interest-bearing bonds in their stead, thus contracting the currency.

NEW BRICK YARD

On May 15, the "News" announced that "Bricks will soon be in fashion in this town M S Green, Esq, and others have discovered excellent clay northeast of Loon lake, adjoining the village, and have commenced to open a brick yard"

This discovery of clay was where Mr. Messerknecht now has his brick yard Esquire Green burned one kiln of brick, but for want of capital to develop it and from other causes abandoned the business

THE COLORADO BEETLE

Potato bugs were then new to the people of this country. Very few people had ever seen one prior to 1865 This year, (1868) the Mankato Record (now Review) remarked that "those striped bugs which, for the past three years have so seriously damaged the crop west of us, have already made their appearance in large numbers" Other papers noticed their appearance, and our paper remarked that "we have not heard of any of these pests in this immediate vicinity but doubt not they will soon visit this section" We remarked that they should be "attacked at first sight and exterminated if possible" As we soon after learned, this was more easily said than done

ARREST OF A FORGER

Quite a sensation was created, May 22 1868 both at Waseca and in Wilton by the arrest of one "Prof J C Lewis" who was quite generally known as a very polite and agreeable singing master He made his appearance in Waseca early in the spring and appeared to be a very Christian-like and honorable man He had nearly finished a term of singing school in Wilton, and was soon to have commenced his labors in Waseca when the arrest was made and the game was up He was charged with having forged the name of Wm E Jones, of La Crosse Wis., to a receipt for $1,000 00 which he put in his own pocket The money had been sent to him as agent of an insurance company to pay off Mr Jones' claim for loss of property insured The forgery occurred the previous December at which time he was arrested but made his escape during his examination. He was arrested in Steele county by A H Hawes general agent of the insurance company assisted by John Martin, then sheriff of Winona county, and Seth W Long then sheriff of Waseca county He was one of those sleek rascals that wear the livery of heaven the more effectually to serve the devil He was afterwards convicted and served time at Waupun prison Wis

FIRST WORK OF CITY FATHERS

The first proceedings of the then Waseca village board of trustees were published May 27 1868 The following officers were appointed by the trustees A E Dearborn, clerk Maj W T Kittredge, treasurer H P Norton marshal, Charles Dunn, street commissioner, and F Y. Hottstott, fire warden

Let it be remembered by future generations that H P Norton who is still with us, was the first city marshal to guard the lives and property of our citizens—and who could have done it better!

The first ordinance passed was signed by "W G Ward, president," and "A E. Dearborn, clerk," and appeared in the Waseca News on the 27th day of May, 1868, and was entitled "An Ordinance Regulating Shows, Theatricals, and Other Exhibitions" This ordinance prohibited all sorts of shows not properly licensed, and fixed the license fee as follows· For a circus $25, for theatricals $5 each, for jugglers, sleight-of-hand performers, vocal or instrumental concerts, and all other shows or entertainments charging an admission fee, $5. * * * Six ordinances in all were published on the same date

Maj Young and D L Whipple then contractors and builders, built the Swede church in the Charles Johnson neighborhood, in Otisco, this season It was a model church in a model farming community

PIONEER CLERGYMEN

Among the early workers in the moral vineyard of Waseca, was Rev W W Satterlee He was a thorough, fearless, Christian worker, not only mentally but physically He did not hesitate to work with his hands six days in the week and preach on the seventh He was one of the ablest ministers of the gospel that ever preached in Waseca During the winter of 1868, he was instrumental in the organization of a Good Templar lodge He was untiring in all good work Rev. G. C Tanner, of the Episcopal church, was an earnest worker in the moral and religious field During the winter of 1867-8 and following, six different denominations of Christians held regular services in Waseca namely. Congregationalists, Rev E H. Alden, pastor; Presbyterians, Rev J G Patterson, pastor, Methodist Episcopal, Rev W W Satterlee, pastor; German M E church, Rev Uhl, pastor; Baptist church, Rev S T Catlin, pastor, Episcopal church, Rev G C. Tanner, pastor. These were the pioneer clergymen of the town and county

HEAVY RAINS AND MUD

The last week in May and the first ten days of June, 1868, brought very heavy rains The streets were then ungraded and without drainage, and were so many lines of almost bottomless mud That was true not only of the village streets, but it was very nearly true of all the highways leading into the city. The poll tax, which was all that was available that season, amounted to four days' work or $6 for each man—the whole amounting to about $600 00 It was determined by the village board to expend $200 on the roads leading north and northwest, $200 on the St Mary and Wilton roads, and $200 in the village The town of Woodville, was liberal, and expended considerable money on the roads from the east. Mr Trowbridge was especially liberal in helping to grade Second street Charles Dunn was street commissioner that year, and put in a good deal of hard work, making the streets quite passable Under date of June 17, we find this record "Road Commissioner Dunn has been doing good service on the roads during the past week He has not only put the main street in good condition, but has made North street passable for the heaviest loads from the village to Clear Lake Wood street has been materially improved and other streets made passable '

FOURTH OF JULY 1868.

Although there was no formal celebration of the Fourth the first year of our village life the records show that a large number of people collected in the place from the surrounding country and held a sort of impromptu celebration It appears that the great day was ushered in by the firing of a brass piece, brought over from Berlin, Steele county Quite an excitement was created early in the day by two young Americans that celebrated by engaging in a knock-down scrap in settlement of some old grudge Then Marshal Norton put in a hot job and broke up that part of the celebration Then came a horse race between O Neil's sorrel, and Smith's brown—the brown appearing to be the better trotter And next came the most exciting of all—a foot race between Geo Dreever and "Dad" Sweet—the latter winning the race and the money by a close rub Waseca then had a character known as "Uncle Tom " He was engaged that day in selling drinks of various kinds, and having an eye single to profits he hastily built a platform in front of his business place and secured two or three local speakers to make the eagle scream Among the speakers that day we call to mind our departed friends, M S Green, Esq, and Hon Wm. Brisbane Then followed numerous wrestling matches and the day closed with the firing of the brass piece and a fire-cracker fusilade which lasted long into the night

THE VILLAGE COW AND PIG

The running at large of cattle in Waseca village was the subject of early and much debate among the people and with our city fathers. On the 22d of July, 1868, the trustees passed an ordinance that cattle, horses, mules, or sheep found running at large within the village between the time of one hour after sunset and before sunrise should be taken up and impounded, and the poundmaster, marshal, street commissioner, and constable were especially enjoined to enforce the law. This was better than no law, but it was poor protection for gardens and lawns.

THE FIRST WASECA PICNIC

The first Waseca picnic was a picnic, and no mistake. It came off July 24, 1868. It was a glorious harvest day, with golden sunshine and a cool, refreshing breeze from the northwest. All nature was entrancing in its sunshine and shadow as it smiled upon our beautiful Clear lake, with its surrounding timbered slopes and wooded hills. It was a gathering of all the first families of the town—which included almost everybody—and the village was almost entirely deserted for the time being. Some of the picnic party went around on the west side of the lake by carriage, as far as Mr. Coon's place, and walked the remainder of the way, while a large number gathered at what was then known as the Kittredge boat-landing and took rowboats for what was then called Maple hill on the north shore of Clear lake. No one then lived on the north shore of the lake, the locality being then clothed with the majestic forest trees planted by Nature's own hand. The boat ride across the lake occupied nearly three-quarters of an hour, and furnished the highest enjoyment for all the company. A few steps up the slope brought us to the picnic grounds. The large primitive maples and elms, with their great, spreading tops formed a perfect shade. The land sloped each way, so that the grounds selected were dry and in fine condition. There was very little underbrush, while the lake with its surroundings furnished a picture of natural beauty unsurpassed anywhere. Here, amid the monarchs of the primeval forest, the pioneers walked and talked, swung, gathered flowers, chatted, drank lemonade, played "Miss Johnnycake" and other games, and enjoyed a royal good time generally. Every one belonged to the elite "Sets" and "pushes" and "classes" were then unknown, and pure, American equality and generosity were at the front At the feast there were no regular toasts with impromptu responses written out in advance; but it was a jovial, joyful, happy occasion, where full justice was done to the inner man After lunch the tables were cleared and Judge Baldwin led off in a regular game of "pull-away," the ladies all joining in the game Between 6 and 7 o'clock p m all hands embarked on board the row boats manned by the jolliest crews that ever sailed the lake, and, just as old Sol was disappearing beyond the western hills, the happy company reached the village in condition to enjoy a night of refreshing rest The local paper, in writing of the party said "Such recreation is good for the health, pleasing to the senses, innocent in its nature, democratic in its tendencies, and calculated to make life worth the living We trust that this excursion may prove an introduction to many more of the same sort Nature has given Waseca the amplest means of enjoyment, and it will be our own fault if we do not frequently use and enjoy them"

DEATH OF AN EARLY SETTLER

The "News" of August 5, 1868, contained an obituary notice of the death of C O Norton one of the pioneer blacksmiths of the county, who died of inflammation of the bladder at the age of 39 years He was one of the most jovial and companionable men and his death was felt as a personal loss by a large circle of acquaintances He was buried with Masonic honors and sleeps in the quiet graveyard known as the Wilton cemetery

FIRST FATAL ACCIDENT

The first fatal accident on the new railroad occurred August 3, 1868 The train coming in from the east some three miles before reaching the village ran over a young boy, cutting off one of his legs near the ankle, and the other near the body Some of the child's fingers were cut off and a piece of the scalp was missing The boy belonged to the family of Mr Fetterly, a brother-in-law of Mr A Wert, of Waseca He was about four years old, and, while at play, fell asleep on the track He was not discovered by the engineer until too late The little fellow died within two hours after the accident

ATTEMPT AT SUICIDE

On the 31st of August, 1868, a great excitement was raised in Waseca by an attempt or pretended attempt at suicide About 10 o'clock a m. of that day an old gentleman by the name of McIntosh, living in an old house near the present residence of ex-Mayor Moonan, attempted to shoot himself. The first intimation the public had of the matter was the loud report of a gun, followed by the screams of a woman Many ran to the spot, and, upon arrival, found McIntosh lying upon the ground, face downward, and Mrs McIntosh screaming wildly. It transpired that his son, in connection with another boy, named Douglass, had stolen some $40 from the grocery of Jo Gatzman, the Saturday evening before, and the old gentleman became very much excited upon hearing of it Early that Monday morning he drank very freely at the saloons, and, just before the shooting, when the Douglass boy passed his house, he chased him with a fish spear and threw it at him He threatened to kill himself —a matter not unusual with him, it was said, when he was excited with liquor. After chasing the boy, he ran into the house, swearing that he would shoot himself. He seized his loaded gun and cocked it but his wife interfered to prevent his designs A scuffle ensued, during which the gun was discharged, making a ghastly wound in his left side, tearing the flesh from the lower ribs the size of a man's hand, and tearing away the end of one of the old lady's fingers Drs Young and Satterlee dressed the wounds, and the old man raved like a madman during the day However, as soon as the whisky and beer worked off, he became quite meek, and, in due time, recovered from his self-inflicted injury

"A MONSTER YEARLING!"

Under this heading the Waseca News of August 26th, 1868, published the following.

"Waseca village is one year old this month It contains over one hundred business and residence buildings, and a population of seven hundred souls Clear Lake City—adjoining on the south, and virtually a part of the town—contains some twenty buildings By actual count, both places contain one hundred twenty-nine buildings Nearly all of these belong to the class denominated "good structures" Several other buildings are now being constructed and will be completed before winter Where there was only a wheat field or native prairie, one year ago, we now have a live town of nearly one thousand wide-awake people and a business center for a wide extent of country Wheat is quoted at $1 25 here, which is certainly 15 cents lower than its actual value In Milwaukee and Chicago it is quoted at $1.88 Forty-eight cents for freight and margin is quite enough, and No. 1 wheat should bring to-day $1 40. At present there is but one buyer in the market, next week there will be several, probably, when we hope to see wheat kept up to the market value at this point"

But the people were disappointed The next issue of the paper had the following·

"Our market report shows that wheat No 1 is selling for $1 15 That is the price to-day. What it will bring to-morrow or next day, no one here can give any information The men who own the means of transportation in this state have concluded to shave the producers out of all that a bountiful harvest has given them Three or four men control the markets of the state Into every town along the railroads they send buyers that are by them instructed, from day to day, as to the price to be paid This is all legitimate enough, but the joke comes in when we learn that outside buyers are charged ten cents more on a bushel for transportation than they were charged last year, thereby enabling the men that own the roads and boats to bid higher than any other person Thus all opposition is driven out and the combine is secured a monopoly of the grain markets"

RAILROAD EXTENSION

During the month of September, 1868, the contract for building the Winona and St Peter railroad, from Waseca to Janesville, was let to Col Degraff & Son, and work commenced upon the extension in October. The building of the road west gave great temporary prosperity to the business men of Waseca as well as to many other residents of the county.

BIG SHIPMENTS OF WHEAT.

The amount of wheat received from farmers, at the railroad elevator, in Waseca, the first week in September, 1868 was 11-072½ bushels, the amount shipped out was 10,560 bushels, and the price was $1 25 per bushel. The total receipts of wheat at the railroad elevator, during the month of September, amounted to 53,326 bushels—the receipts of the last week in that month were 18,558 bushels

THE WHEAT YIELD IN WASECA COUNTY

This year, 1868 was one of the great wheat seasons for Minnesota Mr H W. S Hinkley, who was then a noted thresherman of the county, reported yields as follows: John Byron, of St Mary, threshed 440 bushels of wheat from 13 acres—a yield of 34 bushels per acre. Wm Byron, same town, threshed 917 bushels from 34 acres—an average yield of 27 bushels per acre Anthony Gorman, Esq, same neighborhood, got 578 bushels from 24 acres—a yield of 24 bushels to the acre Wm Priebe, of the same town, got 40 bushels to the acre The average yield throughout the county that year was a trifle over 20 bushels to the acre, and those who were fortunate enough to market their wheat in September got from $1 00 to $1 30 per bushel.

MISCELLANEOUS ITEMS.

Then as now, people were married and given in marriage. The first marriages in Waseca were reported as follows:

Married, by Rev. W. W Satterlee, Dec 9, 1867, at the Trowbridge House, Waseca, Minn, W. G Ward, Esq, to Miss Ella C. Trowbridge, Also at the same time and place, J. H Jenkins, Esq, to Miss Augusta M. Trowbridge. On the 26th of the same month, Hon. P. C. Bailey and Miss Lurinda C. Dodge were married by Rev E. H Alden, at the residence of Mr. D L. Whipple

A Presbyterian church organization was effected in this place on the evening of September 8, 1868—the trustees being Maj. W T. Kittredge, I. C. Trowbridge, Wm Everett, S. H Drum D L. Whipple, Mr Murfin and Mr. Sutliff. Preparations were soon after made for the building of a church edifice which resulted in the erection of what is now known as the Baptist church—the first church erected in the place. The contract for building this church was let to Messrs Whipple & Young—both since deceased—and work was commenced thereon early in November. The building was completed and dedicated December 20.

Here is an item that appeared Nov 25, 1868 "Venison is beginning to find its way into our market. Several deer have been shot in this section within the past few days Some of our sportsmen killed one in the timber bordering on Clear lake, a few days ago" No live wild deer have ever been seen in this section since

NARROW ESCAPE FROM DEATH

On the 10th of December, 1868, Mr Samuel Leslie, now of

Otisco, and Mr. Jones, both then of Waseca, commenced hauling wood across Clear lake It was a bitterly cold day They tried the ice in several places, and believing it was strong enough to hold a team and load, drove across and got one load of wood, returning safe and sound Upon coming back with the second load, when near the center of the lake, one horse broke through the ice. Mr Jones unhitched from the sleigh and succeeded in getting the horse out upon the ice He then concluded to leave the load and take the team home, as the one horse was wet and very cold, and Mr Jones himself was already quite wet He therefore mounted one of the horses and started for shore They had gone but a short distance, however, when both horses went through the ice at once Mr. Jones succeeded in getting out of the water on to the ice but was thoroughly wet After an ineffectual effort to get the horses out Mr Leslie came to Waseca for help, Mr Jones remaining with the horses to keep their heads above water It was an intensely cold day and an hour passed before help arrived to get the horses out By that time, Mr Jones' feet and hands were badly frosted The horses were at last gotten out of the water on to the ice, but they were so thoroughly benumbed and chilled that they would not stand upon their feet, and showed little signs of life They were given up as lost and left upon the ice, the men returning to town The next morning Mr Douglas found one of the horses alive and wandering around his dead mate, apparently loath to leave him Had the weather not been so intensely cold, or if the horses had been blanketed no doubt both could have been saved It was a mystery to all why the horses broke through the ice where they had three times before the same day passed safely over It was a sad loss for Mr Jones who depended much on his team to earn his living Our people, however, with their accustomed liberality and goodness of heart contributed somewhat to his relief

THE FIRST BRASS BAND

The new town of Waseca was up with the times in many ways Among the other enterprises we recall the fact that a brass band was organized at Christmas time, and a concert and a festival were held to raise funds to help the boys get started The receipts of the two evening entertainments, December 25 and 26, amounted to over $100. The entertainments were well received and highly enjoyed. S H Preston and his sisters Mrs Young and Mrs. McIntosh, took leading parts in the entertainments, and Mr Preston became leader of the band, sacrificing both time and money for which he has never received proper consideration Messrs Preston, Willsey and Bennett were elected as financial committee, and H D. Baldwin as treasurer

ROUND UP OF THE YEAR.

The year 1868 closed with what ought to have been one of the most prosperous epochs in the history of the nation The crop yields had been much above the average The returned soldiers North and South, had added their productive labor to the great storehouses of national wealth. But, notwithstanding all these means of prosperity, hard times seemed to be settling down upon the nation Wheat that readily commanded $1 25 per bushel in September, went down to 75 cents in October where the price substantially remained for many months While the price of wheat in Milwaukee and Chicago was $1 88 per bushel, buyers at Waseca were paying only $1 25—a difference of sixty-three cents on a bushel Allowing a margin of three cents a bushel for handling, there was sixty cents a bushel for railroad freight.

The fall in the price of wheat held good also as to barley and other farm products Very soon the business men of the country commenced to fail The commercial failures which had numbered but 485 in 1863, 520 in 1864, 530 in 1865, and 632 in 1866, suddenly increased to 2,608 in 1868 and to 2,799 in 1869. In 1866, the average price of wheat, in New York was $2 19 while the price in 1869 had dropped to 94 cents And what caused the drop in the price of wheat? Let us reason!

Some said that the extortion of the transportation companies was the cause of the trouble, but the fact was that prices everywhere and of everything in the United States came tumbling down.

The historian should present facts, and government reports show that in 1865, the amount of money in circulation, including greenbacks, was $1,180,197,147 In 1868, greenbacks had been called in and destroyed under the refunding acts of congress until the money in circulation had been reduced to $906,091,245—a total destruction of greenbacks amounting to $274,105,902. Very few people then knew the cause of the hard times in the midst of abundant harvests, but most men of sense and intelligence have since learned that the supply of money has more to do with prices than the supply of any other one article in the commerce of the country Hence the business failures and the hard times of 1868-9 The money kings were getting in their secret work. Is it any wonder that farmers rebelled and organized the Granger Movement?

CHAPTER XXXVII, 1869.

THE WEATHER—FIRST BANK FAILURE—SEVERE WIND STORM—STAGE OVERTHROWN—VERY COLD MARCH—DEPOT BURNED—SCHOOL HOUSE CONTEST—JAIL AND COURT HOUSE BURNED AT WILTON—INCOME TAX—THE DARK DAY—SHOCKING DEATH OF MURPHY—RAILROAD TO JANESVILLE—WASECA CATHOLIC CHURCH

The year 1869 was ushered in by a heavy rainstorm, followed by a week of cold, unpleasant weather The remaining three weeks of January brought mild, warm weather. There was quite a fall of snow in February and March, and early in April the snow disappeared with a heavy rainfall, causing very high water The spring was backward, and seeding did not commence until about the middle of April

About harvest time, the country was visited by heavy storms of rain and high winds, making the harvest a long, tedious, and expensive one. Grain also suffered somewhat from blight and rust, but the yield was large, much larger than the prices, for on the 15th of November, 1869, wheat, in Waseca, brought 57 cents for No 1, and No. 2, which was the grade of this section, brought only 52 cents.

FIRST BANK FAILURE

In accordance with the fashion at that time Waseca had a bank failure which proved to be a very great damage to the whole community It came to the surface January 29, 1869 Like a thunder clap on a clear, January morning, or a conflagration at midnight, or a mighty whirlwind on a cloudless summer day, or a sudden and murderous Indian outbreak on a defenseless, frontier town, so came the first bank failure in this county as the report flew from ear to ear that Baldwin & Kittredge had failed The failure was a bad one The assets amounted to only $32,000, while the liabilities footed up to $31,000 One-half of the assets consisted of real estate, considerable of it village lots, and did not sell for the estimated value when sales were made. It was a terrible blow to our young village, leaving many of our citizens in very bad shape financially The failure took with it the bank at Blue Earth City, conducted by S P Child under the firm name of Baldwin & Child That failure, in turn, caused financial distress to many people in Faribault county, although every creditor there was finally paid in full, dollar for dollar, while here the assets did not pay over sixty cents on the dollar The late Mr Wm Everett was appointed assignee, in the bankruptcy proceedings, and managed the estate to the satisfaction of all concerned

A SECOND NEWSPAPER

W D Palmer and A J Clark started a paper at Wilton called the "Courant," which continued some six months and then failed. Palmer remained only two weeks Mr Clark having charge of the paper the remainder of the time Clark recently died, in Texas, we think His last newspaper enterprise (and he started many) was at Roseau, in this state He was a very congenial, companionable man, but whisky was his bane and kept him in the slough of poverty and despondency

SEVERE WIND STORM

There was a very severe wind storm on Friday, March 5 1869 Al Long, then one of Burbank & Co s stage drivers, between here and Mankato, had his stage upset and rolled over and over down a hill as though it were a paper kite The horses were thrown down and badly tangled up, and one of them was badly injured There was but one passenger aboard, and, fortunately he was not injured although he asserted in language strong that the stage coach rolled over twenty times

DEATH OF A BRAVE SOLDIER

The death of William Bliven occurred on the 8th of March He was one of the boy settlers of the county His marriage to the only daughter of W H. Young against the wishes of her parents, was somewhat romantic Mr Bliven enlisted at the mustering-in of the Tenth Minnesota regiment and served with it until the close of the Rebellion as a brave and faithful soldier While in the service, he contracted that lingering and dreadful disease, consumption, which finally closed his earthly career His was another name added to the long roll of those honored patriots who gave their lives that this nation might live as the home of free men.

THE COLDEST MARCH DAY ON RECORD

Waseca News, March 17, 1869

We give it up' We stand corrected' We have always stood by Minnesota and Minnesota weather, but now we feel shocked. Our potatoes and other small supplies of vegetables are frozen in the month of March' Can we stand that? Thermometer down to 20 degrees, can we call that blessed? We can't see the propriety of hot weather in January and such monstrous weather in March If anybody wants to emigrate, we say, 'let 'em go' Our feelings have been exceedingly outraged Wonder if the torrid zone is 'froze up?' Is there no way of getting up a change?"

DEPOT BURNED

On the 17th of March, '69, the city saw its first very destructive fire The following is the description given at the time. "About one o'clock in the morning our citizens were startled from their slumbers by the fearful cry of fire! fire!! fire!!! which rang out with dreadful clearness on the still, morning air Flames were seen issuing from the W & St P R R station-house, which, being of wood, was, with nearly all its contents, soon a mass of smouldering ruins. It is impossible to learn the exact origin of the fire, but it is supposed to have originated from the explosion of a kerosene lamp which was left burning on the table in the office. A large amount of freight was stored in the building—much of it belonging to merchants in Mankato and other towns to the west and southwest of us The books and papers of the office were all destroyed Some 2,000 bushels of wheat belonging to Troost & White, millers of Minnesota City, were consumed The estimated loss was from $12,000.00 to $15,000 00 " * * *

The railroad company rebuilt at once, constructing what is now (1904) the C & N-W freight depot It was completed May 10th following

FIRST SCHOOLHOUSE CONTEST IN WASECA.

On the 27th of March, 1869, there was a lively annual school meeting—the question being to build or not to build a schoolhouse Those in favor of building elected the following officers: James E Child, director, Eri G Wood, treasurer, G. N. Taylor, clerk After a lengthy and stormy debate the meeting adjourned to April 10th. On the evening of the 10th, after a long and heated struggle, the majority of the voters of the village selected lots one and two of block three, First addition, as the site for the schoolhouse Bonds bearing 12 per cent interest were issued, and a resolution was formally adopted directing the officers of the district to let the contract for building the schoolhouse, to the lowest responsible bidder at any price not to exceed $2,000 The present High School building now stands upon the site then chosen The building of the first schoolhouse was a struggle from start to finish, but the first building was completed October 1st, 1869, and school opened on the 4th of the same month

The total expense of the public school that year, including rent, blackboard, stoves and pipe, lightning rod, fuel and incidentals, with two teachers, Prof. Carman and Miss Lizzie Smith, amounted to only $775 80

It is proper to note in this connection that March 26th, 1870, at the annual meeting, Child and Wood were re-elected, and Dr. L D McIntosh was chosen clerk The opposition finally carried a motion to adjourn for one week, hoping thereby to defeat a motion to levy a tax for eight months of school At the adjourned meeting, however, the motion carried and the school board was fully sustained

DESTRUCTIVE FIRE AT WILTON

On the 3d day of April, 1869, as if to aid the rapid decline of the doomed village of Wilton, then the county seat, a disastrous fire occurred. The fire originated, it was thought, either from the stove pipe, which led from the jail stove to the chimney, or was set fire by a prisoner, named Shea. The fire was not discovered until about eight o'clock, when it had reached the roof and spread far and wide on the inside, between the roof and ceiling over the adjoining court room Heroic work was done to save the building, while men, women and children, with much presence of mind, worked bravely in saving the books, papers, records and furniture of the county offices The venerable old court house soon fell in, and Mr. Henry J Meyer's building, which contained LaDow's Hall, J. H Wightman's stock of hardware, Powers & LaDow's library, and G A LaDow's household effects next fell a prey to the devouring flames Hall's saloon next met its doom and in the space of an hour and a half the whole block was but a mass of smouldering ruins Each building was insured for $200, which did not cover a tenth part of the loss The people of Wilton cared for those made homeless and the county commissioners met April 12, to arrange for county offices—the county offices being temporarily located in the wagon shop of B. Bundsho. The prisoner Shea, who was serving time for robbing a drunken man in Waseca, was rescued without serious harm, although he was terribly scared.

FIRST FINANCIAL REPORT.

The first financial report of the village of Waseca was published April 21, 1869 This report showed no real or personal property taxes collected, but the total receipts amounted to $396, and were derived from the following sources, to wit

Jerome Madden, saloon license	$50 00
Thos White, same	50 00
T E Marshall, same	50 00
Jos Gatzman, same	50 00
W S Libby, same	50 00
G Liek, same	50 00
John Maloney, same	50 00
W S Libby, billiard license	15 00
T. E Marshall, same	15 00
A Wert, dray license	5 00
De Castro, show license	5 00
Fines Collected	6 00
Total	$396 00

Then followed itemized expenses amounting to $391.69, leaving a balance on hand of $4 31

Saloon license fees and corporation expenses were light in those days compared with the present

THAT INCOME TAX

In those days, (1863-9)) before the gold-buggers had gotten

control of the Republican party, the supreme court, and the government, there was an income tax—and a very just tax it was too, although there were some queer pranks about taxpayers then as now Here is a little article which went forth from the sanctum of the Waseca News, May 12, 1869, viz.

"Ward, Child—Child, Ward'"

'INCOME TAX FOR WASECA COUNTY FOR THE PRESENT YEAR"

Child, J E income $1,547, tax . . . $17 35
Ward, W G, income $1,065, tax . 3 25

One a civil engineer for the Winona & St Peter Railroad company the other a scrub of an editor on a country newspaper'

What a tremendous loss there must have been in business circles for less than a thousand dollars a year' Heavy men laboring for less than a thousand dollars a year''

"Where is Hunter with his bonds and farms and merchandise? and Bailey and Watkins with their hardware? and Libby with his United States bonds and liquor profits? and Addison & Everett with their tremendous sales? and Wadsworth with his salary and lands? and the Smiths, and Johnsons, and McCues, and Castors, and doctors and lawyers, and hosts of other equally worthy gentlemen in this county? Are they dying in poverty and obscurity? What have they been doing the past year? Have they been gnawing at their original capital?

It is a glorious thing, Brother Ward, to have an income, but it is excruciating to look upon the poverty (?) of our friends around us' Only two persons, in Waseca county pay income taxes—poor, degraded, 'Black Republicans,' at that'

"Brother Ward, let us call a meeting and get the Democrat Whangdoodle to deliver a speech of condolence'

The man that has an income can and ought to pay his proportion of the taxes; the man that, on account of misfortune or otherwise, in any year, has no income ought not to be called upon to pay taxes The farmer that has a good crop can afford to pay taxes The farmer whose crop is totally destroyed by a tornado or drouth is not able to pay taxes and ought not to be called upon to pay any for that year There is no other plan of taxation so fair and so equitable as taxation based upon income

BASE BALL OF YEARS AGONE

Perhaps it will interest some of the people of to-day and of the future to read and learn something of the first prominent baseball organization of Waseca county It was christened the "Clear Lake Base Ball Club" and was organized Wednesday evening,

May 5, the following officers were elected: B S Lewis, president, W M Murfin, vice president, W O Nanscawen, secretary Lewis Brownell, treasurer, J. W Johnson, P. P. Smith and M H Helms, directors It was organized with a membership of 18—afterwards increased to 27 The next Saturday evening, at a regular meeting, the following were chosen as the first nine viz Mike Murphy captain, M H Helm, pitcher, Wm Wood, catcher, I W Johnson short stop, M Murphy, first base, B S Lewis, second base, Dan Haines third base, W M Murfin, center field, Charles Vincent, right field, Roger Wood, left field The members met every evening, Sundays excepted, upon the grounds now occupied by the court house and jail, for practice It was little more than an amateur club until it absorbed the "Blooming Grove nine," and made Martin Healy captain and pitcher It finally became the champion club of the state and won the silver bat The base ball excitement about that time became almost universal throughout the country and even aged men would leave their business to broil in the hot sun while they watched the ups and downs of the game But, like every other fad, it had its day, and our Waseca people, after one year of excitement, loss of time and cash outlay, concluded to give the game over to less practical men and boys

CONGREGATIONAL CHURCH

On the 11th of May, 1869 members of the Congregational church met in what is now the Baptist church building of Waseca, and adopted articles of incorporation in accordance with the laws of the state The following gentlemen were chosen trustees· Ezra Wood, A E Dearborn, Austin Vinton, J H Stevens L Hummiston, Ed Bennett and G A Rowland Ezra Wood was elected president and A E Dearborn secretary At this meeting there was considerable discussion regarding the erection of a church edifice at an early day, but nothing decisive was accomplished until the following September. About the 22d of that month the committee had secured $1 700 00 for the purpose, and about October 1, D. L Whipple and Maj Young commenced work on the construction of the edifice. The building was completed the next spring, and constitutes the main part of the present church

TOTAL ECLIPSE—THE DARK DAY

There was a total eclipse of the sun on the seventh day of August, 1869, at 3 43 p. m This eclipse of the sun was one of the most awe-inspiring sights ever beheld Long prior to the obscuration, almost everyone had prepared his smoked glass and was watching intently for the phenomenon that astronomers had foretold years and years before. Exactly on time the moon was seen to intrude between the earth and the sun Slowly and surely darkness covered the face of the sun, the obscuration growing more and more, and then was seen the approach of the moon's shadow in the air The heavens were darkened The stars and planets shone forth as in the night. The air grew sensibly cooler Animals became strangely agitated. Birds seemed bewildered and fluttered in the treetops A strange gloom covered the earth. Buildings, trees, animals, and all other objects had a peculiar and unnatural appearance. The human face assumed a pallid, ghastly shade, and as the eclipse reached totality or near it, all grew silent and meditative; and a feeling of profound awe not to say dread, took possession of the beholder.

COUNTY POLITICS

The Republican county convention was held at Wilton, September 2, 1869 At this convention Waseca secured the nomination of Maj W C. Young, who was well known to favor the removal of the county seat to Waseca. The nominees were as follows: Maj. W C Young for representative, J B Hill, sheriff, J. A Canfield, judge of probate, Lewis Brownell county attorney; C E Crane, surveyor, P. C. Bailey, court commissioner; Dr M S Gove, Coroner

The Democrat county convention was held September 18 1869, and put in nomination the following candidates Kelsey Curtis for representative, B S Lewis, county attorney, H. A Mosher, register of deeds, Philo Hall treasurer; S W Long sheriff, Dr. R O Craig coroner, John Bradish, judge of probate The result of the election gave certificates to W C Young, S M Long J A Canfield, B S Lewis, C E. Crane, P C Bailey, H A Mosher and Dr M S Gove Hence, as will be seen in the result, honors were divided between the parties even at that day, when party feeling ran high.

SHOCKING DEATH BY ACCIDENT

One of those shocking accidents that sometimes occur, happened September 24, 1869 Mr John Murphy an early settler of Byron, accompanied by one of the Messrs Linnihan of the same town, in returning home from Waseca in the evening, and while crossing a bridge over a runway on the Geo T Dunn farm in Wilton, met with a fatal accident. While crossing the pole bridge, the off horse slipped one hind foot through the bridge. The horse commenced to struggle and Mr Murphy, as was supposed, took the near horse by the bridle and tried to quiet the team. The off horse, however, struggled and plunged about until Mr Murphy and both horses were thrown from the bridge, on the east side, the man falling underneath and both horses on top of him It was so dark at the time that nothing could be seen any distance. Linnihan, who was in the wagon, called to Murphy but got no answer He then got out of the wagon and felt around until he discovered Murphy beneath the horses Linnihan cut the harness from the horses and the off one got out. Murphy was fast under the other horse and under water, and Linnihan found it impossible to extricate him He then mounted the live horse and aroused the neighbors, who came with lanterns They drew out the body of the horse in the creek under which they found the lifeless form of Mr. Murphy It was a very sad affair.

SHOOTING DEER AND CHICKENS ON THE RAILROAD TRACK.

Among the railroad incidents of that day, we recall the story of Conductor Denny Keeler, and Engineer Nichols It was the first week in December, 1869, when going east, that they had a novel experience Just after pulling out of Dover Center, they discovered a fine deer upon the track some distance ahead Crowding on steam they gave chase The road at this place was fenced on both sides of the track, so there was little chance of escape for the frightened animal but to outrun the fiery horse behind him The train gained steadily and rapidly upon the deer, and, when within gunshot, both Keeler and Nichols fired, both shots taking effect and disabling the deer, but not killing it. The train was stopped and Denny, with knife in hand, cut the deer's throat, and took the carcass aboard without even a pass or the payment of fare, and proudly landed it in Winona as indisputable evidence of their prowess as hunters

It was not unusual in those days when Waseca was the western terminus of the road, for the boys to stop a train between Owatonna and Waseca long enough to bag a few chickens.

RAILROAD EXTENDED TO JANESVILLE

The village of "East Janesville," as the present Janesville was then called, was surveyed and platted by S H Mott in August, 1869 The people of the "Old Village of Janesville," which was situated on the west side of the outlet at the south end of the beautiful Lake Elysian, had anticipated the building of the road to that point and the new village was well under way before the first train reached that point J W Sprague, general manager of the W & St P Ry at that time, was proprietor of the new town and reaped a harvest of shekels The first building was erected by Judge Baldwin who went from Waseca It was built in August, "Jim" Cummins hauling the first load of lumber for it This building was opened as a boarding house and hotel It was afterwards known as the "Johnson House" Hon J O Chandler came over from the old town and opened a stock of general merchandise A W Jennison and Frank A Miner from Waseca also opened a store with a general assortment of goods Hon D J Dodge, from Waseca, opened a hardware store under the firm name of D J Dodge & Co J D Andrews, also from Waseca opened a drug store in the new town Hon R O Craig came over from the old town and opened a doctor's office Other buildings followed in rapid succession and when the first train arrived Oct 10th 1869, East Janesville was a bustling little town

As soon as regular trains made Janesville, the daily stages of Burbank & Co ceased to arrive at Waseca from the west but made their headquarters at Janesville For ten years the Burbank stage lines had been our sole dependence for mail facilities on the main thoroughfares, and when these stages ceased their daily visits it seemed much like the death of an old friend in the community

MISCELLANEOUS NOTES

Mrs E Fisk, one of the very early settlers of Wilton, and highly respected, died June 20, 1869

The first Mrs Peter Lindsay, who had been ill of cancer of the breast for three years, had it removed about the first of February, 1869 by Drs Coe Gove and Brubaker. She died not long afterwards

The "News" of March 31, 1869, contained a four column legal notice of application for right of way through Waseca county by the W & St P R R Co It had to be published six weeks and was what printers call a "fat take."

The Fourth of July was duly celebrated this year on July 5th at Waseca Rev E H Alden was the orator of the day Capt M H Helms acted as marshal, Hon Sam B Williams served as president, and Lewis Brownell read the Declaration of Independence The base-ball ground was the center of attraction during the afternoon There was a big dance at McCue's hall in the evening and a display of fireworks was made by the village The day was very pleasant and passed off without an accident

September 17, 1869, Wm W Casey of Elysian, stole a pair of oxen from Erick Larsen, of Iosco, traded them to a Mr Wilson residing on the Des Moines river, for a horse, and then sold the horse to one Scott, of Morristown Casey was soon after arrested and later convicted of the crime The oxen were recovered through the efforts of Hans Hanson

September 22 1869, Henry Willyard shot a pelican which was sailing over Waseca It measured eight feet from tip to tip of its wings It was sent to a taxidermist at Winona and mounted, and for a long time stood in one of the drug stores of Waseca

For the year ending September 1, there had been received and shipped from Waseca 480,000 bushels of wheat—almost a half-million bushels. The receipts of June amounted to 43,381 bushels, and for July, to 32,189 bushels During the year there was a large trade in agricultural implements The sales for the year ending Sept 1 amounted to $86,935 The wheat crop of that year, although mostly No 2 amounted to 300 882 bushels, as returned by the assessors The crop was fair but prices ruled low

In the fall of 1869, Mr. John Bierwalter, since deceased, was made night watchman of Waseca—the first ever employed in the place.

C A Wright came to Waseca from Winona in December of

this year, and succeeded Henry Willyard as manager of the grain elevator of the W. & St. P. R. R. Co.

There was a meeting of prominent Catholics at the house of Thomas White, October 24, to devise ways and means for erecting a church building. This was the beginning of efforts which culminated in the erection of the first Catholic church in Waseca. This building has since given way to the present magnificent edifice, the largest and most costly in the county.

CHAPTER XXXVIII, 1870.

COUNTY SEAT CONTEST—ATTEMPTED HANGING BEE—M & ST L RY NEW COURT HOUSE IN WASECA—W B MORRIS DROWNED BANK BURGLARY COUNTY SEAT REMOVED—UNITED STATES CENSUS—FIRST COUNTY FAIR—GRANGE MOVEMENT—C K. DAVIS FOR GOVERNOR

The year 1870 was an exciting one in Waseca county The county seat contest—a bank robbery—the attempted hanging of "Date" Smith and Frank Waters, suspected of horse-stealing—the first county agricultural fair held in the county, and the Grange organizations kept the people of the county on the qui vive.

LEGISLATION FOR THE COUNTY

The legislature in 1870 convened Jan 4 and adjourned March 4 The constitution then limited the pay of legislators to sixty days.

At the beginning of the session of the legislature in 1870, a bill was introduced by Maj Young, our representative, to submit the question of the removal of the county seat from Wilton to Waseca to a vote of the people

At an early date in the session, he also introduced a bill authorizing the village of Waseca to issue bonds in the sum of $5,000 00 for the erection of a court house to be donated to the county of Waseca, in case the county seat should be removed from Wilton to Waseca

The question of the removal of the county seat was the all absorbing subject of discussion during the year As early as February, in a discussion of the question, the "News" of Waseca said:

"It has become almost an axiom in this state that every village or city must bleed or die, and Waseca can not expect to escape entirely the lot of others. In order to obtain the county seat, it will be necessary for this village to offer a bonus to the county. A bill has already passed the legislature authorizing the people to issue bonds for this object.

"Harmony among ourselves is essential to strength, and passion should have no place in the considerations of matters pertaining to local interests. So far as we are able to learn, it is generally conceded that the county seat will be removed to this place, this fall, by a large majority.

"It is much better for the farmers of this county to settle this question now, than to have it hanging in the balance of uncertainty for several years to come, with the certainty of its removal to this place eventually."

On the 7th of March 1870, the board of trustees of the village of Waseca ordered a special election for the voters of the village to be held at Bennett's hall on the 19th day of March to vote upon the proposition to issue the bonds of said village in the sum of $5,000.00 bearing interest at the rate of 12 per cent. for the purpose of erecting county buildings in said village for the use of the county of Waseca, as authorized by an act of the legislature approved February 24, 1870. The resolutions to be voted upon read as follows:

"Resolved, that bonds of the village of Waseca, with interest coupons attached, be issued for the purpose named in the act, in the sum of $5,000, bearing annual interest at the rate of 12 per cent. per annum.

"That the denominations of said bonds, and the time or times when the same shall be payable, be such as the board of trustees may hereafter direct, provided that no bond shall be issued running more than 10 years from the date thereof, and the faith and credit of the village are pledged to the punctual payment of the interest and principal of said bonds."

The resolutions were unanimously adopted, and, early in the season, a brick court house was erected.

MINNEAPOLIS AND ST. LOUIS RAILWAY

During the early months of this year the question of the building of the Western railroad, now known as the M. & St. L. railroad, was very thoroughly discussed. At that time the writer in the Waseca News said:

"To the people of this place this road is of the utmost importance.

and anything that they can do to assist in its early completion will be cheerfully done The city of Minneapolis by a vote of its people has decided to issue bonds to aid in the construction of the road to the amount of $300,000 00 The business men of that city have also subscribed $100,000 00, making a total of $400,000 00 from Minneapolis. The whole stretch of country through which this road will pass is unsurpassed in richness and fertility of soil, and is as densely populated by thrifty farmers as any portion of the state. By means of this road, Minneapolis, with her large flouring mills and manufacturing establishments, may command a larger trade than any other city in the state, and we are glad that the people of that city so view it Take, for instance, the matter of pine lumber, the villages along this road can get lumber transported from Minneapolis to Owatonna, for $16 00 per car load, but from there to Waseca, a distance of 15 miles, we must pay $20 00 a car load, virtually driving the Minneapolis lumber from our market, and, for that matter, driving our lumber dealers out of business Besides, the wheat market is far behind what it would be if this north and south railroad were built

"We again urge the people of this place to take united action to promote the interests of Waseca."

In connection with this railroad matter, the citizens of Waseca met at Bennett's hall, March 11, 1870 H P. Norton was called to the chair and Esquire Bennett was chosen secretary Hon S B Williams stated the object of the meeting, and made some remarks upon the great importance of the road to this locality Short speeches were also made by Messrs Latham, Brownell, Lewis, Bennett and others Messrs. Williams, Everett, and Trowbridge were appointed a committee to confer with the officers of the railroad company in regard to the location and building of the road Mr Latham then offered the following resolution which was unanimously adopted:

"Resolved, that we, the citizens of the village of Waseca, consider that this railway, running from Minneapolis to Albert Lea, through this village will be of great benefit to us, and we are willing to do everything in our power to further the interests of said road"

THE THEN NEW COURT HOUSE.

The contract for building the court house was let to Marble & Dresser of Owatonna early in the spring, and the management of the business, at the election of May 3rd, was somewhat in issue. Wm Everett and S B. Williams were elected trustees, who, with H. P Norton, elected in 1869, constituted the board of trustees for the ensuing year. At the first meeting of the trustees, after election, it was "Resolved, that the bonds of the village, (to be) issued for the building of county buildings, be issued so as to be payable, one thousand dollars in three years, and one thousand dollars in each year thereafter until the whole $5,000 shall become payable, and that they be issued in denominations of not more than $1,000, nor less than $100 each." The same day the board issued "Bond No 1" due three years after date, for $1,000, bearing interest at 12 per cent. Bond No. 2, for $500, due four years from date, and bond No 3 for $500, due in five years, with coupons attached, were issued to Marble & Dresser, of Owatonna, who had entered into contract to construct the court house for $5,000 But before the bonds were delivered, Bond No 1 was surrendered or rescinded and bonds numbered 4 and 5, for $500 each, were issued in lieu thereof, May 10, 1870 At the same time, bonds numbered 6 and 7, for $500 each, were issued to the same persons On July 1, the third installment of bonds was issued—the same being bonds numbered 8 and 9 for $500 each On July 12 the court house being completed, the last two bonds were issued, the same being for $500 each, and due in seven years from the date thereof.

DROWNING OF W B MORRIS

Mr Morris was one of the early settlers of Alton township and an energetic enterprising citizen, highly respected by all who knew him He was drowned May 25, 1870 It was a time of high water and he attempted to swim his horse across the Le Sueur river, near Mr Markham's place But when the horse reached the north bank and attempted to ascend it he fell back into the boiling flood, throwing Mr Morris into the stream, where he soon drowned. He was an upright man and his loss was deeply felt His widow, a highly respected lady, still resides on the farm at this writing, 1904.

ATTEMPTED HANGING BEE

There was great excitement in the county about the first of June, 1870, in regard to horse-stealing Two horse thieves from Winneshiek county, Iowa, had been traced through this county and "rounded up" at Waterville, where two of the horses were also found Many of the people of the county suspected that "Date" Smith and Frank Waters were connected with the gang of horse thieves which operated in Iowa and Minnesota It was of frequent occurrence prior to that time for men with stolen horses to congregate in Waterville where for many years these two men resided. But at the time we speak of, "Date" Smith and family had resided in Waseca for about a year. At the time of the arrest of the two thieves from Iowa, near Waterville, both these men fell under suspicion, and a large number of farmers from the northern and western portions of the county got together in a body and visited Waseca with the avowed intention of hanging Smith and Waters to the nearest tree or telegraph pole. Whether the crowd really intended to hang them, or only to give them a scare, has never been determined to this day. But certain it is the crowd caught both men and took them out on the railroad track, near the old round house, east of the depot, and had rope enough to hang half a dozen men James E Child was at the time justice of the peace and knew nothing of the mobbing until a lady friend of Mrs Smith went to him with much anxiety and implored that he do what he could to save the men—especially Smith. Mr. Child did not find it an easy matter to get citizens to face the mob and release the prisoners, but he finally secured the volunteer assistance of H A Mosher, M H Helms, Asa Mosher, C. A Wright and Henry Willyard, and proceeded to the place where the crowd had assembled. Without saying a word, these men elbowed their way through the excited crowd until they reached the accused men who were entirely surrounded Mr. Child, as justice of the peace, then ordered the crowd, in the name of the state of Minnesota, to fall back and allow the men to pass out The crowd at once fell into a hubbub, some being in favor of law and order, and others demanding that the men should be hanged. One farmer of giant frame, flashing black eyes, and a fog-horn voice, said: "We ought to hang the whole d——d outfit."

The rescuers, without parleying or awaiting the action of the excited masses, at once pushed through the crowd with the trembling men to Second street, thence down Second street to what was then the Vincent hotel, where Smith and Waters were rushed upstairs, and guards placed at every door and stairway Mr. Child, as justice of the peace, warned the excited crowd that any man that should attempt to force an entrance or that should aid and assist in disturbing the peace, would be arrested and punished to the full extent of the law He appealed to their love of law and good order and implored them to disperse and resort only to lawful means for the punishment of crime Every man of the rescuers presented a bold front, and the excited crowd soon discovered that Smith and Waters would not be given up without a struggle in which some men would get hurt The cooler heads and more reasonable ones in the crowd soon prevailed upon their companions to disperse. It certainly was a time of much excitement and had the men been armed with guns or revolvers, there might have been very serious results As it was, about a half-dozen determined men prevented what might have been a double murder. Smith and Waters, although the latter indulged in some drunken bravado the next day when there was no danger, undoubtedly realized the seriousness of the situation Smith sold his property here, and both he and Waters soon after left this portion of the state This episode, too, served the purpose, no doubt, of frightening thieves from this section; for it was generally believed that there would be a hanging bee should any more horse thieves venture this way for some time to come

FOURTH OF JULY

Waseca celebrated the Fourth of July, 1870, in a formal and enthusiastic manner. It was then considered the great day of days in this republic. It was seldom that a Fourth of July passed without appropriate public exercises during which the great, underlying principles of the equal and inalienable rights of all men to life, liberty and the pursuit of happiness were rehearsed and emphasized This year, Hon Gordon E Cole, of Faribault, delivered a very able address

THE FIRST BANK ROBBERY

After the Baldwin-Kittredge bank failure of Jan 29, 1869, Kinyon Bros, of Owatonna, opened a bank in Waseca On the 24th of August, 1870, some burglars broke into the bank, blew open the safe by means of gunpowder, and stole the sum of $3,000 in cash, besides valuable papers They left, as mementos of their visit, a linen coat, some whisky in a bottle obtained from a druggist, a piece of bologna sausage, and a variety of tools used in their burglarious operations.

Sheriff Toher, of Steele county, with D L. Whipple, who was sheriff of this county, organized a detective force and soon found one of the burglars, tracking him to St Peter, and back to Mankato, thence to Janesville, and back through Waseca to Owatonna. The evidence upon the examination disclosed the following facts in connection with the arrest of John T Howard, alias Thomas Gale, charged with the robbery of the bank·

He first came to the Arnold House, at Owatonna, on Sunday evening, August 21, and remained over night The next morning he left, and returned in the evening with a span of horses which he put into Hastings' livery stable. On the next Tuesday morning, by depositing $200 with Mr Hastings, he obtained a team and carriage and drove to Waseca, arriving here about 10 o'clock in the forenoon. He got a ten dollar bill changed at Kinyon's bank reconnoitering the premises, and then drove on to Janesville, arriving at the Baldwin House about noon, where he took dinner The same evening he arrived at Mankato and put up at the Clifton House He ordered his team to be ready the next morning at four o'clock In accordance with this order the team was ready, but the accused man was not there After waiting half an hour, the team was again put into the stable and fed About this time Howard came to the barn considerably out of breath, with perspiration on his face, as though he had been exercising violently He then remained until after the early breakfast, and finally started away at 5 30 alone About 10 o'clock in the forenoon of Wednesday he again appeared in Janesville, in company with another man designated as the "gray-bearded man" The two drove to the express office, and the latter took a valise into the office and expressed it to one Hubbard, of Osage, Iowa They then went to the Baldwin House and took dinner—the gray-bearded man paying the whole bill. They left Janesville about noon together, and were next seen and noticed by Mrs. Julius Ulrich and Mrs. Pat McCarthy, of St Mary, a few miles west of Waseca, with another stranger, there being three in the carriage when the women saw them. Dr. Brubaker saw them the same afternoon near W H Gray's farm, about a mile west from Waseca A short time after this, Mr Ed Bennett saw the team, with Howard alone, pass his slaughter house, west of town, coming towards Waseca Howard was next seen by Mr. Terwilliger near Clear Lake, going towards Owatonna with the Hastings team, which was well known to many of our people. Soon after passing Mr Terwilliger, he was seen to stop near the Woodville cemetery, and a man came up to the buggy Howard was next seen at Owatonna that evening, where he delivered the team and put up at the Arnold House He went to bed about 8 o'clock, remarking that he was very tired.

That night the bank at Waseca was robbed, and the next morning about 5 o'clock, he was seen on the sidewalk near the Arnold House About one o'clock in the afternoon he was arrested on suspicion and searched by Sheriff Toher, who found upon his person about $230 00, in cash, some pistol cartridges and some other minor articles In his satchel was found a book descriptive of banks and safes, a revolver, and a peculiar cap. Shortly after this arrest, Toher went to Dubuque in pursuit of the valise which had been expressed from Janesville to Osage, Iowa. On opening it, he found a kit of burglar tools a very strong and peculiar brace, two bits or drills for boring steel or iron, a steel punch, two steel wedges of peculiar shape, some powder, a coil of fuse, a cap similar to the one found in Howard's satchel, and a peculiar instrument for fastening to and turning a door key from the outside when the door is locked and the key left inside in the lock.

Some of the paper wrapped around the bits in the valise corresponded in quality and color with pieces of paper found in the bank in Waseca the next morning after the robbery The two steel wedges found in the valise corresponded exactly with the two wedges left in the Kinyon bank by the burglars Experts testified that they must all have been made by the same man about the same time, and, probably, from the same bar of steel He was examined before a justice of the peace, and held to await the action of the grand jury

Afterwards two other men were arrested, and Howard, to save himself from state prison, turned state's evidence and sent an old man and one other to the penitentiary, his only punishment being about one year in the county jail awaiting trial He was an accomplished scoundrel and liar, and ought to have been sent to prison for at least ten years

COUNTY SEAT CONTEST OF 1870.

The year 1870 was one of the most exciting, in a political way, of any in the history of the county since 1857, when the county seat question was first voted upon. As heretofore stated, Waseca built a court house early in the season, at a cost of $5,000 The Wilton advocates, for some time, contended that the offer of the court house, by Waseca, was a fraud, but this contention was not successful before the people, and the managers at Wilton themselves at last, pretended to make an offer of $5,000 in bonds for the building of a new court house, provided the people of the county should vote to retain the county seat at that place But as there was no authority in law for the issue of such bonds, the people gave no heed to their offer.

As the season advanced, the canvass for the removal of the county seat increased in interest and intensity. Waseca, as never since, stood solidly together, shoulder to shoulder, and worked most effectively Every man in the county was "sounded" and for some time prior to election day, the work for that day was planned, and every man was alloted his position in the ranks of the workers Two men were sent to every polling place in the county on election day, to work for Waseca, and especially to bring in, as soon as possible, on the night of election, the exact returns of the vote cast on that question. The writer well remembers the day He, in company with Mr John Crain, then a blacksmith of Waseca, was detailed to attend the polls in the town of Byron Each man at Waseca voted early and started for the several stations assigned A few days before election there had been several days of heavy rain storm which closed with a very light fall of snow and freezing weather. The day was cold and the roads very rough. We could drive only on the walk, and much of the way a slow walk at that The election that year, in Byron, was held in a small house, in the western part of the township, near the Christy McGrath place. The polls were held open until a late hour, and the canvassers seemed provokingly slow in counting the ballots; but as soon as we had the figures we started for Waseca, arriving about 11 o'clock that night Only one town more was then to be heard from (Vivian) and every man in Waseca then knew that the county seat contest had been decided in favor of Waseca.

Those who had faced the storm and cold of the day and been jolted over thirty miles of rough, frozen road, were excused from further service, but there was a select company of "secret service men" that had been chosen to carry out the will of the people by an actual removal of the property and of the offices of the county from Wilton to Waseca before daylight the next morning And sure enough at daybreak, the sound of music by the cornet band, the huzzas of the people, and the shouting of boys announced the arrival of the register of deeds and his office furniture, the clerk of the district court and his office records, and the county treasurer with the furniture and books of his office The county auditor and others came over during the morning, and before noon, the day after election, the county seat was fully established and the officers all doing business at the new court house The Waseca News announced the arrival of the offices the next day after the election and said.

"The thing 'is did' That big lawsuit over the removal of the county seat will be held at Waseca—when it comes off Any one having business at the county seat will find the 'machine' in full blast at the court house The struggle is over The billing and cooing, the coaxing and hiring, the drinking and treating, the threatening and flattering, the work and excitement on both sides are at an end The question is settled—forever settled The matter has been thoroughly discussed and fairly understood, and the result is the untrammeled voice of the people Politics is over, too, for this year, and now let us bury the hatchet, renew personal friendships, and devote our energies and strength to the building up of our material interests and to the cultivation of fraternal feelings and good fellowship'

UNITED STATES CENSUS

The United States census was taken during the months of June and July this year. The north half of the county was enumerated by James E Child, and the south half by S J Willis The following statement was published at that time The increase in population was shown by the following figures

June 1, 1855, number of people	70
June 1, 1860, number of people	2,601

June 1, 1865, number of people 4,786
June 1, 1870, number of people 7,857

These figures show an annual increase from 1865 to 1870 of 614 Comparing the wealth of the county, the result was equally satisfactory. The amount of wheat produced in 1864 was 61,050 bushels, while the product of 1869 reached 393,811 bushels In connection with this subject we find that 28,000 bushels of wheat were marketed in Waseca during the month of August, and 28,136 bushels in the month of September, for which the farmers received $41,947 00

The number of horses in the county increased from 825, in 1865, to 2 055 in 1870 Horned cattle increased from 4,565, in 1865, to 6,263, in 1870 In 1865 there were 533 cultivated farms, and in 1870 there were 1,028 The census value of all the property of the county was estimated at $2 205,284, in 1870.

THE FIRST COUNTY FAIR

The first county fair was held in Waseca, at the new court house, October 6 and 7 Among the exhibitors that drew premiums, the following names appear J W Hosmer, of Janesville, finest honey, Mrs B F Weed and Mrs R R Howard, then of Wilton, fine dairy butter, Daniel Pierce, then of Freedom, apples and vegetables, Hon Joseph Minges, of Otisco, and Hon Wm Brisbane, of Wilton, best potatoes, R R Howard, of Wilton, fine Chester White swine . The display of horses was quite large while the number of cattle was small in comparison. The Misses Gallagher, Riegel and Landers displayed much skill in horseback riding on the race course In classes A and B, horses, Ole Everson, J A Wheeler A Dewing, W H Young, S S Phelps, Wm Byron, Jas A Root, W L Wheeler, H Vincent, Henry Behne, Albert Remund and P O. Houg received premiums In class C, cattle, Martin Hackett, Patrick Healey, R M Middaugh, S H. Talbut, and C W. Hensel were the premium takers In class D, sheep swine and fowls, the lucky ones were J A Claghorn, Peter Eckert, Patrick Healy, J A Root, J G Greening and R. R Howard In class E, there were twenty entries and those who won prizes were Daniel Semple, Daniel Pierce, E G Wood, and J. Erno. Class F, vegetables, ten entries, gave premiums to Patrick McDermott, Wm Brisbane,

Daniel Pierce, S H Talbut, J W. Altenburg, and Jas. A Root In class G, B. F. Weed got the premium on sorghum syrup, and John Buckhout on flour Among the other premium takers appear the names of Valentine Butsch, G A Roland, A Wert, Mrs O Powell, Mrs M. S Gove, Mrs G P. Johnson and Mrs. Myrick.

Hon Wm Brisbane delivered an excellent address

He dwelt upon the wholesome and honorable calling of the farmer, and eloquently urged the importance of a more liberal education for farmers' sons and daughters, and especially in regard to their own calling He said the trouble was that too many persons were farming who knew little or nothing of the business. Farms were poorly cultivated—machinery was allowed to rust and rot—cattle died for want of proper food and care, and in many ways farmers lost money and time, more because they did not understand the business than for any other cause.

THE GRANGER MOVEMENT

It was during this year, 1870, that heavy railroad extortions had called forth a strong protest from the farmers of the country as well as from every justice-loving citizen The cost of shipping a bushel of wheat from Waseca to Chicago was then from 25 to 30 cents. Discriminations of the most outrageous character were practiced throughout the West The doctrine of government control was stoutly and strenuously denied by all the railroad corporations, their agents attorneys and hireling editors, and especially by their dupes all over the country. On the other hand, intelligent and independent attorneys and editors, and intelligent and independent men of common sense in all callings claimed that the state, the government, had the right and the power to fix reasonable rates of transportation for passengers and commodities This issue, for the time, overshadowed all others, notwithstanding the efforts of corporations, then as now, to prevent the question from becoming a party issue The daily papers of both parties, all over the country, were employed to denounce the true friends of the masses as "demagogues," "ignoramuses," "fanatics," "blatherskites," "socialists" and "anarchists" The corporations even tried to enlist the efforts of priesthood to break up the grange organizations and, in some localities, succeeded to some extent Nevertheless, the work of education and organization went forward rapidly in this section, and the Grange became a great, non-partisan, political power that finally gave the country what was known as the "Grange laws," and forced into the courts the question of the right and the power of the government to control the railroads The supreme courts of the states and the nation decided in favor of the people, and it was learned, among men capable of learning, that the "demagogues," "ignoramuses," "socialists," "anarchists" and "fanatics" knew more about law and fundamental rights of man and property than all the corporations with their paid attorneys, their agents, their boodlers and their hireling editors And yet there are mullet heads to-day that will tell us that to regulate the transportation rates on railroads so that every person and every locality shall enjoy just and equal rates would destroy the railroads and bring anarchy to the whole country. What fools we mortals are in this world!

It was in this year that a Grange was organized in almost every neighborhood in the county There was one in Waseca But, as it does in all great and popular organizations, the spirit of rivalry and jealousy crept in. Men of small calibre, little intelligence, and narrow jealousy sowed the seeds of discord by insisting that none but actual farmers—men who tilled the soil with their own hands—should be members. This narrow view of the organization drove from it much of the intelligence necessary to direct any movement successfully. This, together with the fact that I Donnelly managed to disrupt it for his own personal ends, soon destroyed one of the best and most useful educational agencies ever introduced into our farming communities The organization still lingers in some places, but its power for good is broken

Hon C K Davis was nominated and elected by Granger sentiment, a law to control rates was enacted the first year of his administration, the next year the railroads secured control of the legislature and repealed the law. And the singular part of it all was that the very men who would be the most benefited by the government control of roads were the mullet-heads in the community to vote with the corporations No wonder that Cush Davis, when the law was repealed, exclaimed—"I am sick of the people They desert their best friends. I am done with them As soon as I am through with this governor business I shall go back to my office and my law books. As Vanderbilt said, 'the people be damned,' for they don't appreciate honest, self-sacrificing men who work to save them from the slavery of modern feudalism.''

FALL ELECTION OF 1870

Party lines were loosely drawn at that time Major Wm C Young, Republican candidate for senator, received a majority of 402 over James Jones, his opponent, Hon Wm Brisbane, Democratic candidate for representative, received 233 majority over Mr S C Dow, his opponent, who was a very good citizen and a Republican. E Cronkhite, Democratic candidate for auditor, was elected over Fred Kittredge, Republican, by a majority of 324 The democrats elected Wm. Lee, of Iosco, and H G Mosher, of Otisco, county commissioners The majority in favor of the removal of the county seat to Waseca was 215

SHORT NOTES OF 1870

January 19, 1870, No 1 wheat brought only 48 cents per bushel

The creditors of the defunct bank of Baldwin & Kittredge realized only 25 cents on the dollar

May 2, the house of Mr. Chas San Galli was consumed by fire It was fully insured

On June 2, 1870, under the auspices of the Farmers' club of Blooming Grove, the first monthly fair was held in Waseca The fairs were held on the first Thursday of each month, a few times, but were finally discontinued

On July 29 1870, the village board of Waseca made a deed of the then new court house to the county of Waseca, to become absolute upon the removal of the seat of justice from Wilton to Waseca

Whitney L Wheeler, about forty-eight years of age and one of the very early settlers of the county, died November 4 1870, after a somewhat severe illness. He and his family settled first in St Mary, afterwards moving into Wilton He was a staunch, prominent republican, who was active in every campaign. He was the owner of some valuable horses and practiced as a veterinary surgeon At the time of his death he was treasurer and captain of riders of the Waseca County Horse-thief Detectives The society at its next meeting passed resolutions to his memory, commending him for his "zeal, efficiency, capability and honesty."

CLOSE OF THE YEAR.

The year 1870, on the whole, had been one of prosperous conditions for the county The weather had been mild. There was a heavy snow storm on the 14th, 15th and 16th of March, the snow remaining until the last days of the month. Seeding commenced about April 8 The last three days of June were excessively warm and closed with a cyclonic storm of not very heavy proportions A similar storm of July 19, was much heavier and more severe, especially southwest of this county. In this county much of the grain was injured, and some light buildings were unroofed, but there was no wide-spread damage or fatalities

The season had been reasonably productive, and the fall weather was the finest in the history of the state, before or since Our grand, salubrious, and charmingly beautiful Indian summer continued long into December, and gave the farming community ample time to clean up all the fall work In the Waseca News of December 6, appeared the following

> "Plowing and grading in December! Was there ever before anything like the present weather in Minnesota? So warm, so mild, so pleasant! From our office window we notice several plows running on the farms adjoining this village. At this date, December 3, men are engaged in plowing and grading Lake Avenue, east from our office Just think of it, away up here in Minnesota, men plowing with their coats off—houses being built and plastered—house plants growing in the open air—all in the state of Minnesota, during the month of December Is this the result of building the Pacific railroad, or of removing the county seat?"

The first hard freezing of the ground was Dec. 18th, and the first heavy snow storm of the season was on Christmas day The year closed with a "Merry Christmas," followed by a "Happy New Year."

LAST SESSION OF OFFICIALS AT WILTON

The county commissioners of 1870, Wm Byron, Robt Earl, O.

Powell, John Buckhout, and R. F. Stevens, held their last session at Wilton Sept 10, and their first session in Waseca Nov 17, at the new court house

CHAPTER XXXIX, 1871.

AGRICULTURAL SOCIETY—STATE R R BONDS, $5,000,000 SWINDLE—LOREN G WOOD SHOT—YEAR OF STORMS AND FIRES—CHICAGO CREMATED—WASECA COUNTY FIRES—FIRST LIBRARY ASSOCIATION—ELECTION RETURNS—DEATH OF FIRST SETTLER, A G. SUTLIEF

The Sabbath day, bright and still, with blue skies and a balmy atmosphere, ushered in the New year, 1871. It was one of the very few years in the history of civilization when the year began and ended on Sunday or the Sabbath day, for, whether properly or improperly, both names are used interchangeably

Amidst the earthiness of life,
Vexation, selfishness and strife,
Sabbath! how sweet the holy calm,
Comes o'er the soul like healing balm.

We digress a little to remark that, aside from all religious views or creeds, Sunday should be observed as a day of rest, not, perhaps, for the sake of the Sabbath, but for the sake of man For years past, the nation has recognized the fact that laboring men engaged in public work and for great corporations have no Sabbath—no day of rest that they can call their own. It is pretty well settled that the day of rest, prescribed by the law of Moses, was based upon the fact that such rest, as a rule, is essential to, and promotes health The day ought to be kept quietly, reverently, studiously, and thoughtfully. Always remember that "the Sabbath was made for man and not man for the Sabbath "

The year opened auspiciously so far as the weather bureau was concerned. The first heavy snow storm of the year came on the eleventh of January and continued two days With the exception of this rather severe storm, the winter was comparatively a mild one, and favorable to farm work and general business.

AGRICULTURAL SOCIETY

At its annual session in January the Waseca County Agricultural society held an interesting meeting and elected the following officers president, J B Smith, vice president, P. C Bailey, treasurer, J W Johnson, secretary, B S Lewis, executive committee, O Powell, Simon Smith, H Vincent James A Claghorn and M H Helms

MARCH MEETING OF COUNTY BOARD

At the March meeting of the board, very little aside from routine business was done Seventy-five dollars was appropriated for the grading of the hill at McDougall Creek on the Wilton and Waseca road The old court house lots in Wilton belonging to the county, were deeded to the village of Wilton. The sum of $156 was appropriated to build a fence and a walk around the new court house grounds

The annual report made at this session showed the balance of cash on hand to have been $473 48, with uncollected taxes amounting to $8,645 87

THE $5,000,000 RAILROAD BOND SWINDLE

In territorial days, 1857-8 when the times were hard and people were very much depressed, the territorial legislature without any lawful authority, submitted a so-called constitutional amendment to the constitution that had been submitted and adopted the fall before but that was then held up by congress The so-called amendment was submitted to the people April 15th and adopted, but Minnesota was not admitted as a state until May 11, 1858 As soon as the people realized what a flood of fraud and corruption and deception had deluged the young community, they denounced and repudiated the whole thing The legislature of 1859-60 submitted an amendment providing that no more bonds should be issued—$2,500,000 having been already issued—and that no part of those issued should ever be paid without first submitting the question of payment to the voters of the state Thus matters stood until the winter of 1871, when the legislature was prevailed upon to provide for paying the bonds and submitting a proposition to the people authorizing the same

As showing that bribery and corruption are not confined alone to the present day, an extract from the Waseca News of April 5, 1871, will be appropriate On that date it said

"We were aroused to a realizing sense of the iniquities of the scheme, last week, by a contemptible offer of the sum of $100, provided we would abandon our honest convictions regarding this bond measure and advocate its adoption by the people And we were further awakened to a realizing sense of the danger of this proposition by the assurance, on the part of the tempter, that the proposition would surely carry, as nearly all the leading papers of the state had found it to their interest to advance the measure, either directly or indirectly In a word, those interested in the scheme are prepared to spend a large amount of money to corrupt the people—or, rather, those who discuss public topics through the newspapers and on the stump

'As the bondholders have the temerity to send their agents about the country with offers of bribery to editors, publishers and lawyers, they certainly will not scruple to use all the appliances that brains and money can command to corrupt the governor, the commissioners, and the attorneys that are, under the proposed law, to present and pass upon their claims

"This offer of bribery is, of itself, sufficient evidence upon which to condemn the bill."

After a hot fight the bill was defeated by a fair majority

LOREN G WOOD SHOT

April 13th Loren G. Wood, and Allen Scott, son and nephew respectively of the late Eri G Wood, started on a duck hunt across Clear lake They secured a boat belonging to a Mr Green and crossed the lake Shortly afterward, Mr Green desiring to use the boat, went and got it, leaving the boys to return afoot While on their way home, traveling single file over a narrow path, on the east shore of the lake, with Scott in the rear carrying a loaded gun, Scott stumbled and fell, bringing the muzzle of his gun to the front, on a line with Wood's right foot While in this position the gun was accidentally discharged, and Loren received the whole charge of the gun in the hollow of his foot. Mr. Green, who was within hailing distance on the lake, hastened to the scene of the accident, and assisted in conveying the wounded boy home Some of the shot passed entirely through the foot, but Dr. Young, who dressed the wound, took from it some shot and a quantity of wadding Loren never fully recovered the use of his foot

FOURTH OF JULY.

The day was formally celebrated at Janesville, Hon Amos Coggswell, of Owatonna, being the orator of the day Waseca also had a celebration of all home talent There was a baseball game between Waterville and Blooming Grove, and a boat race on Clear lake

DESTRUCTIVE STORMS

The Waseca News of July contained the following

"The pleasures and festivities of the Fourth of July were not ended when, over a large portion of southwestern Minnesota, the Storm God wheeled his chariots into line and devastated a large extent of country along the rich valley of the Minnesota river. The storm swept across a large region of country between Madelia and New Ulm, crossing into Nicollet county, sweeping in great fury down the Minnesota valley, and thence through Mankato, Le Ray and Jamestown

"Last Friday afternoon, July 7, 1871, while the people were talking and lamenting over the news of the destructive storm of July 4th, in adjoining counties, dark clouds appeared in the southwest and the northwest and apparently joined in battle array some miles west of here The storm came on rapidly, the wind blew a gale, some hail fell, but no serious damage resulted in this village - North and west of this place, however, in the towns of Janesville, Iosco, and Blooming Grove, the destruction of crops was total over a large extent of country. Mr McDermott, of Blooming Grove, informs us that the crops in his neighborhood are almost totally destroyed—that the trees, even, are stripped of their foliage. From Mr. J. E. Jones, of Iosco, we learn that the crops are wholly destroyed for several miles north of his place his own with the rest The house of Mr Larsen, in the Riley neighborhood, was blown down, and the fences generally were prostrated"

Thousands of acres in this county were laid waste, and the people were left in very distressing circumstances. The course of the storm was from west to east and laid waste a strip of country from two to four miles wide across the northern tier of townships. Many of the hailstones were as large as hen's eggs and, in many places, the ground was covered with them. The destruction to crops in the state that year, by wind and hail, was so far-reaching, that the legislature, at its next session, made provision to furnish a loan of seed grain to the suffering farmers the next spring Some of our farmers of the stricken townships were aided in that way

At Janesville, on the 7th, lightning struck the barn of Darling Welsh, setting it on fire and killing one of his horses.

RELIEF FOR THE STORM STRICKEN.

Hon Warren Smith was appointed by Gov Austin as state commissioner to ascertain and report in regard to damages by storm or prairie fire to settlers of this county during the season, and about Dec 20th, he received $425 00 from the state to be distributed equally among seventeen of the most destitute families In addition to this amount, the citizens of Waseca had contributed $100, and the county commissioners had received $200 in state funds, making in all $725 00, besides some clothing, which was distributed among the needy.

YEAR OF TERRIBLE FIRES.

The year 1871 was one of very destructive fires in several localities in this country, the most noted being the great Chicago fire of October 8, 9 and 10 The fire originated in a cow-stable at 9.30 o'clock, Sunday evening A strong west wind drove it rapidly through seventy-three miles of streets till it covered three and a half square miles of the doomed city, destroyed 200 lives, 17,450 buildings, and property valued at $200,000,000—the number rendered homeless being 98,500 people.

At the same time a devastating sheet of fire, ten miles wide, swept over the country bordering Green Bay, Wis, causing the death of one thousand people and destroying property to the value of $3,000,000

In the same month many lives were lost and much property destroyed by fire in Michigan

The first week in October, a great prairie fire originated near Breckenridge, Minn, and was driven eastward by strong winds a distance of about one hundred and sixty miles It left in its track a scene of desolation unparalleled in the history of the state. Buildings, fencing, grain and hay stacks, and cornfields, were swept away by this roaring, crackling, consuming monster of the prairie. Fortunately no lives were lost though a number of people had narrow escapes.

October 4 and 5, a prairie fire swept the towns of Vivian, Byron, and Wilton In Byron, Wm Smith's house, stable, reaper, wagon, and household goods were consumed His two dogs were so frightened that they fled to the cellar where both were burned to death. Alex Brisbane's stable, seeder, and much of his fencing were destroyed One of the Messrs McGrath had his one hundred-acre crop all destroyed, but saved his house Mr Quinn lost his house and some other property Granville Barnes, John C. Hunter, and others lost considerable property Almost every farmer in the line of the fire lost more or less fencing

The losers in Vivian were Messrs Poland, Banker, Randall, Hadley, Merrill and Hanks.

September and October were extremely dry months, and when once a fire was started it spread with great rapidity.

FIRST LIBRARY ASSOCIATION

The first library association was organized by adopting articles of incorporation Dec 1, 1871. The incorporators were G P Johnson, Rev E C Starr, James E Child, Fred Kittredge J F Murphy, B. S Lewis, H. A Mosher, Rev F. A Riggin, A E Dearborn, Edgar Cronkhite, E P Latham, Hiram Lanpher, Warren Smith, D. E Priest and Edward Bennett The association started out with one hundred volumes of standard works, and soon after added about fifty volumes more, mostly by donation. The originators of the organization were largely actuated by altruistic motives, hoping thereby to benefit the community at large The library from the start was only partially successful The demand for history, biography and standard literature was slight compared with the demand for trashy stuff of a romantic character In a few years the stockholders dissolved the corporation and divided the books among themselves

THE ELECTION OF 1871.

The local result of the election was a queer mixture—showing a preponderance of local and personal feeling superior to political considerations While the republicans carried the state ticket by majorities ranging from two hundred to two hundred and sixty-three, many of the local candidates on the republican ticket were "left by the wayside." The local candidates received the following votes:

SENATOR

James E. Child, republican	856
Wm Brisbane democrat	514

REPRESENTATIVES

John Thompson, republican	850
John S. McKune republican	622
Kelsey Curtis, democrat	739
L. P. Latham, democrat	579

REGISTER OF DEEDS

H. A. Mosher, republican	780
Geo. Hofeld, democrat	603

TREASURER

Geo. R. Buckman, republican	694
R. O. Craig democrat	697

CORONER

L. D. McIntosh, republican	677

COUNTY ATTORNEY

F. A. Newell, republican	677
B. S. Lewis, democrat	724

JUDGE OF PROBATE

J. A. Canfield, republican	742
Wm. Huse, democrat	645

CLERK OF COURT

S. J. Willis, republican	674
Jas. B. Hayden democrat	696

SHERIFF

M. B. Dolson, republican	511
S. W. Long, democrat	878

SURVEYOR.

C. E. Crane republican	817

For the office of county treasurer, Mr. Buckman instituted a contest that resulted in his favor by a very small margin.

CLOSE OF THE YEAR

The old year, with its crimes and its follies, its virtues and its happinesses, its successes and its disappointments, had passed into history and eternity The terrible conflagrations that swept many places in the West, nearly destroying Chicago and some other places, formed a heart-rending chapter in the history of America In Minnesota, many localities suffered from fire and storm, although the state at large enjoyed general prosperity. The noble generosity of the American people, however, was displayed as never before Throughout the length and breadth of the land, a noble impulse of generous charity furnished the means to clothe the naked, feed the hungry, and furnish homes for the homeless. The afflictions of the year stirred the noblest impulses of the American heart, and, for a time, at least, drove mean selfishness out of sight, and made us more charitable toward all mankind

NOTES OF THE YEAR 1871

Ozias Baker, one of the very early boy-settlers of the county, son of Wm S Baker, died of consumption, Feb 10 1871, aged twenty-seven years. He was one of the heroes of Company G, First Minnesota Regiment, he served three years therein and then enlisted and served in the First Minnesota Heavy Artillery until the close of the Rebellion

Mr Asa G Sutlief, the first white man to make a home in Waseca county, after a lingering illness of some weeks died Oct 13, 1871 At the time of his death he was considered one of the wealthiest men in the county A biographical sketch of him appears elsewhere in this work

The price of wheat during the year 1871 ranged from 95 cents to $1 15 per bushel

CHAPTER XL, 1872.

THE NEW YEAR—COUNTY AND STATE LEGISLATION—DONNELLY'S TRIBUTE TO AUSTIN—RAILROADS AND SALOONS VICTORIOUS—COURT HOUSE FIRE—WESTERN HOUSE BURNED—"GREELEY WAVE" IN WASECA—THOROUGHBRED CATTLE —HANGING OF EASTON—STORM OF AUGUST 6—THE "DOLLY VARDEN"—DRAINING CLEAR LAKE—THE "EPIZOOT"—DECEMBER COLD.

The year 1872 opened on Monday with the usual happy greetings and family reunions "Josh Billings" once commanded as follows

"Git out your brand new cutter,
And git your gal's consent,
Hitch up Dobbin or some other kritter,
And let the animal went"

The wheat market opened favorably the first of the year, the price ranging from $1 to $1 05

COUNTY COMMISSIONERS

The county board for this year was made up as follows O Powell of Woodville, H G Mosher of Otisco, Wm Byron of St Mary, Wm Lee of Iosco, and S K Odell of Vivian. Mr Powell was reelected chairman

The board fixed the bond of the incoming county treasurer at $20,000 Saloon license was fixed at $100 per year, the applicant to pay pro rata for the number of months the license should run Dr R O Craig, of Janesville, resigned the office of county superintendent of schools, and the board appointed in his place Mr H G. Mosher, of Otisco, to serve out the remainder of the term Dr M S. Gove was chosen by the board to be superintendent for the term commencing the first Tuesday in April Nothing further of especial interest was done by the board at its January session

THE FOURTEENTH LEGISLATURE

The legislature opened its session on Tuesday, Jan 2, and closed March 1. Waseca county was represented in the senate by James E Child, and in the house by John Thompson, of New Richland, and Kelsey Curtis, of Alma City. The governor of the state was Horace Austin By the way, he was one of the best governors the state has ever had. Hon I. Donnelly once said of him·

"I do not desire to employ the language of adulation, but I feel justified in saying that he has proved himself a great man—great in the language Tennyson applied to the Duke of Wellington

"'Great in saving common sense,' great in honesty, great in fidelity, great in persistent devotion to the public welfare, great in that firm faculty of the mind which is able to look beyond the pressure of individuals and combinations and all personal hopes and aspirations, and see in the far background only the great people who have placed their destinies in his hands * * * This is an age of vast, almost universal corruption Gray-headed men tell us, with sad faces, that they doubt the perpetuity of our free and noble institutions It sometimes looks as if one universal sea of corruption would swallow up all we hold dear in government.

'When, therefore, in the midst of such a state of things, the people find one honest, truthful, earnest, incorruptible man, who, at his own political peril, does his whole duty, they should stand by him to the last extremity"

And yet, within a few short years, the people forgot their friend, and corporate greed destroyed him politically and injured him financially

The legislative session was a laborious one although but little of general importance was accomplished The lobby, as usual, was filled with the "picked, paid and skilled retainers' of the corporations who are "summoned by the messengers of electricity and appear upon the wings of steam," and all proposed measures looking to the control of railroad rates and the prohibition of discrimination in such rates were defeated

The saloon license question occupied much attention for a

time, and the liquor laws were made a little more stringent by amendment

One commendable act was that providing for the disposal of the 500,000 acres of internal improvement lands granted to the state by congress It provided that the lands should be appraised and sold the same as the school lands, with a proviso that the funds to be derived therefrom should not be expended by any act of the legislature until said act should be ratified by the voters of the state

PERSONAL

The St. Paul Dispatch of February 29, near the close of the session, contained the following note·

"As you enter the senate chamber, the first gentleman on the left is Mr Child, of Waseca, the author of the temperance bill that did not pass He is an ordinary sized man, somewhat pale, and has spoken on more subjects and oftener, probably, than any other member of the senate, unless it be Mr Haven He has a strong individuality, is a ready debater, fearless in presenting his views and, though somewhat eccentric, is a useful and valuable senator. His brief speech on the preservation of game for 'eastern sportsmen' was the finest specimen of irony delivered in the senate this session"

Winona Republican, March 6, 1872

"Senator Child, father of the defeated temperance bill, was heard on almost every question In many things he seemed to stand alone He is a straightforward, upright man, despises the 'Heathen Chinee,' and all his tricks, speaks fluently and forcibly, has nothing to do with cliques or rings, votes an honest, loud 'no' whenever the case is not according to his convictions, knows nothing of the doctrine of expediency. He would make a martyr for the truth He was perhaps the hardest worker in the senate—always ready with amendments to hinder or check unwise legislation; he voted oftener than any other senator"

By act of this legislature, the 200,000 acres of land secured to the state by act of congress, through the efforts of Congressman Donnelly, to aid in making slack-water navigation on the Cannon River, was transferred to the Cannon River railroad to promote its construction The road is now owned and operated as a branch of the Great Western, and furnishes transportation for farmers along the northern portion of this county tributary to Morristown, Waterville and Elysian

COURT HOUSE ON FIRE

On Sunday morning, March 10, Auditor Cronkhite discovered that the floor of the court room was on fire He aroused the people and the fire was soon extinguished The court room had been occupied the Saturday before and the fire originated from the stove The damage amounted to about fifty dollars.

WESTERN HOUSE BURNED

This hotel, belonging to Mr Thomas Barden, of Waseca, was discovered to be afire about 5 30 o'clock a m, April 12, and in a very short time the hotel and the barn belonging to it were entirely consumed. As at that time Waseca had no water supply and no fire company, it was almost a miracle that the dwelling house of Mr. G W Watkins and the store and barn of Dr. Brubaker, near by, were saved from destruction, by the efforts of citizens The wind was blowing a heavy gale at the time and had it not been for the drenching rain of the previous evening, no doubt the fire would have destroyed a large amount of property The burned property was insured for $2 200

THE GREELEY CAMPAIGN

This was the year of the noted Greeley campaign—one of the most unique in the history of the world President Grant was a great military genius, but he was neither a great statesman nor a politician He had ways of his own and a strong will, and during his first administration he offended many of the ablest men in his party—more especially on account of his appointments to office, but also on account of his allowing the gold combine to influence the financial policy of the administration, thus bringing on a financial depression which caused suffering and wide-spread dissatisfaction But the rugged old hero stood by his friends, whether good or bad, and hence the organization known as "Liberal Republican"—although it was the most illiberal, politically, that was ever known in this country The men who led the movement in this state were, most of them, able men—men of brains, some of them men of wealth The more prominent were Judge Aaron Goodrich Samuel Mayall, John X Davidson and Theodore Heilscher of St Paul, Judge Thomas Wilson of Winona Dr. W W Mayo of Rochester, Hon Wm G Ward of Waseca Hon C D Sherwood of Fillmore county, ex-

United States Senator M. S. Wilkinson, and J. R. Hubbell, of Mankato. The national convention of this new party was held at Cincinnati May 4, 1872, and Horace Greeley was nominated on the sixth ballot and on the third day of the convention. B. Gratz Brown, of Missouri, was nominated for vice president. Both had been republicans, and Mr. Greeley had been a life-long opponent of every principle of the democratic party from Van Buren to Buchanan. He was an ultra high tariff advocate, and one of the staunchest opponents of the slave oligarchy. Nevertheless the so-called democratic party of that day met at Baltimore, July 9th, and endorsed the nomination of both Greeley and Brown.

The whole affair was so politically grotesque and ludicrous, not to say farcical, that the cartoonists and the people at large outside the Liberal Republicans themselves enjoyed the campaign more than any other political struggle in the history of the nation.

But not so with Mr. Greeley. It sent him to the mad house where he died Nov. 29th—twenty-four days after his defeat.

It is the opinion of the writer that it was not his defeat at the polls which unbalanced his great mind, but the treachery and meanness of Whitelaw Reid. Mr. Greeley was so great a man that his defeat for the presidency was of small consequence. But he was the founder, and for more than a generation the editor of the "New York Tribune," the greatest newspaper of its day in the world. His paper was the political bible of hundreds of thousands of people. His name was a household word throughout the land. Mr. Greeley had been for a life-time the king of journalism, the great advocate and fearless defender of temperance reform and democratic-republican institutions. He was an American of Americans, believing in the Fatherhood of one God, and the true Brotherhood of All Mankind. While sometimes mistaken in judgment, he was, nevertheless, one of the greatest and grandest men of this or of any other age or nation. He could have survived his defeat with resignation, but the New York Tribune was his idol, his heart and soul, his very life-blood, and when it came to his knowledge that Whitelaw Reid had secured financial control of his paper, and could absolutely exclude Mr Greeley's editorials and was doing so, his great heart broke, his magnificent mind gave way, and he died a maniac. It was a foul, cruel, moral murder of a great and good man. Friend and foe alike mourned his pitiful death, bowed their heads in the most profound sorrow, and forgave and forgot what many thought the mistake of his life—his candidacy for the presidency in opposition to the great party of which he was one of the founders and builders.

THOROUGHBRED CATTLE

The gentlemen who first gave the matter of thoroughbred cattle much attention in this county were Charles A De Graff of Alton, near Janesville, and Hon. W G Ward, of Waseca Mr Ward's farm is situated just west of Waseca a part of it in Woodville and a part in St Mary The De Graff farm was wholly in Alton Their farms were both opened as early as 1870. In April, 1872 Mr Ed Bennett, of Waseca, visited Racine, Wisconsin, in the interest of these gentlemen, as well as himself, and brought back six grade Shorthorn cows for Mr. Ward, and ten grade cows and three calves for Mr De Graff For himself, he brought back a full blood, Shorthorn bull, eleven months old weight 1,000 lbs. At that time Mr De Graff had a thoroughbred Shorthorn bull, two and a half years old, and five thoroughbred Shorthorn and Alderney cows, in addition to those brought on by Mr Bennett Mr Ward had a thoroughbred Alderney bull and a thoroughbred heifer of the same breed, besides the Shorthorns These gentlemen did much in those days to help improve the cattle of this county.

THE HANGING OF EASTON

A good deal of excitement was raised in and about Alma City the last week in June on account of a hanging affray which came off at the farm of John Hoffer, situated near Bulls Run, in Freedom John Hoffer missed $20 in money and accused one Easton, known as the "Old Ditcher," of stealing it Easton, an old man, about seventy years of age, stoutly denied the accusation Hoffer and wife and two hired men, named Brooks and Singer seized the old man and threatened to hang him The evidence on the examination showed that they put a rope around his neck and hanged him to a tree for a few seconds, and then let him down, he still protesting his innocence As soon as he could get away, he disappeared entirely, very soon thereafter it was discovered that a nephew of Hoffer had stolen the money. An investigation was instituted by the neighbors, but the old man, although traced into Iowa, as two witnesses testified, was never found The Hoffers admitted that they tried to scare the old man, but did not intend to hang him Mrs. Hoffer, a young and vigorous woman, also admitted that she whipped him with "a little whip no bigger than her finger" Many of the good citizens of the western part of the county considered the assault upon Easton and the result of the examination an outrage upon justice and the public welfare

THE STORM OF AUGUST 6TH, 1872.

On Thursday evening, August 6th, a very heavy rain storm visited all Southern Minnesota In the southern part of Waseca county, the wind blew a gale Grain shocks were blown apart and scattered in every direction. Fences were blown down and a number of buildings unroofed Several substantial buildings were moved from their foundations. The German Evangelical church building, at Wilton, was moved from its foundation, and Sam Prechel's blacksmith shop at the same place was unroofed

Mr. Theodore D M Orcutt, then a farmer, of Freedom, wrote of the storm as follows

"It commenced to rain about 9 o'clock p m, with a strong wind from the north, when, suddenly, the wind shifted to the west and the storm came with terrific violence Houses, heretofore waterproof, afforded but little protection to their occupants or contents It took the strength of two men to close a door or hold a window if unfastened The roof and a portion of Mr Helwick's house were carried away and badly torn to pieces The roof of Mr Straub's residence was taken off, and the roof and upper part of an unoccupied log house on the farm of Wm. E Heath were carried about six rods and completely demolished A chamber window in the frame house occupied by Mr Heath and his family was blown in and the house inside deluged with water, Mr Heath and family having taken refuge in the basement. The next morning was gloomy enough—cloudy, with a drizzling rain at intervals, all the forenoon Look in any direction you might, and fallen trees, unroofed buildings, dilapidated hay stacks, great gaps in fences, battered and almost leafless cornfields, one or all would mar the landscape But the worst feature was the total demolition of the grain shocks and the uncut grain The latter was flattened to the earth, involving a great amount of extra labor in cutting and a loss of at least twenty per cent of the grain"

Damage by the storm was extensive throughout the county, but the southern half of it suffered more than the northern portion.

THE ELECTION

The contest for local offices in this county attained fever heat. Hon W G Ward, "Liberal Republican," became the candidate of the democrats and railroad interests for state senator. On the ticket with him were Patrick Kenehan, of Wilton, and J O. Chandler, of Janesville, for representatives, and Edgar Cronkhite for auditor The republicans nominated A W Jennison, of Janesville, for state senator, John Thompson, of New Richland, and J. L Saufferer, of Blooming Grove, for representatives, and T. D M Orcutt, of Freedom, for auditor The contest resulted in the election of W G Ward by a vote of 802 for Ward to 778 for Jennison, and 835 for Cronkhite to 748 for Orcutt.

Saufferer and John Thompson, republicans, were elected to the house

NOTES MISCELLANEOUS FOR THE YEAR

A number of deaths occurred this year. Mr David L Whipple an early settler and sheriff of the county from 1860 to 1866 died on the 4th of February of lung fever He was well known throughout the county and highly respected by all conditions of men. His remains lie buried in the Wilton cemetery. His wife survived him, but he left no children

P Brink Enos, a young lawyer of much native ability, but with an unfortunate appetite for strong drink, was one of the early settlers in Wilton He removed to North Platte in 1865, where he died of convulsions April 7th

Augusta A Fratzke, daughter of Mr John Fratzke, of Freedom, aged nine years, was instantly killed in her father's house on April 21st by the accidental discharge of a gun Her head was blown off by the discharge and the walls of the room were literally covered with her brain and pieces of her skull It appears that on the day previous her father had been out hunting and was unable to discharge one barrel of the gun. When he came home in the evening he put the gun into an open closet, behind a lounge. At the time of the accident, Augusta, a brother a little older and a girl named Badc, together with a cat and a dog, were at play, when suddenly the gun was thrown over against the lounge and discharged with the terrible result noted.

Mr. B F. Hanes, one of the very early settlers of Vivian, an educated, bachelor recluse, died the last week in June, of fever.

Mr. E J Hurd, of Janesville, while at work in his sawmill June 28th, was caught by one of the belts and thrown against a post with such violence as to cause almost instant death.

DRAINING CLEAR LAKE

It was during the month of October, 1872, that certain persons in Rice county that owned mills along Straight river commenced ditching with the avowed intention of draining the lakes of Woodville into Crane Creek, hoping thus to supply water for their mills. This movement aroused a strong feeling of indignation and opposition in Waseca, and an injunction was issued to prevent the work During the legislative session of the ensuing winter an act was passed prohibiting the draining of the lakes—more especially Clear lake

OTHER MATTERS.

The first snowstorm in the fall was very severe. The Waseca News then remarked that the "oldest inhabitant" never before saw such a day, so early in the season "Old Winter" howled and screamed and spit snow and made people uncomfortable generally. About five inches of snow fell. The roads and railroads were blockaded, and business was almost suspended

Mr Simeon Smith, of Blooming Grove, one of the settlers of 1855, died on Wednesday, Nov 6, at the advanced age of seventy-eight years.

Frank McKune, son of Capt. Lewis McKune, who was shot and killed at the first battle of Bull Run, died at the residence of his sister, in Lake City, Dec. 16, at the age of twenty years, of hemorrhage of the lungs.

The prices of wheat during the months of November and December ranged from 80 to 98 cents. Sales of wheat at the elevator in Waseca during the last six weeks of the year ranged from 4,500 to 12,000 bushels The crop was a good one throughout the county, although in some places there was considerable loss on account of the August storm

THE "EPIZOOT."

This peculiar horse disease made its appearance in this section in the month of November and soon became epidemic The illness commenced with a half-suppressed cough, which soon became more violent. A fever set in with intense heat of the mouth and a discharge from the nose of offensive mucus, in large quantities The horses attacked refused all food, would not lie down, and, in a few days, became very weak. Many died The best veterinary surgeons described the disease as acute catarrh and influenza The distemper, or disease, originated in eastern Canada where thousands of horses died. It next appeared in the Eastern States and thence came West. The large cities seemed to suffer the most. In some cities the horses would all be taken in one day, as it were, and all business would be brought to a standstill That was before the introduction of electric cars, and when horse cars were being used in all large cities. During the latter part of December nearly all business was brought to a stand-still in this county by the "epizooty." During the week ending December 28, only 358 bushels and 40 pounds of wheat were marketed in Waseca, while during the first week in that month 11,580 1-2 bushels were received by the same elevator Not very many horses died in this section, but nearly all were affected by the disease more or less.

This December was one of the very coldest in the history of the county In many places, the day before Christmas, the thermometers registered as low as 25 and 30 degrees Fortunately, during the coldest days, there was no wind and the atmosphere was dry and crisp. In Chicago the thermometer said 20 degrees below, and at Fort Scott, Kansas 18 degrees below

CHAPTER XLI, 1873.

THE NEW YEAR—THE GREAT BLIZZARD—MANY PERISH—GREAT LOSSES—THE MURDER OF MRS BUSER AND CHILD AND THE SUICIDE OF ANTON RUF—SIXTY-EIGHT DAYS IN A SNOW DRIFT—PATRONS OF HUSBANDRY—ACCIDENTALLY SHOT—CHAMPION BASEBALL TEAM—BIG SNOW STORM OCT 24—THE ELECTION—RAILROAD DISCRIMINATIONS—THE PANIC OF 1873 AND ITS CAUSES—DEATHS AND ACCIDENTS—HON WM BRISBANE VISITS SCOTLAND.

The New Year's Day of 1873 was very fine indeed After the terribly cold week about Christmas time the sunny, pleasant ushering in of the new year was very acceptable The Waseca News of that day contained the following:

"The old year, with its hardships, wrongs, crimes, wickedness; with its joys, pleasures, successes, advancement, and plenteous harvests, passed into historical eternity last night. To-day we commence anew.

"Has the experience of the past given us brighter hopes of the future? Life is what we make it Each can help to make it a heaven or a hell Each individual must advance No one can stand still One's progress is either for better or worse To-day many will degrade their manhood and disgrace their families. Many a father will set a bad example before his sons. On the other hand, many sons and daughters will commence the new year in a manly, womanly, and sensible way They will not get drunk themselves nor give drunkenness to their friends The 'coming man and woman' will not drink wine nor any other intoxicating beverage

"How many of our readers will to-day resolve to inaugurate a new fashion, one which shall do away with the damning effects of the barbarous, useless, and expensive custom of tippling? Let the wealthy and those high in office set an example worthy of imitation Wishing our readers, one and all, a 'Happy New Year' we close our 'forms' and say goodnight."

COUNTY COMMISSIONERS

The county commissioners this year met on the 7th of January and organized by electing Mr O Powell chairman for the third time. Little business outside of the ordinary routine was transacted

The county auditor was directed to procure field notes of surveys and meanders from the surveyor general. The auditor was also "authorized to record in the road calendar the plats field notes, and road orders of all county and state roads in Waseca county legally laid out during the last five years, and to employ an assistant to do the work, if necessary"

STORM ON THE 7TH AND 8TH

The 7th of January opened warm and pleasant. In the afternoon the wind came strong from the northwest and before dark a blinding snow storm raged over the whole of Minnesota. It continued through the night and during the following two days and nights The cold was rather severe and a number of people in the state lost their lives Seventy persons were reported frozen to death in the entire state, and thirty-one badly injured by frost The loss of live stock in the state was reported as follows· horned cattle 250, horses 25, sheep and hogs 10, mules 3. No doubt the loss of stock was larger than was reported

We copy the following from the Waseca News of Jan. 15 1873:

"A man named Avon Aleckson was chopping in the woods near Lake Watkins, in Woodville, Tuesday When the storm came on he started for home, got lost, was out all night and all the next day till near evening, before he found a house. His feet were so badly frozen that they are black, and it is feared they must be amputated Otherwise he was not badly frozen. But the poor sufferer was so weakened by exposure that he died some three weeks later of hemorrhage of the lungs

"Mr J G Greening, of Otisco, who came from Blue Earth City, last Friday, informs us that a Mrs Sultz, living near Wisner's Grove, Faribault county, was found dead after the storm, about half a mile from her house It appears that her husband went to Delavan that morning, and that the woman let one of her children go to a neighbor's house When the storm came on she went to her neighbor's place to get the child, leaving her other child in the house The neighbor prevailed upon her to return, bring her other child and remain over night The poor woman started for her home, lost her way in the blinding storm and perished The child left at home—about three years of age—was found in bed alive."

Mr. James Ivers, of Byron, lost fifteen sheep out of twenty-three. Mr Bevans of the same town lost an ox. Mr. Mayne, of Wilton, also lost an ox. Several head of cattle perished on H J. Wadsworth's farm in Wilton.

Mr. Rodney Hanks, then a resident of Vivian, was returning home from Janesville on the afternoon of the 7th, with a span of mules. He had great confidence in his mules, and believing that they would take him home in due time, gave them their own way. They finally got tired of tramping snow and stopped short on the prairie, refusing to go further in such a storm. Mr. Hanks had on a small load of wood which he piled up on the windward side as a protection, and turned his wagon box bottom side up as a protection Here he sheltered himself as best he could from the howling, pitiless storm until Friday morning, when he made his way home Although considerably frosted he was not permanently injured. But the wonder is that the man and the mules did not all perish.

No weather can suppress some newspaper men The next week after this storm the following appeared·

"When the cold wind blows, take care of your nose, that it doesn't get froze, and wrap up your toes in warm woolen hose' The above, we suppose, was written in prose by some one who knows the effect of cold snows, and the further this goes, the longer it grows, each telling what he knows about writing in prose, when it snows and it blows, as it so often does."—Ex.

To which the Winona Republican added.

"Ere the ditty we close we must tell of our Mose, who indignantly rose, and proceeded to expose the substance of our woes, where the Mississip' flows. He positively knows that the river is froze, without regard to zero's from its head to its toes."

And the Waseca News continued·

"'Pat' don't propose to favor those who read this prose with what he knows of wind and snows, and frosted toes, and tattered clothes, and all the woes that follow those who won't repose at home and doze when it snows and blows"

A BLOODY TRAGEDY.

One of the most terrible crimes known in the history of the county came to light on the 17th day of February, 1873. On that fatal Monday morning, Anton Ruf, residing in the eastern part of Woodville, deliberately murdered Mrs Alexander Buser and her youngest child, evidently with Mrs Buser's connivance and consent. The evidence showed that he first cut the child's throat, then killed the woman and laid the lifeless form of the infant upon its mother's arm on the bed Ruf then cut his own throat and lay down beside them, but, in his death agony, turned over and fell upon the floor face downward A large butcher knife had evidently been sharpened for the occasion as such a knife was found near the bed

The history of this affair if fully written, would fill many pages and rival the awful stories of the romances of the last century The facts are revolting enough and are given here as they were brought out at the time of the awful tragedy

Anton Ruf, a German by birth and a single man, several years before the tragedy, bought a piece of land in the eastern part of Woodville, and erected a house He then wrote to an acquaintance in Wisconsin, Mr Alexander Buser, a married man, and invited him to come with his family and live with him Mr. Buser accepted the invitation, and came on from Wisconsin in April, 1869, bringing with him his wife and three children Mr Buser bought a half interest in the farm and moved into the house with Ruf For a time matters went along smoothly, but after a few months, Mr. Buser suspected that Mrs Buser was at least dividing affections with Mr Ruf Quarreling ensued, and matters went from bad to worse until in October 1871, Buser attempted to expel Ruf from the house A fight ensued in which Buser came out second best and was driven away entirely Ruf and Mrs Buser remained on the premises, and, so far as known, lived agreeably together, the children remaining with them, until district court convened Feb 11, 1873 At this term of court, information was placed before the grand jury accusing the parties of criminal intimacy The Waseca News of February 19 and 26 contained substantially the following account of the bloody tragedy.

"The history of the affair, as near as we can learn is as follows. Mr Alexander Buser, lawful husband of the woman, moved into the house with Anton Ruf, a single man, in April, 1869 Mr and Mrs Buser had three children at that time, two boys and a girl, the eldest, a boy, being about thirteen years of age at the time of the murder A fourth child was born to the woman about two years before the tragedy In October, 1871, as Mr. Buser claims, he was driven away by Ruf, and after this time the latter and Mrs Buser lived together in undisputed possession of the premises, the children remaining with them

"On the morning of the fatal day, when the children started for school, the mother told them that she was going to Waseca The children remained at school throughout the day, and when they returned home in the evening, found the door fastened Supposing that their mother had not yet returned from Waseca, they went to the house of Mr Michael Spillane, Sen, about a quarter of a mile away, and remained over night The following morning, the elder boy and T. Tynen, another lad, went to the Ruf house, and, finding the door fastened, looked in at the window when they saw Ruf lying on the floor, covered with blood, dead. These boys, frightened at the awful sight, hurried back to Mr Spillane's place and got Michael Spillane, Jr, to go over to the house with them Messrs Waldo and Whitman also visited the house but no one broke open the door or entered the house at the time. One of the Spillane boys then drove to Waseca and notified the coroner, Dr McIntosh, who summoned a jury and proceeded to the house where they found the woman and her youngest child dead on the bed, with their throats cut square across, and Ruf dead, lying upon the floor with his throat also cut across almost from ear to ear The bed and the room presented a horribly bloody appearance

"It appeared that the triple murder was committed with the utmost deliberation Both Ruf and Mrs Buser wrote letters which they left upon the table in the room

"These letters showed some sentimental affection between the two, and accused others of their troubles Neither one seemed to realize the moral depravity of the two as exemplified in their lives

"The following are correct translations of the letters found in the house by Coroner McIntosh

"Dear Mine'—Hear the last painful cry of your friend! By the time you receive this I shall be before the Heavenly Judge He may judge me I was hounded to death I got one to ask Alexander (Buser) to save me He did it not I will not go to state prison

"I pray you to make it possible to get my poor, dear Mina to you I beg you to do it You know that I wept when she was born, and that I had a sad presentiment of something bad. O, my time is short I s̄ ffer agonies for my children which are terrible Judge not You know that I love my children, that I would do so longer, but circumstances do not leave me in condition to do so

"Thine, Anna'

The foregoing was folded and addressed to Salome Duerft, New Glarus, Green county, Wis

On another sheet of paper she wrote.

"Farewell, poor children Your father ought to have saved me, but he could not or would not do it You, my dear, dear Mina, follow your mother as soon as you can The world is a hard place.

"My soul entreats you, even after death, not to curse your poor, unfortunate mother.

(Signed) "Anna."

On the same page, in Ruf's handwriting was the following·

"Dear Anna has fully determined to die rather than be dragged before a court, together with those horrible folks, and afterwards to be ridiculed and despised"

Mrs Buser again wrote as follows, signing her maiden name:

"No man should ascribe the cause of this deed to Ruf, but to —— —— and Alexander Buser They wanted to hound Ruf to death I follow him of my own free will that the world may see that our affection for each other was no misdemeanor (kein unfug) All of you together shall not triumph. (Signed) "Anna Ritter"

Then in her writing was added·

"Here I write my last testimony" (then Ruf continues) "Alexander Buser and —— —— are the murderers of dear Anna We are willing to die. I swore I would follow her Only God, the Judge, or the Judgment day can make all things right.

(Signed) "A Ruf"

The following on the inside of the door was evidently written by Ruf after having murdered the woman and child:

"No one parts love save Death I wanted to take Mina along too A few words of sympathy would have saved the mother and her child from being murdered. I waited till 12 o'clock noon"

To make the letters and writing more intelligible in some respects it is proper to state that Ruf and the woman had been informed that their past conduct was being investigated by the grand jury This information no doubt alarmed them. On Saturday Ruf visited Waseca and conferred with an attorney It appears that his attorney made a written proposition to Buser, who was then in the neighborhood, asking him to consent to a divorce Ruf and the woman probably expected that Buser, if willing to consent to a divorce, would write or call immediately and let them know his intention As they received no word from him, they no doubt believed that they would be arrested and sent to prison.

The appearance of the victims at the coroner's inquest was

most shocking and horrible The child's head was nearly severed from the body at one stroke of the knife The woman received a severe gash across both shoulders and the throat—probably from one powerful blow. It was evident that Ruf drew the knife twice across his own throat

Mr. Buser soon after returned to Wisconsin, taking the children with him. So far as known, Ruf had no relatives in this country

"SIXTY-EIGHT DAYS IN A SNOW DRIFT AND STILL ALIVE"

An article with the above heading appeared in the Waseca News of March 19, 1873, and read as follows:

"Two fat hogs belonging to Wm. Bevans, of Byron, that were lost during the snow storm of Jan 7th, last, were found alive and healthy on the 14th inst, in a snow drift adjoining a straw stack Sixty-eight days under a snow drift and yet alive is doing pretty well Messrs Carmody and Covell, of Wilton, who are responsible for this information, remarked that it was the 'cheapest way in the world to winter hogs.'"

THE PATRONS OF HUSBANDRY

This organization, which had been at work for several years among the farmers of the country, especially in the West, organized a county grange in Waseca, May 3, 1873 It was run on the narrow-gauge plan, but it nevertheless accomplished a great deal of good The call for the meeting was signed "Wm A Erwin, secretary," by order of committee

The temporary organization was effected by the election of I. D Beaman, of Blooming Grove, temporary chairman; and W D Armstrong, temporary secretary. After the election of a committee on credentials and one on permanent organization, a recess was taken till afternoon

At the afternoon session, the committee on credentials reported the following gentlemen entitled to seats. J S Abell, Joseph Minges, Adam Bishman, A L Warner, and Sam Leslie, of Pomona grange, C E Graham, S Hydorn, D D Green, P. Vanderwarka, and C Bates, of County Line grange; A Keyes, S. C. L. Moore, and S C Dow, of Alma City grange, Hugh Wilson, R F. Stevens, J Turnacliff, Noah Lincoln, and Geo. H Woodbury, of Wilton grange; Philo Woodruff, David Wood, M Dewald, and J R Davidson, of Hazel Dale grange; I D. Beaman, S. F. Wyman, Albert Remund, Patrick Haley, and Wm Habein, of

Blooming Grove grange, W. H. Gray, D Riegle, James Bowe, F. Brossard, P. McDermott, and W. A Erwin, of Toboso grange, H W S Hinkley, Wm Runnels, W. D. Armstrong, M F Connor, and Nicholas Fox, of Connor grange; M Haley, Patrick Murray, H Haley, John McWaide, and James Jones, of Hibernia grange.

Waseca grange No 49 elected three delegates to the council, who presented their credentials The committee to whom they were referred disagreed as to the propriety of admitting any Waseca men The matter was referred to the council and by a majority vote it was decided that Waseca grange was not entitled to representation in the council on the ground that some of the members of that grange were not practical farmers.

The following permanent officers were elected I D Beaman, master, M F. Connor, overseer, W. D. Armstrong, secretary S. C L Moore, gate keeper, John S Abell, lecturer, A. Keyes, chaplain.

A business committee of one from each grange was appointed, namely Hugh Wilson, P Woodruff, A L Warner, M Haley A Keyes, P McDermott, W D Armstrong, Patrick Haley, and S. Hydorn.

This organization was kept up for about two years, when owing to dissension among the members, it gradually disappeared

FOURTH OF JULY

The weather was grand, and there was a general observance of the day in Waseca Hon M D L Collester was the orator of the day and delivered a very fine address

The baseball game between the Blooming Grove Champions and the Mankato club, was the absorbing entertainment of the day Blooming Grove won by a score of 62 to 13 A few slight accidents were reported Some one drove into Mr Thos Barden's buggy and overturned it, throwing Mrs Barden out and bruising her somewhat, though not seriously Mr. Thomas Lynch, of Wilton, had a runaway in which he and his wife were thrown out of the buggy without suffering serious harm.

ACCIDENTALLY SHOT

On August 29th, Mr John Bowe, of Blooming Grove, was

accidentally wounded by the discharge of a shot gun in the hands of one of the Bowe boys, the hammer of the lock accidentally slipping from his hand The wound though painful, was not dangerous.

CHAMPION BASE-BALL TEAM.

The Northfield base-ball club challenged the Blooming Grove Champions to a match game of ball at the fair grounds, in Northfield, on the 18th of September The Northfield club held the silver bat of the state, and this was offered as the prize for the winning side The Blooming Grove boys won the prize by a score of forty-six to nineteen The Northfield boys suffered three whitewashes, Blooming Grove none. Martin Haley was the captain and pitcher, Jas Johnson, catcher; Wm. Johnson, first base, Frank Haley, second base; C. D Todd, third base, R W Jacklin, short stop, G. Donaldson, right fielder; F Collins, center fielder, John Blowers, left fielder Some years after, the club, having lost some of its best players, lost the prize in a game with the Winnebago City club The last heard of the silver bat it was in the hands of the college boys of Winnebago City.

FIRST SNOW OF THE SEASON.

There was a snow storm on the night of Oct 24 that continued through the night and into the forenoon of the 25th. Snow fell to the depth of about ten inches, and the drifts, in places remained until spring The strong wind accompanying the snow swept it from most of the plowed fields, so that considerable fall plowing was done after the storm, but fall work was very much interfered with on the farms

THE ELECTION.

This was the year when the anti-monopoly sentiment was very strong throughout the nation The order of the Patrons of Husbandry had established a "Grange" in almost every farming community, and its teachings had aroused a very strong opposition to the extortions and unjust discriminations practiced by the transportation corporations The high rates of interest charged throughout the West also caused much hardship and loss of property The people were thoroughly aroused and, to a certain extent, joined hand in hand for self protection The people of Waseca county were never more thoroughly aroused than during the campaign of 1873 Hon C K. Davis, republican, and Hon Ara Barton, democrat, were the opposing candidates for governor Mr Davis carried the county by a majority of 166 The result of the votes for county representatives and officers was as follows

REPRESENTATIVES	
L D Smith, rep	967
J E Child, rep	765
Kelsey Curtis, dem	478
David Wood, dem	599

TREASURER.	
Warren Smith, rep	986
M Sheran, dem	381

JUDGE OF PROBATE	
J A Canfield, rep.	774
Neri Reed, dem	617

COUNTY ATTORNEY	
F A Newell, rep	502
P McGovern, dem	898

COURT COMMISSIONER	
J B Smith, rep	1403
Geo McDermott, ind	24

REGISTER OF DEEDS	
H A Mosher, rep	845
Louis Krassin, dem	562

SHERIFF	
G H Woodbury, rep	512
C Cunningham, dem	196
S W Long, ind	696

CORONER	
L D McIntosh, rep	1402

COUNTY COMMISSIONERS	
R O Craig, dem	193
H P Packard, rep	112
H K Stearns, rep	217
Frank McLane, dem	69

Quite an effort was made throughout the state by the corporations to defeat Hon C K Davis, but he received a majority of about 5,000 The issue that absorbed public attention more than any other was that of railroad discrimination. The "Grangers" of Waseca county, at their county council, held July 12, 1873, "resolved that the charge of $20 by the W & St P. R R. Co (now C & N.-W Ry Co) for simply hauling a loaded car of lumber or lime from Owatonna to Waseca, a distance of fifteen miles, when the regular charge for hauling the same car load from Winona to Waseca, a distance of one hundred and five miles, is only $20, is an unjust discrimination and an outrageous extortion that calls loudly for a stringent legal remedy "

In Rice county complaint was made that a carload of lumber shipped from Minneapolis to Faribault cost the Faribault dealer

$31 50 in freight, while the same carload of lumber shipped to Owatonna, fifteen miles further, over the same road, cost only $22 freight—a discrimination against Faribault of $9 50 on every carload. The same carload, shipped forty-eight miles further south to Austin, cost only $24 freight—discrimination of $7.50 per carload. In the matter of through rates from the east, the same wrong was manifest. The railway rates on goods from Chicago to Faribault were, per 100 pounds, for first class goods, $1 10, second class, $1 00; third class, 75 cents, fourth class 55 cents. The rates charged on the same classes, transported by the same road through Faribault to St Paul, fifty-six miles further, were 80 cents for first class, 70 cents for second class, and 35 cents for third class.

In view of these unjust discriminations, practiced everywhere in the state, the people in every farming community demanded the enactment of a law prohibiting the charging of a greater freight rate for a short distance than was at the same time charged for a longer distance over the same road and in the same direction.

It was contended by the Grange men that, in view of these undisputed facts, the law ought to require the railroad corporations to charge equal rates to all men, and to carry freight a short distance over the same road at a fixed rate for a short haul which should not exceed the charge for a longer haul They claimed that this demand was no more than fair and reasonable, and that no sane or reasonable person desired to injure the railroads nor require them to perform service at unfair or unreasonable rates. Notwithstanding this fair and just request, there was and is the very strongest opposition to any law which shall honestly and effectually carry out the principle of equal and reasonable rates.

THE PANIC OF '73

The year 1873 was considered by many as one of the worst, financially, ever experienced by the country up to that time Waseca county suffered much less than many other localities, owing, doubtless, to its very productive soil and convenient markets. The spring time brought disappointment to farmers on account of the cold, wet weather. There was considerable warm weather the first week in March, and most of the snow disappeared, but about the middle of that month there commenced a series of rain and light snow storms with cold, freezing nights, which kept the fields in bad condition until the middle of April. Flat, wet lands could not well be seeded, and where seeded gave no crop Some of the early sowed grain rotted. On the 17th of May a heavy rainstorm visited the country and continued for several days off and on, making the roads of this county almost impassable and seriously delaying corn planting. Owing to the hard winter, the cold, wet spring or some other cause, many of the fruit trees, though putting forth their leaves in the spring, withered and died during the summer. Only those in the most favored locations and of the hardiest varieties survived the season The summer season from the first of June until October, however, made up to a great extent for the disagreeable and discouraging spring The crops were fairly good, especially the wheat and hay crops, and the favorable harvest weather enabled the husbandmen to save everything in good shape.

Notwithstanding these fairly good conditions, agriculturally, times were close Judge Kiester, in his history of Faribault county, asserts that "money was extremely scarce and rates of interest very high Everybody was more or less in debt, and everyone to whom money was due was urgent, persistent for his pay. The county newspapers were filled with notices of mortgage foreclosures and sales of land under execution During this and several subsequent years, many homes and farms passed away forever from the hard-working pioneers for a very small proportion of their real value In the fall there came upon the nation a great money panic—a tremendous financial crash. The great failure of Jay Cook & Co., led off in this dance of financial dishonor and death Banks were suspended, thousands of individuals of supposed great wealth, and great moneyed corporations of all kinds went down to ruin and bankruptcy Great manufactories and mines were closed down, and great public enterprises were brought to a sudden close The number of defaulters in both public office and private station was legion. The army of the unemployed swelled to hundreds of thousands, and great privation and distress prevailed throughout the country. This was the visible beginning of one of the greatest financial disasters in the history of our country, and one which continued its work of ruin and distress for several years."

The causes of this wide-spread disaster, as claimed by one set of economists, were over-production, wild speculation, extravagant and wasteful living, contracting debts for what we did not need, borrowing money to build railroads where there was nothing for them to do, and the building of villages and cities with no farming country to back them.

Another set of economists urge upon our attention the fact that, notwithstanding our enormous national debt, then payable in greenbacks and silver dollars, congress, in the month of February, at the instigation, and through the corrupting influences of English and European capitalists, who were large holders of our bonds, bought for greenbacks and made payable in greenbacks, silver or gold, passed an act, ostensibly relating only to the national mint and coinage, but which really and actually demonetized silver by destroying the silver dollar and providing that silver money should not be a legal tender for any greater sum than five dollars. The work of demonetization was accomplished without the knowledge of the people at large, and a great majority of the members of congress afterwards declared that they did not know, when the law was passed, that it demonetized silver. These economic writers claim that the destruction of our silver money doubled the debts of the debtor class, or poor people, while by the same act the bonds of the bondholder were doubled in value. In other words that values of actual property and labor were, by the act, so depreciated that it would take, for instance, two hundred bushels of wheat to pay the debt which, when contracted, called for only one hundred bushels.

Whatever the cause may have been, the depression was universal and the suffering wide-spread, especially in the large cities.

MINOR NOTES OF THE YEAR

There were several prominent deaths during the year. Robert Woodrow, one of the early settlers of Woodville, died February

3, 1873, after an illness of several months He left a wife and two children

Mrs. Michael Kinney, one of the pioneer women of Iosco, died February 8 and was buried February 10 Her funeral was very largely attended, the large Catholic church being entirely filled.

There was a very heavy snow storm February 26, so heavy that the roads and railroads were badly blockaded for two or three days

John Toole, section foreman at Janesville, aged 64 years, was killed March 7, 1873, by being thrown from a hand-car by a freight train

Nettie, four-year-old daughter of Mr. Alex Brisbane, then of Wilton, was so badly scalded by falling upon a kettle containing boiled potatoes that she died March 9, after twenty-four hours of great suffering

Henry Adolphus Trowbridge, highly respected son of Hon I C Trowbridge, of Waseca, died April 20, 1873

A daughter of Mr and Mr John Forest then of Wilton, died April 22

Mrs Wm Orcutt, of Freedom, after a severe illness, died April 23.

On June 3, Wm Bluhm, a lad about fifteen years of age, son of Henry Bluhm, then of Meriden, accidentally shot himself while hunting in the woods In drawing his gun over a log the gun was accidentally discharged, its contents striking him in the neck and throat He died soon after

A young child, aged one year and eight months of Mr. and Mrs Isaac Ballard, of St Mary, fell into a pail of hot water on Saturday and was so badly scalded that it died on Sunday, July 5

Albert M Smith, of Waseca, son of J B Smith, died July 4, at the age of twenty-seven years, of consumption.

A child of Mr D A Erwin, of St Mary, two years old, met with a sad accident Sept 29. It upset a dish of hot starch, prepared for ironing purposes, and was severely burned upon its breast, abdomen and legs It lingered until October 8 when death came to its relief

Samuel, son of Anthony Sampson, of New Richland, a boy about nine years of age, fell from a wagon Oct 10 1873, and was so badly injured that he died within a few minutes after his fall.

On the 17th of the same month, a son of John Byron, of St Mary, about seventeen years of age, got caught on the tumbling rod of a threshing machine and was so badly injured that he died the following Monday, the 20th Both of these families were among the very early settlers of the county

On the 15th of October, Mr Henry J. Meyers, then of Freedom, had his left arm torn off in a threshing machine His arm was amputated at the shoulder and although he was otherwise injured to some extent, he soon recovered

An elderly gentleman named Tosten Tostenson was found dead on the north shore of Clear Lake, Oct 22 He was found with his face in the water and his body on the shore It was thought that he knelt down on the shore to get a drink of water, that he fell in with his face down, and had not sufficient strength to raise himself out of the water.

The salary of the county superintendent of schools, for the first time in the history of the county, was made somewhat commensurate to the labor required of the officer On the 21st of March the county board having theretofore appointed one of its members superintendent, raised the salary to $720 per annum.

There was a heavy snow storm this year, April 9, when six inches of snow fell.

The tax list for the county, this year, filled over ten columns of a seven-column paper, set in brevier type. The list was the smallest it had been for five years. The tax lists of the early days were the main support of local newspapers in each county

On May 8, this year, Hon. Wm Brisbane started on his journey to visit the scenes of his childhood in his native Scotland

During the months of September and October, of this year, the Waseca railroad elevator received 86,898 bushels of wheat, of which 13,524 bushels graded No 1—71,817 bushels graded No 2, and 1,567 bushels went rejected

On the 27th of November Mr James Gearin, of Wilton, had the misfortune to lose his dwelling house and all its contents by fire. He carried only a small amount of insurance but the members of the grange to which he belonged, known as Connor Grange, at once clubbed together and erected a new house for him

CHAPTER XLII, 1874.

COUNTY AND STATE LEGISLATION—BIG RAILROAD CONTEST—GENERAL EDGERTON, SENATOR COGGSWELL—TAXING RAILROAD LANDS—EXCITING LOCAL ELECTION—THE SALARY GRAB—GRASSHOPPER A BURDEN—DEATHS, ANDREW JACKSON, JERRY HOGAN, WM BAKER, MRS L D HOCANSON AND CHILD, MRS ANDREW LYNCH, MRS HICKS, ISAAC BIRD, DR GOVE, WM ACKERMAN, N WOOD.

The year 1873 closed with a pleasant day, and the new year 1874 was introduced by the most beautiful winter day ever seen in Minnesota The sky was cloudless The sun shone in all its beauty during the whole day. There was almost a perfect calm, and the atmosphere was as warm and balmy as in spring time.

The county commissioners assembled at the court house January 6th, and organized by electing Wm Byron, of St Mary, chairman for the year.

License for the sale of liquors was fixed at one hundred dollars

The following road and bridge appropriations were made $150 to aid in building a bridge across the Le Sueur River, where the Freeborn and Owatonna road crosses said stream, $50 to help finish the bridge and grading at McDougall creek where the Waseca and Wilton road crosses the same, $100 to be used in reparing the road known as the Wilton and Faribault highway at the Chesterson and Bowe hills $145 to repair the road and bridge near Alma City, across the Le Sueur River, on the Janesville road.

H G Mosher was re-appointed county superintendent of schools at a salary of $720

THE LEGISLATURE OF 1874.

This body assembled Jan. 6, and adjourned March 6. Waseca county was represented in the senate by W. G. Ward, and in the house by L D. Smith and James E. Child It was dubbed by the corporation men "the Grange legislature," not an inappropriate designation. No legislature of this state has ever contained a greater proportion of true, tried, honest, and capable men, than that of 1874 The battle between the true representatives of the people and those influenced by the corporations was carried from the polls, at the fall election, to the halls of legislation. The choice of speaker of the house turned upon the issue—"Shall the state control the railroads in the matter of rates for the transportation of freight and passengers?"

As in all issues of his kind, it was found that the railroad lobbyists were the loudest "reformers" The corporations induced such men as the late Hon I. Donnelly to urge the election of Hon. John X Davidson, of St Paul, a "Liberal Republican," as against Hon A R. Hall, who represented a farming community in Hennepin county, and who had been speaker in 1872 and 1873 In the hope of dividing the real anti-monopoly forces in the legislature, the corporations attempted to work up a contest for speaker among them and finally defeat both by electing a speaker of their own

The "Minneapolis Sunday Mirror" was chosen especial champion of this move, and after the defeat of the scheme, published the following screed

"Last summer 'Pat' (James E) Child, editor of the Waseca News, made an herculean effort to become a member of the Grange at that place, and by virtue of the fact that he owned a farm in that vicinity, succeeded As a consequence he was elected to the legislature, where he was expected to labor, first, last and all the time in the interests of the Anti-Monopolist party But what was the result? The Grangers, on gathering together on the eve of the session, counted noses and concluded their force was strong enough to elect the speaker, and they set their pins accordingly 'Pat' was confidently counted as one of them, and they relied upon him to take a prominent post A caucus was called, and to the unqualified astonishment of the clan, 'Pat' was found in the ranks of their opponents. He was in favor of the election of Hall as against a reform candidate Wonder-struck, several of the Grange party interviewed him. 'What's the matter, 'Pat?'' said they. 'Well," he evasively replied, 'I find myself so mixed up that I must support Mr Hall for speaker'"

Then this organ of plutocracy went on to insinuate that Mr Child had been bribed to support Hall, and urged as proof the fact that Child was appointed "chairman of the most responsible committee of the house—that on railroads"

The paper containing this article was not one of general circulation in the state, but very many copies of it were mailed to people of Waseca county before Mr Child knew anything of it, and when it was called to his attention he dismissed it as unworthy of notice

But he soon after learned that innocent people had been imposed upon by the story, and at the urgent request of friends, gave out the following statement·

"It is not true that 'Pat' Child became a member of the Grange last summer, (1873) but it is true that he and a number of other persons started the first Grange in Waseca county It was organized under a special charter, or dispensation, issued by Wm Saunders, Master of the National Grange, and duly certified to by O W Kelly, National Secretary and one of the organizers of the association, and is dated May 14 1870 Mr Child is still a member of the same Grange Before the meeting of the legislature, Mr Child had declined to be a candidate for speaker, and was one of the very first to advocate the election of Mr. A R Hall, and that too, without any communication with Mr Hall whatever on the subject When Mr Child arrived at St Paul, he found that the corporations, through their lobby, had induced many of the country members to urge him for the speakership, and soon after his arrival a so-called committee waited upon him and urged him to become a candidate for speaker Mr Child promptly informed them that he did not desire the speakership, and that he had already decided to support Mr Hall, believing him to be a man of ability and integrity and anxious to deal honorably and fairly with all the people and all the interests of the state He also pointed out to the members that called upon him that the men back of the move were railroad lobbyists, as he believed, and that their object was to divide the anti-monopoly forces and then elect one of their own men—thus getting control of the machinery of the house It is true that Mr Child has been appointed chairman of the railroad committee It is also true that one hundred and six other gentlemen were appointed upon various committees by Speaker Hall, and the insinuation that there was bribery in the appointments made by the speaker, is characteristic of the lobbyists and corporation managers, who know of no higher incentive than a money or personal consideration'

The author records this affair, not on account of its intrinsic importance, but that people may see how easy it is to smirch the character of any man in public life and to make many believe that honesty and integrity do not exist among men. And these corruptionists make these assaults upon honest men, not because they object to corruption in office—but to drive honest men from public life so that they, the monopolists, may have an opportunity to plunder the people undisturbed.

Whether the "Mirror" published the assault upon Mr Child because its editor was misinformed and misled, or for a money consideration, the author does not know, but sixty days thereafter, the same paper, for reasons known only to its editor, published the following, sending Mr Child a marked copy·

"James E Child, (better known as 'Pat' Child) sits in the 'no corner,' he cares for nobody and nobody cares for him No man can approach him, no man could corrupt him, no man could convince him, he knows how it is himself—He is generally right, and stands well among the members, notwithstanding his eccentricities, and has made an excellent member—If every legislature had a 'Pat' Child there would be less foolish legislation'

THE LEGISLATIVE BATTLE

The railroad battle opened in the senate the first week of the session, when Senator Coggswell, of Steele county, introduced "A bill for an Act to create a board of railroad commissioners and to provide rules for the management of all railroad corporations and railroads in the state of Minnesota" The friends of the bill did not feel sure of the senate, but had more confidence in the house, so a few of the trusty, hardworkers of the house, with the assistance of Senator Coggswell and of Gen Edgerton, railroad commissioner, took the Coggswell bill, revised and amended it in some respects, and had it introduced in the house by Hon C S Crandall, of Owatonna. The move was non-partisan so far as its friends could make it so—Senator Coggswell being a democrat, Representative Crandall a republican, and both from the same county of Steele.

The bill, as introduced, was substantially a copy of the Illinois law enacted in 1871, and now (1904) in force in that state It prohibited discriminations and made it the duty of the commissioners to fix all rates on all the roads It gave the commission entire control of the roads subject to the decision of the courts in certain cases. The bill was stubbornly fought at every stage of the proceedings both in the house and senate The first test vote in the house resulted as follows

Ayes—Adley, Berry, Beals, Brown, L Buell, Burlison, Child, Clark, Crandall, Daniels, Dickerson, Doesdall, Eppel, Gilmore, Gillick, Graling, Greer, Halvorson, Hanson, J N Hanson, A R Harrington, Healy, Hill, How, Hoyt, Hughes, Hyslop, James, Kenworthy, Lafond, Martin, J, Manning, Meyerding, Melrose, Metcalf, Morgan, Morse, Nelson, Norton, Olds, Ottun, Parmerlee, Passon, Pease, Pond, Pratt, Rice, Shellman, Sloan, Smith, L D Smith, Isaac, Stanton, Taylor, D, Taylor, J, Tirrell, Trask, Truwe, Treadwell, Walker, West, Wells, White, Willston, Woodbury and Mr Speaker —65

Nays—Adams, Auge, Babcock, Barns, Benz, Benson, Becker, Brown, L. M, Davidson, Delaney, Denny, Dilley, Drury, Eckdall, Fletcher, Groetsch, Hansing, Jordan, Lawrence, Langley, Lord, Loomis, Martin, J, McArthur, McCluskey, McDermid, Pettit, Rahilly and J K, Smith —20

Those not voting were Messrs Barron, Fiker, Foss, Fleming, Hechtman, Jones, Kletchka, Mason, McDonnell, Peck, Rieland and Swanstrom

This vote demonstrated that the people had a working majority of twelve in the house, and yet so persistently was the bill opposed that it did not finally pass until next to the last day of the session for the passage of bills, when the senate learned that none of its bills would pass the house until the railroad bill should be acted upon finally in the senate On the final passage of the bill in the senate, only two votes were recorded against it—those of I Donnelly, granger, and Senator Drake, of St Paul, president of the St Paul, Minneapolis & Omaha Railroad Company This result was so comical that Senator Drake crossed over from his seat and shook hands with Senator Donnelly amidst the uproarious laughter of the Senate, Mr Donnelly saying "We clasp hands across the bloody chasm "

This railroad legislation, although acquiesced in, apparently aroused all the animosity of the corporations and of the favored shippers in the large cities, and every prominent anti-monopolist in the legislature of 1874 was retired at the next election Enough men were colonized in every county, by the railroads, ten days before election, to defeat objectionable men—the people, as a rule, being more partisan than sensible Not only were the legislators retired, but Gov. Davis was driven out and kept out until he surrendered to the corporations ten years afterwards

From the adjournment of the legislature of 1874 until the ensuing election, no money or exertion was spared to secure the repeal of the law, and the repeal was accomplished in 1875

RAILROAD LANDS

Another matter which was of great importance to the people at the time was the taxation of railroad lands. A large amount of land granted by government to the Winona & St Peter Railroad Company had been clandestinely sold to the Winona and St Peter Railroad Land Company, and under the terms of the grant the lands had been liable to taxation for a number of years, but by shrewd management the company had escaped taxation. In the session of 1874, Senator Ward introduced a bill taxing the lands and it became a law Under its provisions, Waseca county was entitled to some $10,000 in back taxes And this, like the railroad law prohibiting discriminations, was repealed at the session of 1875, and the people were cheated out of their just dues by the legislative action of the railroad combine The total taxes due upon the lands in the state amounted to $61,500.00.

INTENSE POLITICAL STRUGGLE

An extract from the Waseca News of that date will illustrate the methods resorted to during the campaign of 1874. This county was then republican by majorities ranging from 125 to 200.

The News commenting upon the election returns said:

"There never was a more barefaced and outrageous insult ever offered to the resident voters of any county than was perpetrated on last election day in this county. The week before election the superintendent of the Winona & St Peter Railroad came to this place, and while here stated in substance that he should have votes enough here to defeat the republican candidate for state senator at any rate

"How well he kept his word, let the facts prove The total vote last year, with a full state and county ticket, was 1,408 The highest Democratic vote on any state officer (Dike) was 660 The highest Republican vote on any state officer was 787—Republican majority 127 Now mark the vote this year! Republican candidate for senator 749, democratic candidate, 875—the latter receiving 215 more votes than were cast the year before by the same party.

"Then look at the vote of last year and this, outside of Waseca and Janesville Last year the total vote of the county, outside of the two towns named, was 905, and this year only 952—an increase of only 47 votes Now take the two towns containing the villages of Waseca and Janesville the increased vote in Waseca is 108, and the increased vote at Janesville is 61, a total increase of 169 votes But this is not all In St Mary there were railroad men enough to increase the vote in that town ten over that of last year, making a total increase in the three towns of 179 votes

"Is there anybody who pretends that the men who were sent to this county to carry the election are bona fide residents of the county? No, they were simply colonized here for ten days to carry the election for the railroad company and the saloonists, and the next day they disappeared like a fog on a June morning * * *

"We admit that the majority against us in Janesville and Waseca, where the railroad concentrated its votes, where its money could purchase the riff-raff, where its power could terrify the weak was 192 We admit that among the farmers, outside of Janesville and Waseca, where money could not bribe, where threats could not intimidate, and where principles are not for sale to the highest bidder, our majority was 48. We admit these facts and admit them with the utmost satisfaction The votes which we received were the free and untrammeled offering of freemen, without being bribed or intimidated We sacrificed no principles, we neither furnished nor guzzled whisky; nor did we cringe before the power, the money, nor the threats of the railroad kings

We admit that the political agents of the railroad, with the aid of their tools, and the saloons, defeated the whole county Republican ticket, with one exception We admit that we were defeated because we would not endorse the salary-grab, and because we are unalterably opposed to railroad extortion and discriminations, and because we are in favor of protecting women, children, and society against the injuries resulting from the rum traffic. But defeat, under such circumstances, is not at all discouraging to one who would rather be right than to hold the highest office in the state Others may cringe before the hands that smite them, if they choose, but we shall not The principles which we have advocated we believe to be right and thus believing we shall continue to act."

Two weeks after the election, the same paper, under the title, "Railroad Misrepresentation," said

"It seems to be one of the strong points of those who are at work for the railroad interest to misrepresent those who believe that railroad corporations should not be above the laws of the country One of our exchanges labors through a long article to show that the editor of this paper is an enemy of the railroads Nothing could be further from the truth, as every sensible man must know who has been a reader of the paper. Railroads are essential and important aids to the development of the country, and any man who would intentionally destroy them would be an enemy to his country. This we have always maintained, and any effort to destroy the just rights of railroad corporations would be opposed with all the zeal that we possess.

But while we cheerfully accord to railroad corporations all their just rights, we are not blind to the fact that these corporations have far exceeded their rights in the past, and heaped numerous abuses upon the people who have generously aided them We have denounced and opposed the abuses of railroad corporations, and shall continue to do so while those abuses exist

What are and have been the issues between the people and railroad corporations? The corporations claim the right to charge such rates as they please. For instance, a company in this State, prior to the passage of the law last winter, charged for carrying wheat fifty miles, twelve cents per bushel, and for carrying the same commodity, over the same road, a distance of one hundred miles, only eight cents per bushel In one county where there are two villages, only a few miles apart, and where there is no railroad competition, one town was charged for shipping wheat twelve cents per bushel, and the other still farther on, only eight cents per bushel In the matter of lumber, the same kind of discriminations were practiced all over the country As between individuals these discriminations were carried on to a great extent Governors, state officials, senators, representatives, judges, ministers, editors, merchants, and leading lawyers were carried over the roads at half fare, and often times free of charge, while Jack, the hod carrier, Sam, the carpenter, Kate, the kitchen maid, Molly, the washerwoman, Jones, the farmer, and Bill, the blacksmith, were charged five cents a mile. A merchant inside the ring could get his goods shipped below cost and on time, while an outsider had to pay high rates and await the pleasure of the company as to time These and many other abuses that might be enumerated, we have sought, both as an editor and a legislator, to correct, but that we ever sought to injure the railroads is a mistake, to designate it by no stronger word

But the railroad rings are not satisfied with the great power which they naturally possess, they must go further. They must control the legislation of the state and nation in their interest Having learned, during the past two years, that the courts will not sustain their theory that the legislature has no control over their rates and charges, they now go to the polls to control the election of legislators To do this they resort to the most arbitrary means Their workmen must vote as they dictate or leave their employ Every man along the lines of their roads, at all dependent upon them, is made to feel their power unless he submits to their political dictation The liquor-traffic, always corrupt and wicked, is their ready accomplice in influencing and controlling elections

During the past two years the people have made considerable progress towards checking the abuses which had become almost unbearable, but now the companies, having failed in the courts, propose to undo the work which has been accomplished, and, unless we are much mistaken in the signs of the times, they will succeed for a time But their victory will be short lived No such power as they claim should ever be tolerated in this country any great length of time

So far as we are concerned, we propose to continue to battle for the right, fully understanding the tremendous power of the companies and of their saloon allies to crush out all who oppose them. We shall do this, not as an enemy of railroads, but as an opponent of the abuses which the railroad magnates practice upon the masses of the people"

"THE GRASSHOPPER SHALL BE A BURDEN"

Verily the people of Western Minnesota, in 1873-4, probably for the first time, realized the magnificent description given by the prophet Joel of the grasshopper invasions of his day when he said:

"The land is as the garden of Eden before them, and behind them a desolate wilderness. Yea, and nothing shall escape them. Before their face the people shall be much pained; all faces shall gather blackness * * * They shall march, every one on his ways, and they shall not break their ranks. Neither shall one thrust another * * * They shall run to and fro in the city, they shall run upon the wall; they shall climb up upon the houses, they shall enter in at the windows like a thief"

They first made their appearance about June 1873 Vast swarms of the insects appeared suddenly in northwestern Iowa and shortly afterwards in southwestern Minnesota They came with the west and northwest winds by the millions They settled upon all kinds of crops, and destroyed whole fields in a day. The people were taken entirely by surprise. They knew not what to do. In fact they were utterly powerless before this vast and innumerable insect army of invasion. Gardens were destroyed and whole farms were devastated While the grasshoppers left the wild grasses, they devoured the tame grasses and all kinds of grain. This year (1873), while they did not destroy all the fields they deposited their eggs by the million and then disappeared

Since the settlement of the state there have been five grasshopper invasions—1856, 1857, 1865 1873-4-5 The insects in 1873 sowed the land from the Blue Earth River west full of eggs Many people fondly hoped that the frosts of winter had destroyed the eggs and that we should see no more of them. How vain were all these hopes! About the 9th and 10th of May, 1874, the weather being warm, the little pests began to hatch and come out of the ground They were about the size of fleas, but they had the appetite of a full grown hog, and they forthwith commenced their work of devastation. They were ceaseless workers. Neither frosts, nor heat, nor wet weather, nor storms, nor tempests, seriously affected them They ate almost everything in sight where they hatched out in 1874 Fortunately no eggs, to amount to anything, were deposited in Waseca county But in Faribault and Blue Earth counties, adjoining, the destruction of crops was very great. The writer, in driving from Blue Earth to Mankato, July 5, 1874, realized as never before, what is meant by the words, "the grasshopper shall be a burden," and that, as Joel said, "the land was as the garden of Eden before them, and behind them a desolate wilderness, nothing did escape them "

Gardens were totally destroyed. Vast fields of splendid growing grain were eaten to the roots—not a vestige left

Various methods of fighting the pests were resorted to with little effect The most effective instrument or method of destruction was called the "hopperdozer". It consisted of a common piece of sheet iron, six or eight feet long, with small strips of board along the two longer sides, to give it stiffness, and a string or wire to draw it, extending from the two front corners The whole sheet was then covered with coal tar. By drawing this "hopperdozer" over the field or garden while the insects were wingless, they would hop on to the tar in great numbers where they would be held fast and soon die. Hopperdozers were used extensively during the last year of the invasion throughout the infested regions Large quantities of tar were purchased at public expense by towns and counties and almost every farmer had his hopperdozer. But it is generally believed that none of the appliances could avail against such an invasion as that was. The troublesome creatures disappeared as suddenly and mysteriously as they came The exodus finally occurred on the 20th of July, 1877. The day was oppressively warm, the thermometer indicating 102 degrees in the shade with very little or no wind About ten o'clock a m it was discovered that the air overhead was filled with flying grasshoppers. They were in swarms of millions, flying high and going rapidly southeast. For more than an an hour they swarmed past while all over Southwestern Minnesota millions of the insects rose from the ground and joined the passing hosts. Whither they went remains a mystery, but their departure was a great and lasting relief for which all men were devoutly thankful

It was estimated at the time that the following acreage was ravaged by the insects, to-wit 150,000 acres, or 2,500,000 bushels, of wheat, 40,000 acres of oats, equal to 1,320,000 bushels, 20,000 acres of corn, equal to 340,000 bushels, besides large quantities of rye, barley, buckwheat, potatoes, flax and other crops.

Great numbers of worthy people were impoverished by this grasshopper raid Many farmers were left without bread or seed in the western portion of the state Without state aid or aid from some source they must leave their farms and seek employment elsewhere, leaving the land desolate Fortunately the state authorities, under Governor Davis' able advice, came to the rescue and most of the people courageously remained upon their farms and won a victory for themselves and the state

DEATHS NOTED DURING THE YEAR

Mr Andrew Jackson, one of the early settlers of Woodville, died Feb 5, from exposure He left an estimable family to mourn his departure

Jerry Hogan, a single man, living alone, one of the early settlers of the county, was found dead in his cabin March 11 Those who found him judged that he had been dead several days when the body was found, and that he died of disease. For some time prior to his death he had been considered partially insane. His team was found in the stable nearly starved

A sad and fatal accident caused the death of Mr William Baker, of Freedom, March 13. While in the flouring mill of Stokes & Kimball, at Janesville, his clothing caught on an upright shaft and he was drawn on to it, breaking one arm in several places from the hand to the shoulder. While being whirled around by the revolving shaft his legs came in contact with a post, one of them being entirely severed below the knee, and the other nearly torn off The poor man lived some three hours after this horrible mutilation of his body

A sad and fatal accident befell the family of Rev L. D Hocanson, of Otisco, March 20, 1874 in the evening Mr Mose Johnson and wife, his brother and brother's wife and two children, and Rev. Hocanson, wife, and child had been to attend a funeral in New Richland In returning home they had to cross the LeSueur river at the Michael Anderson bridge. The water was so high as to run over the bank at the south end of the bridge, and when the team reached the bridge, one of the horses became frightened and threw itself off the bridge, dragging the other horse and the sleigh with it into the swollen stream All except Mr Mose Johnson and wife and Mrs Hocanson and her two-year-old child, got out without difficulty Mr Johnson and wife clung to the wagon box until they were rescued by a man living near by Mrs Hocanson and child were drowned and their bodies were not recovered until the day following. Mr. Hocanson was pastor of the Swedish Lutheran church, in Otisco, and the sad accident caused deep sorrow in the whole community.

Mrs Lynch, wife of Andrew Lynch, died of pneumonia, April 17, 1874. Mr. and Mrs Lynch were among the early settlers of the county, having settled in St Mary in 1856 She reared a large family of children and was an estimable woman

Mrs Hicks sister of Mr. E G Wood, and one of the very early settlers of this county, a widow lady, died April 24, 1874, of a complication of diseases, while under treatment at Minneapolis She was a native of Vermont and married a man named Scott, who died a few years after the marriage. She came to Minnesota in 1858, a widow, with two children, a son and a daughter She was married in 1859 to Rev Mr Hicks, who died soon afterwards

Mr Isaac Bird, of Wilton, one of the early settlers, died July 29, of kidney trouble, from which he had suffered for years. He was a native of England, coming to this country when a boy.

Dr M. S Gove, the pioneer physician of the county, passed to the Great Beyond on the 1st day of December, 1874 His sudden and unexpected death was a great shock to the community. While he himself realized from the first that death was near, none of his friends could believe it He died of blood poisoning contracted in the line of professional duty. He was born in the town of Strafford, Orange county, Vermont. He studied medicine and surgery in his native state, and, after graduating in 1849 came West, settling in Indiana where he practiced until 1858, when he came to Minnesota and took up his residence in Wilton, then the county seat He moved to Waseca about 1870. He was a public-spirited man and took great interest in all public matters He was a member of the county board during the supervisor system in 1859-60, and was at one time superintendent of schools under the township system. He took an active part in the organization of the Waseca County Anti-Horse-Thief society, and was its president many years. A large concourse of people followed his remains to the grave, the members of the Anti-Horse-Thief association, mounted on horse-back, paying their last respects to their presiding officer by joining in the funeral procession. At the next meeting of the association it resolved: "That we will ever cherish his memory with feelings of consideration and respect as a man of scholarship and ability in his chosen profession, a kind neighbor and good citizen." A year or two after his settlement in Wilton he married Miss Sarah Dodge, then a teacher in the public schools of the county and a very estimable young woman.

Shortly after the death of Dr. Gove, a shocking death occurred at the crossing of the Le Sueur river near the St Mary farm of Thomas J Kerr A man named Wm Ackerman, of Medo, Blue Earth county, came to Waseca with two other men and four teams, on December 9 for lumber In the afternoon they started home, and when near the crossing of the Le Sueur river, at Mr Kerr's place, the lumber on one of the wagons got shoved forward against the team, and the men stopped to fix it Ackerman's team, which was ahead of the others, started forward while he was aiding the others. He ran to his wagon and made an attempt to catch the lines, but missed them, and fell in front of one of the wheels which passed over his body. By this time all the teams were on the run, and the team next to Ackerman's also ran over him He was taken to Mr Kerr's residence, where he expired within a few minutes He left a widow and four children.

The death roll of the year closed with the name of Nathaniel Wood. Father Wood, as he was generally called, died at the residence of Mr. G R Buckman, his son-in-law, in Waseca, Dec. 23, 1874, aged seventy-eight years He had suffered for several years from a cancer on his under lip, and for many months had been confined to his bed. His death was not, therefore, unexpected. He was one of the earliest settlers of Woodville, and was universally respected for his Christian devotion and uprightness of character. His Christianity was not of that India-rubber character which is sometimes used for selfish purposes, but the real article, which entered into his everyday life—his business and his politics

ELECTION FIGURES

The following figures show the result of the election in the county in 1874

STATE SENATOR	
P McGovern, dem	875
J. E. Child, rep	720

REPRESENTATIVES	
Jos Minges, rep	968
H P Packard, rep	748
M H Lamb, dem	827
John Thompson, dem	666

COUNTY AUDITOR	
Edgar Cronkhite, dem	955
H J Wadsworth, rep	698

COUNTY COMMISSIONERS	
Wm Burke, dem	93
Chris Melchior, rep	49
Wm Byron, dem	70
Geo Hofeld, dem	104
C. H. Newell, rep	110

SHORT NOTES FOR THE YEAR

Among the marriages of the year we record the following Mr W H Taylor, one of the early boy-settlers of Blooming Grove, and Miss Emma Barnes, one of the early girl-settlers of Wilton, were married March 5, 1874 They were very worthy, industrious, energetic and frugal young people They now carry on a sheep ranch in Montana and are among the wealthy, well-to-do of that state

Mr August Pream, of Alton, and Miss Augusta Hollander, of Wilton, were married June 10, 1874, and began married life in Alton where they have been engaged in successful farming

August 25, 1874, Mr Rudolph Jacoby, then a recent arrival from Germany, a bright and well-informed young man, was joined in marriage with Miss Annie Schmidt, daughter of Mr Edward Schmidt, one of the very early settlers of Otisco She was the only child and inherits her father's fine estate They own one of the finest farms in Otisco.

On the 10th of January, 1874, the dwelling house of Anthony James, one of the early settlers of Woodville, together with nearly its entire contents, was destroyed by fire His eldest daughter, while carrying a small child from the burning building, fell and broke one of her legs near the knee The fire was caused by the accidental breaking of a kerosene lamp

On Nov 30, 1874, the house of Gottlieb Prechel, of St Mary, on his old farm, was destroyed by fire. The old house was not worth much, but unfortunately for Mr. Peter Hund, who occupied it, his household goods, with considerable grain, were all destroyed.

Under date of June 17, 1874, the Waseca News published the following.

We are pained to learn that Wm R Brisbane, son of Hon Wm Brisbane of Wilton, was dangerously injured last week The cattle having broken into his field, he mounted a large horse and rode into the field to drive them out While on the gallop, the horse ran against a cow with such force as to knock himself down, Mr Brisbane falling under him The horse, a very heavy one, made several attempts to rise, each time falling back upon the body of the unfortunate man Mr Brisbane vomited for several hours afterwards, and suffered great pain, but finally got better"

Mr Brisbane has never fully recovered from the effects of the fall and the injuries he then received.

On the 17th of June, 1874, the county board passed a resolution appropriating $1,000 for the building of a vault to the court house for the safe keeping of the records, books, and papers of the county, especially the records of the office of the register of deeds It was to be 16x20 feet, one story high, and built of brick, with heavy iron doors O Powell S K Odell, and H K Stearns constituted the building committee to oversee the work

The Waseca News of October 7, 1874, contained the following:

"A sad accident happened on Thursday last, in the town of Otisco. John Peterson, commonly known as "Little" John Peterson, while at work around a threshing machine was caught in the side gearing by the right arm near the elbow His arm was drawn in up to his body and torn off, lacerating the flesh about his shoulder and side in a horrible manner"

He slowly recovered and lived a number of years afterwards, dying a year ago of heart failure

The year 1874 was the last year of the second decade in the history of the county The white population had increased from nothing to over eight thousand A railroad had been built through the county, wagon roads had been improved, sloughs and streams bridged, and the country covered with improved farms owned by intelligent freemen

CHAPTER XLIII, 1875.

THE RADICAL—COUNTY LEGISLATION—A HARD WINTER—SALOON TROUBLES—SPELLING SCHOOLS—NEW CHURCH BUILDINGS—RAILROAD BOND PROPOSITIONS—GRANGE WAREHOUSE—OLD SETTLERS ORGANIZE—DEATHS OF THE YEAR—MAN FROZEN TO DEATH—COUNTY POLITICS—BAD STORMS—BUILDING OF TURNER HALL—DIED, KITTREDGE, MRS FETTERLY, MRS TAYLOR, MRS H J. CARLTON, JOHN L. WERDIN, MR BRANDT, MRS BOUCHER, MINNIE FARRINGTON.

The first week of 1875 ushered in the "Minnesota Radical," edited and published by James E Child It succeeded the "Waseca Weekly News" which had been published by the same man since 1863. It published as its platform the following.

We look upon the saloon traffic, in all its departments, as a crime against humanity, and a burning disgrace to our boasted civilization, as the one great cause of business failures, of crimes of every grade, and of the poverty and misery which go to make up so large a portion of the world's history This traffic levies upon the tax-payers of the state seven eighths of the expense of the state prison, over one-half the expense of the reform school, and a large portion of the immense costs annually paid for criminal prosecutions It habitually violates the laws of both God and man It makes paupers and slaves of women and children It murders our citizens, depraves the young, and destroys the weak It corrupts voters and contaminates the ballot box

We believe that the producing, commercial, and industrial interests of the country should have the best and cheapest modes of transportation possible, and while capital invested in such means of transit, whether by railroad, or otherwise, should be permitted the right of reasonable and just compensation, all abuse in management, excessive rates of toll, and all unjust discriminations against localities, persons or interests, practiced by them, should be prohibited by law, and the people should be protected from the improper and arbitrary use of the vast powers possessed by railroad and other transportation companies; and that it is the duty of the state and nation, each in its legitimate sphere, to enact laws which will limit to just and reasonable rates all tolls, freights and charges of transportation companies, and protect the people from extortion and imposition

Let us unite as one man in an honest effort to suppress the liquor traffic, to prevent extortions and unjust discriminations by corporations, to drive corruption and bribery from high and low places"

COUNTY LEGISLATION

The board of county commissioners met Jan. 5, 1875 The members present were Dr. R O Craig, H K Stearns, Wm Burke, Maj. Wm. C. Young, and C. H. Newell. Dr. Craig was elected chairman M D L. Collester was appointed county attorney in place of Mr P. McGovern, who had resigned to accept the position of state senator. The board petitioned the legislature to enact a law authorizing the commissioners of the county to issue county bonds not exceeding ten thousand dollars, for the purpose of erecting a county jail.

A HARD WINTER

On the 8th of January, there was a Minnesota blizzard, lasting all of one day. On the 2d and 3d days of February there was another fierce snow storm, and on the 10th and 23d of the same month severe storms again deluged the country with snow The first week in March a very heavy snow storm from the northeast covered all the northern portion of North America.

It was a hard winter in Minnesota, but light compared with the visitation in Canada That country was covered with such mountains of snow as to make travel impossible Large districts there were isolated for months and trade was paralyzed The appearance of spring weather was welcomed by all the people of the North

DEATH OF FREDERICK W KITTREDGE

Mr Kittredge was born in the State of Ohio, in 1841 He was the son of Dr Kittredge of that state, and a half brother of Maj W. T. Kittredge, one of the early settlers of Wilton Fred came to this county in 1861 and taught school in Wilton one term Soon after he went to Mankato where he took an active part in defense of the town during the Indian outbreak Shortly after the Indian outbreak he married Miss Elizabeth L Baker, of Ohio, and they began wedded life on a farm near Okaman His health failing, he moved with his family first to Wilton and then to Waseca where he engaged in the drug business in company with N E Strong He was an honorable, upright, intelligent gentleman and highly esteemed He was sick for nearly a year of heart disease, and died Jan 4, 1875 He was an honored member of the Masonic fraternity and his brethren were kind and attentive to him during his long illness. He left surviving him his widow and three daughters. His remains were taken to Ohio for burial

"WASECA COUNTY BANK ASSOCIATION"

This banking association was formed the first of the year by twenty-four of the citizens of this county and eleven residents of Faribault Rice county The officers of the association were the following President, Geo. W Newell, cashier, Frank A Newell; directors, P C Bailey, J W. Johnson, R M Addison, S S Phelps, J A Claghorn, E G Wood, of Waseca, H M Matteson, W B Brown, and L Emmett, of Faribault, Rice county

SALOON TROUBLE

On March 4 1875, an exciting affair took place The "Radical" made a record of it, as follows:

Some time within the day, Charlie Blank, Lansing Blank and Curtis Sucker, commenced to fill up on rot-gut whisky, in accordance with the statute in such cases made and provided—at least, we suppose so About five o'clock p m they went into Roeder's and took a horn or two of legal tangle-leg, and were about to leave, when Roeder demanded prompt payment. Lansing, who, it appears, had called for the licensed fluid, told Roeder that he would pay him on Saturday Whereupon Roeder clinched Charlie's hat off his head, and said he would keep it until his bill was paid This aroused the animal on the part of all hands, and a general clinch ensued The old lady of the mansion gave a screech and a scream, and, like a catamount or some other animal, gently placed her fingers in Charlie's curls Curt and Lansing embraced old Roeder, opened the door and gently deposited him in the street Curt then stepped to the door, reached in and brought forth the presiding female of the house and Charlie who were fondly or otherwise clasped in each other's embrace As they struck the sidewalk, the embracing business ceased. The old lady stood on end, placed her gentle hands upon her heaving bosom and screamed a scream of angry defiance that would have done credit to a female panther By this time there was hurrying to and fro, and eager enquiries as to the cause of all the commotion In the mean time the boys had walked up town, making loud talk Presently Marshal Willyard appeared upon the scene and arrested Curt, whom he placed in charge of Constable Stevenson He then made for Charlie, who took a run for home The marshal met a team which he pressed into his service, and soon ran down his man Lansing was not found until morning, when he, too, was arrested On Friday morning the three young men were brought before Justice Baker, on a charge of drunkenness They all plead guilty, and were fined $10 each and costs—the latter amounting to $4 75"

This affair was followed by a number of arrests Roeder was arrested for selling liquors and Justice Baker requested the county attorney to appear and prosecute the case This the county attorney refused to do, claiming it was a village and not a county affair

Mr. Brownell was then employed to prosecute the case, and Roeder was convicted by a jury—the case being a very plain one and the evidence clear and conclusive The saloon attorney then went before an ignorant court commissioner, got out a writ of habeas corpus, and, upon the hearing, the court commissioner set aside the verdict and the judgment of the justice and set the prisoner free That such a proceeding could take place among civilized men shows the power of the liquor traffic at certain times and in certain places But so indignant were the law-and-order people of the county that when the grand jury convened, the following March, indictments were found against the following persons for the unlawful selling of intoxicants, viz., W T Cronkright, of Alma City, John Deeth H W Zeller, Christian Hansen. Jule Egge, Roger Hanberry, and David Carey, of Waseca The jury also presented an informal indictment or presentment against the county attorney for refusing to prosecute Roeder for selling liquor before Justice Baker The judge of the district court upon his own motion, set aside the indictment against the county attorney on the ground of informality

SPELLING SCHOOL.

During the winter of 1874-5 spelling schools became very popular in the county, and the contests were interesting and instructive The following record of one of the contests is from the "Minnesota Radical" of April 28, 1875

"The school was organized by the choice of Rev Mr Shedd, as president; Messrs Latham and Brownell, as judges, Mrs. Latham and Mr Jamison, as captains, and Major Young, as teacher

The winner of the sack of salt, the foot prize, was Mr G Parks, who could not master "pigmies" Mrs James Claghorn couldn't get along with "jockeys," and took the pepper box. "Noxious" was altogether too noxious for Mrs Garland Rev Lorin was poor at "seizing" and Capt Jamison went down on a "mattress" Mr McCormick spelled "chimneys" with nies for the latter syllable Esquire Bennett couldn't get along with a "prude," and Mr. S. T. Lewis experienced a slip of the tongue on "hen-hawk" "Cougar" took down Mr S O Sherwin, Miss Abbie Kittredge could not manage a "canoe," Mr Spencer was no good on "rummage," and the bird "albatross," was the wrong bird for J F Preston "Cochineal" brought the color to Mr Dearborn's face, and Miss Hollister was disgusted with "cinnamon' S N Sherwin was taken from the field by a "hurricane," J. L Claghorn was caught "joking," H A Mosher was slightly "embarrassed," and Mrs S N Sherwin couldn't reach the "eldorado" of her anticipations

At this point only three of the contestants remained upon the battle-field, viz Mrs Shedd, Mrs Latham and Miss Annie Child Mrs Latham couldn't handle a "lariat" and Mrs Shedd didn't know any more about "vaquero" than some others did. Miss Annie Child got caught in a "chaparral," but won the prize—Holland's Mistress of the Manse"

It is a pity that the American people can not devise a system of orthography more in accord with common sense than the present barbarous one which occupies so much of the time of pupils to the detriment of other studies

THREE NEW CHURCH BUILDINGS

This was a year of new church buildings. The Episcopalians, the German Methodists and the German Evangelical association, each erected a new house of worship The German Methodist edifice then erected is still standing and received a new roof in 1904 The German Evangelical church then built gave way to a new and larger building erected in 1904 The Episcopalian chapel still serves the people of that church and is in a good state of preservation

RAILROAD PROPOSITION

Preliminary to the building of the M & St L railroad through this county, there was considerable strife between the people of the old village of Wilton and the people of Waseca. About May 10, 1875, a gentleman by the name of Barnum, representing the Minneapolis, St Paul & Iowa railway company, came through the county and called a meeting before which he had an offer to lay The meeting was held May 15, at the old court house, in Waseca At a preliminary meeting, a committee had been appointed to report upon the matter A local paper reported as follows:

'On motion of Hon W G Ward, James E Child was called to the chair and H A Mosher was chosen secretary A motion was made by Mr Ward that "It is inexpedient for the town of Woodville to vote bonds to aid in the construction of a railroad or for any other purpose."

At the suggestion of Mr G P Johnson, by consent of the mover, the chairman decided to wait a reasonable time before submitting the motion, for the report of a committee previously appointed

Within a few minutes the committee entered, and S B Williams, Esq, proceeded to call the meeting to order, but was himself called to order at once by Mr Ward, who took evident pleasure in informing him that the meeting was fully organized and ready for business Friend Williams took in the situation and commenced to give his views on the subject of railroad bonuses

Mr Ward, again interrupted, and said the gentleman was out of order as he was not talking to the motion Without insisting upon a ruling, Mr Williams took a seat

Mr Barnum, of Iowa, who was then called for, remarked that he had nothing to say until the pending motion was disposed of—then he had a proposition to make

Mr Ward then stated that he had no desire to take any advantage of the friends of the bonus proposition, and would withdraw his motion and allow the meeting to proceed de novo, simply retaining the chairman and secretary No objection being made, Mr Barnum proceeded to state his position on railroad matters in general, and made quite a speech, saying that, on general principles, he was opposed to subsidies to railroads, except where it could not be helped, but that the present question of granting aid was one of the cases where it could not very well be helped We could have the road if we wanted it and would pay for it, and if not, we need not have it

He then made the following proposition

"That the Minneapolis, St Paul & Iowa R R company propose to the citizens of Waseca county to locate, grade, iron and operate their railway from the south line of said county to the village of Waseca, and to have the cars running thereon at the earliest practical moment, provided that said county raise for said company in town bonds, reliable subscriptions, or money a sum equal to $25 000, and place the same in pledge for said company subject to their order, as follows one-half when the cars are running to the town of Wilton, one-fourth when the cars are running to the village of Waseca and one-fourth when the cars are running to the north line of said county—bonds to draw 7 per cent interest payable semi-annually, and that said county furnish right of way, free of cost to said company, of 50 feet on each side of the center line, as the same is or may be located, and depot grounds 300x2,000 feet, in the village of Waseca"

Mr Ward then addressed the meeting in opposition to the proposition He argued that Waseca was the natural point of junction for the proposed road and that it would come here He stated that the bonus would make no difference with the company, and cited the case of Mankato and St Peter The Winona & St. Peter company had decided to build a branch into Mankato, and after that decision, the officers of the road went to the citizens of Mankato and obtained a bonus which they put into their own pockets, but bonus or no bonus the branch would have been built At St Peter after the plans and specifications for the bridge had been made and approved and after the contract for building the bridge had been let, operations were suspended for ten days, by the officers of the road, in order to get a bonus out of St Peter, when, as a matter of fact, the bridge would have been built bonus or no bonus

Mr Barnum said in reply that nearly all the roads in the West were land-grant roads, while this one was not He had come here in good faith, and should be pleased to co-operate with the people here, but as there seemed to be strong opposition, and as there was no motion before the meeting, he would withdraw the proposition, and leave the people here to take such action as they might deem for their best interests.

S. B. Williams, Esq, addressed the meeting in favor of voting a bonus He thought that under the circumstances it would be money well invested

On motion of Hon P McGovern that a committee of ten be appointed to canvass the matter, the chair appointed as such committee, P McGovern, W. G Ward, Thos Bendure A Vinton, B S. Lewis, I C Trowbridge, W. C Young, S B Williams, G P Johnson, and S H Foster

The meeting then adjourned to meet on Saturday, May 22 at 2 o'clock p m

Excitement ran high during the week, so high indeed that timid souls did not attend the adjourned meeting At the time of the adjourned meeting, the chair called the meeting to order, and the committee appointed at the previous meeting, through the chairman, Hon P McGovern, reported that they had no suggestions to make

Mr Lewis then offered the following resolution, and moved its adoption:

Resolved, by the citizens of Woodville township, Waseca county, that we will give to the Minneapolis, St Paul and Iowa railroad company, or the railway company which shall first construct and build said line of road, to aid in the construction of said road, through said town, the sum of $25,000 in the bonds of said town, drawing seven per cent interest payable semi-annually, payable in thirty years from their date, said bonds to be delivered when said company shall have constructed its road to a junction with the W & St P R R in the village of Waseca, and shall have the same in running operation

On motion of B. S. Lewis, the meeting decided to vote upon the resolution by ballot The chair appointed as tellers to receive the votes Messrs W G Ward, W C Young, and Lewis Brownell.

W G Ward took the floor and made a speech in opposition to the resolution. He was replied to by Mr Brownell, who favored its adoption

Fifteen minutes was agreed upon to allow parties to prepare ballots, the polls to remain open one-half hour

One hundred eighty-five votes were cast—95 for, and 90 against the resolution, and the resolution was declared adopted

Although the contest was very spirited, it really decided nothing as it was only an informal expression of opinion; but it aroused a discussion which, in 1876, resulted in the bonding of the township in the sum of $30,000

The town of Wilton had on the 17th of May 1875, voted to issue bonds to the amount of $25,000

GRANGE ORGANIZATIONS

The first Grange in Waseca county was organized May 14, 1870, under a dispensation issued by William Saunders Master of the National Grange, and certified to by O W. Kelly, the first national secretary of the order As early as May 3, 1873, there were ten granges in the county ready to co-operate with one another for the benefit of all, and a county organization was effected at that time This organization was more for discussion and mutual instruction than for business, and it was finally deemed advisable to create a company, or corporation, for the purchasing and handling of grain. This was accomplished Oct 19, 1874, at Waseca The records of the town of Woodville for the year 1874, contain the articles of incorporation of the Grange association The following were its managers

"H W. S Hinkley, W D Armstrong, R R Howard, L D Smith, Hugh Wilson, J J Wilkins, Robert Earl, Samuel Hodgkins, and J Penfield

The capital stock was fixed at $2,000, and each share was $25 The name of the organization was Waseca County Grange association, and its principal place of business was at Waseca Its business was to erect or lease a grain warehouse, and to operate the same, to receive handle, buy, ship, store, and sell grain and farm products It commenced operations that fall, and, for a time, appeared to be doing a good business The price of wheat was at once raised by the combine buyers, and the farmers of the county, outside the men that formed the organization and were fighting the Chicago wheat ring, reaped a rich harvest But the association after a time learned with considerable loss of money that the man they had entrusted with the management of the warehouse was one of the many unfortunates that can not be trusted Although a man of many good qualities, he possessed the fault of drinking liquor, and the wheat men soon managed, indirectly, to keep him under the influence of the dram shops. The final outcome was a loss of the entire capital invested by the stockholders, leaving the wheat combine with a stronger hold than before The experiment revealed the fact that farmers, as a rule, are not yet ready to stand by one another in a fight against organized monopoly"

OLD SETTLERS ORGANIZE

No attempt was made to create an old settlers' organization until November 10, 1875, when a number of the early settlers joined in the published call for a meeting to be held at the court room in Waseca on the evening of Nov 19, 1875 At that time twenty-five men came together and made a preliminary organization. The following officers were elected James E Child, president, H. A Mosher, secretary Geo R Buckman, treasurer; H P Norton, O Powell, and George P Johnson, executive committee.

A constitution and by-laws were adopted and it was determined that a public meeting and a picnic supper should be held at Turner Hall, Dec 15, to which all persons who settled in the county prior to 1865 should be invited Pursuant to this determination, the executive committee issued its call, and on the evening of that day two hundred persons assembled and participated in the festivities of the occasion

After adding a large number of new names to the membership and calling the roll, some slight amendments were made to the by-laws The entrance fee was 25 cents and the annual dues, 50 cents The following was the published program

1 Music by the band

2 Calling of the roll, adding new names thereto, and the consideration of propositions for the more nearly perfect organization of the association

3 Music by the band

4 Address by the president, giving a history of the first year's settlement of the county by white people

5 Music by the band
6 Refreshments
7 Volunteer addresses and historical sketches of frontier life

EXTRACTS FROM THE PRESIDENT'S ADDRESS

"We have met here to-night for a twofold purpose—that of pleasure and that of perpetuating the early history of the county Ancient history is more or less shrouded in mystery, and in all the accounts of the origin of the older nations, cities, and empires, fiction is so interwoven with facts that it is difficult to separate truth from fable Even the history of one of the greatest nations and empires of the world commences with a statement more fictitious and romantic than truthful or sensible

It relates that a daughter of a certain king who had been appointed by that king priestess of Vesta, in which capacity she was to lead a life of single blessedness devoted exclusively to religious services finally became the mother of twins—two bouncing boys The king, fearing that these little fellows might some day dethrone him or his, ordered one of his servants to murder them Pursuant to this order, the servant put the little fellows into a sap-trough and went down towards the river with a design to cast them in, but seeing that it was very rough and running with a strong current, he was too much of a coward to approach it He therefore deposited the two boy babies near the bank of the river and hurried away. The flood increasing continually set the trough afloat and carried the children gently (of course they went gently the historian says they did) down to a pleasant place where they were landed safe and sound

Under the guidance and influence of the goddess Rumina, who presided over the nurseries of the ancients, and whose rites were celebrated without wine or whisky but only with libations of sweet milk, the infants as the story goes, were suckled by a she-wolf and fed and taken care of by a woodpecker These animals were sacred to Mars and the woodpecker was always held in high honor and veneration by that nation of great warriors, orators, and statesmen

Such wonderful events, say the historians, contributed not a little to give credit to the mother's report that Mars, the god of war, was the father of the children

I shall not follow the history of these boys real or fictitious, this evening Suffice it to say, that they were the founders of one of the greatest empires of the earth Rome and the Roman empire owe their name and origin to Romulus and Remus, and these were the twin brothers whose early lives were so shrouded in darkness that the historian could only give this ridiculous legend of their early lives

The early history of Waseca county of course, will not be embellished with the story of any such fabulous or miraculous event yet the record of its early settlement and the experience of those who came here at an early day to make homes in the prairie wilderness will not be entirely destitute of interest nor wholly without a touch of the romantic I shall this evening confine my remarks to the first settlement made within the limits of the county It was made during the summer of 1854" [Then followed an account of the settlement of Mr Sutlief and family as detailed in chapter two of this history.—Author]

Hon. Wm Brisbane was called out and gave a graphic description of the company that went from Wilton to the Winnebago agency, in 1862 to protect the white settlers from a threatened massacre by the Indians He closed with an eloquent plea in behalf of virtue, morality and Christianity.

Hon. S B. Williams, Mr J W Wheeler, Hon Joseph Minges, Hon. Job A Canfield and others were called upon and made appropriate remarks There were over two hundred in attendance and the occasion was one of much enjoyment

The following vice presidents were chosen at this meeting: Wm Lee, of Iosco, W H Harmon, of Vivian; Job A. Canfield, of Otisco; C.H Newell, of Byron, George H. Woodbury, of Wilton, J R Davidson, of Blooming Grove, W. D Armstrong, of Freedom; Hon Wm. Brisbane, of Wilton, Samuel Remund, of Blooming Grove; Thomas J Kerr, of St Mary

Mr. Wm. Lee, of Iosco, favored the audience with a description in rhyme of his early experiences.

The organization continued for some three years, when it was allowed to die out The last record of the organization to be found by the author shows the following as its officers: Hon Warren Smith, president, Eri G Wood, Austin Vinton, Job A. Canfield, Michael Anderson, J D. Andrews, J W. Tefft, J H Wheeler, William Lee, J R Davidson, Samuel Remund, Wm. Hover, W H Harmon, H. K Stearns, E E Verplank, A E. Crumb, C H Newell, G. H Woodbury, Hon. William Brisbane, Thomas J Kerr, John White, and W D Armstrong, vice presidents, H A Mosher, secretary, H G Mosher, treasurer. Of the foregoing, only five are now living

DEATHS OF 1875

The following deaths are noted: Mr Fred W Kittredge died of heart disease Jan 6 Mrs Fetterly, a very aged woman, died in January Mrs A L Taylor, wife of Mr G N Taylor, died quite unexpectedly Feb 2 She had been ailing for three weeks, but was not considered dangerously ill until about an hour before her death She was born in August, 1835, married Mr. Taylor in 1852, came with him to Rochester, Minn, in 1855, and to Waseca county in 1865 She was one of the pioneer Baptists of the city of Waseca Mrs H J Carlton, of the town of Wilton, one of the very early settlers of the county, died of apoplexy after an illness of only a few hours She and her husband were among the oldest settlers of the state She died Feb 21, 1875. Mr John L Werdin, of Iosco, father of Mr H J Werdin, of Alton, after several weeks' illness, died Jan 24, 1875 He was among the early settlers and highly respected

Mrs. John Boucher who, at an early day, settled in Blooming Grove with her husband, died March 9, 1875 leaving a large family to mourn her departure

Miss Minnie Farrington, daughter of Mr S A Farrington, of Woodville, who was born in Otisco, Sept 4, 1857, died December 10, 1875 of measles She was taken ill at Mankato, where she was attending school, and, not knowing the nature of the disease, started for home Arriving at Waseca, she went to the residence of her aunt, Mrs Blatchley, where she went into convulsions from which she never recovered Her death cast a gloom over the whole community.

MARRIAGES

There were marriages near the close of the year 1874, reported in January 1875 The following are noted John F Preston to Miss Etta M Taylor, of Waseca Dec 30, 1874; Martin E Parmelee, of Waseca to Miss Ada C Dearborn, of Lowell, Wis, Dec 28, 1874, G W Soule of Blooming Grove, to Miss Nancy B Canfield, of Otisco, Jan 2, 1875, E A Erwin, to Mrs M F Wilson, both of Wilton, Jan 18 1875, Aiken Myene and Addie Harmon, both of Vivian, Nov 25, by Rev A Cressy, Walter Hunter, of Dakota county and Miss Phoebe Coulthart, of Waseca, Nov 23, 1875

COUNTY POLITICS

The interference of railroad managers in the local politics of the county, in 1874, aroused a feeling of opposition in the county which took definite form in 1875 The agitation had continued since the election in 1874, and took form Sept. 15, 1875 when a number of prominent citizens of both the old parties joined in a call for a county convention to be held Oct 9, 1875 As soon as this call appeared, the republicans called a convention and the democrats followed Excitement ran high and discussions resulted in some bitterness of feeling that has not been entirely effaced, even at this day, in the minds of the implacable

The delegates that attended the convention of the Reform Party were the following· Edward Brossard, D A Erwin, Gustus Brossard, and W A Erwin, of St Mary, W H Stokes, J J Headly, A J Hurlburt Jerome Dane, A R Willsey, and C. B Allen, of Janesville, Henry Gray L D McIntosh, A Blatchley, J E Child, S. A Farrington, Samuel Hawkes, B H Taylor, A H Wellman and Nathan Wood, of Woodville, Thomas Barden, Peter Burns, John Kenehan, Hale Kinyon, and John Campbell, of Wilton, I D Beaman and E R Conner, of Blooming Grove, and M L Devereaux, of Alton The following candidates were nominated for representatives, Samuel Hawkes and Kelsey Curtis, for treasurer, Warren Smith, for sheriff, M F Connor, for register of deeds, E G Pierce, for clerk of court, James Vandermade, for county attorney, Lewis Brownell for surveyor, C E Crane, for coroner, Dr. L. D. McIntosh, county commissioner, first district, H Vincent The following central committee was chosen Capt A H Wellman of Waseca, T D M Orcutt of Freedom, Capt J J Headley of Janesville, Thomas Barden of Wilton, Dr H D Cobb of Vivian, S W Franklin of New Richland E G Pierce of Alton, Albert Remund of Blooming Grove, H P Chamberlain of Iosco, L E Francis of Byron, and Samuel Leslie of Otisco

The following platform, after considerable discussion, was unanimously adopted.

"In severing our connection with the Republican and Democratic parties, we give the following as some of the reasons therefor

1st. That these parties, acting in unison, have repealed the only railroad law of the state, that of 1874, which has ever given protection to the people by requiring the companies to do business at reasonable and uniform rates, and in its place have substituted a law which permits the companies to resort to extortion and unjust discriminations, affording to the public no adequate remedy for the wrongs which the companies may see fit to perpetrate, thereby practically denying the right of the people to be protected from the grasping avarice of wealthy corporations.

2d That these parties, at the last session of the legislature, repealed that portion of the tax-law of the state which provided for the collection of back taxes upon the lands of the Winona & St Peter railway company, whereby Waseca county has lost about $8,000 and other counties in proportion

3d. That the older parties, by their platforms and by their legislative acts, stand pledged to the liquor-dealers of the state to perpetuate one of the worst monopolies of modern times, viz the exclusive right to make drunkards For a paltry sum of money these parties authorize a few conscienceless men the legal right, by the use of alcoholic poison, to rob weak men, their helpless wives and children and to spread broadcast crime and pauperism for the support of which the people are burdened with taxation

4th Throughout the state, almost without exception, the old parties elect men to office that neglect or refuse to execute and enforce the laws that prohibit the sale of intoxicating liquors on Sundays, to minors, students, or intemperate persons

5th. The old parties of this state, in nearly every locality resort to corrupt practices to control caucuses, conventions and elections Wealthy men and corporations join hand in hand with the liquor dealers, and money and whisky are freely used to influence the weak, the mercenary, and the corrupt.

In view of these facts, we believe the time has fully come when every voter, who is opposed to these wrongs, should unite in the organization of a Reform party for their overthrow: therefore,

Resolved, That we fully endorse the platform, and cordially support the nominees of the State Reform convention held at Minneapolis, June 10th, 1875

Resolved, That it is the duty of the legislature to pass a law for the control of railways, embodying the principles of the railroad law of 1874, with such modifications in detail as experience may have demonstrated to be necessary

Resolved, That it is the duty of the state to protect its citizens from injury, and the people from unjust taxation, and that to accomplish these, the legislature ought to pass a law requiring dealers in intoxicating liquors to pay the damages resulting from the sale and use of such liquors

Resolved, That common fairness requires the legislature to extend the local option law, now applicable to municipal townships to all cities and villages, thereby giving to the voters of every locality the right to vote no license

Resolved, That it is the duty of the next legislature to provide by law for the levy and collection of all back taxes on the railroad lands of this state, not especially exempted by chartered law sustained by the decision of the supreme court

Resolved, That we are unalterably opposed to the sale and use of alcoholic liquors as a beverage, and denounce as unworthy of our suffrages, any man who engages in the sale or use of such liquors, and we believe that the best way to discountenance intemperance in the community is by a refusal of all good citizens to support intemperate and liquor-guzzling men for official positions or places of trust

Resolved, That, in our opinion, a more efficient law should be passed for the prevention of bribery and corruption at elections, and that any elector, offering or accepting a bribe, be disfranchised and disqualified for office for a term of years"

The Republican convention, which had been pushed in one day ahead of the Reform convention, nominated a mixed ticket—saloon and anti-saloon men

The Republican convention nominated the following ticket:

For representatives, Robert Earl and Gullick Knutsen, sheriff, J D Andrews, treasurer, Warren Smith, register of deeds, H A Mosher, clerk of court, B A Lowell, judge of probate, J A Canfield, county attorney, M D L Collester, surveyor, C E Crane; coroner, Dr. McMahan; county commissioner first district, H Vincent.

The Democratic convention was held on the 16th of October, 1875, and the following candidates were named:

For representatives, Kelsey Curtis and Wm Brisbane; sheriff, Daniel Murphy; treasurer, Thomas White, register of deeds, George Hofeld; judge of probate, Caleb Halleck clerk of court, James B Hayden, county attorney M D L Collester (Republican nominee); surveyor, Frank Hoffstott, coroner, Dr McMahan, county commissioner first district, Patrick Healy.

The campaign, though short, was hissing hot The following appeared in a local paper Oct. 27, 1875.

"Last week the Whangdoodle vomited forth the following

"Oh! James E Child, the venomous, blackhearted and utterly dishonest demagogue, it astonishes us, even us, who have studied your slimy, treacherous course for years, that you can have the cheek, the brassy impudence to stand up before this people to proclaim and practice your vileness Does your conscience never flatten you to the dust and rend you? does not the shadow of that dark time pass before you, when you will pray for the rocks and mountains to fall upon you and forever conceal you from the eyes of an avenging God? But, we feel thankful that some of the people are getting their eyes open to your political chicanery You were plainly invited by the people last fall to take a back seat, and we are sure the day is not far distant when you will inhabit the byways and back streets of life, shunned by all true men, an outcast from, and a byword in society, as other blatherskites have done and been before you"

To which the author replied:

Poor "us!" It is to be hoped that he feels better since getting so much bile off his stomach Why, bless your poor soul, when you came down to Waseca about a year ago on a drunk, you shunned us, and we expect that "all true men" of your habits of life, and your way of thinking, will shun us simply because their deeds are evil, but that is really no reason why you should make a blackguard of yourself, and call us pet names You are not of half as much importance as you seem to think, for, ever since you wilfully, maliciously and knowingly published the slanders of "One who knows" against Warren Smith, without cause or provocation simply as the hireling dog of the railroad and whisky ring of Waseca county, and recommended the liar as a man "strictly reliable and eminently respectable," your falsehoods and blackguardism are estimated at what they are worth

We have long hoped that you might lay aside your selfish animosity toward us, and that you might learn wisdom in your advancing years In fact we could wish that you might be happier

Last fall you witnessed our political defeat, on the Republican ticket by the railroad and whisky ring, which you are kind enough to refer to occasionally, and you got the little post office as a reward for your political treachery and self-stultification Why, with all this success, are you not happy and contented? Is it because that now, as of old, "the wicked flee when no man pursueth?"

Your calling us a "venomous, blackhearted and utterly dishonest demagogue" may be pleasing to the little ring of politicians by whom you are employed, but to the people at large it sounds very much like the hissing of a slimy serpent pierced with a sharp instrument Why should a little truth concerning your real character make you hiss out such vileness? Keep cool, dear one, and be a little more truthful Quit forever those base practices which have brought sorrow upon the gray hairs of your parents, have pierced with grief the heart of her whom you swore to cherish, and have brought to shame those whom you have begotten

> "While the lamp holds out to burn
> The vilest sinner may return"

We know very well that it is not of your own free will and

accord that you make these false and brutal assaults upon our character, but simply because you are the hired tool of a little gang of unprincipled and unscrupulous politicians Now, why do you not break away from these men and paddle your own canoe? Why do you not purchase the material with which you print your paper, and become a free man once more? How much better you would feel then, and how much easier it would be for you to be a decent man

The county was thoroughly canvassed by local speakers and the Republicans brought in a number of prominent speakers from abroad in order to counteract the reform movement The reform leaders were handicapped to some extent for the reason that the Republicans had nominated—with one exception—a most excellent ticket, and the Democats had nominated two of the reform candidates However, the battle was fought to a finish with the following result:

Governor, Reform vote 334, Republican 547, Democrat 546, representatives—Kelsey Curtis 820, Robert Earl 587, Gullick Knutsen 562, William Brisbane 541, Samuel Hawkes 266, treasurer—Warren Smith 886. Thomas White 523, register of deeds—H. A Mosher 821. Geo Hofeld 453, E. G Pierce 145, clerk of court—J. B Hayden 646. B A. Lowell 374, James Vandermade 302, sheriff—S W Long (Ind) 466, J D Andrews 429, Daniel Murphy 399, M F Connor 127, judge of probate—J. A. Canfield 649. Caleb Halleck 626, county attorney—M D L. Collester 712, Lewis Brownell 680, surveyor—C E Crane 937, Frank Hoffstott, 489, coroner—Dr J C McMahon 1,098, Dr L D McIntosh 321, county commissioner—H Vincent 281, Patrick Healy 214 The straight Reform or prohibition vote was 334, the number received by Prof Humiston.

JOSEPH A WHEELOCK.

In the contest of 1875 the following was quoted as from the pen of Mr. Wheelock, then editor of the St Paul Press

"We consider tippling houses, saloons, or retail groggeries where rotgut whisky, or whisky of any sort, is sold by the glass or dram as public nuisances, schools of intemperance, and fruitful sources of vice We are inclined to believe that, upon grounds of public order and decency, the lawmaking authority has the right to prohibit the exposure and sale of spirituous liquors in this most seductive and dangerous of forms, and to abolish this nuisance and snare of tippling houses and groggeries

"If it be not criminal, it is, to say the least, internally mean business, and a full grown man who cannot find a better avocation than to stand behind a bar and pander to a vicious custom of idle tippling, that soon grows by what it feeds on, into a scorching curse—is a nuisance to society, and the sooner his avocation is abolished the better. There is however, a case in which liquor selling is, upon every principle of ethics or of law, unquestionably a crime—and that is when the seller commits the twin crimes of fraud and slow murder upon his customer, by selling various forms of poison under the names of whisky, brandy, &c"

MISCELLANEOUS NOTES.

The winter of 1874-5 was more than usually stormy. On January 8, there was a blizzard and on Feb 2 and 3, and again on the 16th and the 23d days of the month occurred severe snow storms On the 16th railroads and wagon roads were badly blockaded The weather during harvest was especially bad for harvest work There were heavy rainstorms August 3, 8, 14 and 31, and much of the grain was injured in both shock and stack One of the local papers of September 8, said

"The recent rain storms in this section have been enormously destructive. What was once the best wheat crop ever produced in this section is now so badly damaged that very little of it will go number one Along the LeSueur river bottoms the crops are nearly all under water, and much damage has been done to crops and fences It is simply impossible at present to estimate the amount of damage that has occurred. We learn that much of the wheat in stack is badly damaged"

The weather cleared the first week in September and the fall months were pleasant, enabling the farmers to do their fall work in good shape

Turner Hall, now Ward's opera house, was built in 1875, and dedicated the 2d and 3d of December Dr. Schmidt of Jordan, M D L Collester of Waseca and Col Pfaender of New Ulm, delivered addresses, Mrs Wm McIntosh and Miss Gerlicher presented a flag, the latter making the presentation speech The hall was built by subscription, but owing to poor management, it was not a financial success and finally became the property of the late Hon. W G Ward.

At the October term of the district court, Frank Conway, of Elysian, having stolen horses from H A Waggoner, was convicted of horse-stealing and sentenced to five years' imprisonment in the Stillwater prison. Frank was a peculiar man. He was possessed of many good qualities. When sober he was a good neighbor, a kind husband, an affectionate father. He was a man of fair intelligence, and, for a number of years, was one of the county commissioners of LeSueur county. But he had a craving for liquor, and was, no doubt, afflicted with both dipsomania and kleptomania.

And now the year draws to a close. Old Boreas has come down from his frozen home in the unknown North. The birds have flown. The trees are stripped of their foliage. The grass and the flowers of the prairie are dead. The white mantle of the Snow King covers the land and the year has passed into eternity.

"All ends are hid in God."

CHAPTER XLIV, 1876.

CENTENNIAL YEAR—DEATHS OF JOHN HOFFER, MRS WM RODDLE, MRS S W LONG, ELDER SMITH, CHRISTIAN KRASSIN, ROBERT MURPHY, MRS ECKENBECK, MRS JANE SOULE, MISS MURRAY OF RATTLESNAKE BITE, JOHN DUNN, MINNIE YOUNG —B H TAYLOR DROWNED—SHOOTING OF YOUNG FULLER—HOT CITY ELECTION FOLLOWED BY LIBEL SUIT—GOPHERS IN BLOOMING GROVE—BRISBANE'S CENTENNIAL ADDRESS—NORTHFIELD BANK ROBBERY—CAPTURE OF THE YOUNGER BROTHERS—RAILROAD BONUS OF $30,000.

Hail! All hail!! the great Centennial year
Of the great Republic—A year of jubilee

The weather in Minnesota was magnificent At twelve o'clock midnight, all over the land, the Centennial year was welcomed by the ringing of bells, the firing of guns, music of all kinds, especially of the brass band sort In every village and hamlet there was great public rejoicing

To signalize the great event, preparations had been made on an extensive scale during several preceding years for a World's Exposition at the historic city of Pennsylvania The great fair opened on the 10th of May, and closed on the 10th of November On the Fourth of July there was held, in that city, the most magnificent and extensive celebration ever held in the Union. The story of the Exposition is as entrancing as a splendid romance, and it was in all respects a fitting and worthy commemoration of the one hundredth anniversary of the adoption of the great Declaration of Independence

Should one ask, what meant the midnight ringing of bells,

the shrill notes of the fife, the thunder of the big bass drums the shrill notes of Young America, the sunrise salute of thundering cannon and the grand display of flags and bunting, the answer is, it is the great anniversary of the birth of the American nation—the most memorable event, save that of the birth of Christianity, in all the history of mankind

In their influences upon the future destinies of mankind, the doctrines of the Declaration of Independence, enunciated by the Fathers, in 1776, stand forth in true statesmanship mountain-high beside the selfish doctrines of plutocracy and kingcraft.

The Fourth of July, 1776, was the birthday of a great nation and of grand doctrines The old doctrines of the divine right of kingcraft, bolstered up and defended by a hireling priestcraft, received a rude shock that day.

The great truth that all men are created with equal rights—that by the great God of the universe, they are endowed with certain inalienable rights, among which are life, liberty, and the pursuit of happiness—that to secure these rights, governments are established among men—that government derives all of its just powers from the consent of the governed—that whenever any government becomes destructive of these ends, it is the right of the governed, all the people, to alter or abolish it and institute such government as will secure these rights and the safety and happiness of all the people—this great truth should be imperishable.

No such doctrine, in its entirety, was ever before enunciated. Never before 1776 did men dare to make it and stand for it Men before had preached the doctrine of civil and religious liberty in isolated instances, and had suffered martyrdom, but this was the first great uprising for equal rights and privileges And our young men and women should study these doctrines and get clear ideas of the nature and the character of this sublime event in the history of our country and in the history of the world—for America is a great world power.

The doctrine upon which this government is founded should cover the whole earth Everywhere it should be established that all government should of right be by the people and for the people, and not the people for the government This is the grand idea of our nation—liberty regulated by laws enacted by citizen sovereignty—equal rights and privileges for each guaranteed by all.

Let us hope that this nation of American freemen shall exist while time shall last, and that the hallowed principles of the Declaration of Independence may spread abroad throughout all the world and prove a blessing to all mankind. Let every American remember that it is "righteousness that exalteth a nation" and that "injustice will destroy any people"

> "Columbia! Columbia! to glory arise,
> The queen of the world, the child of the skies."

THE WINTER OF 1875-6.

As a rule, the winter of 1875-6 was pleasant in Minnesota. There was quite a severe snow storm Jan 25, 1876, followed by pleasant weather until February 29, when there came a heavy fall of snow followed by cold weather until the last of March The snow did not melt away until the last days of March, when it went suddenly, causing floods and washouts in many parts of the country. April was a favorable month and seeding was done at the usual time

DEATH OF JOHN HOFFER

Saturday, Jan 6, 1876, Mr John Hoffer residing near Alma City, met with a fatal accident near Capt Dickerson's mill on the Agency road, not far from Mankato He was returning home from Mankato with a load of lumber and was driving a pair of spirited young horses They became frightened by an attempt of other men and teams to pass them on the road and ran a short distance, Mr. Hoffer falling off, and the horses continuing on with the forward part of the wagon. They were finally caught without being much injured Mr Hoffer was found unconscious and was carried into Mr Marble's house. He was apparently in a dying condition, with blood running from his mouth, nose and ears. Doctors were called, but the unfortunate man remained unconscious until his death about thirty-six hours after the accident The physicians said that he had sustained a fracture of the skull at the base It was claimed that the racing was the result of too much whisky.

DEATH OF MRS WM RODDLE

Mrs Wm Roddle one of the pioneer women of our county and mother of Hon W. H Roddle, late secretary of state of South Dakota, died Jan 21, 1876, of congestion of the lungs. She was sick only a short time. She was the mother of Mrs. G W. Watkins, Mrs. Buel Welch, Mrs Stephen R Child, Hon Wm H and Benjamin Roddle, and Mrs. C. E. Root, who died some years ago She was a good neighbor and an exemplary woman

MISCELLANEOUS HAPPENINGS OF THE YEAR.

Mr Alvah Kinney, of Woodville, Feb 20, 1876, met with a sad accident near Elysian He was thrown from his wagon by a sudden jolt, and in his fall broke both bones of his right leg between the knee and the ankle One of the bones protruded through the flesh when he was brought home.

The residence of B. S Lewis, Esq, now occupied by Cashier J. B Sullivan, was built during the Centennial year by Mr Silas Barnard, since deceased.

The Sons of Temperance, one of the oldest total abstinence societies in the United States, organized a division in Waseca, March 3, 1876. It is claimed that this is the oldest temperance society of this country, the first Division having been organized as early as Sept 29, 1842, in the city of New York. That it has accomplished a grand work in the uplifting of humanity, is admitted by all. Several Divisions were organized in this county by Dr M T Anderson, a very earnest advocate of total abstinence

DEATH OF MRS SETH W. LONG

The following is from the Waseca Radical of March 15, 1876

'The citizens of this place were surprised and shocked last Wednesday to hear of the death of Mrs Sarah Long, wife of Sheriff Long, of this city, who died in Janesville, on Wednesday morning, March 8, 1876, of congestion of the lungs, after a few days of illness The funeral services were held at the Episcopal chapel, in Waseca, last Friday; Rev Mr Young, of Mankato, officiating, and the remains were buried in the family lot at Wilton She was fifty-four years of age last June She came to Okaman with her husband in 1856, and had an extensive acquaintance in this county. Deceased was a member of the Episcopal church and was held in high esteem by all her acquaintances. She leaves a large family to mourn her death At the time of her sickness and death, she was visiting her daughter, Mrs D J Dodge, of Janesville"

SHOOTING OF YOUNG FULLER.

The following account is from a Waseca paper of March 29, 1876

"A sad and lamentable affair occurred in the town of Janesville, last Friday evening, March 24 Mr James Ash, an old resident of that town, highly respected, was married last Thursday The married couple went to St. Peter that evening where they spent the night. The next day they returned to his farm in Janesville Just after the couple retired for the night, some of the boys and young men of the neighborhood opened the charivari by firing guns, drumming on tin pans, jingling bells, &c He took down his shot gun and fired into the crowd The shot struck a boy about fourteen or fifteen years of age, a son of Orlando Fuller, some of the shot striking him in the breast and penetrating into the lungs, and others striking him in the abdomen"

Fortunately the wounds did not prove to be mortal and the lad soon after recovered The evils of the barbarous charivari were made prominent in this case, as several protracted law suits grew out of the affair.

DEATH OF REV. ELIJAH STORRS SMITH

Elder Smith, as he was familiarly called, was a pioneer clergyman of Wilton He was a native of Rutland county, Vermont and was born June 18, 1805 He was licensed to preach the gospel at the age of twenty-eight. He married Roxana Laws in 1829 For twenty years he was pastor of the Baptist church at Elba, Genesee county, N Y He then removed to Indiana where he spent nearly three years, thence to Illinois, where he preached until 1859, when he came west to Wilton as a home missionary He was a very faithful and patient clergyman He and his good wife participated in all the hardships and deprivations of frontier life with Christian cheerfulness They had no children born to them, but had two adopted daughters One of them, Mary, became the wife of Dr York, of Kansas, who was murdered by the notorious Bender family of that state Mr Smith died of paralysis, April 7, 1876, in his seventy-first year and his remains lie buried in the Wilton cemetery of which he took especial care for several years prior to his death

DROWNING OF BURT H TAYLOR.

One of the truly sad events in the history of Waseca was the drowning of Burt H. Taylor, April 15, 1876. On that date, at the northwest shore of Loon Lake, within the city limits of Waseca, a son of Mr. Glidden, a lad ten or twelve years of age, took a small skiff and ventured out into an open space of water between two fields of ice While he was paddling around, all unconscious of the dangers awaiting him, the wind from the west drove down some floating ice, which closed in between the boat and the shore The ice rapidly accumulated and the boy found it impossible to make his way out He became frightened and hollooed for assistance To add to his alarm the boat leaked some, and he had nothing but his cap with which to throw out the water. Mrs Glidden soon discovered the perilous condition that her boy was in, and supposing the boat would be crushed by the ice and her son would be drowned, became very much alarmed and excited and cried piteously for help to rescue her boy.

Young Taylor, with the generosity and courage for which he was noted, stripped off all but his underclothing, plunged into the ice-cold water of the lake and swam to the rescue of the boy A number of persons intently watched him as, with strong arms and noble spirit, he reached the floating ice and commenced the perilous effort of breaking through it and gaining the boat. He successfully broke through the first barrier of ice, and it seemed for a time that he would really accomplish his object He then struggled heroically through the ice and slush which was tossed madly about him by the fierce wind until within thirty feet of the boat.

What a grand effort! Could he succeed? It seemed so, but no! He was chilled to the vitals, or injured by the floating ice cakes, or taken with cramp! He sank to a watery grave

The citizens were soon aroused, and the utmost excitement prevailed Morris Landers, with his team and wagon, took Daniel Murphy, Will Blowers, and others and went around on the south side of the lake, taking with them a boat As soon as they reached the west side of the lake, where it was clear of ice, they launched the boat and went to the rescue of the boy who was still fast in the ice In the mean time, Emil Sandretzky and Dr McIntosh came around on the north side of the lake with another boat, and and made their way through the ice, both boats reaching the boy about the same time. The ice, driven by the strong wind, immediately closed in about the boats, and it required the united strength of all on board to break their way out of the ice-gorge against the wind.

Having set the scared and chilled boy on shore, the boats then returned, with poles and grappling irons, to search for the body of young Taylor. The search was kept up until a late hour Saturday night, but owing to the high wind and the weeds and grass which cover the bottom of the lake in that vicinity, the body was not found The search was continued all day Sunday, but without avail. There was more or less search for several days, but the body was not discovered until May 7, following, when Mr A G Bush, brother-in-law, of young Taylor, found the remains near the west shore of the lake, southwesterly from the place of the accident Mr Taylor was a Master Mason and his remains were interred with Masonic honors.

A LIST OF DEATHS

Mrs Charles Eckenbeck, one of the earliest settlers of Waseca, died on the 19th of April, 1876, at the age of forty-five years, of cancer of the bowels She was a native of Germany, but had resided in America for many years She was mother of Mr S C Eckenbeck, well known to all the early settlers and now in the milling business at Appleton, Minn

Mr Christian Krassin of St Mary, aged sixty years, died on the 23d day of April, 1876 He was born in Prussia and came to America about the year 1852 He settled first in Wisconsin, but came to this county in 1856 and opened a farm in St Mary township Some four years prior to his death, he was injured severely by a ferocious bull After this accident he never saw a well day He was a whole-souled, industrious and prosperous farmer, a quiet citizen, a kind husband and father, and a true friend

Mr Robert Murphy, of Alton, was accidentally killed at Janesville, by a runaway team of horses, May 26 1876

Mrs. Christensen, wife of Nels Christensen, residing in the eastern part of New Richland township, met with a fatal accident on Saturday, May 13, 1876. She had been down to Le Sueur river washing some clothing, and while passing a colt, on her way to the house, was kicked by the brute in the stomach and abdomen so severely that, after lingering for several days in intense pain, she died on the 25th of the same month She left a large family of children

July 11, 1876, Mrs Jane Soule died at the residence of her son, William, in Morristown Mrs Soule, a widow with eight children, came to Minnesota in 1855 and settled in Morristown near our county line She was the mother of Mr George Soule, for a long time a resident of this county She was one of God's noble mothers in Israel

A sad and heart-rending death occurred at the home of George Murray, of Iosco, July 20, 1876 A daughter of Mr Murray, five or six years old, was bitten by a rattlesnake on one of her feet, Sunday evening, July 16, near the house of Richard Dreever The snake was killed and had six or seven rattles. The child lingered until the 20th, suffering great pain, when death came to her relief

John Dunn, of Woodville, brother of J M Dunn and one of the early settlers, died July 21, 1876 of inflammation of the membranous lining of the skull near its base His suffering was intense He was about twenty-four years of age, and highly respected

Hon Henry Goodspeed died of consumption October 19, 1876, aged forty-five years (See biographical department)

SOME MARRIAGES

There was a double wedding July 3 1876, at the residence of Mr and Mrs Noah Lincoln, of Wilton, the ceremony being performed by Judge Canfield. The high contracting parties were Mr A D Scullin and Miss Elva Lincoln and Mr I F Scullin and Miss Louise Lincoln Both gentlemen were then residents of Oakland, Freeborn county

Mr S C Eckenbeck and Miss H E Parmelee were married July 8, 1876, by Rev Alfred Cressy

The last marriage of note of the year was that of Mr Clarence T. Ward, since deceased, to Miss Annie E Baldwin, then of Redwood Falls, Minn The bride was the well-known daughter of

Judge H. D. Baldwin, one of the prominent and early settlers of the county, the groom was the eldest son of Hon W G Ward, late of this city Clarence died some years ago, but his widow still resides at Redwood Falls

A HOT ELECTION.

The Waseca village election of 1876 occurred May 2 and was one of the most exciting ever held in the place A strife had arisen between Hon W G Ward on one side and B S Lewis, Esq., on the other Each had his friends and each had pluck Mr Lewis had control of a paper then published in Waseca, called the "Leader" To offset the Leader's influence or supposed influence, Senator Ward empolyed the "Minnesota Radical" to publish a large edition of extras which he sent to every voter in the village The language used on both sides was more emphatic than elegant, and out of that contest grew a strenuously conducted libel suit by Mr Lewis against Mr. Ward It resulted in a judgment of one dollar damages and costs of suit. It was some years before harmonious relations were re-established between the contending factions

GOPHER DAY IN BLOOMING GROVE

For a number of years, the voters of Blooming Grove at their annual town meeting voted to appropriate $25 a year for the killing of gophers June 26 1876, was gopher day, and $23.34 was distributed among the "gopher boys" that day Samuel Remund received the highest award, $4 75, and Charles Wolf the lowest, 30 cents The boys produced satisfactory evidence of having killed 1,548 striped gophers and 171 pocket gophers

THE CENTENNIAL FOURTH OF JULY

The fourth of July, 1876, was celebrated in almost every village and hamlet in the United States, and many of the citizens of this county met at Waseca to observe the day Rev. Loring offered prayer, Mrs Willsey read the Declaration of Independence, Hon Peter McGovern delivered the oration, and Hon. Wm Brisbane was county historian of the day After referring to the general history of the country, Mr Brisbane spoke as follows of the

COUNTY OF WASECA

On the second day of February, 1855, about 3 o'clock p m , a weary, halfstarved party reached the recently erected shanty of Mr Sutlief, about ten miles south of the now thriving young city of Waseca Need I tell you how grateful they felt for the cheering warmth of that humble shanty? Hitherto, for several nights, they had spread their straw beds upon the snow, and you could have followed their trail by the blood in the cattle tracks, for there was a hard crust on the snow at that time which cut the cattle's legs

How strangely inconsistent is the human mind! That night in the humble shanty the hearts of the little party swelled with gratitude, and they thought they were happy But, on the morrow, the country presented such a forlorn and desolute appearance that a sort of despondency began to creep over them The country was covered with snow, and even the trees looked short and stunted The weather was intensely cold Neither houses nor barns nor sheds nor fences could be seen anywhere Like Robinson Crusoe, they were monarchs of all they surveyed They received no letters to tell them of absent friends at home, nor newspapers to instruct or while away an hour, for the nearest postoffice was at Mankato There was no neighbor to drop in and tender a word of comfort, for their nearest neighbors were at Owatonna, twenty miles away Such were the surroundings of the oldest settlers in Waseca county, twenty-one years ago last February

The scripture says that we ought not to take our flight in the winter or on the Sabbath day, yet the oldest settler of the county took his flight in the winter Perhaps he was not well versed in scripture or else he disregarded its teachings Be that as it may, he has learned wisdom from experience, and has now become a teacher of men by publishing a paper of commanding influence in this village And as everything connected with the history of that individual must be interesting, it may not be out of place to mention the difficulties he had to overcome even in getting married In those early days when the oldest settler made up his mind to take unto himself a wife, he went to consult with the man who could make two into one, viz , Esquire Jenkins, a man of rather eccentric character In talking the matter over grave doubts arose whether John Jenkins was really a bona fide justice or not Here was a rather unlooked-for dilemma To solve the problem, John started and actually did walk on foot all the way to St Paul to get Governor Gorman to confirm him as a legal justice of the peace, and thus empower him to bind in the holy bonds of matrimony the oldest settler of Waseca county "

[The statement that there was doubt about Mr Jenkins being a qualified justice and that he walked to St Paul is romance —The Author]

"But now all is changed Instead of traveling thirty-five miles on foot to reach a postoffice, we have plenty of them near at hand Instead of being compelled to send East for a paper and wait four or five weeks after its publication before receiving it, we have three published in the county, and the telegraph to inform us instantly of all matters of importance. Society here, too, will bear favorable comparison with that of any other part of the country.

It is seventeen years last month since I came to Waseca county, and I have sometimes thought I was as great a fool to start in summer as the oldest settler was to start in winter. There was a track, to be sure, but nothing that could be called a road. Bridges, like angels' visits, were few and far between. I thought the clouds that floated over Minnesota were rotten and couldn't hold water, for the rain fell in torrents. I was just a month to a day coming three hundred miles.

In those days we had to go seventy miles to market—often wallowing through the mud, often through the snow—compelled at times to camp out when the thermometer ranged ten degrees below zero. I have often thought that it is a blessing that there is to be no resurrection of the brute creation, for if there were, all eternity would be spent in lawsuits for assaults and batteries upon the poor, dumb animals that hauled our wheat to Hastings. Then we had little or no time for fall plowing. The year before the railroad was built to Waseca I was nine weeks on the road to market with two teams. And what did we get a bushel for our wheat at Hastings? From forty to fifty cents. If we hired the wheat hauled, we had to pay from twenty-five to thirty cents a bushel, which left us the magnificent sum of twenty to twenty-five cents at home. This is no wild and imaginary statement. I recollect selling to Mr Hunter four hundred bushels of wheat at thirty cents a bushel, taking it all in "store pay." I have seen the time when a pound of pork would buy only a pound of salt, in Wilton, and when butter brought only six cents a pound, and—will you believe it—the wagons still screamed for grease. We couldn't afford to grease our wagons for it took much grease to bring a little money, and yet it is just as far to New York now as then. Still we grumble, although we get from three to four times as much now for wheat as we got then. It may be asked, 'How do we get so much more for our wheat now than then?" The question is easily answered. The power of capital and the skill of the engineer and of the mechanic have annihilated distance and brought New York to our doors. In plain language, cheap transportation has doubled and trebled the value of our wheat. * * *

I think I have alluded to the struggles and contests of rival villages and localities for the location of county seats. Waseca county has had her share of these contests. When the county was set off from Steele some four or five places contended for the honor of having the county seat, but Wilton finally won the prize—at least every one thought so. But establishing county seats is something like nominating candidates for the presidency. One or two prominent candidates feel quite sure that they will be nominated, but the various factions can not harmonize, and the consequence is some obscure individual steps to the front and wins the prize. It was just so with Wilton. She thought it was all 'hunkadora' with her so far as the county seat was concerned, but one day an engineer came along with his staff and said he wanted to locate a railroad through Waseca county He did, and he left Wilton out in the cold A station was established about five miles north of her, and then it began to be whispered that it would be better to have the county seat where the county market was This generated a terrible local storm The lightning flashed, the thunder rolled, and the elements jarred so that the Second Adventists declared the crack of doom had come

"When the firing ceased and the smoke of battle cleared away, they began to look around for the dead and wounded, but not a soul was to be found While the Wiltonians slept, the garrison fled, carrying the archives and munitions of war with them They threw up fortifications and entrenched themselves at a place called Waseca, and then swore by the 'Great Jehovah and the Continental Congress' that they had come to stay, and stay they will Now there is not a man in the county but is proud of the county seat And as this is the centennial birthday of our nation, we can not do better than to banish the recollection of past feelings of animosity from our hearts, should any still linger there Let us throw the mantle of forgiveness over all men and stand erect before God and the world, thus proving our title to true manhood Let us forgive those who have wronged us. It is not worth while to hate when so few years are given us in which to love Let our affections and good intentions be strengthened, that our hearts may be lighter and our hands stronger for the life work before us"

HORSES STOLEN AND BARN BURNED

On August 14, 1876, Mr Fred Schultz, residing in Freedom, had a span of young horses stolen from his stable, and the stable, together with another horse and some grain, was consumed by fire Several haystacks were also burned. A fellow named George Buck was caught with the stolen horses at Minnesota Lake the next day and arrested He was afterwards sent to prison.

THE NORTHFIELD BANK ROBBERY

On the 7th of September, in our Centennial year, the James and Younger gang of cutthroats, from Missouri, invaded Northfield, Minn

About 2.30 p m of that day, three armed men entered the bank in Northfield, where Heywood, cashier, Bunker, assistant cashier and Wilcox, clerk, were present They immediately jumped over the counter, through a space of about two feet left for the use of the teller, and cried out, "Hold up your hands! We are going to rob the bank." One of the robbers starting to go into the vault, Heywood followed him and partially closed the vault door The robber pushed Heywood back, and one of the other robbers came to his assistance and struck Heywood on the head with his revolver The two then dragged Heywood again towards the vault, cursing him and telling him to open the safe, the inner door only of which was closed At this time they drew their knives, and one of them drawing his knife across the cashier's neck, making a scratch, again ordered him to open the safe Just at this moment Bunker attracted their attention by starting for the back door One of them immediately fired at him, striking him in the fleshy part of the shoulder. He however, did not stop, but ran out, giving the alarm Failing to make the brave Heywood open the safe, and hearing firing out of doors the robbers started out. The last one jumping over the counter, turned, and placing the muzzle of the revolver within a foot of Heywood's head, shot him in the right temple, killing him instantly

About the time the three robbers entered the bank, six others, three of whom advanced from opposite ends of Main street ,commenced firing revolvers promiscuously right and left, and yelling furiously and profanely ' Get out you s— of a b— !'' The first two shots they fired into Lee & Hitchcock's front windows cutting smooth holes through the glass and tearing great holes in the shelving inside Most of the windows for five hundred feet on both sides of the street bore evidence of the reckless shooting In a few moments quite a number of citizens opened fire on the robbers. A R Manning and Henry Wheeler shot two of the robbers dead and wounded one or two others The people were thoroughly frightened and the robbers soon left, taking with them their wounded

They passed through Dundas and thence into the timber west of Cannon River

The whole country was thoroughly aroused Armed men in this county and throughout Southern Minnesota guarded the highways and watched every avenue of escape until most of the bandits were killed or captured September 27th The following account of the capture of the Younger brothers is from the Mankato Review, which said

"Soon after arriving at Madella we were fortunate in capturing Capt W W Murphy, one of the gallant captors, who rendered valiant service in the memorable fight. From him we learn that the first intelligence was brought to town by Oscar Suborn, a lad about seventeen years old, son of Ole Suborn, who lives in Linden township, Brown county. It seems that the four robbers came to his father's house, on Thursday morning, and asked for breakfast. They were told it was not ready, but if they would wait it would be furnished them. They said that they could not wait, and got some bread and butter, went off some distance from the house and sat down to eat it. They represented themselves as a hunting party, but the family suspected them as being the robbers, and after they left, the boy took a horse from the team his father was using to haul hay, and brought the information to Madelia, four and one-quarter miles distant. The location is in the vicinity of Armstrong lake. Sheriff Glispin was one of the first to receive the intelligence, and within five minutes he and several others were mounted and started. Others were directed to go in other directions to intercept them in their retreat. The first sight Glispin's party had of them was at the right hand outlet of Hanska lake, six miles west of Madelia. Here Glispin called upon them to surrender, but they continued to retreat and shots were exchanged.

"A horse owned by a Norwegian in the pursuing party was wounded, and it is thought fatally. The robbers then waded a slough, Glispin and his party being mounted could not follow them, but had to go round—a distance of several miles. After crossing the slough the robbers made straight for the Watonwan river, which they struck and crossed, at the bend, six miles west of Madelia, and near the house of Andrew Anderson. Glispin and party crossed about a mile east and got in front of them. They saw the robbers, and drove them back into the brush of willows and plum trees lining the bank in that vicinity. By this time horsemen and teams from town and elsewhere began to arrive, and there were probably fifty persons occupying the bluffs. Here the horsemen were dismounted, and recruits called for to charge the brush. Only seven persons responded. James Glispin, sheriff, Ben Rice, son of the ex-senator, of St. James, Capt. W. W. Murphy of Madelia, Geo. Bradford, Chas. Pomeroy, jr., T. L. Vought, of Flander's House; and Jas. Severson, clerk in Yates' store. Others were called for but they refused to respond, and the gallant little band of seven, charged the robbers, passing through the thick brush in a northerly direction until striking the river, when they deployed as skirmishers, their line being formed about five feet apart. Then moving westward, up the river, after going about fifteen rods, they ran upon the four men, secreted in thick willows. Glispin was on the extreme right of the line, advancing in an open path, and being seen by the robbers, a shot was fired at him, which he dodged by falling on his knee, at the same time returning a well-directed shot from his carbine. Seeing Glispin fall, Murphy next at hand supposed him to be shot and he opened fire with his revolver, the rest of the party following suit in rapid succession. Glispin kept up a rapid fire and Murphy having exhausted the six chambers of his revolver, Glispin handed his revolver to Murphy, the party steadily advanced sending volley after volley at the robbers All stood up manfully, not flinching, but each and every one doing his whole duty In the hottest of the fray assistance was called for from those in the rear, but no one responded Then the order to charge was given The man who seemed in advance of the robbers was hit, ran two rods in a cornering direction from the attacking party and fell mortally wounded Cole Younger and his brother were seen to fall and were heard groaning, and the other brother, wounded at Northfield, stepped out of the brush, saying 'Don't fire any more, we are all shot to pieces' The pursuers ordered him to hold up his hands, which he did, and fearing that it was a plan to decoy them, Glispin told his men to take aim at the man, and then commanded him to advance and deliver his pistol to Murphy, which he did The firing ceased, and Glispin's men advancing, found one man dead, and Cole Younger and his brother lying together on the ground badly wounded"

Two of the gang, supposed to be the James brothers left the other murderers and escaped to Dakota on stolen horses As often as their horses tired out they would turn the tired ones loose and steal others. The two were never captured The captured ones plead guilty, thereby under a peculiar statute, escaping hanging They were sent to state s prison for life One of the brothers died in prison, a second committed suicide after being paroled, and Cole, the worst of the brothers, has been pardoned—to the everlasting disgrace of the state

The Pioneer Press of November 23, 1876, paid these cutthroats the following compliment

"The three Missouri bandits and cutthroats—Cole, Jim, and Bob Younger—made their last appearance in St. Paul yesterday At least it is hoped that we may never look upon their ugly mugs again Sheriff Barton, of Rice county, assisted by his son and J. H Passon and Thomas Lloyd, accompanied the convicted scoundrels to the state prison, where they have been sentenced to remain for life * * * Three vulgar and brutal ruffians, every one of whom richly deserves a gibbet, have passed from their reception rooms at Faribault,—where they have been flattered and pampered for weeks, (by the foolish,) and where they have received their visitors with a benignity and patronage that was something royal in its style—to the penitentiary in Stillwater Now let the warden of the prison see that they are kept there The legislature of Minnesota has given these wretches their miserable lives—and it is hoped that an insecure prison will not give them their liberty also"

THE FALL ELECTION.

There were three tickets in the field and the campaign was a very earnest one The Prohibitionists cast five hundred votes straight The following officers were elected

P C Bailey, state senator; Anthony Sampson and Fenton Keenan, representatives, Edgar Cronkhite, auditor, C G Parke, court commissioner, H K Stearns and R O Craig, county commissioners

RAILROAD BONUS

The year closed with an election in Woodville and Waseca in which the people decided by a vote of 266 to 51 to issue the bonds of the town in the sum of $30,000 to aid in the construction of the M & St L railway, the bonds to be issued upon the completion of the road.

CHAPTER XLV, 1877.

COUNTING IN OF PRESIDENT HAYES—LINNEHAN HOUSE BURNED, ALSO HOUSE OF GEO. KLINE—JOHN HABEIN INJURED—DEATH OF MRS BENNETT, MOTHER OF SIXTEEN CHILDREN—BUILDING OF THE M & ST L RAILWAY—DEATHS OF THE YEAR—COMPLETION OF M & ST L RAILWAY, BANQUET AND ADDRESS

The strenuosity of the people of this county during the Centennial year was followed in 1877 by a calm The most exciting affair of the year was the counting in of President Hayes and Vice-president Wheeler At one time anarchy was feared, and even at this time men of the highest intelligence and integrity are wont to speak of the affair between the North and the South at that time as keenly critical The commission that the matter was referred to was composed of five judges of the supreme court, five senators and five representatives—eight Republicans and seven Democrats To the regret of many, the commission divided on party lines

HOUSE BURNED

The house of Mr John Linnehan, of Byron, was destroyed by fire Feb. 4, 1877 Mr and Mrs Linnehan were visiting a brother in the neighborhood at the time In the evening the boys built a fire and went out to do the chores In a short time the house was discovered to be on fire Everything was lost except one feather bed In addition to the loss of household goods, fifty bushels of seed wheat and a harvester were consumed There was an insurance of some $200 on the house.

On the 9th of the same month George Kline one of the "boys" of the First Minnesota, residing in St. Mary, lost his home by fire He awoke about midnight and found his house all on fire His children had a narrow escape from being burned with the house All the household goods, clothing, and everything else in the house were totally consumed He carried insurance to the amount of $500

John Habein, of Blooming Grove, son of Wm Habein, while blasting rock, April 24, 1877, met with a serious accident He was charging a rock, and while driving in brick to confine the powder, it exploded, inflicting a deep wound in the flesh between the thumb and first finger of the right hand, and a severe one on the cheek, just below the eye, carrying away the flesh from the outside corner of the eye nearly to the top of the nose, and blowing his face and hands full of powder and small pieces of brick Fortunately his eyes were not injured He soon recovered

MOTHER OF SIXTEEN CHILDREN

Mrs Esther Bennett, mother of Ed Bennett, Esq, of Waseca died at Tivoli, Blue Earth county on the 14th of May, 1877 Deceased was the mother of sixteen children, fourteen of whom attained their majority—ten males and four females The Bennett family located in Blue Earth county in 1856, and maintained a prominent position in its early history. The deceased was a most estimable lady, highly esteemed by a large acquaintance.

BUILDING OF THE M & ST. L RAILWAY

The Minneapolis and St Louis railroad was construted through Waseca during the year 1877 Thomas White, of Waseca, had the contract for building four miles of the road on each side of Waseca The road was completed to Albert Lea Nov. 7.

MARTIN KRASSIN, OF ST MARY,

Who first visited Waseca county in 1854, and who located here with his family in 1855, died June 1, 1877 Martin Krassin was the son of Gottlieb Krassin, Sr., and was born in Prussia in the year 1821 He came to America with his aged parents and young wife in July 1854 He stopped for a month or two with relatives, near Princeton, Wis, and then made a trip of exploration through Minnesota in company with Mr. John Greening, as noted in the "First Settlement of St. Mary."

OTHER DEATHS

Mrs. Eleanor M Helms, wife of Hon M H. Helms, passed to rest June 30, 1877 She was one of the daughters of Samuel Dodge, who settled near Wilton in 1857. Her age at the time of death was 25 years, nine months. She left surviving her husband and two daughters.

COMPLETION OF MINNEAPOLIS AND ST. LOUIS RAILROAD.

This important line of road, for which the people of Woodville had voted $30,000, was completed in the fall of 1877, and on the 11th day of December of that year, the managers of the road, in connection with the business men of Minneapolis, gave a free ride and a free banquet to five hundred invited guests along the line of the road. Addresses of welcome and responses were delivered, each village and city being represented on the program. To the toast "Waseca," the response was reported by the Minneapolis Tribune as follows·

Mr Child said

"Mr President Waseca rejoices at the completion of the connecting link of road which unites Lake Superior with the lower Mississippi. This is a happy day for Waseca county Her humblest citizen may well feel proud of this grand festal occasion Waseca county, with her streams of pure water, her numerous silvery lake-gems, scattered here and there in every township, her thriving villages, her school houses, her mills, her mercantile enterprises, her banks, her forests and groves of timber, her herds of cattle, her thirteen hundred farms, her granaries crowded with a million bushels of wheat ready for your mammoth mills, her twelve thousand happy and prosperous souls, reaches out her hand to-day across the intervening prairie and woodland, and warmly clasps that of Minneapolis, who, with her palaces of brick and granite, with her merchant princes, with her inexhaustible water power, with her mills of world-wide reputation, with her men of indomitable pluck, with her warm hearted hospitality, has become noted throughout the nation—aye, throughout the civilized world.

"Twenty-three years ago today, the oldest male inhabitant in Waseca county, now living within its borders, belonging to the 'red shirted brigade,' and was engaged in 'swamping' at a lumbering camp on the north branch of the Oconto, in northern Wisconsin. He was a wild, fanatical fellow. One evening by the camp-fire, after reading a friend's letter descriptive of Southern Minnesota, he made up his mind to pack his 'turkey' and make a winter trip to the land of promise.

"On the 6th of January, 1855, he and two other venturesome men, one of whom now sleeps in the Wilton cemetery, and the other of whom, poor fellow, is engaged as assistant postmaster in the United States senate, started for Minnesota with ox teams On the 2d day of February, 1855, they arrived in what is now Waseca county, having camped two nights in the open air, on Minnesota snow banks One lone shanty was all there was of civilization to break the native solitude of the prairie and woodland, from Straight river to the frontier town of Mankato. What a change in these twenty-four years! This occasion will not permit even a glance at the hardships, the privations, the struggles, the heroic labors of those who first broke the prairie sod and started civilization in a new country But the people of Freeborn, Waseca, LeSueur, Rice, and Scott counties, who a few years ago were seen carting their wheat to Hastings, camping at night by the roadside, in fair weather and in storm, need not to be reminded of these scenes, for they have been written upon the tablets of memory by the hand of experience; and that experience prompts every heart to rejoice that to-day we may visit the metropolis of the state, in palatial railroad cars—going in the morning and returning to our own firesides in the evening The day of slow coaches, foundered horses, and brave (sometimes tyrannical) stage drivers has passed, and in place thereof we have the iron horse with his train of rolling palaces—the grandest production of American capital, skill and ingenuity Waseca joins with Albert Lea, Hartland, Richland, Waterville, Kilkenny, Montgomery, New Prague, and Jordan in accepting the hospitality of this city, on the 'Minneapolis plan,' and will contribute her full share toward the upbuilding of the dual city at the head of navigation, on the grandest river of North America

"But this is a digression Waseca is the theme. Well, Waseca is noted for many things She is noted for a variety of statesmen She has more 'honorables' to the square mile than any other county in the state Some are as wisely silent as Gen Grant, while others are as noisy—if not as wise—as 'Sunset' Cox or Wendell Phillips She boasts of six hundred men who, with clear heads and untainted breath, at the last election, cast their ballots in favor of 'destroying the destroyer of millions' and freeing our land of a slavery more intolerable than that which drenched Southern soil with the blood of our fathers and brothers

"She is noted for her rich and productive soil, for her industrious and well-to-do farmers, for her No 1 wheat, for her pleasant and comfortable homes, for her four newspaper offices, for her numerous churches and numerous saloons, almost equaling Minneapolis, and for her enterprising business men in every branch of trade

"In 1876 she produced from 47,877 acres 475,177 bushels of wheat That was the lightest crop ever raised in the county This year from fifty thousand acres, she has produced one million bushels of wheat She boasts of over three thousand work horses, thirteen hundred beef and working cattle, four thousand milch cows, thirteen hundred farmers' families, sixty-nine thousand acres of plowed land, and numerous cultivated groves containing 265,000 forest trees

"The sheep of Waseca county in 1876 produced 9,089 pounds of wool; the cows produced 283,250 pounds of butter, and 4,288 pounds of cheese, the bees, 136 hives, produced 1,629 pounds of honey, the apple trees in bearing, numbering 5,629, produced 2,325 bushels of apples The total amount of hay saved was 27,384 tons

"It is a glorious, good county, a near relation to the garden of Eden, and, as its Indian name implies, is a 'land of plenty,' 'abundant in food' and contains as much solid mud to the square mile, on a rainy day, as any county in the state

"But on this occasion we may all look beyond the limits of our several localities and join in congratulating one another upon the national importance of the completion of the thoroughfare that now unites the great unsalted seas' of the North with the never freezing waters of the Sunny South And we do not and should not forget that the success of this important enterprise is due to the energy and labors of President Washburn and his Minneapolis co-workers To the ability and courage of such men the people of the state owe a large debt of gratitude Without doubt all will join in expressing the hope that the fraternal relations now existing between the North and the South, the East and the West, may grow with our growth and strengthen with our advancing years, and that ere the close of another decade the people will have cast aside all local prejudices so that our great natural highway by way of New Orleans may be utilized to the fullest extent by the millions that are to possess the great valley of the Mississippi

Waseca is proud to be represented here to-day by so many of her citizens, and rejoices in the fact that Minneapolis and St Paul are now within a few hours ride of our happy hunting grounds We cordially invite our friends of these cities to visit our goodly land that flows with the milk of human kindness and the honey of Christian charity—except about election time—and to learn how good and how pleasant it is to dwell in the land of plenty where every one sits by his own fireside and calls no man master"

CHAPTER XLVI, 1878.

MILD WINTER—SOCIAL AND MORAL WORK—MRS FOSTER'S TEMPERANCE REVIVAL—MRS STEVENSON FOUND DEAD—LINES ON THE DEATH OF MRS STEVENSON BY MARY DAYTON—BUILDING OF THE COUNTY JAIL—COURT SCENE, LAUGHABLE AND DISGRACEFUL—RICHARD TONER AND ANNIE McCANN BURNED TO DEATH—NEW JAIL BROKEN—JIM JOHNSON SHOT—D C FREELAND—FIRE COMPANY ORGANIZED

The winter of 1877-8 was one of the mildest in the history of the state Frost came out of the ground in January so that plowing was done in some localities during that month There was very little snow all winter and no sleighing For several weeks the roads were dry and dusty Some farmers sowed wheat in February The Mississippi River from St. Paul to New Orleans was free from ice as early as March 8.

SOCIAL AND MORAL

Owing to the mild weather, no doubt, there was considerable doing in the way of lectures and social gatherings during the season. The month of January, in Waseca, brought a great temperance revival Mrs J Ellen Foster, then a noted lecturer and attorney, of Iowa, delivered a series of powerful lectures, or addresses, in Waseca

THE LECTURES

The local paper, speaking of Mrs Foster's work, said "Mrs. Foster has taken the town by storm She has started a good work The "Blue Ribbon" is a success Mrs Foster's lectures, delivered in this place since last Thursday, together with the terrible death of Mrs. Stevenson, whose body was found last Sunday morning, have created an emotional temperance sentiment in this place which we hope may settle down to something sound, substantial and practical.' The death of Mrs Stevenson was detailed in the local paper of Jon 9, 1878, as follows·

TERRIBLE DEATH OF MRS. STEVENSON.

"It is with a sad heart that we record the fearful death of Mrs S J Stevenson, wife of the late deputy sheriff of this county, who was found within thirty feet of the Catholic church of this village and only a few rods from her own home, last Sunday morning, frozen to death, with an empty bottle in which there had been whisky. There is no reason to doubt that she came to her death while in a drunken condition, as for years she had been more or less addicted to the use of liquor—was, in fact, a slave to its power

"She was found by Mr Breen's son and James B Hayden, clerk of the court When first discovered the body was in a kneeling posture, the face, knees, and toes resting upon the ground and the body bent as though she had fallen while on her knees, thus her spirit passed beyond the vale.

"She leaves four children—two daughters, who have reached womanhood, and two little boys

"When sober, she was one of the kindest and best of women, especially in sickness, and with the exception of this fault was a respectable, kind-hearted woman She was about fifty years of age"

The death of Mrs Stevenson brought forth the following lines from Miss Mary E Dayton, then a young school teacher, afterwards Mrs Shepard, now deceased The lines were so sincere and true that the author offers no apology for reproducing the following extracts from the poem

LINES ON THE DEATH OF MRS STEVENSON

"Gone to the earth, returned to dust!
Gone to her maker, too, we trust
Her life is done, her work is o'er,
Now she will rest forever more
She knew no happiness in life
But much she knew of toil and strife,
She once was young and very fair—
Alas! she knew not then the snare
That would enfold her in its grasp,
Till human power and help were past
She fell into the tempter's power,

He met her in an evil hour
She sinned and fell, 'tis plain to all,
She lost her pride, her hope, her all
She yielded to the demon rum,
Not thinking of the harm to come,
Until too late, his grasp she felt
Ah, where's the heart that would not melt
Before a scene so sad, yet true?
Picture the agony she knew!
Not ours the right to judge, but learn
From sin and evil now to turn,
Oh! man, Oh! youth, beware, beware,
We're all beset by many a snare,

* * *

When tempted oft to turn astray,
Remember God, the living way
Think well before one glass you take,
Before His holy law you break,
Think of that creature once so pure,
Think of the woe that came to her!
Think of her lying stiff and cold,
Think of her poor immortal soul!
'Tis true she sinned, but who is he
Who sinneth not? If such there be,
His is the right to judge of one
Who sitteth now before God's throne."

DEATH OF MRS NATHANIEL WOOD

Mrs Amelia Wood, wife of Mr Nathaniel Wood, who settled in Woodville in 1855, died Feb 6, 1878, at the advanced age of seventy-six She was a native of Vermont, and was the mother of Messrs. Eri G., Loren C and Luman Wood, and Mrs. J. K Meyers, Mrs Scott, Mrs G R Buckman, and Mrs. R. M Addison

COUNTY JAIL BUILDING.

For several years the county commissioners, under the wise counsel of Auditor Cronkhite, had been creating a fund for the building of a jail, and on the 20th of March, 1878, the contract for building the same was let to W B Craig & Co , their bid being $9,333. Conrad, Bohn & Co. bid $9,445 The contract required the completion of the building on or before the first of the following October.

WHOLESALE INDICTING

The temperance people of the county were very active in 1878 At the March term of court, thirteen indictments were found by the grand jury against as many different persons in New Richland for selling liquor unlawfully. Nearly all of them plead guilty and were fined $50 and costs of prosecution

THE FOURTH OF JULY

this year was celebrated by our people quite generally Public meetings were held in Blooming Grove, Otisco, Janesville, New Richland, and Waseca Rev R Forbes and James E Child delivered addresses in Blooming Grove, Hon Wm Brisbane delivered the oration at New Richland, Rev. Gilbert Shaw addressed the people of Otisco, there was a circus at Janesville a picnic at Waseca, and a church celebration and dinner at St Mary

LAUGHABLE AND DISGRACEFUL

As far back as 1878 it was not unheard of for attorneys, while under the influence of liquor, to try cases

The following actually occurred in Waseca—names alone being fictitious The affair is given as reported at the time

"A laughable and at the same time a disgraceful scene occurred in Hon B Smyth's court, last Wednesday The plaintiff was a man named Taylor, a lithe, supple, plucky chap, and the defendant, a Mr Gove. Lawyer Cole appeared for plaintiff and Lawyer Jones for defendant. The plaintiff was put upon the stand and all went as usual until the cross-examination, when some sharp words ensued Jones called the witness a d——n gambler, whereupon the witness told Jones he was a d——n liar

"That was too much for Jones, he seized a chair and raised it, threatening to knock the witness' brains out Taylor, not to be outdone in politeness, as quick as a flash also presented a chair Cole rushed to a corner and called for a revolver, the jurors ducked their heads, one behind another expecting every moment the crash of arms, the justice commenced gathering up his papers, men from the street rushed wildly to the scene of conflict, everything was in suspense until two seconds rushed in and prevented the flow of gore by parting the combatants Lawyer Jones, being disarmed, paced up and down like a caged lion, asserting that he was a respectable citizen of Waseca, and that he would not take such an insult from a tramp Whereupon Taylor informed him that he (Taylor) was not a tramp, and moreover that Lawyer Jones was not even a respectable citizen And then the valorous Jones again approached Taylor with clenched fists and flashing eyes threatening a terrible lesson in pugilism Taylor again assumed a fighting posture, and no one can tell how much blood might have flowed had not Constables Roddle and Stevenson rushed between them. Disgusted at his failure to cross-examine the witness over the head with a chair, Jones left the court in contempt After his departure the court held the scales of justice in equal poise and finished the trial—peace and harmony prevailing"

RICHARD TONER AND ANNIE McCANN BURNED TO DEATH

One of the saddest occurrences in the history of the county transpired August 27, 1878 The following account was given at the time by John J Toner, son of Richard Toner:

"The inmates of the house were Mr and Mrs Toner, the parents, who slept below, John J. Toner, their son, a young man, and two hired men, two daughters, young women, and the girl, Annie McCann, all of whom slept in rooms upstairs Mary Toner, the older daughter, first discovered the fire about fifteen minutes after one o'clock, Tuesday morning, in the southeast corner of the building, upstairs, next to the kitchen She at once gave the alarm John, as soon as awakened, went below and called to his parents, and then went out with one of the hired men, thinking to extinguish the fire He soon found that the fire was beyond control and went back to the front door of the main building His sister then told him that the McCann girl was still upstairs He sent for a ladder whereby they might reach the chamber window Just then one of the daughters said 'father is still in the house' John then went to the open bed-room window and reached into the bed but could not find his father He then called him. At this time the smoke and heat were stifling and he turned his head to get a fresh breath When he turned again he found his father prostrate with his head in the window By this time, the fire was over head and all around them One of the men came to assist, but both were unable to succeed in removing the old gentleman and were driven back by the fire The other man also made an attempt to reach the window, but was driven back by the fire Nothing more could be done, and, Mr Toner and the girl perished in the flames Nearly everything in the house was consumed Mr Richard Toner was one of the oldest settlers of the county, having settled in Iosco in 1856 He was about 65 years of age He leaves a large family and an extensive circle of friends to mourn his sad death Of late years he has been a sober, exemplary citizen, and universally liked and respected on account of his generosity and neighborly deportment

"The origin of the fire is unknown One of the men, desiring to use some warm water, as late as eleven o'clock the evening before was in the kitchen, but saw no fire

"It is a sad affair, and casts a gloom over the whole community"

THE ELECTION OF 1878

The campaign of this year was one of intense feeling and excitement There were four tickets in the field—Temperance, Greenback, Democrat, Republican The vote on state senator was as follows: S B Williams, temperance, 729, P C Bailey, republican, 464, Fenton Keenan, democrat, 443 W D. Armstrong, greenback, 274 John S Abell temperance, received 570 votes and was elected representative, while John Thompson, republican, was elected by a vote of 553 over Ira D Beaman, temperance, who received 505 votes Mr E Cronkhite, candidate on both the temperance and democratic tickets, was re-elected by a vote of 745. The total vote of the county this year was 1,922

NEW JAIL BROKEN

Scarcely had the new jail been completed when the four inmates came very near making their escape They cut off one of the bars with a common, steel table-knife, unlocked the scuttle door leading into the attic with an old key went into the attic and knocked a hole through the brick wall, on the north side, close to the cornice Sheriff Keeley's attention was attracted by the noise, and he and Jailor Long proceeded to drive the culprits back into their cells Evidently the jail was not burglar proof

MARRIAGES, DEATHS, AND MISCELLANEOUS EVENTS

The marriage of Mr Martin Haley and Miss Ellen Collins, at Waseca, by Father Christie, Feb. 25, 1878, was quite a society event Mr Haley had been captain of the champion baseball club of the state, and was son of Mr Patrick Haley, one of the well-to-do and early settlers of Blooming Grove Miss Collins was a sister of Sheriff Collins, of Waseca Mr John Kahnke and Miss Mary Matz, of St Mary were married the next day—Feb 26 Mr. Kahnke is one of the young old settlers of the county. Mr H N Carlton, one of the earliest boysettlers of Woodville, married Miss Lovica Smith, daughter of A C Smith October 1878 The bride was the first white child born in the town of Woodville.

Mr A E Crumb, of Byron, an early settler, died Jan 30, 1878, of lingering consumption, aged fifty years He had resided in the county about fourteen years

Mrs Louise A Ballard, the first woman married within the

limits of Waseca county (then Blue Earth county), died August 15, 1878, aged forty-one years, at Decoria, Blue Earth county. She left a family of ten children She was the daughter of Mr and Mrs Bernard Gregory, now deceased, who settled in St. Mary in 1855

James Johnson, son of Isaac Johnson, both early settlers in this county, was accidentally shot near Mapleton, Nov 10, 1878 It appears that he had been hunting, in company with his brother William and two others, and was returning home in a buggy He had the butt end of his gun on the bottom of the buggy, and leaned forward to let one of the company have some tobacco When he straightened back, the gun slipped, striking the hammer on the bottom of the buggy, and discharging the contents into his thigh, severing the femoral artery. He only lived a few seconds, and spoke but a few words "Jim," as he was familiarly called, was one of the famous players of the "Champion Base Ball Club" of this county and had many warm friends

Mr D C Freeland, one of the early settlers of Vivian and a man of high character, died of ulceration of the liver, Nov 26, 1878. He was son-in-law of Mr Wm. Hoover He left surviving him a widow and three sons His widow is now Mrs. A T. Wolcott, and his sons are prosperous residents of the Pacific coast at Portland, Oregon

THE FIRST FIRE COMPANY

The following appeared in the local paper June 26, 1878

"We, whose names are hereunto subscribed, propose to start an independent fire company for the protection of all property in the corporate limits of the village of Waseca We respectfully ask the assistance of all property holders.

M V Hunt, M O Forbes, James Wert, C M Oster, F M Smith, Thos Breen, J M Robertson, W H Roddle, C McKenna, Jos Smith, Edward Castor, B. F. Forbes, Wm Blowers, F B Johnson, L C Clug, Gust Schillknecht, C M Baker, Gust Thom, Ed Fisk, Eugene Fisk, H. E Strong Henry Herbst, John F White, E W. Cummings, Walter Child, J Niebels The following officers were elected: foreman, Dr M V Hunt, 1st assistant, E W Fisk, 2d assistant, John White; treasurer, Frank Forbes secretary, C M Baker, executive committee, Dr. Hunt, W H Roddle, L C Klug."

CHAPTER XLVII, 1879.

FINANCIAL DEPRESSION—ROADS AND BRIDGES—DIED, O F. WAGGONER, MRS LUCINA GRAY, MR WARNER, OF OTISCO, MICHAEL BOHEN, REV GILBERT SHAW—REUNION OF THE FIRST MINNESOTA AT WASECA—ADDRESS OF WELCOME BY PRESIDENT McCORMICK—JUDGE LOCHREN'S ADDRESS—"THE CHARGE AT GETTYSBURG"—COPY OF THE "FIRST MINNESOTA"—HEAVY STORMS OF THE YEAR—HORSE THIEF AND HIS REVOLVER—THE FALL ELECTION

Ring out the old, ring in the new,
Ring happy bells across the snow
The year is going, let him go
Ring out the false, ring in the true
Ring out the grief that saps the mind
For those that here we see no more?
Ring out the feud of rich and poor,
Ring in redress to all mankind
Ring out the want, the care, the sin,
The faithless coldness of the times,
Ring in the common love of good
Ring out old shapes of foul disease,
Ring out the narrowing lust of gold,
Ring out the thousand wars of old,
Ring in the thousand years of peace
Ring in the valiant man and free,
The larger heart the kindlier hand,
Ring out the darkness of the land,
Ring in the Christ that is to be—Tennyson

The financial depression which set in about 1868 as a result of the retiring of greenbacks and the refunding of the national bonds, had forced upon the people the utmost economy and economy in living always brings prosperity And thus it was that as a rule the people found themselves in the enjoyment of general prosperity in 1879.

ROADS AND BRIDGES

The board of county commissioners for 1879 consisted of Hon. R. O. Craig, John Brady, Thomas K. Bowe, Wm Burke, and H K. Stearns—all Democrats except Mr Stearns. Hon R. O. Craig was elected chairman The jail having been built the year before, and being nearly or quite all paid for, the board became fairly liberal in appropriating money for roads and bridges At the January session $43 21 additional was appropriated for replanking the bridge across Bull Run in Freedom At the March session, appropriations were made as follows: $150 to build bridge across Le Sueur river in New Richland, $80 for building road on line of sections 24 and 25, in New Richland, and $70 for building road through section 8 of same town, $249 49 for a bridge across the Le Sueur river near Markham's town of Alton, $53 for planking Alma City bridge, $50 for grading hill on road between the towns of Iosco and Blooming Grove, near McWaide's, $50 for grading hills on Faribault road in Blooming Grove, $50 for repairing road near Alfred Smith's in Blooming Grove, $25 for making road across slough, on section 14, town of Iosco, $40 for improvement of road between W Timlin s place and Iosco creek; $35 for building road near Martin Dewald's place in Iosco, $200 for constructing road on line between sections 22 and 27, 23 and 26, and 24 and 25, in town of St Mary, and between sections 19 and 20 in Woodville The county surveyor was ordered to make plans and specifications for building a bridge across McDougall creek, in the town of Otisco At the session of the board May 20, 1879 ,the following additional appropriations were made: $314 to J J Headley for building the McDougall creek bridge, $14 81 additional for replanking the Alma City bridge, $200 for building road in the town of Byron on the line of the Vivian and New Richland county road, $25 for road near John Keeley's farm in St Mary, $75 for repairing Waseca and Morristown road near Rice Lake, $300 to assist in building road across the outlet of Lake Elysian on town line between Janesville and Alton, provided $300 be first expended on said road by the towns of Alton and Janesville or by citizens thereof, $25 to aid the construction of a road on line between sections 23 and 25, in town of New Richland

THE DEATH LIST OF 1879

Mr. O. F. Waggoner, who came to this state at a very early day with the Winnebago tribe of Indians, died of convulsions, Jan 6, 1879, at the age of about sixty years He settled on the Winnebago Indian reservation in 1855, and when the Winnebagoes moved west, he located near Alma City. His son, Mr John Waggoner, at this writing, 1905, resides in Alton near Alma City.

Mrs. Luema Gray, widow of Wm M Gray, deceased, of Blooming Grove, died March 25, 1879 She was one of the earliest settlers of the county, having come here in the early summer of 1855 She was about seventy years of age and left a large family of children and grandchildren to mourn her departure

Mr Michael Bohen, one of the early settlers of St Mary, died of hemorrhage of the lungs, August 16, 1879 He arose in the morning feeling as well as usual, went to the barn to do his chores and while there commenced coughing and spitting blood Soon blood flowed in a stream from his mouth and he died in about ten minutes He left a wife and five children.

Rev Gilbert Shaw, then postmaster at Wilton, died October 25, 1879, of hemorrhage of the lungs Mr Shaw was an active, earnest Christian minister

THE FIRST MINNESOTA REUNION

The veterans of the "Old First Minnesota Regiment of Volunteers" held their twelfth annual reunion at Waseca, June 18, 1879 It occurred on one of those beautiful Minnesota days when it is just warm enough to be comfortable and just cool enough to be agreeable The morning opened with the firing of artillery and a general display of flags on most of the buildings A large flag, with "Welcome, First Minnesota," inscribed upon it, was suspended over the street between the McCue and Trowbridge blocks, and wreaths of oak leaves decorated with flags were stretched across the streets at various points. Turner Hall was decked with flags, flowers, and wreaths of green leaves, the whole presenting a pleasing and attractive scene

At 2.30 p m a procession was formed at the union depot.

under the direction of Maj Young, and marched in the following order.

1 Waseca Hose Company.
2 Band and Drum Corps.
3 Mayor and City Council
4 Committee of Reception
5 Veterans of the First Minnesota Infantry
6 Artillery.
7 Carriages and Citizens

The line of march was through the principal streets to Oak Grove, just northeast of Turner Hall The veterans bore the tattered remnants of their old colors, followed by one piece of artillery captured by the First Minnesota battery at Cheraw, South Carolina, and another gun presented by the United States minister to Belgium to the First Minnesota regiment for gallantry in the first Bull Run fight

Arriving at the grounds, the people were seated, and R L. McCormick, Esq, president of the village board, delivered, in an eloquent manner, a well considered address of welcome to the First Minnesota, in which he tendered to the boys the hospitalities of the city

The following extracts from his welcome are worthy of permanent record

The War of the Rebellion is over Its history is daily receiving accessions. Its incidents are still fresh in our minds, and its battles are as familiar as the names of the cities of our own state Upon this field, to which others can do much more complete and ample justice, I will not trespass further than to say that Bull Run, Ball's Bluff, Yorktown, West Point, Fair Oaks, Peach Orchard, Savage Station, Glendale, White Oak Swamp, Malvern Hill, Antietam, Charlestown, Fredericksburg, Haymarket, Gettysburg, Bristow Station, and Mine Run, carry with them their story of the struggle and of the honorable part taken in it by the First Minnesota Before our posterity we would compare Gettysburg with the equally decisive battle of Waterloo. Vicksburg with Salamis, Lookout Mountain with Thermopylae, and Sherman's famous march to the sea with the retreat of Xenophon's immortal ten thousand, and high in the annals of military achievements, side by side with the names of the most illustrious commanders of ancient or modern times, Caesar, Alexander, Napoleon, Frederick of Prussia, or a Wellington, we would point with pride after the immortal Washington, to the record of our Grant, our Sherman, and our Sheridan, who attained their proud eminence and fame by the unflinching courage of regiments like the First Minnesota, whose cheeks did not blanch and whose hearts did not quail when they met the shock of battle. When the Congress was set on fire by the Merrimac, in the mouth of James River of the 434 men of her command, only one-half responded to their names the next morning at Newport News The dead were buried at that place and their remains lie among those of scores of Union soldiers On a board in the form of a cross at the head of the grave of one of these latter, whose name and history were unknown, was placed the most touching, beautiful, and poetical epitaph "A soldier of the Union mustered out" Soldiers of the First Minnesota, your term of active service is completed You have been honorably discharged, but at each year's annual reunion you find some of your number have been again and finally mustered out. This year, with others of the First, whose names are familiar to me, the gallant Sully has gone to join the brave who lost their lives when he led your regiment at Savage Station and Malvern Hill On the roll of Company K, of your regiment, is the name of a cousin of mine, through whose correspondence I received my most vivid and practical ideas of army experience in camps, on the march, and in the heat of battle From him I learned the story of the two days' fight at Gettysburg, the thrilling narration of the crisis in the second day's battle, when Hancock, pushed to extremity to gain five minutes time, ordered the First Minnesota alone and unaided to charge a whole division of the rebel army To-day history points with pride and admiration to the unquestioning and unflinching courage of the four hundred men of the Minnesota First, marching to certain death against and into the fire of 6,000 of the Rebel army Against such overwhelming numbers that, as you met them in your invincible strength you could only hold their center, while to the right and left of you they swept around your flanks, enfilading your ranks with terrible death To the surprise and rage of your enemies, as well as the admiration of unborn generations, you held your advance until the supporting columns of Hancock's Corps wheeled into position and relieved and rescued you

"Out of the jaws of death,
Out of the mouth of hell,
All that were left of you,
Left of four hundred"

The day was saved, and the few survivors of that terrible sacrifice were enrolled among the immortal heroes of the ages * * *

Homer was unknown and unhonored by the age he lived in, he was a stranger to the men he walked with and talked with as if his very nearness in outward presence diverted their gaze from his rare genius, but in after times he moved in upon the world like a great orb of light through the open portals of reflection and communion, and those who sat under the magic of his far-shining beams were the first to know and honor his title to the laurel wreath of fame The scholar of to-day with a long reach of centuries coming in to fill the space between him and old Rome, knows

Rome more minutely and more broadly than Rome knew herself; comprehends more fully Roman law, Roman literature and Roman life, and understands more clearly the direction and scope of Roman influence. And when that day comes when honor will be fully done to whom honor is due, the soldiers of the First Minnesota will be found among the immortal throng of those to whose fame poets will vie in singing praises and to whose memory, affection and admiration will erect in the hearts of the citizens of this broad commonwealth monuments even more enduring than towering shafts of polished marble Soldiers' welcome to Waseca"

Hon Alexander Ramsey, who was governor of Minnesota at the outbreak of the Rebellion in 1861, was present and gave a short history of the mustering in of the regiment and of its glorious record

The following answered to roll call

COMPANY A

Stephen Lyons, Wayzata
E J Palmer, Jordan
W Mattheis, St Paul
John Halstead, St Paul

COMPANY B

Myron Shepard, Stillwater
A A Capron, Stillwater
John P Dunsmore, Stillwater
William Darich, Stillwater
C A Bromley, Stillwater.
James Cleary, Stillwater
Adam Marty, Stillwater
John Cooper, Bloomington
Chas Valentine, Minneapolis
Ed A Stevens, Minneapolis

COMPANY C

M Sherman, St Paul

COMPANY D

A A Laflin, Maple Grove
Wm Garvey, Kasson

COMPANY E.

Wm Lochren, Minneapolis
M Taylor, Dayton
J. B Ellison, Minneapolis
E B Lowell, Minneapolis
G S Lewis, Lake Crystal

COMPANY F

W H Hoyt, St Paul

COMPANY G

S G Flanders, Faribault
Geo F. Johnston, Janesville
John Rohrer, Morristown
Benj Buck, Morristown
E Phillips, Owatonna
C B Jackson, Morristown
Geo Thom, Brownton
E Hollister, Warsaw
E E Verplank, New Richland
I DuBois, Owatonna

E Z Needham, Farmington
J. H. Johnston, Minneapolis.
G R Buckman, Waseca
Philo Hall, Waseca
C M Benson, Morristown
Samuel Reynolds, Waterville
J S Bemis, Waterville
W. W Brown, Kilkenny
L J Mosher, New Sharon, Ia
E D Haskins, Faribault
H C Whitney, Faribault
George Magee, Faribault.

COMPANY H

Chas. Mansfield, Mankato.
John C Shaffer, Chicago, Ill
Chas. Shatts, Minneapolis

COMPANY I

Richard L Gorman, St Paul.
A E. Rider, Oak Centre
James Cannon, Mankato
Geo Klein, Janesville
Omer H Sutlief, New Richland
Theodore Golden, St Paul
Milo S Whitcomb, Faribault

COMPANY K

M McEntyre, Mankato
W H Churchill, Stockton.
Gus Coy, Mankato
C H Andrus, Mankato

COMPANY L

A J Underwood, Fergus Falls
Evans Goodrich, Mankato
J T Dahl, Waseca.

NON-COMMISSIONED STAFF

Frank Dickinson, Redwood Falls
J W Pride, Jr , Shingle Creek

The first day of the reunion was spent by the veterans, after listening to the address of welcome and to the congratulatory speech of ex-Governor Ramsey, in social chat and in getting acquainted with the people of Waseca In the evening there was a big campfire, attended by nearly all the people in Waseca. On the second day the great attraction was the address of Hon William Lochren, at this writing one of the United States district judges of Minnesota Judge Lochren's address was really a condensed history of the regiment The following extract is a gem in the record made by the men of the "First" After mentioning the other battles in which the regiment participated he described the great battle of Gettysburg, and concluded as follows

"During the forenoon of the second day we were in reserve except that three companies were detached for the support of batteries Still we were within the range of artillery and some of our men were wounded from shells.

"After noon we were moved to the left to support a battery on the position from which Sickle's corps had advanced against the enemy. There on the crest of a slight ridge we could see about a half mile in our front the conflict between our forces under Sickles and the enemy who were giving away before him. Seldom had we such an opportunity of viewing a battle, in which we were not engaged, and great was the anxiety as to the result, as our men would at times seem to press the enemy, and at other times to yield to superior force. At length the vastly increased volume of musketry told plainly of stronger reinforcements on the side of the enemy, and soon we saw with alarm that our men were overpowered and retiring, at first slowly, but soon in confusion and disorder and presently in full retreat, passing our position, while the bullets from the enemy begun to whistle past us as they advanced steadily in well-formed lines of battle, apparently fifteen or twenty thousand strong, and had nearly reached the dry run at the foot of the ridge. Had they succeeded in getting to our position they would have turned the left flank of our army and been in its rear and must have forced the position, if supported by an attack in front, and won the battle. At that moment Gen. Hancock, our corps commander, galloped up to our little band which was about three hundred strong, and calling to Col. Colville, asked, "Colonel, will your men charge these lines?" A glance showed what was meant.

"It was necessary that the regiment should be sacrificed to save the army, by delaying for a short time the advance of the enemy until the Sixth corps, in reserve, could be moved to the position. Every man saw the necessity and knew what was expected. It was apparently certain death, but there was no faltering. The Old First had never failed to go where ordered, and never had retired without orders. As Napoleon's Old Guard at Waterloo threw itself in front of the whole allied army to save the emperor, every man was nerved at the instant, and stepped off promptly, as the command "Forward" came from our gallant colonel. "Double-Quick" followed the next instant, and down that declivity rushed the handful of devoted men, the speed increasing with every stride, but the numbers melting away under the storm of lead such as men never faced before, which was poured into us from the enemy's whole force. Rapid as was our pace, it seemed as if none would reach the enemy, but the survivors struck them with the force of a projectile, just as they were beginning to cross the run. The suddenness and vigor of the charge and prompt use of the bayonet, caused a recoil, and soon cleared the run of ten times our numbers, and the first line of the enemy broke to the rear in confusion. Sheltering ourselves as well as we could in the run, we opened fire on the enemy in front, having to sustain not only the fire from the front, but from both flanks, as far as they could reach us. But the enemy's whole advance was checked. How long we held this position I could never estimate but for a sufficient time to enable the reserve to occupy the position, and until we were commanded to fall back. But of the three hundred who made that charge, not more than seventy-five returned scathless, and when our dead and wounded were gathered, not a man was missing"

Immediately after Judge Lochren's address, a public banquet was served, followed by toasts and short speeches. In response to the toast, "The Press," a well preserved copy of "The First Minnesota," printed and published by the boys while in the service, was presented by the speaker This copy, the only one known to be in existence, was furnished by Neri Reed, of Iosco, in this county This paper was published at Berryville, Va, March 11, 1862, by the boys of the "First." It was edited and published by Ed A Stevens, Frank J Mead, T H Presnell and two others whose names I do not call to mind Mr. Stevens gave a short history of capturing the printing office and issuing two editions of a loyal paper on the "sacred soil" of old Virginia Ex-Governor Ramsey secured the paper and deposited it in the archives of the State Historical Society.

HEAVY STORMS

There was a terrific hail storm on the 12th of May, 1879, which did much damage The fruit trees and small fruit were badly injured The window glass on the south side of nearly every building was broken more or less Hail stones as large as ordinary hens' eggs covered the ground in many places, while those of an ounce in weight were numerous J F Murphy measured one chunk of ice, which was two inches in diameter Many a window looked as if it had been riddled with bullets The post office building, in particular, received considerable damage The sky-lights to Palmer's photograph gallery were almost entirely destroyed

The public buildings injured were · The Baptist church, 21 lights of glass, the school buildings, 47 court house 13, English M E church, 54, Congregational church, 19 Turner hall, 13 There was scarcely a dwelling in the village not injured more or less The grain was not far enough advanced to be materially injured

Another storm visited the county May 27, 1879 There was a heavy rainfall, accompanied by a strong wind Weak fences were blown down, out-houses were upset, shade trees were injured, some shanties were unroofed, lumber piles suffered, and chimney extensions flew around with perfect looseness The marshes and streams filled with water and the whole surface of the country was pretty well wet down.

Speaking of the storms of July 1 and 2, a local paper said

"Last week, Tuesday and Wednesday night, terrific rain storms visited a large portion of the state In some places west of us the wind and hail entirely destroyed the small grain, and did much damage to other crops In some parts of Nicollet county, buildings were blown down, and some cattle injured In Blue Earth county, near the Waseca county line, west of Freedom, considerable damage was done Mr. Gunzolus, of this county, had his granary blown down and his house partly unroofed. In Steele county, many buildings were torn in pieces, some persons injured, and some cattle killed At Vassa, Goodhue county, dwellings were torn in pieces, seven persons killed outright, and thirty others more or less injured. News comes from all portions of the state of local tornadoes doing more or less damage. In this county, with the exception of a small tract in Freedom, no serious damage was done to the crops The rainfall was very heavy, probably as heavy as in other portions of the state, and there were local dashes of hail, but the wind, with the exception noted in Freedom, was not heavy"

FOURTH OF JULY

The Catholic society of Waseca held a picnic for the benefit of their church—the net receipts being $200 New Richland held a formal celebration, Hon William Brisbane and Hon. M. D L Collester being the orators of the day Blooming Grove did herself proud, as usual, Rev William Pagenhart and James E. Child being the speakers. The Erwin family and neighbors, in St Mary, observed the day in a formal manner—the venerable P. A Erwin, then eighty-two years of age, presiding The ladies furnished a most appetizing dinner and all fared sumptuously

HORSE THIEF AND HIS REVOLVER

On July 16, 1879, Mr Finger Fingerson, of Blooming Grove, had a horse stolen, and on Thursday a man, giving his name as Frank Carr, stopped at Esquire Northrup's on the road between Waterville and Morristown, to borrow a saddle Mr Northrup being suspicious of him, questioned him pretty closely, and finally concluded that he had stolen a horse, and ordered his arrest by three or four men who were there. Mr Carr took to his legs and ran toward Morristown, but Messrs Brooks and Purrington, with a horse and buggy, soon overtook him. Then the thief stopped and drew a revolver on them While Carr was standing there with drawn revolver, Mr Benson, who had cut across the field on foot, came quietly up behind him, in the brush, and threw his arms around him, but the man, being quick and quite muscular, threw Mr Benson down Before the thief could again run the two men in the buggy were upon him, he was taken back to Mr Northrup's, and committed to the Rice county jail. In a short time after he was sent to Faribault, Sheriff Keeley, who had been pursuing him arrived at Mr Northrup's and identified the horse as the one stolen and returned it On Sunday the thief was turned over to Mr. Keeley, brought to Waseca, and lodged in jail He was afterwards convicted and sent to prison at Stillwater.

ELECTION OF 1879

At this election there were three tickets in the field—Democratic, Republican and Prohibition. The following candidates were elected C McKenna treasurer, Matthew Keeley, sheriff, Charles San Galli, register of deeds, M D L Collester, county attorney Orson L Smith, surveyor, J B Hayden clerk of court, H C Woodbury, judge of probate, Dr M V Hunt, superintendent of schools, Dr. D. S Cummings, coroner, Philip Purcell and N M Nelson, county commissioners

CHAPTER XLVIII.

WASECA COUNTY HORSETHIEF DETECTIVES.

This mutual protection organization is one of the oldest in the state, having been organized in 1864 In every sparsely settled farming community, horse stealing is almost a profession. The summer of 1862 revealed the fact that we had in our midst a gang of horsethieves. In the month of June, Orrin Pease, who had just settled in the town of St Mary, had a pair of fine horses stolen After considerable search by Sheriff Whipple and others, the horses were found in the possession of three men named Erno, Beatty, and a colored person called Anderson, all three of whom were convicted of larceny, but, pending an appeal to the supreme court, broke jail at Wilton and made their escape The stealing of these horses, the escape of the thieves, and the expense attending their arrest and trial, created a strong feeling of indignation on the part of our people against thieves in general and against horsethieves in particular, and was the primary cause of the organization of the Waseca County Horsethief Detective Society that still exists. The names of the Pioneers who brought forth this organization are as follows

W L Wheeler,	Eri G. Wood,	Henry Watkins,
Asa G. Sutlief,	M S. Gove, M. D,	Myron Blackburn,
Wm Brisbane,	Eugene A. Smith,	J K Myers,
Geo. E Brubaker,	W H Young, Sr,	Q A Heath,
Noah Lincoln,	Joseph Bird,	Wm Roddle,
B A Lowell,	D L Whipple,	James E Child.

The minutes of the first few meetings will be of interest The first, or preliminary, meeting was held at Wilton in the court room, February 16, 1864 The minutes read as follows

"Wilton, Feb 16, 1864

"A meeting of citizens of Waseca county was held at the court house this date for the purpose of organizing an anti-horsethief association. William Brisbane was called to the chair and E A. Smith elected secretary Motion was made and carried that the chair appoint a committee of three to draft and present a constitution The chair appointed as such committee D L. Whipple, B A Lowell, and E B Stearns The committee presented a constitution which, after slight amendments, was adopted and reads as found on pages 1, 2, 3, and 4 of this (record) book On motion a temporary organization was effected by electing Dr M S. Gove president, Wm Brisbane vice-president, and E A Smith secretary. The following named persons then each paid one dollar to the secretary and signed the constitution, thus becoming members of the association" (Then follow the names hereinbefore given, and the record continues)

"On motion, the society proceeded to ballot for four temporary riders, which resulted in the election of Henry Watkins, D L Whipple, W L. Wheeler, and E G Wood The riders-elect then chose D L Whipple captain The following persons were elected viva voce as a vigilance committee, viz B A Lowell, J K Myers, A G Sutlief, and Joseph Bird

On motion, the meeting adjourned till Saturday at one o'clock, Feb 27, 1864

(Signed) E A SMITH, Secretary"

Evidently several men that did not have a dollar with them that day took an active part in organizing the society But they paid in their dollar at the next meeting Portions of the constitution, as adopted, are given as follows

"We, the citizens of Waseca county, to secure our property against thieves and marauders, do form ourselves into a company to be known as the 'Waseca County Horsethief Detectives,' and will be subject to the following rules and regulations.

"Art 1 Any resident of Waseca county, being recommended by five of his townsmen that are members of this society may be admitted to membership by a vote of the company upon signing this constitution and paying into the treasury one dollar" (At the next meeting this was amended to read "two dollars.")

"Art 2. The officers of this association shall be a president, a vice-president, and a secretary, who shall be ex-officio treasurer These officers shall be elected annually on the Tuesday following the third Monday in February, at Wilton" (This was afterwards changed to Waseca.)

'Art. 6. There shall be twelve riders elected from among the members of this company, who shall be elected for the term of one year, or until others are elected * * *

'Art 7 One of the riders shall be elected captain He shall be the leader of the riders and shall control and direct all their operations

There were twenty-one articles of the constitution as originally adopted, and within the year three others were added, making twenty-four in all

At the adjourned meeting, held February 27, 1864, eleven more members joined. The temporary organization and officers were made permanent, and the following additional riders were elected W. H Young, Sen, L. S Wood, E Plummer, J. K. Myers, Jos Bird, Peter Vandyke, Wm Roddle, Sen, and Austin Vinton.

The meeting then adjourned until the third Saturday in March, 1864. At the March meeting John Anderson, L. F. Peterson, Chas Johnson, Edw Sehmitt, and O Powell joined the association

The first man of the association to die was the secretary, Mr. Eugene A Smith, who died at Wilton, of typhoid pneumonia, Sept 19, 1864

A meeting was held Nov. 27, 1864, for the election of a secretary in place of Mr Smith, deceased Dr Gove presided, L S Wood served as secretary pro tem, and James E Child was elected secretary to fill the vacancy. John G Greening was elected a member at this meeting.

Evidently, from the records of the society up to the annual meeting in February, 1900, many persons had been elected, had paid their fees, and yet had neglected to sign the constitution. The membership was carried along in this loose condition until the annual meeting in February, 1900 At that meeting, upon motion of Mr Adam Bishman, it was ordered that all the names of the members of the association, residing in the county and in good standing, be published in the Waseca County Herald as a part of the report of the meeting. In accordance with this motion, the secretary, Mr. E P. Latham, gave a list of the members of the Waseca County Horsethief Detective Society, in good standing and residing in said county, Feb 17, 1900

Obadiah Powell,	Thos Johnson,	Patrick Farrell,
James E Child,	James Bowe,	Geo Matthews,
G E Brubaker,	Michael Gallagher,	Hugh Healy,
B. F Weed,	Wm R Brisbane,	Christy McGrath,
Jos Manthey,	M H Helms,	N J Breen,
C C Comee	J H Wightman,	John Curran,
James M Dunn,	W J Fitzgibbon,	E P Latham,

Thos Barden,
W D. Armstrong,
Gil Peterson,
J S. Abell,
Jacob Dane,
Chas Konrad,
Wm. Lindsay,
John Radloff,
J. W. Cleland,
Gottlieb Krassin,
S H Drum,
John Olson,
John P. Whelan,
Wm. Trahms,
John Blowers,
Siegfried Lawin,
Michael O'Brien,
Jos. T Dunn,
Henry Gehring,
Sam Hodgkins,
R. Miller,
J. A Taylor,
Nicholas Weller,
Wm Buker,
Geo H Wood,
B G. Sutlief,
E A Everett,
S J. Krassin,
Herman Gehlhoff,
Archie Johnston,
Louis Klessig,
A D Goodman,
Chas Rudolph,
Robt Schwenke,
Martin Collins,
R O. Swift,
Wm Bartel,
Aug Summick,
O H Sutlief,
J J Dinneen,
Hiram Powell,
John J Diedrich,
J A Tyrholm,
L. W Sterling,
Iver Iverson,
Dr J B Lewis,
Thos Collins,
W F Schank,
Henry Reynolds,
Knute Jameson,
Thos. Fitzgerald,
F O. Peterson,
John G Arentsen,
Adam Bishman,
E. G Wood,
Ed Schmidt,
Wilfred Vinton,
Wm. H. Gray,
Ole Olson,
Christy Hefferon,
John Carmody,
Wm Byron,
John Byron,
Gottfried Gehring,
Henry Meyers,
Thos. Ratchford,
John McWaide,
Barney McAnany,
Mike Smith,
A. Lynch,
T. J Kerr,
Wm Mettzler,
Fred Betner,
R P Ward,
S Hawkes,
John Bouchier,
Phil Bishman,
Sam Leslie,
C Fettie,
E. Bauman,
Ed. F Hayden,
I Ballard,
Chas K Wheeler,
Gus Slaack,
Wm Coulthart,
C McGuigan
W. H. Gillis,
Guy Evans,
James Curran,
David Zimmerman,
Wm A Henderson,
Henry Buker,
John A Krassin,
Chas Clements,
H. L. Hoyt,
A Guyer,
H F Lewer,
H A. Waggoner,
G H Goodspeed,
Tim McGuire,
J. W Aughenbaugh,
B J Chapman,
Alfred Wood,
John Y Brisbane
Frank Domey,
B. M. Gallagher,
F A Swartwood,
H. Roberts,
M. J Swift,
Jacob Echternach
Chris Hansen,
H F Hass,
Henry Schwenke,
Michael Heffron,
Julius Gehring,
Walter Child,
Andrew Liane,
Carl A Sampson,
John Zimmerman,
Malachi Madden,
David Fell,
P. C Bailey,
Henry Blaeser,
Ole Brack,
Robt. Collins,
Nora Armstrong
Joseph McCarty

Some of these members have since died, and many new names have been added

There is no doubt in the minds of the men of this association that the organization has been the means of putting almost an entire stop to horse-stealing in this county

During the forty-one years of the life of the organization only one horse has been stolen from any member of the organization and not recovered—and even in that case it was a question with some whether or not the horse was the property of one of the members The thieves probably thought it was not. In that case the most strenuous efforts were made to find the property and the thief or thieves

While the horse then stolen was never recovered, it is a well-known fact that at least two families then stopping in this vicinity found it convenient to move out of the county a short time afterwards on account of the close watch put upon all their movements It is believed that the gang has not tried to operate in this county since.

CHAPTER XLIX, 1880.

PARTY TOMAHAWK BURIED—ROUND HOUSE AND MACHINE SHOPS OF C. & N W. RY. CO—GREAT CONTEST BETWEEN WARD AND DUNNELL FOR CONGRESS—A RED HOT CONVENTION—ELECTION RESULTS—TERRIBLE SNOW STORM OCT 15—SOME STOCK PERISHED — ANN HAYDEN KILLED BY A DRUNKEN MAN—DEATH OF H F BIERMANN—WOLVES KILLED

In 1880 Waseca was still a village, but rapidly approaching the statue of a city The village election in 1880 fell on May 4. Evidently the political tomahawk had been buried and the combatants had smoked the pipe of peace, for at this election only 259 ballots were cast of which R L McCormick received 209 votes, B. S Lewis 204 and Wm McIntosh 62—McCormick and Lewis being declared duly elected The new board met and organized May 21 1880 R L McCormick was elected president. M D L Collester clerk, F A Newell treasurer, Wm Blowers marshal, Wm Coulthart street commissioner The new board started out by instructing the marshal to notify all saloon keepers that the laws and ordinances regarding the traffic would be strictly enforced The board went so far as to have the ordinance printed and posted in the saloons The number of persons to whom saloon licenses were issued this year was seventeen

ROUND HOUSE AND MACHINE SHOPS.

On July 12, 1880, a very important move was made to secure the location of the C & N W Ry. roundhouse and shops at Waseca A petition signed by nearly one hundred of the prominent men of Waseca asked the village board to appropriate $1,000 to

HON. WM. G. WARD.

purchase twenty acres of land of W G. Ward to be deeded to the railroad company for a round house and repair shops There was considerable excitement at the time, and the trustees, the same evening, passed the following resolution

"Whereas, W G Ward has conveyed to the W. & St P (C & N W) R R Co a strip of land 400 feet in width for the purpose of an engine house, etc, containing 24 and 50-100 acres of land, now, therefore,

"Resolved, that there be paid to said W G Ward, from any funds in the village treasury the sum of $1,225 00 upon the executing and delivering to the clerk of the village his personal bond to refund said amount to the village, less reasonable damage for the disturbing the surface, use and occupation of said land, in case said land shall revert to him by the conditions of said deed"

Thus was accomplished, in a very short time, an important undertaking which did much to increase the population and the business of our young city It was also in evidence that in really very important matters our citizens are a unit. The pay roll of the C & N W in Waseca, amounts to at least $10,000 a month, on an average The new, or present, round house was erected in 1880-1, and constitutes an important factor in the business prosperity of Waseca

AN EXCITING CONGRESSIONAL CONTEST.

The year 1880 will long be remembered by the people of Waseca county on account of the very exciting congressional contest of that year, in which one of our citizens was a contestant For years there had been a strong feeling against Congressman Dunnell on account of his "salary grab" record, and his general subserviency to corporations and combines The district was then composed of the counties of Winona, Houston, Mower, Fillmore, Olmstead, Steele, Freeborn, Waseca, Blue Earth, Watonwan, Rock, Pipestone, Murray, Nobles, Martin, Jackson, Faribault, Dodge, and Cottonwood Dunnell had created a machine which was strong throughout the district. But there were many able and determined men who thought it could be smashed The plan was to bring out favorite sons from a number of counties and in that way get control of the convention as against the salary grabber. And thus it was that Freeborn county instructed for John A Lovely, Fillmore for H. S. Barrett, Houston for James O'Brien, Faribault for J. B. Wakefield, Blue Earth for E. P. Freeman, Waseca for Hon. W. G Ward. The convention was to consist of one hundred and twenty-five delegates and was to meet at Ward's Opera House, July 7, 1880. Every county was represented and a number of counties had two sets of delegates The tricks of the politician were visible throughout the district. Jackson and Mower counties both had double delegations. Freeborn county, which was overwhelmingly for Judge Lovely, worked up a Dunnell delegation on cheek. It was admitted by non-partisan men of unbiased judgment that Dunnell was beaten on a fair vote by fifty-four to fifty-six delegates. Both factions held caucuses the night before the convention, and each faction declared it had a regular majority of the fairly elected delegates Dunnell's friends had the central committee, and when the hour arrived every delegate was at his post W Holt, chairman of the district committee, mounted the platform and called the convention to order He arbitrarily announced that Freeborn, Mower, and Jackson counties, having contested delegations, would not be allowed to vote until the committee on credentials had been appointed and reported He also stated that the district committee had instructed him to call Earl S. Youmans to the chair as temporary presiding officer Holt had scarcely commenced to make this announcement before S. P Child, of Blue Earth, was standing on the floor in front of him shouting, "Mr. Chairman," at the top of his voice. "Sim," when in good condition, can be heard a mile away, under ordinary conditions But Holt was wilfully both deaf and blind on this occasion, and went right along as though Child were not in existence. But Child was not to be silenced When Holt refused to hear, he mounted a chair, nominated Hon W. W. Braden temporary chairman, put the motion to vote, and above the yells of both factions declared Mr Braden elected. Braden and Youmans both reached the platform at the same time. D. F. Morgan of Albert Lea, anti-Dunnell, was chosen secretary and E C Huntington, of Windom, was declared elected secretary by the Dunnellites It is said that the anti-Dunnell men had the greater lung power and the excitement was intense The Dunnell men ranged on one side of the hall (it was then a hall) and the anti-Dunnell men on the other. Braden and Morgan of the anti-Dunnellites captured the only table and chairs, the other officers being compelled to stand. The excitement was at fever heat, but the coolness and good nature of both Youmans and Braden probably prevented a disgraceful physical encounter, which several times seemed likely to occur The shaking of fists and loud denunciation finally satisfied the more strenuous

The Dunnell faction had everything "cut and dried," and Dunnell was put in nomination by General Miller, of Worthington, in a whooping speech He received sixty-eight votes out of the seventy-one cast on informal ballot. The anti-Dunnell men at the same time were balloting The candidates named were J A. Lovely, H S. Barrett, J. B Wakefield, and W. G Ward. It took six ballots for these delegates to agree upon a candidate On the sixth and last ballot, Hon. W. G. Ward, of Waseca, received all the votes, seventy-five in number, and was declared the nominee amid cheers loud enough to awake the dead if the dead could hear. Dunnell's nomination was ratified on the street in front of the hotel, while a monster meeting at Ward's Opera House ratified the nomination of Mr. Ward At first, everything looked favorable for the election of Senator Ward, but, soon after the nomination, the state and national central committees sided with Dunnell and the campaign closed disastrously for the Ward faction. Mr. Ward had been a prominent Greeley man, and the cry of "party" was effectually raised against him throughout the district While he carried his own county by a plurality of 882 and a majority over both his opponents of 415, he received only 7,656 votes in the whole district He was everywhere slaughtered except at home by the party men But the seed had been sown, and at the next congressional election it was Hon Milo White and not Dunnell who was nominated and elected.

It was in the campaign of 1880 that Mr Ward became proprietor of the "Minnesota Radical," which he afterwards sold to C. E. Graham, then of Janesville

THE FALL ELECTION

For president, Gen. Garfield received a majority over Gen Hancock of 418 The following local candidates were elected: R L. McCormick, state senator, Christopher Wagner and D. J Dodge, representatives; C. E Crane, county auditor; F. A. Newell, court commissioner, A. J. Jordan and W. D. Armstrong, county commissioners—all Republicans, except Jordan.

TERRIBLE STORM IN OCTOBER

The worst October storm known to the white people of Minnesota commenced Oct. 15, 1880. A heavy rain from the Northwest set in about two o'clock p m An hour afterward it changed to a blinding snow storm, known in this section as a blizzard. Everyone was caught unprepared for such a storm Many cattle and especially sheep suffered severely in the western portion of the state A farmer at Heron Lake, Jackson county, lost a large number of sheep in the lake They were driven into it by the blinding storm of snow and wind and were drowned. Another man had about fifty head of cattle on the prairie that night with nothing but a few haystacks to protect them from the fierce blasts and no fence to keep them from straying away He and his faithful dog watched the herd all night, some of the leading cattle being fastened to posts, and yet three head of young stock got away during the night and were found in a big grass marsh the next day after the storm subsided The storm continued until about ten o'clock on the 16th, when the sky cleared Many of the railroads had to suspend operations on account of the snow blockade Within a week, however, the snow disappeared and the weather remained mild until Nov 8, when winter came in dead earnest Cold weather, with frequent snow storms continued throughout November and December

TERRIBLE CONSEQUENCES OF DRINK

John Meagher, a man about twenty years old had been at work for several months for Ed Hayden, of Alton township. On the 26th of October, 1880, he came to Waseca with a load of wheat for his employer, and while here he got drunk When he started home towards night, he was unable to sit up on his wagon, and lay down with his face downwards He had no box on the wagon, only some boards laid on the bed part of a common hay rack. As he drove out on Elm street, two of his boon companions were with him They were pretty noisy, and attempted to get the team to run It seems that these two companions left him before going very far, and Meagher proceeded on his way alone.

Arriving at the residence of John Keeley, on section 7, of St Mary, Mrs Ann Hayden, aged about eighty years, mother of J B and Ed Hayden, came out and got on to the rack to ride home with him, she having been visiting a sick girl at Mr Keeley's She stated that Meagher lay on his face and that he said he was sick, and that he would occasionally vomit They had proceeded not more than a mile or so, when they came to a ravine over which a bridge was built In attempting to cross the ravine, or gully, without crossing the bridge, the horses became entangled, and, turning around too short, upset the wagon. Meagher was pitched to the ground head foremost, his face striking in the mud Mrs Hayden stated that he made no groan or sign of distress, and the probability is that his neck was broken by the fall and that he died almost instantly Mrs Hayden was thrown to the ground, under the feet of the horses, and either by their trampling upon her or by the falling of the rack upon her, her left limb sustained a very serious compound fracture about midway between the knee and ankle, her right fore arm was broken, and she was otherwise more or less bruised This occurred about seven o'clock in the evening, and the place was at a considerable distance from any house There Mrs Hayden lay, helpless and in extreme distress, for the space, probably, of nearly an hour, when John Keeley came along on his return from Janesville Hearing her cries of distress, Mr Keeley went to her aid. The team was cut loose from its entanglement, and the suffering woman conveyed to her son's, about a mile distant Dr Craig, of Janesville, and Dr Cummings, of Waseca, were summoned, and attended to the wounds of the unfortunate woman as best they could The coroner, Dr. Cummings, did not deem it necessary to hold an inquest on the body of the dead man, so he was laid out to await the orders of his relatives, who lived in Deerfield township, Steele county Meagher was not known to be a man of drinking habits prior to this time The unfortunate lady lingered until Oct 30, when she died of her injuries

DEATH OF H. F BIERMANN

On Tuesday morning, Dec 21, 1880, Mr. H F Biermann started for Waseca with a load of wheat. When he reached the top of the long hill north of Michael Sinske's, he stopped and locked his wheel, and at the foot of the hill stopped again to unlock it It is supposed that while he was working at it, his feet slipped and he fell partly under the wagon, and that before he regained his footing the horses started and drew one wheel of the heavily loaded wagon directly across his breast, crushing him in a terrible manner The unfortunate man was found soon after by Mr McDougall and Michael Sinske, who took him home A doctor was immediately sent for, who did all in his power to alleviate his sufferings, but all efforts were of no avail, and he lingered until Wednesday when death came to his relief Mr Biermann was one of the 1855 settlers of this county, as elsewhere detailed in this volume.

WOLVES KILLED

A large number of wolves killed in this county on which bounty had been paid during the years 1876-80 is as follows For the year ending Nov 15, 1877, eleven, 1878, thirty-six, 1879, thirty-three; 1880, thirty; total, 130 The county bounty, $2.00 each, and the state bounty, $3 00, making $5.00 bounty on each scalp, gave an aggregate sum of $650 paid for exterminating the wolves in Waseca county during the time mentioned.

CHAPTER L, 1881.

VERY STORMY WINTER — RAILROADS BLOCKADED — HARRY READ'S STORY—NEW CHARTER FOR CITY OF WASECA—TORNADOES IN JUNE, JULY, AND AUGUST—DESTRUCTIVE FIRE IN WASECA OCT. 20—MURDER OF CHRISTIAN SCHIEFNER NEAR NEW RICHLAND—C & N. W ROUND HOUSE AND MACHINE SHOPS BUILT THIS YEAR—RESULT OF ELECTION—WASECA FIRE COMPANIES—DIED, J K. MAYNE, PATRICK CALLAHAN

With the opening of the year 1881, the county fathers met, Jan 4, the following being present· Thos Bowe, A. J. Jordan, Philip Purcell, N. M. Nelson, and W. D. Armstrong. Philip Purcell was elected chairman Only routine business was transacted, except that a new desk was ordered for the judge of probate.

THE WINTER WEATHER.

While the winter of 1880-1 was by no comparison the coldest ever known to Minnesota, it was by all odds the stormiest, the longest and the most disagreeable. The Southern Minnesota railroad was blockaded from Winnebago City west from the middle of January until the first week in April On the 5th and 6th of April, that year, in Jackson county, the snow was three feet deep—on the level—and a heavy span of horses could be driven over it, the crust of the snow being so hard as to bear the weight of the team About the 7th of April the weather became warm and the snow rapidly disappeared.

WINTER STORY BY HARRY READ

The following appeared in the Waseca Herald, Jan 14, 1881·

"Engineer H A Read came home Wednesday night, having been on duty up on the west end of the road He relates some of the charms of railroading in winter Having recently been to Winona and procured a new engine for the Western division, Mr Read was commissioned to break it in Last Sunday, with the thermometer down to 35, and roads more or less blockaded, he was making his way to Watertown, having a freight train and a caboose of passengers The water tanks along the road had either gone dry or frozen up, and Mr Read's supply of water was rapidly being exhausted When within half a mile of Goodwin, his train became stalled in a snow bank He succeeded in getting his engine through and pulling on to the station Here the citizens turned out and, with buckets and tubs, brought water to fill up his tank He then went on to Watertown, some twenty miles, and remained until Monday, when he came back and, with help, the train was extricated from the drift, where it had remained all night Fortunately two of the cars were loaded with wood, which had enabled the passengers to keep themselves warm On Tuesday night, as Mr Read was coming down the road between Lamberton and Walnut Grove with two engines on the train, and in front of them a train with a snow plow, the head train became stalled Before Read's train was signalled, it ran into the caboose, raised it up, and tipped it fairly on to the head engine An engineer and fireman jumped off and were considerably hurt It takes a host of nerve and pluck to follow railroading on the Western prairies"

A New Richland correspondent on Feb 18 wrote

"Railroading this winter is not one of the pleasant occupations Six engines and crews, including the southward bound passenger train, were snow bound at Hartland six days, and as this place is but a small village, its facilities for accommodating so many were insufficient, and a good deal of suffering ensued The passenger train fortunately had but eight passengers aboard It was stalled in a drift one mile north of the station, and was detained there and at the station seven days One lady and her daughter were on their way to Boston, and were in quite ill health As the passengers were compelled to stay in the car, it was exceedingly tiresome and unpleasant for them"

The body of J. K. Mayne, who died in Wilton, Feb 11, 1881, was buried temporarily in a snow drift near his home, the snow being so deep that it was impossible to gain access to the cemetery

PATRICK CALLAHAN.

This gentleman settled in Freedom with his family in 1865. He died March 22, 1881, aged about sixty years He had been an invalid some two years as the result of a sun-stroke Alderman Callahan, of Waseca, is his son

NEW CITY CHARTER

On March 26, 1881, Waseca received, at the hands of the legislature, a new charter Under its provisions the city was divided into five wards The first election under the new charter was held May 3, 1881. The first city contest was a battle royal The candidates were Hon Warren Smith, and Hon M D L Collester The total vote for mayor numbered 373 Mr Smith received 219 votes, and Mr Collester 164 In the First ward, H H Sudduth was elected over C A Wright by a vote of 45 to 34. In the second ward, Dennis McLoughlin received 110 votes, and Dr M V Hunt 40 In the Third ward, James B. Hayden was elected without opposition by a vote of 32 The Fourth ward elected Theodore Brown by a vote of 33, to 15, cast for E W Fiske The Fifth ward cast 30 ballots for Thomas Coleman, and 26 for John Gutfleisch H G Mosher was unanimously elected assessor, and Hon John Carmody and Hon B A. Lowell were elected justices of the peace without much opposition Samuel Stevenson was elected constable by a vote of 234 to 115 for G H Zeller The first city council met at the office of the clerk of court in the old court house, May 10, 1881, and was called to order by Mayor-elect Smith Aldermen present, Theodore Brown, James B. Hayden, H H Sudduth, D McLoughlin, and Thos Coleman James B Hayden was elected president of the council, and the mayor made the following appointments which were confirmed, namely: Jerome E. Madden city recorder, Frank A Newell treasurer, C E Leslie city attorney, and Lucius Keyes marshal

One of the bills allowed by the council this year was accompanied by the following entry

"D Welch, for standing around with his hands in his pockets and looking on while the men were excavating cistern at the court house corner, $19 00."

TORNADOES AND HURRICANES.

The year 1881 was noted not only for its winter storms and blizzards, but also for its summer tornadoes On the 11th of June a destructive tornado started near Blue Earth, in Faribault county traveled northeasterly and passed near Minnesota Lake Its pathway was strewn with the wrecks of houses, barns, grain, stock, etc. The farm house of Mr Chaffey was entirely blown away, killing both himself and wife, an aged couple The fine large barn of T. J Probert was blown down, seriously injuring his daughter, who was in the barn at the time, also killing one horse, blowing his machinery all to pieces, besides scattering about 500 bushels of grain. The county bridge at Grady's, on the Maple river, was blown entirely away, and the house of John Grady was also blown away The lady that was living in the house felt it moving, and opened the door to jump She landed in the cellar all right. The house of Geo Harrings was unroofed, house of Robert Jones blown away with its contents, his wife being badly injured, barn of E Curtis blown down, house of D Matterson blown from foundation and three of his family injured, house of August Zabel blown entirely away together with its contents, and he and one son were injured Much other damage resulted in the vicinity.

Another terrible storm struck New Ulm July 15, at 4 48 p m., and in twelve minutes had destroyed property to the value of $300,000, killed four persons in New Ulm and fifteen in the adjoining townships, and wounded eighteen severely The tornado was terrible Houses were taken up bodily, carried considerable distances and then crushed as they were dropped to earth Three churches were completely destroyed, as were numerous business houses

August 30, a severe storm visited Waseca county, although it did not amount to a tornado The Janesville Argus noted that, "The rain was a deluge and the wind a cyclone Very little damage was done in Janesville, but east of the village sad havoc was made with the grain stacks and cornfields. We first hear of trouble at A P Wilson's place, northeast of the village, where twenty grain stacks were leveled Mr Wilson says the fall of water was tremendous, it standing in his yard from six to ten inches in depth, and over his plowed field a boat might have sailed without fear of grounding. Mr McHugo had a setting of stacks blown down, Mr Lilly, southeast of the village, seven stacks, some of them entirely blown away, Pat Lilly, eight stacks, Mrs. McDonough, twelve, Sam Lambert, six Keeley boys, fifteen, D. Glynn, ten, C. Flynn, four, M Lang, seven, Pat Foley, four, C. Guyer, several Fences were leveled generally in the track of the storm."

The Waseca Herald noted that Isaac Ballard had a cow killed by lightning. At M. Spillane's place, near Meriden, the storm came with such force as to burst in the windows and doors The blinds to the windows were as completely broken as though a man had taken a hammer and smashed them to pieces One immense mass of hail fell, many of the pieces of ice being fully as large as a man's fist Mr Spillane had forty acres of corn driven into the ground. A dozen or so of pigs and hogs and many turkeys were killed The storm throughout the country was severe

A DISASTROUS FIRE

The most disastrous fire that has ever visited Waseca occurred on the night of Oct 20, 1881. The Herald of that date contained the following account.

"A midnight fire broke out in the Dr Brubaker building, corner of Second and Oak streets, and before it was subdued a dozen buildings were burned to the ground, a half dozen families rendered homeless, and thousands of dollars worth of goods and household property devoured by the flames or badly injured

Roger Hanbury was working around some cars near the W & St Peter freight depot, and discovering the fire, gave the alarm, which was immediately taken up by two locomotives In a few minutes many hundred men were on the ground with such means of fighting fire as could be obtained, but they consisted only of pails, axes, ladders, and the long cable with hooks for tearing down buildings The first efforts were to tear down the small building owned by J Halvorsen and used for a shoe and harness shop This had hardly been accomplished before the Kraft hotel caught fire, when it became evident that the entire row of buildings must go Efforts were then devoted mostly to removing the contents of the several buildings to safe distances

The buildings burned were the two-story structure belonging to Dr Brubaker, occupied below by Adolph Schildknecht's drug store, and one room above by Dr. Cleary for an office, the shoe and harness shop of J Halvorsen, the large two-story hotel occupied by Mrs Kraft; the saloon building owned by Wm Herbst, and occupied by Miller & Weishar, A Wert's two-story restaurant and dwelling, including his bakery, etc; Karstedt's harness shop, the capacious furniture store and manufacturing rooms of Comee Bros , Preston's jewelry store, the shoe shop occupied by Anton Anderson, and owned by H A. Karstedt, the store occupied by D McLoughlin, and owned by John Anderson, of Otisco, Craven's machine buildings, and other minor adjoining buildings and store rooms. The losses were estimated at $25,000 At the time of this fire the city had no fire company nor any means of fire protection"

MURDER OF CHRISTIAN SCHIEFNER.

The trial of Christian Henniger, for the killing of Christian

Schiefner on the 3d of June, 1880, near New Richland, was held at the fall term of the district court, and Henniger was found guilty of manslaughter in the second degree. The men involved in this tragedy were two farmers residing about two miles west of the village of New Richland. For a number of years they had been at enmity with each other, and had several times resorted to the law to settle their difficulties Their last trouble, which resulted so seriously, was with regard to a small strip of land that each claimed Henniger was breaking up the disputed land, and Schiefner determined to prevent him from doing so. On the day in question, Henniger secreted himself in a wagon and was driven to the scene of the tragedy, where his son and hired man went to work plowing Schiefner soon came out and forbade their breaking up the land. Henniger immediately came from his hiding place in the wagon, and after some words, got his gun and shot Schiefner dead, the charge passing through both lungs. Judge Buckham sentenced Henniger to the penitentiary for five years. It was generally thought that the ends of justice were partially thwarted

At the same term of court one Pettengill was convicted of stealing a horse from Mrs Reed, of Iosco He was sentenced to three years and six months in the penitentiary, as was also John Duff, for stealing Pheiffer's horses.

ROUND HOUSE AND MACHINE SHOPS OF THE CHICAGO AND NORTHWESTERN RAILWAY COMPANY.

It was during this year, 1881, that the C & N-W Railway Co expended about $100,000 in the construction of the round house, machine shops, coal houses, etc, in Waseca. The round house is built of brick and contains twenty stalls for engines The building is circular, and occupies two-thirds of an entire circle The outside wall is 520 feet in length, and the inside wall 240 feet in length, the width is 66 feet the area of the floor is 36 400 square feet, the walls are 20 feet high From one end of the main building is partitioned off six stalls, to be used for the general overhauling and repair of cars and engines The turntable is in the center of the circle formed by the round house, and from it engines can be run into any stall The machine and repair shop is 52x100 feet in size with eighteen-foot walls In one end is situated the immense boiler which is used to generate steam to heat the entire structure, operate the steam pump, etc.; in the other end are the forges and other arrangements for repairing cars and engines In this building are found, also, the offices and a large fire and frost proof vault for storing oil There are five forges in the blacksmith shop The boiler is constructed of locomotive steel, and is 6 feet in diameter and 21 feet long The chimney, with which the boiler pipe connects, is 7 feet square at its base, and towers to a height of 52 feet A ladder, constructed of iron rods, extends from the bottom to the top, on the inside.

The water tank is one of the very largest that is built, and holds 2,500 barrels It is 22 feet from the ground to the bottom of the tank, and the tank is 18 feet in height, by 30 feet in diameter The entire space below the tank is boarded up, battened, and painted The pipes that connect with the tank are thoroughly protected from the action of the frost, at all places

The coal shed, separate and apart from the other buildings, is 460 feet long, 26 feet wide, and 14 feet high, and will hold 2 500 tons of coal. It is built entirely of wood, and is a mammoth building. Derricks are provided at two places, from which coal may be supplied At one end of the coal house is a sand house 16x60 feet in size In the construction of the buildings there were used 500 cords of stone, 550,000 brick, 150 cars of sand, 1,600 sacks of cement, 800,000 feet of lumber and six carloads of lime. The plant is a large one and contributes much to the permanent prosperity of the city of Waseca

ELECTION OF 1881.

The county officers elected Nov. 8, were as follows · treasurer, C McKenna, democrat, superintendent of schools, Dr D S Cummings, democrat, register of deeds, Charles San Galli, democrat, sheriff, Hugh Wilson, republican, county attorney, W R. Kinder, republican, judge of probate, S D Crump, republican, county surveyor, Orson L. Smith, coroner, Dr R O. Craig, county commissioners, I C Trowbridge, of Waseca, and Geo W Soule of Blooming Grove

WASECA FIRE COMPANIES.

The very disastrous fire of October 20 and 21, of this year, emphasized the necessity for organizing fire companies, and the year 1881 was appropriately closed by the organizing of an engine company and a hose company.

MEMBERS OF FIRST ENGINE COMPANY

Jesse Reese,	John Maloney,	M D L Collester,
John Lortis,	Walter Child,	Fred Clayton,
Peter Coles,	Samuel Strohmeier,	Gus Staack,
E Morrison,	C Christopherson,	C M. Oster,
H V. Davis,	Ellsworth Goodspeed,	D McLoughlin,
Sumner Wood,	E B Collester,	Wenzel Kruezer,
Charles Platt,	Geo W Smith,	A J Lohren,
C Ebbinghausen,	J M Robertson,	J. A Lilly,
John Roland,	J W Aughenbaugh,	Wm Miller,
Allan Goodspeed,	Thomas Breen,	John F. Murphy
S Swenson,	Wm Schlicht,	

MEMBERS OF THE FIRST HOSE COMPANY

John Locke,	Ed Goetzenberger,	H E Strong,
Ernest Ramsdale,	E L Fiske,	D S Cummings,
Ed Forbes,	A Schildknecht,	C D Ward,
Ed. Cummings,	E W Fiske,	Jake Niebles,
Ed Castor,	J E. Madden,	M O Forbes,

The year 1881 closed with very pleasant weather. The fall months had been delightful with "December as pleasant as May."

CHAPTER LI, 1882.

COUNTY COMMISSIONERS—GOLDEN WEDDING OF HON. AND MRS WM. BRISBANE—A CENTENARIAN DIES—SUICIDE OF ICHABOD WEST—BUILDING OF GRANT HOUSE AND WAVERLY HOTEL—DEATH OF MRS KIMBALL—PROSPEROUS YEAR

The county commissioners for this year were Ira C Trowbridge, Geo W Soule, Philip Purcell, N. M Nelson, A. J Jordan, and W D Armstrong, with C E Crane as county auditor Philip Purcell was again elected chairman Nothing special occurred except the awarding of the county printing without having given notice to the publishers in the county asking for bids This action was a violation of law

A GOLDEN WEDDING

Hon Wm Brisbane and wife, of Wilton, celebrated their golden wedding Jan 20, 1882 Their children, grand children, and great grand children then numbered seventy-three, and nearly all of them were present. There were also present some two hundred other persons, who participated in the celebration of the anniversary One very noticeable—and to Mr and Mrs. Brisbane a very interesting feature—was the presence of Mr and Mrs. John Gillis, of Wisconsin, who were married on the same day and at the same place that they were Mr Gillis came with his aged companion on purpose to celebrate their Golden Wedding with their friends of "Auld Lang Syne" He brought with him a picture of the humble, thatched cottage in Scotland where they commenced their married life. It is seldom that two couples, who married on the same day in the same place, and afterwards emigrated to a foreign shore, are permitted to celebrate their golden wedding together

DEATH OF A CENTENARIAN

A paragraph in a local paper, dated April 14, 1882, read as follows. "Died, at her home in Wilton, on the afternoon of the 6th inst, at 4 o'clock, Mrs Boyer, in the one hundred and fourth year of her age She had been confined to her bed all winter, but did not appear worse than usual until a few hours before her death The funeral services on Saturday afternoon were conducted by Rev Thos Hartley of Otisco" She cared far very kindly by her son, James, who went west soon after her death

SUICIDE

Mr Ichabod West one of the early settlers of Vivian, aged 83 years, on the 8th day of August, committed suicide by hanging himself to a bed post in his room Mr West had been living with his son's family and had been growing blind for some time This greatly annoyed him, and caused him to express fears that he would become entirely helpless This seemed to him an unbearable calamity On Tuesday forenoon he went to his room Soon after, his daughter-in-law had occasion to go in there when she found him suspended to the bed post by means of a handkerchief He had evidently passed the handkerchief around the bed post and then around his neck and deliberately strangled himself to death.

BUILDING OPERATIONS.

During the summer of 1882 several substantial buildings were erected in Waseca Among them were two large hotels—the Grant House and the Waverly,—the Anderson block—now known as McLoughlin Bros.' Store,—the brick building at the southeast corner of Second and Wood streets, and other smaller buildings

DEATH OF MRS KIMBALL

At a very early hour Sunday morning, Sept 2, 1882, at the residence of her daughter, Mrs. H. P. Norton, of Waseca, Mrs Nancy Kimball quietly passed from earth. Mrs. Kimball was the daughter of a soldier of the War of the Revolution, Gen Eliphalet Gay, of New London, N H At this place Mrs Kimball was born on the 25th of June, 1795 She was married to Jonathan Kimball in the year 1820, and continued to reside in New London till 1839 The family then emigrated to McHenry county, Illinois, and settled in what afterwards became Woodstock, the county seat After nine years of pioneer life her husband died, and she lived a widow thirty-four years. Till about ten years ago, she retained her property in Woodstock, and made that place her home. She afterwards resided with her daughters, spending most of her time in Waseca with Mrs Norton.

ELECTION RESULTS

The election, which was held Nov 7, 1882, gave the following local results state senator, Dr R O Craig, representative, John C White, of Waseca, county auditor, C E Crane, coroner, Dr H J Young; county commissioners, Philip Purcell, and N. M. Nelson Messrs. Crane, H J Young and N M Nelson were republicans—the others democrats

CLOSE OF THE YEAR

On the whole, the year 1882 was a quiet one for Waseca county The weather, as a rule, had been mild, and the crops better than average The people generally had been prosperous, and the holidays found them happy and contented.

CAPTER LII, 1883.

COUNTY PRINTING STRUGGLE—DIED, AMANDA GREGORY, EDITOR S M ROSE, MATTHIAS MALONEY—MAPLEWOOD PARK DRIVEWAY—CITY OF WASECA ISSUES BONDS TO BUILD STREETS—STEAMBOAT LAUNCHED ON CLEAR LAKE—MAPLEWOOD PARK ASSOCIATION ORGANIZED—TORNADO JULY 13—PASSENGER TRAIN BLOWN FROM TRACK—ARM BROKEN—PROPERTY DESTROYED—RESULT OF ELECTION

The county commissioners opened their session this year Jan 2. Mr Purcell was again elected chairman As usual in those days, there was an unseemly squabble for the county printing, and more or less favoritism was shown The report says

"Bids for the county printing were considered The Argus bid only for the proceedings of the county commissioners at 25 cents per folio The Radical put in a bid for the delinquent tax list at 2½ cents per description, the proceedings free, and suggested that the financial statement be published in all three papers, and each paid 25 cents per folio The Herald proposed to print the delinquent tax list for $40, the financial statement for $25, the proceedings of commissioners including the proceedings of the board of equalization, for $35, and all other notices at 10 cents per folio In disposing of the county printing, the bid of the Argus was accepted, also that of the Radical with the exception of the financial statement which was awarded without stating the price The proceedings of the board of equalization were awarded to the Herald at 25 cents per folio"

MRS. AMANDA GREGORY

This lady, who was one of the very early settlers of St Mary, died Feb 28, 1883, at the age of seventy-eight years She had been feeble for a long time and died of old age

DEATH OF EDITOR ROSE.

Salem M. Rose, senior editor and publisher of the Waseca County Herald, departed this life at 4 30 o'clock Tuesday morning, March 13th, aged fifty-one years, and three months. Mr. Rose was one of the pioneers of Minnesota, removing to this state about 1860 from New York. He settled in Dodge county, where he afterwards married Abbie F Bunker, and for the years that intervened previous to his removal to Waseca, he was successful in obtaining the reward of an industrious, honest and well ordered life. He was one of the early editors of Waseca and highly respected

DEATH ON THE RAILROAD

Matthias Maloney, brother of the late John Maloney, of Waseca, and of Thomas Maloney, of Iosco, was found dead by the side of the railroad track He was one of the early settlers of the county and lived with his four children a short distance east of New Richland, where he owned a farm Friday night, March 16, he started for Waseca, having in his possession about $45 in money and several valuable papers. At New Richland he took a freight train, arriving at Waseca about the hour of 1 a m Very shortly thereafter his dead body was found lying on the railroad track a short distance south of the M & St L depot He was terribly mangled and cut, which indicated that a number of cars had passed over him Coroner Young was immediately summoned, but he did not deem it necessary to hold an inquest, as the manner of Mr Maloney's death was entirely plain. Whether he was crawling under a car and the train started meanwhile, or whether he was standing on the track and first run over by the engine, can only be conjectured One thing, however, seemed a little curious When his body was found, which was immediately after his death, there was no money or papers about his person No satisfactory explanation of the mystery ever came to light. He left surviving him three girls and a son, the last having then attained to manhood.

MAPLEWOOD PARK DRIVEWAY AND STREETS

During the legislative session of 1883, the city of Waseca asked for and secured an act of the legislature authorizing the city to issue bonds in any sum not exceeding $6,000 00 for the purpose of constructing highways—more especially a driveway or road around Clear Lake and to the grounds known as Maplewood Park Immediately upon the passage of this act, Mayor Collester called a special meeting of the city council Upon petition of numerous citizens, the council adopted the following resolution

"RESOLVED. That the common council of said city of Waseca hereby order a special election to be held by the legal voters of said city on the 19th day of March, 1883, at the court house, in said city, commencing at 9 o'clock a m, and closing at 5 o'clock p m, for the purpose of voting on the question of issuing such bonds as provided by law; and that a copy of this resolution be published in the Herald and the Radical of said city"

The records further show that, at a special meeting of the common council, held March 29, pursuant to the call of the mayor, it was moved and carried "that the recorder be directed to purchase eighteen blank printed bonds in denominations of $500 00 each, said bonds to run ten years with interest coupons attached, bearing a rate of interest of six per cent per annum, interest payable semi-annually, and said bonds to be issued June 1, 1883 ' There was much discussion before the matter of bonds and streets and driveways in and about Waseca was settled. On May 30, following, the council ordered the issuance of two bonds, of $500 each, the money to be derived therefrom to be expended in the construction of the driveway around Clear Lake On June 5, the council awarded the job of grubbing and clearing the road bed around Clear Lake to James Tripp for $165 00 The contract for hauling and putting upon the streets one thousand loads of gravel, from the farm of Mike Tomoski, was let to Mr Patrick Kelly, he being the lowest bidder At the council meeting of June 15, Alderman Robertson introduced a resolution to immediately issue four more city bonds, numbers 3, 4, 5 and 6, of $500 00 each, for the construction of drives around Clear and Loon Lakes. Alderman Wood moved to amend by making the total amount of the bonds $4,000 00, one-half the amount, $2,000 00, to be used in making stone gutters along Second street The amendment was lost by a tie vote—Wood and Broughton voting aye, and Madden and Robertson nay The vote being taken on the original motion it was lost by the same vote June

20, Mayor Trowbridge called a special meeting of the council to take action in regard to the construction of stone gutters on Second street, and also the construction of the driveway around Clear Lake

This meeting resulted in the adoption of a resolution to issue city bonds to the amount of $3,000—$1,500 of which was to be expended in the construction of stone gutters on Second street, and the rest in the construction of the driveway around Clear Lake At the council meeting held Nov 20, of the same year, the mayor and the recorder were directed to issue two more road bonds, each of $500 00 It appears from the records that only $5,000 of the authorized $6,000 in bonds, was issued that year. This was a year of many improvements in and about the city The Clear Lake road was graded in excellent shape as was the Loon Lake drive The stone gutters on each side of Second street were put in this season This last was one of the most useful public improvements ever made by the city up to that time.

STEAMBOAT LAUNCHED.

A small steamboat, called the "Commodore," was successfully launched on Clear Lake, June 16, 1883 The boat was formerly in use on Lake Minnetonka, Minn, and was purchased by Ira C Trowbridge and A P Jamison for $1,200. It served as a pleasure boat for a number of years, especially during the Chautauqua sessions at Maplewood Park. It was finally sold to parties in the western portion of the state, much to the regret of many in this locality

INDEPENDENCE DAY

Great preparations had been made for a public celebration of the Fourth, at Waseca, but a drizzling rain, which set in at 5 o'clock a m and continued till between 9 and 10 o'clock sadly demoralized the arrangements that had been made As soon as the rain ceased, however, the people gathered at Court House Square, where Rev R Forbes delivered one of his characteristic addresses

MAPLEWOOD PARK ASSOCIATION.

During the month of July, this year, steps were taken to

organize this association The temporary officers were Rev. C N Stowers, of Faribault, president, Rev. H C Jennings, secretary, and Mr A. P. Jamison, treasurer Nearly all the leading citizens of Waseca took stock and became interested in what was popularly known as "The Waseca Cautauqua Assembly" at Maplewood Park It was one of the finest resorts in the state and was maintained for fifteen years consecutively—the last assembly being held in July, 1898. Financially, the enterprise was never a success; but morally, socially, and intellectually it was worth more than it cost It is much to be regretted that the people at large did not contribute more liberally to its maintenance

TORNADO EXTRAORDINARY

This was the year of tornadoes in Southern Minnesota, and Waseca had a foretaste of what was a terrible disaster at Rochester, Minn, about a month later

The worst storm that ever visited this section occurred July 13, 1883 About 10 o'clock a m, dense, black clouds rolled up from the southwest and overcast the sky Lightning flashes followed each other in quick succession and heavy peals of thunder shook every building and made the earth tremble Rain soon commenced to fall, and then, for a few moments, there was a death-like calm, when, all at once, the wind came from the northwest with all the force of a hurricane, and the rain came in blinding sheets, accompanied by hail So dense was the falling rain and so fierce the wind that one could not discern objects across the street This terrible storm lasted about an hour, during which time the strongest mind shuddered with fear at what might happen

Although much damage was done to property no person was killed or seriously injured Trowbridge's brick building, now occupied by Mr. Gallien, was unroofed, the tin roofing being carried some distance The top of the south wall was torn down and the rain drenched the interior of the building. His loss was estimated at $1,000. The furniture factory, since destroyed by fire, was entirely unroofed and the body of the building badly wrecked Willyard's planing mill and machine shop was badly torn to pieces—almost a complete wreck. Father Christie's barn at the Catholic parsonage was moved from its foundation The wind totally wrecked the warehouse on the west end of the W & St P. elevator, and moved a number of barrels of cement and salt several rods, but left them standing uninjured. The large wheel of Roland's windmill and portions of the tower were carried away. The top of the front wall of the Simon Smith brick store was blown down The "Priest hotel" lost its chimneys and the barn was totally wrecked. The plateglass front windows of the building now owned and occupied by McLoughlin Bros were broken by flying debris One corner of the old courthouse was unroofed and portions of the wall blown down. One freight car was blown from the transfer track and upset, while many of the cars were unceremoniously moved about the yards. The German M E church was racked out of position and considerably injured. The old "City Roller Mill" of Everett & Aughenbaugh received the full force of the storm as it swept unimpeded across Loon Lake The roof was torn off and the entire building very much twisted out of shape Their machinery was badly disarranged and somewhat damaged. Their warehouse was partly unroofed and five hundred sacks of flour were exposed to the rain. The Grant house had a portion of its roof torn off and some damage was done to inside rooms

The passenger train that left Waseca, going east, just before the storm, was blown from the track, about three miles this side of Owatonna, and several passengers were more or less injured. Among the passengers were Rev. H C. Jennings, Misses Fanny and Etta Forbes, and Max Forbes, all residents of Waseca at that time Miss Etta Forbes had an arm broken by the fall, and all were badly shaken up. After reaching Owatonna, Mr Jennings procured a team and carriage and returned to Waseca with the Misses Forbes

There was one amusing incident during the storm which served to relieve the sadness that was so universal in the community just after the storm subsided There lived in the city at that time a ponderous gentleman by the name of Kelley, a wood sawyer by occupation. He was undoubtedly the largest man in the county. "Brother" Kelley lived alone in a small house just east of the W. & St. P. elevator At the time of the storm he was at his house, and being the heaviest man in the county, he undoubtedly felt that he would be able to hold his own house down under all circumstances But alas! the Storm King was no respector of weights and measures, and, in a jiffy, his house was torn in pieces and scattered to all the winds of heaven. Kelley seized hold of the stove as an anchor, but he was soon torn from that and carried bodily with portions of his domicile into a pond of water near by with part of the roof of his house upon him As soon as he struck the ground and recovered from his surprise, he threw off the piece of roof and waded ashore, where he sat down upon the ground and meditated upon the weakness of human habitations until the storm subsided. Aside from a bad bruise on his head he was not much injured, except in his wounded dignity, for he was a very dignified man.

The German Lutheran church, in Iosco, was moved from its foundation and racked to some extent S S Phelps' large barn, in St Mary, was all torn to pieces, and his granary moved from its foundation In the same town the new residence of James and John Keeley was blown down A cow belonging to Wm Oesterreich was killed by lightning. E. Brossard's barn was unroofed. Julius Papke lost his granary, corn cribs, sheds, and other property

In Blooming Grove, Malachi Madden had a large new barn demolished Two of his small boys were in the barn at the time and were carried quite a distance, but safely landed in a slough. His crops were badly damaged Roger Garaghty living near Madden's, had his log house, his barn and sheds entirely blown down, and his crops badly injured The storm was fearful at Ole Sonsteby's place. He went into his cellar as the storm struck, and immediately his house, built of logs, was taken up and carried away Large oak trees near his house were broken off and some torn out by the roots.

In Woodville, Mike Spillane's granary was blown down and his crops badly injured Charles Hensel had thirty-five tons of hay destroyed, his crops and buildings badly injured, and a quantity of growing timber ruined

At Meriden the German Evangelical church was badly wrecked A very large barn on the farm of H Palas was torn down At the station, a blacksmith shop was torn down, and the flouring mill was unroofed and otherwise seriously damaged.

The damage throughout the towns named was very extensive, and few there were who did not suffer some loss

RESULT OF THE ELECTION

A. Bierman, democrat, for governor, carried the county by a majority of 203 For other state officers, the republican majority was about 165. The democrats elected Charles McKenna treasurer, M B Keeley clerk of court, P McGovern county attorney, and Dr D S Cummings superintendent of schools Hiram A Mosher, independent, was elected register of deeds The republicans elected S D Crump judge of probate, B. A Lowell court commissioner, Orson L Smith surveyor, and Dr. H. J Young coroner. The democrats also elected two county commissioners —M. F. Connor and A J Jordan.

VERMONTERS

The Vermonters held a meeting at the Grant house in December, 1883, and Mr. P. A. Erwin, of St. Mary, was present, although eighty-eight years of age.

WILTON LODGE NO 24.

The first Masonic lodge organized in the county was located in Wilton, and was instituted Jan. 8, 1858 . After the removal of the county seat from that place to Waseca, Wilton gradually faded away, and on Dec. 20, 1883, the lodge was removed to Alma City At the time of its location at Alma City it contained a membership of twenty-five Its membership was soon after much increased.

CHAPTER LIII, 1884.

COUNTY PRINTING DIVIDED—ECKENBECK RESIDENCE BURNED —LIFE AND DEATH OF JUDGE CANFIELD—S. S PHELPS KILLED BY RAILROAD—VICE-PRESIDENT COLFAX ON THE FOURTH—ATTEMPTED JAIL DELIVERY, PRISONER SHOT—J G COOLEY KILLED—PRESIDENTIAL ELECTION.

The county "Fathers" met Jan 1, 1884, those present being N M Nelson, A J Jordan, Philip Purcell, G W. Soule Ira C Trowbridge, and M F Connor The board organized by electing Philip Purcell chairman The county printing was divided among the papers of the county and peace reigned supreme Only the ordinary routine business of the county was transacted

ECKENBECK RESIDENCE BURNED.

Shortly after 4 o'clock on Feb 24, 1884, the residence of Charles Eckenbeck, corner of Wood and Fourth streets, Waseca, was discovered to be on fire. The fire started between the ceiling and roof of the rear part, as near as could be determined, and was first discovered by the hired girl, who rushed out in her night clothes, barefooted, giving the alarm of fire. George Eckenbeck was sleeping up stairs His father, who was still very feeble from a long illness, was also up stairs George took his father in his arms and carried him below. By this time the house was rapidly filling with smoke, and it was with much difficulty that he partly dressed his father and carried him out. Miss Effie Winters was staying over night with Miss Louise Eckenbeck, and as George stepped to the porch with his father in his arms, Miss Winters also passed out, and all fell, but received no injury. Carrying Mr Eckenbeck to a place of safety, George went back to look for his sister, whom he supposed to be in the burning building, but she had previously escaped. While in the house this time George was severely burned on his head The entire building was now on fire and in a very short time burned to the ground Mr. Eckenbeck suffered the loss of a large number of valuable papers, notes, etc.; Louise, many valuable paintings of her own handiwork, besides all her clothes Sylvester and his father also lost their clothing. George saved a portion of his clothes, his gold watch, which was afterwards found in the street, and $50 in money that was in a bureau. He lost $300 worth of books. The value of the property destroyed was about $4,000, most of it covered by insurance

DEATH OF A PIONEER.

Job A Canfield, who settled in the town of Otisco in 1856, was a lifelong pioneer. He was born in the state of Ohio, his parents having been pioneers in that state About the year 1845, when a young man, he settled with his young wife in Dodge county, Wisconsin, near Waupun His wife was a daughter of Obadiah Mosher, also a Wisconsin and Minnesota pioneer Mr Canfield was the first judge of probate in this county, holding the position from 1857 to 1860, and again from Jan 1, 1870, to Jan. 1, 1878. August 12, 1862, at the age of thirty-eight years, he enlisted in Company F, Tenth Minnesota Infantry, and served until May 18, 1865 He died of apoplexy Jan 28, 1884, and was buried with Masonic and Grand Army honors

DEATH OF S S PHELPS

The following account of the sad death of Mr Phelps is from the pencil of Mr. G. W Morse, editor of the Waseca Herald, at the time of Mr Phelps' death·

"Mr. Phelps was in town on business and started for home a few minutes before 6 o'clock, driving a span of horses attached to a pair of sleds with wagon box on same At the time a very fierce blizzard was raging from the northwest, the snow coming in blinding clouds, and the temperature being very cold. About one mile west of here the road that he must travel is crossed by the Winona & St Peter railroad. Each side of the railroad track, at the crossing, for perhaps four rods were banks of snow from three to six feet high, the same having been thrown from the track to keep it clear The snow came in such gusts and the wind roared so loudly that no one could see or hear an approaching train for but a short distance Mr Phelps drove his team down the embankment on to the track, but found the bank on the opposite side too steep and high for his team to climb, and so turned up the track, thinking, no doubt, to get through the fence and so back onto the road He had passed not more than fifty feet up the track before a freight train of two cars and a caboose came dashing along from the west at a speed necessary to pass through drifts that were liable to be found H A Read was the engineer, and did not nor could not see the approaching team until within sixty feet of them He saw the driver rise up and, as he thinks, make an attempt to jump, but such an effort was quite useless, as no person could have got out and up the steep bank of snow in time to escape Mr. Read reversed his engine immediately and did everything possible to stop, but all in vain, until he had gone at least thirty rods Getting off from his engine and looking for the results of the accident the mangled body of Mr Phelps was found under the second car, where his clothes had been caught by projecting bolts and he dragged the distance The top of his head had been taken off, both feet cut off, and he had received many other cuts and bruises, so that he was quite beyond recognition Both horses were killed instantly and thrown from the track after being dragged, one of them five or six rods and the other a little farther The sleds were carried on the pilot until the train stopped Removing the body from under the car, Mr Read detached his engine and came down to the depot Getting Coroner Young and others, he went back and brought the remains of the unfortunate man to the depot, where they remained until morning, when they were placed in a casket and removed to the residence "

THE FOURTH OF JULY—VICE-PRESIDENT COLFAX

Undoubtedly the most elaborate celebration of the national holiday ever held in this county occurred this year. Maplewood Park was then in its youthful glory and all Waseca joined to make the occasion memorable. The day was very fine and the program was fully carried out Vice-President Colfax was at his best and delivered a fine address

The oration ended, the next thing in order was dinner, and again the park was one vast picnic The G A R boys pooled their provisions and enjoyed an army picnic, and many were the jokes and pleasantries that passed around. The drum corps with two fifers, supplied an abundance of martial music At 2:30 the concert began in the pavilion, under direction of Prof. Raymond The attendance was very fair considering the fact that, as a general rule, out door sports are preferred on the

Fourth of July A thunder shower chorus was added to the concert program, which somewhat disturbed the same The rain effectually ended further doings at the park and those who were not encamped there made their way to town, where the two bands were already engaged in making the air resonant with music About 6 o'clock another and heavier shower came, still further dampening the ardor of the celebrators The sky soon cleared and the cool evening was acceptable to the merry dancers of the G A R ball at the opera house and the concert-goers at Ward's Hall. Both were largely patronized and generally pronounced successful There was a brilliant display of fireworks in the evening both at the park and in the city

ATTEMPTED JAIL DELIVERY

On July 14, an attempt was made by the three prisoners then in jail to make their escape About 9 o'clock in the evening, the deputy sheriff, H H Evenson, went to lock the cell doors of the prisoners, the door of Martin Wallace's cell was open, and as Wallace had gone to bed, Mr Evenson very kindly stepped inside of the corridor to shut it As he did so Wallace made for him and dealt him a heavy blow in the face At the same time the other prisoners rushed from their cells and passed out the first door Wallace and one of the others passed into the office and endeavored to get out the outside door, but it was locked They were about to jump through the window when Mr Evenson fired his revolver at Wallace, the ball entering his shoulder. This called a halt, and the prisoners all hurried back into their cells and were securely locked in It was found necessary to call in the county physician to dress the wound of Wallace

SUDDENLY KILLED

Mr J G Cooley, who was among the early Wilton settlers, while hauling wheat to Waseca, Nov 24 1884, lost his life in the following manner. About noon, as he was driving up the hill on the Wilton road about a mile south of Waseca, the wagon, by some means, suddenly went into a deep rut, and Mr Cooley was thrown from the load to the ground, a sack of wheat falling on him As he fell, his body lay in such a position that the hind wheel of the wagon passed over his neck, killing him instantly

The team passed on a short distance and stopped. His son, Josiah, a boy about sixteen years old, was some thirty rods behind his father, with another load of wheat. He saw his father fall and hastened to the spot as soon as possible, finding his father dead. Mr. August Schulz and others soon came up, when the body was placed upon a wagon and taken to Waseca, and thence to the family home in Wilton.

PRESIDENTIAL ELECTION

Grover Cleveland was elected president in 1884 for the first time Waseca county gave James G Blaine 1,189 votes, Grover Cleveland 867, and John P St John 97 The local candidates elected were as follows. M D L Collester, representative. S Swenson, auditor, Austin Vinton and M Craven, county commissioners

CHAPTER LIV, 1885.

DEATH OF J. M. ROBERTSON—COUNTY BOARD—DEATH OF NANCY MOSHER—OFFICE OF MUNICIPAL JUDGE—CRANE CREEK IMPROVEMENT, REPORT OF AUDITING BOARD—ST. MARY CHURCH BURNED—BUILDING STATISTICS

Soon after the "Happy New Year" greetings, Jan 5, 1885, a gloom was cast over the community by the death of J. M. Robertson, a prominent citizen of Waseca He was born in Liberty, Sullivan county, N. Y, May 23, 1852 Two years later his parents moved to Illinois, and thence to Winona in 1856 He grew to manhood in Winona county and came to Waseca about 1879, engaging in the hardware business with Bailey & Watkins He left a wife and two small children. His wife was the accomplished daughter of Hon Burr Deuel, of Quincy, Olmstead county, Minnesota Mr Robertson died of pneumonia It is said that while returning from Chicago, about three weeks prior to his death, he took a severe cold The night was cold, and on the train was a poor woman and child who suffered from lack of warm wraps. To relieve them Mr. Robertson let them have his overcoat The result was he received a cold that brought on the fatal result. For this self-sacrificing act his memory should be preserved.

THE COUNTY BOARD.

The county commissioners this year were N M Nelson, Austin Vinton, M. Craven, Philip Purcell, M. F. Connor, and A. J Jordan. Mr Purcell was again elected chairman. The county printing this year was divided and let to the several papers designated at legal rates A movement was made at this meeting for the building of a bridge across the Le Sueur river at the John Carmody farm, in Wilton, and at the March meeting, $300 was appropriated for that purpose

WINTER WEATHER

The winter of 1884-5, while not as prolonged as some winters, furnished some very cold weather, especially during the month of January

AN AGED PIONEER.

The 87th anniversary of the birthday of Mrs Nancy Mosher was celebrated on the 29th of January by a surprise party for that lady at the residence of her daughter, Mrs W S Baker, of Waseca. There were present twenty-five persons who were the children, the grandchildren, and the great grandchildren of the venerable lady The occasion was one of decided enjoyment Mrs Mosher was born in Vermont in 1797 She was mother of Hiram A, Asa, and "Jim" Mosher, pioneers in this county

MUNICIPAL JUDGE

It was at the legislative session of 1885 that the office of municipal judge was created by special act for the city of Waseca—the offices of justices of the peace for said city being abolished by the same act The new court had jurisdiction throughout the county the same as a justice of the peace, with this addition: in all civil actions where the amount in controversy did not exceed $300. Otherwise its jurisdiction was substantially the same. John Carmody, Esq, was the first judge elected under the new law, and was one of the best who has ever held the position

CRANE CREEK IMPROVEMENT.

The drainage of large tracts of land situated in Steele and this county was undertaken and partly accomplished in 1885 The following report is here reproduced

Messrs. S B Williams, T. H Griffin, and W C Young, appointed by the governor to examine the work and audit the accounts for widening and deepening Crane creek, have submitted their report to State Auditor Braden, in which they say

"The channel in many places has been straightened, widened, and deepened A uniform width of eighteen feet has been preserved for the channel along the whole excavation, and in some places the excavation has been five feet in depth In the opinion of this committee the work already done would be more than doubled in value if the work could be continued to the source of the creek at Watkins lake, and some straightening of the channel below the mouth of the creek

The cost of such improvements to complete the work in a permanent manner, would not exceed, in our opinion, the present outlay of $1,500, additional, as the whole engineering is now complete and nothing but excavation is required This would reclaim thousands of acres of land, a considerable part of which, as this committee is informed, belongs to the state, and is now nearly valueless because of the overflow for want of a free, open channel

"In auditing accounts the committee found all bills reasonable and just except those for surveying, which were considerably above the legal rate of $4.00 per day allowed county surveyors The committee reduced them thereto, bringing the whole outlay within the appropriation Therefore we recommend that there be allowed as follows For surveying, $399, for sundries such as tools, hardware, lumber used, etc, $120.10, for pay roll of laborers on excavation, $748.35, for services of the commissioners of Steele and Waseca counties and mileage, $202 65, for paying the commissioners on behalf of the state, $30 00, total, $1,500. In conclusion the committee wish to say that the work of excavating the channel has been done very much below the lowest bid received by the county commissioners for the said work"

ST MARY CHURCH BURNED

The Catholic church people of the St Mary parish met with a heavy loss Dec 19, 1885. The new Catholic church, which was erected at a cost of $15,000, was entirely destroyed by fire Services were held in the morning and in the afternoon the building was consumed. Very few things were saved. The statue of St Joseph, presented to the church some two months prior by Peter Burns and Christie Hefferon, at a cost of $125, and the statue of the Blessed Virgin were removed without any material damage The chalices were also saved The church members were under lasting obligations to Thomas Garaghty and James Byron for their heroic services in rescuing the altar furniture. Mr Garaghty at one time became so bewildered in the smoke that he probably would have perished had it not been for the assistance of James Byron in going to his rescue. The building was 44x86 feet, and 26 feet high It was insured for $7,000 The burned edifice was replaced with a new one early the next year.

BUILDING IMPROVEMENTS.

The building improvements of the city of Waseca for the year 1885 footed up to $69,600.

CAPTER LV, 1886.

COUNTY PHYSICIANS—HERALD REMOVAL—ANOTHER DESTRUCTIVE FIRE—ROAD AND BRIDGE FUNDS—THE ST. CLOUD TORNADO, TERRIBLE DESTRUCTION OF LIFE AND PROPERTY—A BURGLAR SHOT BY ED GOETZENBERGER--MURDER AND SUICIDE NEAR NEW RICHLAND—THE FARMERS' ALLIANCE—NOTABLE MEETINGS IN THE YEAR—EDITORS, W C T U, OLD SETTLERS, MAPLEWOOD PARK—DIED, JOHN BALLARD, SILAS BUCKMAN, GEO SMITH, HONORA BURKE (KILLED BY R R)—FALL ELECTION—EARLY WINTER—BUILDING STATISTICS

The annual meeting of the county commissioners this year commenced Jan 5 Philip Purcell was again chosen to preside The members of the board were N. M Nelson, Philip Purcell, M F Connor, Austin Vinton, and Milton Craven The county physicians for this year were Dr. H. J. Young for the First district, Dr M J Taylor for the Second, Dr John Nutting for the Third, and Dr. W A Lang for the Fourth The county printing was disposed of as follows The contract for publishing the delinquent tax list was awarded to the "Herald," the contract for publishing the proceedings of the county board went to the Janesville "Argus," and the contract for publishing the financial statement and the proceedings of the board of equalization was given to the "Radical."

REMOVAL.

On the 29th and 30th of January, 1886, the Waseca County "Herald" outfit, was moved into the upper story of the brick building now owned by Hon. C. A. Smith, and adjoining the A.

15

Grapp furniture building, where it remained until September 21, 1900, when it was removed to its present commodious rooms.

A $6,000 BLAZE

On Feb 11, 1886, about 2 30 o'clock a m fire was discovered in Tom Moonan's wooden building, next to the brick store of S. C Eckenbeck & Co, in the rear or kitchen part That part of the building was all ablaze when discovered, and Mr and Mrs. Southworth, who occupied the building, barely escaped with their every-day clothing The fire alarm was given and the members of the fire company and many citizens promptly responded By the time the firemen got out their engine and put on a stream of water, the Moonan building was nearly consumed, and Jos Gatzman's wooden building was well under way The flames soon reached Ward's building, known as Brubaker & Smith's meat market By the most courageous efforts the fire was confined to the latter building, and although Helms building, occupied by Sproat, several times caught fire, it was as often extinguished The loss on buildings was $3,500, and on goods about $2,500 Brick buildings were promptly built the next spring to replace the burned ones

ROAD AND BRIDGE FUNDS

At the March session of the board of county commissioners the following appropriations were made

"Ordered, that $200 be appropriated for repairs on roads and bridges in the first commissioner district, to be expended under the supervision of Austin Vinton; that $200 be appropriated for repairs on roads and bridges in the second commissioner district, to be expended under the supervision of Philip Purcell, that $200 be appropriated for repairs on roads and bridges in the third commissioner district, to be expended under the supervision of N M Nelson, that $200 be appropriated for repairs on roads and bridges in the fourth commissioner district to be expended under the supervision of A. J. Jordan, that $200 be appropriated for repairs on roads and bridges in the fifth commissioner district, to be expended under the supervision of M F Connor"

THE ST CLOUD TORNADO

On the 14th day of April, 1886, Sauk Rapids and St Cloud were visited by a tornado which killed fifty persons and wounded more than one hundred others At St. Cloud, in the track of the storm, stood the Manitoba freight house and cars filled with freight. Down on them the whirlwind pounced, lifted them from the tracks and cast them in shapeless masses Iron rails were torn from the ties and twisted like wires Telegraph poles were torn up and wires twisted into masses The freight house was totally wrecked and over $3,000 worth of freight was whirled through the air and thrown into heaps and scattered over an area of a quarter of a mile Fifteen freight cars were demolished. The cries and shrieks of the wounded rent the air, and the ground was strewn with the bodies of the dead.

The Sauk Rapids disaster was described by an eye witness as follows

"The tornado struck this city at 4 o'clock, and in six minutes the town was in ruins Not a business house was left standing on the main street, and many residences were demolished The wind came from the southwest and swept everything before it for a width of about four blocks The stormcloud was as black as night, with a bright clear sky on either side The courthouse was made a heap of ruins The union school house, two churches, the postoffice, flour mill, and large machine shop were all converted into kindling wood The Northern Pacific depot was blown away, and a large number of freight cars overturned At the present time twenty-two dead bodies have been recovered from the ruins and a large number of persons are injured

"A wedding party of thirty persons were in a building about four miles from Rice station when the storm came, and twenty-two of the party were killed and the others all injured The dead were strewn about for a distance of fully six hundred feet, presenting a ghastly spectacle The situation is a sad one, the living being not only deprived of their friends, but of all their earthly possessions at the same time The total loss of property is not less than $300,000, without a dollar of tornado insurance."

Upon receipt of a report of the terrible affair in Waseca, a public meeting was called at the courthouse Hugh Wilson was chosen chairman, and James E Child secretary A resolution offered by Mr. Lewis Brownell, asking the common council of the city to appropriate $300 to aid the sufferers, was unanimously adopted At the suggestion of Judge Crump, seconded by Hon W G. Ward, the chair appointed a committee of three—Judge Crump, Senator Ward, and James E Child—to solicit funds to aid the sufferers The amount donated by the city was $300, and the amount paid in by private persons was $346 75 All of this was forwarded to the governor of the state to be used for the relief of the sufferers In addition to this amount, the

German Evangelical churches of the county contributed as follows The Waseca church $28, the Meriden church $22 10, Wilton church $11 40, and the Iosco church $42 25

ROAD AND BRIDGE FUNDS

At the May meeting of the board of county commissioners, it was ordered

That $200 be appropriated for work on road on sections 20 and 29 in town of Alton, between the house of P Morrissey and Buffalo Lake, and that A J Jordan and M F Connor be appointed a committee to expend said appropriation, and report at the next meeting of the board that $400 be appropriated for the construction of the Lamb bridge; that $150 be appropriated for repair of roads and bridges in the sixth commissioner district to be expended under the supervision of M Craven, that $100 be appropriated for the construction of the Stewart creek bridge, on section 7, Otisco

At the July meeting it was ordered·

That $75 be appropriated to pay the remainder due for building the Stewart creek bridge, and that $195 be appropriated to pay for replanking the Cobb river bridge

August 20 it was ordered

That $150 be appropriated for repairs on roads and bridges in the first commissioner district to be expended under the supervision of Austin Vinton, that $200 be appropriated for repairs on roads and bridges in the second commissioner district, to be expended under the supervision of Philip Purcell, that $150 be appropriated for repairs on roads and bridges in the third commissioner district, to be expended under the supervision of N M Nelson, that $150 be appropriated for repairs of roads and bridges in the fourth commissioner district, to be expended under the supervision of A J Jordan, that $150 be appropriated for repairs of roads and bridges in the fifth commissioner district, to be expended under the supervision of M F Connor

A BURGLAR SHOT

On the night of June 3, 1886, a man named Ed Menck, a tailor, and a stranger, who refused to give his name, broke into the hardware store of P C Bailey between 11 and 12 o'clock Ed Goetzenberger and Francis Breen had gone to bed a short time before, in the office, adjoining the store They heard the report of the glass breaking, and Ed got up and looked out but saw nothing As there were many people on the streets and some in the saloons, he thought little of it. Presently they heard more noise, this time in the store They arose cautiously, put on their pantaloons, lighted a lamp, Ed. taking his revolver and Francis the lamp, and suddenly opened the door between the office and the store, where they discovered two burglars. The thieves beat a hasty retreat, notwithstanding Ed.'s invitation to them to halt, and as they said something about shooting, Ed went into practice while young Breen bravely held the light Ed emptied his revolver at them as they retreated by crawling through a window, and then he shouted for the police There was a general search instituted, and the men were soon found and arrested by Marshal Keeley Both of them had their hands cut considerably by the glass in the window, and the stranger received a bullet wound, the ball striking him in the back, following a rib, and lodging in front Dr Hunt took out the bullet and dressed their wounds Some of the citizens chipped in and presented Ed Goetzenberger and Francis Breen each a gold watch and chain as evidence of their appreciation of the courage displayed by the young men on the occasion Both offenders were convicted of burglary at the fall term of court and sent to prison.

MURDER AND SUICIDE

The people of New Richland were thrown into a state of great excitement on the evening of July 6, 1886, by the murder of Miss Anna M Discher and the suicide of her murderer The following report was published at the time:

Henry Young was a German whose relatives reside in Wisconsin He had been around here for several years, was always considered a steady young man, not of vicious habits, tolerably well to do, and owned an interest in a thresher, which he ran in season The other victim, Anna M Discher, was the daughter of W F Discher, justice of the peace, and a well-to-do farmer In the afternoon Young was around town and seemed to be drinking heavily. Then he went out to the Discher farm Mrs Discher and daughter were sitting on the porch sewing. He walked up to the girl and after a few words drew his revolver and shot her twice, the bullets taking effect in or near the heart She died in a few minutes in her mother's arms Thrusting the revolver into his mouth, he fired and killed himself instantly It is rumored that he had wanted her for some time to marry him, which she declined to do This is undoubtedly correct, as it seems to be reasonably well founded"

FARMERS' ALLIANCE

This organization became very strong this year throughout

the state On the 15th of May, 1886, there was a meeting of Alliance men at Waseca, George W. Sprague, president of the state alliance, being here to address them Mr W D Armstrong announced that there were now five alliances in the county, and that they might organize a county alliance, if those present thought it advisable; but before doing so he should like to hear from the state officers that were present He introduced George W. Sprague, president of the state organization, who addressed the meeting at considerable length After the address, on motion of M F Connor, the five alliances represented proceeded to the formal organization of a county alliance The president and the secretary of each alliance signed an application to the state alliance for a charter Messrs W D. Armstrong, H A Wagoner, Patrick Kenehan, and Thomas Barden were chosen to act as a committee to draft by-laws for the county alliance, to report to an adjourned meeting to be held May 29 At the adjourned meeting, constitution and by-laws were adopted and the following officers elected. President, L. C. Remund, of Blooming Grove, vice-president. M F Connor, of Wilton secretary, W D Armstrong, of Woodville, treasurer, Jas. E Jones, of Iosco

The regular meetings of the county alliance were to be held on the first Saturday of January, April, July and September The meeting of May 29 adjourned to meet again June 26, 1886 At this last meeting there were present delegates from eight alliances

NOTABLE MEETINGS

There were several notable meetings in Waseca during the summer months On the 15th of June the Southwestern Editorial convention of Minnesota was held in Waseca The editors were entertained at Hotel Maplewood at noon and in the evening a banquet was tendered them at the Grant House.

The W C T U societies of the county held a county convention in Waseca, June 17, 1886 The convention was held in the English M. E. church, Mrs. D. J. Bickford presiding

The old settlers of Freedom and Alton, met on the 10th day of June, in the cultivated grove on the beautiful farm of Prof F D Seaman The day was an ideal one for such a picnic and there were three hundred and fifty persons present. The feast was all that could be desired, and then followed toasts and responses A synopsis of the response by Judge Crump, then of Waseca, is here given:

He said he was the first one, as usual, to make a fool of himself, and he proposed to do it well. He deemed it a compliment to be called upon to address them, although it would be unfortunate both for them and himself "I can remember," said he, "when I became an old settler here It was in 1865 I also remember the first old settler I met here, who is now in Wisconsin He was neither naked or clad, and had twenty-five cents in his pocket—now he has nothing I can appreciate and you can appreciate those who have come here and why they have come. You know that we came here to eat—especially Graham and myself—and we have enjoyed ourselves, especially Graham He knows when he has a good thing We have all enjoyed ourselves on this occasion.

"I can remember when we had myriads of mosquitoes here as big as sheep and kept hogs on them We have driven them out, but alas! the book agents and the lightning rod men have taken their places

"I can remember, too, that the rattlesnake infested this region He, too, has disappeared before the old settler, and the local editor rattles at the passer-by

The Indian, too, I am told, once roamed over these prairies with tomahawk and scalping knife, but he is gone, and the politicians and office seekers now scour the country in search of spoils

"I now come to the defense of my friend, Jim Cummins He has been lied about Somebody has said he is no old settler I know he is He has told me so He broke the prairie sod here in 1858, and camped here with another Indian at that time, and I want it entered in the minutes

"The old settlers set good tables, they are good eaters and long eaters

"I started to say something serious but I have failed—I generally do

"As the pioneers grow older, as the wrinkles in their faces grow longer and more numerous, as the hair gets whiter, as the numbers grow less, from year to year, these reunions will be more valued, and your children will thank you for having subdued this wilderness and built these pleasant homes

"We honor and ought to honor the soldier who defended the country in the hour of peril, but I think the men and women who braved the hardships and dangers of frontier life are entitled to some credit for their courage and fortitude, and ought to be congratulated for coming here

"I don't think I'll talk any more There are editors here who are full of talk, the only trouble is they will lie so"

The sessions at Maplewood Park, this year, were well attended.

Among the noted speakers was Gen Howard, who delivered his famous lecture on the battle of Gettysburg

DEATH OF JOHN BALLARD.

John Ballard, of Iosco, on the afternoon of July 13, 1886, started out with a hay rake, just after supper, to rake hay There was no breeching to the harness, and the rake ran on the heels of the horse, causing him to run. The horse became unmanageable, ran into a grove, and Mr Ballard was thrown against a tree with such force as to break several of his ribs loose from the backbone He was a great sufferer until August 31, when he passed into rest He was about fifty years of age, and settled in this county in 1858 He married about 1861 and left surviving him his wife and ten children, the eldest twenty-four years of age and the youngest three He owned a farm of one hundred and twenty acres, and a ten-acre timber lot, besides considerable personal property He was a Union soldier in the War of the Rebellion and was a member of McKune Post G A R, which attended his funeral, paying the last sad honors to their departed comrade

NOVEMBER DEATHS

Died, Mr. Silas Buckman, in his seventy-eighth year, at 3 o'clock, a m, Nov 9, 1886, of diarrhoea and congestion of the bladder He had been failing since the latter part of August He was a native of New Hampshire, removed to Crown Point, New York, when a boy, and resided there until 1867, when he settled on a farm in Woodville township His wife died some years before Since that time he had lived with his son, G R Buckman.

Died, George Smith, elder son of Hon Warren Smith Nov 10, 1886, at 2 o'clock a m, of congestion, in his twenty-third year George had suffered for a year or more from diabetes and was much reduced in flesh and strength He attended the Saturday evening entertainment at the opera house, and took a severe cold, which caused congestion and death He graduated the spring before with distinction at Dartmouth college and had chosen civil engineering as his profession

DEATH OF MISS HONORA BURKE

A sad and fatal accident occurred at the Phelps' crossing, about a mile and a quarter west of Waseca on the Winona & St Peter railroad, December 24, 1886, about 7 o'clock in the evening Mr Philip Brown and wife, of St Mary, came in to meet Miss Honora Burke, daughter of Michael Burke and sister of Mrs Brown Miss Burke was coming from Minneapolis to spend Christmas with her parents and friends According to Mr Brown's evidence before the coroner's jury they left the depot about 7 o'clock Miss Burke sat on the righthand side of the sleigh, Isabella McCabe, a girl some twelve years of age, next to her, Mrs Brown on the left side, all on the same seat, with Brown sitting on his wife's lap He was driving along on a fast trot and did not see or hear the freight train coming from the west until within thirty or forty feet of the track His wife then said "There comes the train" He tried to stop the team one horse and one mule, and had them nearly stopped within perhaps five feet of the track, when the horse gave a plunge and dragged the mule with him over the track At the same instant the engine struck the sleigh and threw them all out. He and his wife fell near together, the McCabe girl a little way from them, near the fence, and Miss Burke still further from them partly under the wire fence He got up immediately and went to his wife who was hurt some, then to the McCabe girl who seemed to be stunned,—he thought she was dead He next went to where Miss Burke was and drew her from under the fence. He could not see that she was alive, so he put his ear to her mouth and found that she did not breathe Dr Young, who examined Miss Burke, said that she died of concussion of the brain, caused by being thrown against a fence post, and that death was probably instantaneous

THE FALL ELECTION

For the first time in years, the democrats carried the county for state candidates by pluralities ranging from 137 to 504—the latter number being for "Doc" Ames, of Minneapolis—his total vote in the county having been 1,442 The following local candidates were elected: senator, W. G. Ward, representative, M. W. Ryan, treasurer, Chas McKenna, auditor, S Swenson; register of deeds, A F Kruger, clerk of court, M B Keeley, sheriff, A C Krassin, judge of probate, Wm C Young, county attorney, P McGovern, superintendent of schools, J B. Dye, court commissioner, G R Buckman, coroner, M V Hunt, surveyor, O. L. Smith, county commissioners, Austin Vinton, Philip Purcell, J O Sunde, James Conway, Charles Deyling, Oliver Peterson

EARLY WINTER

The following announcement appeared in the Waseca Herald of Nov. 19, 1886

"The beautiful Indian summer of this month came to a sudden close on Tuesday Snow commenced to fall in the morning, with the wind northeast, and continued to fall through the day Tuesday night the wind veered to the north and blew a continuous gale for twenty-four hours, the snow falling continuously and drifting into great heaps. The roads were blockaded in every direction, and railway trains were suspended on both roads The passenger from Minneapolis got stuck in a snow drift between Waterville and Waseca, and no mail arrived during the day It was the heaviest snow storm for years in the month of November, but, fortunately, the weather was not very cold Thursday morning the wind was in the northwest, the snow still falling and drifting The outlook for winter travel was discouraging"

On December 3, the same paper said:

"The deep snow that now covers this part of mother earth is becoming a barrier to trade—a serious obstacle to business"

BUILDING STATISTICS

The people of Waseca in 1886 expended eighty-eight thousand, four hundred eighty-five dollars in constructing new buildings and making improvements. The largest and most important building erected this year was the Catholic Seminary built on lots adjoining the Catholic church, in Waseca, by the Sisters of the Holy Child Jesus Their headquarters in this country are Philadelphia The central building is 30x60 feet, and each wing, east and west, is 40x66 feet, all two stories high Only the west wing and its basement were completed this year and cost $10,-000 The basement of the part completed this season is 11 feet high and divided as follows A play room in the south end 24x40 feet, next a furnace room 12x20, a cellar 10x12, and a wood room 8x12 In the center is a well of water, then a kitchen 13x15 and a laundry 13x15, separated by the stairway hall. At the north end of the building are two dining rooms, one on each side of the hall, 13x15 feet. The first story over the basement is 16 feet high, and divided as follows Entrance hall 7x30, the first room on the right, 14x16, is the parlor; opposite this is the reception room, the same size, the next room on the right, as you enter the hall, is the music room, 14x16, and opposite that is the chapel, 14x16 feet, then comes a hall the whole width of the building seven feet across, and next, two school rooms, separated by folding doors, each room 20x30 feet The second or upper story is 15 feet high, and contains two school rooms, each 20x16 feet; three sleeping rooms, 14x16, one sleeping room, 9x16 feet, a bath room and water closet, 8x9 feet, and two small closets. This is one of the important educational institutions of the state and has done much for the people of Waseca and surrounding country.

The following is a list of structures costing $1,000 and over

Catholic Seminary	$10,000 00
Pugh & Goodman, new brick store . .	8,000 00
Everett & Aughenbaugh, engine boiler house and machinery . .	7,500 00
Joseph Gatzman, new brick store	3,600 00
W G Ward, new brick store . .	3,500 00
Thos Moonan, new brick store .	3,500 00
Pat Solon, new house and barn .	3,500 00
Chicago & Northwestern Railway, round house improvements .	3,000 00
P McElroy, new residence	2,500 00
Van Dusen & Co, improvements to elevator	2,000 00
W D Abbott, new house	1,800 00
H Britten, new house and improvements	1,600 00
W E Scott, new house	1,700 00
Adolph Schmidt, new house . .	1,500 00
H Hoyt, new house .	1,500 00
R M Middaugh, new house . .	1,500 00
B Hassing house and barn	1,200 00
Hans Borelson, new house	1,200 00
School House, improvements	1,100 00
Waseca Iron Works, machinery and improvements .	1,000 00
Waseca Furniture Company, new machinery and improvements	1,000 00
W G Ward, improvements on buildings and house	1,000 00
Thos Flynn, new house	1,000 00

CHAPTER LVI, 1887.

NEW YEAR CALLS—COUNTY LEGISLATION—THIRTY THOUSAND DOLLAR FIRE AT JANESVILLE—WEATHER NOTES—DIED, ROBERT McDOUGALL, W S BAKER, ROBERT EARL, ZABINA CHILD, M D L COLLESTER

New Year's day was ushered in clear and fair on the north end of an iceberg, the thermometer registering thirty-four degrees below zero, at day-break In the afternoon, some twenty-six gentlemen made the customary New Year calls Messrs E A Everett, B U Dye, W A Swift and Geo F Tallon composed one party and were drawn about town by Connelly's matched team of white ponies, hitched to a fur-covered sleigh—pampas grass plumes adorning the horses heads Messrs H W Bird, Jos Truax, and Arthur Jamison went together, riding about town on an inverted crockery crate drawn by Charlie Clement's hybrid horses W. J Jennison, J. A Stemen, F. V Hubbard, H H Sudduth, A D Goodman and Ellsworth Goodspeed composed another party Drs Cummings and Davidson E A White and C C. Griffin constituted a lively quartette G W Eckenbeek, J. D. Walworth, and N S Gordon drank together Oysters, fruits cake, and coffee were generously served and disposed of with much zest

COUNTY LEGISLATION

The commissioners this year were Austin Vinton, Philip Purcell, Jonas O Sunde, James Conway, Chas Deyling and Oliver Peterson The board organized by electing Mr Purcell chairman The question of county printing came up as usual, a portion of the board desiring to let the whole of the work to the lowest bidder, while the majority, led by the chairman, decided to let only four items, to wit proceedings of board of county commissioners proceedings of board of equalization, delinquent tax list and financial statement The Radical offered to print these items for one cent, and received the contract.

The county fathers were very liberal this year, making appropriations for roads and bridges At their January meeting one hundred dollars was appropriated for corduroying slough on town line road between section 6, Alton, and section 31, Janesville, to be expended under the supervision of Messrs Purcell and Conway Thirty-five dollars was appropriated for work on road between sections 17 and 18, Iosco, to be expended under the supervision of Mr Purcell

At the March meeting appropriations were made as follows·

The sum of $200 was appropriated for the repair of roads and bridges in the first commissioner district, to be expended under supervision of J O Sunde The sum of $220 was appropriated to be expended in the repair of roads and bridges, in the third commissioner district, under supervision of Philip Purcell The sum of $250 was appropriated to be expended by Commissioner Peterson—$200 of the same to be expended outside the city of Waseca on roads, and not to exceed $50 inside the city limits Three hundred and fifty dollars was appropriated for roads and bridges to be expended under the supervision of James Conway in the fourth district, and $225 to be expended in the fifth district under the supervision of Mr Deyling.

The board received and accepted the report of the committee on the Krassin bridge, and appropriated $339 to pay for the work. The report of the committee on the Boot Creek bridge was made and accepted, and $53 50 appropriated to pay for the work.

At the May meeting, money was appropriated as follows.

The sum of $400 was appropriated to build a new bridge at St Mary in place of the old one, and Messrs Purcell, Conway and Deyling were appointed to superintend the construction thereof The sum of $400 was appropriated to build a new bridge across the LeSueur river on section 34, in Otisco, and Messrs Peterson and Sunde were appointed to oversee the construction of it. $400 was appropriated to build two new bridges on the outlet of Lake Helena—one on section 36 in Janesville, and one on section 19, in Iosco The sum of $120 was appropriated to build a bridge across the Little Cobb river, on section 33, town of Freedom $125 was appropriated to build a bridge across the LeSueur river, between sections 24 and 25, town of New Richland, and the sum of $100 was appropriated to each commissioner district for the repair of roads and bridges

On July 25, 1887, the board appropriated $1,000 for building the Wilton bridge and making the approaches thereto; and an additional sum of $325 for completing the St Mary bridge, purchasing the right of way for the same and grading the approaches thereto

At the August session of the board the sum of $250 was appropriated for completing the unfinished work on new bridges and caring for material of old bridges in the several commissioner districts.

$30,000 FIRE AT JANESVILLE

The worst conflagration which has ever visited Janesville village, occurred on the night of April 12, 1887 The fire was first discovered bursting from the roof of the barn of the Northwestern hotel, standing east of that building It originated in the hayloft, and was discovered about eight o'clock The horses in the barn were taken out without difficulty The flames spread rapidly to the adjoining buildings, and each new blaze gave impetus to the devouring element To add to the sad situation the big mill had been shut down for some time for repairs, and no water could be obtained from that source, and all other water supplies were soon exhausted Everything was dry and the flames soon spread to the Northwestern hotel, McCabe's hotel, and Kleeman's saloon By this time, the fire was beyond control, spread rapidly each way, and soon crossed to the west side of the street The Johnson house, barn and out-buildings, at the northern limit of the fire, were totally destroyed Mr Church, the landlord, removed most of his furniture and goods It was a hard blow to Janesville, but the plucky men of that energetic town soon rebuilt the waste places

WEATHER NOTES

The winter of 1886-7 gave more than the average fall of snow and cold weather A local paper of Jan. 28 said.

"The boys on the railroad are having a hard struggle with snow The road between Sleepy Eye and Lake Benton makes costly work for the Northwestern during the winter season Much of the time a snow plow has to be run ahead of passenger trains, from station to station, telegraphing back that it is safe for the latter to go on another stage With four or five such outfits between Huron and St Peter the expense is great, the work hard, and the delays vexatious. One or two winters of such expense would almost rebuild the line"

The snow was deep all winter and remained upon the ground until the middle of March The last snow storm of the season was recorded as follows Let it be recorded that on the 22d day of April, A D 1887, a fierce snow storm from the regions of the unsalted sea visited this section, that snow fell to the depth of two or three inches, that, on the morning of the 23d, ice had formed to the thickness of half an inch The next day the snow disappeared."

NOTED DEATHS DURING THE YEAR

Robert McDougall passed from life into the sleep of death, on the evening of Jan 15, 1887 in the sixty-sixth year of his life Robert was born in the highlands of Scotland, in 1821 His parents left their native hills and settled in Canada, near Guelph, where they opened a farm in the then wilderness when he was a small boy Robert spent the years of his minority at home, and encountered all the hardships and hard work incident to a new, timbered country Sometime about 1854, Robert and his brother Hugh came to the "States" They stayed in Iowa for some time, then came to Waseca county, in the fall of 1855 Each made a claim where the McDougall farm now is, and commenced keeping "batch" There were two other young men near them, from Canada, named Robbins—George and William All of them had made claims in good faith, none of them knowing that it was necessary to declare their intentions to become citizens, supposing that they could do that at the time of proving up During the winter of 1855-6, men from Owatonna, who had laid out and platted the village of Wilton, brought in several persons to jump the claims of these men This outrage aroused all the settlers in the neighborhood A meeting was called and it was decided that the intruders must go. Robert was passionate and impetuous, Hugh was cool and determined The claim-jumpers were ordered to leave at once, and so strong was the feeling that they discreetly stood aside while the "boys," as they were then called, left not one log upon another. The claim-jumpers then went to Owatonna and caused the arrest of every settler in the neighborhood except one or two, on a criminal warrant Several of the settlers, including Robert, were found guilty of destroying property The verdict was given by a packed jury; on appeal the judgments were set aside Contests were also instituted in the land office, then at Winona, regarding the claims Matters became so warm that the men from Owatonna dared not be seen on the LeSueur alone, and when the land cases came on at Winona, the "claim-jumpers" were so well convinced that their lives were not secure that they virtually withdrew their claims, with the understanding that they might peaceably take other claims near by Notwithstanding this patched-up truce, the feeling did not die out, and on the night of the 19th of April, 1856, several house-bodies which had been put up on the village site were torn down and demolished Wilton never recovered again until a year after, when the Owatonna proprietors, sold or pretended to sell their interests to other persons The McDougall brothers, a year or so afterwards, proved up on their claims and perfected their titles. Not long after this, Hugh returned to the old homestead in Canada, where he now resides, and Robert took his horses and wagon and started for the mining regions of the Western mountains He spent one winter near the head waters of the Saskatchewan river, then crossed the mountains into Washington Territory, worked in different mines some time, and returned in 1860 After a short visit here, he returned to Canada, where he remained until he was married Shortly after his marriage, in the year 1866, he settled on the farm where he died. Had he lived until the following March he would have been sixty-six years of age He left with his wife nine children—six girls and three boys He owned two hundred acres of land and quite a stock of horses and cattle, at the time of his demise. Some eight or nine years prior to his death, he was badly injured by a horse, one of his arms being broken A quack doctor pretended to reduce the fracture, but it was done so poorly that he suffered much from it Mr McDougall was an honest, conscientious man, and although high-tempered and sometimes very passionate, he was a kind-hearted man and a true friend His remains were deposited in the quiet Wilton cemetery, where he sleeps the last long sleep.

Died, at his home in Waseca, March 6, 1887, Wm S Baker, in the seventy-ninth year of his age. He was born in the state of Maine April 28, 1808 He was a pioneer from early manhood, coming to the state of Ohio in early life He was married to

Clarissa B. Mosher, at Marion, Ohio Dec 30, 1841 He became a member of the M E church in 1842, by conversion, and remained such during the remainder of his life He moved with his family to Dodge county, Wisconsin, as early as 1844 and was among the first settlers of that locality. After out-living the pioneer days of Wisconsin, the family came to this county in 1856, and settled in Otisco At an early day in this county, he took quite an active part in public affairs, being the first treasurer of Waseca county

Died, Oct 10, 1887, Minnie Smith, elder daughter of Hon Warren Smith, of this city, aged 28 years, of lingering consumption She had been an invalid for some time, and everything that wealth and affection could do had been done to prolong her life, but the disease was incurable, and she finally passed from life unto death.

Capt Robert Earl, of Alton, one of the early settlers of Freedom, dropped suddenly dead while butchering hogs, at his farm, on Monday, Oct 17, 1887, of apoplexy Deceased was born in Jamestown, Pa, Aug 10, 1832, and was a little over fifty-five years of age (See biographical sketches)

Died, Zabina Child, Nov 5, 1887, at the residence of his son, S P Child, of Blue Earth City, Minn, of dropsy and inflammation of his stomach. He was a contractor and builder by trade and was a life-long pioneer He was born in Windsor county Vt, November 22, 1808 At the age of twenty he went to St. Lawrence county, New York, working at his trade in the village of Canton and vicinity He made his home with his father, Daniel Child, in De Kalb, St Lawrence county, until his marriage to Orrilla Rice, of Jefferson county, N Y., Feb 14, 1833. In 1834 he removed to Ohio by horse team and wagon, with his young wife and one child, and settled near Medina, then a pioneer settlement. He remained there until about 1837, when a failure of crops and the general hard times of that period induced him to return to his old home in the state of New York There he settled on a small farm with his family, where he remained until 1843, when he again went to Ohio, remaining in Perry, Lake county, about a year. He then removed with his family to the territory of Wisconsin, stopping at Sheboygan a few weeks, and afterwards locating in Dodge county, Wis, near

Waupun He afterwards lived in Herman, Dodge county, and later settled in Outagamie county, near Appleton Afterwards he spent some time with relatives in Pierce county, Wis, lived a while with his brother Simeon in Washington county, Iowa, and in later years resided in Blue Earth City spending a portion of his time in Jackson county, Minn He sleeps in the Blue Earth cemetery

Hon M D L Collester, then of Mankato, died of pleuro-pneumonia, Dec 17, 1887 He was buried from the Episcopal church of that city under the auspices of the I. O O F, of which he was a member He caught cold while taking testimony in the boiler inspection matter at Litchfield, about Nov 22, and was confined to his bed one day while there He returned to Mankato. Nov 25, and on the Sunday following was taken sick with pleuro-pneumonia, of which, after a very painful illness of nearly three weeks, he died Mr Collester was born in Marlboro N H, Jan 26, 1840 He graduated with high rank at Middlebury college in Vermont in 1865 He then read law at Newport, N H., and came West and commenced the practice of law at Minneapolis in 1867 Shortly afterward he accepted a professorship of Greek and Latin languages in Shattuck school, at Faribault, and continued in this position until 1872, when he came to Waseca and again entered upon the practice of his profession While at Waseca he was five years county attorney; one year mayor of Waseca, and one year, 1885, respresented Waseca county in the state legislature, in which he was chairman of the judiciary committee of the House In the spring of 1885 he moved to Mankato, where he lived at the time of his death. He left surviving him. a wife and one child, a son Mr Collester, for many years a resident of Waseca, had many warm friends The writer certainly had opportunities equal to any to know the true character of the man In his business affairs he was honorable, upright and prompt. In his intercourse with his fellowmen he was generous, and his gratitude for favors shown him had no end Such a feeling as enmity or personal revenge was unknown to him While his ambition led him at times to pander to the ignorant prejudices of class, he never failed to respect virtue and honest worth Both on the rostrum and in the field of journalism we have met him in opposing argument, and yet his generous spirit never gave way to that vulgar enmity and personal animosity which too often result from differences of opinion on public questions He was a ripe scholar and an able advocate He believed in the universal brotherhood of man, and his charity for the frailties and faults of others command a like feeling of generosity in his own behalf

CHAPTER LVII, 1888.

COUNTY PRINTING—CROOKED WORK—WINTER STORM—STORM REMINISCENCES BY FRANK A NEWELL AND MIKE RYAN—FIRST FARMERS' INSTITUTE—TORNADO IN VIVIAN—ROAD AND BRIDGE FUNDS—DIED, S FARRINGTON, MIKE ANDERSON, ALEX JOHNSTON, MRS WM BRISBANE, J. S. G. HONNER, A D MONROE, A J AND MRS WOODBURY, JACKSON TURNACLIFF, DENNIS SHEEHAN (KILLED)—POLITICS, DEFALCATION OF MCKENNA IN THE SUM OF $6,694 64—RESULT OF THE ELECTION

The board of county commissioners met in annual session, Jan 3, 1888 Philip Purcell was again chosen chairman—the members present being Jonas O Sunde, James Conway, Philip Purcell, Charles Deyling, and Oliver Peterson. The matter of county printing was again a subject of contention The following history of the affair is from the Waseca County Herald:

"January 13, 1888—On Tuesday evening of last week we were informed that a portion of the county printing would be let on Thursday afternoon and that sealed bids for the same would be received by the board There was no written or printed notice—simply an oral one Neither does it appear on record that the board would receive bids—it was only a slip-shod, informal invitation for bids, the board in no way agreeing to let the county printing at all—either to the highest or lowest bidder

"In response to the invitation, however, the Herald offered to do the publishing and advertising for the year as follows Proceedings of the county board, 5 cents per folio, financial statement (three weeks) 20 cents per folio; proceedings of the board of equalization 5 cents per folio All miscellaneous notices of the county board and of all the officers of the county to be paid for by the county, at 10 cents per folio, first publication, and 5 cents per folio each subsequent publication

'C E Graham, the only other bidder, offered to do the work for the following Publish all the proceedings of the county board during the year for 1 cent, financial statement (three weeks) 45 cents per folio, proceedings of board of equalization 5 cents per folio He did not bid on any other county work—evidently having an understanding in some way that the treasurer's notice and all other notices would be given out, from time to time, at full legal rates, 75 cents a folio for one insertion and 35 cents for each subsequent publication ,

"Upon the opening and reading of the bids, silence reigned for a moment, and then the chairman brought out some bids for forfeited lands and nervously asked what should be done with them. After some talk, the land bids were finally laid over to the March meeting, and then Mr Sunde suggested that the printing bids ought to be considered The chairman thought they would have to estimate as to which would be the lower bid, and, in reply to a question, said the estimate could be made from the last year's work The other members seemed to agree to that, and then took an adjournment to 7 o'clock in the evening

'At the evening session a representative of the Herald went before the board and stated that he had measured all the work of the last year and found that all the published proceedings of the county board, for the year, measured forty-eight thousand ems (192 folios) which at 5 cents a folio, (Herald bid) would be $9 60 The financial statement of last year measured twenty-one thousand five hundred ems (86 folios) which, at 25 cents a folio—Graham's bid being that much higher than ours—would amount to $21 50 That would be $21 50 minus $9 60, leaving the Herald bid $11.90 less than Mr Graham's bid for the same work

'The Herald man also asked the board, if any member of it had any doubts as to the measurement given, to employ an expert to measure the type

And yet the majority of the board, without measuring the type or giving the matter the least investigation, as we are credibly informed, awarded the printing to the ring organ of the county * * *"

'In our last issue, we gave the substance of the proceedings of the board of county commissioners during their session last week, from Tuesday to Thursday afternoon, our time of closing the forms. Saturday afternoon, a representative of the Herald called at the auditor's office for the purpose of obtaining from the public records the further proceedings of the board Our readers may judge of his surprise and ours when informed that Mr Purcell, chairman of the board, had taken possession of the records, and forbidden access to them, or their publication, until after the adjourned meeting, which is to be held, as the auditor says, on Wednesday, the 25th inst

"When asked the reason of such a strange proceeding, the auditor said he could not give any It seemed to be as much of a surprise to the auditor as to others, and when asked if he did not consider himself the lawful custodian of the county records, he said he did not know, but had supposed heretofore that he was

"As a matter of law, Mr Purcell, as chairman of the board, or in any other capacity, has no more right or authority to take possession of the county auditor's records and secrete them from the public than the editors of the Herald have.

"The statute says 'The county auditor shall, by virtue of his office, be clerk of the board of county commissioners of his county, and keep an accurate record of their official proceedings, and carefully preserve all the documents, books, records, maps and other papers required to be deposited or kept in his office' Nowhere in the statute can be found any authority for the county board, as a body, or for any member of the board, even the chairman, to take possession of the county auditor's records, or any portion of them, and secrete them, or deprive the public of the right of access to them

"The proceedings of the county commissioners, as recorded by the auditor, constitute a portion of the public records, from day to day, and every citizen has the right—the legal right—of access to them in accordance with the statutes.

"We think the auditor erred in allowing Mr Purcell to illegally take from his possession these records of the county and secrete them, although under the circumstances he may have a reasonable excuse He says he was not certain that he had a right to refuse the chairman of the board

"Of course, being a county commissioner, and especially chairman, in the eyes of some people, make a 'mighty mucky-muck' of very poor timber sometimes But suppose that the chairman of any county board in the state should become suddenly insane, or drunk, and in such condition should come into the auditor's office to carry off the county commissioners' record book? Would the auditor be justified in allowing him to do so?

"Can the people of Waseca county imagine what has caused the chairman of the board to resort to this unlawful and, heretofore, unheard of act?"

A WINTER STORM

The terrible wind and snow storm which, on Jan 12, 1888 swept the country from Manitoba to Texas seems to have been more destructive of life than any other in the history of the country Nearly two hundred persons were reported frozen to death in Dakota, Nebraska, Kansas, and Texas Two deaths from freezing were reported in Minnesota The storm seems to have been much worse west of Minnesota than within her borders. In this locality it was not nearly so bad as the great storm of 73, though it was bad enough The harrowing details of suffering and death would fill a whole paper. The thermometer in many places north and west of us registered sixty degrees below, while the government record in Minnesota says it was forty-seven degrees below This storm set the old settlers to talking of old times Asa Mosher, Frank A Newell, Geo Watkins, and others had gathered around "Bill" Johnson's comfortable grocery-store stove, and, among others, Mike Ryan, of Byron, one of the old settlers, dropped in Said Newell

"This reminds me of the great storm of '73, Jan 7 Egad! I shall never forget it. I was over at Morristown that morning The forenoon was mild As the day wore on, the increasing moisture made us think that the back bone of winter was broken About 3 o'clock p m, Sam Stevenson and I started for Waseca Dark clouds began to gather in the west, and about the time we reached Blooming Grove, the wind was blowing a gale, producing a change in the atmosphere that chilled the marrow in one's bones The air was filled with blinding snow, so dense that you couldn't see the horse-whip in your hand The sun seemed to withdraw its light, and the earth seemed to tremble beneath the terrific fury of the continuous, howling blast An impenetrable darkness soon settled upon the earth like a funeral pall, bringing with it intense cold, made doubly so by the driving, penetrating, piercing force of the wind I felt as though I were tied down and a thousand imps were shoveling snow into my ears and mouth Sam drove for all that was out, but when I got home I was nearer dead than alive Egad! I wouldn't take another such chance as that of a winter funeral for all the wealth of a Vanderbilt"

"Well," said Mike Ryan, standing with his overcoat on and his whip in hand, "I mind that storm, meself. I was in Waseca that day, and three others as was with me, and one o' them was 'Black Tom,' as we call 'im, an' we started nigh on to 3 o'clock, maybe, to git home. About the time we got to the LeSueur, the wind was a howlin' worse nor the prairie wolves, an' it wasn't long afore it was as black as a stack o' black cats. I drove a pretty good team o' them days, an' so I went ahead, but we hadn't got far on the prairie afore we was afther losin' the road And, says I, one of us must be afther goin' ahead, so as not to lose the track So one was afther goin' ahead, but divil the bit could we see of him, and so we told him to holler once in a while, which he did Finally, when we came to a turn in the road, near a bridge over a slough, the man went straight on and we lost the track Hole' on, says I, we're off the road So we stopped, an' two staid with the horses, an' two of us looked for the road. I soon found the bridge an' shouted the others to come on I got me horses over the bridge all right, but I soon got them down in a drift as high as their heads an' then I took them from the sleigh and said I would lead 'em One of the men didn't come up, so we hollered and hollered, but we couldn't hear nothin' He could hear us, but the wind howled so we couldn't hear him So I went back to the bridge an' found him His team had got off the bridge an' couldn't get up, an' he couldn't get the tugs loose So I let loose the hames, an' we got the horses out, leavin' the sleigh. Then we went on afut, leadin' the horses. Once in a while it would lighten', an' once when it lightened, I seed tnat we were off the road. Then we stopped an' consulted what we would do So two staid by the horses, and the other two of us went lookin' for the track, an' we were to holler once in a while so as not to lose each other, an' afther a time we found the road, an' then we knew we had got on to a cross road that led to Murphy's place So then we went on again, an' afore long we were off the road again We could hardly see at all—the snow an' ice covered our eyes two inches, more or less But as I was afther sayin,' we had to hunt the road again, an' so we did as before, two spread out an' was to holler when they shud find the track An' sure enough, the two fellers as found the track shouted an' we shouted but divil the bit could they hear us So we went toward them, and after a time we couldn't hear them again Howsumever we struck the track, an' then we hollered, but divil the word could we hear, an' after listenin' awhile we thought to go on—so we went—an' would ye belave it now? afther goin' a mile or so we found we were going the wrong way, d'ye see? an' we had to get back over the same road again Well, as I was afther sayin', we finally got to my house just as the wife and children were cryin' their eyes out, for them other two fellers had got in ahead of us Faith, it was a terrible storum, sir One of the men, the feller that got his team off the bridge, was nearly dead—in fact I think he never was as good a man again

"The stable door was all drifted over and we had to shovel a hole through the drift to get the horses in I've been more nor thirty years in Minnesota, an' never seed such anither storum as that, an God grant I niver may."

FIRST FARMERS' INSTITUTE

The first state farmers' institute ever held in the county was opened on Monday, March 12, 1888, at Ward's Opera House in Waseca It was largely attended and highly satisfactory to all concerned It was conducted by Superintendent Gregg and six or seven assistants

A SMALL TORNADO IN VIVIAN.

A whirlwind visited the northern portion of the town of Vivian on May 4, 1888 destroying a school house, a dwelling house and a barn Mr Abraham Abrahamson, living in the track of the storm, started out to save his hay which was being blown away. He had gone but a few steps when the storm struck him, carried him some rods and then placed him very gently on the ground He was picked up later for dead, but in a few hours he recovered consciousness It was found that his hip and shoulder were dislocated, together with other injuries. His friends tried to get a physician but the high water had swept away the bridges and they could not obtain medical aid till Friday night The tornado gathered immediately after a shower of rain and seemed to come from all directions It went sweeping across the prairie at a fearful rate The machine house of Mr Wm. Born was carried some rods away, and his machinery, plows, and wagon were badly injured. About the same time the newly built horse-barn of Mr H Long, 28x16 feet, was blown away, some parts of it being carried a mile distant The lucky part of it all was that his horses got loose at the the same time and went out uninjured. Smaller damages were done to much other property A door came flying through the air from the northwest, high up in the air, and landed in Mr. Ryan's field People were alarmed and took refuge in cellars and groves, watching the flying timbers until the storm passed over.

ROAD AND BRIDGE FUNDS FOR THE YEAR.

The following road and bridge appropriations were made by the county commissioners within the year At the May meeting two hundred and fifty dollars was appropriated to each commissioner district to be expended under the personal supervision of the commissioner of each district, on roads and bridges At the same meeting it was ordered that $120 be appropriated for bridges in the town of Vivian to be expended under the supervision of Mr Devling Also that $100 be appropriated for bridges in the town of Janesville, to be expended under supervision of Mr Conway Seventy-five dollars was appropriated to repair Boot creek bridge between sections 13 and 14, town of Byron, to be expended under the supervision of Mr Sunde Messrs. Purcell and Conway were appointed a committee to build a bridge and grade across the outlet of Lake Elysian between section 4, in Alton, and section 33, in Janesville, and $400 was appropriated therefor to be expended under their supervision

The following appropriations were made by the board July 23

For Markham bridge, $434 00 for new bridge and repairing old, on section 24, New Richland, $220 00, repairing and grading St Mary bridge, $94 00, rebuilding bridge on sections 16 and 21, St Mary, $70 00 repairing bridge on Little Cobb, Freedom, $101 00, repairing Lamb bridge, $19 00, building Iver's bridge, Boot creek, $185 00, building B Weed bridge, Otisco and Wilton, $251 00, building McDougall bridge, $207 00, repairing Wilton bridge, $62 75, repairing Krassin bridge, $32 25, building bridge on Cobbee, Freedom, $75 00, repairing Carmody bridge, Wilton, $76.72.

NOTED DEATHS OF THE YEAR

The first this year to cross the river Styx was Mr Serenus Farrington, one of the early settlers of Otisco He was born in Maine, September 30, 1799, and died at Minneapolis, January 31, 1888 He settled in Otisco in 1857, where he lived thirteen years He then moved with his wife to Owatonna, where they lived till December, when they went to Minneapolis to live with his son Frank Mr Farrington was in comparatively good health, and said grace at the supper table the night of his death, which occurred at 1 o'clock a m He left a widow, eighty-eight years of age, six children, sixty grandchildren and great-grandchildren He had been married about sixty-five years, and had been a member of the Baptist church for a much longer period

Wednesday evening March 14, at 10 05 o'clock, Michael Anderson, an old pioneer of Waseca county, died at his home in Norman county, Minn He had been sick about two years prior to his death, of progressive muscular atrophy For a year and a half he had been obliged to stay in bed and most of that time he suffered terribly He was born November 29, 1828, in Norway, whence he emigrated in April, 1845, to Rock River, Dodge county, Wis. Within a year after arrival here, his father and grandfather both died, and the struggle with penury was a severe forming of the young boy's character At the age of twenty-one years he was married to Elizabeth A Stromme, who survives him They had nine children, all boys, four of whom are living In 1856 Mr Anderson left Wisconsin with his wife, two sons, and his aged mother to seek a home farther west He settled in Otisco early in the summer It was two years before he raised a wheat crop of any account His early threshing was done by driving the oxen over the grain and cleaning it by dropping it from an elevated platform when the wind blew briskly

Alexander Johnston, who died at St Paul, May 9, was one of the very early settlers of the ancient village of Okaman, now extinct He came as a young lawyer and opened an office in that village in 1856 He was born in the year 1833, in Orange county, N Y, and came to Minnesota with his father-in-law, Mr John N Buckhout, who built the Okaman flouring mills. Later, about 1859, Mr Johnston took up his residence in Wilton, and, in 1861, drifted into the newspaper business. March 1, 1861, he and Mr S J Willis issued the first copy of the Home Views, printed and published at Wilton In less than a year after buying Mr Willis' interest he removed the plant to Faribault and continued publishing the Home Views and the Northern Statesman until about October 1863, when he disposed of the plant From Faribault he removed to St Paul and went to work in the office of the old Pioneer In 1866 he started a Democratic paper at Hastings, calling it the Union In 1868 he went to St. Paul again and worked as a reporter on the Pioneer He was also at divers times connected with the Press, the Pioneer Press, the Dispatch, and the Globe He was a man of much ability, and had it not been for the demon of intemperance, would have been useful to society He was by nature generous and honorable, and many of the old settlers felt a pang of sorrow when they heard of his premature death at the age of fifty-five

The sudden death of Mrs Janet Scott Brisbane, the estimable wife of Hon Wm Brisbane, of Wilton, startled the whole community She expired, almost without a struggle, June 14, 1888 Mrs Brisbane was born in the parish of Minto, Scotland, September 10, 1810, being in her seventy-eighth year at the time of her death She married Mr Brisbane January 2, 1832, and in 1839 came with him and their children to America, and settled in the state of New York Ten years later they removed to Fond du Lac county, near Waupun, Wis., where they resided ten years In 1859 they again moved, this time to Wilton, their home at the time of her death She was the mother of twelve children, eleven of whom survived her She was truly a helpmeet.

Much of the success of her husband and family, financially and otherwise, was due to her unselfish devotion and untiring industry. She was unusually well informed for a person so burdened with care, and her business shrewdness was of a high order She was kind, gentle, and affectionate, a good neighbor and a staunch defender of what she believed to be right Few persons were ever held in higher esteem than was she by all her neighbors.

Hon J S G Honner, county treasurer of Redwood county, died at his home in North Redwood, after an illness of two weeks, June 21, 1888 Mr Honner was born in the state of New York in 1831. His parents removed to Canada where he lived until fifteen years of age and then went to Michigan In 1856 he came to Minnesota, and settled in Iosco, this county He was elected county commissioner in this county in 1862 and served two years He removed to Redwood county in 1864, and was one of the first settlers there He was one of the first commissioners of that county, was the first register of deeds and for a number of years was assessor of the town of Honner which was named in his honor He was elected to the legislature in 1866, again in 1870 and in 1872 was a member of the state senate He held the office of county treasurer at the time of his death. He was married in Waseca county in 1858 to Antoinette Green, who survives him They had six children, three of whom survived him

Arden D Monroe, son of H C Monroe of Waseca aged twenty-four years, seven months and ten days, was killed by a runaway team, near Elmore, Minn, Thursday evening, the 19th of July, 1888 The deceased, who was married to Miss Mix, of Waseca, December 1, 1887 and lived near Algona, Iowa had been in the county with his wife visiting for a few days He had also purchased some cattle to take back with him They stopped with his brother in Vivian a day or two and then continued their journey, he driving the cattle, and his wife the team The horses were young, and as they were driving along near the railroad track, about two and a half miles from Elmore, in the evening, a train came along Young Monroe held the horses by the head until the train passed, and then went ahead to look after the cattle, telling his wife to follow with the team at her leisure. He had gone ahead some distance when she started the team One of them commenced to kick and plunge, and got one leg over the tongue, when both commenced to run. Mr Monroe came back to stop them and was instantly run over The horses ran but a short distance when the tongue fell down and ran into the ground, throwing Mrs Monroe out of the wagon She went back to her husband and found him senseless Some hay-makers near by came to her assistance and Mr Monroe was taken to Elmore, where he died the next day. There was a depression of the skull, near the temple, as though a horse had stepped on his head, and his jaw bone was broken. His father was notified by telegram and went immediately to Elmore, returning with the body to Janesville on Saturday. The remains were buried in the Alma City cemetery

Mr and Mrs A J. Woodbury, among the very early settlers at Wilton, died at Jamestown, N D, Sept 3 and 4, 1888, of typhoid pneumonia. Mrs Woodbury died on Monday, at 1 30 p m, and Mr Woodbury at 6 30 Tuesday morning. According to the best information of the writer Mr Woodbury was born in 1808, in Massachusetts, and was therefore about eighty years of age The telegram announced that Mrs Woodbury was about ninety They settled in Wilton in 1856, and built and kept what was known as the Washington House, where they continued to reside until 1882, when they went to Dakota

The death of Mr Jackson Turnacliff was announced in the Waseca County Herald of Nov 30, 1888, as follows·

"Ever and anon, as the years glide along, the hurrying throng of life's duties comes to a sudden halt, and we stand beside the yawning grave, that great leveler of mankind, where the proudest and strongest are but dust, where the weakest and poorest enjoy equal privileges in God's great laboratory of nature This week we are called upon to record the death of Mr Jackson Turnacliff, of Wilton, who died Tuesday night or Wednesday morning of cancer of the bowels. Mr Turnacliff had long been a sufferer from some internal disease which had baffled the skill of our best physicians In order to determine the disease, Drs Young and Cummings made a post mortem examination on Wednesday which clearly demonstrated that he died of cancer of the bowels Jackson Turnacliff was the son of Mr Ferdinand Turnacliff, residing in Wilton He was born in the state of New York, May 6, 1835, and while a child was taken by his parents to Ohio, where he remained until twenty years of age, when he went to Iowa, where he sojourned only a short time In December, 1855, in company with a Scotchman, by the name of Wm Young, and Dr Ambrose Kellogg, he came from Jackson county, Iowa, on snowshoes to Minnesota, arriving at Sutlief's place about New Year's He made a claim on section seven, town of Otisco, which he pre-empted He afterwards bought land in section twelve, Wilton, adjoining it, where he has ever since resided He married Miss Lucia E Barber, of Ohio, in 1858 His wife and a family of eight children, several of whom are married, survive him He lived here through all the hard times of the early settlement of the country, but was in such circumstances financially that he was not only able to live comfortably himself, but to lend a helping hand to some less fortunate He was a good citizen and neighbor, an industrious and frugal man, and a kind and indulgent parent The date of his death was Nov 27, 1888

Mr Dennis Sheahan, of St Mary, was killed by accident Dec 2, 1888 A local paper gave the following account·

Last Saturday evening, as Sheriff Krassin, Mr. John Madden, assistant road master, and Mr D Connell were going to supper, about six o'clock, at the crossing of the M & St L road, on Elm street, they discovered a broken oil-can, a lap robe and other indications of an upset Upon looking around they found the body of Mr Dennis Sheahan, about two rods east of the railroad track, beside the street. He was stretched at full length on his back, in an unconscious condition They carried him to the city engine house and summoned Drs. Cummings and Christie After an examination, Mr Sheahan was carried to the livery stable office of Sheahan & Baldwin, where he remained until he ceased to breathe, about 5 o'clock Sunday morning He remained unconscious up to the time of his death As he was alone at the time of the accident, it is not known just how it happened His horses and buggy were found in the west part of the city not seriously injured It is not known that any bones were broken, and only a slight bruise was found on one elbow It is supposed that death resulted from concussion of the brain. Mr Sheahan was among the early settlers of St Mary, having taken up his residence there in 1856. By his own industry and that of his family, he had accumulated a large property as a farmer He was about sixty-two years of age, and left surviving him a worthy wife and ten children.

POLITICS

Politically speaking, 1888 was an exciting year For some time corruption had run wild in the county, and even the corruptionists themselves fell out with one another. The head boodler was Charles McKenna who "could smile and smile and be a villain" Matters came to a head, Sept 22, 1888, and the following record of events is taken from one of the local papers published at the time:

AUGUST C. KRASSIN.

"The democratic convention was called to order by Hon R O Craig, chairman of the committee, who read the call On the instant of the closing word in the call John Moonan nominated Thos Bohen for chairman Some one moved to amend by substituting the name of Martin Laudert, of New Richland On a vote the amendment was declared lost, then Bohen was elected He thanked the convention, and announced the election of a secretary in order

"On motion of John Moonan, James Timlin, of Iosco, was elected, without opposition. Mr. Moonan escorted him to the table

"A committee on credentials was appointed and as soon as its report was received and adopted, Mike Murphy moved to proceed to nominate by ballot a candidate for sheriff. As a result of the balloting, Krassin received 48 votes, Maloney 20, and Keeley 2 The chair declared Krassin nominated The convention then proceeded to the nomination of representative which resulted in the choice of J L Hanson of Otisco Matters were getting warm, when Pat Spillane moved to nominate county treasurer next John Moonan moved to amend by substituting auditor for treasurer. The amendment was declared carried The first ballot gave J. E. Madden 46 votes, and Daniel Murray, Jr, 21. The former was declared the nominee.

"McKenna's friends began to get excited and several of them moved to nominate treasurer next; but McKenna's Nemesis, John Moonan moved to amend by substituting superintendent for treasurer and the chair, amid much confusion, noise, and tobacco smoke, declared the amendment carried Dr Christie was nominated by acclamation, loud and long, for county superintendent

"Then pandemonium in a mild form (mild for this convention) reigned supreme for a few moments

"Dr Craig moved the nomination of P McGovern for county attorney by acclamation The motion prevailed.

"By this time there was 'blood on the moon,' and John Madden moved to proceed to ballot for county treasurer.

"Hon Wm Brisbane nominated McKenna, and Darling Welch nominated Henry Chase The ballot was taken, and the whole convention crowded around the tellers' table to watch the result. Pretty soon John Moonan gave a whoop, and declared there was a fraudulent vote cast by McDowell, who was not a delegate. The tellers announced the vote as follows McKenna 37—Chase 37.

"Quick as a flash some one moved that 'Henry Chase be declared the nominee of this convention' The chair put the motion amidst the wildest confusion and declared it carried, while at least one-half of the delegates and many others were yelling in a way that would have excited the jealousy of a Modoc band of braves on a scalping expedition

"The decision of the chair added fuel to the fire, and the excited McKenna men rushed to the table, shook their fists in the face of the chairman and demanded a second ballot The chair vainly pounded the table with a cane and shouted 'Order, gentlemen, order.'

"Old men with gray hair, young men and middle-aged men, all joined in a pandemonium such as the old court house never saw before

"The sheriff finally mounted the table, armed with a cane, commanded the peace, and ordered every man outside the railing except the officers of the convention He pleaded and commanded by turns until partial order was again restored

"Some one then moved to take another ballot for treasurer The chair decided the motion out of order John Moonan moved the nomination of C. Deyling for register of deeds Then the floodgates of Babel were again opened, and, amid the wildest yelling and hooting, the chair put the motion and declared it carried

"By this time it began to look as though there might be something more serious than chin music, and Hon Wm Brisbane, declaring that he never before saw in all his life such a disorderly crowd, moved to adjourn Thos Bohen, the chairman still 'full of sand,' put the motion for adjournment and declared it carried, while the McKenna men were still shouting 'ballot!' 'ballot!' 'We'll have a fair ballot or bolt' 'Give us a ballot,' etc, etc

"By this time the platform inside the railing was crowded with excited and angry men, and the sheriff had to call in the whole police force of the city to get the surging crowd back outside the railing At last partial order was restored, and Mike Murphy mounted the table, stating that the president of the convention had abandoned his position, and advising that the delegates present choose another chairman and proceed to fill out the ticket That seemed to please those remaining (many having left the hall) and Hon Wm Brisbane was elected president He accepted the election, remarking that although the convention had adjourned on his motion, he hoped that there might be a fair ballot at last

"Mike Sheehan moved that they proceed to ballot for treasurer, that the name of each delegate be called, and that each vote in response to his name This motion seemed to prevail Then there was a hunt for a list of names, the secretary having left the hall. The list was finally secured As a result of this ballot, McKenna received 39 votes and Chase 12

Without seeming to comprehend the ridiculousness of the proposition, Pat Spillane moved to make McKenna's nomination unanimous, and the motion prevailed. Without acting upon the nomination of court commissioner, county surveyor, or coroner, the convention came to a close by common consent"

After the convention there was much excitement on the streets and it was evident that the "war" would continue The following appeared in the Herald of Oct 5, 1889.

"Before the last Herald was published there were rumors upon the street that Mr. McKenna, county treasurer, had left the country and was a defaulter in thousands of dollars These rumors were stoutly denied by his friends, who claimed that he and his wife had gone to Faribault on a visit, and would return in a few days The Herald, ever careful of publishing damaging statements about anyone without proof of facts, refrained from making public the rumors

"It has since come to light that, on Saturday evening, after the Democratic convention, McKenna at once commenced arrangements to leave He sold his interest in the store to his partner, Mr Bell, arranged some other matters very privately, and, on Tuesday morning, engaged a livery rig and took his wife with him to Faribault, giving out that they would visit friends there a few days. That allayed suspicion, and if any were in the secret they kept it. Mrs McKenna did not return until Friday evening, which gave the treasurer plenty of time to join the boodlers in Canada before anyone here was aware of the facts

"On Friday, the board of audit met to examine the accounts and funds of the treasurer They found a defalcation, and a special meeting of the county board was called The state examiner was notified, and came down on Monday He made examinations, results of which appear of record as follows

"Board of county commissioners met in special session, October 1, 1888, at 2 o'clock p. m, for the purpose of examining into the condition of the county treasury—members were all present

"The board of audit, consisting of Philip Purcell, chairman of the county board, S. Swenson, county auditor, and M B Keeley, clerk of district court, reported that on the 28th day of September, 1888, they met for the purpose of examining the books and vouchers of said office Their examination resulted as follows

July 14th, 1888, county funds on deposit in Bank of Waseca, as reported by the bank to board of audit		$13,744 71
Amount of deficiency in Bank of Waseca, Sept 28th, 1888, or not accounted for ...	$3,727 04	
Amount drawn on private checks	1 863 39	
Amount of private accounts on memorandum book	1,096 19	
	$6,686 62	

Add together the sum unaccounted for, $3,727 04, the amount drawn on private checks, $1,863.39, and the amount credited to his private accounts, $1,096 62, and the total is $6,686 62, which is only $11 98 less than the defalcation which is reported to be $6,694 64 We are informed that the Bank of Waseca explains that matter by saying that the bank officer July 14, made a mistake in giving the amount of the county money deposited—the mistake being the amount of $3,727 40

"The commissioners adjourned to meet Oct 2 At this time the board met with the members all present.

"The board approved of the report. The public examiner being present, stated that he had sent a dispatch to Governor McGill, and the board adjourned until 1 30 p m

16

"Upon the reassembling of the board, a dispatch was received from Governor McGill to the effect that Chas McKenna had been removed from office. Thereupon the county commissioners proceeded to the election of a treasurer to fill the vacancy.

"The ballot resulted in three for H C Chase and two for J B Hayden. Mr Chase was declared elected treasurer ad interim

"The bond of Mr Chase was fixed at $30,000 Mr Chase appeared and filed his bond with R O. Craig, J O Chandler, John Finley and W W. Day as sureties.

"In the evening the board of commissioners met and instructed the county auditor to cause an action to be commenced against Chas McKenna and his sureties, in district court, for the recovery of moneys belonging to said county"

Mr McKenna never returned or made good the defalcation, and his bondsmen had to make good the loss to the county There was universal sympathy for his bondsmen, all of whom were farmers and hard working men that had made their property by hard work and close economy The brutality of thus betraying the confidence of friends is worse ten times over than ordinary stealing.

THOSE ELECTED

The fall election was an exciting one and resulted in the election of the following officers representative, Otto Hanson· county auditor, S Swenson, register of deeds, A F Kruger, treasurer, Emil Dieudonne, probate judge, Hon W C Young, sheriff, A C Krassin, county attorney W D Abbott, school superintendent, J B Dye, court commissioner, G R Buckman, surveyor, Orson L Smith, coroner, H J Young county commissioners, J O Sunde, Albert Remund, Hon H M Buck

CHAPTER LVIII, 1889.

DIED WITHIN THE YEAR, E K CARLTON, P A. ERWIN, SAM KIRSTE, MAJ W C YOUNG, NATHAN WOOD, MRS McDONOUGH, WM BEVANS, SAM MANTHE—COUNTY GOVERNMENT—ROAD AND BRIDGE APPROPRIATIONS—TAKEN TO PRISON, FRANK CONWAY OF ELYSIAN.

With the opening of the year came death and sorrow as well as mirth and happiness Mr E K Carlton, of Woodville, well known to older residents, died Jan 1, 1889 He was born in Otsego county, New York, Feb 5, 1811, was married to Miss Mary Curdick, July 31, 1842, at Hornellsville, New York Soon after he removed to Wisconsin and settled in Dodge county In 1854 he sold his farm there, and the following summer came to Minnesota and settled on East Prairie in Rice county He soon sold out there and came to section five in Woodville in June, 1856 He remained on this farm until the fall of 1877, when he sold it Thereafter he resided in various places in the state, but finally returned in 1881, to this county Mary his wife, died July 27, 1879 Mr Carlton left a twin brother and three children to mourn his death

That old veteran, Mr. Prudin A Erwin, of St Mary, peacefully breathed his last on Wednesday morning, Jan 2 1889, about 8 o'clock Mr Erwin was born in Fairhaven, Rutland county Vermont, Oct 16, 1797. In 1802 he was taken with his father's family to the wilderness of Franklin county, New York He enlisted in the last war with Great Britain, in 1813, and served in the United States army until the close of the war He continued to reside in Franklin county until 1863, when he came to

Minnesota, and opened a farm in St. Mary. His wife died in 1867 Mr. Erwin was a most excellent citizen and a kind neighbor His death was as peaceful and quiet as if he were going to sleep He will long be remembered by those who knew him for he was one of God's noblemen

COUNTY GOVERNMENT.

The county commissioners met this year in annual session Jan 1, the members being Messrs Peterson, Sunde, Conway, Purcell, Devling, and Buck Mr Peterson was elected chairman The county printing was divided among three papers—the Herald got the tax list, the Radical, the financial statement, and the Argus, the proceedings of the board Nothing more than the ordinary routine business transpired at the January session

At the March meeting nothing more than ordinary transpired At the May meeting the following appropriations were made

One hundred and fifty dollars was appropriated to build a road on the town line between St Mary and Woodville, to be expended under the supervision of Commissioners Remund and Peterson, $75 00 was appropriated to build a new bridge between sections 22 and 27, St Mary, to be expended under the supervision of J Conway, $100 00 was appropriated to grade approaches to the Markham bridge, and to grade slough on section 5, Alton, to be expended under the supervision of Commissioners Conway and Buck, $250 00 was appropriated for roads and bridges in the First district, to be expended under the supervision of J O Sunde, $250 00 was appropriated for roads and bridges in the Second district, to be expended on roads outside the city of Waseca under the supervision of O Peterson, $250 00 was appropriated for roads and bridges in the third district, to be expended under the supervision of A Remund, $250 00 was appropriated for roads and bridges in the Fourth district, to be expended under the supervision of J Conway, $250 00 was appropriated for roads and bridges in the Fifth district, to be expended under the supervision of H M. Buck

A SAD RECORD

The following appeared in a Waseca local paper August 2 1889

Frank Conway, of LeSueur county, many years ago convicted of stealing a pair of H A Wagoner's horses, was again arrested last week, and will be taken to Stillwater next Monday afternoon, by the sheriff of this county, to serve out the remainder of his term of five years—four years and nine months, we hear After his conviction of this horse-stealing crime, he obtained bail, after being in Stillwater some three months, pending an appeal to the supreme court His case was argued before the supreme court and that tribunal took six months in which to decide the matter Frank says that when the case was argued he understood that he was discharged However that may be, he went to Illinois and also to Kansas, and when the supreme court decided against him his bail was forfeited Shortly after going to Kansas, he was arrested and put in jail, where he remained some nine months Next he was arrested in Illinois, convicted of passing counterfeit money, and sentenced to ten years in the penithentiary of that state Some months ago his term expired in Illinois, and he returned to his old stamping ground, near Elysian, where he was arrested and brought to Waseca Conway is now sixty-two years of age, and begins to think the way of the transgressor is hard Between twenty and thirty years ago, he was a very popular man in LeSueur county, and was county commissioner for several years From his youth he was steeped in crime, but his jolly ways and honest speech, together with his native shrewdness, threw the community off his track, and only now and then a man suspected his true character Like most men of his class, he was somewhat of a gambler, and a hard drinker at times It is claimed that he was, for many years, the leader of a gang of thieves and counterfeiters extending from Illinois to the extreme Northwest Whether that be true or not, certain it is that some young men in the West took their first steps in dissipation and deviltry under the influence and leadership of Frank Conway. It is wonderful how vice will pull down and degrade a man This man had native ability for almost any position in life He was naturally kind-hearted and knew how to be honorable and upright, and yet he has followed a life which has brought his gray hairs in sorrow and remorse to the verge of the grave in a felon's cell

NOTABLE DEATHS OF 1889

From the Herald

"For a number of years a remarkable family lived in the town of St. Mary, section 32, between the farm of Roger Garraghty on the east, and the old Christian Krassin farm on the west The members of the household were Samuel Kirste, and his two sisters, Rose and Justina Kirste They were very oddly acting people Although German born and surrounded by their own country people, they never associated or mingled with them The land was held in the names of the women Samuel was a miller, by trade, and for several years was employed in the Okaman mill Rose Kirste died over two years ago, and Justina died on the 15th of March, 1887, leaving her property by will to Samuel It appears that the eighty acres of land upon which they lived became the property of Samuel Kirste upon the death of his two sisters

Prior to the death of the two sisters and since, scarcely any one was ever admitted inside the miserable log cabin in which they lived They seemed suspicious of every one, apparently afraid of being robbed

It is stated that when the sisters died, Samuel procured the coffins, performed the duties of undertaker himself, and buried them without any public ceremony whatever

Since their death he had lived entirely alone, accompanied only by three dogs that kept watch over the premises For some weeks he had been in the habit of making occasional visits to his neighbor, John Sell, and exchanging newspapers with him

As Kirste had not been around for several days, Mr Sell went to his cabin Sunday afternoon, April 14, and rapped on the door. The only response was a moan He looked in at the window and saw Kirste, on the floor between the stove and bed, evidently in a dying condition. He became alarmed and went immediately for Mr Menke, half a mile away When Menke and Sell returned, they raised a window, reached inside, turned the door key and went in A sorry sight met their view. The poor man, sadly emaciated, lay upon the floor, gasping for breath and unable to speak They laid him upon the bed where he breathed his last within a few minutes

Soon after Kirste's death, Sell and Menke concluded to lock the house leaving everything as they found it, notify some of the other neighbors and get some one to go to Waseca to notify the coroner They locked the house and went to Mr Menke's farm Shortly afterward, Menke heard a terrible outcry among the dogs at the Kirste place and, thinking it singular, went back to see what the trouble was. When he reached the house he found the window open and, upon looking in, saw Dan Naughton, about twenty four years of age, ransacking every thing in the house Menke unlocked the door and asked Naughton what he was doing there? Dan, at first tried to escape, but Menke prevented him, and after some dispute about the money Naughton had taken, it was agreed that they should go together to the house of James Naughton, Dan's father, and there count the money They did so, and Dan had $908 30 Menke noted down the kinds and amount of money as it was counted over Soon after this, the same day, Menke, Sell, and others went to Kirste s place and made further search, finding another pocket book, or purse, containing over $240

Coroner Young, as soon as he received notice, went out to the place and examined the body and premises Mr Menke turned over the money he found and the keys of the house to the coroner Dr Young then proceeded to James Naughton's, and, as coroner, called for the money that young Naughton had carried there The Naughton family seemed unwilling for some time to turn over the money, and only concluded to do so after the coroner threatened to arrest one of them

Coroner Young brought the money to town, deposited it in a bank, and engaged A Grapp, undertaker, to proceed to the farm and bury the body

Mr Grapp said the cabin and the man presented a sickening and disgusting sight. The man was emaciated as though he had died of starvation He was covered with filth and his garments were stiff with dirt The floor was dirty and covered with boxes, pails, trunks and old truck of one kind and another Mr. Grapp and his assistants washed and dressed the body, put it into a decent casket, depositing beside him his musket, sword and ammunition, and consigned the whole to mother earth in the St Mary burying ground.

So far as known none of the three had relatives in this country Samuel Kirste, somewhat over a year before, had made his will wherein he devised all his property to two grandchildren, sons of his deceased son, supposed to be somewhere from ten to fourteen years of age, and residing in Germany

Very little was known of the history of the deceased, but there were many indications that he was well educated and had moved in refined society The closing scenes of his life can only be accounted for upon the theory that his mind had become unbalanced"

Maj Wm. C Young, then judge of probate of this county, fell dead of heart disease on the sidewalk, near the corner of Elm and Second street in Waseca on the 9th day of May, 1889 Maj Young and family came to Waseca county in 1866 and opened up a farm in Woodville Soon after the founding of Waseca, he moved with his family to that city He was born in Madison county, N Y, August 10 1826 He married, July 12, 1846, Miss Caroline Kingsley, a native of Chautauqua county, N Y, and a sister of Bishop Kingsley of the M. E church In 1854, they came West, residing first in Fitchburg and afterwards in Madison, Wis At the breaking out of the Rebellion, Mr Young raised a company and was chosen captain It was designated Company E, Eighth Wisconsin infantry In 1864, he was promoted to major of his regiment and served in that capacity until the close of the war Soon after his settlement in this county he became prominent in politics He was elected to the house of representatives of 1870, and to the senate of 1871 In 1876, he was appointed postmaster of Waseca and held the position until about 1885, when he was elected judge of probate He was re-elected in 1888, having no opponent, and received 1,653 votes. He was the father of four children · William H, Eugene W, and Mabel A. living, and Luna E, deceased His widow and Mrs. Mabel Bensel are residents of Waseca.

Mr Nathan Wood, although not an old settler, came to Waseca county with his family in 1871, and settled on a farm in Woodville. He was a native of Winchendon, Mass, but emigrated to Pennsylvania, where he carried on a farm until he came to this county He enlisted as a private in Company A, 211 Pennsylvania volunteers, in September, 1864, and was honorably discharged by general order of the war department June 2, 1865. He was mustered into McKune Post G A. R, May 17, 1884. He lost his health in the army and never fully recovered, although he was somewhat better after coming to Minnesota The last time he was out, he attended Maj. Young's funeral, May 11. He soon after had an attack of pneumonia which culminated in what is termed quick consumption His death occurred June 16, 1889, in his sixty-seventh year His end was peaceful and his mind unclouded to the last He left a widow and seven children, the youngest nine years of age, the eldest being Frank A. Wood, cashier at the C & N-W depot

Mrs Rose McDonough, daughter of Andrew Lynch, of St. Mary, and one of the earliest settlers in the county, died June 22, 1889, of typhoid fever, aged thirty-two years and six months She left a husband and five small children, the youngest about six weeks old

William Bevans was one of the very early settlers in Byron He died at his residence July 11, 1889, very suddenly of heart disease He was a native of New York, enlisted in the Tenth Minnesota in 1862, and was discharged in 1864 for disability. He left a large family, having been married twice. His widow survived with two of her children

Waseca Herald, Sept 13, 1889 Just as we were about to close our forms we learn that Sam Manthey, of this city, son of Joe Manthey of St Mary, was instantly killed yesterday afternoon, Sept. 12 at the M & St L gravel pit, in the town of Otisco He was at the time on top of a loaded car of gravel, leveling it off, when some other cars were let loose and came down against the car he was on with great force The shock threw him off He fell upon the track and two trucks passed over him, breaking his neck,and one arm, and otherwise bruising him He died almost instantly His remains were brought to the city by Mr Herman Rieck He leaves a wife and three or four children in rather poor circumstances He was born in this county and was about thirty-two years old

Nothing of importance occurred during the closing months of the year except the warm, rainy weather of the closing week, which gave the country a very muddy Christmas

CHAPTER LIX, 1890.

COUNTY GOVERNMENT—COUNTY POLITICS—DEATHS OF JOHN COLLINS, F L. GOETZENBERGER, HON WM BRISBANE, ASA ROBBINS, OLE K KINN

The county commissioners met this year Jan 7. Mr Oliver Peterson was elected chairman, the other members being Messrs. Sunde, Buck, Conway, Purcell and Deyling

The county printing was divided among the three leading papers of the county, at legal rates The Herald took the tax list; the Radical, the financial statement, and the Argus, the proceedings of the board

Upon the petition of McKenna's bondsmen and many others asking the board to settle with said bondsmen at fifty cents on the dollar,—

It was ordered that the county attorney be instructed * * * to receive the sum of $6,500 as payment in full and in settlement of all liability of the sureties in such case, including costs, interest, etc, provided said settlement be made on or before March 1, 1890. Commissioner Sunde was authorized to expend $25 on slough in Richland township; Commissioner Buck to expend $25 on highway in Wilton township; and Commissioner Peterson, $100 on Johnson hill, Otisco

There was nothing of an exciting character in the summer except the Chautauqua Assembly at Maplewood Park, in July This was well attended and very interesting. One of the noted speakers was Rev. Talmage, of New York.

POLITICAL PARTIES.

The Republican county convention this year was held Sept. 20 The principal contest in the nominating convention was on senator, Hon Chris Wagner won by a vote of 36 to 13 for Hon. I C Trowbridge. Hon. Otto Hanson was nominated for representative by a vote of 34 to 16 The following were the other candidates named: W D Abbott for county attorney, Emil Dieudonne, for treasurer, S Swenson, for auditor, A F Kruger, for register of deeds, E. B. Collester, for judge of probate O L Smith, for surveyor, Dr H J Young, for coroner; and G R Buckman, for court commissioner

The Democratic county convention was held Oct 4. The following candidates were nominated For senator, Dr R O Craig; representative, M H Helms treasurer, A C Krassin, clerk of court, John M Byron, register of deeds, John Wollschlaeger, sheriff, Nic Jacobs; county attorney, F B Andrews, auditor, Henry Murphy, school superintendent, J S Abell, probate judge, Jerome Madden, and coroner, L P Leonard Disgruntled republicans and railroad and saloon influences had much to do with politics that year, and in some respects the contest was a lively one The following gentlemen were elected Dr. R O Craig senator M H Helms, representative, A C Krassin, treasurer. S Swenson, auditor, John Wollschlaeger, register of deeds, F B Andrews, county attorney. John M Byron, clerk of court Henry Reynolds, sheriff, E B Collester judge of probate J S Abell, superintendent of schools; Orson L Smith, county surveyor, Dr L. P. Leonard, coroner. G R Buckman, court commissioner, Oliver Peterson and H C Chase, county commissioners

THE WEATHER

On the whole, the weather for the year 1890 was pleasant, and favorable to farming operations The first installment of snow in the fall came Nov. 8 It snowed gently nearly all day and covered the ground to the depth of about four inches On Sunday many persons were out riding in cutters The snow remained on the ground all the week, but the next week it disappeared and the weather remained mild the rest of the year

NOTED DEATHS OF 1890

The following notices are clipped from the Waseca County Herald of the dates noted

Jan 2, 1890 We were surprised and pained to learn of the death of our esteemed friend Mr John Collins, of Woodville. It occurred about 6 o'clock p m, on New Year day He had been ill of kidney complaint some four weeks, but had not been considered dangerously so to within a short time of his demise Mr Collins was one of our most industrious and successful farmers, having a well-improved farm of four hundred and forty acres He came from Ireland to America when about five years of age He has lived twenty-one years on the farm where he died He has raised a family of five boys and four girls, who are prominent citizens of this vicinity. We are informed that he was seventy-four years of age last June

Jan. 17, 1890 Mr Franz L Goetzenberger, of this city, died at Minneapolis last Tuesday, Jan 14, of pneumonia, in the seventy-fifth year of his age. A few days ago he went to Minneapolis on a visit, and was taken with the prevailing influenza, which terminated as above stated The body was brought to Waseca, on Wednesday, accompanied by his family Mr Goetzenberger was a native of Wurttemberg, and came to this country early in life He lived first in New York, then came west and settled in Otisco somewhat over thirty years ago, on a farm

July 25, 1890 The not unexpected death of Hon Wm Brisbane, of Wilton, occurred Wednesday, July 23, 1890 He was born at Glasgow, Scotland, Dec 11, 1811, and was consequently, aged seventy-eight years seven months and twelve days He had been ill for many weeks, having had an attack of influenza shortly after town meeting, last spring For a week prior to his death he refused food, and at times his mind wandered He suffered much during his illness His funeral, which took place yesterday, was very largely attended, and his remains rest in the Wilton cemetery beside his patient and loved Janet Mr Brisbane came from Hawick, Scotland, to America, in 1839, and settled in Delaware county, New York, where, owing to his natural sympathy for the poor and the unfortunate, he took an active and prominent part in the anti-rent troubles of that period and suffered in consequence Ten years afterwards he bought a farm in Alto, Fond du Lac county, Wisconsin, near Waupun, where he became prominent in political circles, and also accumulated quite a property for a farmer

In 1859 he came to Minnesota and purchased the farm where he ever afterwards resided He was a careful manager and by the assistance of his very frugal and estimable wife and family he accumulated a handsome farm property besides materially aiding his sons in various ways In politics and religion he was, without acknowledging it, a liberal in thought and sentiment He was a rough diamond—somewhat warped and illshaped by surrounding circumstances and early habits—but still a diamond of no mean value His ambition was great His mind never ceased to work upon the problems of life, and he loved to study and discuss the principles of the government of his adopted country. No American ever had a greater love for our American institutions than he While some of his ideas were crude, owing to a want of early educational advantages, he was nevertheless honest in entertaining them and fearless in giving them expression He was always public-spirited and patriotic He was invariably honest and upright in his dealings He was a good neighbor, and although a man of strong passions, he could easily forgive He held many minor offices during his life, and twice represented Waseca county in the State legislature—in 1867 and in 1871 He left a large number of children, grandchildren, and great-grandchildren to mourn his departure He was a Master Mason and an active member of Wilton Lodge No 24 while it remained at Wilton He will be mourned as a brother by nearly all the early settlers of the county, and his memory will be treasured in many hearts long after his body shall have mouldered to dust. Old neighbor and friend, adieu! And may you forever progress and enjoy the spirit realms assigned to the departed

Oct 31, 1890 Another old settler has gone to his long home Saturday morning, Oct 25th, at the home of G H Woodbury, near Jamestown, N D, Mr Asa Robbins, of Otisco, this county, died of typhoid pneumonia, after an illness of one week. He was born in Montgomery county, New York, in 1811 and came to Waseca county in 1861, settling on a farm in Otisco Mr Robbins was one of the hardy, energetic, honest pioneers of America He came of New England stock and inherited and practiced the virtues of the New England people His remains lie buried in Woodville cemetery

Dec. 5, 1890 Mr Ole K Kinn, of Blooming Grove, died Nov 28, of old age, his funeral occurring Monday afternoon at the Norwegian Lutheran church, Rev O A Mellby officiating Mr Kinn was born in Eidsvold, Norway, July 17, 1796, and settled in this county in 1857 He was buried in the Norwegian cemetery by the side of his wife, who died four years ago He was in his ninety-fifth year, and up to within a short time of his death had enjoyed good health He left surviving him several sons and a large number of grandchildren

CAPTER LX, 1891.

AGRICULTURAL SOCIETY—COUNTY BOARD—"EACO" MILL BURNED—WASECA'S NEW CHARTER—WASECA HOUSE BURNED—BIG SALOON FIGHT—DEATH ROLL CONTAINING THE NAMES OF MATTHEW CONNOR, SILAS GROVER, A C KRASSIN, B S LEWIS ESQ, JUDGE HALLACK, JAS A ROOT, SIMON SMITH, AUSTIN VINTON

The year opened with very fine weather—at least warm weather. The Waseca County Agricultural, Mechanical and Industrial Society, at its annual meeting elected the following officers President, Joseph Dunn, first vice president, Isaac Vickere; second vice president, M. W. Ryan; secretary, John Moonan, treasurer, J. A Krassin, board of directors M. Sheeran, J. M Dunn, A Vinton, H J Young, S Leslie, H. Wagoner, A Hawkes, delegates to annual meeting of the State Agricultural Society Joseph Dunn, H J Young, and S. Leslie George Remund was elected general superintendent of the fair grounds for 1891 At that time the society was in a very prosperous condition

COUNTY COMMISSIONERS

These gentlemen, constituting an important branch of our local government, met on the sixth day of January this year The board consisted of Oliver Peterson, of Waseca, Jonas O Sunde, of New Richland, Henry C Chase, of Janesville, H M Buck of Wilton, and Albert Remund of Blooming Grove. At this session of the board, the following entry was made:

"Bid of People's Bank to pay 2 per cent on monthly balances of county funds was accepted, and said bank was declared the depository for all public funds coming into the hands of the county treasurer, with bonds at $60,000, W. G. Ward, I C Trowbridge, D E Priest, Geo Buckman, and Warren Smith, as sureties"

This was the result after an agitation of four years carried on by the Waseca Herald demanding that the county funds be deposited as the law directs. Prior to that time, the election of county treasurer depended upon the wishes and desires of the banks of Waseca, and bribery and corruption had marked each election

J F Murphy of the Herald, got off the following on county printing

"The county printing and publishing, for the current year, has been let and all is quiet and serene, like a gently-flowing river Graham and Murphy and Henry and Bronson came to an understanding and agreed to work for the county at the same rate they would charge private individuals—the price fixed by law Murphy publishes the tax list, Graham the financial statement and proceedings of board of equalization, and Henry and Bronson the proceedings of the board of county commissioners Psalm cxxxiii"

Very little was done during the year, aside from routine business The county road and bridge appropriations were made at the meeting of June 22, 1891 The following is a summary

Ordered that $100 be appropriated for repairs on roads and bridges between sections 17 and 20, 14 and 23, 13 and 24, and on section 15, all in the town of Byron, that $100 be appropriated for repairs on roads and bridges in the town of New Richland, that $75 be appropriated for repairs of roads and bridges in town of Iosco, that $100 be appropriated for repairs of roads and bridges in town of Janesville, that $50 be appropriated to the town of Wilton for replanking the Wilton bridge, that $100 be appropriated for repairs of roads and bridges in town of Blooming Grove, between sections 4 and 9 and on section 23, that $100 be appropriated for repairs of roads and bridges between sections 6 and 7, 19 and 20, 28 and 23 and 1 and 2, in town of Alton, that $45 be appropriated to the town of Otisco for repairs on road, sections 8 and 20, said town, and $25 for repairs on the Burgoff Olson bridge

The proposition to lay out and improve the road from Deerfield through Blooming Grove and Woodville to Waseca was discussed, and preliminary steps were taken which culminated in the establishing of the road the next year

MILL BURNED

On Sunday afternoon, Feb 1, 1891 the city roller mill was wholly destroyed by fire About 1 o'clock smoke was seen issuing from around the cornice at the top of the building The alarm was sounded and the fire department soon had a stream of water on the burning building For about an hour it was difficult to tell which would prove the victor—the fire fiend or the firemen, but when the flames burst out of the building all thought of saving the mill was abandoned and every effort was made to save the flour and other movable property in and around the premises. The safe, office furniture and about four car loads of flour were saved There were nearly 200 tons of coal, 150 barrels of flour and from 8,000 to 10,000 bushels of wheat destroyed, besides a large quantity of bran and shorts and several large bales of flour sacks The firemen and citizens were untiring in their efforts to save the property and to prevent the fire from spreading Had it not been feared that the fire would reach Breen & Sons' oat meal mill, the coal, large engine, and other valuable machinery might have been saved, but Messrs Aughenbaugh and Everett did not wish to take any chances and the hose was moved further south and brought to bear on the bran house, the fire was stopped here before the building was consumed The origin of the fire was a mystery Messrs Everett, Aughenbaugh & Co estimated their loss as follows On stock, $10,000, on building and machinery, $20,000 to $25,000 Loss over insurance on stock $5,000, on building and machinery, $10,000 to $15-000 Mr Ward, who owned part of the building and some machinery stored therein placed his loss at $10,000 * * * Before the embers were cold Everett, Aughenbaugh & Co, had plans prepared for a new structure more elaborate than the one burned It was a severe loss to the proprietors, but with commendable courage, which admits of no failure, they soon replaced the mill and were ready to handle the fall crop of wheat

NEW CHARTER

A number of the citizens of Waseca, early in the year desiring some changes in the Waseca city charter, met together and chose Dr Cummings, John Moonan, and James E Child a committee to revise the old charter After much labor the revision was made, and a new charter passed by the legislature and approved by the governor, April 6, 1891.

BURNING OF AN OLD LAND MARK

The Waseca House, of Waseca, was burned to the ground on

the morning of April 20, 1891, between 1 and 3 o'clock The fire caught in the second story In a few minutes after the alarm was given the firemen were on the ground with their apparatus Water for the fire engine was obtained from the tank of the switch engine. The fire had gained such headway, however, that it could not be extinguished Most of the furniture and goods on the lower floor were saved The house was known to the old settlers of this city as the Waverly House and was completed and opened to the traveling public in December, 1867, by Mr. R. B. Johnson It then stood in the southwest part of Clear Lake City, near Mr San Galli's home. It was built by a townsite syndicate, and was of large proportions, the main part being 26x50 feet, with an addition 26x40 feet and a second addition 16x40 feet, all two story Mr Coleman valued the house and contents at $5,000 there was an insurance of $2,800 on building and contents The hotel occupied the site where the water and light plant now stands

THE SALOON FIGHT.

At the spring election the people of Waseca elected aldermen that favored the enforcement of the liquor laws They also elected "Col " D E Priest mayor upon his pretensions that he would have the laws enforced especially as to liquor-selling As early as June 2, the council, by a majority vote passed ordinance No 64 which required that each saloon should have and maintain a clean, clear glass-front without screens or other means of obstructing a clear view of the whole of the inside of the saloon, in order that officers might the more easily know whether or not the laws were being violated To the surprise of many, this ordinance created much feeling, and the following petition was extensively circulated and was signed by one hundred and twenty-eight citizens The petitioners set forth that·

"The undersigned citizens of the city of Waseca, hereby petition your honorable body to amend ordinance No 64, of the city so that the same shall require keepers of saloons to remove blinds and other obstructions to the public view, during the time only when they are required by law to keep said saloons closed Respectfully representing that we regard the exposure of saloons and other drinking places to the public view during business hours, as unnecessary for the purpose of enforcing the laws, and that such exposure will be offensive to many people and especially so to ladies who generally have no desire to see into or study the saloon business, and demoralizing to the young whose childish curiosity leads them into mischief and will surely induce them to gather and linger around the saloon doors and windows. That people who choose to patronize saloons should have the right to do so with the same privacy with which they attend to their other affairs And that a business sanctioned by law and requiring so large a license fee as is exacted from saloon-keepers, and is under so many strict, legal restraints, should not be subjected to any unnecessary burdens"

The circulation of this petition caused much excitement and a counter petition was put in circulation It was signed by sixty-seven courageous men and read as follows

To the Honorable Mayor and Board of Aldermen of the City of Waseca, Greeting

We, the undersigned, your petitioners, do most heartily congratulate you, upon the passage and approval of the late ordinance, regarding the regulation of the saloon traffic in this city, and more especially upon that section of said ordinance, which requires the removal of all screens, partitions or blinds from before the bars in said saloons We believe the saloon business to be an unmitigated evil, so that while, under present laws it must be endured, yet that it should not be allowed to hide itself behind any sort of a defense, but should be compelled to stand out in all its hideousness, that the public may know, just what means are being used to entrap our young men, and to destroy the moral life of our community; also that the officers of justice may be able to detect any violation of law, and so bring to justice the offenders We, your petitioners, do therefore humbly pray that you will allow the present ordinance to remain as it is, nor allow any offender to escape the penalty provided therefor

The struggle was not confined entirely to laymen. Some of the clergy and many good women took an active part in the contest. On the Sunday while the contest was on some of the clergy preached upon the subject One of them taking for his text, "Men loved darkness rather than light," (John 3 19) said in substance that ever since Adam and Eve hid behind the trees of the garden, men who have committed sin have sought for some kind of a screen for their sin Men who do right are not ashamed. A proper business does not want screens, but publicity A business that is right, honorable and manly, seeks the light The liquor business seeks to hide itself, it is ashamed of its conduct, it caters to debased and degraded appetites; it panders to the lowest passions of men, it never benefits, but always injures, hence it sneaks behind blinds, curtains, stained glass, etc. Now our aldermen, wisely or otherwise, have passed an ordinance prohibiting blinds, curtains, stained glass, etc. This meets with opposition. Those opposed to the ordinance claim that women will stop before the saloons, and children, out of curiosity, will collect in front of the places, and the sights they might see and the sounds they might hear would tend to demoralize them. Then so much the more need of exposing such a business to the light of day. A place that is not fit for a mother to look upon is not fit for a son to visit.

At the meeting of June 16, when the foregoing communications were presented to the council, there was an evident wavering among some of the aldermen. The petitions were referred to the committee on ordinances, and at the next meeting, June 19, the committee recommended a repeal of that ordinance and the passage of another modifying the screen provision and increasing the license fee from $500 to $1,000. This raised a storm of denunciation on the part of the saloon men and a combined refusal to take out licenses under the ordinance. The liquor interests were so strong and united that they induced sixty-three firms and business men to sign the following:

"The undersigned, a committee of citizens of said city of Waseca, would respectfully represent to your honorable body, that we have become fully satisfied, that there is no possibility of any saloon license being taken out in this city, while the fee asked therefor remains any higher than the sum of five hundred dollars ($500), and we are well aware that on account of no saloon license being granted, we are injured very materially in our business, and all classes of business will suffer, as many of our best patrons go to other towns to do trading, for which reason we are prompted to, and do earnestly request you to reduce the saloon license fee to five hundred dollars, as the only remedy to restore our failing business."

In addition to this legitimate appeal to the council for a return to the license fee of $500, threatening letters were sent to the mayor until he was alarmed for his personal safety. In order to let some of the aldermen and the mayor down easy, the council upon the question of changing the license fee from $1,000 back to $500, cast a tie vote, and the mayor was called in to give the casting vote, which he gave in favor of the $500 fee.

vote, which he gave in favor of the $500 fee

From July 1 to July 31 the saloons sat with closed doors—at least in front.

A gentleman that was familiar with the facts as to the saloon men made the following statement:

"About the first of June it became evident that fourteen men would make application for license to sell liquor in this city, (Waseca) and the council thinking that number altogether too many for a place of this size, concluded that by putting the license up a notch, fewer men would take out licenses Some of the saloon men fell in with the scheme, but when it was decided who should be refused license then the trouble commenced As a compromise measure the no-screen ordinance was passed, the two saloon keepers on the council voting for it But this did not please the high-license saloonists and one of them objected and circulated a petition asking that the ordinance be amended so as to require the screens to be down during the time when the saloons are required by law to be closed He carried his point, and the council put the license up to $1,000 Then the saloon keepers combined and refused to take out licenses themselves or allow any one else to take one out, and entered into an agreement that the first saloon-keeper who should violate said agreement and take out license, should pay $100 to each of the others in the combination And that was why no license was taken out at $1,000 and why the saloon men won at last"

OLD SETTLERS THAT PASSED AWAY

The death roll of this year showed an increase over former years The following are taken from the files of a local paper

Matthew F. Connor, of Wilton township, died March 15, of consumption, aged forty-five years. He had been in poor health for several years. Mr. Connor was born in Ireland, Dec 24 1846, came to Waseca county in 1857, with his parents, they settling in Wilton township He married Alice Dolan in 1873 and was the father of eight children He served a term as county commissioner and filled many local offices He was a prominent member of the Farmers' Alliance and an upright man.

Mrs. Silas Grover, one of the early settlers in this county, died May 8, 1891, in Waseca She was born in the state of Maine, Feb 26, 1805, and at the time of her death was in her eighty-seventh year. Moving to Livingston county, New York, she was married to Silas Grover in 1823. They afterward moved to Wisconsin where they lived a number of years and then came to this county, settling in Otisco in 1856. She was the mother of fourteen children, seven of whom are now living There are now living forty grandchildren and forty great-grandchildren—her descendants, living and dead, numbering nearly one hundred Her late husband was a soldier in the war of 1812 Mrs Grover had been ailing all winter, but an acute attack of influenza was the immediate cause of her death

August C. Krassin, then county treasurer, died August 9, 1891, and Benedict S. Lewis, Esq., died May 16, 1891. Sketches of their lives will be found in the biographical department

Hon. Caleb Hallack, of Janesville, died June 20, 1891. He had been American Express agent in Janesville for many years He was judge of probate of this county from Jan 1, 1878, to Jan. 1, 1880 He was a very honorable, upright man and one of the leaders of temperance work in this county. He was about eighty years of age and had been ailing some time prior to his death He was a Master Mason and buried with grand Masonic honors

James A Root, of Wilton, died August 23, 1891—see biographical sketch.

Austin Vinton passed away quietly, Saturday, Oct. 24, 1891 He was conscious to the last and was surrounded by his children and other relatives His death was caused by an attack of influenza the winter before, and had been anticipated by his friends for some time Mr Vinton came to this state in the spring of 1856 and settled on the farm where he resided at the time of his death. He was seventy-five years old. He was a firm friends, a kind neighbor, an da good citien, always alive to the best interests of his town and county He filled many positions of trust in this county and was almost always in some town office. Probably no man has served his town more faithfully and acceptably. He was elected a county commissioner in 1886, and served one term with great credit He sleeps in Woodville cemetery. His two sons reside in Owatonna

Simon Smith died Dec 26, 1891 The Herald said.

"It is our sad duty this week to announce the death of an honored and aged citizen Last Saturday afternoon, Mr. Simon Smith and his grandson, Roy Brubaker, went out to the farm in Iosco, after a load of hay Mr. Smith complaining of feeling tired, pitched on very little hay, the little boy doing most of the work. While both were engaged in fastening the binding pole, Mr Smith fell forward and expired without a struggle. Heart disease was probably the direct cause of his death, and it is thought that the ride out in the country, and the intense cold of that afternoon hastened it He was carried into the house and John Kahnke hastened to town after a physician. Mr Smith was born in Darmstadt, Germany, May 13, 1817 He came to America in 1832, at the age of 15, settling in Crawford county, Pennsylvania He went to Milwaukee, Wis, in 1842, and was married in February of that year. In 1867 he came to Waseca, and after putting up the brick store building adjoining the Bank of Waseca, engaged in the mercantile business He retired from business some years after, and since that time has led a quiet life, farming on a small scale, as his health would not permit much hard labor The remains were interred in Woodville cemetery The world was better for his having lived in it, and may the memory of his life be the means of causing many others to follow in his footsteps and become worthy and respected citizens"

CHAPTER LXI, 1892.

THE SHOOTING AND KILLING OF FRED WEBBER IN THE TOWN OF JANESVILLE—COUNTY BOARD PROCEEDINGS—STORM SWEPT, CYCLONE JUNE 15—COUNTY FAIRS—FALL ELECTION—DIED PATRICK MURPHY, A C SMITH, H H SUNDE, FRANCIS WESCOTT, DR McINTOSH, FRED WOBSCHALL, JOHN AMERSON, WM EVERETT, E E AND JAMES HOLMES, COL. W F DRUM, HON W G WARD, JOHN BUNAGLE, CHAS SAN GALLI

Immediately after the holidays, Jan 5, a man by the name of Wm Koebnik, residing in the town of Janesville, near Elysian, about 2 o'clock in the morning, shot and killed a man named Fred Webber The evidence showed that Webber was a single man, living with Koebnik, that he came to the latter's house in a drunken condition; that a quarrel ensued between the men, one accusing the other of making too much noise They finally came to blows when Koebnik went to his granary got his gun, returned to the house and, after more wrangling, shot Webber and killed him. Koebnik was arrested and bound over to appear at the next term of court, but the grand jury failed to indict on the ground that he shot Webber in self-defense

ANNUAL MEETING OF COUNTY BOARD

Mr Peterson was again elected chairman of the board—the members being the same as in the preceding year, viz Messrs Chase, Buck, Remund, Sunde, and Peterson Two important matters were settled at this meeting—the McKenna matter and the purchase of fair grounds.

In the matter of the fair grounds, it was resolved that the said board purchase fair grounds for the use of the Waseca County Agricultural, Mechanical and Industrial Society, pursuant to the power granted said board so to do in chapter 468 of the special laws of the state of Minnesota for the year 1891, and further that the chairman of said board appoint a committee consisting of three members of said board to procure prices and select location, and report the same to said board at the next meeting thereof. The chairman appointed as such committee Messrs Chase, Buck, and Remund As the result of this action, the present fair grounds were purchased of Mr I C Trowbridge

The last of the McKenna defalcation was disposed of at this session, by the adoption of the following·

Whereas, a resolution was passed by this board, Aug 24, 1891, agreeing to receive a certain sum of money in full settlement with Timothy Sullivan, Christie McGuigan, John Keeley, Peter Burns, and the estate of Dennis Sheehan, bondsmen in the McKenna bond case, and,

Whereas, Oliver Peterson, chairman of this board was duly authorized to act for and in behalf of said board of commissioners in making settlement with said bondsmen; and,

Whereas, said Oliver Peterson did make settlement in full with said bondsmen for and in consideration of the sum of $6,600, which sum was duly paid by the said bondsmen to E Dieudonne, county treasurer, on the 1st day of December, 1891 Now, therefore, be it

Resolved, That this board fully approve of the action of said Oliver Peterson and that the sum of $6,000 be accepted as payment in full to satisfy judgment entered against said bondsmen, and that the above named bondsmen be hereby released from further obligation

At this session the following sums were appropriated $70 to New Richland to replank two bridges between sections 14 and 23 and between sections 24 and 25. and it was ordered that the sum of $800 be allowed for ditching, draining and bridging on sections 2 and 3, Woodville, and sections 25, 26, and 35, Blooming Grove, said amount having been appropriated by the state to be paid back to the county upon the proper certificates.

STORM SWEPT

A terrible cyclone swept across Southern Minnesota June 15, 1892 With a roar equal to the din of twenty railway trains running over a score of iron bridges, a great cyclone swept over the Southern Minnesota counties of Jackson, Martin, Faribault, Freeborn, Blue Earth, Mower. and Fillmore Wednesday afternoon The storm began about seven miles west of the village of Jackson, moved eastward over the villages of Sherburne and Wells in Martin county, passed lightly over Faribault county, caused great havoc in Freeborn and spent itself in the two counties farther east Mr Z M Partridge gave us a list of casualties, in the neighborhood of Freeborn, the result of the great storm as follows: S Keen, two children killed, two injured, and everything gone; Joy Tellet, two barns destroyed; Sam Lowry, barn and machinery, all but house destroyed, Mike Everson, two children killed, four hurt, house and all gone, J. A. Shequeen, everything destroyed, wife badly hurt, horses injured, Oliver Vertby and E McCauley, everything gone, Sam Johnson, granary and barn destroyed, and house unroofed, Hans Omerson, house and machinery all gone and six of the family badly injured, John Heckes, wagon, buggy, and corn crib, Polander, name unknown, his house lost, L. Drake, house and corn-crib destroyed; F. D. Drake, barn, granary and machine shed unroofed, Paulson house, everything gone. Vivian, Byron, and New Richland suffered to some extent but without serious damage.

COUNTY FAIRS

For six years the people, especially the farmers, had been interested in county fairs, and one had been held each fall. This year extra efforts were made by the officers, and the result was a very successful fair It was held Sept 29 and 30, and October 1, and was largely attended There was received from the sale of tickets, $449.75, from the state, $210 52, from privileges, $79.00, from entrance money, $42 10; from subscriptions, $39, from Everett, Aughenbaugh & Co., special premium, $10, grand stand receipts, $22 50; membership fees, $6 00—total $858.87 The fair paid out $389.80 in premiums and $475 30 in expenses The receipts were overdrawn $5 23, but the surplus of the year before, $19.61, still left the treasury with $14 38 on hand That year, Joseph T Dunn, now deceased, was president, and Hon. John Moonan, secretary, both of them very energetic men We regret to say that from that time forward interest in the county fair has waned, and for the years 1903 and 1904 there has been no attempt to hold a fair.

THE ELECTION.

There were only two sets of local candidates this year, Republican and Democratic, except for county treasurer For this office the Republican candidate was Capt. Walter Child, the Democratic candidate, Joseph T Dunn, the People's candidate, George T Dunn, and the independent candidate, Emil Dieudonne On treasurer, the contest resulted in 896 votes for Child, 843 for Joseph T. Dunn, 427 for Dieudonne and 253 for George T Dunn. The other candidates elected were A J. Lohren, county auditor, Peter McGovern, county attorney; Henry Reynolds, sheriff, John S Abell, superintendent, John Wollschlaeger, register of deeds; E. B. Collester, judge of probate, Dr L P. Leonard, coroner, O L Smith, surveyor, E P. Latham, court commissioner, Henry F Lewer, of Woodville, Henry W. Bluhm, of Vivian, and Thomas Boucher, of Waseca, county commissioners Dr. R. O Craig was elected to the state senate, and H M Buck to the house of representatives

THE DEATH ROLL OF 1892

With each succeeding year, the death roll of the old settlers increases in length. The first to be called this year was Patrick Murphy, one of the very early settlers of Blooming Grove. He died of influenza at the residence of his son Thomas, in Minneapolis, Jan 10, after an illness of four days, aged eighty-three years Mr. Murphy was born in Kilkenny, Ireland He came to this county in 1856, where he lived many years, moving to Minneapolis in November, 1891. He was the father of fifteen children, eleven of whom, with his wife, survived him His remains were brought to Waseca for burial and lie at rest in the Waseca Catholic cemetery

Mr. Alfred C. Smith, one of the 1855 settlers of Woodville, after an illness of nearly two years, died Jan 28, 1892 His history is noted at length among the early settlers.

The Herald. "One by one the early settlers of Minnesota pass away. Died, Feb 4, 1892, at Northfield, Minn., Hans H. Sunde, aged sixty-six years and eight months. He was one of the eight families who first settled in New Richland in 1856 He came to America in 1854 and resided in New Richland up to 1883, when he removed to Northfield His remains were brought to New

Richland on the 5th inst., and were buried the 9th, in the churchyard of the Norwegian Lutheran society, which he was instrumental in forming and of which he was a worthy member."

Francis Wescott came to the township of Wilton, this county in September, 1865, where he resided eight years, when he moved to Yellow Medicine county. After living there seven years he moved to Lyon county, where he lived up to the time of his death, which occurred Feb. 29, 1892. He died of pneumonia, after a short illness. His wife and three children survived him. He was an honorable, upright man in every walk of life.

Dr. L. D. McIntosh, who came to Waseca in 1868, died at De Funiak, Florida, Feb. 28, 1892, of heart failure. He went there for the purpose of giving a two-weeks' course of instruction at the Florida Chautauqua. He was a native of Bethel, Vt., and a graduate of the medical college at Castleton, in that state. He came West in 1860 to Sheboygan, Wis., where he married Miss Rebecca Preston and resided until 1868. He was assistant surgeon for a short time in the Forty-seventh Wisconsin Infantry in the Rebellion. He was a very ardent temperance man and prohibitionist during his residence in Waseca. He was a resident of Chicago at the time of his death. The doctor stood high in his profession. At the time of his death, he was holding a professorship in the Chicago dental college, also a professorship of Electro-Theropeutics in the Chicago Post-Graduate Clinic. He was at the head of the Emmert Proprietary Co. of Chicago, and was also appointed assistant superintendent of microscopy at the World's fair.

Ernest Frederick William Wobschall was born the 6th day of January, 1822, in Colmar, Province of Posen, Governmental circuit of Bromberg, Prussia. He came to America in 1853. After spending about two years in Indiana and Wisconsin, he arrived in Minnesota, and settled in St. Mary on the farm where he died, in June, 1855. He came in company with Fred. Proechel, (Big Fred.) Gottlieb Proechel, Martin, John F., and Gottlieb Krassin, Sr., and John G. Greening. He had a yoke of oxen and a home-made wagon, money enough to pre-empt one hundred and sixty acres of land and improve it. In those early days he was a very industrious and frugal man, and soon became one of the wealthiest farmers in the county. In those early days, too, he was companionable and hospitable The writer often made the trip to Hastings with him, camping by the roadside, and eating potato soup from the same kettle Fred probably had some faults—and who among us has not—but on the whole he was an old-fashioned German of honesty and solid worth By his first marriage he had four sons and one daughter, and by his second wife, seven sons and two daughters His last sickness commenced in November, 1891, and terminated the 29th day of April, 1892, at 7 o'clock a m. His death was caused by stomach trouble, known as gastritis He left one brother, a widow, and fourteen children surviving him

On the 22nd day of May, 1892 John Emerson, after a long struggle, died of typhoid pneumonia, in the eighty-ninth year of his life He was born in the state of Vermont, and lived in Windsor county, that state, until 1866, when he came as far west as Wisconsin, where he remained until 1868, when he came to Minnesota. He was married to Dr Young's mother over forty years before By his former wife he left surviving him a son and two daughters The son is a resident of California He was a model Yankee farmer, a strong, upright man, and a good citizen If the world had no worse men than "Uncle John Emerson," it would come very close to the ideal marked out by the gospel of peace

The death of Wm Everett, of Waseca, occurred in California, June 21, 1892. He died of diabetes at the age of sixty-four. He was born July 6, 1828, in Sussex county, New Jersey An extended notice of his life appears in biographical sketches and in the account of the Indian massacre at Lake Shetek

There were two deaths by drowning, July 3, 1892, on section 34, town of Freedom, in the north branch of the Little Cob—Edward Eugene Holmes, fourteen-year-old son of John Holmes, Jr, and James Holmes, aged thirty-two years, uncle to the boy Edward and some other boys were in the stream bathing, the water at that place being ten or twelve feet deep Edward, while swimming across the stream, sank out of sight. This frightened his Uncle James, who plunged into the stream to save the boy Both sank to rise no more in this life. It was thought that both got into the eddy or whirl, near the old bridge, and were whirled around until drowned The bodies were recovered some two hours afterwards, the remains lie buried in the St Mary cemetery.

Died. Col W F Drum, U. S A, at Fort Yates, N D, at 9 o clock p m, July 4, of apoplexy Col Drum, brother of S H Drum, of Woodville was about fifty-nine years of age, and was a man of sterling worth and full of patriotism He was a graduate of West Point, served during the Rebellion with eminent ability, and remained in the service until his death. He was one of the earliest settlers near Meriden, Steele county

Hon W G Ward, whose life and death are noticed at length elsewhere, died Sept 21, 1892, of dropsy

One of the early settlers in St Mary and Freedom, Mr John Bunagle of the latter town, died very suddenly of heart disease Oct 4, 1892 He had been at work with his team in the field, plowing out potatoes, when he said to his wife and daughters, who were with him, that he felt bad They suggested that he go to the house and take a rest When they went to the house, about noon, he was found dead in the barn Apparently he had died without a struggle His first settlement in this county was at the old village of St Mary, where he opened a small country store He finally closed out his store and devoted himself to farming.

After a long and painful sickness, Mr Charles San Galli died Oct 5, 1892, of stomach trouble Mr. San Galli was seventy years of age, having been born in Prussia, July 9, 1822 Upon attaining his majority he engaged in the mercantile business which he continued until 1849, when he came to America, settling in New York, where he remained about twelve years He married Miss Emily Shepherd in 1859 by whom he had four children His wife died in 1869 After twelve years spent in New York, he returned to Prussia for eight years, and then came back to America, residing in Albany, N Y He came to this county in 1869 and bought the Gruhlke farm, adjoining Waseca on the south, where he resided with his family up to the time of his death. He was elected to the office of register of deeds in the fall of 1879, by the Democrats, and re-elected in 1881, serving four years. In addition to his other accomplishments he was an excellent portrait painter He left surviving him two sons and two daughters of mature years

CHAPTER LXII, 1893.

COUNTY MATTERS—CITIZENS STATE BANK—DEEP SNOWS—CITY WATER AND LIGHT PLANT—SEVERE STORM—DIED HON B A. LOWELL, ORRILLA CHILD, DR SATTERLEE, S. W. LONG, WM MARZAHN, LARS SELLAND (KILLED), I C. TROWBRIDGE, MRS C BAKER, J B JACKSON—AN EARLY WINTER—DAIRYMEN'S ASSOCIATION—AGRICULTURAL SOCIETY

The county commissioners this year opened their session Jan 3 Henry C Chase, of Janesville, was elected chairman, the other members being Jonas O Sunde, of New Richland, Oliver Peterson, of Waseca, Henry F Lewer, of Woodville, and Henry W Bluhm, of Vivian The county printing was divided among the several papers of the county as it had been the previous year

The records of this county, and presumably of every other county occasionally show some inconsistencies and this meeting of the board revealed quite an assumption of power on the part of the board of commissioners.

The board of audit of the county, on Jan 2, —

"Ordered that the Citizens State Bank of Waseca be designated as depository of such (county) funds, the sum not to exceed $10,000 at any one time, said bank to allow interest on monthly balances at the rate of 2½ per cent. per annum, and to furnish a bond in the sum of $20,000 to be approved by the board of county commissioners of Waseca county

And it was further ordered That the Peoples Bank of Waseca be designated as depository of the public funds of Waseca county except such amounts ($10,000) as are to be deposited in the Citizens State Bank, said Peoples Bank to allow interest on monthly balances at the rate of 2¼ per cent per annum, and to furnish a bond in the sum of

$60,000 to be approved by the board of county commissioners of Waseca county

The board of county commissioners accepted and approved the report of the board of audit, and also accepted and approved the bonds of both banks So far everything seemed to be well understood and fair, but on the last day of the session, the county commissioners, after reciting the order of the board of audit,

Resolved, That the county treasurer, Walter Child, be and is hereby instructed to deposit forthwith in said banks, all the funds now in his hands, as such treasurer, and also all moneys which shall from time to time come into his hands for state, county, town, city, village, road, bridge, and all other purposes for a period of two years, in such amounts as designated by the board of audit, and

Resolved, That said county treasurer be and is hereby further instructed that whenever the amount of public funds in his hands shall be less than $20,000, he shall keep the amounts of deposits in, and the amounts of drafts on said Citizens State and Peoples Banks as nearly equal as practicable

How could the treasurer obey both instructions?

At the meeting of September 12, it was ordered that $50 be appropriated to the town of Blooming Grove, to be expended for grading hill on road between sections 29 and 30 that $100 be appropriated to the town of Alton, to be expended on a bridge on section 18, across outlet to Lake Elysian and that to the town of Freedom be appropriated $225 for a bridge between sections 13 and 14, of said town

CITIZENS STATE BANK

The Citizens State Bank of Waseca, since changed to the First National Bank of Waseca, was organized the first week in January, with a paid-up capital stock of $25 000 The stockholders and the amount of stock of each were as follows

Names	Residence	No Shares
Willis J Jennison	Minneapolis, Minn	10
William E Scott	Waseca, Minn	10
E A. Everett ..	Waseca, Minn	4
J W Aughenbaugh ..	Waseca, Minn	5
James E. Child	... Waseca, Minn .	10
A Z Conrad .	Worcester, Mass .	10
Alpha D Cadwell	. Sioux Falls, S D.......	148
Chester H Cadwell	Waseca, Minn..	20
Reinhart Miller	Waseca, Minn	1
S Swenson	Waseca, Minn	2

I L Hunt . . .	Waseca, Minn	10
F N Hunt	Waseca, Minn	10
W. A. Henderson .	Waseca, Minn ..	10

The following were chosen directors Willis J Jennison, James E Child, William E. Scott, A Z Conrad, Reinhart Miller, A D Cadwell, F N Hunt, W A Henderson, and E A Everett Mr. A. D Cadwell was its first president, and Dr F N Hunt, its first cashier

DEEP SNOW.

Within the month of February, 1893, snow fell to quite a depth, and on Feb 27, there was a heavy fall of snow The Waseca Herald remarked

> That was a grand display of "the beautiful" that came down in great swirls and gusts and chunks, last Monday. The storm commenced gently on Sunday and got fairly under way during Sunday night It put in a good day's work on Monday, and that night the storm "did itself proud ' Great drifts were piled up in every direction and in every conceivable shape The streets were in picturesque condition, while some of the walks were four feet under the hard-packed snow The scientific (?) appliances of the city for cleaning the sidewalks and opening the streets so that women and children could pass and repass, were all brought into requisition The street force must have been buried out of sight, as none of its members were visible Our city system of dealing with the "beautiful," when it comes in such magnificent chunks, is heroic and self-supporting The schoolma'ams and other young ladies of this city, who have to travel our highways going to and from their labors, are about to hold a meeting, we hear, to pass a vote of thanks to the male rulers of this part of the universe for their efficient method of opening the highways of the city immediately after such a deluge of snow as visited us last Monday

Another snowstorm visited this section on April 20 A local paper made the following note.

> We have had and are having weather, this week, that beats the recollection of the oldest settler Tuesday morning, long before daylight, a rain set in from the southeast and continued until evening, when the wind veered to the northeast and a heavy snow storm set in Yesterday noon the snow was about fourteen inches deep and melting fast At this writing, Thursday afternoon, the wind is in the north and snow still falling The indications are for a clearing up

WATER AND LIGHT PLANT

This was the year of agitation for a water and electric light plant in Waseca As early as March 17, the following was published in the Herald:

"The question of water and water works forces itself upon the people of this city from year to year It must be admitted by intelligent and thoughtful men that the safety of property, the health of citizens, and the general welfare of the people of Waseca demand water works The supply of water, in case of a large fire, is wholly inadequate In connection with a good water supply, or closely allied to it, is the lighting of the city. It is true that we have an electric light plant, but it is owned by a private company Each city can and ought to own its water supply, its electric light plant, its street cars, and other public conveniences In every city where these public works are owned and operated by the city itself the people are served better and at cheaper rates than in cities where they are the private property of corporations The reason for this is obvious Where the city owns and operates these public works there is little chance for bribery and corruption, but in cities where private corporations own and operate them it becomes necessary for the private corporations to also own, control, and operate a majority of the aldermen, mayor, city attorney, and other officers Their interest is to fleece the people, and in order to do it, they must control the city government If they desire to steal the city funds to improve their private property, they must first get control of the city officers—especially of the aldermen, the city attorney, and the mayor Generally the mayor is placed at the head of the plundering gang If the city were the owner of these public works, every taxpayer would be interested in making them self-sustaining and efficient It would seem as though this is a good time to take the subject into serious consideration If the city is to engage in a system of improvements, as herein mentioned, then it behooves our citizens to select for the next mayor a man who, by education and disposition, is qualified to handle and direct such enterprises"

This subject was investigated and discussed more or less for a long time, as the following report to the common council of Waseca will show. On May 11, 1893, there was held a meeting of the common council and of citizens, and a committee consisting of Mayor Cummings, Hon P. C. Bailey and Alderman Martin Hanson made report as follows

"We have visited the cities of Tracy and Albert Lea and carefully examined the water works in operation at both places These points were selected as being nearly identical with us as regards absence of natural elevations which can be used as locations for reservoirs in their source of water supply, as well as in other particulars We desire in this connection to refer to the courtesies extended to us by officers and other citizens of both places. Every opportunity was offered us to inspect their plants, and such information as they have accumulated in the building and operating of the same was freely given us The result has been the noting of numerous details which will prove useful in the event of our city putting in such works

"The plants in operation in both cities are practically identical and consist, briefly, of a deep well with pumping station and ground reservoir in connection, an elevated tank, watermains and hydrants. The well at Tracy is six hundred feet deep; at Albert Lea, seven hundred The quality of the water furnished by each is first class, practically inexhaustible, and suitable for domestic uses The well at Albert Lea, being artesian, flows directly into the ground reservoir, thereby saving the deep-well pumping which is required at Tracy. From the ground reservoir the water is pumped into the elevated tank which, at Tracy, is of wood; at Albert Lea, of steel The bottoms of these tanks are elevated eighty-five feet from the ground level They have proved to be frost proof and in fact no trouble has been had with either plant from freezing These tanks furnish a constant pressure of forty pounds at the hydrants; an amount great enough to control all ordinary fires in two- or three- story buildings To supplement this, the station is fitted with a large steam pump connected with the mains which will furnish any pressure the pipes will sustain

"We are satisfied that the plan above outlined is practical in every way and economical in operation, and that a similar system, in connection with a plant for electric lighting, could be built and operated in the city so as to be self-supporting.

"It is impossible to estimate exactly the cost of such a system in the absence of plans and specifications, but the following estimate is believed to be approximately correct. Deep well, depending on depth, from sixteen hundred to two thousand dollars; pump station, house, boilers, pump, smoke stack, etc, seven thousand dollars, water plant complete, with about two miles of mains, twenty-eight thousand dollars. From eight to ten thousand dollars would be needed if we include an electric light plant

(Signed.)

D S CUMMINGS,
P C BAILEY,
MARTIN HANSON

On May 16, 1893, a petition for a special election to authorize the city council to increase the bonded indebtedness of the city $30,000 for water works and electric lighting was presented to the council, and formal resolutions were adopted that the bonds of the city be issued, bearing six per cent interest, due in twenty years—that a special election be held at the engine room, June 6, 1893, and that the ballots shall contain the words· "In favor of water works and electric light bonds," or, "Against water works and electric light bonds" The result of the special election of June 6 was as follows

Whole number of votes cast	332
In favor of the bonds	242
Against	89

Work on the plant was commenced soon after On June 11, 1893, the contract for putting in the well was let to J T McCarthy—the same was to be an artesian well, ten inches at the ground surface and eight inches after striking the lime rock

The well was completed in 1894, and the water mains were laid the same year The contractor was Mr E T Sykes and the contract price $24,252 58 The electrical department, as near as can be ascertained, cost $5,605 73, the engineers' work $400 00 cost of well, $5,003 03—a total of $35,261 34

SEVERE ELECTRICAL STORM

On the 14th of June a very severe storm passed over this section The Waseca Herald said of it "The destruction of property by lightning was very extensive Mr J McCracken says James Cunningham, of Freedom, had ten head of cattle killed in the pasture, all in one bunch Charles Root, of Byron, had two horses killed H J Werdin, of Iosco, has also informed us that August Keiser, of his town, had six horned cattle and one horse killed in pasture, and that Pat Farley, of the same town, lost three head of cattle We also learn that Julius Kakuschke a tailor of this city, had a cow killed in one of the pastures south of town"

CALLED FROM EARTH.

The death roll in the county during the year was shorter than usual, although some prominent persons were called hence The first of note was the demise of Hon. B A Lowell, who died in a North Dakota hospital May 12, 1893, of general paralysis At that time his home was at Gardner, N. D Deceased was one of the early settlers in this county, first engaging in mercantile business in Wilton, and afterwards living on a farm in Otisco He was, at an early day and during the war of the Rebellion, an earnest and active Republican, and was elected state senator in the fall of 1864. He served during the sessions of 1865-6 very acceptably to our people He came to Waseca at an early day in its history and for many years held the office of city justice He also carried on a small vegetable farm in the western suburb of this city for years, and until his health failed Some years prior to his death he went to live with relatives in North Dakota.

Mrs Orrilla (Roice) Child died May 23 at 11.40 o'clock p m, at the residence of her son, James E Child, of Waseca, aged eighty-three years, two months and twenty-one days She was born in Jefferson county, New York, March 2, 1810 Her father, Enoch Roice, was of Scotch blood, and served in the American army during the Revolutionary struggle Her mother, Sarah Palmenter, was of English descent Both parents came from the state of Connecticut to the state of New York soon after the Revolutionary war Mrs Child's grandfather was also a Revolutionary soldier She married Zabina Child, Feb. 14, 1833, and resided with her husband in the town of De Kalb, St Lawrence county They emigrated to Ohio in 1834, making their home in Medina county. They afterwards went back to St Lawrence county, then returned to Ohio and spent a year, and then came west as far as Wisconsin, where they resided until 1862 Mrs Child then came to Waseca county where she made her home most of the time The latter part of July, 1892, she went to Nebraska to visit her daughter About the time of her journey she contracted a cold, and was quite sick while there She returned to Waseca about the first of December, and gradually declined from that time until her death Dropsy set in a short time before her death, and although she suffered much pain at times, her mind remained clear, and the close of life was a dropping to sleep without an apparent struggle She reared a family of seven children—five sons and two daughters—five of whom survived her

Dr. W. W Satterlee, one of the noted and devoted clergymen of this state, died at Minneapolis, May 27, 1893 The following account appeared in the Waseca Herald at the time

"The deceased was born on May 11, 1837, at the then small village of La Porte, Ind, where he lived with his parents and secured a common school education. He studied medicine while very young, and practiced some years in Wisconsin, before coming to Minnesota, at the same time preaching the gospel as a local minister of the Wesleyan Methodist church. He came to Minnesota, we think, in 1863 or 1864 We first saw him as he was crossing the LeSueur river, at the Wilton ford, with ox teams and covered wagon He soon after located at Elysian where he practiced medicine and preached the gospel until 1867, when he came to the embryo city of Waseca, as the regular pastor of the M E. church. He was the first and one of the ablest and best Methodist ministers ever in charge of the church here

"To know a man thoroughly we must know him in the days of his poverty—at the time when he is struggling for the right against popular clamor. First, he was an uncompromising anti-slavery man when pro-slavery Democracy was in the ascendant After the great struggle which destroyed slavery, he became an anti-saloon advocate While uncompromising in his views, he was a man of unbounded charity for those who differed from him Every impulse of the man was noble and self-sacrificing.

"Some twenty years ago he went to Minneapolis and has served as pastor of several churches there The Minneapolis Journal says

'Six years ago he accepted the chair of political economy and scientific temperance at Athens College in Tennessee, which position he held at the time of his death While teaching in the South, he has been accustomed to come to this city, where the larger portion of his children and family live, to spend his summer vacations, and for this reason he was at Minneapolis at the present time Last Tuesday evening he took a slight cold at the lake, where he was staying, and owing to this he came back to the city to the residence of his daughter, Mrs Pye

"'The next morning he awoke with a severe pain in his left side, indicating pneumonia, and from that time he began sinking very fast until Saturday morning, when he breathed his last at about 10 o'clock The early settlers of this section of the state join with Minneapolis friends in mourning the unexpected death of a noble and true man—a brother of suffering mankind the world over"

Mr Satterlee was a great worker Starting in the world without capital or a "pull," he became a power for good in the land In early days, in Waseca, he found it necessary to resort to manual labor to support his family This he cheerfully did until he finally had a church strong enough to afford him a living He early espoused the temperance cause and became its leader in this state He was also the author of several books—one a reply to "Looking Backward," by Bellamy His reply was well written and showed marked ability He was the personification of true moral courage Whatever his judgment and conscience said was right he believed in, and no offer of personal gain or desire of promotion could swerve him from it He was one of those described by Holland.

Men whom the lust of office does not kill,
Men whom the spoils of office cannot buy
Men who possess opinions and a will;
Men who have honor, men who will not lie,
Men who can stand before a demagogue,
And damn his treacherous flatteries without winking

Seth W. Long was one of the 1856 settlers of this county, having moved that year to Empire in the town of Iosco He came to this county from Ohio, with his father, William Long, and his brother George, who were accompanied by M S Green, Algerine Willsey, James Chadwick, and others. After the decline of Empire he removed to Okaman and kept hotel for a number of years He afterwards removed to Wilton during the war and carried on the Globe Hotel for a number of years. In 1867 he was elected to the office of sheriff of this county, and was re-elected in 1869, 1871, 1873, and 1875, serving in all ten years During his last term of office his wife died After the expiration of his term of office as sheriff he resided most of the time in the western portion of the county For many years he had been in poor health and his death was not unexpected to his intimate friends Seth W. Long was an honest, upright citizen and highly respected by the people of this county The immediate cause of his death was paralysis of the throat and tongue He was stricken on Sunday, May 29, and from that time to the time of his death, June 5, he was totally unable to swallow nourishment of any kind Neither could he speak or converse orally We are told that he died apparently without much pain or suffering His remains lie buried in the Wilton cemetery beside those of his wife and some other members of his family

Died, in Waterville, Tuesday morning, June 27, 1893, Mr William Marzahn, in his seventy-third year. The deceased was born near Berlin, Germany, Dec 9, 1820. He was united in marriage to Miss Caroline Kanne, who survived him. In 1855 Mr Marzahn, wife and four children started for America, three of the children and a brother dying on shipboard of cholera—August Marzahn, of Waterville, being the surviving child Mr Marzahn moved to a farm in Iosco in 1856, and by strict attention to business and hard work accumulated a fine property His son Robert occupies the old homestead and is a prosperous farmer

The Waseca Herald of Sept 8, contained the following

"A horrible death is reported from Blooming Grove. Dr. Leonard, and City Constable George H. Goodspeed, on Tuesday last, were called to the farm of Lars Selland to investigate the death of that gentleman The facts as we gather them are as follows: Mr. Selland arose last Tuesday morning, Sept 5, 1893, and went out about seven o'clock Nothing more was seen of him until about ten o'clock when his lifeless body was found about four feet outside the pasture fence. His hat and a pitchfork were found a few feet inside the fence His body and limbs were bruised and discolored, in almost every part, and his ribs and breast bone were broken in many places The body was found by an old gentleman named Ole Egelson, who lives on the farm There was blood on the ground inside the fence and on the fence, and the conclusion is that he was killed by a two-year-old bull that was in the pasture, and then thrown over the fence by the animal. The bull hung constantly about the place pawing and bellowing It was a very sad affair."

Hon I. C Trowbridge, who laid out the original plat of what is now the city of Waseca, died rather suddenly of heart failure, October 3, 1893 Among other biographical sketches appears a sketch of his life

Mrs Clarissa (Mosher) Baker widow of W. S Baker of Waseca, died on Friday, Oct. 20, 1893, of pneumonia. She was born Feb 18 1819, in Marion county Ohio, where she resided until 1845 She was married Dec 30, 1841, and came West as far as Dodge county, Wis., in 1845, with her husband, where they resided until 1856, when they came to Waseca county and settled in Otisco They afterwards lived for a time in the west part of this county, and finally moved to Waseca when the town was first platted She was the mother of seven children: Ozias, Samuel, Charles, Scott, Cassius, Lucinda and Carrie Ozias, Samuel, and Charles, served in the Union ranks during the Rebellion, Ozias dying soon after his return Lucinda married Chauncey Gibbs and died before the death of Mrs Baker Five children survived her.

The following notice is taken from the Waseca Herald

The Gilmore City Globe, of Iowa, brings the sad news of the death of one of the early and most honorable settlers of this county, Mr. Jesse B Jackson Mr Jackson came to Wilton, in this county, in 1857, and was county commissioner for a number of years He was born in Jefferson county N Y, March 24, 1823 He went to Lorain county, Ohio, in 1847, and in October of the same year was married to Harriet N. Dudley. They were the parents of seven children, four daughters and three sons, five of whom are now living In 1868 they removed to Hardin county Iowa, and in 1871 moved to Pocahontas county where he has since resided, with the exception of two winters spent in California. The nervous disease from which he suffered for many years was contracted partly from a fall from a barn on which he was at work His collar bone was broken and he never entirely recovered from the shock. He passed peacefully away on the 29th of November, 1893, and his remains were buried on the 30th, Thanksgiving Day.

DAIRYMEN'S ASSOCIATION

The sixteenth annual convention of the state dairymen's association was held at Waseca, Minn, December 12, 13, and 14, 1893 The officers present were Hon John L Gibbs, of Geneva, president; Hon A P Foster, of Plainview, vice-president, and Prof T. L Haecker, of St Anthony Park, secretary. The following notes are condensed from the report published at the time in a local paper·

Tuesday was a bitterly cold day, but Father Benson, of Anoka, Secretary Haecker, of St Anthony Park, Treasurer Short of Faribault, and others were here early in the morning Messrs Samuel Leslie, G H Wood, Samuel Hawkes, and other local dairymen were on hand to assist, and in the afternoon and evening many came in from abroad, among them President Gibbs, of Geneva, Freeborn county, and Prof O C Gregg and his corps of institute lecturers The meeting on Tuesday evening was held under very unfavorable circumstances The weather was cold enough in the open air, but the temperature inside Ward's opera house was away below the comfort mark, and many were forced to leave on account of the severe cold But cold as it was the dairymen carried out their program Rev E C Clemans made a unique prayer for good butter, honest butter, sixteen ounces to the pound, and at such prices that God's poor might get a taste now and then

President John L Gibbs presided. He introduced Hon John Moonan who delivered the address of welcome in a very pleasing manner Mr C L Smith, of Minneapolis, a very fluent and entertaining speaker made response The secretary and the treasurer then made their written reports James E Child, of Waseca, and Hon O C Gregg, president of the Farmers' state institute workers, were called upon and made short addresses the first evening. The association was in session three days and much good work was done. The next week this paper reviewed the meeting as follows.

"The holding of the Dairymen's annual meeting in this city, last week, was a matter of great local importance as well as of general interest. It is a fact, which can not be too often urged, that dairying and the raising of hogs and cattle, together with the growing of grain, are of the utmost importance to all the farmers of Minnesota, north as well as south All these should go together wherever circumstances make it possible, and the discussions and papers at the Dairymen's meeting threw much light on the subject Take for instance, the statement that a separator creamery, with 800 cows, a small number for each township, had a clear income of $40,000. That is $50, on the average, for each cow, and each farmer took back with him seventy-five per cent of the whole milk in sweet, skimmed milk, beside his proportion of butter milk with which to feed calves and hogs This amount was realized from the "average cow," while the farmer had only to milk the cows, strain the milk and cart it to the factory—the churning, salting, packing, and marketing being done by the co-operative factory

"Under this system, the poor man, with only two or three cows, can realize as much per cow as his wealthiest brother, while, under the home system of making butter, the farmer, with two or three cows, could not compete at all with his richer brother having a large herd ot cows and all the necessary appliances for butter-making.

"Our German and Scandinavian Americans, to the east of us, along the Steele county border and in Steele and Freeborn counties, have caught on to the fact that even the 'average cow' will give a return of from $45 to $60 a year under this co-operative plan Why should not every farmer in Waseca county do as well?

"There is another consideration in this co-operative creamery plan it does away with the cutthroat practice of speculation which is a necessity where the manufacturer, (creamery man), must take his chances on the market By co-operation, both the manufacturer of the butter and the producer of the milk get just what their joint product is worth in the market, while, under any other plan, the manufacturer and dealer must keep down the price to the farmer in order to cover possible losses and make money."

WASECA AGRICULTURAL SOCIETY

The annual meeting of this society was held at the court room, on Tuesday, Dec 23, 1893 Reports of the secretary and the treasurer were read, showing at length the financial condition of the society The total receipts during the year amounted to $877.02, and the expenses, including premiums, to $856 59, leaving a balance on hand of $20 43 There was outstanding an order for $250 borrowed money, which was made necessary to pay premiums, the weather having prevented the holding of the last fair on two of the appointed days.

The following resolution was unanimously adopted

Resolved, That the commissioners of the county of Waseca be, and they are, hereby requested to purchase our present fair grounds for the purpose of holding an annual county fair, under and by virtue of the power vested in such commissioners so to do by an act of the legislature of the state of Minnesota, passed in 1891

CHAPTER LXIII, 1894.

COUNTY FAIR GROUNDS—PROCEEDINGS OF COUNTY BOARD—CLAGHORN DEFALCATION—A DYNAMITE EXPLOSION—ELECTION RESULTS—DIED HON WARREN SMITH, PETER BURNS, MRS A C SMITH, BYRON SMITH, MRS MYRICK, JOHN REMUND

The year 1894 opened clear bright, and cold The county board assembled on Jan 5 Mr Chase was re-elected chairman—the other members present being Messrs Sunde Peterson, Lewer, and Bluhm Messrs John Moonan, S Leslie, M Sheeran, and O Powell, of the Waseca County Agricultural Society, presented the resolution of the society asking for the purchase of fair grounds, and also addressed the board urging the purchase of the land

The committee of the board appointed to confer with the owners of the fair grounds reported that the land could be purchased at $100 per acre for twenty-five acres The report was accepted and the committee discharged

Mr Peterson then offered the following resolutions which were adopted

Resolved, That the county commissioners of the county of Waseca, Minnesota, purchase twenty-five acres of land lying just east of Second street, and north of Clear Lake road, in the southwest quarter of section 8, township 107, range 22, in the city of Waseca, the same being lands heretofore used by the Waseca County Agricultural Mechanical, and Industrial society for county fair grounds and other lands in the vicinity thereof as and for use as a county fair ground

Resolved, That the title of said lands shall be vested in and remain in said Waseca county, but that the said Waseca County Agricultural * * society shall have the exclusive use thereof for an annual rental of $25 per year, to be paid into the county treasury of said county, on or before the first day of January of each and every year

Resolved, That the board of county commissioners of Waseca county shall not be called upon or required to make any improvements or repairs on the premises as long as the same remain in the possession of the society aforesaid

The roll was called and all voted in favor of the adoption of the resolutions except Mr Jonas O Sunde

The author deems it unfortunate that the people of this county, and especially the farmers, have allowed the fair grounds to lapse into disusage during the past few years May we not hope that very soon again the people will take up the subject and rejuvenate the agricultural society of the county

On May 26 1894, $100 was voted the town of Iosco for a bridge between sections 17 and 18, $20 for repair of bridge sections 18 and 19, $85 town of Alton for repair of Alma City bridge, also $100 town of Janesville for bridge sections 27 and 34

At the May 22 meeting the following appropriations were made from the county road and bridge fund·

"To town of New Richland, $200 to aid in building a new bridge on the river, between sections 24 and 25, and $50 for road grading on sections 23 and 26, to town of Byron, $90 for a bridge over a creek on sections 5 and 8, and $10 for road grading on sections 4 and 9, to town of Otisco, $50 to aid in rebuilding the Walstrom bridge on section 33, $25 for repairs on the Holz bridge on section 7, and $25 for repairing the Hanson bridge on section 35, to town of Freedom, $125 to aid in rebuilding bridge on Bull Run at section 18, to town of Woodville, $25 for grading road on section 19, $50 for grading road on sections 17 and 28, $20 for grading road on sections 5 and 6, and $30 for grading road between section 6 of Woodville and section 1 of St Mary, to town of Iosco, $75 to aid in grading road on sections 8, 10, 11, and 26

At the July meeting the following appropriations were ordered

"To town of Alton, $50 for repairing Alma City bridge and $15 for grading road between sections 26 and 35 of said town, to town of Wilton, $125 for replanking the Wilton bridge, $25 for repairing St Mary bridge, on section 4 of said town, and $25 as aid in building bridge on section 35, of said town, to town of Blooming Grove, $75 for grading road between sections 2 and 11, and $50 for grading road between sections 8 and 17 of said town, to town of Otisco, $215 as aid in building the Holbrook bridge, on section 31, of said town, to town of Freedom, $25 as aid in building bridge across Bull Run, on section 18, of said town, to town of St Mary $35 for grading road between sections 24 and 25 $40 for grading road between sections 1 and 2 $25 for grading road between sections 12 and 13, and $20 for grading road between sections 20 and 29, of said town

At the September 7th meeting the following appropriations were made from the road and bridge fund

To town of Wilton, $20 additional for replanking the Wilton bridge, Blooming Grove, $50 for a bridge on section 25, of said town, Woodville, $20 for grading road on sections 18 and 19, of said town; Janesville, $50 for grading road on section 20, of said town, New Richland, $200 for a bridge on LeSueur river, section 10, of said town

J. L CLAGHORN'S DEFALCATION.

J L Claghorn, who for many years had been a prominent citizen of Waseca in church, society and local politics, failed in business about the first of February, 1894 On the 14th of that month he was arrested on a charge of embezzling $450 belonging to the Hartford Fire Insurance company This came as a thunderclap of surprise to the citizens of the county. He had been trusted by almost everybody Farmers, widows, school teachers, servants, money loaners in the East—all had entrusted him with their funds to handle and loan as he saw fit As soon as he was arrested, it was discovered that the funds were all missing For years he had been spending more than his income, and for a long time he had been "robbing Peter to pay Paul"—borrowing from one friend to pay another He had stood high in the Congregational church, was prominent as an Odd Fellow and a Mason, and had served a number of years as alderman of the "Puritan ward" of Waseca He and his wife had both been great temperance workers and were prominent in every good work That a man can thus serve Good and Evil at one and the same time is one of the mysteries of this mysterious universe At the March term of the district court he was indicted for the crime of embezzlement--larceny—finally pleaded guilty and was sentenced to one year at hard labor in the Stillwater penitentiary He served his time and as soon as released moved to the state of Washington His life emphasized the doctrine—"Trust no man in business matters without security in some form "

BOARD OF TRADE

In the latter part of the winter of 1893-4, the business men of Waseca organized a "Board of Trade " Articles of incorporation were adopted May 11, 1894, and duly published and filed The organization ran well for a few months, but very soon men would come in very late others not at all, and at the end of the first year the association was laid aside as rotten timber. It died of too much apathy or laziness

A DYNAMITE EXPLOSION

The Herald of August 3 contained the following·

"Dynamite! The most fiendish outrage ever perpetrated in Waseca took place on the evening of July 30, 1894, about 10 25 o'clock The Grant House 'bus had just made the 9:50 M & St. L. train and been returned to the barn The horses stood on the west side of the barn, and the 'bus on the east A dynamite bomb was evidently placed in the bottom of the 'bus with a fuse attached which reached to the door Within fifteen minutes after the team had been put into the barn there came an explosion which tore the 'bus into fragments and made the barn look as though a cyclone had struck it The south end and the southeast corner were torn all in pieces, the north door was thrown out into the street, the upper floor was badly demolished, and the roof badly broken Strange to say, the horses were not badly injured Evidently they were knocked down by the concussion, for when found they had changed sides, one evidently having fallen over the other The destruction was sudden and complete So far as is publicly known, at least, there is no clue to the perpetrator"

No clue was ever found, and the perpetrator of the terrible crime will probably die, if not already dead, with this guilt upon his soul

THE ELECTION RESULTS

The election campaign of 1894 was an exciting one The Populists polled their heaviest state vote that year The result in this county was as follows state senator, E B Collester, rep 1,608, R O Craig, dem, 705, Geo T Dunn, pop, 364 representative, H M. Buck, rep, 1,475, M H Helms, dem 852 Keyes Swift, pop, 341 county auditor, A J Lohren, rep, 1,674; J B Ungerman, dem., 944: treasurer, Walter Child, rep, 1 551, Thos Boucher, dem, 1,109 sheriff, Geo H Goodspeed, rep, 1,331, Frank Collins, dem, 1,310· register of deeds, A E Bishman, rep., 977, John Wollschlaeger, dem, 1,708 judge of probate, Geo A Wilson, rep, 1,553, F B Andrews, dem, 1,072· attorney, L D Rogers, rep, 1,370, P McGovern, dem, 1,298· coroner, Dr. W L. Sterns, rep, 1,335, Dr D D Smith, dem, 852, Dr J. P. Corry, pop, 382· school superintendent, C. W Wagner, rep, 1,523. J S Abell, dem, 1,136· Orson L Smith was elected county surveyor, and P C Bailey and Herman Ewert were elected county commissioners.

DEATHS OF THE YEAR

The first old settler called to the Great Beyond this year was Hon Warren Smith, beloved by all our people He died of stomach trouble, after a long illness, March 1, 1894, in his seventy-third year A sketch of his life appears in the biographical department of this work

Mr Peter Burns, of Wilton, one of the early and prominent settlers of this county, died on Wednesday evening, May 23, 1894 The Herald of that date said

"Mr. Burns was born in Ireland in 1837, and came to America in 1851, stopping first in the state of Ohio From that state he came to Minnesota in 1856 and settled in this county In 1862 he was married to Miss Anna Howlan and eight children have been born to them By industry, economy, and good management they secured a competency, and he leaves his family in comfortable circumstances He was a lover of good stock, and kept some very fine cattle and horses He was a man of much energy, and a good citizen. He was one of the pioneers that helped to make this county what it is, and cheerfully endured the hardships incident to frontier life He died of inflammation of the bladder."

Mrs A C Smith, of Woodville, died Friday morning, June 29 1894, after a brief illness Her maiden name was Arminda C Fuller, and she was born in Cayuga county, N Y in 1832 When she was but a little girl, her parents moved to Cataraugus county Western New York, and when she was twelve years old, with quite a number of emigrants from that and adjoining counties, they took boat and came up the great lakes to Wisconsin, settling at Magnolia Here she lived with her parents till about her eighteenth year when she began the life of a teacher, and when she was twenty years old, while still engaged in teaching, she was married to Alfred C. Smith, and moved soon after to Iowa, where they remained till the spring of 1855 when they moved, with four other families to Waseca county, Minn, arriving June 20 of the same year She resided here till the time of her death She left a family of eight daughters and three sons to mourn the departure of a good mother

Paul Billiard s hotel in Waseca took fire on the night of March 22 1894 The fire was soon put under control but not until one of the firemen, Byron Smith, was so injured that he died the next day He belonged to the hook and ladder company and, while working to subdue the fire, sustained a fracture of the skull from a falling chimney He died the next morning, mourned by the whole city Byron had been a lifelong citizen of the county and city He left a wife and one child, who were dependent upon his daily toil for a livelihood His sad death cast a gloom over the whole community

Mrs S W Myrick, daughter of Mr Silas Grover, deceased,—both of these were Wisconsin and Minnesota pioneers,—passed to her final rest Oct 22, 1894 Mr and Mrs Myrick were very early settlers at Minnesota Lake and opened the first hotel there They came to Waseca at an early day in its history and opened a millinery store She had no children of her own, but was survived by her aged husband and many relatives

Mr John Remund died Nov. 26, near Wilmot, S D., aged sixty-four years He was a native of Switzerland and came to Waseca county in 1856, where he remained until 1882, when he and his family removed to his farm two miles east of Wilmot A Wilmot paper says "Deceased was accounted one of the most careful and successful of men that ever did business in Wilmot During his residence here he had also been engaged in farming and had always been regarded as a prompt and square man by all with whom he dealt He was married in Switzerland in 1855 to Miss Mary Minder who survived him They were the parents of ten children, six boys and four girls, seven of whom are now living His sons are Fred, John, Sam, Will, and Julius, and his daughters are Mrs Louis Yonker, of this town, and Mrs. H. W Bluhm, of Vivian, Minn He was a brother of Messrs Chris Sam, and Albert Remund, of Blooming Grove

THE WEATHER

In striking contrast with the year before, warm, pleasant weather was the rule all the fall and continued until after the holidays The year had been a favorable one in the line of farm productions, and, aside from the financial craze that had paralyzed the business of the country, the people of this county were as prosperous as usual. The depression of prices had caused a scarcity of money, but so far as the real necessities and comforts go our people were well provided for.

CAPTER LXIV, 1895.

PROCEEDINGS OF COUNTY BOARD—THE NEW COURT HOUSE—CROPS AND WEATHER—DIED MRS JOHN BROWN, WILLIAM TAYLOR, G GRAMS, J R DAVIDSON, LOUIS W KRASSIN, ASA FRANCIS, PETER McELROY, JEROME MADDEN

The annual meeting of the county board came on the 8th day of January this year Hon P. C Bailey was elected chairman of the board. The other members of the board were: J. O Sunde, H F Lewer, H Ewert, and H W Bluhm Nothing more than the ordinary routine of work was transacted at this meeting

At the meeting of May 20, the following appropriations were made from the road and bridge fund Otisco, $100 for a new bridge on LeSueur river, section 35, $40 for replacing the Anderson bridge on section 34, $50 for grading road between sections 18 and 19, $25 for ditching for the road across Bauman slough on section 5, New Richland, $200 for a new bridge on LeSueur river between sections 2, New Richland, and 35, Otisco, Byron, $30 for replanking and repairing Boot Creek bridge between sections 13 and 24, Wilton, $115 for building two new bridges on the line between St Mary and Wilton, between sections 6 in Wilton and 31 in St Mary, and sections 5 in Wilton and 32 in St Mary Iosco, $100 for grading road between sections 7 and 18, and on section 14, St Mary, $35 for grading road on section 16, and $35 for grading road between sections 13 and 14, Woodville, $70 for grading road between sections 21 and 22, Vivian, $30 for grading road on section 28; $50 for grading road between sections 11 and 14

At the meeting of July 8, 1895, it was ordered that $100 be

appropriated to Blooming Grove, of which $50 was for grading road between sections 1 and 2, and $50 for grading between sections 11 and 12, $35 was appropriated to Vivian for a new bridge on section 10, $30 was appropriated to St Mary for a stone culvert on the Phelps road between sections 10 and 15.

At the meeting September 3, 1895, appropriations were made as follows. to town of New Richland, $25 for a bridge on LeSueur river between sections 14 and 15, $60 for two bridges between sections 21 and 28, and $40 for grading road between sections 16 and 17, New Richland; to town of Vivian, $50 for replanking the Cobb river bridge between sections 31 and 32, of said town, to town of Woodville, $50 for grading road on section 16 of said town, to town of Alton, $50 for grading road on west side of section 6, and $75 for a stone culvert on Janesville and Alma City road on section 32 of said town, to town of Iosco, $75 for grading McWaide hill

October 15, the following appropriations were made to town of Janesville, $150 to aid in rebuilding old town bridge over outlet of Lake Elysian, to town of Otisco, $50 for aid in rebuilding the Ivers bridge on section 31.

The proposition to build a new court house had been discussed considerably for more than a year. and at the meeting of the board Dec. 9, 1895, a petition containing over one hundred signatures of voters and freeholders was presented asking for the erection of a new courthouse, and that a special election be appointed for the purpose of raising funds, not exceeding fifty thousand dollars, for the erection of the same The petition was taken under consideration and the next morning action was taken thereon by the board as follows·

"Whereas, a petition has been heretofore duly filed with the auditor in and of the county of Waseca, Minnesota, signed by more than one hundred legal voters and freeholders of said county, addressed to the board of county commissioners of said county, setting forth that it is the desire of such petitioners that said county shall erect and construct a courthouse in the city of Waseca, in the county of Waseca and state of Minnesota, the said city of Waseca being the county seat of said Waseca county, and that the amount of money to be raised and expended in the erection and furnishing of said courthouse shall be and not exceed the sum of fifty thousand dollars; and said petitioners thereby pray that the proposition expressed in their petition be submitted to the electors of such county at a special election to be held at a time to be designated as provided by law, and,

"Whereas, upon the presentation of said petition, it becomes the duty, imposed by law on said board of county commissioners, to cause the proposition therein expressed to be submitted to the legal voters of said county as therein prayed for,

"Now, therefore, it is resolved by the board of county commissioners of said Waseca county, that a special election be held in said county on the 10th day of March, A D 1896, between the hours of 9 o'clock a m and 5 o'clock p m, on said day, for the purpose of submitting to the legal voters of said county the proposition expressed in said petition"

The proposition was submitted on town-meeting day so that no extra expense was incurred in voting upon the proposition

CROPS AND WEATHER

The year was blessed with as fine weather as was ever known in the county, and the crops were magnificent The wheat yield was more than the average, and the quality was number one, but the price was the lowest ever known in the history of Minnesota On Dec 27, 1895, No 1 wheat sold at 44 cents The highest price paid during the month was 47 cents for No 1 The fall weather was very fine, Indian summer continuing until Nov 18, when there was quite a snow storm, followed by colder weather The year, as a whole, was free from excitement in this county

SAVINGS AND LOAN ASSOCIATION

After considerable discussion through the local papers, a savings and loan, or building, association was organized April 26 1895 Its first directors were Dr D S Cummings D McLoughlin, E A White, E C Trowbridge, Dr F A Swartwood, W E Scott, S Swenson A D Goodman and James E Child The officers were Dr F A Swartwood, president E C Trowbridge, vice-president, A D Goodman, treasurer, and Wm A Swift secretary The association proved to be of great benefit to the people of the city, and is still doing a good business

CALLED HOME IN 1895

Mrs John Brown, of Waseca who died Feb 21, was born at Point's Pass, county of Down, Ireland, in 1812 She was married to John Brown in 1830, and soon afterwards they came to America and settled in the state of New York where they remained until about 1836, when they came as far west as Walworth county in the then territory of Wisconsin They remained there until 1870, when they came to Waseca county Mrs Brown was the mother of eleven children, four of whom survive her Her husband died some five years before.

Mr Peter McElroy, roadmaster of the entire M & St. L railway system, died at his home in Waseca, May 17, 1895, of stomach trouble, aged about sixty-eight years He came to this country from Ireland when a boy, and, for many years, lived in Montreal He had been a resident of Minnesota for about fourteen years

Mr Wm Taylor, one of the early settlers of Blooming Grove, died in Waseca, May 17, 1895 On Saturday morning he was in his usual health. In the afternoon he was taken with pneumonia from which he never got better. He was born in Rothwell, England, Nov 17, 1819 He was married and came to America in 1841; returned to England in 1843, and again came to America in 1846, settling in New Orleans In 1850 he moved to Missouri, going thence to Illinois in a short time, where he lived until 1857, when he came with his family to Waseca county and bought a farm in Blooming Grove. Some years prior to his death he sold his farm and became a resident of Waseca. Seven sons survive him

A very sad death occurred April 23 in Waseca The Herald give the following account of it.

"Last week was one of sadness for many of our people First came the death of Mr Peter McElroy, well known and highly respected, and next Mr Wm Taylor, a long time settler whose friends were numerous, and finally, Mr J. R Davison, one of the early and prominent settlers of the state and county Mr Davison had started on foot to attend Mr Taylor's funeral, Friday afternoon, when, in crossing the railroad track, near Mr Wyman's place, he was struck by an engine This was about 2 o'clock p m, and, although the injuries appeared to be slight, he never recovered, dying about 6 o'clock the same evening, at the residence of Mr S F Wyman, his son-in-law, of this city Mr Davison was an intelligent, useful citizen, and highly esteemed for his many good qualities. He was born in Nova Scotia in 1810, and was married to Miss Eunice Jenks in 1833 In 1848 he left the land of his nativity and moved to Maine, but having started westward he went to the new state of Indiana in 1850 That locality not proving a healthful one, he emigrated to Minnesota, leaving a newly-made grave in each of these temporary homes He settled near Morristown in 1856, but eight years later crossed the county line and built the "Traveler's Home" in Blooming

Grove He was well known to the traveling public till the infirmities of age came on He moved with his wife in 1884 to Waseca to spend the remaining days in the home of their daughter, Mrs Wyman His wife died in 1885 One son and four daughters are still living to treasure his memory"

About the first of November, 1895, Louis W Krassin died at Minneapolis of strangulated hernia He was one of the early settlers of Waseca county. At the breaking out of the Sioux Indian massacre, he enlisted as a member of Capt Austin's company of mounted rangers and participated in the whole of the Indian campaign He was injured while in the service and never fully recovered—finally dying of it. He left a large family of young men and women surviving him At the time of his death he resided at Montevideo

Mr Asa Francis, better known as "Doc" Francis one of the early settlers of Minnesota and of this county, was born May 6, 1800, at Goshen, Conn. At nine years of age he left his home and moved to central New York, and cared for himself ever after At the age of seventeen, he drove a wagon and peddled tinware in New York State, continuing this until 1835 when he settled on a stock farm in the Black River country, where he remained until the spring of 1856, when he moved to the territory of Minnesota He was married in 1828 to Miss Eliza Jones in New York Three children were born, two of whom died in infancy —the youngest, a son, Marshall, lost his life in the War of the Rebellion in 1863 Mr Francis' wife died in 1846 He married Electra Post in 1847, and she died in 1851 in New York, Hon Orin W Francis being the only child of this marriage In 1852 he married Hannah Bailey in New York State, two children being born, one dying in infancy, the other, Lyman E, now deceased, being remembered as a prominent lawyer at Hillsboro N D. Dr Francis first settled in Rice county, in this state, in 1856, and two or three years after came to Waseca county taking a farm in Byron, where he resided until 1879 when he removed to North Dakota and took a homestead in Cass county, where he resided until 1886 That year he and his wife removed to Fargo, where they made their home until the time of his death It appears that about a year prior to his death he had the grippe from which he never fully recovered He was up and about, however, until the Tuesday before his death, which occurred December 2, 1895, at the age of ninety-five years and six months, less four days His wife survived him, at the age of eighty years, having been his companion for some forty-three years

Mr Charles Domy, of Woodville, another old settler, about ninety years of age, passed over the river Jordan, Dec 17, 1895, honored and respected by all his acquaintances. He was of French parentage and was a native of Canada

Mr Jerome Madden, of Waseca, whose early life is noted elsewhere, died this year, Nov 18

CHAPTER LXV, 1896.

PROCEEDINGS OF COUNTY BOARD—THE VOTE ON COURTHOUSE—CONTRACT FOR BUILDING COURTHOUSE LET—WASECA CREAMERY—TERRIBLE SUFFERING AND DEATH OF SOL MIDDAUGH—MASONIC HALL AT ALMA CITY BURNED—"EACO" MILL BURNED—CREAMERIES ESTABLISHED—DIED: JENNIE GASINK, JULIENNE MINSKE, HANNAH BUCKMAN, JOHN PETERSON, JUSTINA KRASSIN, JOHN JORDAN, P H SPILLANE, MARY DONOVAN—THE ELECTION

The legislative branch of the county government met in annual session Jan 7 and organized by electing Hon P C Bailey to preside The county printing was let as follows The tax list to the Herald, the financial statement and the report of board of equalization to the Radical, and the proceedings of the county commissioners to the Argus—all at legal rates

At this session fifty dollars was appropriated to the town of Alton for repairing the Lamb bridge

PROPOSITION TO BUILD COURTHOUSE

The following figures show the vote of March 12 1896, upon the proposition to build a new courthouse at Waseca

	Yes	No
New Richland, town	22	64
New Richland, village	42	68
Byron	28	51
Vivian	54	24
Otisco	33	115
Wilton	48	48
Freedom	28	107
Woodville	77	26

Waseca, First ward	229	8
Waseca, Second ward	178	9
Waseca, Third ward	160	8
St. Mary	46	65
Alton	11	114
Blooming Grove	34	45
Iosco	33	92
Janesville, First precinct	101	31
Janesville, Second precinct	22	62
Totals	1,146	937
Majority	209	

At the meeting of the county board April 23, after a very lengthy and laborious examination of the eleven plans submitted, the commissioners accepted the plan submitted by architects Orff & Joralemon of Minneapolis, the cost of the building not to exceed $35,000 It is 68x91½ feet in size, two stories high with a stone basement. It fronts on Second street, is built of St. Louis mottled brick, and is heated by steam The first floor is fire-proof The tower and dome are one hundred feet high and furnish a fine look-out over the city and surrounding country

After ordering the publication of advertisements for bids for constructing the proposed building, the board adjourned

At the May meeting, the board proceeded to open the proposals for erecting the new courthouse The bids, twenty-one in number, ranged from $48,000, made by Keefe Bros of Waseca, to $34,765 96, made by J D Carroll, of St Paul Park, the latter bid was accepted

The following appropriations were made to towns To Freedom, $75 for stone culvert on county line road on section 7, and $25 for grading road on slough between sections 27 and 34, to Vivian, $40 to be used for building bridge between sections 21 and 28, $20 for a bridge on road between sections 22 and 27 and $40 for bridge on road between sections 1 and 2, to Iosco, $50 to be appropriated for grading road on section 10, to Alton, $100 for a stone culvert between sections 9 and 10

At the board meeting of May 18, 1896, the contract for furnishing the heating apparatus for the new courthouse was awarded to Pond, Hasey & Co, of Minneapolis, for $2,150 W F Porter & Co, of St Paul, also had in a bid at $2 325

In the afternoon the board ordered the purchase of sixty feet front of the Priest land, adjoining the courthouse grounds, and appropriated $2,500 to be paid upon receipt of proper conveyance of land

The following appropriations were made from the road and bridge fund Town of New Richland, $30 for two bridges and approaches on road between sections 17 and 18, $30 for grading road between section 2 in New Richland and section 35 in Otisco, and $40 for two bridges between sections 15 and 22 in New Richland; to town of Otisco, $35 for a bridge and grading on section 10; $45 for repairing the Walstrom bridge, and $20 for repairing bridge on section 9

At the September meeting, the following appropriations were made from the road and bridge fund Town of Byron $25; town of Janesville $100, town of St Mary $50

The erection of the courthouse progressed slowly during the year 1896 The contractor finally failed entirely, and the American Surety Company, his bondsmen, were compelled to take charge of the building and complete it Great credit is due to the board of county commissioners and to Hon A J Lohren, then county auditor, for this very complete edifice It is of much credit to the county. The American Surety Company and Hon S P Child, its state agent, are also entitled to credit for honestly carrying out the contract

THE WASECA CREAMERY

got its start the first of this year. A joint meeting of farmers and business men was held the Saturday before New Year s day and a subscription for stock started John Diedrich headed the list with fifty shares, or $500 Committees were appointed to solicit stock and also to ascertain the number of cows that would be pledged to the enterprise At the adjourned meeting held Jan. 3, there was a large attendance and the following officers were then chosen for the first year Thomas Bowe, president, W H Wheeler, vice-president, James Conway, secretary Wm Mittelsteadt, treasurer, Cornelius McGonagle, Fred Mahler, and D A Erwin, directors The officers were also elected directors

On motion of John Diedrich, the chair was authorized to appoint a committee on articles of incorporation and by-laws, and the chairman appointed Messrs John Diedrich, W. H Wheeler, James Conway, Wm Mittelsteadt, C McGonagle, Fred Mahler, and D. A. Erwin as such committee

The meeting then adjourned to meet at the same place Thursday, Jan 9, 1896, at 1 o'clock p m.

The committee on articles of incorporation and by-laws met on Monday and drafted articles and by-laws for the association

Forty-six farmers subscribed for stock, the total amounting to $3,080 Members of the association met again Jan 9, selected a site for the building, adopted articles of incorporation, and made arrangements to perfect the organization and to erect a creamery building The enterprise proved to be an entire success, and the association is doing good work to-day The liberal business men of Waseca subscribed to the enterprise $365.

TERRIBLE SUFFERING AND DEATH

Solomon Middaugh, one of the early settlers of Meriden and Waseca, about 1875, moved with his family to Jackson county, Minn On Jan. 15, 1896, in returning from Estherville to his home, his team ran away, throwing him out and breaking both his legs His brother, R M. Middaugh, of Waseca, went to his brother's assistance and wrote the following letter describing the closing scenes of the sufferer's life:

Petersburg, Jackson Co., Minn, Jan 27, 1896

To the Editors of the Waseca County Herald:

It is evening and the doctor has just left us giving no hope that dear brother Sol will live through the night While I am writing this he is resting quietly, but has passed a very hard afternoon Ah! but how he has suffered ever since the awful Monday night, just two weeks ago, when, lying upon the prairie, he vainly called for help that did not come.

Poor fellow! He lies helpless upon a high bed, with both legs strapped to the ceiling and walls to keep them in place

How he has lived through it all is a mystery The particulars of the sad accident, so far as I can learn, are these He was coming home from Estherville with a horse team attached to a lumber wagon loaded with some lumber and tin roofing When about one mile from home the ring on one of the singletrees broke, letting the tongue down The horses ran, striking the wagon tongue against a stone which threw the wagon high in air, and this was the last poor Sol knew until he found himself on the prairie, some distance from the road, with both legs broken close below the knees He must have fallen with both legs into a wagon wheel The track showed that one of the wheels must have been clogged for some distance, as it dragged on the ground

When he recovered his senses he crawled some twenty rods, leaving a trail of blood all the way Pools of blood in places show that he must have stopped to rest several times At last, when near the road, his strength gave out, and he had to give up He gathered his broken legs under him as best he could, and there remained all the long night calling for help About 8 o clock the next morning he was found, more dead than alive, by some school children on their way to school.

The team did not go home, but ran across the fields through a wire fence, and, when found the next morning, one horse was still attached to the front axle, with only one wheel on, and some of the fence wire hanging to it Both horses were cut some, but not seriously. The wagon was a total wreck, scattered in every direction

Many wonder why Sol. did not bleed to death during the night, and the only answer is that his leg froze and this stopped the flow of blood Although he had on warm felt boots, they were frozen solid and had to be cut open to get them off.

These are the disconnected facts concerning my brother Sol, and, if you can fix them up, they may be of interest to his many friends in Waseca county

Later—Poor Sol. passed away this (Tuesday) morning at 2 o'clock

Yours in sorrow,

R M MIDDAUGH.

LODGE ROOM AND RECORDS BURNED

On the night of May 23, 1896, the Masonic lodge room, at Alma City, was burned The lodge occupied rooms over Daniel J Bickford's blacksmith and wagon shop The cause of the fire is unknown to the public It seems that there was lodge meeting that night until after 10 o'clock within two hours afterward the whole building was in ashes Mr Bickford lost nearly all his tools and stock on hand, and the hall and all its contents, including the records, were consumed The records of the lodge were the oldest in the county, being "Wilton Lodge No 24," organized in 1859 Most of the older Masons in the county took their first Masonic lessons in that lodge while it was located at Wilton Many of the "boys in blue" were initiated into the mysteries of the order preparatory to taking their chances on the Southern battle fields After the old village of Wilton had shrunk out of sight, as it were, the archives of the lodge, retaining the old name and number, were removed to Alma City

"EACO" MILLS, WASECA, MINNESOTA.

BURNING OF THE "EACO" MILL

At about twenty minutes after 3 o clock Tuesday morning, Aug. 25, 1896, the fire alarm and mill whistle aroused our citizens and it was soon discovered that the old and long-vacant coffin factory, on the west side of the M & St L railroad track, nearly opposite the flour mill of Everett, Aughenbaugh & Co., was on fire It made a terribly hot fire, but soon burned to the ground, and the people were just congratulating one another that the fire was no worse, when the cry went forth that the flour and bran house on the south of the mill was on fire

Undoubtedly the heat upon the sheet iron covering had set the woodwork inside on fire. Every effort was made by the fire department to keep down the flames, but the high wind and the bursting of a watermain in the south part of the city at that time, reducing the pressure, combined to aid the flames which were carried directly into the windows of the mill It was short work for the consuming element to destroy one of the best mills in the state, the accumulation of years of industry, economy, and safe business management Two cars loaded with flour were also consumed The total loss of the Eaco Milling Company was estimated at $70,000, and the property of the mill was insured for $45,000 The old coffin factory was of little value and had been, for a long time, the tramps' paradise There is no doubt that the fire was either the work of incendiarism or the carelessness of tramps The mills were at once rebuilt on a more elaborate plan than before, and are, at this day, doing the best of work

SEVERAL CREAMERIES.

Several farmers' co-operative creameries were established in the county this year In addition to the Waseca creamery, the following are noted

In the month of January, the farmers of St. Mary and adjoining towns organized a co-operative creamery association by adopting articles of incorporation and subscribing stock to the amount of $3,500 The following officers were chosen Patrick Campion, president, James Byron, secretary, M W Keeley, treasurer. M Gallagher, manager, George Kahnke, Steven Priebe, Michael Sheeran, and Michael McGonagle, Jr, directors

The last of January, the farmers of Otisco and vicinity, organized a creamery association and elected as its first officers, Hon. H. M Buck, president, Joseph Fromlath, treasurer; R. Jacoby, secretary; W R Brisbane, Louis Anderson, Amil Weckwerth, Chas J Johnson, John A. Johnson, board of directors The amount of capital stock was fixed at $3,000

The Janesville creamery had been running a year, and the Argus reported it as follows "Total number of pounds of milk received, 1,077,905, pounds of butter fat, 41,839, pounds of butter made and sold, 48,923, average price per pound, twenty cents plus a fraction. The officers for the ensuing year are P. G Ayers, president; J H Murphy, vice-president, James Sullivan, secretary; J. W. Jennison, treasurer, Ed Hayden, A Gunn, H Hugunin, H O. Thrall, and the officers named, constitute the board of directors

DEATHS OF 1896 AS NOTED

Mrs Jennie Gasink, about eighty-three years of age, mother of Albert, John, and Gradus Gasink, died Jan 28, of old age and the grippe She came to this country from Holland in 1847, and settled first in Milwaukee, Wis She and her husband moved to Sheboygan, the same state, in 1853 and came to Waseca in 1869, where she has since resided Her husband died some nine years before She left surviving her seven children and a large number of grandchildren

Mrs Hannah Buckman, wife of Augustus Buckman died Feb 26, at Waseca. She was born in Crown Point, state of New York, March 20, 1840. She was married in December, 1863, and came to Minnesota in 1869 She became the mother of seven children, five of whom survive her She was first taken with pleurisy, and typhoid pneumonia followed She had passed the critical point in her illness, it was thought, and she appeared much better But later she was taken with congestion of the stomach and rapidly sank into the sleep of death Mrs Buckman was a kind-hearted, good neighbor, ever ready to share her scanty fare with those in need She was one of God's noble workers who somehow so often fail to receive a fair share of the comforts of the life which they work so hard to produce Hers had been a life of toil and care on behalf of her children, and may her memory and industrious example be to them a monitor and guide through life.

Mr John Peterson, of Otisco, one of the very early settlers of the county, died Aug 27, 1896, of cancer of the liver He was born in Sweden, Feb 6, 1828 He came to America, stopping at Chicago, in 1853 He worked in Chicago six months, going thence to La Fayette, Indiana, where he worked until he came to Minnesota via Red Wing, in 1857. He at first secured 120 acres of land on section 28, Otisco, and afterwards bought 40 acres more Soon after his settlement here he married Miss Carolina Hokanson, of the same town They had nine children Mrs Peterson came from Sweden with her parents in 1858 Mr Peterson had the misfortune to lose one arm in a threshing machine, in October, 1875

Mrs Justina Krassin, widow of Martin Krassin, after long years of poor health, passed peacefully away, Aug. 31, 1896, aged sixty-one years She was born in Germany, in 1835, married Martin Krassin in 1851, and came with him to America in the year 1854 She reared a family of six children, all of whom are living except August C, who died Aug 9, 1891.

Another old settler departed this life, Sept 1, 1896 The Herald noted his departure as follows

Mr John Jordan, a single man, of St Mary, was found dead in his bed on Wednesday morning. He arose about 4 o'clock and was about the house for a short time, and then retired to his room where he was soon after found dead Mr Jordan was born in Ireland, June 4, 1835, and came to America with his family in 1849. He first landed in New Brunswick, afterwards lived in Massachusetts, and came to Minnesota in 1856, settling on section 16, in St Mary, where he had since resided He remained single, having upon his farm a renter family at the time of his death. Mr Jordan was a jolly, easy-going, pleasant man, with numerous friends. It is supposed that he died of heart disease.

Patrick H Spillane, Esq, of Woodville, after a severe illness, died December 19, 1896, at the age of fifty-five years He was a native of Framore Ireland, came to America at the age of ten years, lived near Waupun, Wis, enlisted in Company D, Third Wisconsin infantry in February 1864, marched with Sherman to the sea, was engaged in the battle of Averysboro N C, where he was shot through the body, just above the hips, and from which he never fully recovered He married Miss Charlotte

Lang, in 1867, and the same year came to this county. The next year he took a homestead in Faribault county, where he remained some eight years, and then returned to Waseca county. He was, for several years prior to his death, justice of the peace of Woodville, and a prominent member of the G A R post of Waseca He was honorable and upright in his dealings, and possessed high qualities of good citizenship His funeral took place with military honors at the Catholic church, Father Treanor officiating He left surviving him a widow and five children —three boys and two girls

Mrs Mary Donovan, of Woodville, passed to her long rest, Dec 22, 1896 She was the widow of the late C. Donovan, and had been sick for many months of cancer She was a native of County Cork, Ireland She and her husband came to this county from Wisconsin over twenty-five years ago She left five sons and two daughters to mourn her departure

THE GENERAL ELECTION

This year saw the great struggle between plutocracy, or the gold standard advocates, and democracy, or the bimetallists of the country, and plutocracy won by an overwhelming majority In Waseca county the gold standard won by a majority of six hundred and forty votes The local candidates received the following votes

Representative, John Wilkinson, rep, 1,940, Keyes Swift, populist, 1,315, auditor, A J. Lohren, rep, 1801, John S Abell, dem 1 448, treasurer, W H Roesler, rep, 1,913, E R Krassin, bimetallist, 1,366, sheriff, Geo H Goodspeed, rep, 2 101, P H Kenehan, populist, 1,198, register, Chas San Galli, rep, 1,202, John M Wollschlaeger, dem, 2 131, judge of probate, Geo A Wilson, rep, 2 145, John Madigan, dem, 1,117, attorney L D Rogers rep, 1 559, P McGovern, dem, 1 739, clerk of court, Henry Reynolds, rep, 2,009, John M Byron, dem, 1 290, school superintendent, C. W. Wagner, rep, 2,227, Dr J P Corry, populist 1,171 Orson L Smith, for county surveyor, E P. Latham, for court commissioner, and Dr M J Taylor, for coroner, were elected without opposition Joseph Fromlath, of the first commissioner district, Henry F Lewer, of the third, and Raymond

Doyle, of the fifth, all democrats, were elected county commissioners

THE WEATHER.

As a rule, the weather was favorable throughout the year The heaviest rain storm of the season commenced Nov 25, and continued three days The long drouth which had prevailed in the Northwest for two years was broken The sloughs and low places were filled with water and the high lands were thoroughly soaked. While November was cold and stormy, the first half of December was mild; but the latter part of the month was stormy, and in the last week of the month a very severe sleet storm visited Southwestern Minnesota, extending into this county

CHAPTER LXVI, 1897.

COUNTY PRINTING—COUNTY BOARD—CONTRACTOR CARROLL DISCHARGED — COUNTY APPROPRIATIONS — NEW COURT-HOUSE COMPLETED—TORNADOES—WILLIAM HARDING'S 100 YEARS—DIED J W HOSMER, WILLIAM VON SIEN, ESTHER M YOUNG, J C HUNTER, R F STEVENS, CORNELIUS McGONAGLE, THOMAS CAWLEY, C M READ, MATTHEW COLEMAN, CHARLES M SMITH, W H IVERS—DECORATION DAY—SHORT CROPS—HOG CHOLERA

The year was ushered in with a January thaw which lasted about a week and closed with a sleet and snow storm and then colder weather

COUNTY COMMISSIONERS WORK.

The board of county commissioners met in regular session Jan 5, 1897 Members present, Joseph Fromlath, P C Bailey, H F Lewer, H Ewert, Raymond Doyle. The board organized by the election of Mr. Lewer as chairman The board of audit made a report designating the Citizens State Bank of Waseca and the Peoples Bank as depositories of county funds for the ensuing two years.

The publishers of the newspapers of the county having failed to come to any agreement regarding the county printing, the whole of it was awarded to the Waseca County Herald at five cents a description for publishing the tax list, and one cent for all the other publishing

John D Carroll, the courthouse contractor, having failed to carry out his contract on time, the county commissioners met in special session Feb 2, 1897, and resolved "that the said contract and said modifications therein with the said John D Carroll is hereby declared forfeited by him, and that the same be and is hereby terminated and ended as to performance thereof by him and that he is hereby required to cease any further work on said courthouse and all charge or control of the construction of the same" On Feb 6, the board again met and by arrangement with S. P. Child, agent of the American Surety Company, the contract for finishing the courthouse structure was let to C F Haglin, of Minneapolis, for $10,000.

The board of commissioners, at their session, May 21, 1897, received proposals for building a steel bridge instead of the old Markham bridge in the town of Alton from the Gillette, Herzog Manufacturing Company, of Minneapolis, the Wisconsin Bridge and Iron Company, of Milwaukee, the Massillion Bridge Company, of Ohio, the A D Wheaton Bridge Company, of Chicago, and the N M Stark Bridge Company, of Des Moines, Iowa, ranging from $1,100 to $975 These proposals were all rejected. The members of the board, in company with the bridge builders present, proceeded to the Wilton bridge for the purpose of examining as to the condition of said bridge, and upon the return the board concluded to auction off, to the lowest bidder, the building of two steel bridges in place of the old Wilton and Markham bridges Thirty-five bids were received, ranging from $2,000 to $1,299, for building the Wilton bridge Then eight bids ranging from $2,200 to $2,195 for building the two bridges named were received The lowest bid was made by the Gillette, Herzog Manufacturing Company, of Minneapolis This bid was accepted, and it was ordered that the contract for the building of said bridges be awarded the said Gillette, Herzog Manufacturing Company, of Minneapolis, the Wilton bridge for $1,260, and the Markham bridge for $935

On May 22 it was ordered that the following appropriations be made from the county road and bridge fund: To town of Vivian, $50, for grading road on marsh between sections 6 and 7 in said town; to town of Iosco, $50, for the new road between sections 27 and 28 of said town, to town of Blooming Grove, $50, for grading road between sections 14 and 15 in said town, to town of New Richland, $100, for a bridge on section 31 of said town; to town of Alton, $60, for a stone culvert on road between sections 13 and 14 of said town

On June 16, 1897, bids having been received by the board—

It was ordered that the contract for the building of a combination bridge, on section 1, of Janesville, be awarded to the Gillette, Herzog Manufacturing Company, of Minneapolis, for the sum of $445 It was also ordered that the contract for the building of a combination bridge on section 33, of Otisco, be awarded to the said Gillettte, Herzog Manufacturing Company for the sum of $450 Commissioner Ewert was appointed to oversee the building of the bridge on section 1, of Janesville, and Commissioner Fromlath was appointed to oversee the building of the bridge on section 33, of Otisco

At the same meeting, appropriations were made as follows

To Lars Syverson, $25, for damages on land caused by the change of location of the Wilton bridge; to town of Freedom, $50 for grading approaches to the bridge on road between section 1, of Vivian, and section 36, of Freedom The town of Freedom was also allowed to expend an appropriation made May 7, 1896, on the Bull Run bridge on section 13, of said town, to town of St Mary, $50, of which $25 is to be expended on road between sections 13 and 14, and $25 for grading road on section 1 of said town

At the meeting of Sept 6, the following appropriations were made from the county road and bridge fund·

To town of Janesville, $30, for grading approaches to the new bridge on section 1, of said town, to town of Freedom, $50, as aid in the building of a new bridge across Bull Run, on section 13, of said town, to town of Woodville, $65, for grading road between sections 13 and 14, and 21 and 22, of said town

At an adjourned meeting held Oct 22, 1897, it was ordered that the new Wilton bridge be accepted, and that the contract price, $1,260, less $35, be paid to the Gillette Herzog Manufacturing Company It was also ordered that the Markham bridge be accepted and the contract price, $935, be paid to the Gillette, Herzog Manufacturing Company, conditionally that the little sag in said bridge, now appearing, be straightened by said firm free of charge within one year from date, which order was accepted by the representative present from said firm

THE NEW COURTHOUSE

The new courthouse was completed about the 1st of August, 1897, and was formally dedicated, Sept 23 The following account is from the columns of the Waseca County Herald·

"The recent completion of our grand, new courthouse, with its nicely graded grounds and pleasant surroundings, calls to mind the courthouse history of this county, which may be of some interest to the present generation.

"The county of Waseca was organized by act of the territorial legislature, dated Feb 27, 1857 By that act the voters of the county were authorized to hold an election on the first Monday of June, 1857, to choose the county seat and elect county officers Three villages, Wilton, St. Mary and Empire, were candidates for the county seat, and Wilton won Strange as it may seem, nothing is left of these "ancient towns' except the lands upon which they were built

"The first courthouse was a store building, about 24 feet wide, 60 feet long, and two stories high The record of its purchase reads as follows

"'At the session of the board of county supervisors, Oct. 12, 1859, M S. Gove, H. G Mosher, and J W La Paul were appointed a committee to purchase the store building owned by Thos L Paige, in the village of Wilton, for a courthouse, with the county certificates of tax sales of lands sold in 1858, and bid in by the county—the amount of said purchase not to exceed $700 E A Rice, register of deeds, was ordered to assign the certificates upon receiving deed'

"The building was purchased and used as a courthouse until it was destroyed by fire, April 3, 1869

"The same year of the purchase of the courthouse, a jail, costing about $500, was built adjoining it on the north end. This was also burned by the same fire that consumed the courthouse

"The records were nearly or quite all saved, and the county officers took temporary quarters in the wagon shop of Bernard Bundschu. The county board at that time consisted of R F. Stevens, John S McKune, Robert Earl, Wm Byron, and John Buckhout. They met in special session April 15, 1869, and finally purchased the John C Hunter building for $500, to be paid from the insurance money on the old building This was the second courthouse, worth much less than the first, but serving the purpose after a fashion, until the pending county seat conflict should be permanently settled

"Waseca had been platted in 1867, and was already a large and thriving town That it would eventually secure the county seat was inevitable

"At the next session of the legislature, February, 1870, an act was passed authorizing the village of Waseca to issue bonds in the sum of $5,000, the proceeds to be used in the building of a new courthouse for the county of Waseca, upon the removal of the county seat to Waseca The people of Waseca voted in March to issue the bonds and before fall the then new courthouse was completed.

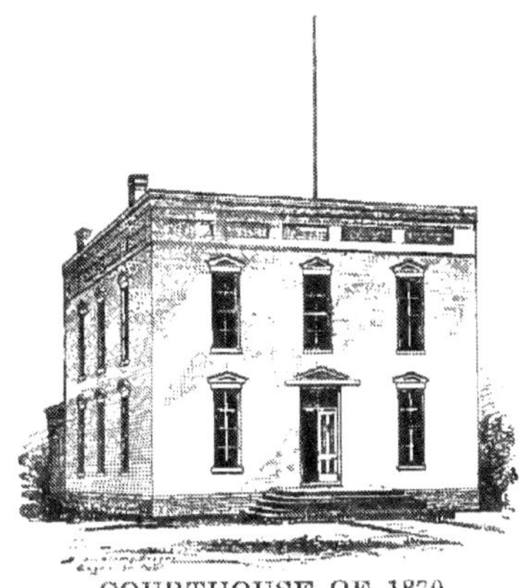
COURTHOUSE OF 1870.

"This courthouse, removed last spring, was a fine brick structure, 40x50 feet on the ground, and two stories high. The lower floor was divided into four offices, and the second floor was used as a court room. At that time, 1870, it was one of the best and most commodious courthouses in Southern Minnesota. The building was for years poorly cared for by the county board and left to decay.

"The history of the present new and elegant courthouse, just completed, is current history, fresh in the minds of our people. It is 74 feet north and south by 92 feet east and west. The tower is 100 feet high, with a flag staff 30 feet in length. Its total cost, including land, furniture, burglar-proof safes, etc., as reported by Auditor Lohren, is $55,833.07. In all its appointments it is most ample and complete. The vaults are large and roomy, and most of them well lighted. The county offices are all on the first floor, the second floor being devoted to the court room, jury rooms and judge's private room.

"Though there are more costly courthouses in the state, it is believed that there is not one of its size so complete and ample in its arrangements.

COURTHOUSE AT WASECA 1896-7.

TORNADOES.

There were two severe storms in the summer—one on the 10th of June, the other July 6. The Cream correspondent of the Herald wrote as follows:

June 10, Cream and vicinity were visited by high winds, electrical disturbances, rain, and hail, about half past four o'clock p. m. There were several hurricanes formed. They were perpendicular cloud columns reaching from the upper clouds to the earth.

The one south destroyed Postmaster Oleson's home and its contents, his barn and grove. Some of the contents of the office were picked up two miles away. The column passed just south of Mr Hydorn, picked up the Wm. Davidson school house, and whirled it all into pieces The register and some of the library books were picked up east of Plum Valley, near Sam. Hodgkin's place, in Vivian It just brushed Mr Krause's new house, which is being constructed, but left it unharmed People that were near say the roar was deafening The hurricane that passed north tore down a barn northwest of Alma City There were four horses in the barn which escaped unharmed. A cow near by had a leg broken Coming in just east of the village of Alma City, it caught the creamery building and twisted it into pieces Mr Bickford's nearly new, large house was moved from its foundation, the roof injured, and porch and kitchen torn away. Mrs. Bickford had over a hundred chickens before the storm, the next day she had but one and that had been blown into the house The storm passed thence east, doing much damage near Peddler's Grove.

The Alma City correspondent described the storm as follows

It started northwest of Alma City, visiting Mrs Gleason's place and tearing down the ice house. A new barn, built last summer, was carried out into the road and left in splinters From there the tornado went to John Markham's and moved his new barn the carpenters had just commenced, off its foundation. From there it went to the creamery and left the building nothing but a wreck, carrying some parts of it a long distance From there it went to Brother Bickford's and just riddled things Some hogs and chickens were killed and one horse considerably injured, but he will live. Fences were torn down, trees broken off and torn out by the roots Mr Bickford was knocked down and hurt, but is now at work. The family saved their lives by being in the cellar It unroofed Mr Le Selle's granary and tore his fences down It was a terrific storm and the wonder is that no one was killed or seriously injured in the vicinity.

The Otisco correspondent related that the storm twister of the 10th struck Otisco, Thursday afternoon, at the Le Sueur river bridge, near Ed. Weed's place, moving directly east No buildings happened to be in its path until Mr John Carlson's place was reached There the machine shed, and new barn were blown down and dashed into splinters, not enough whole lumber being left to make a chicken coop Mr. Carlson and two sons were in the barn at the time, and were blown away with the building All were more or less hurt, but strange to say, none seriously Most of his machinery and his wagon and buggy were also destroyed

Other reports showed that while the rain was general throughout the county, the high winds prevailed only in the central portions The large barn of Mr. Wm Meyers, on section 31, St Mary, was lifted from its foundation and broken all in pieces For a wonder the ten horses in the basement of the barn were uninjured His wind mill was shattered, and the porch to his house was torn off The roof of one of the barns on the Lamb farm, in Alton, was torn off Gus E Vogel, on section 3, Freedom, had his buildings torn down, and his face considerably cut. His family went into the cellar and escaped injury. It is reported that the wind mills of Nic Fox, James Kaiser, and Julius Meyers, in Meyers' neighborhood, were badly shattered The cyclonic portion of the storm, in this county, was confined to narrow limits; but near Lyle, Mower county, many buildings were torn down, several persons killed, and a number wounded

THE JULY STORM.

On July 6, 1897, many counties were visited by destructive hail and wind storms A large territory at Sleepy Eye was devastated by hail Delhi, Redwood county, Fulda, Murray county, Glenwood, Pope county, Marshall and Minneota, Lyon county; St Cloud, Stearns county, Northfield, Rice county, Adrian, Nobles county, Anoka, Anoka county; and Claremont and West Concord, Dodge county, were all more or less injured by terrible hail storms The most disastrous of the many storms was a tornado at Glenwood, Pope county, in which several people were killed and injured, a score or more seriously The storm tore down buildings of all kinds and killed stock in great numbers.

A local paper contained the following regarding this county

"The storm of last Tuesday did much damage to the M & St L railroad tracks north of here A freight train containing goods for this city was ditched The passenger trains yesterday were compelled to go around by way of Mankato Regular trains resumed to-day"

The Palmer correspondent of the Herald wrote of the storm as follows.

"Tuesday night, this section was visited by the heaviest and most fearful rainstorm the oldest inhabitants ever saw or ever wish to see again. People were awakened from their slumbers by the force of the storm to behold the heavens ablaze with lightning and one vast, white sheet of rain all around The water fell in torrents It was as though the skies had opened and a sea of water was pouring down It was a cloudburst of the fiercest kind There is no way of estimating the amount of rain that fell. A kerosene barrel that stood away from any building, where no water could run into it from the roof, and about one-fourth full of water the day before, was full to overflowing after the storm. Every slough, meadow, and little hollow was full of water the next morning For over a week the farmers had been laboring under difficulties in making clover and timothy hay Tons of the finest hay were caught out in cocks or windrows The hay is practically a total loss A few had succeeded in getting a good lot of hay in stack only to find, after the storm, that the tops had been washed or blown off and the stacks water-soaked to the bottom The loss in hay will be heavy Aside from the loss of cut hay, the soil has been washed off corn fields and higher lands onto the grass lands, completely burying the grass, or making it so dirty it is unfit for hay Many of the sloughs and meadows are still under water from one to three feet, and the grass seems to be rotting There are, as yet, only small areas free of water.

WILLIAM HARDING'S ONE HUNDRED YEARS

Mr Wm Harding, of the town of St Mary, in this county, with the aid of hosts of friends, celebrated the one hundredth anniversary of his birthday, April 1

Mr Harding first saw light in East Orsley, England, one hundred years ago—the year that John Adams was inaugurated president of the United States, and more than two years before George Washington died at Mt. Vernon At the age of about fifteen years Mr. Harding became, for a short time, a British soldier in the war of 1812 between Great Britain and the United States He remained in Canada, at different places for fifteen years, and then settled in Milwaukee, where he remained some five years. He next went to Burlington, Vermont, where he remained until the breaking out of the Mexican war with the United States, which lasted from the latter part of 1845 to the beginning of 1848 He served the United States during the Mexican struggle, and afterwards resided in Chicago, where he remained until about 1858, when he came to Minnesota and settled in Iosco Prior to the War of the Rebellion he lost his wife January 24, 1862, he enlisted in the Fifth Minnesota regiment and served until September 13, 1862, when he was discharged for disability He married Mrs Reibling, Nov 20, 1867, and by this marriage he had three children—Prof Everhard Harding, of the State University William Jr, and Miss Caroline, now Mrs George Phelps It is said that he was the oldest G A R. man in America He enjoyed his usual health until about the first of September, 1897, when he seemed to be overcome by the extreme warm weather, and sank peacefully to his final rest and to an honored grave, Sept 7, 1897

DEATHS NOTED DURING THE YEAR 1897

The first to cross the river of Death this year was Mr J W Hosmer, one of the first permanent settlers in the town of Janesville. He died Feb 24, 1897 He was born in Genesee county N Y, May 19, 1824 He came as far west as Wisconsin when eighteen years of age and remained there until 1856, when he came to Minnesota and lived for a short time in Empire (Iosco), where he opened a store He remained there but a short time, when he disposed of his store and, at what was known as Old Janesville, built a sawmill which was very beneficial to early settlers in the county He also engaged in mercantile enterprises and did a thriving business as Indian trader—there being many of the natives on the Winnebago reservation near by. He also engaged extensively at one time in the production of honey, owning the largest apiary in the West He became known nationally as an expert in the management of bees and the production of honey It is said that in one year his bees produced nine tons of honey He died of paralysis, and at the time of his death was one of the oldest settlers remaining in the township

Mr. William Von Sien was born in Mecklenberg, Schwerin, Germany, Aug. 28, 1832 He came to America about 1861, and worked for some time near Waukesha, Wis Coming to Waseca county in 1867, he settled south of Waseca. By his first wife, who died in 1870, he had one daughter, since married. He married Catharine Theis, in 1872, by whom he had ten children all living He died on Tuesday night, April 6, 1897 of heart disease

Mrs Esther W Mosher Young died of Bright's disease, April 25, 1897, at Minneapolis, Minn, aged sixty-nine years She was born in the state of Ohio, October 13, 1827 Her parents removed from Ohio, to Wisconsin, about the year 1845, and lived in the town of Chester, Dodge county, some six miles south of Waupun. She remained with her parents in Wisconsin until about 1854, when she married Mr. Parthian Young She came with her husband to Minnesota in 1855 or 1856 and with him made a claim on what was long known as the Peter Lindsay farm, on the south line of Woodville township They sold to Mr Lindsay and returned to Wisconsin Some time afterwards, most of her people living here she returned to Minnesota with her two daughters, where she remained until her death Minnie, the older daughter, died when about fifteen years of age, and Nellie, the younger, is now a prominent teacher in the city schools of Minneapolis

Mr John C. Hunter, an early and prominent settler of this county, died at his Duluth home on Thursday evening, May 15, 1897 Mr Hunter was for years a prominent merchant of Wilton, and well and favorably known by all the early settlers of the county He had an attack of grippe in early winter from which he never recovered He was a brother of Mrs W A. Henderson, of this county His wife, two sons, and three daughters survive him It is said that he left large property interests in the northern portion of the state

Mr Royse F Stevens was born in New Portland, Somerset county, Maine, August 29, 1817 His wife's maiden name was Lucinda M Spaulding They came to Minnesota in 1863, and first lived in Vivian on a farm Afterwards the family moved to Wilton, and Mr Stevens engaged in the work of blacksmith Later he bought a farm in Wilton, where he lived with his family until about 1881 He was county commissioner during the years 1868, 1869, and 1870 and again in 1873 He sold his farm in Wilton and removed with his family to the vicinity of Lake Benton, Minn There his wife died Oct. 16, 1881 Thereafter he lived with his children in Dakota and western Minnesota. About 1896 he returned to this county and lived with his son Edwin He was taken ill the 18th of January, 1897, and soon became unconscious He remained in this condition with only lucid intervals until his death which occurred May 27, 1897, in his eightieth year He was a good citizen and a kind neighbor His remains were taken to Lake Benton and buried beside those of his wife

Mr Cornelius McGonagle, of St Mary, passed to his last rest July 19, 1897, after an illness of about two weeks He died about 10 30 o'clock of stricture of the bowels He was born in this county 38 years before, being the son of Mr Michael Mc-

Gonagle, Sr, one of our oldest settlers He was a communicant of the Catholic church, a member of the Ancient Order of Hibernians and of the Foresters of America, and an honorable, upright citizen, held in high esteem He left surviving his wife, an infant daughter, and numerous other relatives to mourn his early departure

Mr Thomas Cawley, of Blooming Grove, who came to this county in 1866, after a long illness, died Sunday night, Aug 15, surrounded by his family His funeral, which was very largely attended, took place at the Catholic church in Waseca and his remains were laid to rest in the Catholic cemetery south of that city

Mr C M Read, the aged father of Conductor Harry A Read, died suddenly Sept 18, 1897 He had been in his usual good health, and was coming in from his carpenter shop, when, as he opened the screen door to his son's residence, he fell dead upon the floor He undoubtedly died of heart disease He was born in New Haven Conn, October 20 1813 At the age of twenty-two years, he came as far west as Cleveland, Ohio, where he resided for many years He was one of the aldermen of that city in 1848 In 1854, he came to Tama county, Iowa, where he lived until he came to Waseca, about 1883

Mr. Matthew Coleman, for many years a resident of this county, died at his home in Waseca, Sept. 26 1897, at an advanced age He first settled on a farm in the south part of the county in 1862, and about 1868 came to Waseca and opened the "Waseca House," where the electric light plant now is He and his son conducted this hotel for several years He was in poor health for more than a year prior to his death

Mr. W H. Ivers, of New Richland, met a sudden death on Wednesday, Nov 3, 1897 He had carried his milk to the New Richland creamery and had nearly reached home when he suddenly fell from his buggy and broke his neck, dying almost instantly It is supposed that he fell in a fit, as he was subject to such spells Mr. Ivers was among the early settlers of the county, and owned a fine farm on section 6 The farm has a flowing well and an artificial lake well stocked with carp

DECORATION DAY

The thirtieth day of May, held sacred to the memory of the

brave men and the devoted women that served this country during the days of the wicked Rebellion of 1861-5, was duly observed in 1897 The day in Waseca was observed more appropriately and with greater propriety than on any previous occasion There was an earnestness and thoughtfulness quite commendable on such an occasion The addresses were good Mayor Moonan voiced the patriotic sentiments of the younger generation, while Rev S G Updyke re-kindled the fires of patriotism that burned in every loyal heart during the "sixties," when the traitor horde, led by that arch conspirator, Jeff Davis, assailed the national life and, with traitor hands, attempted to destroy personal liberty throughout the world. While neither address was partisan, Mr. Updyke's side statement that, although corporations and trusts seemed now to be uppermost, still he believed that the people would yet triumph and hand down to future generations our glorious government unimpaired, was thoughtful, truthful, and appropriate. Such words from a veteran of the War of the Rebellion—a man of education, of extensive historical research, of conscientious convictions, of unselfish love of humanity—give us hope for the future, hope for our country, hope for the great brotherhood of toiling humanity in the days to come when, regardless of wealth, "A man is a man for a' that."

SHORT CROPS

The crop of wheat this year was a partial failure in yield, and was considerably injured by the heavy rains of July The hay crop was also injured by heavy rains The wheat crop of India being also a failure that year caused a rise in the price of wheat so that our farmers received about as much this year from their poor crop as they did the year before from a much better crop

HOG CHOLERA

Hog cholera was brought into this county from Iowa in 1896 by the importation of a few carloads of hogs to be fed and fattened The importation proved to be a calamity Nearly half the hogs in the county died of the disease in 1896-7-8 In fact the disease still lingers in some neighborhoods, and the utmost care is required to prevent its spread The importation of hogs and cattle at any time from the South is a great mistake on the part of Minnesota farmers

CHAPTER LXVII, 1898.

COUNTY PRINTING—ROAD AND BRIDGE APPROPRIATIONS—DEATHS HELENA CLARK, PETER BECK, FRED PROECHEL, MRS MARTIN KAISER, L F. PETERSON, S SWENSON, GOTTLIEB PRECHEL, C. KELEHER, WILLIAM BURKE, O W FRANCIS, S W. FRANKLIN, WARREN GATES, JOHN BAILEY, J F PRESTON, AUGUSTA KRASSIN, FRED REDESKE—WEATHER AND STORMS—NEW CATHOLIC CHURCH—FRED METZLER'S LEGS CUT OFF—ELECTION

The board of county commissioners of Waseca county, Minn., met in regular session, at the office of the county auditor, of said county, on the 4th day of Jan 1898 Members present H F Lewer, Joseph Fromlath, P C Bailey, Herman Ewert, and Raymond Doyle. Commissioner H F Lewer was elected chairman for the ensuing year Only the usual routine of business was transacted, except the following It was ordered that $50 be appropriated to the town of Wilton for graveling the Wilton bridge grade For the first time in the history of the county all the county printing was let to the lowest bidder The Herald was awarded the publishing of the financial statement, the county commissioners' proceedings, the proceedings of the board of equalization, and the official ballot of the next general election The Radical got the tax sale notices, and also all the stationery printing and the court calendars and the Journal was awarded the tax list, the official blanks, and the printing of the official ballots

At this meeting the county commissioners accepted the offer

of McKune Post Grand Army of the Republic to plant its cannon on the courthouse grounds

At the session of March 15, 1898, it was ordered that the appropriation made to the town of Freedom, July session, 1896, be used for grading between sections 28 and 33 and between sections 27 and 34, of said town Also ordered that the appropriation to the town of Freedom, made at the June session of 1897, be used for a stone culvert on county line road on section 7 of said town Appropriations were made to the town of Wilton, $20 60 for repairing the Turnacliff bridge in said town, and to town of Otisco, $50 for grading county line road on section 12 of said town.

At the meeting of May 20, the following appropriations were made·

To the town of Byron, $35 for repairing bridge between sections 13 and 24 $25 for a new bridge between sections 29 and 30, and $40 for new bridge and grading between sections 25 and 26, all in the town of Byron, to the town of Vivian, $40 for grading and repairing bridge between sections 22 and 27, and $40 for grading and repairing bridge between sections 6 and 7 all in the town of Vivian, to the town of St Mary $150 for a stone or steel bridge on section 16 and $46 63 for replanking the Keir bridge, all in the town of St Mary to the town of Alton, $75 for a stone culvert on section 17, and $25 for grading new road on section 27 all in the town of Alton, to the town of Blooming Grove $30 for grading road between sections 10 and 11, $30 for grading county line road on section 25, and $40 for grading road between sections 17 and 18, all in the town of Blooming Grove, to the town of Iosco, $15 for grading road between sections 7 and 18, $40 for grading road between sections 24 and 25, $20 for ditching road between sections 22 and 27 and $15 for grading road on section 13, all in the town of Iosco"

At the session of July 12, 1898, it was ordered that $315 00 be paid to the Gillette Herzog Manufacturing Co on contract for the new St Mary bridge It was also ordered that the expense for placing the cannon on the courthouse grounds to the amount of $185 96 be paid from the county revenue fund.

At the July meeting it was ordered that the new St Mary bridge built by the Gillette, Herzog Manufacturing Co, of Minneapolis, be accepted, and that the balance of the contract price, $1,000 00, be paid

At the meeting of October 20, 1898, it was ordered that the pay roll presented by Commissioner Fromlath in the sum of

$237 00, for grading the approaches to the McDougall, Holz, and Weed bridges, be approved. that the pay roll presented by Commissioner Doyle for grading at the St. Mary bridge, in the sum of $90 80 be approved, and that the pay roll presented by Commissioner Ewert, for grading approaches to the Lamb bridge, in the sum of $23 25, be approved There was allowed to Mr Peter McLin, for material and work on the Shaughnessy bridge, $20 40

On motion, it was ordered that $75 00 be paid to one Mrs Gleason, of Alma City, for a strip of land at the Alma City bridge to be used for road purposes At the same meeting appropriations were made as follows to A Bird for a strip of land for road purposes, near the St Mary bridge, $5 00; to the Gillette, Herzog Manufacturing company, on contract for bridges, $2,000, to Mr Ramble, for two piles for Markham bridge, $6 00, to town of Wilton, as aid in repairing the Carmody bridge, $92.39

At the meeting of the board, Dec 28, 1898 it was ordered that the pay roll for grading at the Alma City bridge in the sum of $179 38 be approved and that said amount be paid from the county road and bridge fund. It was also ordered that $13 35 be appropriated to the town of Janesville for the straightening of a bridge on the county road

CALLED HENCE DURING THE YEAR

Mrs Helena Clark, wife of Wm Clark, residing on section 4, Janesville, a short distance from Elysian, died Jan 10, 1898, after a long and painful illness The funeral was held on Wednesday, Rev Father Sullivan, of Waterville, officiating

From the Herald, Jan 14, 1898 "The funeral of Mr Peter Beck, of Waseca, took place from the Catholic church, last Saturday, and was largely attended by sympathizing friends and neighbors He was born in Prussia, May 26, 1830, and came to Sauk county, Wisconsin, where he married Miss Anna Lehnertz, in 1856 They came to Minnesota in 1867"

Mr Frederick Proechel, of Waseca, died of inflammation of the bladder Monday night, March 21, 1898 He was born near Posen, Prussia, Dec 18, 1826, and came to America about the year 1852-3 He spent some time working in St Louis and then went to Princeton, Wis From there he came to Waseca county in June, 1855, in company with Martin Krassin, and others He then made a claim in St Mary where he resided alone until the breaking out of the Rebellion He enlisted in Co B, Brackett's Battalion, Nov 24 1861, with which he served until Nov 24 1864—just three years He then made a trip to Germany and soon after married He sold his old home, after a time, and bought other lands until he became quite wealthy The liquor habit got the better of him, some years ago and he was finally sent to the Rochester asylum, where he remained until about a year ago, when he was discharged He left surviving a worthy widow and several children He had many good qualities, and will be remembered by many of the old settlers as "Big Fred" to distinguish him from Fred Wobschall and Fred Krassin, who came to Minnesota with him in 1855

Mrs Martin Kaiser, of Freedom (nee Jane Connor, daughter of widow Simon Connor) died April 23 1898 of grippe She had, only a short time before recovered from the effects of having one leg amputated on account of cancer from which she had long suffered She left surviving seven children with her husband to mourn her departure She was a sister of Mr Simon Connor, and was highly respected by her neighbors Her father was one of the pioneers of Wilton

Mr L F Peterson, a sketch of whose life appears elsewhere died April 25, of this year

From the Herald. The announcement of the sudden death of Mr S Swenson, Tuesday morning, May 10 1898, was a great shock to every one in this community He was so well and so favorably known to almost every person in this county that his sudden demise was felt as a personal bereavement

He was born in Fredericksvoern, Norway, Sept 3 1849 where he enjoyed the advantages of the high school of his town At the age of fifteen years, he shipped as a sailor lad and visited nearly all lands He was at one time shipwrecked off the coast of Africa

After following the sea for four years, he came to America, and lived at Rochester, Minn, where he worked at blacksmith work He came to Waseca about 1865, and entered the employ of the C & N W Ry Co, at the roundhouse During all these years of toil, at the blacksmith trade, he spent his spare moments in studying the English language and those branches which qualify a man for business and official duties In 1881, he was appointed deputy auditor of this county and so well did he perform his duties that he was elected county auditor in 1884 This position he held for four successive terms He was one of the most popular officers of the county

In 1893, he became the efficient cashier of the Citizens State Bank of Waseca, the position which he held at the time of his death

In 1882, he was married to Miss Julia Anderson, who survives him He had two adopted children, Clara, now grown to womanhood and a young girl adopted last year.

He was a Master Mason and had also attained the most excellent degree in the Chapter He filled the Master's chair of Tuscan lodge very acceptably for several terms. He was a most courteous and exemplary citizen, an honorable and upright business man, a true husband, kind and affectionate toward his family, charitable to the needy, and a favorite in the social circles, to which he gave considerable time

Gottlieb Prechel, of St Mary about seventy-one years of age, died May 24, about noon, of inflammation of the bladder—having been ill some months Deceased was one among the first settlers of the county, having located in St Mary June, 1855 He was a native of Prussia and came to this country about 1853—first stopping in Wisconsin, where he remained until the spring of 1855 when he came to Waseca county in company with Fred Proechel, Fred Wobschall and others, and settled where he has since resided Deceased was an industrious frugal man and a peaceful citizen He left surviving him two sons and two daughters—Lewis Prechel, of Woodville, Emil H Prechel, of St Mary Mrs Julia Monter, of Deerfield, and Mrs Dora Grunwald, of St Mary

Mr Cornelius Keleher died July 13, 1898, in Minneapolis at the residence of his daughter, Mrs Crow, of heart failure, aged seventy-eight years, four months and fifteen days He was born in the county of Cork, Ireland, and came to America in 1846, landing in Newburyport, Mass He afterwards resided in Wisconsin and then came to St Mary, in this county, in 1856 He was an industrious hard working man one who always paid his honest dues and kept his contracts He was a man of strong will, and had a mind of his own on all subjects He was at one time prominent in St Mary town-site affairs, but for many years he had abandoned all ambitions and quietly spent his days with his children and grandchildren He was the author of a book regarding church affairs, compiled some fifteen years before His remains were brought to Waseca, taken to the St Mary Catholic cemetery, and there deposited beside those of his wife, who died many years before

Mr William Burke, of Alton, died August 13, 1898 of what is

called the "Hotchkiss" disease, which shows itself by inflammatory swellings on different parts of the body. The malady defies the skill of physicians Mr Burke was born in Oneida county, N Y, February 15, 1844 He was the fourth son of Michael and Catherine (Kelly) Burke, both from county Roscommon, Ireland At the age of seventeen, William enlisted in company E, Sixteenth Wisconsin infantry, in 1861 He was discharged in June, 1862, on account of sickness, but re-enlisted in the same regiment again as soon as he recovered, participating in the battles of Shiloh, Atlanta, Jonesboro, Dalton, Resaca, and Corinth He was discharged July 16, 1865 and returned to Wisconsin Shortly after he went South and spent some time there, coming to Minnesota, however, in 1867, and settling in Alton January 28 1867, he was married to Joanna Quirk, born in Middletown, Connecticut, her parents being natives of Cork and West Meath, Ireland Mr Burke was chairman of the board of supervisors of Alton for several years, and in 1875, was elected a member of the county board, a position which he held for six years He was at one time assessor and for many years he was school director He was a man of decided opinions, but nevertheless charitable toward those who differed from him

Hon O W Francis, son of Asa ("Dr") Francis, one of the early settlers of Byron township, died at Fargo N D, of appendicitis Aug 16, 1898 At an early age he studied law with Batchelder and Buckham, of Faribault Soon after reaching his majority, he removed to Fargo, N. D, where he entered upon the practice of his profession, and was very successful He was a member of the Dakota legislature at the time of his death He invested largely in farming lands and other real estate, and is said to have become quite wealthy

Mr S W Franklin, early settler in New Richland, a sketch of whom is given elsewhere in this volume, died of erysipelas after an illness of two days August 21, 1898 He was one of our best citizens

Mr Warren Gates, of Alma City, died suddenly, Sept 5 1898 He was taken with a cough which resulted fatally in a few minutes He was born in Bennington county, Vt January 31, 1828 He was a wagon maker by trade and first opened shop in Erie county, N Y He came as far west as La Crosse, Wis, in 1864

He began his residence in Alma City, in the fall of 1865, being one of the first of her settlers He married Miss Helen M Canfield, of New York State April 25 1852 They were the parents of six children

"Mr John Bailey, of Medford, who died at Rochester, Wednesday morning, December 7, at 5 o'clock, was one of the old and respected settlers of Waseca county He was born at Franklin, New Hampshire and was about sixty-eight years of age at the time of his death. In the spring of 1855 he came West and first located in Waseca county He was one of the proprietors of the townsite of St Mary which made a strong fight for the county seat of Waseca county In September, 1862, he moved to Faribault, and later to the village of East Prairie, remaining at the latter place until 1865, when he moved to Medford In 1876 he was appointed postmaster, which office he held about twelve years

Mr John F Preston, at one time a prominent citizen of Waseca, and a brother of S H. Preston, died suddenly of heart failure, near his home in the suburbs of Knoxville Tenn, Dec 14, 1898 Deceased was born in Pittsfield, Vt about 1850, and came to Waseca county about 1869 Some time afterwards he married Miss Etta Taylor He was engaged in the sale of musical instruments and jewelry in Waseca until about the close of 1889, when he went to live near Knoxville, Tenn His wife and two sons survived him, but the younger son has since died

Died, on Sunday, December 18 1898, Mrs Augusta Rieck Krassin, wife of Gottlieb Krassin, of Waseca Deceased was born in Germany, October 22, 1867, and came to Minnesota about the year 1882. The immediate cause of her death was blood poisoning

Mr Fred Redeske, of Otisco, passed away Dec 28, 1898. He died of stomach trouble, having been sick a long time He was a native of Prussia, sixty-one years of age, and came to Chicago in 1873, thence to this county in 1881 He left surviving him his wife, two sons, and three daughters His funeral was held under the auspices of the "Deutcher Krieger Verein" of which he was an honorable member

WEATHER AND STORMS

The year as a whole was one of few storms and much pleasant weather The winter of 1897-8 was especially free from severe storms The following appeared in a local paper, Feb 18 1898

"This has been a wonderful winter for weather From the middle of December to the 11th of February there was mild and pleasant weather, almost without a ripple of cold Early on the morning of the 11th inst, there was a fall of some three inches of snow, nearly all of which disappeared the next day The first of the week, Monday and Tuesday, there was a fall of more snow, but the temperature was very mild and not to exceed four inches of snow came"

April 29 1898, the same paper sang the following

"O, the mud, the terrible mud, in we go with a sickening thud. The horses shy and pull and plunge, as through our streets they heave and lunge And then the sun comes out a-glint, and makes the mud as hard as flint We all stand by with none to soothe without a move the streets to smooth A little wisdom, now and then exerted by our councilmen, and duly used upon each street, would bring to all a glad heart beat"

The first snow storm in the fall of 1898, was noted as follows. Nov 21

"That was a regular, old fashioned "northwester," last Monday and Monday night Six or eight inches of snow fell, we judge, and was blown into huge drifts as fast as it came. The weather became very cold Tuesday morning and the snow drifted badly during the day The highways are in very bad shape—neither sleighing nor wagoning, with heavy drifts all along, especially where there are groves or fences It is seldom we get so severe a storm thus early in the season This was the beginning of real winter

NEW CATHOLIC CHURCH

This year plans were made for a new church building by the Catholics of Waseca It was planned to be 50x134 feet—the architecture to be Romanesque in treatment to be constructed of pressed brick the tower to be 125 feet in height, the total seating capacity 1,000, and to be one of the finest churches in southern Minnesota

WASECA COUNTY CREAMERIES

Waseca county, at a comparatively early day organized a number of farmers co-operative creameries In 1898 this county contained in proportion to its geographical size and population, more creameries than any other county in the state In 1898 the local papers published the following

"Here is the list of the creameries accredited to this county with location and number of patrons.

Freedom, (Cream P O)	120	Palmer	70
Vivian	126	Hamburg, (Minnesota Lake P O)	60
Alma City	135	St Mary, (Waseca P O)	71
Blooming Grove, (Morristown P O)	42	Smith's Mill	99
New Richland, (private)	75	Byron, (New Richland P O)	46
Otisco	100	Plum Valley, (Vivian P O)	75
Janesville	120	Waseca Co (New Richland P O)	70
New Richland	90	Plainview, (Iosco)	50
Waseca	115	Southeast Otisco	60
Oakwood, (Waseca P O)	50		

Freeborn county, with twenty townships, then had twenty-nine creameries, Faribault county, with twenty townships, had twenty-eight creameries, while Waseca county with only twelve townships, had nineteen "

A TERRIBLE ACCIDENT

From the Waseca Herald, Sept 3, 1898 "About half past five o'clock, last Saturday afternoon, Fred Metzler, of Wilton, was thrown from his wagon, by an engine, on the C & N W Ry, at the Second street crossing, and both his legs were cut off just below the knees. The bones were so badly crushed and mangled that both legs had to be amputated above the knees It was a fearful maiming!

It appears, from what we can learn, that Metzler had just unloaded his grain at the Farmers' grain elevator, and was coming over to the business portion of the town When he reached the crossing, he found a threshing outfit, with a steam engine, just south of the tracks, which made his horses a little shy and attracted his attention as he drove on to the right of way Just as the wagon was on one of the tracks, the engine struck the front of it, throwing him out, with the result stated As the wagon was struck by the engine, the horses broke loose from it and ran astride an electric-light pole, breaking the neck yoke They then ran down Second street as far as the Grant House near which they were captured

Mr Metzler was taken up by James E Shanesy and Emmons H Smith and conveyed to the Waseca House where Drs Cummings, Swartwood, and Blanchard dressed his wounds It is said that he is doing as well as possible under the conditions

This is a terrible affair, and not everybody is guiltless The Herald has many, many times urged upon the proper authorities the grave importance of providing at this, and the M & St L crossing, safeguards against just such terrible and cruel accidents"

THE ELECTION OF 1898

The contest in the Minnesota election this year was only second to that of 1896 in deep and intense interest The leading candidates for governor were W. H Eustis and John Lind Ex-congressman Lind was the candidate of the Silver Republicans, the Democrats and the Populists, while Mr. Eustis was the candidate of the Republican party and the gold combine The result on governor in this county was as follows: John Lind received 1,315 votes and W. H Eustis 1,118, giving Lind a plurality of 197—the normal republican majority being a trifle over 300 Local candidates received the following votes senator, E B Collester, rep, 1,167, P. McGovern, dem, 1,373, representative, John Wilkinson, rep, 1,309, H C Chase dem, 1,169, W C Wobscnall, ind, 63, auditor, A J Lohren, rep, 1,149. P J McLoone, dem, 1,313, treasurer, W H Roesler, rep, 1 288 J. T Dunn, dem, 1 280, sheriff, Geo H Goodspeed, rep, 1,199. Frank Collins, dem, 1,387, register of deeds, A F Kruger, rep, 1,163, J M Wollschlaeger, dem, 1,427, judge of probate, Geo A Wilson, rep, 1,623, W S Miner, dem, 904, county attorney, B F. McGregor, rep, 1,039, John Moonan, dem, 1,532, superintendent of schools, C W. La Du, rep, 1,031, F J Remund, 1,611 county commissioner, 2d district, W L Herbst, rep, 252 M. H Helms dem, 276, county commissioner, 4th district, Herman Ewert, rep, 368, James Vaughn, Jr, dem, 335 O L Smith, for county surveyor, and Dr E J Batchelder, for coroner, were elected without opposition

CHAPTER LXVIII, 1899.

COUNTY GOVERNMENT AND APPROPRIATIONS—MASONIC REMINISCENSES—WEATHER AND STORMS—FIRE IN WASECA—DIED URSALENA REMUND, MICHAEL SPILLANE, MRS MICHAEL McGONAGLE, NELS A NELSON, W C JOHNSTON, ANDREW MATZ, HON L. D SMITH, SAMUEL LAMBERT, G R BUCKMAN ANDREW LANG, JOHN L GRAHAM, E B STEARNS, ADNA CARPENTER, CLARISSA NORTHRUP, GRANDMA BAILEY, H H SUDDUTH, CHARLES HANSON (KILLED), ANNIE REBSTEIN, THOMAS BRADY, JOHN DALTON, ALBERT ELTON (SHOT)—BISHMAN GOLDEN WEDDING.

The county commissioners this year met on Jan 3, Mr Joseph Fromlath being chosen chairman of the board and purchasing agent for the county The county printing of the year was let to the lowest bidder and was divided among the papers of the county as follows. the publication of the delinquent tax list went to the Radical, proceedings of the county board of equalization, to the Janesville Argus, proceedings of the county commissioners, to the Janesville Democrat; the financial statement to the Waseca Herald, the printing and furnishing of stationery and county blanks, to the Waseca Journal

At the meeting of March 21, only routine business was transacted except the small appropriation of $45 07 to satisfy the bridge balance claimed by the Gillette, Herzog Co

At the meeting of May 5, it was ordered that the county build seven new steel bridges, and that the auditor be instructed to advertise for bids for building the same. It was also ordered that the purchasing agent purchase five No 2 Austin & Weston wheel road scrapers for use of the county that $150 be appropriated to the town of Blooming Grove, to be expended as follows $75 for grading roads between sections 10 and 11, $75 for grading road between sections 15 and 21, that an appropriation of $100 be granted to the town of Wilton for grading road between sections 19 and 30, that the town of Freedom be granted $40 for replanking bridge over Cobbee creek in section 34, that the town of Alton be granted $150 to be expended as follows $100 for grading on new road in section 34, and $50 for grading on road in section 37

At the meeting of May 19, the contract for building seven steel bridges was awarded to the Gillette, Herzog Manufacturing Co, of Minneapolis, for the sum of $3,997 The sum of sixty dollars was appropriated to the town of Freedom for steel for repairing bridge between sections 1 and 12 The sum of $200 was appropriated to the town of Janesville to be expended as follows: $50 for grading on county line road on west line of section 19; $25 on bridge at Wm Jamison's in section 15, $65 on bridge on new road in section 22, and $60 on bridge on east and west road in section 12 An appropriation of $170 was made to the town of Woodville to be expended as follows $30 to grade hill on center line of section 21, $50 to grade new road in section 23; $40 to grade road between sections 5 and 6, and $50 to grade road running south from Waseca in sections 29 and 30 An appropriation of $100 was made to the town of Vivian, $50 of which was to be expended for grading road in section 26 and $50 on road leading to New Richland between sections 11 and 14

At the meeting of July 10, appropriations were made as follows

To the town of Janesville, $150 to be expended on north and south quarter-line road on section 22 in said town, and the supervisors of said town were also authorized to expend the $50 appropriated to said town at the May session of the board, to Byron township, $195 to be expended as follows $135 for bridge over Boot creek, between sections 24 and 25—$20 for repairing bridge between sections 27 and 28—$35 for repairing bridge between sections 17 and 20, to the town of New Richland, $200 to be expended as follows $50 for grading on road between sections 23 and 24—$50 for grading road between sections 15 and 21, $50 for grading road between sections 18 and 19, and $50 for grading road between sections 7 and 18, also $200 to St Mary to be expended as follows $150 to build new bridge on road running east and west between sections 21 and 28, $25 for grading road between sections 18 and 19, and $25 for grading on town line road between St Mary and Woodville, on section 1, to Otisco the sum of $150 to be applied as follows $80 to build a new bridge over the Little LeSueur, in section 8, $50 for grading road between sections 17 and 20, and $20 for grading on east and west road across section 22, to Freedom, $40 to build bridge between sections 1 and 12, in said town

At the meeting of August 26, the sum of $90 was appropriated to the township of Iosco for grading and excavating for the Murray bridge.

At the meeting October 17, 1899, the county commissioners under whose supervision various bridges had been built in the county by the Gillette, Herzog Manufacturing Company, having reported the work as about completed in a satisfactory manner, it was ordered that $3,517 00 be appropriated as part payment for the same, to be paid at once, the remaining $500 to be paid when the bridges were completed and approved by the commissioner having each bridge in charge

At the same meeting the following appropriations were made from the road and bridge fund:

To Strunk and Gaehler, for building stone foundations for the "Guse' bridge, as per contract, $67.50; to Ludwig Guse for furnishing fifteen cords of stone for the "Guse" bridge, $90 The pay roll submitted by Commissioners Lewer, Fromlath, and Doyle for superintending the building of steel bridges and labor performed in grading approaches to the same, amounting to $239 50, was approved and allowed.

MASONIC REMINISCENCES.

In February, 1899, the following paper was prepared and read on Washington's birthday anniversary commemoration in Masonic hall, Waseca.

"Among the early organizations of this county that have quietly exercised more or less influence upon society, none exceeds in importance or merit that of the Masonic fraternity The ideal objects and purposes of Masonry are brotherly love, equal rights and privileges, charity and good citizenship, honesty, sobriety, purity, and the protection of the homes of its members Ancient Free Masonry has no sectarian creed save one—a belief in God—the Great Architect of the Universe, the brotherhood of man, and the equal rights of all mankind

"The first permanent settlement of the county commenced in 1855 In 1857, Col John Calvin Ide built a steam sawmill at Wilton, on the west bank of the Le Sueur, just below where the present Wilton bridge spans that stream He finished off the upper part of the mill for use as a lodge room, and on the first day of June, 1857, the first lodge in the county was organized, 'under dispensation,' with Jesse I Stewart, worshipful master, John C Ide, senior warden, H P Norton, junior warden, E A Rice, treasurer, H S Edmondson, secretary, Thos. L Paige, senior deacon, Buel Welch, junior deacon, and John Magill, tyler The other members of the U D lodge, as far as we could learn, were Isaac C. Price, W. S. Baker, J. R. West and H P. West There may have been others, but the lodge records having been destroyed by fire, we are unable to give more definite information. Wilton lodge No 24 received its charter on January 8, 1858, or, at least, it was instituted on that day, with Col John C Ide worshipful master, Thos. L Paige senior warden, Buel Welch junior warden, P C Bailey treasurer, H P West secretary, I C Price senior deacon, J R West junior deacon, D D. Stevens, tyler This was the only Masonic lodge in the county from that time until December 11, 1868, when Tuscan lodge No. 77 was instituted in Waseca The Wilton lodge membership extended throughout the county The lodge remained at Wilton until November 21, 1883, when it was removed to Alma City, where it now has a habitation. It contained many relics of the early days and its records were valuable as a portion of our early history, but they were all destroyed by a fire which occurred May 23, 1896 There is a third lodge at Janesville which commenced work under dispensation August 10, 1875, with Dr R. O Craig worshipful master, E. H Gosper senior warden, F H Miner junior warden, R M. Redfield senior deacon, J. W Tefft junior deacon, S C L Moore senior stewart, C. H Younglove junior stewart, R Heritage tyler The other members were R N Sacket, Kelsey Curtis, Darling Welch, and J O Chandler

"As to Tuscan Lodge No 77, of Waseca, we learn that as early as December 11, 1868, the first formal meeting of Masons was held in the hall, in the upper story of what was known for many years as the 'Radical" building, on the corner of Second street and Lake avenue, occupying the lot where the Koerbitz bakery and restaurant building now stands Those present at that meeting were Maj Wm T Kittredge, Capt E M Broughton, N E Strong, E G Wood, Lewis Brownell, H, P Norton, B S Lewis, Frank Miner, Judge H D Baldwin, and James E Child—ten of us Of these, Major Kittredge, Lewis Brownell, and B S Lewis have been transferred to the realms of space 'from whose bourn no traveler returns' Capt Broughton moved away some years ago N E Strong resides in Pomona, California Judge Baldwin is at Redwood Falls, Frank Miner resides in Janesville Norton, Wood and Child are now the only ones of the original organizers left in the city

"This meeting was held to accept a charter under dispensation from the Grand Master, C W Nash, authorizing Wm T Kittredge, as worshipful master, E M Broughton, as senior warden, and N E Strong, as junior warden, to organize a lodge for 'work and instruction' The master appointed as subordinate officers, H P Norton, secretary, Lewis Brownell, treasurer, B S Lewis, senior deacon; E G Wood, junior deacon, James E. Child, tyler.

"At that meeting, regular communications were appointed for the second and fourth Thursdays of each month, at 6 30 o'clock p m.

"It was also ordered that Bro Strong supply the lodge with a copy of the 'Holy Bible' and necessary stationery—that Bro Lewis see to procuring a suitable altar and other necessary wooden furniture—and that Bro Broughton procure aprons and lodge jewels

"The petitioning members, not mentioned hereinbefore, were James O. Chandler and Jesse W Tefft, then of Janesville, Orin T. Roice, Jonathan Shaw, and Henry Willyard—fifteen in all on the lodge roll.

"The lodge, under dispensation, 'rode the goat' and did active work, and on the 14th of January, 1869, a charter was issued by order of the grand lodge On the 21st of the same month the members elected their first officers, as follows: Wm T Kittredge, worshipful master, E M Broughton, senior warden, N E Strong, junior warden, Lewis Brownell, treasurer, James E Child, secretary The appointed officers were B. S Lewis, senior deacon, Eri G. Wood, junior deacon, Frank Miner, tyler.

Right Worthy Deputy Grand Master, C W Daniels, assisted by Rev Dubois, both of Faribault, came over, instituted the new lodge and installed its officers in a very impressive manner

"Their first public banquet took place on this occasion, the same being served by Mr Vincent, at what was then known as the Vincent hotel situated on the northwest corner of Second and Wood streets

"Wm. Everett, the first man to build a dry goods and general assortment store, in Waseca, was the first candidate for Masonry in the new lodge Following immediately after, came Henry J. Wadsworth, A E Dearborn, Edward Bennett, and W S Libby, none of whom are now with us The expense to each member of maintaining the organization at that time may be judged by the fact that the membership dues were four dollars a year, payable quarterly

"The lodge records show that from the organization of the lodge until the year 1879, it was the custom to have a banquet at the time of the installation of officers, generally the latter part of December, but since then the fraternity have held an annual banquet in honor of the 'Father of our country,' who was a distinguished master mason of his day

"Tuscan lodge No 77 has a valuable piece of furniture, the Master's chair, which is covered with nearly all the emblems of Masonry carved upon it It is a master piece of workmanship, and was conceived and manufactured by Mr George Webb, late of Waseca He informed us that he commenced work upon it in 1868, and completed it in 1881 He was offered $40 for it, but concluded to present it to Tuscan lodge It is charming and unique in its workmanship and is more admired by masons than any other object in the lodge room"

From the "Radical" building the lodge moved first to the Trowbridge block hall over the clothing store of Leuthold Bros —next to what is known as Odd Fellow's hall, and last to the hall in the Hendrickson building, corner of Second and Wood streets The order is in a flourishing condition in Waseca and has a very convenient lodge room, occupied jointly by the Chapter, the O. E S and the Master Masons.

WEATHER AND STORMS

"That was a mighty cold streak of weather that struck Minnesota, Friday night, May 12, 1899 Ice formed a quarter of an inch thick in a tub of water at our house. Saturday was raw and cold, and Sunday morning there was a sprinkle of rain mixed with snow. Monday opened with a cold, northeast thunder storm although there was very little rainfall. While small grain is looking fine, corn is kept back by the cold weather"—Herald of May 19, 1899

Only one severe storm was noted this year. On May 30, this county suffered to some extent, especially the southwestern part Wilton suffered more than any other locality heard from.

Mr. Tim Linnihan's granary and sheds, on his farm, were torn down. Mr Martin Sheran, Sr, sustained considerable damage to his house and machinery At the farm of Andrew Lynch, trees were twisted off and considerable damage done Mrs Frederick's windmill was torn down, and the chimneys on her house demolished Patrick McDonough, Jr, found his barn wrenched from its foundation and damaged to some extent The machine shed, hen house, and buggy of Eugene Bird were shattered, and some of his trees broken down Mr Wm Van Loh also suffered severe losses. The storm was heavy throughout the county, but no other serious damage resulted

The following newspaper note of Dec. 1, 1899, is reproduced:

On the night of the 21st of November, last year, we received an old-fashioned "nor'wester" Over six inches of snow fell, and the next day was very cold with a high wind which drifted the snow very much. The roads were left in bad shape, as there was neither good sleighing nor wagoning Quite a contrast with this year, as we are now enjoying most beautiful weather—more like early October than December The snow of Nov 21, last year, remained during the winter

DESTRUCTIVE FIRE

There was but one very destructive fire during the year At the early morning hour of two o'clock, Feb. 27, 1899, the sharp clang of the fire bell rang out upon the night air, and the hoarse thundertones of the city plant whistle vociferously proclaimed a great fire in what was known as the McCue building, one of the first large buildings constructed in Waseca. It was built about 1868, and was occupied, at the time of the fire, by several persons. The hall in the upper story was rented to McKune post, G A R Nearly all of the post property was consumed except the guns which were not materially injured All the pictures, relics and keep-sakes were destroyed. The ground floor was occupied by Mr Ed. Castor's jewerly store, August Santo's saloon, and Kast Bros' barber shop Adjoining, on the north of the McCue building, was a house occupied by Mr and Mrs P W Hagan, as residence and millinery shop The burned buildings belonged to the W G. Ward estate.

CALLED HOME IN 1899

The death roll was longer than usual this year The first to be called was Mrs Ursalena Remund, wife of Samuel Remund, of Blooming Grove. She was born at Canton Grisons, Switzerland, Feb 22, 1845, and died at the Samaritan Home, Waterville, Minn, January 9, 1899, at 6 30 o'clock a m., after a somewhat prolonged illness. She came to America in 1866, locating at Alma, Wis., where she was united in marriage with Mr Henry Rover They afterwards came to Winona, Minn, where they remained two years, moving thence to Faribault, Minn, where Mr. Rover died. On the 30th day of July, 1874, she was again united in marriage with Samuel Remund and assumed the duties of mother in a family of ten children, the youngest of whom was less than two years of age It is the least that could be said, to say that she performed her every duty and was a most thoughtful, self-sacrificing and loving mother.

Michael Spillane, Sr, aged eighty-nine years and five months, died at his home in Woodville, Jan 13, 1899, of old age and grippe He was born in Waterford, Ireland, in September, 1809 He came to New York in 1847, where he remained until 1851, when he came west and settled in Waupun, Wisconsin There he married Mrs. Stockfleeth, a widow He came to Woodville in 1867, and settled on his farm near the east line of the township

Mrs Michael McGonagle, Sr., who died at six o'clock a m, Jan 19, 1899, was born in county Dinegal, Ireland, in 1829, and came to Boston, Mass, in 1843 In 1851, she married Michael McGonagle They came west to Iowa in 1855, remained there about a year, coming to St Mary in 1856 She was the mother of nine children, eight of whom survive her—four sons and four daughters She was sick only about a week and died of heart disease She was one of the brave, pioneer women of Minnesota and worthy of all honor Her remains rest in the St Mary Catholic cemetery.

Died, Jan 24, 1899, Mr Nels A Nelson, of Blooming Grove. He was the son of Mr Andrew Nelson, one of the honored early settlers of that town Deceased was born in the town where he died, March 22, 1865, and was engaged in farming. He died of typhoid fever

From the Herald Another early settler and a G A R veteran has passed to the "Great Beyond" W C Johnston received a telegram last Friday announcing the death of his father, Charles W. Johnston, in San Francisco, Cal, on that day, Feb 17, 1899, of Bright's disease Mr Johnston was among the first to enlist in Company F, Tenth Regiment Minnesota Volunteers. He was mustered in August 18, 1862, and was honorably discharged May 16, 1865 He was a faithful soldier and was highly esteemed by his officers and comrades

Mr Andrew Matz, Sr, died at the home of his son George, in St. Mary, April 9, at 5 46 o'clock, at the age of seventy-six years He came to this county about 1869 Five sons and one daughter survive him, all of them wealthy farmers.

Died, Hon L D. Smith, of Alton, on Friday, April 14 1899, in his sixty-ninth year, of a complication of diseases His parents were pioneer settlers in Ohio, and he was born in Medina county June 29, 1830 He was married June 14, 1858, to Lucinda R Lamb who survived him He came to Minnesota in an early day and first settled in the neighborhood of Hopkin's station, near Minneapolis. He came to Alton, in the early days of that township, and became conspicuous as farmer and successful apiarist and honey producer. In the fall of 1873 he was elected a member of the house of representatives of this state, a position which he filled with honor, fidelity, and ability He afterwards sold his farm and engaged in the cooper business at Albert Lea He next removed to Tennessee, where he did not remain long, returning to this county some three or four years prior to his death, with his wife and two sons. He was a good citizen, a true man, an unselfish patriot

Died, April 17, 1899, at 11 o'clock p. m, of neuralgia of the heart, George R. Buckman, of Waseca, Minn, aged sixty-six years, three months and twenty-four days An extended sketch of his life and public services may be found elsewhere in this work.

Mr Andrew Lang, of Wilton, died April 27, 1899 He came to this county about 1868, and first settled in the town of Janesville. He afterwards removed to Wilton where he had lived a number of years. He was well and favorably known to a large number of citizens, and a large concourse of people attended his funeral He was buried in the Janesville Catholic cemetery. He left a widow, two sons, and two daughters.

May 13, 1899, death called another old settler to cross the river Styx, and this time it was no less a personage than John L. Graham, of Janesville He was born in Pennslyvania, August 31, 1810, and was nearly eighty-nine years of age He was married to Miss Emma Heemans in 1841, and came West in 1863, first stopping in Houston county In 1865 he and his family settled in Freedom He had three sons, C E, of the "Radical," Arthur, a prominent farmer in Freedom, and Ernest, of Hayward, Wis. He was an outspoken, upright man, and thoroughly honest, even in his prejudices, which were many and strong

Mr. Ebenezer B Stearns, a sketch of whose life appears elsewhere, died May 15, 1899, at the age of eighty-six years, seven months and fourteen days.

Herald, Waseca The death of Adna Carpenter, of Janesville, is announced by the Argus. It appears that he died Tuesday afternoon, at 2 o'clock, June 29, 1899, at the Astoria, in St Paul, of stomach trouble. He was receiving treatment from a specialist there, and died rather unexpectedly Mr Carpenter was one of the pioneer settlers in Alton, adjoining Janesville, and was known as a Janesville man He was well known as an extensive stock buyer at one time, and both made and lost money in the business He left a wife and two daughters to mourn his departure

Mrs Clarissa Northup, widow of Caleb Northup died July 25, 1899, at 8 o'clock a. m, at Balaton, Minn, aged eighty-six years Deceased was born in Rhode Island in 1813, and when she was very young her parents removed to Alleghany county, New York. She married Mr Caleb Northup in 1833, at

Hornersville in that state In 1843, they came west to Dodge county, Wis, some three or four miles east of Horicon This was a timbered country, and it was at their home in that place where the writer first met deceased This was in the month of April, 1845 Mr Northup had chopped and cleared several acres of land, built a log house and a log stable The family was then busily engaged in manufacturing maple sugar and syrup which constituted about the only crop that brought any money to the timber settler As bedtime approached the family gathered about the big fireplace, the father read a portion of the Scriptures and the mother poured out her soul in genuine prayer We have always remembered the kindness and hospitality extended to us by this "mother in Israel." There may be what some people term more genteel religion or worship, but there can be no truer devotion than that which was manifested on that occasion in the log cabin in the then frontier settlement of the great West They remained in Wisconsin until 1856, when they came to Minnesota and settled on section 36 in the town of Wilton Here they endured all the hardships incident to pioneer life until about 1866, when they removed to Warsaw, Rice county. Nine years afterwards Mr Northup died and was buried there After his death Mrs Northup lived with her children, six of whom survived her Her remains were taken to Warsaw, Minn, and laid beside those of her husband

"Grandma" Bailey, almost ninety-six years of age, was one of the really old settlers of the county She was born Oct 13, 1803, and went to her final sleep about midnight, August 25 1899 She was a New Yorker and resided near Utica Her husband died in 1854, and she came West with her daughter, afterwards Mrs West, in 1857, where she joined her son, Hon P C Bailey, at Wilton. Since that time she always made her home with him. Physically she was a very remarkable woman having enjoyed good health nearly all her life. For a number of years prior to her death, except for a few months immediately preceding her death, she made regular calls upon her old acquaintances to whom she would tell over and over some of her life experiences. She was always a welcome caller She was "short" on professions but "long" on good works all her life

The old Wilton settlers, with many others, will cherish her memory

Mr H H Sudduth, partner of Mr S H Preston, of Waseca, in the drug business, died suddenly Oct 7, 1899 He was apparently in his usual health all day, and about 10 o'clock in the evening called at the residence of F A Roth, by appointment, as Mrs. Roth had arranged to go over to stay with the Sudduths that night, Mr Roth being absent. As he entered, Mrs. Roth noticed that he looked very pale and, in surprise, asked if he was sick He faintly replied, "Just tired out," and fell to the floor Mrs Roth called in the immediate neighbors, sent for Mrs Sudduth and Dr Swartwood, and all was done that could be done, but to no avail He breathed his last about 1 o'clock Sunday morning His wife, a son and a daughter survived him

From the Herald: "A dispatch of Nov 1, brought the heart-rending news that a head-end collision between a passenger and a freight train occurred a mile and a half west of Courtland village about 6 o'clock The locomotives of both trains were ditched, a number of cars were derailed, and Charles Hanson, engineer on the passenger train, was fatally injured, dying about four hours after the accident The freight train, going west, was in charge of Conductor Chapman, with Engineer Lindell and Fireman Williams The conductor and engineer both live in this city Williams, we learn, is of Winona, Conductor Moses Gage, of Winona, had charge of the passenger train coming east, with Charles Hanson engineer and Wm Cleary fireman—the two latter being residents of Waseca Mr Hanson was an old resident of this city, one of the oldest railroad employes on the Northwestern system, and was well known throughout the Northwest"

Mrs. Annie Rebstein, of Waseca, died Nov 13, 1899, in her eighty-first year She had been ailing for a year or more with physical disabilities incident to old age She came from near the city of Baden, Germany, about 1858 and settled in Otisco. Some years after this, she married Mr Rebstein After living on the farm for many years they sold it and removed to Waseca Mr Rebstein died a few years prior to this, and since then she had resided alone most of the time Mr Joseph Fromlath, of Otisco, looked after her business affairs

Another old settler suddenly joined the great majority on the Eternity side of the River of Death, Nov 28, 1899 Mr Thos Brady, an early settler in Byron, on that day, about 4 o'clock p m, while walking on the street in New Richland, near Newgaard's corner, suddenly fell, dying almost instantly without a parting word. It seems that he had been a sufferer from heart trouble for several years but on this occasion he had no warning of the sudden change Only a few seconds before he had been talking with friends, and appeared to be in the enjoyment of his usual health. He was about fifty-two years of age and had been a resident of Byron about thirty-two years

Mr John Dalton, a prominent farmer of Iosco died of paralysis Dec 8 1899 He was one of the pall bearers at the funeral of Mr Patrick Moonan, and at that time contracted a cold which, it is claimed resulted in progressive paralysis He was a man highly respected among his neighbors and acquaintances

Near the close of the year a very sad death occurred Mr Albert Elton, about twenty-five years old, son of August Elton, of Woodville, was accidentally shot, Dec 27 1899 by Gustof Ziesman, aged about thirty years, while they were hunting rabbits The accident happened about noon and Albert died about five hours afterwards Drs Cummings and Blanchard were called, but the unfortunate young man was beyond the help of surgical aid It appears from all that can be learned, that Ziesman was trying to put a cartridge into his gun, that Elton was standing some eight or ten feet away, and that, in some way the cartridge exploded driving the charge through Elton's right arm and into his body The shot penetrated his lungs and caused his death in a few hours.

A GOLDEN WEDDING.

The golden wedding of Mr and Mrs Adam Bishman was duly celebrated by a large family reunion, Sept 2 1899 Aside from the children and grandchildren there were present Capt John Brandt (brother of Mrs Bishman) and wife and Capt John Knapp and wife, the latter being a sister of Mrs Bishman These relatives reside near Syracuse N Y The occasion was one of much pleasure to all the participants.

CHAPTER LXIX, 1900.

NEW BRIDGES—COUNTY AFFAIRS—SUNSHINE AND STORM—SEVERE DROUTH—TERRIBLE STORM, NINE PERSONS KILLED—RATTLESNAKE IN WASECA—NEW PRINTING BUILDING—BURNING OF UNITED STATES MAIL—DIED CHARLES GORMAN, ANN J TAYLOR, JOACHIM HECHT, MISS MARGARET McGUIGAN, P. LAVELLE (KILLED), MICHAEL MADIGAN, E P LATHAM, JOHN BYRON, AIKEN MYCUE (SUICIDE), DR H J YOUNG, MYANDA E HILL, MRS JOHN MORGAN MRS CHRISTIAN KOESTER, MRS HARRIET E IDE, THOS BURNS, ALLEN GOODSPEED, STEPHEN McBRIDE, MRS J. K MEYERS MRS. THOMAS MALONEY, CHRISTY HEFFERON, W F CARROLL (KILLED), W KREUZER, MRS B F WEED, WM GIBBS, SON OF B D ARMSTRONG (SHOT), ANDREW LYNCH ANDREW R HENDERSON (KILLED)—ELECTION

The county commissioners met this year Jan 2 Mr Fromlath was again elected chairman and purchasing agent The board designated the Waseca County Herald as the paper in which the delinquent tax list and all other official matters and proceedings of the county should be published during the year, at the rates established by law.

The board met again March 20 1900, but transacted nothing more than the usual routine business

On May 4, 1900, a contract was entered into by and between the Gillette-Herzog Manufacturing Co. of Minneapolis, Minn., and the board of county commissioners for the construction and completion of six steel bridges for the sum of $3 025 00, said bridges to be completed and ready for travel on or before the 1st day of August, 1900

At the meeting or May 24, 1900, it was ordered that $350 00 be appropriated from the county road and bridge fund to each of the 1st, 3d, 4th, and 5th commissioner districts

At the board meeting Aug 22, 1900, the contract for placing a steam heating plant in the county jail building was awarded to The New Prague Manufacturing company, for the sum of $545 00, they being the lowest bidders

SUNSHINE AND STORM.

As a rule, the people of Waseca county enjoyed favorable weather during the season Although it was an unusually dry season, the wheat crop was very fine. The Herald of June 22 said:

> Never before, since white men settled in Waseca county, has there been at this time of year, such a drouth Everything green, except the trees, has been seriously injured in growth The grass crop except on the wet sloughs, is almost a total failure. The upland pastures at this writing, June 18, are as bare as we ever saw them in October We are glad to hear of copious showers all around us, but so far, since the first of April, we have not had in Waseca, all told more than an inch of rainfall Our wisest farmers are putting in corn and millet for feed, and it behooves every man to prepare for the worst If we get rain this week or within a few days there may be some crops to save, but a few more days of hot, dry weather will wither everything Let every one who has tillable land put in root crops, late corn and millet Every one should save everything eatable for man and beast

Fortunately the country was visited by a few light showers, and fairly good crops were produced.

A DESTRUCTIVE STORM

One of those unaccountable atmospheric disturbances that occasionally destroy life and property made its appearance in Iosco, Sept 24, 1900, about 5 p m. It first demonstrated its power at the farm of Wm Mittelstead, where it tore down his new barn It next visited the residence of Mr Wolter, tearing off a portion of the roof It moved toward the northeast, doing more or less damage At Superintendent Remund's farm, in Blooming Grove, the barn was injured and the roof taken from his machine shed A little further northeast, at the Goar farm, a young man was killed and much property destroyed It made straight for the village of Morristown, where it tore down a brick building, occupied as a saloon, and killed eight men. Mr Jackson's barn, at Palmer, was blown down, and there were other losses.

A RATTLESNAKE IN WASECA.

Killed a rattlesnake! That is what Mrs E. A Everett did September 4, 1900, at her residence, at the corner of Lake Avenue and Tenth street, in the yard near the house As she was walking in the yard she heard a peculiar rattle, and discovered the snake not far from her feet She lost no time in getting a stick and killing the serpent. It had five rattles and was well developed.

NEW PRINTING HOUSE

During the summer of 1900, Mr J E Child erected a new brick building especially for the Herald newspaper and job printing business. It is 24x75 feet, built of brick, with stone basement, one story above basement It was occupied Sept 21, 1900.

BURNING OF UNITED STATES MAIL

From the Herald of Nov 9, 1900

"Last Friday evening, November 2, 1900, one of our postoffice clerks, a young man, was seen burning a quantity of papers in the rear of the postoffice, near the alley. Some lads, at play near by, gathered up some of the papers, which were partly burned, and took them to Judge Devine's house. Glancing at them the judge discovered that they were marked 'Sample Copy,' that they were addressed to some of our well-known citizens Each of the papers was a copy of 'The Evening Democrat,' of Winona, October 29, 1900, containing a fac simile of the West Hotel register, of Minneapolis, of Saturday December 26, 1896, whereon was registered the name of J A Tawney, as well as the names of some of the lumbermen then and there present

"This paper, thus destroyed, contained, among other matter, Mr Tawney's statement at Lanesboro, to-wit

"'That I attended a meeting of the lumber barons of Minnesota at the West Hotel immediately after my election in 1896, or that I attended a meeting of lumbermen there or at any other place where the lumber schedule was discussed or prepared, or taken by me to Washington to be incorporated in the Dingley tariff law, is a lie from the beginning to the end'

"It also contained, in addition to the fac simile of the West Hotel register, extracts from the 'Mississippi Valley Lumberman,' showing that his (Tawney's) statement, as quoted at Lanesboro, was wholly false There was much other matter of importance bearing upon the political issues of the day.

"We are informed that three hundred copies of the paper (the Democrat) were mailed to persons here How many were wholly destroyed we do not know

"On Saturday morning, Judge Devine, Tony McDonald, and the writer visited the remains of the bonfire of newspapers, in the rear of the postoffice, and found the remains of several other papers, not wholly consumed Among the charred remains we found packages addressed to the following well known names P F Gallagher (firm of Boucher & Gallagher), Wm Oestrich McMahon, Wm, T R Bowe, J O Neff (of the Round House), T B Ryan, Edward Remund, Louis Rabe, Wm Von (remainder of name gone), James Bowe, Gallo Bros, Anton Oswaldson, John Crawley, and Peter Featherman

"On the next train north, Messrs P F Gallagher, of Waseca, who was one of those who had his mail burned, and J T Jordan, of St Mary, went to St. Paul, for the purpose of making a complaint before a United States commissioner and securing a warrant for the arrest of the accused party

The United States officials refused to act

The St Paul Globe of Sunday morning said

"On reaching here last night, Messrs Gallagher and Jordan, in charge of a big bundle of half charred papers, hunted up United States Commissioner Spencer, and were courteously received by that official, but he informed them that he could do nothing, as District Attorney Evans, who had been informed of the matter, left instructions that no warrant should be issued for the present

"A visit to Chief Postoffice Inspector Kimball, who was found at the Windsor hotel, after a long search, was less fruitful of results, according to Messrs Gallagher and Jordan, that official giving them anything but a civil reception

"They were informed, so they say, by Mr Kimball, that it was too near election for such a proceeding They were told that no warrant could be issued at present, and that unless they saw fit to await the going through of the customary red tape they might as well go home"

Postoffice Inspector Lance, who investigated the matter, said that the information taken by him showed beyond a reasonable doubt that copies of the Evening Democrat were properly mailed at Winona and received at the Waseca postoffice that day, November 2, and burned by one of the clerks the same evening

But for some reason, known only to government officials, the matter was never prosecuted

Politics, Politics, how many crimes thou art guilty of!

MANY OLD SETTLERS PASS AWAY

From the Herald A sad and fatal accident befell Mr Charles Gorman, an old settler of St Mary, last Monday afternoon, Jan 8 We are informed that he was engaged in hauling wood, wagon length, and had just hauled a load into his yard He stepped in between his horses and the front end of his wagon to throw off the wood It appears that one of the horses must have kicked him, as there was a mark just back of his right ear The horses then ran and one wheel of the wagon passed over his chest crushing in the bones, and another wheel evidently passed over his abdomen He was insensible when found, and died about five hours afterwards He leaves a family and numerous relatives to mourn his untimely death He was a brother of Anthony Gorman, Esq, of the same town

Died Jan 19, 1900, at the residence of her son near Saco, Montana, Mrs Ann J Taylor, aged about eighty-one years, of pneumonia Mrs Taylor was born and bred in England, and came to this county with her husband Wm Taylor deceased, many years ago They first lived in New Orleans but owing to slavery in the South, at that time, they were not satisfied there and came North and settled in Blooming Grove on a farm at an early day Mr Taylor died some years before, but Mrs Taylor continued to reside in Waseca until the fall of 1898, when she went to Montana with her son, Mr W H Taylor Her remains were brought to Waseca and buried beside those of her husband in Woodville cemetery

Mr Joachim Hecht was born in Germany, in 1825 and came to America about 1856, settling in Blooming Grove He died after a well-spent life, Feb 22, 1900, being at the time seventy-five years of age He left surviving two sons, John and George, and three daughters, Mrs Adolph Mahler, Mrs Gus Eichorst, and Mrs C J Voge His widow is still living at this writing, 1905

On Feb 23, 1900, occurred the death of Miss Margaret McGuigan, daughter of Mr C McGuigan, of Iosco. The lady had been ill for a long time, but her death was not expected so suddenly Deceased was born in Lafayette county, Wisconsin, in December, 1858 The family came to this county and settled in Iosco in 1867

A fatal railroad accident happened in Waseca, Feb. 24, 1900, causing the death of Mr Patrick Lavelle He was yard master and had just received orders at the freight depot for the next day, when on his way to his home, which was east from the depot, and near the old round house, for some unaccountable reason, he stepped from one track to another immediately in front of a moving train, which ran over him, killing him instantly Mr Lavelle had been in the service of the company here some 20 years His wife had died the previous November, and he left a family of six children

Edward Payson Latham came to Waseca upon the completion of the road to this point, in the fall of 1867, and was station agent for two years On Jan. 1, 1868, he was united in marriage with Miss Mary S Banks, at Norwalk, Conn After a time he resigned his position as railroad agent, and engaged in the drug business. He afterwards was engaged in the hardware business, a meat market, and various other enterprises He had at various times served as city assessor and in several other official positions, being at the time of his death court commissioner of the county, and contractor for carrying the rural mail over what is known as the Wilton and St Mary route Upon his return home the Tuesday evening prior to his death from delivering the mail, he was taken with a chill. Although ill, he went to the postoffice Wednesday and Thursday mornings to sort out the mail for his son, who took his place as carrier On Thursday he grew rapidly worse, and it became evident that pneumonia had set in. Notwithstanding his strong and vigorous frame, he was unable to cope with the disease, and grew steadily worse until death came to his relief the following Wednesday morning. March 28, 1900 He was born Nov 12, 1831, at Thetford, Vermont, and was one of a family of seventeen children He was educated in the public schools of his native state, and came West as far as Winona, in 1866, where he served as paymaster on the W. & St. P. R. R. for some time He was the father of eight children, six of whom survived him For several years prior to his death he held the position of secretary of the Waseca County Horsethief Detective society

Mr. John Byron, an old settler of St Mary, a sketch of whose life is given elsewhere, died April 14, 1900, in the city of Waseca. mourned by all

Mr Aiken Myene, of Vivian, died by his own hand April 17, 1900. It appears that he deliberately shot himself through the head with a revolver, in his cattle barn, at milking time Two of his boys were near by and heard the report of the revolver and soon after found their father dead His wife died September 16, leaving eight children ranging from two to eighteen years of age It is thought that brooding over his situation brought on a fit of insanity Deceased was born November 25, 1848, and came to this county with his father, Aiken Mycue, Sr, in 1864 They first settled in the village of Wilton. About 1866, the family moved to Vivian, where Aiken resided. His father died March 9, 1896

Dr Henry J. Young was the first physician who located in Waseca—he having come here in the fall of 1867 He was born in Vermont, June 9, 1831, and remained in his native town until 1851, when he commenced the study of medicine with Dr E A Knight, of Springfield, Vt After two years' practice in Vermont and New Hampshire, he came as far West as Sheboygan, Wis, where he practiced until 1862, when he was commissioned as assistant surgeon of the First Wisconsin cavalry and went to the front with that regiment At the end of a year, he resigned on account of sickness and returned to Sheboygan In the fall of 1864, he received the appointment of surgeon in the Forty-seventh Wisconsin infantry He served in this capacity until the regiment was mustered out, when he was placed in charge of the general hospital at Tullahoma, Tenn, where he served until the hospital was closed He then returned to Sheboygan, where he remained until the fall of 1867, when he came to Waseca As a physician and medical adviser he had few superiors He was kind and considerate to the poor, always ready and willing to aid the distressed even though there was no hope of reward for his services Near 1898, he removed to Alabama, where he remained about a year, and then went to Lebanon, Oregon, where his life closed April 23, 1900, at 11:30 o clock in the evening

Mrs Myanda E, wife of Mr J B Hill, was born in Ridgebury, Pa, in 1826 She married Mr Hill in August, 1846 They came West as far as Green Lake county, Wisconsin, in 1850 They came to Minnesota in 1857 and lived on the south bank of the Cobb river, in Vivian Mrs Hill had the honor of being the first white woman to settle in that township In common with the pioneers of this county she endured many of the privations and hardships incident to the early settlement of this state, although she never experienced the pinching poverty incident to a large majority of the early settlers When the writer first knew her, she and her husband kept almost an open house to all comers, and were very kind and obliging. About 1889 she had a stroke of paralysis which weakened both body and mind, and from that time to the day of her death she was a confirmed invalid The family removed from Vivian to Minnesota Lake, in 1872, where she continued to reside until her death, April 26, 1900

On May 21, 1900, Mrs John Morgan, of Iosco, passed away, after a very short illness—the cause of her death being neuralgia of the heart Mrs Morgan was a sister of the late Mr Christie McGuigan, of this county, and was born in Ireland, in 1826 She came to America in 1848 first stopping in Philadelphia and afterwards living for some time in St Louis, Mo She afterwards, in 1855, married Mr John Morgan, and, with him, became one of the early settlers of Iosco, where they have since resided She left surviving two sons and three daughters namely: James B and J. C Morgan, Mrs John Bruce, Mrs John Devine and Mrs Lige Wesley

Mrs Harriet E Ide died at the home of her daughter, Mrs N E Strong, in Pomona, Cal, June 19, 1900, aged eighty-nine years and ten months She had lived in Pomona fourteen years Col John C Ide and his wife, Harriet E, were characters in the early history of Minnesota and especially of Waseca county Col. Ide and family came to Minnesota in 1855 first living at what is known as East Prairie, in Rice county He served as a member of the territorial legislature in 1856 In the fall of this year he and his family came to Wilton He built the first saw mill in the county and did much in the way of upbuilding and improving Wilton, then a new village and the county seat In the fall of 1857, he was a candidate for lieutenant governor on the Republican ticket with Gov Ramsey—both being defeated. Col Ide afterwards met with financial reverses He was appointed county auditor in 1863, holding the position until his death by heart disease in the fall of 1866 During all the vicissitudes of prosperity and adversity Mrs Ide remained devoted to her husband and family. She was a kind neighbor and full of charity She was the last of a trio of "grandmas" who were the most aged of the old settlers of this part of the county—Grandma Bailey, Grandma Child, and Grandma Ide They all lived beyond the three-score-years-and-ten limit, and enjoyed the highest esteem of hosts of friends If the spirits of mortals recognize each other on the other side of the Styx no doubt there was a happy reunion of congenial souls as that of Mrs Ide took its flight to the land of shadows on the 19th of June, 1900

On the 23d of June. 1900, Mr Thos Burns, of Wilton, started up the stairway to Dr Chamberlain's office, in Waseca, and when about half way up fell on the landing, gave a groan and breathed his last within a few moments He was a long-time resident of Wilton and was a brother of B Burns, now living, and Peter Burns, deceased

Allen Goodspeed, a brother of Geo H Goodspeed, of this county died at his residence in California, July 8, 1900, after a prolonged illness He was born January 21, 1860, came to Minnesota with his parents at an early day in the history of Waseca, and moved to California some twelve years prior to his death

Stephen McBride of Iosco, died at his home, July 13, 1900, from injuries received in a runaway some few weeks before The injuries resulted in dropsy and expert medical attendance failed to bring any relief

The Ventura, California, Free Press of August 3 1900, states that Mrs J K. Myers died at the age of seventy-five years nine months and eleven days She was born in Vermont, October 15, 1824 Her father, Nathaniel Wood, moved thence to Malone, New York, where he remained until 1844, when he and his family came West to Iowa There she met Mr Jacob K Myers, of Virginia, and they were married in 1845 In 1856, Mr Myers and family came to Waseca county and pre-empted the quarter section of land constituting the original plat of what is now the city of Waseca Here they remained, successfully carrying on a farm, until 1867, when they sold the farm to Mr. I C Trowbridge. They went from here to Monona county Iowa, where they resided until about 1874, when they removed to California Her husband, one son, and two daughters survived her.

Mrs Thos Maloney of Iosco, after an illness of only one week, died August 9, 1900 On Friday previous to her death she complained of weakness and of stomach trouble, but was somewhat better Saturday. On Sunday she thought she was getting better, but on Monday she did not feel so well, and when bedtime came she thought it too warm to sleep in her room on the lower floor and wished to go upstairs, where she thought it might be cooler She started upstairs and when she reached the top step she fell backwards to the floor below, receiving injuries to her spine and about the head from which she did not recover She lingered until 7 o'clock p m, Thursday, when God was pleased to take her to enjoy her reward Mrs Maloney was born in County Mayo, Ireland, fifty-nine years prior to her death She came to the United States with her parents when a small girl They lived near Scranton, Pa, where she married Mr Maloney in 1862 They came to Iosco in 1863, where she had since lived. Surviving her were her husband, four sons, and four daughters The sons are John G, James, Richard, and Frank, and the daughters were Misses Anna and Cecilia, Mrs John Costello, and Mrs P Kane

Christy Hefferon, another of the toiling heroes of earth, was called to his final home at 10 o'clock p m, Thursday night, August 23 1900 He was one of the pioneers of the county, first settling in the old village of St Mary He afterwards resided on a farm until the death of his wife, a few years ago, when he moved to Waseca to live He was a native of Ireland, born November 16, 1823, and came to this country when a young man His remains were conveyed to the St Mary cemetery and interred beside those of his wife He left no children

There was a bad railroad wreck on the 1st of September, 1900, in which W. F Carroll, of Waseca, lost his life. The following particulars were at the time condensed from the Mankato Free Press:

A freight train going east, with a double header to help it up the grade was ready to depart and was backing into the siding to await the arrival of the St Peter and New Ulm passenger at 7 50 o'clock A flagman had been sent up the track to flag the New Ulm train, but he passed up on the outside of the Omaha track Just at that moment an Omaha freight train pulled along, which obscured the flagman from the C & N W passenger, and the latter rushed on to its doom The engine on the passenger was backing in, and was in charge of W F. Carroll, engineer and C O Sisco, fireman They hadn't time to jump from their engine had they attempted to do so after the danger they were in was discovered. The tender of the passenger engine struck the forward freight engine as it was on the open switch just before it had cleared the main track, and there was a fearful crash The wreck was one of the worst that ever took place in or near the city As the cloud of steam which escaped from the two disabled engines and completely enveloped the wreck, cleared away, the awfulness of the crash revealed itself The two engines were piled up together, a mass of twisted and broken iron. The freight engine was completely dismantled, the cab being entirely carried away Had not the engineer and fireman, Chas Densil and William Sherman, jumped, they would doubtless have been instantly killed Engineer Carroll was found on the west side of the wreck on the ground on his hands and knees He was fatally injured, the lower portion of his abdomen being laid completely open, bones badly crushed and his jaw was broken He was conveyed immediately to his home, where he died shortly before 10 o'clock

Mr Wenzel Kreuzer, the well known wagon manufacturer and blacksmith, died at his residence in Waseca, about noon, Oct 7, 1900. He was born March 22, 1851, in Germany, and came to this country in 1868, when only seventeen years of age He first stopped in Milwaukee where he worked at his trade for three years, and then came as far west as Mankato There he lived for four years He married Miss Elizabeth Renther, at Mankato, in 1873 In 1875 he removed with his family to Waseca, where he had afterwards resided When in good health he was a stirring, successful business man, and accumulated quite a property He was a liberal-minded, good citizen, and an honest, upright man He had been in poor health for a long time, and his death finally resulted from consumption He left surviving him a widow and six children.

From the Waseca Herald of Nov. 9, 1900 Another old settler has gone to her long rest, has "joined the silent majority" Her death was sudden and unexpected We learn from her sister, Mrs Maggie Turnacliff, of this city, that, although Mrs Weed had been failing in health for some time, she was as well as usual Thursday evening when she retired for the night About 4 o'clock Friday morning, her husband was awakened by a gurgling noise, and when he spoke to her and raised her head her spirit had departed The fact is recalled that her mother, Mrs. Wm Brisbane, died in almost the same way, a few years ago Helen Brisbane Weed was born in Hawick, Scotland, June 21, 1836. Her father, Hon Wm Brisbane, came to America with his family in 1839, and resided in the town of Andes, Delaware county, N. Y., on what was called the "Holland purchase" In 1849, the family went to live in the town of Alto, Fond du Lac county, Wis. Ten years later, 1859, they moved to Wilton, in this county But prior to this time, while living with her married sister, in Preston, Jackson county, Iowa, Helen married Mr Benjamin F Weed, December 6, 1855 In the summer of 1856, Mr and Mrs Weed settled on section 23, Wilton She left surviving her besides her husband, four sons, one daughter, five brothers, and four sisters She was a most estimable woman, a kind and hospitable neighbor an affectionate and devoted mother, a good wife, and a true friend None knew her without feelings of respect and admiration. She was so good, so kind, so gentle in sickness and distress among her neighbors, that her memory will be held dear while life remains with them

Waterville Advance William Gibbs died at his home in this city on Saturday, November 12, 1900 after a brief illness of five days The deceased was born on the 9th day of March, 1824 at King's Kipton, Huntingdonshire, England He was married to Miss Mary A Howell on December 25, 1848 They came to America in May, 1854 remaining in New York until November of the same year They went from there to Wisconsin, and thence to Hastings On May 31, 1856, they settled in Blooming Grove, where they resided until November 11, 1892, when they removed to Waterville

Mr Andrew Lynch one of the very early settlers in the town of St Mary died Dec 10 1900 at 4 o clock, at an advanced age He settled on the farm where he died, in the summer of 1856, and lived there continuously until his death He left surviving him three sons and five daughters

An account of the sad death of Andrew R Henderson, Dec. 19, 1900, was given in the Madelia Times as follows

"On his return from dinner, Mr Henderson dropped into the mill office and chatted a few moments, and then went over to the engine room to resume his duties about the mill He had noticed that the fan shaft of the condenser was loose and called the attention of the engineer to the fact, saying he thought a collar in the water tower must be loose Mr. King turned the water off the tower and asked if he hadn't better throw off the belt Mr. Henderson said he didn t need to, so they both went into the fan room of the condenser, a small space about five feet high They found the collar all right and oiled the bearings. On leaving the chamber Mr King preceded He had just stepped out of the door when he heard a terrible pounding behind him and, turning saw the body of Mr Henderson whirling about the shaft the pounding sound being produced by his limbs striking the roof King ran into the engine room and shut down the engine, but it was too late The shaft on which the poor fellow was caught revolved at the rate of four hundred and fifty revolutions a minute and by the time it had ceased to revolve, life was beaten out, and only a mangled, mutilated mass remained The shaft was far enough from the floor and ceiling so his head didn't strike. His death was in all probability instantaneous and painless When the machinery was stopped it was found that nearly all his clothing had been torn from his body At the time of the terrible accident, his father, W. A Henderson, was at the ranch near Dickinson, N D, taking care of another son, James, who was ill. Mrs Henderson, his mother, was quite ill at her home in St Mary, and Mrs Andrew R Henderson, wife of the deceased, was with her married sister who was sick and resided near Echo in this state"

Deceased was born in the town of St Mary about 1869, his father being Wm A Henderson well known in this county and state as an extensive and successful farmer Andrew attended business college for some time, and in April, 1895, he associated himself with C S Christensen, forming the firm of Christensen & Henderson, proprietors of the Madelia Roller Mills He represented the milling company as a traveling salesman for four years He was most happily married to Miss Nancy H Phelps, of St Mary, on the 30th day of August, 1899.

THE ELECTION OF 1900

The election this year was an exciting one—the struggle being substantially the same as it was in 1896 The local result was as follows. Wm. McKinley's majority was 589 John Lind, for governor, dem, and populist, received a majority of 33 For representative G E Brubaker, rep, received 1,675 votes, and Raymond Doyle, dem, 1,439, county auditor, C H. Bailer, rep., 1 650, and P J McLoone, dem., 1,516, treasurer, Otto C Johnson, rep, 1,543, and Jos T Dunn, dem, 1,610, sheriff, Milo A. Hodgkins, rep, 1,362, Frank Collins, dem, 1,809, register of deeds, Walter Child, rep, 1 417, and John M Wollschlaeger, dem., 1,760 judge of probate, G. A. Wilson, rep, 1,905, and Chris. Strunk, dem, 1,203, county attorney, F L Farley, rep, 1,241, and John Moonan, dem., 1,934, clerk of court, Henry Reynolds, rep, 1,577, and W H Stearns, dem, 1,546, school superintendent, L J Larson, rep, 1,656, and F J Remund, dem and populist, 1,643, county commissioner, First district, H J. Hanson, rep 283, and John Y Brisbane, ind, 209, commissioner of Fifth district, Herman Weckwerth, rep, 261, and Joe S Root, dem, 254 N M Nelson, court commissioner, O. L Smith, surveyor, and Dr. H G Blanchard, coroner, were elected without opposition.

CHAPTER LXX, 1901.

COUNTY GOVERNMENT MATTERS—FOURTH OF JULY STORM, NARROW ESCAPE FROM DROWNING—DEATH OF BISHOP WHIPPLE—DIED MRS TERRENCE LILLY, JOHN MORGAN, MARY REMUND, O POWELL, ANDREW NELSON, W. H. HARMON, JOSEPH T DUNN, ELLA J. BALLARD, EDWARD MOYLAN, SR, JOSEPH MANTHEY, MRS PETER BECK, MRS J. M WOLLSCHLAEGER, MRS ERI G WOOD, JESSE R WEED, ED I SCHOLER, MRS O. T. HAGEN, GULLICK KNUTSEN, T. K ALLAND, ROGER GARAGHTY, OF BLOOMING GROVE, FERDINAND HOLZ (HANGED), S W MYRICK, A CALLAHAN, MRS A N ROBERTS

The new board of county commissioners of Waseca county, met in regular session at the auditor's office on the 8th day of January, 1901 Members present, H J Hanson, M H Helms, Fred McKune, Herman Ewert, Herman Weckwerth. The board organized by electing Commissioner Herman Ewert, chairman. The Radical of Waseca, was chosen as the official paper of the county for the year

At the meeting of May 18, it was ordered that the bid of Gillette Herzog Manufacturing Co, of Minneapolis, Minn., for the construction and completion of two steel bridges for the sum of $911 25 be accepted, and also that $100 be appropriated to the town of Woodville to be expended in grading in section 13

NARROW ESCAPE FROM DROWNING JULY FOURTH, 1901

Loren Wood wife, daughter, Luman S Wood and their sister, Florence, narrowly escaped drowning during the terrible thunder storm of the afternoon of July 4 They were rowing for the north shore of Clear Lake, Waseca, when a sudden storm arose as they were off Maplewood Park. They started for the shore, but the storm overtook them, and their boat swamped and capsized. It was fortunate indeed that both Loren and Luman were good swimmers, level headed, and familiar with the lake The women, too, evinced the most wonderful courage and good sense Several persons at the park saw them as they went overboard, and among the number were W L. Grapp, and E. A. McAdams, who immediately manned a boat and started to their assistance Unfortunately one of the oar locks to the boat gave out and the rescuers were forced to make for the shore, landing at the foot of Von Sien's hill They sprang ashore and ran as fast as possible back to the park where they found another boat and immediately started out again This time they reached the shipwrecked persons, who were bravely clinging to the sides of their half-submerged boat. They took Mrs Wood and her daughter safely to land, returned at once and took Miss Florence ashore, Loren and Luman insisting upon remaining for fear of overloading the rescuing boat In the meantime, Prof. George Alden had secured a boat and started to the rescue. Being near sighted, and the rain coming down in sheets, he passed the Wood boat and searched for some time before finding it He finally found the Wood brothers shortly after Miss Florence had been rescued, and took them on board Several times different ones of the Wood party were separated from their boat by the force of the terrible gale and it required the utmost skill and coolness to regain their hold. Many times the waves rolled over and entirely submerged them, requiring all their strength and courage to maintain themselves. Very few persons would have lived through such an experience Messrs McAdams, Grapp, Alden, and Peterson were entitled to all the credit that could be bestowed upon them for their courage in facing such a storm to go to the relief of the shipwrecked. There was general rejoicing as the news spread that all were saved

DEATH OF BISHOP WHIPPLE

Henry Benjamin Whipple, bishop of the Episcopal diocese of Minnesota, died at his home in Faribault at 6 o'clock, on the morning of Sept. 16, 1901 He had been ill only a few days The week before he suffered a severe attack of inflammation of the throat and lungs, but rallied and was considered out of danger Sunday evening there was a serious relapse, followed by death early Monday morning Bishop Whipple was born at Adams, New York, February 15 1822 In his early manhood he engaged in mercantile business In 1847 he relinquished business and became a candidate for orders in the church, and in 1849 was ordained deacon In 1850 he was ordained priest and served as pastor of different churches until June 30 1859, when he was elected bishop of the diocese of Minnesota As bishop he was eminently successful Seabury Divinity school, Shattuck military school, and St Mary's hall, all at Faribault, are among the institutions founded by the dead prelate He was a good man, and his influence, as a rule, was for higher moral living, for nobler aims in life He died full of years and good deeds and will be mourned by the old settlers of this state, regardless of sect or creed He brought honor upon our state and nation, and his name will be revered by coming generations

THOSE WHO CROSSED THE RIVER OF DEATH IN 1901

Jan. 4, 1901, Mrs Terrence Lilly, an old settler of this county, quietly fell asleep at the residence of her son, B J Lilly, of Waseca She was born in Ireland, seventy-seven years before, came to this country in 1847, and lived first in Cincinnati, Ohio, She and her husband afterwards removed to Illinois, where they remained two years They came to Minnesota in 1856 and settled in the town of St Mary, where she experienced the hardships incident to frontier life Her husband, many years her senior, died nine years before, at the age of eighty-two She was a good Christian neighbor, a devoted wife, a kind mother. Funeral services were held at the Catholic church in Waseca and her remains rest in the Janesville Catholic cemetery beside those of her husband

Mr John Morgan, of Iosco, passed to his long rest Jan 25, 1901. He had been ill of heart trouble for some time, but the evening before his death he sat up for a few hours, talked with all in the house and, after going to bed, slept soundly and naturally The first signs of death occurred about 7 o'clock next morning, when he seemed to be in a stupor This lasted about an hour, when he went to sleep as easily as a child, to sleep the long sleep of death. He was born in the county of Derry, Ireland, in November, 1830 At the age of fifteen he went to Scotland and there secured work in an iron mine He was employed there until 1849, when he sailed for the United States, landing at New Orleans after a seven weeks' voyage. He pushed on up the Mississippi river to his destination at Shellsburg, Wisconsin, where he engaged as miner in the lead mines There he saved his scanty earnings until he had enough to send for the rest of his family, a father and five sisters He next found employment as a boatman on the Mississippi river for a number of years He also had the honor of working on the boat that went from St Paul to Traverse on the Minnesota river, and carried the commissioners, including Gov. Ramsey, that made the treaty with the Indians for lands west of the Mississippi river, on July 23, 1851

Mrs Mary Remund, widow of the late John Remund, was one of the oldest settlers of Waseca county She was born in Switzerland and married Mr. Remund in that country In February, 1856, she and her husband moved to section 15, Blooming Grove, where they lived until 1876 Then they went to Vivian, where they remained until 1882, when they sold their farm and removed to Wilmot, S D Mr Remund died at that place in 1894 In February 1900, Mrs. Remund came back from Wilmot, and lived until her death with her daughter, Mrs H W Bluhm. She was taken with that dread disease, pneumonia, and died February 28, 1901. She was the mother of ten children, seven of whom, five sons and two daughters, survive her. The sons and one daughter reside near Wilmot, the other daughter being Mrs H. W Bluhm, of Vivian Mr Bluhm accompanied her remains to Wilmot, where they were deposited beside those of her husband

Obadiah Powell, one of the prominent and highly respected old settlers of the county, was born Feb 1, 1828, at Hartsville Steuben county, New York His forefathers were among the early settlers of America and he was a typical American farmer. He arrived in Woodville in 1856, taking the claim where he resided the remainder of his life, May 6, 1856. On July 5, 1857, he married Miss Mary Jane Gray. He helped to organize one of the first, if not the first, school district in the county, was elected its first clerk, and was either clerk or treasurer of the district for many years He was the first chairman of the board of supervisors of Woodville, and for two years, under the supervisor system, represented his town on the county board. He was a member of the board of supervisors of his town most of the time till 1869, when he was elected county commissioner of the first district—Woodville and Blooming Grove He was re-elected, served two years, and then resigned He was afterwards town supervisor for two years and for many years elected and re-elected town treasurer until failing health admonished him to refuse the office longer. He held various offices in the I O. O F organization, of which he was an honored member. He also served two years as a member of the state board of equalization He was an active and highly respected member of the Waseca County Horsethief Detective association, and was its treasurer for a long time and until February 1900 He was sick of dropsy for many months prior to his death which occurred April 3, 1901, at 3 o clock p. m. He left surviving him a family consisting of his widow, five sons and three daughters

On April 11, 1901, Mr Andrew Nelson, of Blooming Grove, went to his long rest Although he had been ill for months, he was able to be up and about the house an hour before he died Just before he expired he arose from his bed and said to his son Oscar that he was about to die He was assisted to a chair and died within a few moments Deceased was born in Sweden, August 29, 1829, and was in his seventy-second year He was among our first settlers and one of the most honorable of men. A sketch is given of his early life elsewhere in this work

W. H Harmon was one of the early settlers in Vivian He was born in Berkshire county, Massachusetts, Jan 27, 1827 At the age of twenty-two, he married Miss Esther Smith, by whom he had eleven children His wife died in Vivian May 14, 1873 He afterwards married Ellen Mycue, of that town, who died a few years ago in Waseca. Deceased was one of the pioneers of the state, having lived first in Blue Earth county, in 1857 and a year later on section 32, in Vivian, where he resided until he removed to Waseca At one time he was quite wealthy, but in the crash of 1892-3 he lost nearly all his property, and became much depressed. He was a member of Tuscan lodge No 77, A F. and

A M, and was always esteemed an honorable, upright man He died at the home of one of his daughters, Mrs John Elmore, near Alma City, April 19, 1901, in his seventy-fourth year

Mr Joseph T Dunn, county treasurer at the time of his death, was born in Park county, Indiana, November 21, 1855. His parents, William and Mary J (Baird) Dunn, were born in Ireland and were of Scotch origin His parents settled in Otisco in 1856, being among the very early pioneers of the county. His mother died in 1871, and his father in 1884 March 21, 1877, he married Miss Lena Beck, then of Steele county, Minnesota, who survives him He had six children, two sons and four daughters For many years he was engaged in buying and selling cattle and hogs, and was very well known to most of the people of the county as an honorable, upright man He was personally very popular Three times he was a candidate on the Democratic reform ticket for county treasurer and each time received many more than his party vote He was for years a prominent member of the Waseca County Horsethief Detective society, and at the time of his death was its captain of riders He was also an honored member of the I. O of O F lodge in Waseca He died of pneumonia, April 18, 1901, after an illness of about a week, at the age of forty-five years, four months, and twenty-eight days

A J. Jordan, for many years of St Mary, and later of Waseca, died April 4, 1901, at his home He was about sixty-four years of age, and died of a complication of diseases He was born in County Mayo, Ireland, and came to this country when about thirteen years old His parents first lived in Massachusetts, afterwards in the state of New York He afterwards went to Pennsylvania, where he married Mary Loftus, July 7, 1856 They came, very soon after marriage, to this county, settling in St. Mary He was quite a politician, in his way, and served one term as county commissioner

Miss Ella J. Ballard died at St Barnabas hospital, Minneapolis, Wednesday, May 1, 1901, at 5 o'cock p m, after an illness of only four or five days Her death was caused by blood poisoning from an internal pelvic abscess, which must have developed very rapidly, as she was apparently in good health nine days before her death when she spent the day shopping with her twin sister, Nellie She was one of the daughters of the late Daniel Ballard

Mr Edward Moylan, another prominent old settler, passed to the Great Beyond Wednesday morning, May 1st, 1901 Mr. Moylan, of St Mary, was born in Kilkenny, Ireland, in the year 1818 He was a wagon maker by trade and remained in Ireland until he was thirty-three years of age He then came to America, and landed in New York on the last day of July, 1851. He worked his way to Rochester, N Y, where he was employed at wagon making for five years. He married his first wife, Miss Mary Burke, from County Galway, Ireland, in the spring of 1852 In the fall of 1856, he removed with his family to Galena, Ill, and thence to Dubuque, Iowa, where he worked during the winter at his trade In the spring of 1857 he took the first boat up the river to St. Paul, and then back to Hastings, where he landed He hired a team and went as far as Faribault with his wife Then he left her and came on foot to the then new and promising village of St Mary, where he bought a lot, intending to open a wagon shop He was in better shape financially than many others, having saved up some $500 in gold He bought a cow for $50, and hired a man for $13 to move the family and goods from Faribault to St Mary His experience in getting settled was like that of all pioneers in this then new country Soon after St Mary began to decline, he went to farming His first wife died in 1869, August 29 He married his second wife, Miss Hannah Gorman, in 1872 He left a nice farm of one hundred and sixty acres besides personal property He was one of our best citizens, prompt and honorable in all his dealings, a peaceable man a good neighbor, a kind husband and father. He was always a rugged, robust man and was seldom sick until the day of his death The morning before he died he did his chores about the farm He died of pneumonia being ill only one day He left surviving, besides his widow, Mrs Charles McLoone, Mrs Charles McCabe, Richard Moylan, of St Paul, married, and William and Edward, of St Mary, single

Mr Joseph Manthey, of Waseca, after a long and painful illness, died May 10, 1901, in his seventy-seventh year. He was born at Adamsheim, Prussia, March 15, 1825 He came to the United States in 1853 and lived first, in Wisconsin, near Princeton, where he married Miss Minnie Krassin, daughter of Mrs Augusta Krassin, in December, 1855. Mr Manthey was a blacksmith by trade, and in 1856, in company with Gottlieb Krassin, Sr., and Christian Krassin, came to this state and settled in St Mary, on the farm where his son now resides There he built a rude blacksmith shop, the first in St Mary township, and also opened a farm He was the father of nine children, eight of whom, with their mother, survived him. Samuel, the eldest son, was killed on the railroad, at the Otisco gravel pit, some years ago leaving a wife and three children Mr Manthey was one of the most genial of men. He excelled as a conversationalist in his native language, and was always kind and generous to his family and neighbors He had troubles enough of his own, yet he was always cheerful and hopeful

Mrs Peter Beck, of Waseca, died Thursday morning, July 5, 1901, at an early hour, of heart disease. She had been feeble all winter She was born in Germany She came to this country thirty-four years before her death and lived in Steele county She and her husband afterwards settled in Waseca Her husband died some months before she did She left surviving her a son, Mr Henry Beck, of Meriden, and three daughters

Mrs John M Wollschlaeger, of Waseca, after an illness of three weeks, died at 7:45 o'clock, Wednesday evening, July 17, 1901. Louisa Ida (Neidt) Wollschlaeger was born in Waseca January 18, 1876. Her mother died while Louisa was very young, and her father Mr. Christian Neidt, died about 1884 She married Mr John M Wollschlaeger, our popular register of deeds, April 18, 1900. She had an attack of cholera morbus, followed by inflammation of the bowels. Abcesses formed which caused much suffering and, finally, death Her trouble assumed a malignant form at the start, and defied medical skill She left surviving her husband, a brother and a sister

The people of Waseca were painfully shocked upon hearing of the sudden death of Mrs Eri G Wood. which occurred about 1 30 o'clock p m, July 23, 1901, her age being sixty-six years, five months and sixteen days She had been indisposed for a week or more, but had been pronounced by her physician much improved She ate her dinner with a relish and was able to be about the house Her death, therefore, came as a surprise to her family and many friends. She evidently died with little or no pain, passed quietly away like one falling asleep. Mary Lovejoy Stevens was born at Haverhill, Grafton County, N. H., January 28, 18[illegible]. With her parents and a colony of friends, she emigrated overland to Medina, Ohio, about the year 1840, where she grew to womanhood. In September 1851, she came to Clayton County, Iowa, and for a year made her home with her sister, Mrs. Charles Watkins. October [illegible], 18[illegible], she was married to Eri G. Wood. Seven children were born to them, six of whom survive: four sons, Loren, Sumner, Lamam and Robert, and two daughters, Isabel and Florence. Mr. and Mrs. Wood moved to the home where she died in 18[illegible] and were among the very early settlers of the county.

Jesse R. Weed, one of the early settlers of Byron, died August 2, 1901. Elsewhere in this volume is given an account of his early settlement.

Mr. Edward Isaac Schuler, who was born July [illegible], 18[illegible], in Waukesha county, this state, died August 31, 1901, of cancer of the stomach. He was married to Caroline Fell, daughter of John Fell, of this county, March 15, 1888. He left with his wife six children, the eldest being a son twelve years of age. He also left five brothers and five sisters to mourn his early departure. His disease had been of long standing, although he was not made aware of the nature of the trouble till about a year prior to his death. Early in the year he was treated at the Mayo hospital in Rochester. The doctors removed the diseased portion of the stomach, as they thought, and for a time he gained strength and appeared to be improving. But within a few weeks the old feeling returned and further examination by the doctors disclosed the fact that there was no help for him.

The long illness of Mrs. O. T. Hagan, of Blooming Grove, terminated in a peaceful death Sunday evening, August 18, 1901. She was the victim of that dread disease consumption. Mrs. Hagan was the daughter of Mr. and Mrs. Gullick Knutsen and was born in Iosco thirty-three years before her death. She left three small girls with her stricken husband.

Mr. Gullick Knutsen, one of the oldest settlers and best citizens of Waseca county, died on Sunday, the 11th of August, 1901, at his residence in Blooming Grove, of diabetes. He was born at

Roldal, Bergenstift, Norway, May 25, 1840; came to America with his parents in 1851, living in Dane County, Wisconsin. His parents remained there until the spring of 1856 when they came to Minnesota, and in the latter part of June settled in Blooming Grove. At the time of the Indian massacre, in 1862, he enlisted in Company B, First Minnesota Mounted Rangers. His comrades from this county were Hon. S. P. Child, Lieut. T. F. West, John Cunningham, J. H. Elliston, Eglo Oleson, W. M. Fay, L. W. Krassin, John Murphy, and Jordan Smith. He was a brave and faithful soldier and participated in all the hardships of the campaign against the red skins. He served his full term and was mustered out at Fort Snelling. In 1866, he was married, June 25th, to Miss Martha Johnson, of Lodi, Columbia County, Wisconsin, who was born in Haugs, Bergenstift, Norway, August 20, 1844, and came to America with her parents in 1850. Eight children were born to them, seven daughters and one son. After their marriage they settled in Iosco, where they lived until 1878, when they sold and returned to section 18 in Blooming Grove. For many years he held town offices being supervisor, treasurer, and town clerk. He was town clerk at the time of his death. He left surviving him Mrs. Knutsen and seven children. All of the children were present at the funeral except Martha, Mrs. Stolee, who is in Madagascar, her husband being a Lutheran missionary in that far away land.

Mr. T. K. Alland, whose death occurred September 13, 1901, of consumption, was born thirty four years before and brought up on the old Alland homestead in section 30, Blooming Grove. He received a good common school education in the school district in which he resided, and of which he was director at the time of his death. About eleven years ago he was united in marriage with Miss Alice Jameson, who, with five small children, the oldest nine years old, survive him.

Mr. Roger Garaghty, of Blooming Grove, first cousin of Mr. Roger Garaghty, of St. Mary, expired at his home, October 1, 1901, of old age. He was a native of Ireland, came to America when a young man, lived for some time in St. Louis, Mo., and came to this county about 1863, settling in Blooming Grove. He was about ninety years of age and his death was peaceful, like one falling asleep. He was an honorable, fair dealing, quiet citi zen, a good neighbor, and highly respected by all his acquaintances

Mr Ferdinand Holz committed suicide Nov 29, 1901, at his home in Otisco. Mr E H Holz, his son, reported the following facts Deceased had complained of ill health for some time. On the morning of the 29th of November, he complained to his wife that he felt ill and desired to go to Waseca for treatment He was assured that he would be taken to Waseca by his wife and son Paul His son, E H Holz, and Mrs E H Holz were milking the cows at the time After the talk with his wife and son, he went out of the house as usual, there being nothing unusual in his manner or actions Soon after, before 7 o'clock a m he was found dead in the granary, having hanged himself with a strap It is believed that his mind had been affected, more or less, since the death of his brother the preceding February and that his disease became suddenly acute that fatal morning Deceased was born in Germany June 14, 1826 He came to America about 1847 He enlisted in the Union army in 1864, came to this county in 1869, and has since resided here He died at the age of seventy-five years, five months and fifteen days He left surviving a widow and eight children.

Samuel W Myrick died December 24, 1901, after a short illness, at the residence of Mr L A Bullard, in Waseca of pneumonia, at the age of eighty-one years, three months and fourteen days Deceased was born in Vermont, September 10, 1820 He married Miss Fidelia Grover, in the state of New York, in 1843 They came West at an early day and resided near Horicon, Wisconsin. It is said that he came to Minnesota in 1854, stopping for a time in Fillmore county He moved to Minnesota Lake about 1857, being one of the first to settle in that locality He afterwards lived in Morristown where he and his wife owned a millinery store They came to Waseca about 1870, where they opened a millinery store which they conducted for many years His wife died some years before The writer's first acquaintance with him was while Mr Myrick and his wife kept a pioneer hotel at Minnesota Lake, in 1858, where "many a weary traveler found refreshment and sleep "

The New Richland Star, Dec 20, 1901

Anthony Callahan, one of the pioneer residents of Byron, died suddenly at his home in this village Saturday afternoon He had been complaining of not feeling well, having contracted a cold and left church Wednesday before services were over because of his feebleness Thursday he was stricken with paralysis at his home losing entire control of his body and limbs, two days later death came, peacefully and painlessly Mr Callahan was born in Ireland nearly sixty-six years ago and came to this country in 1857 first living in Illinois, then moving to Wisconsin, and after his discharge from the army, thirty-five years ago, settling in this county About two years ago he moved from his farm in Byron, where he had spent the previous twenty-six years, and made his home in this village

Mrs Amos N Roberts died Monday afternoon, Dec 30, 1901, at her home in Waterville, after a lingering illness of Bright's disease She was born June 2, 1832, her maiden name being Mary A Christman In early childhood she moved with her parents to Illinois, where she was married to Amos N Roberts in 1854 They came to Minnesota in 1855, and to Waterville in 1877 Eight children survive her For a number of years Mr and Mrs Roberts kept the Okaman hotel and during the years of the Buckhout milling business many an old settler made his home with them while waiting for his grist Mr and Mrs Roberts were well and favorably known to all the pioneer settlers of the county

CHAPTER LXXI, 1902.

WORK OF THE COUNTY FATHERS—MURDER OF PHILIP BISHMAN—BOY ACCIDENTALLY HANGED—DEATH AND DESTRUCTION CAUSED BY TORNADO JULY 5—ELIZABETH AND ADAM BISHMAN, JR, KILLED—OTHER TORNADOES, JULY 15 AND AUG. 30—SHERIFF COLLINS SHOOTS A DESPERADO—GASOLINE EXPLOSION—DIED. "JOKER" JONES, GOTTLIEB KRASSIN, SAMUEL KNUTSEN, THOS BOWERS, JOHN G. FELL, C. HOOVER, MRS G BUCHLER, MRS. L W CONCANNON, MRS C J BLUHM, F. HOLLANDER, MRS FRANK ERFURTH, BENNY SIMONS, GEO. WOSKIE (KILLED)—THE ELECTION.

The board of county commissioners met in annual session Jan 7, 1802, and organized by re-electing Mr. Herman Ewert chairman The Waseca County Herald was chosen the official paper of the county for the year. The board this year consisted of Herman Ewert, H. J Hanson, M H. Helms, Herman Weckwerth, and Fred McKune.

At the March session of the board only routine business was transacted

CHARIVARI AND DRUNKEN BRAWL, FOUL MURDER OF PHILIP BISHMAN, JUNE 18, 1902

On the 18th of June, 1902, Charles Lipke and Mrs Katie Hanson, of Wilton, were married in the forenoon by Judge Geo. A Wilson, at Waseca It appeared in evidence that Lipke invited Philip Bishman and Michael Mulcahy, of Waseca, to attend his reception that evening. These two men secured a keg of beer and drove over to Wilton At the coroner's inquest, Mulcahy testified substantially as follows:

"I am about thirty-seven years of age Knew Philip Bishman in his life time—have known him from boyhood Left Waseca with him Wednesday evening about 9 o'clock. We got a team and buggy from Gallagher, took a keg of beer from Meyer's saloon and drove to Wilton Bishman drove the team. Stopped nowhere on the road till we reached the Kujath place, in Wilton. We took the beer and went out upon invitation of the man who got married (Lipke). When we got there we put team in barn Bishman took keg of beer in house and we went in. We drank some beer. The groom drank with me and then I drank with the bride. There were several people there They were social and drank beer lively After staying about twenty-five minutes I wanted to go home, but they were playing cards and called Bishman back. I went out into the barn and camped down Don't know just how long I was there, but two or three men came to where I was and one of them said, 'Where are you, you —— —— son of a ——' One of them caught hold of me, and I said, 'What is up?' They said, 'We'll use you as we have your partner' There were three of them. One knocked me down and dragged me to the buggy and I got in Then they went toward the house, then they came back and pounded me with a club Bishman was then in the buggy and said, 'Don't, boys, don't' They knocked me out of the buggy and I took a northeast course to get away from them As I left I heard loud talk One man said, 'You ——·—— son of a ——, are you dead? I will kill you' Fred Kujath is the man that swore he would kill me, and E P Bahr is the man that used the club on me.

Albert Sunnick was sworn and testified in substanee as follows·

"I live in Wilton—have lived there five years. I knew Bishman anyway five years I saw him there at Kujath's place Wednesday night I met Bishman and the other man there I was at the charivari that evening, at Kujath's with my brother Some of the folks there had gone before I left My brother and I left between 12 and 1 o'clock I saw some of the fight I saw E. P Bahr knock Bishman down in the house with his fist, and when Bishman got up Bahr knocked him down again Mrs Kujath said they should stop and put Bishman in the buggy and send him home I was outside, but could see in Fred Kujath and old man Kujath were outside, I think Bahr dragged Bishman out of the house to the buggy They said they wanted to get the other man (Mulcahy) They went to the barn and got him, and about then my brother and I left We heard the racket after we got away a short distance. I did not hear striking before I left, but shortly after I heard striking as with a strap or board I heard Bahr ask where Mulcahy was. I heard nothing from Bishman. After I got away I heard Bahr call 'Philip' three times, but I heard no answer. The moon shone and the night was light This was at Carl Kujath's, and Fred is Carl's son Both the Kujaths and Bahr and the others had been drinking and were jaggy"

Ernest P Bahr, one of the accused, at his own request and after being informed by Mr Moonan of his legal right not to make any statement, was sworn and made substantially the following statement.

"I live in Wilton—am twenty-five years old in July, and a farmer I have rented the Jack Turnacliff farm and my mother keeps house for me I have known Philip Bishman since I was a boy I have also known Mulcahy since I was a boy Wednesday evening I was at a neighbor's and heard of the wedding—saw the Sumnick boys and we went over to Piehl's place—in front of Kujath's There were some fourteen or fifteen of us. Services were being held in a church near by, and we waited with our charivari until meeting was out That was about 10 o'clock I was chosen captain Then we went to Kujath's and charivaried the couple As we were about ready to go, Bishman and Mulcahy drove up with a keg of beer They asked us to come back and have some beer, and so we went into the house and commenced to drink beer We probably drank too much Bishman and Mulcahy wanted to drink with the bride Bishman followed her into the kitchen and when he came back in the room he and Mulcahy talked very vulgarly between themselves They talked so we thought they ought to be whipped Bishman sat by Mrs Kujath I told him he was a son of a —— I hit him several blows with my hands Then Bishman came out of doors Fred Kujath said I did just right Fred's mother said we should not hit him again, but put him in the buggy and send them away Then the two Kujaths and myself went to the barn to get Mulcahy We hit him a few blows and took him to the buggy and put him in When we got to the buggy with Mulcahy Bishman had gone—had got out of the buggy While we were looking for Bishman, Mulcahy jumped out of the buggy and ran away Both the Kujaths followed him, but he got away When they came back, Fred said, 'Let's have another drink,' and we drank more Then we found Bishman near the fence by the house I lifted him partly up and about that time Fred Kujath hit him on the head with a water glass and afterwards with a club as I took him to the buggy

"When we got to the buggy I put my ear down to his mouth and found he was dead I said to Fred, 'He is dead' Fred said, 'If he is dead we shall have to report him to the coroner' First we thought to take him to the house, but Mrs. Kujath said we should not bring him in the house, so we took the body to the barn The old man Kujath said we should make up a story that we found him in the barn dead in the morning The old man also said he ought to be killed, and that he hit him himself

"I then went home and told my mother I had to go to Waseca. I didn't tell her the truth Then I went and got Verbitzky to haul my milk to the creamery, after which I hitched up my team and drove to Kujath's Fred was going to Waseca, and the old man said we must both tell the same story, and he would clean up the blood and obliterate the tracks Fred changed his stockings and we drove to Dr. Blanchard's office in Waseca We told him about the death, but didn't tell it all We hitched the horses and pretty soon Sheriff Collins called to me and I went to Dr. Lynn's office where I saw Mulcahy, who said, 'That is the man who used the club' I don't remember striking anybody with a piece of board—don't think I did I know Fred Kujath hit Bishman with a piece of board and kicked him about the head as he was on the ground by the buggy, before we knew he was dead. When I first found Bishman was dead I called 'Philip' three or four times, but got no answer When we found Bishman by the fence, near the house, he was alive and talked, but when we got him to the buggy he was dead I saw no blood on him at the fence I was not at the buggy when Mulcahy ran away. When I was through with the charivari I started and intended to go home, but Fred Kujath urged me to stay and have some more beer. I am willing to tell all I know about the matter"

These statements at the inquest reveal substantially all the facts It was a drunken brawl, just such as may happen at any time among people indulging in intoxicating liquors At the fall term of court, Bahr and both the Kujaths were convicted of manslaughter —the two Kujaths after trial and E P Bahr upon his own confession and plea of guilty Carl Kujath, the elder, received a sentence of one year and six months in the Stillwater prison, and each of the others ten years So far as Bahr was connected with the murder of Bishman, he no doubt was incited thereto by his drunken condition, and it is clear to the mind of the writer that, had there been no intoxication, there would have been no murder

DEATH AND DESTRUCTION—WINDSTORMS, WIDESPREAD AND DESTRUCTIVE OF LIFE AND PROPERTY, RAGED IN WASECA COUNTY SATURDAY NIGHT, JULY 5, 1902.

From the Herald, July 11:

The whole county of Waseca was storm swept last Saturday evening. The tornado in many places destroyed buildings large and small, making a general wreck of windmills and killed two persons and a large number of horses, cattle, sheep, and poultry It was one of the worst and most extensive storms in the history of this county Its general direction was a little north of southwest to a trifle south of northeast, with cyclonic demonstrations here and there quite erratic Everywhere the wind blew a gale and the rain fell in blinding sheets The first reports that reached us here were the sad and fatal results of the storm at the farm of Mr Adam Bishman, of Otisco Adam Bishman, Jr, his two sisters, Elizabeth and Clara, and a lad from the Owatonna State school, were in the basement of the large barn milking cows at the time of the storm It appears that the two large barn doors on the west side of the barn were open, and when the storm came in all its death dealing fury, it blew out the east side of the barn and moved the structure off its foundation, letting the large quantity of hay in the barn fall down upon the people and animals in the basement As we are informed, there were, besides the four persons named, nine horses, a large number of cows and some smaller animals in the basement of the barn at the time All of these were caught fast beneath the hay, lumber and timbers Miss Elizabeth was evidently killed at once, as she was found beneath a piece of timber with her chest crushed in and her collar bone and two upper ribs broken. Her death must have been almost instantaneous. The rescue required time and the herculean efforts of many neighbors When the storm struck the farm, Mr Adam Bishman, Sr, seventy-eight years of age, and his aged wife were in the house, and at first did not realize the force of the storm Mr Bishman first discovered that three large soft maple trees between the house and barn were broken off near the ground He next looked to the barn and found it demolished A glance revealed to him the horrible fact that his son and two daughters were buried beneath the crushing mass of hay and timber, and that he alone was powerless to rescue them He and his aged and heart-stricken wife were alone in that terrible storm What could they do? In a moment Mr Bishman decided to call in his neighbors, as he alone was powerless The rain was still coming in almost blinding sheets, accompanied by the fury of the wind, as he started for Otisco station, about a mile to the southwest, nearly facing the wind He reached the station after much effort There he called upon Mr R Jacoby, who, with promptness and energy, aroused the neighborhood In the meantime, a telephone message was sent to Dr Swartwood, of Waseca, calling him to the scene of the fatal disaster For four hours men with strong hands but tender hearts toiled in the storm and darkness before they were able to rescue the living and give aid to the wounded They were compelled to remove most of the hay with their hands. They found Miss Clara Bishman and the Owatonna State school boy alive and unharmed Miss Elizabeth, as before stated, was dead Adam Bishman, Jr, was fastened beneath the timbers of the barn, still alive, but so crushed and injured that he died Sunday evening

Eight cows were found with the life crushed out, and two others so badly injured that they soon after died Four out of nine horses in the barn were found dead The house was not injured Three trees close to the house were twisted off near the ground The gasoline engine-house between the house and barn was untouched Just north of the barn, east of the house, and west of a cottonwood grove, was a shed, which was untouched The cottonwood grove just east of the shed, was badly injured Adam Bishman, Jr, died of internal injuries, having been caught between timbers which pressed upon the lower part of his chest and back When taken out by the rescuers, he was able to talk, but circulation could not be restored and death resulted He was born in Otisco, and reared on the farm where his young life was crushed out He was a bright, well-educated young man, being a graduate of one of the departments of the State University He was the pride and reliance of his aged parents, having assumed the heavy burdens of carrying on the large farm Miss Elizabeth had been a home girl all her life, never having enjoyed very good health But she had always been a kind and faithful daughter and a great comfort, especially to her aged mother

Words cannot express the sympathy of the whole community for the aged parents and for all of the bereaved family

OTHER DESTRUCTION

"The whole county bears evidence of the destructive force of the storm We cannot name all the losses, but we give the greater ones as they have been given to us

"St Joseph's church, on South Prairie, was so shaken by the wind that the plastering was badly injured Mr George Matthews, of the same vicinity had a span of horses frightened by the storm into a wire fence, and they were so injured that recovery is hardly expected Tim and James Sullivan, of Janesville, who own one of the largest, if not the largest barn in the county, the same being 40x100 feet, write that the barn was moved on its foundations about six inches at one end and three inches at the other—the foundation walls being badly injured Martin Vaughan, in Alton, found the cupola of his barn blown off and the roof injured Joseph Adams, of Freedom reports a severe loss—barn and other buildings torn down and a span of horses killed Mike McGannon, of Byron, had the chimney on his house blown off and other slight damages done T J Adams' big double corn crib was dashed against his house with such force as to break in his roof Henry Linnihan, of Byron, says his house is badly racked and injured by the storm Daniel Linnihan, Sr, had glass broken in his house and a chimney demolished In the village of Otisco and vicinity the following are reported J L Hanson, store front blown in, Otto Bauman, store front badly damaged, Frank Taylor, blacksmith shop blown down and demolished, Hoover's warehouse moved from its foundation, Everett, Aughenbaugh & Co's warehouse moved from foundation, and R Jacoby and W. H Stearns' corn houses were overturned

The Janesville Argus reports that a barn at the west end of town was lifted off its foundation and literally torn to pieces. One side was carried a block or more and landed in the forks of a big cottonwood tree in front of Mr Wentland's residence. The timbers were scattered over a wide area J D Underwood had the roof of his barn taken off and his buggies tangled up in bad shape The horses were caught and were extricated from the ruins with difficulty The roof was taken up and carried quite a distance The greatest damage was done about four miles northwest of this place at the home of J H Jewison where a large barn, erected three years ago, was leveled to the ground Reports from an eye witness are to the effect that from appearances the barn was moved off its foundation and then collapsed in turning over Three cows were killed outright and two others injured Strange as it may seem, the horses, three in number, were not killed They were pressed into a space about three feet high After considerable labor they were gotten out and at present they appear to be all right Mr Jewison lost his hog house and corn crib, but his residence remained without injury

The Herald also learns that Wilton suffered Herman Weckwerth, of Wilton, county commissioner, was one of the heaviest losers by the storm He had two large barns and some smaller buildings totally wrecked His loss cannot be less than $2,000 Diedrich Freeman of Woodville, had his barn moved off its foundation The barn on the Rieck place, east of the McDougall farm, was turned off its foundation and badly damaged Gustof Krueger, the farm tenant, found one of the horses in the barn with one leg so broken and mangled that the animal had to be killed. Several windmills in Woodville, among them Emil Sahler's were torn down Albert Domy's horse barn was torn away, leaving his horses exposed to the storm, but not injured Alfred Wood, no doubt, was the heaviest loser in Woodville It is reported that the cyclone first turned his barn around and then tore it to pieces, scattering the lumber and timbers in every direction Pierce Hacket, of Blooming Grove, reports damage to his house, barn, and granary Some of his smaller buildings were swept away entirely Charles Brush, of the same town, on the Steele county line, section 25 had his barn torn down and a fine span of horses killed

Ten days later, July 15 the county was again visited The Herald said

Tuesday was a very comfortable, pleasant, refreshing day and very few persons indeed suspected a destructive storm that night Even the weather bureau of Tuesday gave no intimation of the storm that was to sweep from the land of Manitoba across North Dakota and Minnesota like a demon that night The storm or a kindred storm was heard of about 8 o'clock Tuesday evening in North Dakota and soon after Borup, in Clay county Minnesota was reported wiped out The storm reached St Paul about 12 40, and a little after 2 o'clock a m, a storm struck Waseca with great fierceness Coming from the northeast, it swept the whole city Every yard was visited, and every lot owner had his favorite tree broken and crushed by the merciless wind The buildings, fences, and sheds on the fair grounds were badly wrecked "Floral hall" was crushed The judges' stand was unroofed and carned southwest across the racetrack The hay that was being made on the premises was scattered to all the winds of heaven One cupola of the high school building was torn off, and the fine shade trees were badly demoralized on the northeast Large trees in all parts of the city were broken down, and the leaves and branches covered all the land Several farmers from Blooming Grove report general destruction to wind mills and the same reports come from Woodville and Otisco It would be an endless task to report the destruction of fruit and shade trees in this county Most of the fruit is torn from the trees and the crop is almost a total loss P. J Kelly's barn was turned one-quarter around From facing the south, it was turned about so as to face the east The plate glass in the side window of the front of Thomas Barden's brick building, on the corner of Lake avenue and Second street, was broken out by the force of the wind, but no other damage resulted A small patch of slate roofing was taken from the court house tower by the wind A portion of the roof was taken off the C & N W round house, and a large number of trees in the vicinity were broken down Ward's large barn on his farm, west of town, was moved slightly on its foundation

ANOTHER DEATH-DEALING TORNADO, AUGUST 30.

In the terrible tornado of August 30, 1902, four persons lost their lives and thirty-one were more or less seriously injured Among the killed were Delmar Peterson ,aged five years, of Waseca, and among the wounded were Mrs Charles Peterson, Mrs John Keegan, News Agent Frank Madden, and young John Keegan, all of Waseca. The Herald of Sept 5, gave the following account of the terrible affair:

"One of the strangest and most heart-rending accidents in the history of this section of country, resulting in the death of a number of persons and the wounding of many others, occurred last Saturday afternoon, about 6 o'clock, some two miles east of Meriden on the C & N-W. railway The train was due at Waseca at 5 50, but was a little late. It was made up of an engine, a baggage car, and two coaches, and left Owatonna for the west soon after 5 o'clock, with nearly sixty passengers on board The storm, which had been raging for some time, had attracted general attention, but no alarm was felt The train was in charge of Conductor W H Kinzie and Engineer J. K Mitchell of Waseca, and was filled mainly with residents of the little towns and cities through which the road runs

"Suddenly there arose in front of the train, and slightly to one side, a huge black cloud, driven forward at racehorse speed by a wind that seemed to have sprung up in an instant Everyone on the train noted with alarm that this cloud was headed directly toward the cars and the conductor was asked to try to outrun the tornado. Engineer Mitchell had also noted the dangerous looking cloud, and had made up his mind that safety lay in getting ahead of it He threw open the throttle Faster and faster ran the train, and faster and faster sped the sullen cloud that menaced the terror-stricken passengers. In an instant the air grew so dark that to see the length of a car was impossible Calling to the brakeman, the conductor instructed him to light the lamps in the car, in an endeavor to reassure the passengers who were in a panic The brakeman responded Jumping on one of the seats he opened one of the lamps, struck a match and applied it to the wick just as the tornado struck the train, which was running at a high rate of speed over a slight embankment, two miles from Meriden With a crash and a jar the train came almost to a standstill, but only for an instant The weight of the engine proved too much for the cyclone, which leaped over the ponderous machine and attacked the baggage car and the coaches with their human freight

The baggage car was lifted bodily from the track, the coupling wrenched apart, and the car piled in a heap against the fence at the edge of the right of way, nearly twenty feet distant The two passenger coaches followed an instant later. They were picked up, high in the air, and then slammed down on the wreckage of the baggage car, bottom side up with a force that broke all the windows and smashed some of the seats into fragments From the mass of wreckage at the side of the track arose the screams of mangled and bruised men and women, hemmed in by debris of all kinds, and groping in the dark for an exit from the overturned cars By herculean effort the train men released several of the male passengers, armed them with axes, and then the real work of rescue was begun Huge holes were cut in the overturned cars, and through these holes the half-unconscious persons were dragged, many of them fearfully mangled and torn by the cruel splinters that filled the cars Suddenly the work of the rescuers was halted by a cry coming from the debris at one end of the car 'My baby! My baby!' The voice of a woman arose above the groans of the wounded There was a rush for that end of the car, where lay Mrs Charles Peterson, reaching out in the dark for her five-year-old son. She failed to find him and perhaps it was just as well that she did His delicate body had been shockingly mangled by the crashing timbers, and the mother might not have recognized in the torn and bleeding form the child that had, a few moments before, been nestling at her side The little fellow was dead, with the head severed from the body Ten feet away was the body of a woman, cut almost in two by a timber that had struck her as the car turned over Tenderly these two bodies were laid on the grass at the side of the track and covered with a piece of cloth, and then the work of searching the wreckage went on In the second car were found three persons who had been so badly injured that they were at first thought to be dead These persons were Miss Eva Richardson, A. C McConnell and an unidentified woman Miss Richardson died later.

"By this time the number of searchers had been materially increased and a systematic attack was made on the wreckage. Rain was falling and the injured, as well as the uninjured, were drenched to the skin in short order Owing to the fact that an oil tank carried by the train had broken and the oil had been scattered around in the neighborhood of the wreck it was not considered prudent to make a fire As soon as the injured had been drawn from the wreckage, Engineer Mitchell ran to Meriden and telegraphed the news of the disaster to Waseca Two special relief trains were hastily made up, equipped with doctors and supplies and rushed to the scene of the wreck By the time these trains arrived the injured and the dead had been taken to a farm house a mile away, where they could receive better attention than could be given them at the track side Every room of the modest little farm house was filled with the injured persons, and all over the floors, made comfortable with quilts and blankets, were the victims of the wind's fury When the special trains arrived at the place where the train had been wrecked the doctors were taken to the farm house, where they dressed the injuries of the wounded Then conveyances were secured, and all of the persons, including the dead and the fatally injured, were taken to the trains and brought to Waseca The injured persons were taken to the various hotels, where they were placed in the best rooms to be had, and every effort was made to make them comfortable

Persons who had been on the train and had escaped injury were generous in their praise of the various members of the train crew, who had done so much to avert a panic. By their rapid work and their calmness they had quieted the excited men and women who were struggling to free themselves and who in their madness, were trampling on the unfortunates unable to aid themselves

The path of the cyclone was from the southwest to the northeast In the vicinity of the accident, farm buildings and windmills were razed to the ground, trees uprooted, and stacks blown over or carried son, New Ulm, Elizabeth Miller, of St Peter, and Almira Bickford, of for rods across the fields.

The killed were Delmar Peterson, aged five, Waseca; Ethel Richardson, New Ulm, Elizabeth Miller, of St Peter, and Almira Bickford, of Albert Lea The last named lingered until Saturday evening, when death relieved her suffering"

A TERRIBLE EXPLOSION

Local paper There was a frightful explosion Friday evening, Oct 10, about 6 o'clock, at the restaurant and residence of Mr Gus Schildknecht, in this city The noise of the explosion was heard half a mile away The south front window in the lower story of the restaurant was shattered and some of the pieces blown across the street The front windows in the second story were blown out and shattered, and the basement was set on fire. Two young men, Hugh McDougall and Gus Schildknecht, Jr, who were in the basement, were severely burned about the face and hands Miss Schildknecht, who was sitting at the supper table near the trap door leading into the basement, was knocked over by the door as it was thrown open by the force of the explosion The building was lighted by gas generated from gasoline in a tank in the ground outside the building and conveyed into the basement and building through pipes Evidently there was a leakage somewhere in the piping, for when Gus Schildknecht, Jr, accompanied by young Hugh McDougall, lighted a candle at the foot of the stairs, in the basement, the explosion was terrific

Both young men were thrown down, but at once sprang to their feet and rushed up stairs, both being considerably burned McDougall suffered more injury than Schildknecht, his face and hands being severely burned. Schildknecht's left hand is in a sling, and he is not able to do much with his right McDougall is confined to his room"

Both young men soon recovered, but it was a close call for them

THE DEATH ROLL OF 1902

Mr James Jones, better known as "Joker" Jones, passed peacefully away Friday morning, Jan 24 1902 Mr. Jones was born in Kells, county of Meath, Ireland, about 1810 In 1848, he was married to Miss Mary Devlin who preceded him to the grave by ten years They left Ireland in 1849 and landed at New York They first moved to Albany, N Y, where they made their home until 1853, when they came as far west as Chicago There he was employed on the waterworks system for three years In the spring of 1856, in company with Richard Croke, John Otis, and their families, he came to Minnesota, arriving at Okaman about the middle of May Here he purchased eighty acres of land, in section 8, Iosco, on which he lived until the time of his death He was a hard working man and also one of the most genial of men, always ready with a joke to make every one feel happy. Even during the days of corn coffee and "Johnny cake," he made the light of joy to shine in desolate places Shortly after the death of his wife, he fell from a horse and broke one of his legs, which left him a cripple the rest of his life His eyesight commenced to fail him about five years prior to his death and continued to fail until he became totally blind With all these afflictions, however, he was the same jolly old soul to the last His health was poor during the closing year of his life, and he required the constant care of his devoted daughter. Two daughters are all the relatives that survive him—Mrs Charles Monson, of Iosco, and Mrs Anderson, of Colorado.

Gottlieb Krassin, Sr, died at the residence of his daughter, Mrs Theodore Pommerenning, of Otisco, Saturday, March 8, 1902, of bladder difficulty and old age He was born in Prussia, May 18, 1818. He was married in that country and came to America with his family about 1851, and first resided near Princeton, Wisconsin They remained there until 1856, when they came to Waseca county, arriving in the town of St. Mary, August 5 of that year He reared a large family of children, six of whom survive him, namely, Gustof, Gottlieb, and John A Krassin, Mrs Henry Meyers, of Waseca, and Mrs. Chas Rudolph and Mrs. Theodore Pommerenning, of Otisco. One brother and one sister also survived him

Mr. Samuel Knutson, one of the pioneers of the county, died May 11, 1902, at the age of seventy-six years Mr Knutson was born in Norway, and came to this country while yet a youngish man He came to this county in 1857, settling in Woodville. He shortly afterwards removed to Blooming Grove, and settled on the north shore of Knutson Lake, named in his honor. He left a large number of relatives to mourn his departure, but they may well feel consoled in the fact that he lived the life of the righteous to a fair old age

Mr Thomas Bowers, one of the very early settlers of Wilton, whose home was on the southeast shore of Silver Lake, quietly and peacefully passed to the Great Beyond, Thursday, May 22, 1902, surrounded by relatives and friends Mr Bowers was born in Scotland, of Irish parentage, in 1822 He came to America in 1847, and first lived in New York, where some of his relatives still reside He afterwards made his home in Dubuque, Iowa, and from there he came to this county about the year 1856 He located at Silver Lake where he has since resided He leaves surviving him two sons and a daughter—one son, Thomas, Jr, having died about a year before the death of his father

After long, weary months of great physical pain, Mr John George Fell, of Waseca, quietly passed away to that unexplored region "from whose bourne no traveler returns" For months he suffered from cancer of the lip and face which finally killed him Mr Fell was born August 24, 1827, at Fautsbach, Wurtemberg, Germany, and was in his seventy-fifth year at his death. He came to America in 1857, and settled in the town of Iosco, in 1858 In 1860, he married Miss Friedericke Schulz Eight children were born to them, one of whom died young Four sons, three daughters, and his wife survive to mourn his loss At the time of his death he had nineteen grandchildren He encountered all the hardships, toils, and privations of pioneer life without a murmur, and was always ready to assist those deserving aid He accumulated a competency and left his family well provided for.

Mrs G Buchler, wife of ex-Mayor Buchler, of Waseca after an illness of two and a half months, died Sunday June 15, 1902, of a complication of ailments She was born in Hessen, Germany, in 1841, and came to America when twelve years of age She married Mr Buchler, May 10, 1862, in Sheboygan county, Wisconsin The family came to Waseca in October, 1869, and she resided here continuously from that time to the time of her death She leaves surviving with her husband three daughters and two sons

Mrs L W Concannon, of Byron, died suddenly of heart disease about 10 o'clock Tuesday morning, Sept 9, 1902 Her husband came to this country from Ireland in 1851, and settled in Illinois. They were married in 1856, and came to Minnesota in 1877 They moved to section 19 in Byron where they have since lived, having a very pleasant home She was the mother of eight children, and enjoyed the respect of all her neighbors

Mrs C J Bluhm, of Waseca, died suddenly and unexpectedly Sunday night, Sept. 20, 1902 Deceased retired Sunday night apparently in good health. Nothing unusual occurred until about fifteen minutes before 1 o clock when Mr Bluhm awoke to find his wife breathing heavily He spoke to her but received no answer He then shook her gently, thinking she had nightmare, but still received no response He then turned on the light and found that she was dying He called the children, but she recognized no one and expired at once Mrs Anna K Hitmeyer Bluhm was born near Milwaukee, Wis, February 28 1861 She came to Minnesota with her parents in 1875, and married Mr Bluhm November 8, 1878. They at first lived on a farm in Vivian, but afterwards moved to Minnesota Lake where Mr. Bluhm engaged in selling general merchandise for five years The family then moved to Waseca where they have since resided Mrs Bluhm was the mother of thirteen children, ten of whom survived her

Mr Florian Hollander, one of the early settlers in the old village of Wilton, died of old age about 11 o'clock, Tuesday night, Oct 28, 1902 He was a harness maker by trade and carried on that business in Wilton until the people of the village deserted the place, when he engaged in farming He was about eighty years of age at the time of his death One of his granddaughters cared for him during the last years of his life.

Mrs Frank Erfurth passed to rest Oct 25, 1902 She was the second daughter of the late Robert McDougall, one of the 1855 pioneers of this county and was about thirty-four years of age She left surviving to mourn her departure, her husband, a daughter, and two sons She was the first one of a family of nine rugged children to be called hence by the Angel of Death

On the 8th of Nov 1902, Benny Simons, son of Mr and Mrs B Simons, of Waseca, was drowned in Rice Lake Benny, a Courtney boy, and Mrs Miller's boy got into an old boat and pushed out into the lake The boat was leaky and soon commenced to take in water The boys, no doubt, became frightened, for Benny and Courtney both jumped out of the boat Benny went beyond the reach of the boat, while Courtney hung to the side of it and finally crawled back into it Benny came to the surface once or twice, but soon sank in the water and soft mud, drowned Messrs Willcox and Foster who were in a boat on the lake, some distance away, heard the cries of the boys and hastened to their relief They soon rescued the Courtney and the Miller boy, and at once proceeded to search for the body of the drowned lad, which they found after some little delay. His death was a sad blow to his parents

Tuesday afternoon, Dec 16, 1902, shortly after three o'clock, the wires flashed the announcement of the almost instantaneous death at Owatonna, of Engineer George Woskie, of Waseca. The dispatch announced that a freight was standing on the Milwaukee track, near the crossing, as Engineer Woskie pulled in, and just as his engine reached the crossing, the Milwaukee train suddenly backed into his cab, killing him almost instantly His head was cut open and he was otherwise injured His fireman was only slightly hurt Mr Woskie was an old and well-known engineer on the C & N-W road, and a long time resident of Waseca. He left a wife and son, the latter about eleven years of age, to mourn his untimely death. Deceased was forty-four years old on the 26th of June previous to his death In an action against the Milwaukee company, Mrs Woskie recovered $5,000

THE ELECTION OF 1902

Hon Peter McGovern, of Waseca was the Democratic candidate for congress in the First district, this year, and carried this county by a good majority The result on local candidates, including congressman, was as follows for congress, James A Tawney, 1,217, Peter McGovern, 1,460, state senator, E B Collester, rep., 1,658 R O Craig dem, 1,031, representative, A J Lohren, rep, 1,385 D McLoughlin, dem, 1,307 auditor, C H Bailer, rep, 1,559 John E Thamert, dem, 1,144, treasurer, C A Wagner, rep, 1,466, Henry W Bluhm, dem, 1,226, sheriff, Milo A Hodgkins, rep, 1,263, Frank Collins, 1,465, register of deeds, F W Roesler, rep, 1,061, John M Wollschlaeger, dem, 1,664 attorney, F L Farley, rep, 1,265, F B Andrews, dem 1,406 superintendent of schools L J Larson, rep 2,027, George V Cunningham, dem, 1,506, court commissioner, Fourth district, Ernest Miller rep, 306 M W Keeley dem, 383 county commissioner, Second district, James H Murphy, rep, 301, M H Helms dem, 216 Dr H G Blanchard, coroner, Orson L Smith, surveyor, and Geo A Wilson judge of probate, were eleeted without opposition

CHAPTER LXXII, 1903.

COUNTY COMMISSIONERS' WORK—THE FIRST NATIONAL BANK OF WASECA—CHARTER COMMISSION OF WASECA AND NEW CHARTER—PAVING SECOND STREET, WASECA—A MURDEROUS ASSAULT UPON JOHN ROCKNEY—A GOLDEN WEDDING—DIED GUSTAV SCHILDKNECHT, PATRICK DOLAN, MRS JOHN POWERS, ERI G WOOD, SAMUEL REMUND, MILO BALDWIN, MARY J PEASE, MARY HACKETT, G C. RUNNERSTROM, MARY DINNEEN, RICHARD PROEHL (KILLED), EDWARD MOYLAN, JR, JAMES W CLELAND, PATRICK KENEHAN, JAMES DOYLE, PATRICK McDONOUGH, SIMON BROWN, MRS A KAIBEL, GILBERT OLSON KIN

The county commissioners met on Tuesday Jan 6, this year, and organized by electing Herman Weckwerth, chairman The county publishing was awarded to the Journal-Radical of Waseca

The county board, at its meeting held May 8, appropriated $225 to the town of New Richland, to be expended for putting in abutments on bridge between sections 23 and 24 in said town, $100 to the town of Blooming Grove, to be expended for putting in abutments on bridges between sections 1 and 36 and sections 4 and 9 in said town, $25 to William Frank to help in erecting a foot bridge across the LeSueur river in section 35, St Mary

At the board meeting of May 28, it was ordered that the sum of $500 be appropriated for building the Blooming Grove and Waseca road, upon condition that the sum of at least $500 be raised by the property owners along the line of road to be built and an additional $500 be raised for the same purpose from other sources, to be expended during the summer of 1903, it being understood that said road is to be built under the supervision of a competent engineer, to be agreed upon by the parties interested; that $500 be appropriated for some one road leading out of New Richland, to be expended in the year 1904, on like conditions as contained in preceding order, that $500 be appropriated for some one road leading out of Janesville, to be expended in the year 1904, on like conditions as contained in first preceding order

The bid of A Y Bayne & Co, of Minneapolis, for the construction and completion of six steel bridges, according to plans and specifications, for the sum of $2,118 30, was accepted

THE FIRST NATIONAL BANK

The first National Bank of Waseca opened its doors for business Jan. 1, 1903. It was the successor of the old and successful "Citizens' State Bank of Waseca," organized in July 1892, as successor to the bank of C Hardin & Sons, which commenced business about 1872 in Waseca The first stockholders of the First National were E A Everett, L A Sloss, Jos Henderson, John McKinzie Otto Hanson, Hans Lavesson, Chas E Lavesson, F E Booth, A A Crane, C P Sommerstad, J B Sullivan Paul Flemming, J J Sullivan, J E. Madden, John L Hanson, Joseph Fromlath, W A. Henderson, and James E Child The first directors were A L Sloss, Otto Hanson J B Sullivan E A. Everett, J E Madden, James E Child, and Wm A Henderson

The first officers of the new bank were E A Everett, president, James E Child, vice-president, J B Sullivan, cashier, C P Sommerstad and Gene Miller, assistant cashiers The paid up capital stock amounted to $50,000

Its official report for the month of January, 1905, was as follows

Report of the condition of the First National Bank of Waseca, at Waseca, in the State of Minnesota at the close of business, January 11th, 1905

RESOURCES

Loans and discounts	$176,712 23
United States bonds to secure circulation	50,000 00
Premiums on United States bonds	2,976 56
Bonds, securities, etc	265 10
Banking house, furniture and fixtures.	18,636 50
Due from national banks (not reserve agents)	5 549 32
Due from approved reserve agents	1,256 90

FIRST NATIONAL BANK OF WASECA

Checks and other cash items		1,229 31
Notes of other national banks		175 00
Fractional paper currency, nickels and cents		35 12
Lawful money reserve in bank, viz		
Specie	$8,341 50	
Legal tender notes	1,000 00	9,341 50
Redemption fund with U S. Treasurer (5 per cent of circulation)		2,500 00
Total		$268,677 54

LIABILITIES

Capital Stock paid in		$ 50,000 00
Surplus fund		2,000 00
Undivided profits, less expenses and taxes paid		176 67
National bank notes outstanding		49,100 00
Due to state banks and bankers..		325 15
Due to approved reserve agents		7,261 24
Individual deposits subject to check	$ 43 765 64	
Demand certificates of deposit	8,409 64	
Time certificates of deposit	107,639 20	159 814 48
Total		$268,677 54

CHARTER COMMISSION, NEW CHARTER

Early in the season, steps were taken by the citizens of Waseca to have a charter commission appointed whose duty it should be to frame a "Home Rule Charter," as provided by the state constitution and by legislative enactment Petition therefor was duly made, and on the first day of May, 1903, Judge Buckham filed his order appointing James E. Child, E B Collester, D S Cummings, F. B Andrews E A Everett, Anton Guyer, Peter McGovern, Dennis McLoughlin, John Moonan, Fred Mahler, Charles Leuthold, Louis A Larson, Charles A. Smith, F A Swartwood, and R P Ward Judge Collester, at the time being state senator, declined to serve, and Prof L Bliss was appointed in his place and served as one of the commission The commission sat at intervals throughout the summer and fall, and submitted a charter to the voters at the spring election The charter, while it received a majority of all the votes cast, did not receive four-sevenths of the vote and was defeated It was again submitted in amended form on May 10, 1904, and duly adopted The labor of framing the charter and securing its adoption was considerable, and the task was, as is generally the case, a thankless one.

PAVING SECOND STREET

The years 1902-3 were among the wettest in the history of the state, and the highways were so nearly impassable everywhere that "good road" arguments appealed very strongly to all our people. Early in the season of 1903 the people of Waseca agitated the question of paving Second street, and as early as August, the common council had decided to have the work done The contract was entered into Aug 9, 1903, and the work was completed before winter commenced Ever since, that street has been in fine condition

A MURDEROUS ASSAULT.

From the Herald " One of the most bloodthirsty assaults ever committed in this county was made Friday afternoon, Jan 23, 1903, at Pat McCarthy's saloon, in this city, by one Gilbert Storle, of this city, upon Mr John Rockney, of Woodville It appears from the best information obtainable that Storle or Olson (he answers to both names) owns a small farm adjoining Mr Rockney's place One day last fall, Rockney's cattle got into Storle's hay stacks Storle demanded exorbitant damages, according to Rockney, and they were unable to agree as to the amount Rockney should pay About two weeks before the shooting on Friday, Storle commenced to quarrel with Rockney and drew an old revolver, snapping it at him several times He could not make the revolver work, so Rockney escaped and got away from him Last Friday, Mr. Rockney and his daughter Clara, came to Waseca, and very soon after their arrival Storle came to them and commenced to abuse Rockney, the latter all the time trying to avoid him. Rockney went to several places and Storle kept after him Rockney, being a cripple in one foot, became alarmed for his safety, and told his daughter to see Marshal McDonough and ask him to disarm Storle In the meantime Rockney went into the saloon and was followed in by Storle The marshal, upon being informed of the situation, at once started for the saloon, but before he got there and without any talk, Storle drew a self-cocking, 32-calibre revolver and shot Rockney three times in quick succession One bullet struck the left side of his face on the lower jaw, another hit him just back of the lower lobe of his ear on the right side, and the third took effect in the back of his neck—the last shot being fired after Rockney had fallen to the floor Just as the third shot was fired Marshal McDonough arrived and arrested Storle He drew his revolver on the marshal and resisted arrest, but the marshal soon disarmed him and, with the assistance of A W Dibble, took him to the county jail, where he made renewed resistance to being locked in. That Storle was insane or crazy drunk was plain That there was "method in his madness" is believed by many, and that he was an unsafe man to be at large is evident"

Soon after the shooting and before an examination of the offender, information was filed in probate court charging Storle with insanity, and, upon examination, he was committed to the Rochester insane asylum where he is still held

A GOLDEN WEDDING

Golden weddings are not so numerous as to exclude them from the notable events of local history Hence this note. On March 3d, 1853, in St Lawrence county, New York, Miss Cephronia A Fetterly and Mr Angus Wert were united in marriage They came to Waseca in 1868 On March 3, 1903, they commemorated the fiftieth anniversary of their wedding Their family, consisting of six daughters and two sons, were all at their Waseca home to celebrate the happy day In the morning, from 11 o clock until 1 o'clock p m, a breakfast for the children and relatives, and in the afternoon, from 3 20 to 6 o'clock, a reception to one hundred or more friends furnished the entertainment for the day The rooms were decorated with yellow flowers—the gold color scheme being carried out There were yellow roses daffodils, carnations and tulips The occasion was one of much enjoyment The venerable couple are still with us and in the enjoyment of good health.

THOSE WHO DEPARTED IN 1903.

After a long and severe illness of cancer of the bowels and several operations performed at the Mayo Hospital, at Rochester Minn, Mr Gustav Schilknecht passed away Tuesday morning, Jan 20 about 2 o'clock Mr Schildknecht was born in Germany, March 7, 1848 He came to Waseca some twenty-five years before his death, and was married to Miss Grapp, sister of A Grapp, in 1881 They have two children, Gustav and Lena Deceased was a member of the I O O F. lodge of this city, and also of the Rebekahs Both these societies had charge of the funeral services

Mr Patrick Dolan, one of the very early settlers of Iosco, died Sunday morning Feb 1, 1903, of old age He was eighty-six years old At the age of twenty-three he came to the United States, landing at Boston, where he remained for seventeen years, working at the mason trade Here it was that he met and married Miss Ellen Hubert, who preceded him to the grave by about five years Mr. Dolan came to Waterville in the spring of 1857 and took a claim in Iosco, on which he lived until his death. He was a very energetic man and had accumulated quite a fortune He had held in his lifetime many places of trust in his town, and was a model citizen and a kind and loving husband and father He left surviving him five sons and five daughters

Mrs John N Powers, one of the pioneers of Waseca county, died at her home in Waterville, Feb 8, 1903, of Bright's disease Mrs Powers' maiden name was Anna Connor, and she was a sister of the late Matthew F Connor of Wilton With her parents, she was among the pioneer settlers of Wilton—enterprising, industrious, honest, worthy Deceased was born in Ireland came to America with her parents in December, 1846, settled in Illinois where they remained until 1857, and then came to this county and resided in Wilton. She married Hon John N Powers in 1868 Her husband died about two years before her death Eight children survive her She was a noble woman and performed well her part in life.

From the Waseca Herald of Feb 13, 1903

"The Angel of Death summoned from our midst, about 5 o'clock a m of Tuesday, February 10, 1903, one of the noblest and best of our citizens, Mr Eri G Wood None knew him but to honor and respect him Mr Wood was taken ill of pneumonia, week before last, and after a manly struggle of several days gave up his spirit and joined the great majority on the other side He was born March 17, 1832, in Franklin county, state of New York He was the son of Nathaniel Wood, who came West and settled in Iowa as early as 1845 There Eri grew to manhood, and in 1855 married Miss Mary L Stevens, who died in July, 1901 He came to Woodville with his wife in 1856 and made his home where he has continued to reside till the time of his death He was a quiet, unpretentious, unambitious man of much more than ordinary ability, and one of the pioneers for whom the township of Woodville was named The township was organized April 5, 1858, and the first town meeting was held at his house, May 11, 1858 Mr Wood served as one of the first judges of election, and was elected the first assessor of his township The modesty and honesty of the man appeared in his first dealings with the public The town record shows the following bill against the town for services, etc

For assessing town of Woodville	$8 00
Service as judge of two elections	2 00
Use of room three days for elections	3 00

His son, Loren G, was the first white child born in Woodville—the date being August 5, 1856 The first religious services held in the township were held at his residence by Rev Moreland, in 1857 He united with the M E church in early life and was ever a consistent member He was the father of seven children, six of whom survive him. Mr Wood was a prominent Chapter and Master Mason, and also a member of the I. O of O F, of this city In all of these organizations, he held for several terms the highest stations He was also a useful member of the board of education of Waseca for many years His first step in Masonry was taken in Wilton Lodge No 24 January 5, 1865. He was passed to the degree of Fellowcraft, January 15 the same year, and made a Master Mason February 2, 1865. His advance was not only rapid, but thorough He became a member of Tuscan Lodge No. 77 December 11, 1868, and remained a consistent member to the day of his death He first became Worshipful Master of Tuscan Lodge January 23, 1873, a position which he filled till January 13, 1876 In politics, he was originally an abolition, prohibition republican, then he affiliated with the prohibition party from 1872 till 1896, when he supported Mr Bryan. Strictly speaking, he was a conscientious independent in politics"

Mr Samuel Remund, of Blooming Grove, breathed his last, Sunday morning, Feb 8, 1903, at 8 10, aged seventy years and twelve days. He was born at Oberamt Laupen, Canton Berne, Switzerland, Jan 26, 1833 He died of dropsy In 1855, he married Miss Anna Jueni, and the same fall came to America landing in New York at Christmas time They immediately came West by way of Buffalo, Cleveland, and Chicago to Dubuque, Iowa They did not tarry long in Dubuque but left there Jan 15, 1856, for Blooming Grove They were detained at Dunleith by sickness and did not arrive in Blooming Grove until the eleventh of February In company with him came his parents, his brothers John, Rudolph, and Albert, and his sister Lina—his brother Christian, having moved to Blooming Grove June 28 1855, furnished them shelter until they were able to build for themselves Samuel made his claim on section nine His first wife became the mother of ten children, and died Feb 23, 1871 beloved by all who knew her. In the fall of 1871, he married Miss Elizabeth Neuhart, of the same town She gave birth to two children, dying at the birth of the second, the child also dying, Feb 6, 1874 This left Mr Remund with ten children, the oldest still in her teens. He again married in the fall of 1874 Mrs Ersulena Rover, whose maiden name was Schneke, became his third wife, and was a kind, good mother to the motherless children She nobly and faithfully performed the duties which she had assumed until Jan 9, 1899, when she, too, passed away from earthly scenes She died as the result of an operation for cancer Her death was sincerely mourned by her husband and children October 20, 1900, he was again married; this time to Mrs Anna B Goelz, whose maiden name was Koch, and who survived him Ten of his children also survive him

Mr. Milo Baldwin, of Freedom, was born in Litchfield county, Connecticut, March 22 1818, and died at his home in Alma City, January 29, 1903 When he reached his majority, he engaged in the painting business in New York He followed this occupation for a short time, and then removed to Medina county, Ohio, where he followed farming for six years, and then went to Indiana, where he engaged in both farming and cabinet making Mr Baldwin then removed to Minnesota and settled in Freedom, where he lived until his death

Mrs Mary J Pease, of Woodville, who was stricken by paralysis on the 13th of February, died Sunday evening, February 22, 1903, at 9 o'clock p m, aged seventy-four years Two children, both married, survive her—Mr Wm. F Eaton, who resides in Otisco by her first husband, and Mrs Viola Patch, residing at Motley in this state Mrs Pease came to this county with her husband about 1862 Mrs Pease was an energetic, business woman, and accumulated quite a property. She was prompt in the payment of all demands, and enjoyed the entire confidence of the community in business matters

Mr. G C Runnerstrom, of Otisco, died Monday night, April 6 He was born in Sweden in 1826. He was married to Miss Christina Johnson, by whom he had five children Three children survive him a son, G R Runnerstrom of Otisco, a daughter, Mrs John Blowers, of the same town, and one other Mr Runnerstrom settled in Wilton as a butcher in 1863, and opened a meat market, which he conducted for some time He finally sold his market and moved to Otisco, where he carried on farming He had not been a well man for thirty years prior to his death

New Richland Star·

"Mrs Mary Dinneen, wife of John Dinneen, died at her home in this village Tuesday May 5, 1903, at 2 30 p. m, after a long illness of kidney and liver disease, aged seventy years Deceased was born in Ireland and came to this country with her parents when a young girl, first settling in St Lawrence county, New York Here she was married to Mr Dinneen Shortly after their marriage, the young couple came to this county, first locating on what is now Henry Bluhm's farm in Vivian and afterwards taking a homestead in Byron About seven years ago Mr Dinneen built a residence in this village and from that time they have lived here Mrs. Dinneen had been in feeble health since she left the farm, and since last September had been confined to the house From January last she has been unable to leave her bed She was a good Christian woman of generous impulses and charitable disposition."

A man killed by drinking intoxicants, was the announcement on June 26, 1903. Richard Proehl, of Byron, accompanied by his wife and daughter and his brother-in-law, who resides near Mapleton, Minn , drove into Waseca with Mr Proehl's team and the brother-in-law's buggy Mrs Proehl, her daughter and her brother took the train for Rochester, Minn , to visit her mother, who had undergone an operation in the hospital there Mr Proehl drank rather freely through the afternoon and evening, and late in the evening started for a visit in Iosco When he reached the M & St L crossing near Mr Wyman's place, instead of crossing the track, he turned his team north on to the railroad track and drove along the track, one horse inside the rails A Mrs Wobschall, whose home is close to this crossing, observing the conduct of the man, and knowing that the 10 o clock passenger was almost due, instantly telephoned to the M & St L. depot the situation Messengers were hastily dispatched, but they were too late The on-coming train, as it neared Charles Ward's residenee, struck the horses, throwing one of them a considerable distance and killing it The other horse was pushed along and literally ground up The carriage also was badly broken The unfortunate man was instantly killed, his head being crushed, his left arm broken twice, and one leg also broken twice

Young Edward Moylan, of St Mary, received an injury by a fall from a load of hay in the fall of 1902 From that time he had been very poorly better at times, then worse again Sunday July 12, he came to the home of his sister, Mrs Charles McLoone, of Waseca, and, feeling very weak, he decided to remain for a few days This weakness grew in intensity until Tuesday morning, July 20, 1903, when his death occurred from heart failure Edward was born Feb 11, 1874, in St Mary township, and was the only child of his widowed mother His father died about three years before.

James W Cleland was born in Delaware county, New York, in 1847 His father was a Presbyterian minister and came West in 1862, living about a year in Steele county, and then settling in Wilton, Waseca county, where he purchased a farm His children were reared on this farm, one by one leaving it when old enough to enter college, until finally only James was left with the old people James had married, meantime, in the fall of 1877, Miss Amanda Connor, of Blooming Grove who had been successfully engaged for several years in teaching school in the county After the death of Rev Cleland and his wife, the old home farm was sold and the present home of the family, on the west shore of Clear Lake, was purchased Mr Cleland had a stroke of paralysis in the fall of 1899, but rallied from it and was able to be about the house until the winter of 1901, when he slipped on some ice, fell and injured his hip From that time he was practically helpless On July 15, 1903, he received another stroke of paralysis, which proved fatal He was the father of seven children four of whom survived him—Edgar, Spencer, Jay, and Ralph

Waseca Herald, Oct 10, 1903

"Another of the noblest of our pioneer settlers, P Kenehan, has gone to his long rest Intelligent, modest, unassuming, honorable, industrious and liberal minded, he was respected and held in high esteem by all who knew him He was born in Ireland March 17, 1823, and emigrated from his native land March 18, 1849, landing in New York May 1, 1849 He afterwards came West, first to Geneva, Wis., then to Peoria, Ill, next to Lacon, in the same state, and finally to Wilton, in this county, in 1856, where he has ever since resided In the early days he held the office of town supervisor for many years and was always an honorable and efficient officer In the Indian outbreak of 1862, he became a member of the company of "Home Guards" at Wilton, and was very influential in helping to prevent a panic among the people at that time He married Miss Bridget Martin, October 24, 1849, and became the father of nine children, three of whom died in infancy While attending the funeral of his friend, M Gallagher, on the 24th ult, at the St Mary church, he had a stroke of apoplexy resulting in paralysis After lingering a few days he departed this life Oct 10, 1903"

Another of the early and enterprising pioneers of Minnesota joined the great majority on the other side, October 13, 1903 at the advanced age of eighty-five years Mr James Doyle resided with his son, Raymond Doyle, of Freedom, at the time of his demise Mr Doyle was born July 6, 1818 at Tinahely, County Wicklow Ireland When nineteen years of age, he left Ireland and spent the eight following years traveling and working in Scotland, England, and Continental Europe He came to America in 1847, living in Niagara county, New York He was married at Providence, Rhode Island, in May, 1851, to Miss Catherine McCormick He came West the following year to Logansport, Ind, and in the fall of 1853 resided temporarily at La Crosse, Wis. In the spring of 1854, he began farming at La Crescent, Houston county, Minn, and spent the following thirteen years there In 1867, he sold his farm there and came to Waseca county, where he resided continuously until his death His wife died April 4, 1901, and from that time he made his home with his son, Raymond, on the old homestead After the death of his wife, to whom he was devotedly attached, his health gradually failed until he passed away

On Monday, Nov 15, 1903, occurred the death of Mr Patrick McDonough at his home in Wilton after an illness of about a year His funeral was held in St Mary and he was followed to his last resting place by a large number of relatives and friends by whom he was held in high regard His wife died some years ago Their family circle contained twelve sons and daughters, all of whom survived the father, and one of whom, M McDonough, was, for a number of years, city marshal of Waseca

Mr Simon Brown, formerly of St Mary, later of Woodville, died on Wednesday night, Dec 8, 1903 Mr Brown was among the early settlers of St Mary, and was noted as a quiet, industrious, peaceable farmer He had been ill for some time of cancer of the stomach, that dread disease which, of late years, has carried so many to the grave He was nearly sixty-two years of age

Mrs. A Kaibel, of Waseca, died very suddenly of general paralysis, Dec 9, 1903 She was born in Concoleva West Prussia, in 1839 At the age of fifteen, she came to America with her parents and settled in Marquette county, Wisconsin In 1855, she married Martin Buscho In 1862 the family came to this county and have resided in or near Waseca since that time After the death of Mr Buscho, in 1870, she married Mr Kaibel.

She was the mother of twelve children, four of whom survived her

Gilbert Olson Kin, of Iosco, died on Sunday, Dec 20, 1903, of stomach disease Deceased was one of our most industrious, temperate, and honorable citizens, and was held in high esteem by a large circle of relatives and acquaintances. He had been quite a sufferer for several years from rheumatism, but his last illness and the cause of his death was stomach trouble, thought by some to have been cancer For some weeks prior to his death he was a great sufferer He was a veteran of the war of the Rebellion, having served in Company K, Fifth regiment, Minnesota infantry He left surviving him his aged companion and twelve children He was some sixty-nine years of age His family were left in comfortable circumstances

CHAPTER LXXIII, 1904.

COUNTY MATTERS—WASECA'S NEW CHARTER—MR AND MRS BARNEY BURNS' GOLDEN WEDDING—ATTEMPTED ASSASSINATION OF A GIRL WHO SOON AFTER MARRIES HER WOULD-BE MURDERER—DIED GEO W ARENTSEN, C E GRAHAM, CAPT C C COMEE, J A KAHNKE, P FARLEY, KATHERINE MURPHY, W. H ROESLER, ADAM BISHMAN, BRIDGET KENEHAN, HON C. WAGNER, MRS. J B SULLIVAN, JOHN CAHILL, PHILIP KEELEY, R GARAGHTY OF ST. MARY, SAMUEL HAWKES, MRS P SPILLANE—RESULT OF ELECTION

This year the county legislators met Jan 5, and organized by electing Herman Weckwerth chairman and H J Hanson vice-chairman Only routine business was transacted at this session

The county publishing and advertising for the year was awarded to the Journal-Radical, of Waseca

WASECA'S NEW CHARTER

At the beginning of the new year, the agitation in Waseca regarding the proposed new city charter was at its height and so continued until May 10, 1904 when it was adopted by the voters at a special election The adoption of the new charter introduced a new theory in city government, namely the control and management of the water and light plant by a board of three instead of by the common council as theretofore This seemed to be a new idea to many, and it was not long before a contest grew out of the new departure as between the mayor and council, on the one side, and the water and light board, on the other As the contention is still unsettled at this writing, the matter must be turned over to some future history

GOLDEN WEDDING

Mr and Mrs Barney Burns, of Wilton, who settled in that town as early as 1856, celebrated the fiftieth anniversary of their marriage Tuesday, Oct 11, 1904 They had eleven children, all living, and thirty-two grandchildren, and their presence made the gathering one of much enjoyment Mr and Mrs Burns are among the very early pioneers of this county, and are to be congratulated upon their continued good health and prosperity May they live long in this land of plenty

MURDEROUS ASSAULT

One of the most tragic events of the year occurred on Sunday afternoon, Nov 27, 1904, at Waseca Miss Alice Ryan, aged nineteen years, daughter of Mr and Mrs Thomas Ryan, was occupied as "central" at the telephone office. A few minutes after 5 o clock, Charles Smith about twenty-six years of age, son of C A Smith, grandson of J B Smith, and brother-in-law of Miss Ryan, came into the reception room of the telephone office, and, with scarcely a word, drew a revolver and fired at Miss Ryan three times, the third time the bullet striking her in the back of the neck and lodging in her body. Smith was overpowered and arrested Miss Ryan was taken to Dr Cummings' office and placed in his care.

The would-be assassin was a young man, who had been engaged for several years as brakeman and freight conductor on the Chicago and North-Western railway Some four or five years before this event, he had married a sister of Miss Alice About a year after the marriage, a babe was born to them, the mother dying some two weeks later The child was cared for by the grandparents, Mr and Mrs Thomas Ryan Meantime Smith desired to marry Miss Alice, but her mother not approving of the union, Miss Ryan refused to wed Smith brooded over his dismissal, and finally became jealous The day of the shooting, he had been drinking considerably It was generally believed that Charlie Smith sober, was not the guilty party, but that Charlie Smith, crazed with saloon liquor, was the criminal Charlie Smith's hands are red with the blood of this innocent girl—and whose hands in Waseca are clean? Smith, full of cruel, murderous, licensed liquor, plans to murder a helpless girl He secures cartridges, marches directly to his victim, and, without the least warning, in open day, in the presence of three witnesses shoots her with murderous intent.

And now as to the sequel. Miss Alice rapidly recovered. Mrs Ryan, mother-like, visited her son-in-law in jail As soon as Alice was able, she also went with her mother to see him As a result, Smith soon obtained bail, and, on the evening of his release, he married the girl he would have assassinated at the March term of court, 1904, Smith was let off with a fine of $100 on a charge of assault in the second degree

CALLED HOME

The death roll of the fiftieth year in the history of the county was not lengthy, considering the number of years since the first settlement was made Several of the old first settlers are still living in the county, while others are living in other localities

The first to cross the Great River this year was Mr. Geo W Arentsen, who died Jan 6, 1904, at Jackson, Minn He was born in Holland, some eighty-three years ago He came to America when a young man, and settled in Wisconsin, at Sheboygan Falls, about 1850, where he married Miss Lucretia E Campbell He was a shoemaker by trade and followed his calling there until 1869, when he came to Waseca He purchased a farm in Woodville where his family resided, but he worked at his trade in Waseca He remained here until 1880, when he removed his family to Jackson county, Minnesota His family lived on a farm, but he opened a shoe shop in the village of Jackson He remained there until 1887, when he returned to Waseca and resided with his son John until the fall of 1903 when he returned to Jackson and remained until the time of his death, living with his son John

Clarence E Graham, editor and farmer, was a noted character in the history of this county He died at his farm in Alton, Jan 11, 1904 The immediate cause of death was dropsy Mr Graham was born in Windsor, Broome county, New York, December 22, 1841, and was the son of Mr. and Mrs John L Graham He was reared in the county of his birth When nineteen years of age, he went to Perry county, Missouri, where he took part in carpentry work on the court house then being built. While there he saw what they termed Lincoln men ridden on a rail for their opinions' sake The following winter ill health compelled him to return to New York He remained there during the winter In the spring of 1862, his father and brother came to Minnesota, and he and his mother followed the same fall, settling in Houston county In 1863, he enlisted in Company D, Second Wisconsin cavalry, known as Washburn's cavalry and remained in the service until December 12, 1865, when he was mustered out, and came to Waseca county January 9, 1866, he moved to a farm in Freedom township, where he resided until 1873 He then removed to the village of Janesville, where he purchased the Argus and was soon after made postmaster of the place In 1881, he sold the Argus to J A Henry and removed to Waseca, where he purchased the Waseca Radical He continued his connection with this paper until it was sold to the present proprietors of the Journal-Radical. Soon after selling the Radical, he engaged in farming so far as his health would permit January 3, 1869, he married Miss Rosetha Helen Stone, who survives him They were the parents of four sons, three of whom are still living

Capt C C Comee, another old veteran, died Jan 15 1904, of a complication of diseases incident to old age He was born in the state of Massachusetts in January, 1827 He enlisted in the Ninety-fourth New York infantry at the opening of the Rebellion, was chosen first lieutenant of his company, and soon after was promoted to captain He participated in many battles, was taken prisoner at the battle of Gettysburg, and was confined in Libby prison for nine months. He was honorably discharged near the close of the war and came to Minnesota in 1864 He was county auditor of this county from 1865 to 1870 He then removed to Tennessee, where he remained for a number of years, returning to Waseca some eighteen or twenty years ago, where he followed his trade of painter Two sons and four daughters survive him

Waseca Herald:

Mr John A Kahnke, one of the early settlers of St Mary, died on the 20th of Jan, 1904, at his home in that township He was eighty-seven years of age and died of a complication of ailments incident to persons of that age He was a native of Germany, but came to this country many years ago He was not only a good man when he died, but he had been a good man for the last thirty years to our personal knowledge, and, we doubt not, all his life He was not only honorable and upright, but also kind, charitable, and obliging If there is a heaven, John A Kahnke will have a place there His children, worthy offspring of honored parents, are four sons, John, Albert, George, and Frank, and four daughters, Mrs John Volz, Mrs Joseph Matz, Mrs Casper Kramer, and Mrs Peter Amberg May their last days be like his

Patrick Farley a prominent farmer of St Mary, died suddenly Feb 2, 1904 Mr Farley had been slightly indisposed from what he supposed was heart trouble, but that afternoon, feeling better than usual, he said that he was going out to pump water for the stock His sons urged him not to do so, but, saying that he needed the exercise, he wrapped up and went out He was gone somewhat longer than usual, causing so much anxiety on the part of the family that James went out to look for him, only to find his lifeless body, still warm, on the ground near the pump A post mortem examination showed that he died of apoplexy Mr Farley was born in Ireland in 1836 He came to Waseca county when twenty-nine years of age, settling in Alton Twenty-one years later he purchased his farm home in St Mary Surviving him are his wife, five sons, and four daughters.

After an illness of several years, during three of which she had been unable to be about the house, Mrs Katherine Murphy wife of Alderman Henry Murphy died at her home in Waseca, Saturday night, Jan. 30 1904 Mrs Murphy was born in Ireland, coming to America in 1853, and to this county in 1875 She was about eighty-four years of age at the time of her death She left surviving, with her husband, one daughter and one son

Wm. H Roesler, of Waseca, died Feb 23, 1904, of heart disease Deceased was born in Marquette county, Wisconsin, Sept 11, 1858 He came to Waseca county with his parents when he was eight years old and resided here after that time In January, 1885 he was united in marriage to Miss Pauline W Kaiser They were the parents of five children After his marriage, Mr Roesler lived on his farm in Wilton until, in 1892, he accepted a position with the Laird Norton Lumber Company in Waseca. In 1896, he was elected treasurer of Waseca county on the republican ticket and filled this office efficiently for two terms For more than a year he had been manager of the Farmers' Elevator in Waseca, and had just been chosen to this position for another year

Waseca Herald, March 18, 1904 -

The sudden death of Mr Adam Bishman, of this city, shortly after 12 o'clock noon, last Monday, March 14, 1904, was a severe shock to his many friends and acquaintances in this county He had been feeling unwell for some two weeks, but neither he nor his friends supposed his illness was serious Mr. Mahler called upon him at dinner time, but did not consider his condition at all critical, and yet, before Mr Mahler reached his store, a messenger overtook him to say that Mr Bishman was dead. Adam Bishmann, as he was christened, was born in Dorn Durkheim, Hesse Darmstadt, Germany, on the 27th day of March, 1824 He came to America in 1846, settling in Monee, Illinois In 1849, he returned to his native town and was married to Miss Anna M Brandt, September 2 They at once came to his Illinois home, where they lived until they came to Minnesota, in 1856, moving to Otisco where they resided until November, 1902 They then took up their residence in Waseca, where they have since lived When Mr Bishman came to Minnesota, he was in much better financial circumstances than most of the pioneer settlers of the West, and he died possessed of a considerable fortune, the greater part of it being invested in land Notwithstanding his comfortable financial standing, he and his now aged companion participated fully in the hardships incident to pioneer life, and never failed to extend the hand of friendship and hospitality to all comers Many of our readers will call to mind the terrible tornado which visited Mr Bishman's Otisco farm in July, 1902, when a son and a daughter were crushed and killed Notwithstanding that fierce storm, Mr. Bishman went to Otisco station, over a mile distant, gave the alarm, and telephoned to Waseca for medical aid It was a terrible ordeal for so aged a person, and he never fully recovered from the shock then received He leaves surviving of his own family a son, George, of South Dakota, and three daughters Miss Clara, at home, Mrs Gus Krassin, of this city, and Mrs Anna Perso, of South Dakota He also leaves surviving three brothers and two sisters Philip of Illinois, Louis of Mankato, Jacob of Otisco, Mrs Christian Klein of Chicago, and Mrs Philip Miller of Rice county Deceased was one of our best citizens In politics he was a prohibitionist In his dealings he was prompt and honorable He was kind to his family hospitable and friendly with his neighbors, and liberal to his church."

Mrs Bridget (Martin) Kenehan widow of the late Patrick Kenehan, of Wilton, died Sunday, May 8, 1904 at the home of her daughters, Misses Mary and Agnes, in Waseca, at the age of seventy-six, of blood poisoning Her ailment commenced in her hands and gradually extended to her body causing death Mrs Kenehan joined Mr Kenehan in holy wedlock, at Geneva Wis., Oct 28, 1849. She was the mother of nine children of whom six are now living, three sons and three daughters

Hon Christoph Wagner passed to his rest June 19, 1904 A local paper of June 24, 1904, noticed his death as follows

The people of this county were surprised and shocked on Monday last to hear of the death of Hon. Chris Wagner, of New Richland, who died of heart failure at 12 45 that morning after an illness of only two days Mr Wagner attended the G A. R encampment in Waseca, last week, and appeared to be in his usual health He was taken ill shortly after his return from Waseca, and passed away a little after midnight, Sunday night

Deceased was born in Prussia, November 7 1842, came to America in 1847 with his parents, who settled in Sheboygan county, Wisconsin There he resided until 1861, when he enlisted in Co A, Ninth Wisconsin infantry, in which he served three years and three months He was honorably discharged in 1864 and returned to his old home in Wisconsin December 10, 1867, he married Miss Mary Zieger and in 1869 came to Waseca county and took up his residence on section 18, town of New Richland, which has been the family home since that time

He was a member of the state house of representatives during the notable session of 1881, when the "Old Minnesota Bond Swindle" was finally consummated That was a session that tried men's souls The man that could be bribed took his price and the people were mulcted in bonds to the amount of $5,000,000, which they still have to pay. Mr Wagner stood firm against the wiles of Selah Chamberlain's lobbyists and the devil of corruption, and came forth unsullied in character Of course plutocracy marked him for slaughter, but he lived and died with an honored name among honest men that are intelligent enough to know an honest man from a boodler.

In 1885, Mr Wagner and his brother C A, now county treasurer, opened a lumber yard in New Richland Afterwards deceased became sole owner, about eight years ago, he sold out altogether. He assisted in organizing the New Richland State Bank, was chosen its president, and continued to hold that position to the time of his death For twenty years, he has been almost continuously town clerk, and for many years has been a member of the board of education of the village For the past two or three years, he has confined his principal activities to the management of his farm of three hundred fifty acres adjoining the village of New Richland

He leaves surviving him Mrs Wagner, his widow, three sons—C W Wagner, editor of the Litchfield Review, Dr Frank J Wagner, and Otto H Wagner, of New Richland, six daughters—Mrs Jacob Echternach, Mrs C G Hauge, Misses Ida M, Alma H, Bertha M, and Elsie E

An honorable, upright citizen and a good man has passed away. His memory will be an inspiration to honorable life

Mrs Gertrude Utley Sullivan, wife of J B. Sullivan cashier of the First National bank of Waseca, entered into her rest Saturday September 3, 1904 She was born February 16, 1875, in Fryeburg, Maine She came West with her parents and lived in Lake Preston, S. D. Here she attended the public school and, later, received instruction in Sacred Heart Academy in Waseca

She was married to J. B Sullivan in Lake Preston November 10, 1892 Two children, John aged eight and Florian aged five, with her husband, mourn her departure

Mr. John Cahill, of Janesville, an early settler, died Thursday night, Sept. 22, 1904. Mr Cahill had been a great sufferer from rheumatism for many years, but had been in his usual health, going to town and back Thursday He went to bed at an early hour As he did not get up at his usual time in the morning, his son-in-law, Thomas Eustis, went to his bedside and was shocked to find him dead Mr Cahill was born in Ireland in 1831. He came to this country in his early manhood, married, and settled on the farm where he lived. His wife and family of eight children survive him

Mr Philip Keeley died very suddenly on his farm in St Mary Friday, Nov 18, 1904 He had started a fire to burn up some rubbish The flames were spreading in the direction of some hay stacks, and Mr Keeley was working with all his strength to keep the fire under his control A neighbor saw him fall to the ground and hastened to his assistance Drawing Mr Keeley out of the smoke, the man ran for help to revive the fainting man, but before aid came, Mr Keeley was beyond help. Deceased was a brother of James Keeley and of Matt Keeley, formerly sheriff of this county

Mr Roger Garaghty of St Mary, died Nov 17, 1904 He had not been as well as usual during the day and his son Thomas had decided to call in a physician A few minutes later, the son entered his father's room and found that the old gentleman had passed quietly away Mr Garaghty had been a prominent citizen of St Mary for nearly forty years having settled upon section 32, in that town, in 1865 He was born July 4, 1833, in Ireland His parents were Peter and Mary Garaghty, who reared a family of six children. Deceased came to America in 1849, when only sixteen years of age. His first two years in this country were spent in Marquette county, Wisconsin He then went into the South where he remained until 1865 when he came to this county. November 16, 1856, he married Miss Catherine Madden, who also came from Ireland in 1849 She was the daughter of Thomas and Honora Madden, and was born August 5, 1833 They were the parents of five children, three of whom survived him. He held the office of town clerk one term, and held school district offices on several occasions.

Mr Samuel Hawkes passed quietly away at his home in Waseca, Wednesday morning Dec 7 1904 In April, 1903, he suffered a stroke of paralysis He partially recovered from this and had been able to be about the city more or less Mr Hawkes was born in Windham, Cumberland county, Maine, September 13, 1838. He lived with his parents until he was eighteen years of age, when he came to Iowa. After a short residence there, he came to Meriden, Steele county, Minnesota, and bought a farm In October, 1865, he was married to Miss Caroline M. Skillings, of Maine He brought his bride to his farm where they lived for nine years He then sold this farm and bought a farm about one and one-half miles northwest of Waseca After he purchased this farm, he and his family lived part of the time there and the remainder of the time in Waseca

After an illness of about a year of cancer of the stomach, Mrs Patrick Spillane passed away at her home in Woodville Saturday morning, Dec 24, 1904 Charlotte Lang Spillane was born August 22, 1847 in Cataraugus county, New York Soon after this the family moved to Waupun, Wis At the age of nineteen, Mrs Spillane was married to Patrick Spillane, and came to Faribault county, Minnesota, where they took up a homestead. In 1874 they moved to Woodville, this county, which was the home of the family after that time. Mr Spillane died in December, 1896. Five children were born to Mr and Mrs Spillane, three sons and two daughters, all of whom survive the mother.

THE ELECTION OF 1904

Although this was presidential year, there was very little enthusiasm and more than the usual number did not vote The local returns showed the following results

For representative, Emil Dieudonne, rep, 1,314, Wm H Meyer, ind, 1,340, treasurer, Fred W Roesler, rep, 1 435, John L. Hanson, dem., 1,269, sheriff, Geo H. Goodspeed, rep 1,360, Frank Collins, dem, 1,384; register of deeds, F J Skoedopole, rep, 1,032, John M Wollschaeger, dem, 1,704, attorney, John J. Isker, rep., 1,332, F B Andrews, dem, 1 363, clerk of court,

Henry Reynolds, rep., 1,517, W. S. Scott, dem., 1,182; superintendent of schools, L. J. Larson, rep., 1,481, Herman A. Panzram, dem., 1,652; county commissioner of the Third district, John S. Johnson, rep., 240, Patrick McHugo, dem., 175. C. H. Bailer, county auditor, Geo. A. Wilson, judge of probate, Dr. H. G. Blanchard, coroner, N. M. Nelson, court commissioner, O. L. Smith, surveyor, H. J. Hanson, county commissioner of First district, and Edward Thompson, county commissioner of the Fifth district, were elected without opposition.

J.F. MURPHY
W.A. CLEMENT
J.A. HENRY
C.W. BROWN

CHAPTER LXXIV.

NEWSPAPERS AND NEWSPAPER MEN OF WASECA COUNTY, PAST AND PRESENT NEWS, RADICAL, JOURNAL-RADICAL—HERALD—ARGUS—NORTH STAR CHILD, MURPHY, GRAHAM, MORSE, HENRY, BROWN, AND OTHERS

NEWSPAPERS

The present newspapers in the county of Waseca are the Journal-Radical and the Waseca County Herald, of Waseca, the Argus, of Janesville, and the North Star of New Richland.

The Journal-Radical is the lineal descendant of the Home Views, which first made its appearance at Wilton as far back as March 13, 1860 That was sometime ago It was edited by J W Crawford, at one time register of deeds of this county, and printed at the office of A B. Cornell, in Owatonna. About the 1st of March, 1861, Alex Johnston and S J. Willis took the paper in hand, called it The Waseca Home Views, and printed it at Wilton on their own press and type They published it in Wilton until the fall of 1861, when Johnston bought the Willis interest and removed the material to Faribault, changed it to a democratic paper, still continuing to publish a Wilton edition with Buel Welsh, Esq, as local scribe at Wilton. In the fall of 1863, Hon H D Baldwin, who had a lien upon the material, brought it back to Wilton James Mowatt was employed as printer, and James E Child served as editor. The first issue of The Wilton Weekly News made its appearance December 8, 1863. It was a six column folio, all home print, and Republican in politics. At the close of the first year of the paper, Mr. Child bought the outfit and assumed control of the

21

paper March 8, 1866, the paper was made one column larger, and in this form it continued for a number of years In October, 1867, Mr Child removed the material to the then new village of Waseca and changed the name to Waseca News In November, 1868, Wm J Graham became half owner of the News, and tried to edit it for some time He remained with the paper until May 31, 1871, when Mr. Child again took entire charge of the office.

On the 1st of August, 1871, Mr. John F. Murphy, now of the Herald, became a partner in the management of the News and continued as such until May 29, 1872, when he retired

July 15, 1874, the form of the paper was changed to a six-column quarto. It was then the largest paper published in Southern Minnesota west of Winona

Jan 6, 1875, the name of the paper was changed to the Minnesota Radical In May, 1878, Walter Child, son of James E, became part owner of the paper and took charge of the mechanical department In October of the same year the Messrs Child bought a portion of the material of the Liberty Blade, of Minneapolis, and took over the subscription list of that paper, calling the consolidated papers the Radical and Liberty Blade It was known as an advocate of the temperance and anti-monopoly interests Incessant toil as attorney and editor for years had impaired the health of the elder Mr Child, and he reluctantly sold his interest in the paper to Hon W G. Ward, in July, 1880 who was then a candidate for congress. Mr. Ward restored the heading, Minnesota Radical, and employed Hon E B Collester as editor, although Senator Ward himself wrote the "savage political articles." In August, 1881, Mr Ward, having tired of the "luxury," transferred it to C E Graham This gentleman continued the paper until the last of December, 1901, when he sold material and good will to a company consisting of Dr F A. Swartwood, P C Bailey, E B Collester, L Bliss, R P Ward, C A. Smith, and W A Clement These men at the same time became the owners of the Waseca Journal, a paper theretofore published by J T Heck, who came here from Washington Recently Mr W. A Clement, who had been business manager from the beginning of the consolidation of the two papers, has bought the other interests, and is now sole proprietor. The Journal-Radical is now somewhat like the boy's jackknife He first broke the blade and had a new one put in Then he broke the back and had it replaced. Lastly the handle came off and he got a new one; and yet it was the same good, old jackknife.

THE WASECA COURIER.

This paper was published by Mrs A. B. Cornell, of Owatonna, in 1862-3. It was a five column quarto, the local editor being Col. J C Ide of Wilton It never had the hearty support of the people of the county, and ceased to exist in the fall of 1863.

WILTON COURANT

Early in the winter of 1867, after the News had been removed to Waseca, A J Clark and W D Palmer, of Winona, were induced to start a paper at Wilton, and they called it the Courant. Mr Clark was "great" on securing bonuses and managed to get a number of pledges from citizens of Wilton and from some of the county officers. His bills for the printing of county blanks were enormous, far exceeding any ever allowed before or since, but the people did not, as a rule, take kindly to the new paper, and about August 17, 1869, Mr. Clark, having secured a bonus from a town in Sherburne county, gathered his material together and removed thither. He was a man of considerable ability, genial, and kind in disposition, but strong drink had so debased his manhood and destroyed his business ability that he died a financial and physical wreck a number of years ago in the South

JANESVILLE ARGUS

The next successful paper to be established in the county was the Argus In the spring of 1873, John L (not "Billy") Barlow prevailed upon the people of Janesville to purchase press and material for a newspaper and turn the same over to him, taking a chattel mortgage back Mr Barlow seemed to be a failure from the start, as a newspaper man, and those who had their money invested foreclosed the mortgage within three months after he started, and the paper was suspended

In the fall of 1873, the Janesville proprietors of the material prevailed upon C. E. Graham, of Freedom, to accept the same and start a newspaper. The first number appeared November 2,

1873 It was a five-column quarto and bristled with odd, quaint sayings, and with witticisms fresh and stale presented in an original manner Mr Graham continued to publish the paper until August, 1881, when he sold it to Mr John A Henry and bought the Waseca Radical Mr Henry has had command of the Argus continuously ever since, although he was ably assisted by Mr C. W. Brown, as a partner, from the fall of 1900 to about June 15, 1903

THE RECORD.

Messrs. W J Graham and A H Carman, in October, 1873, started a small, three-column folio, called The Record. It suspended the next spring

WASECA LEADER.

This was a weekly paper instituted in Waseca, by T F Hollister, from Wisconsin, in the spring of 1876 Mr. Hollister struggled hard to maintain the publication, but with three papers in the village at that time he found it impossible On the 7th of May, 1880, he sold his outfit to Messrs G W. Morse and A F. Booth who consolidated it with the Herald, then owned by Messrs Morse & Booth.

WASECA COUNTY HERALD

Lem Reeves and A J Fullerton came to Waseca from McGregor, Iowa, and commenced the publication of a seven-column folio, the first number of which bore date October 5, 1877 and announced itself as "straight Republican." Oct. 4 1878, it was changed in form to an eight-column folio with "patent inside " That fall Mr Fullerton retired Mr Reeves continued the publication of the paper until May 2, 1879, when he disposed of the outfit to A F Booth. July 1, following, H F. Pond, of Trempealeau, Wis, bought a half interest in the paper, and the firm name became Booth & Pond They published the paper until April 23, 1880, when Mr Pond retired On the 7th of May following, as before stated, Mr Booth "absorbed" the Leader, at the same time forming a copartnership with Mr G W Morse. The next week Mr Booth sold his interest to Mr S M Rose, and on May 14, 1880, the Herald was issued by the new firm of Rose & Morse Under the able management of these two men, the paper became firmly established Mr Rose died about March 13, 1883, and his widow continued her interest in the paper until Dec 1883, when she sold to Mr J F. Murphy her half interest and the business was thenceforth conducted in the name of Morse & Murphy, until Oct 15. 1885, when Mr. Morse sold his half interest to James E Child. The firm name of Child & Murphy was used until about the first of April, 1890, when the name of the firm was changed to J F Murphy & Co This name has been continued to the present time At the beginning of volume XXI, Sept. 21, 1900, the form of the Herald was changed from an eight-column folio to a six-column quarto

THE NORTH STAR.

R. P. Child made the first venture in newspaper work at New Richland, in the fall of 1878. About six months' experience closed the deal Sept 24 1884, Morse & Murphy, of the Waseca Herald, commenced the publication of a paper called the New Richland Review, with L M. Paschall as local editor It was ably edited by that gentleman, but it did not pay and was discontinued Oct 7, 1885 The next venture was the North Star, which made its first appearance Feb 4, 1886, S K Gregg and M. E Goodwin publishers Mr Goodwin retired April 15, 1886, leaving Mr. Gregg sole owner. The latter part of August, 1887, Bronson & Holland bought the paper, O H Bronson becoming editor Their first paper was dated Sept. 5, 1887. Mr. Holland soon after retired, leaving Mr Bronson in sole command. Along in the nineties, Mr. Bronson sold the outfit to B W Graham, nephew of C E Graham, "on time" After about a year Mr Bronson again took charge of the office He was a very competent, bright editor He continued with the Star until June 15, 1903, when he sold the whole plant to Mr C. W Brown, who has continued it with marked business ability ever since

TOWN TALK

A three-column folio paper made its appearance Oct 9, 1879, and was exactly what its name implied. At least, for the time being it was the talk of the town It bore the name of T White, editor, although T. White probably never wrote a word of it The second number, dated Oct. 23, 1879, was decidedly personal, and exhausted the energies of its authors, it is supposed, as that was the end of the publication.

THE CLIPPER,

Oct. 4, 1901, Thos J. Kelley, from Jordan, Minn., started a paper called the Clipper in Waseca He issued six numbers and then threw up the enterprise. No doubt he was deceived by representations made by Waseca men that knew nothing of the newspaper business

CHAPTER LXXV.

WASECA COUNTY IN THE SPANISH WAR—OVATION TO COMPANY K—CAMP RAMSEY AT ST. PAUL—COMPANY ROSTER—TRIP TO CHATTANOOGA—MARCH TO CAMP THOMAS—CAMP LIFE—RETURN HOME.

For years, Waseca county had maintained a military organization, known as Company K. At the time of the breaking out of the Spanish war, in 1898, the company was nearly complete in its number of men, and within a very short time after the call for troops, the company was ready for service. About the last of April, Capt. Walter Child received orders to embark his company for St. Paul the next morning. "There was hurrying to and fro" among the boys to get ready for the sudden change, and the people of Waseca, at the instigation of John Moonan, Esq., also moved in the matter. A local paper said:

CAPT. WALTER CHILD.

"Wednesday evening, Capt. Walter Child received orders for Company K to proceed to St. Paul, via the M. & St. L. railway 7:30 o'clock morning train. Hon John Moonan learned of the order about 9 o'clock the same evening, and immediately set to work to give the boys a decent send off Quietly but effectively he enlisted the services of patriotic citizens and in a few hours, Thursday morning, had everything arranged for a monster meeting and banquet And so it happened that Company K, of this county, received a generous ovation the night before it left. The Waseca Opera House was filled to overflowing, and the street in front of the building was crowded with a swaying, patriotic mass of people who could not gain admittance While a bounteous supper was being prepared in the G. A R hall by the ladies, the crowds outside were being entertained by the Waseca band At the same time, in the opera house, a formal meeting was being held to cheer and congratulate the young men that were about to face the hardships of war in defense of the old flag"

The boys had a little experience to start with. They left Waseca early in the morning, arriving at St Paul a little after 10 o'clock the same morning. Upon arrival the company received orders to leave all grips and packages with detail and teams which would bring them out Consequently all boys without haversacks left their rations, and had nothing to eat until 9 o'clock at night, after marching from St Paul to the fair grounds It was an unfortunate oversight on the part of the St Paul officers The company was finally mustered into the United States service May 8, 1898 The following was the roster of Company K, Waseca:

CAPTAIN, Walter Child
FIRST LIEUTENANT, Milo A. Hodgkins.
SECOND LIEUTENANT, J S Sheehan
FIRST SERGEANT, Geo E Stowe
QUARTERMASTER SERGEANT, E Durston

SERGEANTS

Joseph Dunn	F C Priest
Arthur E Ward	Charles Hemstreet

CORPORALS

Alvis Henle,	A F Bartles,	D. E Cordry,
Carl Lund,	F C Cook,	E R. Connors,
J McLoone,	Henry Gasink,	M W Anderson,
A J. Kurkowski,	P. J McLin,	J D Reynolds.

MUSICIANS

L H Dibble,	H E. Gillam

ARTIFICER

H E Hartson

WAGONER

W A Santo

PRIVATES.

Bostwick, H J
Beers, R W.
Burke, Geo F
Barlow, Geo W
Blomberg Alvin
Blakeslee, W M.
Calhane, W F
Clark, Frank
Chase Ira
Daniels, S B
Dewald, H
Davis, E A.
Ellingson, M E
Erickson, W M
Fritz, D C
Fristad, A
Gibbs, U S
Gasink, Geo A
Gasink, Edward J
Hale, I W
Hanson, Olof
Holzgrove, H C
Hale, John
Healy, Geo
Irons, Frank B.
Johnson, Theo
Koplen, E W
Land, Joe
Larson, O J
Lloyd, T E
Middaugh, R. W.
Middaugh, C A
Mycue, Wm.
McLin, Frank
Mika, C B.
McMahon, W. A
McGinnis, Timothy E
McDonald, James A.
O'Leary, John
Olson, Simon
Olson, Martin
Petran, A. L
Peterson, Fred
Panzram, H A J
Ryan, M A
Reynolds, Wm S.
Remy, W M
Sill, Ransom
Schaumkessel, Aug
Schaumkessel, Al.
Shortell, Henry
Vernon, Wm
Veal, Herman
Wilsey, T. A
Williams, H H
Winship, A F
Webster, Harry
Wichman, Theo
Zerath, F. C

The company remained at Camp Ramsey, the State Fair grounds, until May 16, 1898, when its regiment the Twelfth, was taken to Chickamauga Park in Tennessee The company passed through Waseca, on the 16th of May, over the M & St. L railway, and was furnished coffee and lunch at Waseca, with a grand ovation The following extracts from a private letter written by Captain Child, give something of an idea of the trip.

On train between
Hannibal and St Louis, Mo, May 17, 1898.

Father We broke camp at 6 30 a m Monday, May 16, and took train about 11 a m. Were detained in St. Paul on account of our baggage and stock, and did not leave there until about 2 o'clock p m One man of Company D had his head badly cut in Minneapolis while leaning out of a window He was knocked senseless

Our regiment is in three sections We all have sleeping cars. The officers have a very fine sleeper and the men are comfortably provided for The people of nearly every town along the route are out in force, especially through Minnesota and Iowa We awoke this morning in

Burlington, Iowa, got coffee at Keokuk, and had our breakfast We have been following the Mississippi river all the forenoon, and the country is the most Godforsaken, I believe, that I ever saw

We passed the second section of our regiment at Hannibal They stopped there for coffee, as their engine had broken down The boys are all feeling well at this writing, 12 m, except Geo Gasink, who is a little sick at his stomach from riding on the cars

We have seen, from the car windows, the log huts that we have heard of, occupied by the colored race One small town in Missouri was nearly all log huts

Company K appreciate the eatables and demonstration made by the Waseca people, and are at this time enjoying the lunches Waseca is all O K The merchants there furnished our train with coffee for $7 50, while in Keokuk the same amount of coffee cost us $23 50

We shall be in St Louis at 3 30 p m, and from there we go to Corinth, Miss, thence to Chickamauga We shall probably reach our destination about Wednesday night

Under date of May 21, writing from Camp Thomas, he said.

"We arrived at Chattanooga, Thursday morning at 4.30, and although we were there all the forenoon, we did not leave the depot

"We left Chattanooga about 1 o'clock p m and marched to Chickamauga Park, a distance ot some ten miles. The boys were all in heavy marching order, and a good many of all the companies fell out along the road We got into camp a little after 7 o'clock, and the boys were nearly dead for want of water A detail was sent for water to one of the springs, but found it guarded by an Illinois company. Their guns were loaded with cartridges, and they would let no one get at the spring unless accompanied by an officer, such a cry as went up from the men for water, when we arrived, was enough to make a man sick

"A lieutenant has to go with the water brigade several times a day The reason for this guarding is, that some one had poisoned the springs and wells, a day or two before we arrived, and they had to be cleaned out, so guards are now stationed at each spring and well

"The Park is a fine place. Our regiment has cleaned its camp quarters so that there is no grass or leaves left on the ground We all had a good bath in Chickamauga creek yesterday The water looks dirty but one can wash quite clean in it after all

"This is no play soldier The first night in camp no tents were put up, and we all lay upon the ground in our blankets and were very glad ot the chance to do so and rest A good many of the boys sleep in the open air yet, as one car load of our tents was lost on the way Our boys are all standing camp life pretty well, although the 'grub' is pretty tough at present, as we are just finishing up our traveling rations We expect something better after a little

Under date of June 11, the Waseca Herald correspondent wrote:

"On the 11th of June, Corporal Cordry was detailed to return to Waseca to secure twenty-three recruits for the company so as to bring it up to the number of one hundred and six He arrived at Waseca June 13, 1898, and on the 21st of the same month his recruits had all been secured. The following were the recruits with name, age and occupation of each Anderson, Otto, 31, miller, Axtell, Arthur V, 21, farmer, Borge, Lars K, 22, tailor, Clark, Geo A, 22, saddler, Davis, Thos A, 24, miller, Everson, Sofus, 21, clerk, Hanley, James M, 21, law student, Hanson, Albert, 23, plumber, Johnson, David, 23, laborer, Ketchum, Verner A., 20, farmer, Lindsay, George W, 25, clerk, Leo, Wm, 25, tinner, Smith, Jasper A., 26, farmer, Skaug, Henry M, 21, clerk, Shave, Edwin, D, 23, carpenter, Sand, Ole, 21, mechanic; Smith, Varde, 18, laborer, Starr, Frank E, 19, laborer, Sterner, Wm A., 27, butcher, Thoresen, And C, 23, miller; Waite, Fred A, 22, butcher, Wynnemer, Fred, 31, mechanic, Wickersheim, 24, farmer"

The regiment remained at Camp Thomas, Ga, until August 22, when the men broke camp and started for Camp Hamilton, near Lexington, Ky The Waseca Herald correspondent, under date of Aug 28, 1898, wrote as follows:

"We broke camp at Camp Thomas at 6 30, Monday, the 22d, packed up and started on the march for Rossville about 9 o'clock, after a fast march of nearly seven miles, we arrived there only to find that there were no cars and that we would have to wait until night When night came we were told that the cars were expected any time, so we camped on the ground without even putting up our shelter tents, for we expected to load any time within the night The cars at last arrived Tuesday morning, and at 9 o'clock we were going as fast as steam could carry us away from the place that none of the men can remember with pleasant thoughts. Nothing of any interest happened en route, only that the boys were delighted with the beautiful scenery that was to be seen from the car windows

We arrived at Rossville about 4 o'clock, Wednesday morning, unloaded, marched to our new camp, put up our tents, and Thursday night found us all settled with board floors in our tents A good many of the boys have purchased cots

This place seems to have been made on purpose for a camp—the ground is sloping and it so pleasant and cool here. The grass is green and that is something we have not seen since we came South This is in the heart of the blue-grass country where the best of everything grows If anything does not grow, the people make sure to get it in some other way The people here think there is nothing too good for a soldier, at Camp Thomas all the people thought of a soldier was the money they could get from him, and they got pretty near all of it too

Just think of paying forty cents a gallon for milk, and that not very good Here we get the very best milk right from the farmers for twenty-five cents a gallon"

By this time the war with Spain was substantially at an end and the boys were destined to return home without seeing any actual fighting

After remaining at Camp Hamilton about a month the Twelfth regiment was ordered home, to New Ulm, to be mustered out of service The company arrived in Waseca September 22, and was tendered a banquet and a flag presentation. The banquet was prepared by the Woman's Relief Corps and the old veterans of McKune Post, G A R, with the assistance of lady friends The company men and many of their relatives, with the members of the W R C and G A R, sat down to a sumptuous repast at the G A R Hall, about 7 o'clock p m As soon as the banquet was disposed of, all repaired to the court room where speeches of welcome were made, and a large silk flag presented to the company The flag was the joint work of the ladies of Waseca, Waterville, and Janesville, and was a very handsome gift Short speeches were made by Senator Collester, Hon Peter McGovern, Capt. Walter Child, Editor John A Henry, and lawyers F B. Andrews and John Moonan

The company remained in camp at New Ulm,—most of the men being home on furlough—for a month, when they were paid off and mustered out of the United States service, with the privilege of continuing as a part of the State organization. But after the service the men had seen, they lost interest in the organization and declined to stand the expense of maintaining a company, so they soon after disbanded.

CHAPTER LXXVI.

MISCELLANEOUS MATTERS—WASECA AND ITS MAYORS—COMMISSIONER KEELEY INVESTIGATES AND FINDS "STEALAGE"

WASECA AND ITS MAYORS

The official record book of Waseca, from the organization of the village to the year 1881, has been lost for a long time How or when, no one seems to know After considerable search, were found the following names and dates. Under the village charter there were three trustees, instead of aldermen, and one of the three was made president, who was in fact mayor or chief magistrate.

PRESIDENTS

W G Ward in 1868, Wm Everett in 1870, I C Trowbridge in 1871-2, George P Johnson in 1873, 1874 and 1875, P C Bailey in 1876, 1877, 1878, R L McCormick in 1879 and 1880.

MAYORS

Warren Smith in 1881, M L D Collester in 1882, I C Trowbridge in 1883, 1884, 1885 and 1892, G Buchler, 1886, E B Collester, 1887; D S Cummings, 1888, 1889, 1890, 1893, 1894, 1895 and 1896, D E Priest, 1891, John Moonan, 1897, C A Smith, 1898 1899, 1900, 1901, 1902 and 1903, Wm. C Wobschall, 1904 and 1905

From the Waseca County Herald, Dec 30, 1904

COMMISSIONER KEELEY INVESTIGATES.

"We are informed that the record of the proceedings of the board of county commissioners, at their late session, did not contain all that was done. It is reported to us that the board appointed a committee of two of the county officers to examine certain books of the county, and that no record was made of their appointment. Our informant says that Commissioner Keeley, some time ago, commenced to investigate a little on his own account, being assisted by another He found, first, that the law required all plaintiffs in district court, having jury trials, to deposit with the clerk of court $3, second, that the clerk of court is required, by statute, to "forthwith" pay over the same to the county treasurer; third, upon inquiry of the county treasurer and the county auditor, that no such fees had been paid into the county treasury for years

These findings Mr Keeley presented to the county commissioners and the county attorney at the late session All of the commissioners, save one, were astonished; that commissioner, it is said, at first argued that the officer was all right After considerable discussion by members of the board, the clerk of the court appeared before them, invited them into a back room, confirmed Commissioner Keeley's statement, and agreed to restore every cent as soon as he could borrow the money.

The commissioners then appointed the county attorney and the county auditor to investigate the books of the clerk of court and ascertain the amount of money withheld from the county, and to report at the next meeting of the board

We are informed that the amount collected by the clerk during the past eight years and not paid over amounts to over $500

Subsequent investigations by the state authorities confirmed Mr Keeley's findings, but the attorney general of the state held that since all this stealing had been done prior to the commencement of the clerk's term of office Jan 1, 1905 he could not be removed unless he should be indicted and convicted by the courts The grand jury of the county at the March term of court, failed to indict the clerk and Mr Henry Reynolds continues as one branch of the court which, theoretically, is expected to have clean hands

CHAPTER LXXVII.

LEGISLATORS OF FIFTY YEARS—COUNTY AUDITORS—REGISTERS OF DEEDS—TREASURERS—DISTRICT COURT CLERKS—SHERIFFS—PROBATE JUDGES—COUNTY ATTORNEYS—COUNTY SURVEYORS—COUNTY CORONERS—SCHOOL SUPERINTENDENTS

LEGISLATIVE ROSTER.

On the adoption of the State constitution in 1857, the counties of Waseca and Steele, constituting at that time the Fifteenth senatorial district, were represented in the first legislature, which assembled December 2, 1857, by Senator Lewis McKune, of Waseca county, and Representatives H. M Sheetz, G C Pettie, and Smith Johnson, of Steele county At the election of 1858, Buel Welch, of Waseca county, was chosen representative However, owing to the protracted session of the legislature of 1857-8, there was no session in the winter of 1858-9.

The second legislature convened December 7, 1859, and adjourned March 12, 1860 The Fifteenth district was represented in the senate by W F Pettit, of Steele county, and in the house of representatives by Amos Coggswell, and G. W Greene, of Steele county, and George T. White and Jesse I Stewart, of Waseca county.

In 1860 the counties of Steele, Waseca, and Freeborn were set off as the Sixteenth senatorial district This district was represented in the third legislature by Senator George Watson, of Freeborn county, and Representatives J. E Child, of Waseca county, and W F Pettit, of Steele county

The fourth legislature, assembling January 4, 1862, contained in the senate A B. Webber, of Freeborn county, and in the house

H C Magoon, of Steele county, and P C Bailey, of Waseca county

The fifth legislature opened January 6, and adjourned March 6, 1863. Senator M A Daily of Steele county, and Representatives Asa Walker, of Freeborn county, and Philo Woodruff, of Waseca county, represented the Sixteenth district

Senator F. J Stevens, of Steele county, and Representatives Philo Woodruff, of Waseca county; and J. L. Gibbs, of Freeborn county, represented the Sixteenth district in the sixth legislature, which met January 5, 1864

The seventh legislature came together January 3, 1865 This district was represented by Senator B A Lowell, of Waseca county, and Representatives J. L. Gibbs, of Freeborn county, and J. B Crooker, of Steele county.

The eighth legislature opened its sessions January 2, 1866 This district was represented by Senator B A. Lowell, of Waseca county, and Representatives J B Crooker, of Steele county, and Augustus Armstrong, of Freeborn county

On January 8, 1867, the opening of the ninth legislature this district was represented by Senator Augustus Armstrong, of Freeborn county, and Representatives William Brisbane, of Waseca county, W H Twiford, of Steele county, and J. E Smith, of Freeborn county.

The tenth legislature convened January 7 1868 and adjourned March 6 The Sixteenth district was represented by Senator Augustus Armstrong, of Freeborn county, and Representatives William R Kinyon, of Steele county, J. E Smith, of Freeborn county, and George A La Dow, of Waseca county.

In the eleventh legislature, J B Crooker, of Steele county, was senator, and Augustus Armstrong, of Freeborn county, E Easton, of Steele county, and Warren Smith of Waseca county, were representatives from the Sixteenth district.

The twelfth legislature met the first time on the 4th day of January, 1870 J B. Crooker, of Steele county, was in the senate, and Major W. C Young, of Waseca county, H. W. Ruliffson, of Steele county, and Dr A C. Wedge, of Freeborn county, were in the house

The next year Major W. C. Young, of this county, was elected to the senate, and Dr A. C Wedge, of Freeborn county, F B.

RESIDENCE OF JNO. S. ABELL, SEC. 11, OTISCO TP., WASECA CO., MINN.

Davis, of Steele county, and William Brisbane, of Waseca county, were chosen as representatives from the Sixteenth district to the thirteenth legislature.

Under the apportionment act of 1871, Waseca county was made a senatorial district by itself and was entitled to a senator and two representatives In the fall of 1871, James E Child was elected to the senate, and Kelsey Curtis, of Alma City, and John Thompson, of New Richland, were elected to the house

In the fall of 1872, W G. Ward, of Waseca, was elected to the senate; John Thompson, of New Richland, and J L Saufferer, of Blooming Grove, were elected to the house

The sixteenth legislature convened January 6, 1874. W G. Ward held over, and L D Smith, of Alton, and James E Child, of Waseca, were in the house

In the fall of 1874, Hon Peter McGovern, of Waseca, was elected to the senate, Morris H Lamb, of Alton, and Joseph Minges, of Otisco, were chosen to represent this county in the house

At the legislative session of 1876, Mr McGovern still represented Waseca county in the senate, and Robert Earl, of Freedom, and Kelsey Curtis, of Alma City, represented the county in the house

In 1877, Hon. P C Bailey, of Waseca, was our senator, and Fenton Keenan and Anthony Sampson, of New Richland, were our representatives.

At the twentieth session of the legislature, which assembled January 8, 1878. P. C. Bailey was still senator from this county, and J O Chandler, of Janesville, and Fenton Keenan, of New Richland, represented the county in the house.

In the fall of 1878, S B Williams, of Waseca, was elected to the senate by the prohibition party, and John Thompson, of New Richland, and John S. Abell, of Otisco, were elected to the house

In the fall of 1880, R L McCormick, of Waseca, was elected to the senate, and Christoph Wagner, of New Richland, and D J Dodge, of Janesville, were elected representatives It was in the session of the legislature of 1881 that the old Minnesota state railroad bonds were resurrected and settled

At the fall election of 1882, Dr. R O. Craig, of Janesville, was chosen senator, and J C White, of Waseca, was elected to the house. Under the apportionment act of 1881, Waseca county was entitled to one senator and only one representative.

In the twenty-fourth legislative session, Dr. R. O. Craig was still in the senate, and M D L Collester, then a prominent attorney of Waseca was our representative in the house

In the fall of 1886, W G Ward was again chosen to the senate, and M W. Ryan, of Byron, was elected to the house.

In the twenty-sixth legislature, Mr. Ward was our senator, and Otto Hanson, of Otiseo, represented us in the house

In the fall of 1890, R O Craig, of Janesville, was again chosen to the senate and M H Helms, of Waseca, was chosen representative

In the twenty-eighth legislature, which assembled January 3, 1893, and adjourned April 18, R O. Craig continued to represent the county in the senate, and Henry M. Buck, of Wilton, was our representative in the house

At the fall election of 1894, E B Collester, of Waseca, was elected to the senate, and Henry M Buck, of Wilton, to the house.

Mr Collester continued to represent this county in the legislative session of 1897, and John Wilkinson, of Freedom, was our representative in the house

There was a new apportionment by the legislature of 1897, and the number of this senatorial district was changed from eleven to ten.

In the fall of 1898, Peter McGovern, of Waseca, was elected senator, and John Wilkinson, of Freedom, was chosen representative

Senator McGovern continued to represent us during the session of 1901, and G E Brubaker, of Waseca, was our representative in the house

In the fall of 1902, E B Collester was again elected to the senate, and A J Lohren, of Waseca, was elected to represent the county in the house.

Senator Collester continues to represent this county in the senate of 1905, and William H. Meyers, of St. Mary, is our representative in the house

Biennial sessions of the legislature began in 1881.

COUNTY AUDITOR.

The office of county auditor was not created in this state until

1859. The first to occupy this office in Waseca county was Spencer J. Willis, who entered upon his duties January 1, 1860, and held the position for three years Colonel John C Ide, of Wilton, was his successor, being appointed such in January, 1863 upon the resignation of Mr Willis Colonel Ide held this office until the fall of 1866, when he died suddenly of heart disease. Captain C C Comee then of Vivian, was appointed by the county commissioners to fill the vacancy for the unexpired term. At the election following in November, 1866, he was elected to the office and was re-elected biennially, holding the office until 1870, when he resigned Captain Comee was succeeded by Hon. Warren Smith, who was appointed to fill the vacancy caused by Mr Comee's resignation At the fall election of 1870, Edgar Cronkhite, Esq, of Freedom, was elected auditor, and entered upon the duties of the office March 1, 1871 He was re-elected in 1873, 1875, 1877, and 1879, thus holding the office for ten years most acceptably to the people of the county Mr C E Crane, of Freedom, was the next to fill the office of auditor, being elected in the fall of 1880 He was re-elected in the fall of 1882, and thus served the people of the county for four years. He was followed in the office by Mr S Swenson, of Waseca, who was elected November 4, 1884, and re-elected in the falls of 1886 and 1888, thus holding the position for six years Mr A J Lohren, of Waseca, was elected auditor in 1890, and again in 1892 and 1894 He was succeeded by P J McLoone, of Waseca, who held the office from January 1, 1897, to January 1, 1901 C H Bailer, the present auditor, was elected to this office in 1900, 1902, and 1904 At the last election Mr Bailer had no opponent

REGISTER OF DEEDS

At the time of the organization of the county of Waseca, Governor Gorman appointed Mr Tarrant Putnam register of deeds He entered upon his duties in March, 1857, and held the office until the election in June following, when he was succeeded by Mr. J W Crawford, then of Janesville, who had been elected to the position At the general election in the fall of 1857, Major E A Rice, then of Wilton, was elected to this office, and held the position for two years At the fall election of 1860, Mr. Tarrant Putnam, of the same place, was elected to succeed Major

Rice. In the fall of 1862, Mr Putnam was re-elected, thus holding the office four years in all Mr. H P Norton, then of Wilton, now of Waseca, was elected to succeed Mr Putnam in the fall of 1863, and held the office for two years The next incumbent of this office was Mr Hiram A Mosher, an ex-soldier, who had lost an arm in the service He was elected in 1865, and re-elected term after term, holding the office until January 1, 1880 Then he gave way to his successor, Mr Charles San Galli, of Waseca, who was elected register of deeds in 1879 Mr San Galli served in all four years, when Mr H A Mosher was again elected to this office in the fall of 1883, and served until November 13, 1884, when he suddenly died of heart disease On the death of Mr Mosher, the county board appointed Mr A F Kruger, of Janesville to fill the vacancy In the fall of 1886 Mr Kruger was elected to the office and held the position for four years. John M Wollschlaeger, of Waseca, was elected to succeed Mr. Kruger in the fall of 1890 He has been re-elected each succeeding two years by increased majorities and is our present register of deeds

TREASURER

The first man to hold the position of treasurer in Waseca county was Mr W S Baker, of Otisco, who was appointed to that position at the first meeting of the board of county commissioners, which was held on the 16th of March, 1857 His duties were not arduous, as there was no money in the treasury He held the office until the close of the year, when Jesse I Stewart who was elected in the fall of 1857, succeeded him Mr Stewart held the office for two years, when he was succeeded by Mr J. S Rice, then of New Richland, who held the office for two years In the fall of 1861 Hon George T. White (afterwards Captain White), then of St Mary, was elected to succeed Mr Rice as county treasurer Although he enlisted in the month of August in 1862, he continued to hold the office by deputy during the term for which he had been elected Hon. P. C Bailey, of Wilton, was elected in 1863 to succeed Mr White Mr. Bailey held the office for two years, when he was succeeded by Mr George R Buckman then of St Mary, who held the office by re-election until January 1, 1874 At the election of 1871, the official returns showed that

Dr. R O Craig, of Janesville, received a majority of three votes, but on contesting the matter the court decided that Mr. Buckman was duly elected to the office of treasurer Mr. Buckman was succeeded in 1874 by Hon. Warren Smith, of Waseca, who held the office by re-election for six years In 1879, Charles McKenna was elected to succeed Mr Smith He was re-elected in 1881 and again in 1883 and 1885 He held the office until the month of September, 1888, when he was found to be a defaulter in the sum of $6,694 It is safe to say that Mr. McKenna, during his residence in Waseca county, did more to sow the seeds of bribery and corruption than any other politician that ever flourished here The Democratic county convention, which met on the 22d of September, 1888, broke up in a row, one faction claiming the nomination of H C Chase, of Janesville, and the other claiming the nomination of Charles McKenna Immediately after the convention, and clandestinely, McKenna disposed of all his property, and on the following Tuesday, under pretense of taking his wife to Faribault on a visit, he made his escape to Canada As before stated, it was discovered that he was short of county funds $6,694, which his bondsmen were required to make good H. C Chase, of Janesville, was appointed to the vacancy, and Mr Emil Dieudonne was elected in the fall to succeed Mr McKenna. Mr. Dieudonne held the office for one term and Mr August C Krassin was elected in the fall of 1900 to take his place Mr. Krassin held the office until August of 1891, when he died Mr Emil Dieudonne was appointed to fill out the term In the fall of 1892, Captain Walter Child was elected treasurer and held the office for four years. He was succeeded by W. H Roesler, of Waseca, who also filled the office for four years. In the fall of 1900, Mr. Joseph T. Dunn, of Waseca, was elected treasurer His death occurring April 18, 1901, Hon. D J. Dodge, of Janesville, was appointed by the county commissioners to fill out Mr Dunn's unexpired term Mr C A. Wagner, of New Richland, was the next to fill the position, and Fred W. Roesler, of Waseca, was chosen at the election in 1904, and entered upon the duties of the office January 1, 1905

CLERK OF DISTRICT COURT.

The first district court held in Waseca county was under our territorial form of government in 1857, and Thomas L. Page held the office by appointment. He soon resigned the office, and H P Norton, now of Waseca, was appointed to fill out his term At the fall election of 1857, Mr. Norton was elected to the office for the term of four years. In the fall of 1861, H P. West, then of Wilton, was chosen to the office and held the position for a term of four years Mr. N E Strong, then of the same town, was elected in 1863, and held the office from January 1, 1864, to January 1, 1868 S J Willis was elected in the fall of 1867, and held the office from January 1, 1868, to January 1, 1872. He was followed by James B. Hayden, of Alton, who held the plaee by re-election from Jan 1, 1872, to Jan 1, 1880 M B Keeley, of Waseca, was chosen in the fall of 1879 to succeed Mr Hayden Mr Keeley held the office by re-election until Jan 1, 1892, when he was succeeded by John M Byron, then of St Mary, who held the office until Jan 1, 1897 At the fall election of 1896 Henry Reynolds was elected to the position, and was re-elected in 1900 and in 1904 For a time Mr Reynolds was suspended from office by Governor John A Johnson for having embezzled jury fees paid into court for several years, but was reinstated as elsewhere detailed in this work

SHERIFF.

The first sheriff of Waseca county was Nathaniel Garland, who was appointed to that office by the governor of the territory at the time of the organization of the county by legislative act He was then elected to succeed himself at the special election held in June, 1857 He filled the office until the close of the year 1859 At the fall election in 1859, D L Whipple was elected to succeed him Mr Whipple was re-elected in 1861 and 1863 Captain E. M Broughton, then of Okaman, was elected in the fall of 1865 and served from Jan 1, 1866, to Jan 1, 1868. Mr Broughton was succeeded by his brother-in-law, Seth W Long, who held the office for ten conseeutive years. Matthew Keeley, of St Mary, was elected in the fall of 1877 to the office of sheriff which he held for four years Hugh Wilson, of Waseca was the next incumbent of the office and held the position from Jan. 1, 1882 to Jan 1, 1886 In the fall of 1885, August C Krassin, of Waseca, was chosen to the office of sheriff He was re-elected in 1888, and held the position until January, 1891 Henry Reynolds, of Otisco, followed Mr. Krassin in office, and remained in it until Jan. 1, 1895. Mr Reynolds' successor was Mr. George H Goodspeed, who held the office for four years Frank Collins, of Waseca, was chosen sheriff in 1898 and he has held the office continuously since, being our present sheriff.

JUDGE OF PROBATE

Job A. Canfield, of Otisco, was the first judge of probate in Waseca county and was elected to that position in 1857 He continued in this office until 1860, when H D. Baldwin, Esq , was elected in 1859 to follow him Mr Baldwin held the office for four years In the fall of 1863, P Brink Enos, Esq , of Wilton, was elected to the position, which he held until the close of 1865 James E. Child, then of Wilton, was chosen to the office, which he held from Jan 1, 1866, to Jan 1, 1868 He was succeeded by Hon H D Baldwin, then of Wilton, who held the office until Jan. 1, 1870, when Hon J A Canfield, of Otisco, was again elected to the office Mr Canfield then held the office for eight years Mr Caleb Hallack, of Janesville, was then elected to the position, which he held from Jan 1, 1878, to Jan 1, 1880 H C Woodbury, then of Wilton, followed Mr Hallack and held the position one term. S. D. Crump, of Alton, succeeded to the office Jan 1, 1882, and served in this capacity until Jan 1, 1886 Following Mr Crump, Major W C Young, of Waseca, took up the duties of this office and executed them until his sudden death, May 9, 1889 He was followed by E B Collester, Esq , who was appointed to fill out the unexpired term In 1890, Mr Collester was elected to this office, and again elected in 1892 In the fall of 1894, George A Wilson, of Janesville, was elected to the position and has since executed its duties continuously up to the present time, having no opponent in the election of 1904

COUNTY ATTORNEY

John Bradish, Esq., of Janesville, had the honor of being the first county attorney of Waseca county He received the magnificent salary of $100 a year He held the office one year only, when he gave way to M S (Squire) Green, of Empire, who was elected to that position in the fall of 1857 James E Child, then of Wilton, was chosen to follow Mr Green in the office in 1859, holding the position for one year. H. D. Baldwin, then of Empire, was elected county attorney in the fall of 1860, and performed its duties until Jan 1, 1865 James E Child was then again chosen to the office and held it for two years. Major W. T Kittredge, then of Wilton, was next elected county attorney. He entered upon his duties Jan. 1, 1868, and continued in office two years. B. S Lewis, Esq, of Waseca, was next chosen to this office and entered upon its execution in 1870, holding this position four years. Peter McGovern, Esq., of Waseca, next occupied this office, holding it for two years, when he was succeeded by M. D L Collester, Esq, of Waseca, who held the office until the close of 1881 W R Kinder, of Waseca, then served as county attorney for two years. Mr. P. McGovern then held the office again until the close of 1887 W D Abbott, Esq., of Waseca, was chosen in the fall of 1887, and served a term of two years The next incumbent was Mr F B Andrews, of New Richland In the fall of 1892 Mr McGovern was again chosen county attorney for one term. He was succeeded by Mr L. D Rogers, of Janesville, who served one term, when Mr McGovern was again chosen. In 1898, Mr John Moonan was selected to succeed Mr McGovern, and in 1900 Mr Moonan was again elected to the office. Mr. F B Andrews, the present county attorney, was chosen in 1902 and again in 1904.

COUNTY SURVEYOR

The first surveyor of Waseca county was H W Peck, of Empire, who was appointed March 16, 1857 He held the office about a year, when he removed to Ohio He was succeeded by Eugene A Smith, of Wilton, a brother of Orson L Smith, our present surveyor He held the office until 1862, when George P Johnson, of St Mary, was elected to the office and performed its duties from Jan. 1, 1862, to Jan 1, 1864 H G Mosher, of Otisco, then occupied the office for two years, when he was followed by O. S Canfield, of Freedom, who held the office two years In the fall of 1867, Mr C E. Crane, of Freedom, was chosen surveyor and held the office continuously until the first of January, 1881, when he was succeeded by Orson L Smith, who still holds the position, this being his thirteenth term

COURT COMMISSIONER.

The following gentlemen have held the office of court commissioner in this county since its organization, commencing with 1860, in the order named: W. T Kittredge, Job A. Canfield, James E Child, J B Smith, C G. Park, Frank A Newell, B. A. Lowell, G R Buckman, E. P. Latham, and N M. Nelson, the present incumbent.

COUNTY CORONER.

The early records, if any were made, regarding county coroner, are very deficient. The names of those remembered and of record are given in the order of time in which they held the office: Nathaniel Wood, of Woodville, 1860-1-2-3, W S Baker, then of Otisco, 1864-5, Dr M S Gove, then of Wilton, 1866-7-8-9-'70-1, Dr. L D. McIntosh, of Waseca, 1872-3-4-5, Dr J. C McMahon, 1876-7-8-9, Dr D S Cummings, 1880-1, Dr R. O Craig, of Janesville, 1882-3, Dr H J Young, of Waseca, 1884-5, Dr M V. Hunt, then of Waseca, 1886-7, Dr H J Young, 1888-9; Dr L. P Leonard, dentist, of Waseca, 1890-1-2-3-4; Dr W L Sterns, of Waseca, 1895-6; Dr M J Taylor, of Janesville, 1897-8, Dr. E J Batchelder, of New Richland, 1899-1900; Dr. H. G. Blanchard, of Waseca, 1901-2-3-4-5

SUPERINTENDENT OF SCHOOLS

This, one of the most important offices in the county, was in early days the most poorly paid Prior to 1864, school superintendents were appointed by commissioner districts, and at one time by townships; and oftentimes the superintendent was totally incompetent But the legislature of 1863 created the office of county superintendent to be appointed by the county commissioners The first to be appointed in this county was Rev. Elijah S Smith, who served at a salary of $100 a year until 1867 James E. Child was then chosen at a salary of $200 a year. Think of such an overwhelming salary for visiting sixty schools twice a year and holding two public examinations in three of the most public places in the county each year! Mr Jesse Poland, of Vivian, then served one year. Rev S T Catlin next accepted the position in 1869 at a salary of $300. Dr R O. Craig was appointed in 1870. In 1871, Dr M S Gove was elected by the people, but declined to serve, and the board of county commissioners appointed H G Mosher, one of their own number, to that office He gave such entire satisfaction that he was elected and re-elected, serving until 1880. In the fall of 1879, Dr M. V Hunt was elected and served in a way for two years. In the fall of 1881, Dr D S Cummings was elected and served four years He was followed by J B Dye, who was elected to the position in the fall of 1886 He held the office two terms. Hon John S Abell was chosen in the fall of 1890, and again in the fall of 1892, serving with credit to himself and the schools He was succeeded by Mr C W Wagner, who was elected in the fall of 1894 and again in the fall of 1896. He was an efficient officer Frank J Remund succeeded him for one term, having been elected in the fall of 1898 Mr Remund was succeeded by L J Larson, who was elected in 1900 and again in 1902. In the fall of 1904 Mr Herman A Panzram, the present active and industrious incumbent, was elected and entered upon his duties Jan 1, 1905

CHAPTER LXXVIII.

TOWNS AND TOWNSHIP ORGANIZATIONS—NEW RICHLAND TOWNSHIP AND VILLAGE, TOWNSHIP OF BYRON, VIVIAN AND ITS EARLY SETTLEMENT, OTISCO, WILTON AND ITS VILLAGE, FREEDOM, ALMA CITY, WOODVILLE, ST MARY, ALTON, BLOOMING GROVE, IOSCO AND "EMPIRE," JANESVILLE, OKAMAN, AND VILLAGE OF "EAST JANESVILLE" AND EARLY SETTLEMENTS.

NEW RICHLAND.

This is the southeast corner township of the county, at the headwaters of the Le Sueur river The township was originally all prairie except a narrow skirt of trees along the river The soil is very rich and productive The first settlement in the township was made in 1856 by a colony, as detailed by Hon A Sampson Among the early settlers the following are noted Knute Christensen, Nels Christensen, K O Rotegard, H O Sunde, Anthony Sampson, H H Sunde, Ole K Hagan, W. Anderson, Christian Knudson, and E O Strenge were the first to settle in the township, and they located about June 10, 1856 Of the settlers of 1858, the following are remembered Ole Hogaas, who died in 1885, John Benson, born in Norway in 1833, a prominent and well-to-do farmer; Nels Tyrholm, now of the village, Torkel Lund and Ole H Sunde, H J Hanson, now county commissioner, David Skinner, Hon John Thompson, who recently died at Albert Lea, Eric Christianson, A N Berg, A. J. Stensvad, and Ole Johnson Andrew Berg is one of the wealthy farmers of the town He is father of fourteen children. J H Wightman, now a resident of New Richland, was born in the state of New York Feb. 3, 1822, he settled in Byron in July

1857 went to Wilton and engaged in the hardware business with Hon P C Bailey in 1864 After two years he sold to G W Watkins, and opened a general store at Wilton At the building of New Richland, he moved his stock to that place and continued in trade till 1885-6, when he sold to A. J. Newgard and retired to his farm on section 16, where he still resides. Mr E E Verplank, elsewhere noticed in this work, settled in this town in the "sixties" He married Miss Sophia Hanson Oct 22, 1864. Knute O Hagan, Torkel Lund, E C Sybilrud, and Rev O A. Mellby settled early in this township.

RICHLAND'S "FIRST" ITEMS

Mrs Even Tostensen, daughter of O K Hagan, was the first child born in the township Samuel S Sampson was the first person to die He departed this life Aug 22, 1861 The first school meeting was held at the house of Nels Tyrholm. The officers elected were Anthony Sampson, director, John Larson, clerk; and T. Tidmanson, treasurer. The first church organization was in 1861 The first school house was built of logs in 1862, on land donated by Mr A Sampson, the first teacher was a Miss Northrup The Norwegian Lutheran church on section 11 was built in 1875-6 and cost about $5,000 The first place of worship was built of logs in 1862, and Rev B Muse, of Goodhue county, was the first minister. The Lutheran society was first organized in 1858, by Rev Laurs Larson, a home missionary at the residence of Ole Arneson The first town meeting was held at the residence of John Larson. Hon John Thompson was chairman J S Rice was chosen moderator and S W. Franklin clerk The first township officers elected were as follows. Supervisors, John Thompson (chairman), J S Rice, and David Skinner, assessor, A Sampson, treasurer, Nels Christianson, justices of the peace, J S Rice and John Larson, constables, George W Legg and Andrew Johnson, overseer of the poor Ole Johnson Mr John Larson was not only one of the first justices of the peace, but was also the first postmaster. The thriving village of New Richland, situated upon section 17, was surveyed and platted in August, 1877, by Henry T Wells. There have been four additions to the plat since, one by Charles Zieger, one by Mr Wells, one by Frank McClane, and one by Jane McClane The village grew by leaps and bounds the first two years of its existence Buildings were erected by a Mr Buncho, by Thomas Lynch, J H Wightman, A. J Stensvad, Henry Jaehning, Hugh Wilson, Halvor K Stearns, Murphy & Johnson, C H Brossard, Clark & Swann, Nels Tyrholm & Son, Hon Fenton Keenan, Joseph Smith & Co, E E Ellifson, Hunt Bros., Fred Bettner, Torgerson & Johnson, Newgard & Zieger, O P Olson, T Thompson, P. A Holt, O. S Bokke, N J Robbins, who built the Washburn hotel, Ole Johnson Moe, who built the Commercial house, and Charles Brunnell, who built the American house The Model Roller Mill, now owned by Everett, Augenbaugh & Co, was built in the fall of 1879 by Messrs Dunwoody & Corson at a cost of about $40,000 The plant was bought by the Messrs Everett, Augenbaugh & Co some years since and has been thoroughly repaired and remodeled so that it is an up-to-date plant and is run in connection with the "Eaco" Mills at Waseca The mill does most excellent work, and furnishes a live market for all the good wheat raised in the surrounding country

The Congregationalists erected the first church building in the fall of 1882 at a cost of about $1,500. Rev Wilbur Fisk was the clergyman who then served the people and rustled for the church

The Norwegian Lutheran church was constructed in the summer of 1883 at a cost of about $2,500.

A school building was erected in the north part of town in 1878 at a cost of $1,200 Since that time a new site has been selected south of the business portion of the town, and New Richland now has one of the finest school buildings and school house sites in the state.

Strangers Refuge Lodge No 74 of the Independent Order of Odd Fellows was organized Jan 4, 1880, with the following officers C G Cheesebro, N. G.; E Steinhaus, V. G; F G Schneider, S, Henry Jaehning, treasurer, C Hooper, R S. N G, Charles Brossard, L S N G, W Smith, Jr., W; Charles Brunell, C, and W Luff, I G.

Lincoln Post No 26, G. A R, was organized in 1882 Its first officers were Chris Wagner, P. C, B F Weed, S V C, O H Sutlief, J V C, Fenton Keenan, O D, E E Verplank, A, H J Hanson, Q M, and P. A Holt, O G

New Richland has a good town hall, a beautiful public park, a telephone system owned by Mr Milo Hodgkins, and well graded streets It is surrounded by an industrious, frugal, well-to-do class of farmers.

BYRON TOWNSHIP.

Originally, in 1857, Byron was a part of the Otisco precinct, and so remained until the fall of 1858, when it was organized as a separate township. The early records of the township have been lost, but the oldest settlers claim that the first supervisors of the town were J H Wightman, chairman, Daniel C Davis and Christie McGrath, David Beavins town clerk, and C. S. Weed, assessor

Jeremy Davis and family were the first white settlers in the township Jeremy built the first log cabin in the summer of 1855 It was destroyed by fire in the spring of 1857, and the family was left houseless for a time Mr Davis died in Byron, Sept. 13, 1863.

Daniel C Davis, son of Jeremy, born May 13, 1834, came with his father and settled at the same time, in 1855. July 18, 1861, he was united in marriage with Miss Elizabeth Parvin.

Christie McGrath, a native of Ireland, settled in Byron in 1856, and still resides on his farm He saw many hardships in the pioneer days He has been an industrious worker all his life.

William and David Beavins also settled in this township in 1856. David was a character in his way He was a very kind hearted man and very jovial He was long on profuse promises, but sometimes short on performances. One time he promised Alex Johnston a large number of votes in Byron, upon the strength of which he got many a drink After election Alex chided him for not getting a single vote, and Dave, with a great appearance of sincere sorrow, declared that he was mistaken in the day and didn't get to the polls, and that that was the reason why Alex was short on votes. It was claimed by others that Alex's opponent saw David last on election morning William served in the Union army and died a few years after his return home

Isaac Ling settled in Byron in 1856 He served as a soldier in Company F, Tenth Minnesota infantry, dying at Dauphin Island, March 10, 1865 Mrs. Ling died here the same year, leaving a number of small children. C. S Weed and family also settled in Byron in 1856

J H Wightman, now of New Richland, Richard Ayers (deceased), late of Janesville, William Philbrook, who died in 1865; Jacob W Pierce, still a resident of the town, moved to Byron in 1857

Omer H Sutlief, Garret Hope, and a number of other men and their families, came to this town prior to 1860

Garret Hope, born in county of West Mayo, Ireland, Aug. 15, 1840, came to America in 1852, and lived for a time in Connecticut, he came West to Beloit, Wis., in 1855, and to Byron in 1858. Some years ago he sold his farm in Byron and removed to California

Benaiah Parvin came here in 1860, and after several years' residence, emigrated to Arkansas, where he died soon after

Calista J. Campbell, born in Madison county, N. Y, came West with her parents to Rock county, Wis, as early as 1848 Dec 11, 1849, she married Edwin A Crump. Eight years after they moved to Winneshiek county, Iowa, and three years later came to Byron Some time afterward they spent a few years in the village of Wilton—Mr. Crump running a wagon shop and Mrs. Crump a millinery store Mr. Crump was consumptive, and died Jan 20, 1878 They were the parents of five children—three sons and two daughters. Mrs Crump bravely carried on the farm in Byron, with the assistance of her children until 1880, Feb. 28, when she married Mr John N Wilson, who was born in Canada Sept 1, 1833 In 1854 he came to Wisconsin, later he went to Colorado, where he enlisted in Company G, First Colorado regiment, and served until the close of the rebellion Mr. and Mrs Wilson now have a cozy home in New Richland village

Peter Bumgerten, born in Prussia, June 27, 1832, came to America in 1857, first living in Wisconsin. He remained there until 1869, when he came to St Mary in this county. Six years after he removed to Byron The last few years of his life he resided in New Richland, and died there in the spring of 1905

Lawrence Concanon, born in Ireland, July 20, 1827, landed at New Orleans in 1851, he followed up the river to Illinois, where he lived until 1877, when he came to St Mary After spending three years in St. Mary, he settled on section 19, in Byron, where he still resides

Zalmon M. Partridge, born Jan 15, 1834, in Berkshire county,

Mass, came to Minnesota in 1857, and lived in Dakota county, where he worked at carpentering and farming. Three years later he went to Virginia where he worked as a brick molder In August, 1861, he enlisted in Company H, Fourth Loyal Virginia infantry, and served a little over three years Nov 2, 1864, he married Narcissus Samples, of West Virginia In 1866 he returned to Minnesota with his family, again going to Dakota county In 1870 he came to Byron, where he has since resided and made a good home Mr and Mrs. Partridge have been the parents of four sons and one daughter.

Mrs. Margaret Dwyer, one of the early settlers of Byron, nearly perished in the winter of 1864 She started to visit a neighbor, about four miles distant, was caught in a blinding snow storm, became bewildered on the prairie, and wandered around from Wednesday until Friday afternoon toward evening, when she arrived at her sister's house. She was so badly frozen and so much exhausted that she could scarcely move without assistance Her suffering was intense She lost half of each of her feet and was for a long time unable to walk.

Byron, in early days, was treeless but now it abounds in fine groves of cultivated timber, which give the landscape a very attractive appearance. The township, as a whole, is better adapted to stock raising and dairying than to wheat culture

VIVIAN

This is the southwest township of the county and was known in early days as the "Cobb river country" The land in this township is more nearly level than that of any other town in the county. The "Big Cobb river," running westerly through the southern portion of the town, and the "Cobbee," in the northern portion, furnish the principal means of surface drainage The soil is a dark, alluvial loam, on a heavy clay subsoil, and very rich and productive

E S Woodruff was the first white man to reside in Vivian. He had an Indian woman for his wife He formerly lived near Green Bay, Wis, among the Indians, and afterwards lived in Iowa He settled on section 27, in this town, in the summer of 1856 and lived there until the spring of 1865, when he died He was one of the early mail carriers of that section Later, the same year, two bachelors, B F Hanes and E. A Clark, came here Clark afterwards married and removed to Wisconsin in 1858 Hanes lived on his claim until his death, which occurred in 1872 James B Hill, a sketch of whose life is given elsewhere, moved here with his family July 2, 1857 S. L. Daggett soon after moved near Mr Hill's place He afterwards went to Blue Earth and died there in 1863 Four brothers named Shannahan came here in 1857, but soon after left for the gold mines in Colorado Joseph Thurston and family and W H Harmon and family moved to this township in 1857 Ichabod West and his two sons, Ammi and John F, with their families, and John Dwyer and John Dineen and their families, began their homes in this town in 1858 Thomas Ryan, deceased, settled on section 15 in 1858 John A Wheeler, one of the early settlers in St Mary, took a claim on section 4, in this town in 1858 He was a windmill inventor and manufacturer He at one time built a flouring mill, with windmill power, at Freeborn Lake He was quite a genius He was a Union soldier in the War of the Rebellion His death occurred about 1876 Ole Johnson and his family came from Norway in 1855, lived in Waupun, Wis, for three years, and came to Vivian in 1858 Ole was born Jan. 4, 1824, and his wife, Betsy Nelson, Oct 3, 1826 They were married Feb. 8, 1852 He enlisted in Company F, Tenth Minnesota Volunteer infantry, and served till the close of the war. Mark Moore, Montraville Sias, and three Welshmen (brothers)—Owen M David, and Samuel Jones—also came here in 1858

Vivian was organized as a separate township under an order of the county commissioners dated April 5, 1858 According to tradition—the official records being lost—the first town meeting was held at the house of J B Hill. The first town board consisted of J B. Hill, E S. Woodruff and S. L Daggett—Hill being chairman. E A Clark was town clerk The names of the other town officers are entirely forgotten

The first death recorded in the township was that of a man named Sweeney, who perished near his home in November, 1857 He had been to St Mary, and on his return was caught in a snow storm. Darkness coming on, he undoubtedly became bewildered on the prairie and froze to death Many of our pioneers were thinly clad, and it is not surprising that a man, lost upon the prairie in a blinding snow storm, should perish

The population of the township has nearly all changed since 1860 Very few indeed of the earlier settlers remain The Ryan family and the Ole Johnson family are the only ones remembered to have settled in the township prior to that date The town is now well peopled by hardy, frugal, industrious farmers who are making it one of the richest agricultural townships in the county. Like Byron, it is well adapted to the production of grass, and to the raising of cattle and hogs

As before stated, the early records of the town were destroyed. Mr Edward Thompson, present town clerk, reports the records of the first ten years missing The records of 1868 are the first to be found, and they show the town supervisors of that year to have been as follows J B Hill, chairman, S S Comee, and M Sias

OTISCO

This is one of the wealthiest and most densely populated townships in the county An account of the first settlement of this township, and its first settlers, is given in the fore part of this book The name Otisco, at first, embraced all of Vivian, Byron, New Richland, the south one-third of Wilton and the south one-third of what is now Otisco This continued for a year, when, on April 5 1858 the county commissioners organized the townships of the county in accordance with the government survey The government township 106, of range 22 was designated as Otisco Several villages have been born and put to rest on the soil of Otisco, and only one remains Two pioneer speculators, Watters & Chamberlain, came in 1856, bought the claims of George and William Robbins on the east side of the Le Sueur river, opposite the Wilton village site, and there laid out a village which they called Waterlynn They erected a store and a hotel They did quite a business at their store, but the hotel did not flourish The latter building, which was part logs and part frame, went up in smoke one night in 1858 It was occupied at the time by Dr William Murphy and family—J F Murphy, now of the Waseca Herald, being the eldest son of the family That was about the last of that village and the site now makes a very good farm

The "ancient village of Otisco" was laid out by Warren Bundy and S. S. Goodrich in July, 1857. It soon had a store, a post-office, a blacksmith shop, and a sawmill Dan and Gould Grover built the dam and the sawmill, and for a time the mill did good work The Grovers soon sold to Griggs & Obert. After a time Gould Grover again became owner, or manager, and was soon after killed in the mill by accident It then passed into the hands of Eno & Beatty, who turned out to be professional and practical horsethieves, and were caught stealing the horses of Orrin Pease. Soon after the arrest of Eno and Beatty, the mill dam went out and the village boom soon collapsed Goodrich owned the store and Mr Owen Salisbury was the first postmaster

Since the building of the M & St L railway the present Otisco station has been laid out and is quite a lively little burg with its store, postoffice, blacksmith shop, grain elevator, creamery, etc Its present business will no doubt remain permanently

It is not the intention of the writer to cumber the record with the names of transient persons or those who have come in later years unless they may have been connected in some way with public affairs, for the reason that space and expense forbid There are many such in Otisco Mention is made, however, of all the early settlers.

Silas Grover, an aged veteran of the War of 1812, settled in this town in 1856, and resided in the county till his death, April 12, 1870 H G Mosher settled here Oct. 10, 1856 Mr Mosher, wife and two children, and J S Abell, wife and two children lived the first winter in one cabin, 16x20 feet Mr Mosher and family removed to Kansas in the eighties Uriah Northrup, Sr., and his sons, Benjamin, Uriah, George and Thomas H, settled here at a very early day. The elder Mr Northrup died here and the sons removed to Rice county. Owen Salisbury, the first postmaster at the old village of Otisco, finally moved to Wabasha county, where he died J D. Andrews was one of those restless, energetic pioneers who are always on the move He moved to Otisco, July 3, 1858 He was a carpenter by trade He afterwards entered the drug business at Wilton, went to Duluth and opened a drug store, returned to this county and went into business at Janesville, afterwards removed to Madison, S D, where he died June 11, 1887

Moses Plummer, born at Sanborton, N H, Dec 23, 1817, married Miss Matilda S Cate, who was born at Meredith, N. H, Nov 11, 1824 They came to Minnesota in 1859, first residing in Clinton Falls, Steele county They then came to Otisco in 1860, and purchased a farm of one hundred and eighty acres. Mr Plummer was with a crowd of three hundred people in Meredith hall, in 1850, when the floor gave way, killing several and injuring many Mr Plummer then received injuries from which he never fully recovered For five years previous to his death, he was paralyzed and helpless He died Sept 20, 1883. He left surviving his widow and one daughter, Mrs B L Case They now reside in Owatonna

Roger B Wood, born June 1, 1842, in Ontario, Canada, worked westward until he reached Waseca in 1867, where he opened a wagon and blacksmith shop He remained in Waseca until 1871, when he moved to his present farm in Otisco, which contains three hundred and fifty-four acres He married Miss Parmelia Smith, a bright Western girl, Dec 15, 1869 She was born at Oak Grove, Dodge county, Wis, Feb 1, 1852, and came with her parents to Byron, in this county, in 1866 They have been the parents of six children, five of whom are living

Asa Robbins was an early settler in Otisco He was a native of New York State, born in 1811 February 5, 1838, he married Miss Hulda A Chapman, who was born Jan. 9, 1815, and died Dec 10, 1885

Gustaf Johnson was born in Sweden, Nov 25, 1831 On reaching the United States, he came directly to Otisco His wife's name was Johanna Johnson, and she was born in 1831, in the same country They have a pleasant farm home and six children.

James Irwin, born in Ireland in May 1828 came to America in 1849 He was a Union soldier in the War of the Rebellion He lived in Wisconsin after the close of the war, until 1870, when he came to Otisco and purchased a farm of one hundred and sixty acres He has five sons living.

The first judges of election at the organization of the town are said to have been Owen Salisbury H G Mosher and S S Griggs

WILTON

This was the first township in the county to be settled The first settlers were Asa G Sutlief and family, who pitched their tents on section 35, in the month of August, 1854 The next to

HON. CHAS. A. SMITH
C. N. NORTON
G. W. STRONG
R. D. GARLAND

reach here were S P and James E. Child, who arrived Feb 2, 1855 Chris Scott and family came about ten days later, in February. Others followed and before fall there were some ten families in the township. A precinct election was held in the fall of 1855 at the house of Chris Scott, on the farm now owned by Mr. John Carmody, Sr The first election precincts were formed regardless of town lines, and the township of Wilton, as it now exists, was not organized until the spring of 1858 The first town meeting was held at the house of Joseph Doty, May 11, 1858 P C Bailey was chairman and stated the object of the meeting Buel Welsh was chosen moderator, and Thomas L Paige, clerk. On motion of A. J. Woodbury, the township, like the village, was named Wilton. The following were the first township officers. town board, W W. Robinson, chairman, John Brand, and A J Woodbury, town clerk, Tarrant Putnam; assessor, L Curtis, justices of the peace, J. B Jackson and P. C Bailey; overseer of the poor, A. Miller; constables, Peter Van Dyke and L. Curtis.

The first birth was that of a child born to Mr. and Mrs Plummer in July, 1855 This family soon after removed to Wisconsin, being sick of the country The first death was that of a child of Mr and Mrs William Wells, in the summer of 1856 The first prairie broken was by Asa G Sutlief, in August, 1854. The first sawmill in the town and county was built by Colonel J. C. Ide Rev Mr Hicks, a Methodist clergyman, in 1856, held the first religious service in the township at the house of Caleb Northrup, on section 36 The first school house was erected by Mr. E B Stearns, in what is now the Carmody, or Brisbane, district, in 1858. It was a frame building standing on the bottom land, half a mile south of the present school house site The building was afterwards moved with ox teams over the hill to the present site—a move that caused much excitement at the time

The first Catholic Church built in Wilton stands at the southwestern corner of section 31, where some sixty families—over three hundred people—meet for worship

FREEDOM

The town of Freedom and the west tier of sections in the town of Wilton were held by the Winnebago Indians until 1863 After the removal of the Indians, the lands were sold to white men under sealed bids to the highest bidder, no bid being accepted at less than $2 50 per acre Settlers crowded into the town rapidly March 9, 1864, the people of the two towns of Alton and Freedom petitioned the county commissioners to have the new territory organized as a town, and the board granted the petition The order of the board provided that the electors should hold their first town meeting at the house of Stephen Robinson, situated at the place then known as Peddler's Grove, on the 5th day of April, 1864 At this meeting the voters decided that the name of the new town should be Freedom. It is said that F. D Seaman gave the casting vote making "Freedom" the name

The town early took front rank as one of the prettiest and most productive in the West Its people stand high morally and intellectually, and in wealth they rank with the most opulent of farming communities

Among those who setted at an early day in Freedom the following are noted

Henry Chase was born in 1842, in the Green Mountain state He enlisted in Company E, Ninth Vermont infantry, and was four months in Libby prison, having been captured at the first Winchester battle He was discharged in 1863, went to Freedom in 1864, and remained there until 1869, when he moved to Janesville, this county He is now a resident of Wisconsin, although still interested financially in Janesville.

Luke Chase is said to have been the first white settler in the township

Ed Steele and Steve Robinson moved to a grove of burr oaks on section 3, and, being traveling peddlers they gave the place the name Peddler's Grove

Delos P Young, a native of Massachusetts, born May 11, 1838, came from Wisconsin in 1864, and made his home in this town. He now resides in Mankato. F. D Seaman, now a resident of Alton, came in April, 1864 He is a native of New York, born Sept 8, 1843. He enlsted in Company G, First Wisconsin cavalry, in the fall of 1861, and served a year In the fall of 1864 he again enlisted, this time in Company A Second Minnesota infantry, and served until July, 1865 when he returned to Freedom Sept 23, 1868, he married Phoebe Chase, who was born Sept 24, 1849, in Orleans county, N Y

William Davidson, Sr, now nearly eighty-three years of age, and his two sons—William and J D—were early settlers and still remain here

Willet Tolles (deceased), Daniel Pierce, S C Brooks, Amos Waring, William Reid, Luther Ackerman, Simon Sackett, now of Janesville, John H. Fields, Harry Scoville and Ira Abell were among the settlers of 1864

John J. Wilkins, born in New Jersey, July 13, 1827, William Orcutt, since deceased, Darling Welch, afterwards a resident of Janesville, and later of Waseca, John L Graham, deceased, late of Janesville, Arthur Graham, born in New York Sept 12, 1845; Captain Robert Earl, and others settled here in 1865

Samuel S Rollins, born in New Hampshire, May 1, 1836, F. W Bromaghin, born in St Lawrence county, N Y, June 29, 1820 Hon John Wilkinson, born in Wisconsin, Feb. 28, 1846, John Davis, and C E. Graham were among the 1866 settlers

Sandford Hydorn, another St. Lawrence, N Y, man, born July 24, 1841, who served the Union from 1862 to 1865, settled here in 1868

The Congregational church of Freedom was organized in November, 1878, and Rev Robert S Armstrong was its first pastor.

ALMA CITY

It is generally conceded that Uncle Sam Larabee, now deceased, was the father of Alma City The village was surveyed and platted by S E Stebbins in 1865, for Uncle Sam, who at once put up a hotel, then and for a long time known as the "Larabee House" "Uncle Sam" and "Aunt Patty" were known far and wide Aunt Patty was thrown from a buggy and killed in 1885, and Uncle Sam died in 1900 at the advanced age of eighty-five years, of of heart disease, while eating supper He was with his daughter, Mrs Craig, at Blue Earth, at the time of his sudden death

The same fall Chase and Ames opened the first store. Mary Ann Johnson opened a store about the same time In the spring of 1866 A H. Davis and O P Smith each opened a store. Rineerson & Morton opened a blacksmith shop in 1865

Alma City has always been a thriving village and the center

of business for most of the people of Freedom and a portion of the people of Alton. It has a thriving school and a successful creamery

WOODVILLE

Township No 107 north, of range 22 west, was named after one of its earliest settlers (Mr. Eri G Wood) by resolution of the county commissioners, April 5, 1858 Long before any white man ever viewed the rich hunting grounds of this county the native Indians must have made the town of Woodville one of their principal villages There can be no doubt, in view of the Indian mounds and other relics which have been found upon the shores and in the vicinity of Watkins lake, that the Sioux Indians, for many generations, lived in large numbers in this township Geographically it held a commanding position for the red man From Clear lake he could, with his canoe, descend Crane creek to Straight river, thence to the Cannon river, and on to the Mississippi, or he could drag his light boat across the narrow strip of land that divides Clear lake from Gaiter lake, and there launch it for a journey down McDougall creek, thence down the Le Sueur river to the Blue Earth and the Minnesota rivers, and thus easily traverse vast sections of country abounding in fish and game Later residents may doubt this view of the primitive situation, on account of late dry seasons, but the older settlers of this region remember well when small boats were run and could be run as here stated.

The splendid forests which then existed in portions of Woodville, Blooming Grove, Deerfield, and Meriden, not only afforded comfortable shelter from the freezing blasts of winter, but they furnished plenty of fuel and material for Indian wigwams The woods abounded in game and the lakes were filled with the very choicest fish Barring the sometimes intense cold of winter, it was the ideal land of milk and honey for the native tribes It is no less a land of plenty for the white men that now possess it

The surface is beautifully diversified—gently undulating, as a rule—rich prairies interspersed with timber, lovely lakes, bordered with groves of heavy timber—the groves being adorned in spring with blossoming plum trees, cherry trees, thorn and crab apple trees, and other flowering shrubs and trees in great profusion Of the 23,040 acres of land in the township, over 2,000 are embraced in its lakes. The principal of these is Clear lake, which occupies portions of sections 8, 9, 16, and 17, and is a trifle over a mile and a half in length and nearly a mile wide

In addition to this beautiful body of water, there is Loon lake, a beautiful gem of water within the limits of the city of Waseca, half in section 7 and half in section 18 There is a wooded island in the center of the lake, which, in summer, with its dark green foliage, gives the lake a picturesque and very beautiful appearance, especially during the months of June and July With very little expense Loon lake could be made to rival in beauty and picturesqueness Lake Como, at St Paul, and many other noted places of resort May we not hope that in the near future it may be so improved as to be a "thing of beauty and a joy forever?"

The surface soil is a rich, black loam, resting upon a gray clay and gravel, mixed, which, in turn, rests upon a heavy, blue-clay subsoil, many feet in depth, and almost impervious to water The surface soil is as productive and lasting in quality as any in the known world. Experience has demonstrated that it is capable of withstanding extreme moisture and extreme drouth, for in the past fifty years there has never been a failure of crops At the time of the first settlement and for years thereafter, until pastured and fed down, the native grasses, blue joint and "crowfoot," grew to be from five to six feet in height, and were fully equal to cultivated grasses as food for animals

The first settler in Woodville was Mr A C Smith, deceased Mr Smith died Jan 29, 1892, and his worthy wife died June 29, 1894 O Powell, Eri G and Loren C. Wood, Henry Watkins, E K. Carlton, Jacob Myers, William Dunn, and Austin Vinton settled here in 1856 A part of this township was at first a portion of the precinct of Swavesey, which at that time embraced all of Blooming Grove, Iosco, Janesville, and the north halves of St. Mary and Woodville

March 16, 1857, the county commissioners divided Swavesey precinct,making the precinct of Empire out of the two west townships. They appointed for Swavesey, W H Young, of Woodville, and Lewis McKune, of Blooming Grove, as justices, and Loren Clark Wood, of Woodville, and S F Wyman, of Blooming Grove, as constables

At the fourteenth meeting of the county commissioners, held

at Wilton, April 5, 1858, Woodville was set off by metes and bounds, and J K Myers, William M. Green, and E G Wood were appointed judges of the first election

On the fly leaf of the first town record book, in the handwriting of Loren C Wood, is the following "Township 107 north, Range 22 west, was organized on the 11th day of May, A D 1858, and named Woodville."

The record continues:

"The town of Woodville held its first town meeting on the 11th day of May, 1858" (At the house of E G Wood) Mr J K Myers was chosen to serve as moderator, and L C. Wood, as clerk On motion of Nathaniel Wood, the meeting adjourned one hour for dinner At 1 o'clock the meeting was again called to order Obadiah Powell, J K Myers, and F Glover were elected supervisors L C. Wood was elected clerk, Eri G Wood, assessor, W H Young, collector and treasurer, Nathaniel Wood, overseer of the poor, Lewis C Kate and W H. Young, constables, Amzi Schaffer and Austin Vinton, justices; and Garret Houck, overseer of roads"

Aug 25, 1864, the town held a special meeting and voted to issue soldiers' bonds in the sum of $1,200 Following this record there are three certificates recorded showing that William R Brisbane, Francis Lincoln, and George Nock—all residents of Wilton—were duly mustered into the United States service for one year, and credited to the town of Woodville Dec 19 came the last call of President Lincoln for 300,000 men Woodville promptly called a special meeting Jan 14 1865 and voted soldiers' bonds in the sum of $1,600 Of this amount only $633.30 were afterwards issued. The records also show that Wilfred Vinton and W. H Young, Jr., were mustered into the service to the credit of this town, March 25 1865 Another special town meeting was held March 11, 1865, which ratified and sanctioned the action of the board in issuing bounty bonds As the Rebellion soon after was subdued, there is no further record of the matter.

Loren G Wood, son of Eri G, was the first white boy, and Lovica Smith, daughter of A C, was the first white girl, born in the township

The first school building was a log school house, a short distance east of the present Woodville cemetery Miss Emma Cook, afterwards the wife of Major W. T. Kittredge, was the first teacher away back in the summer of 1859

PATRICK CAMPION.

ST MARY

After being partly in the precinct of Empire and partly in the precinct of Wilton for a year or more, what now comprises the township of St Mary was duly organized in a township by order of the county commissioners on April 5, 1858 The township, 107, range 23, was duly designated as the "town of St Mary," and the tavern of J W. Clark was named as the place for holding the first town meeting. B M Morrill, Warren Smith, and H W Chamberlain were appointed to serve as the first judges of election The first town meeting was held May 11, 1858.

The Catholics of St. Mary, under the leadership of Father Keller, of Faribault, organized in 1856 Religious services were held at the house of Andrew Lynch, near St Mary, at one time. The Catholics built their first church in 1858 They established a cemetery in 1857, and some say that a Mr Crossman was the first person buried in it, but Mr William Byron asserts that the first person buried there was a Mr Morris, and that the next was Michael O'Brien, who was killed by lightning in September, 1858

ALTON.

Township 107, range 24, remained a portion of Freedom until the 27th day of April, 1866, when the commissioners of Waseca county passed an order to organize the town of Alton, the first town meeting to be held at the house of M. L Devereaux, in said township, May 15, 1866 Township officers were elected at that time, and the town started out free from all entangling alliances

Lucius Keyes has the honor of being the first settler in Alton He was born in Medina county, Ohio, in 1837 He now resides near Knoxville, Tenn He moved to Alton, on section 32, in September, 1863. William Wager and Elijah Hills, with their families, came here a few days after the arrival of Keyes The families of Wager and Hills spent the first winter in one cabin built of poles and bark taken from the old Indian wigwams, and a few basswood boards The cabin was only 14x16 feet in size Morris Lamb was another of the early comers At the breaking out of the great Rebellion he was a resident of Cumberland county, Tenn, and was compelled to leave there on account of his Union sentiments. He first lived near Minneapolis, but in 1864 came to Alton He died Dec 31, 1869

His son, Hon Morris H Lamb, born in Ohio, Jan 2, 1837, also came here in 1864 Aug 15, 1864, Morris enlisted in Company F, Eleventh Minnesota infantry, and served until July 11, 1865, when he returned to his home in Alton. Oct 20, 1870, he married Miss Harriet Oldfield, and they at one time, about 1880-85, carried on the largest dairy business in the county Mr Lamb was a member of the house in the legislature of 1875 He and his family have been residents of California for a number of years

C M Campion, with his sons, Patrick and John, came here at an early day, and settled on section 13, where he continued to reside until his death Patrick and Edward Hayden also settled on section 13 in 1864 For further information regarding the settlers of this township, see "Biographical Sketches"

BLOOMING GROVE

This is one of the towns that has preserved its records in good shape At first it was a part of the precinct of Swavesey, and so remained until April 5, 1858.

There seems to be something of a conflict of authorities regarding the organization of this township The county commissioner record shows that the township of Blooming Grove was set off by itself by an order of the board of commissioners April 5, 1858, and that Patrick Healey, James Isaacs, and J M Bliven were appointed judges of election But the records of the town show that the voters themselves had organized nearly a month before The first recorded history of the town reads as follows.

"TOWN OF BLOOMING GROVE

According to an act to provide for township organization, a meeting was held at the house of Patrick Healy, in the town of Blooming Grove, Waseca county, state of Minnesota, March 11, 1858, for the purpose of electing town officers, and enacting such other township business as provided in said act.

The meeting being called to order at the proper time, James Isaacs was chosen as moderator and Morgan Woodruff as clerk The polls were kept open from 9 o'clock a m to 5 o'clock p. m, with one hour adjournment at noon

After closing the polls the votes were canvassed by the moderator, when the result of the election of town officers was found to be as follows.

For chairman of board of supervisors, Philo Woodruff received 52 votes, for supervisors, James Isaacs 25 votes, A Derrin 25 votes After drawing for a decision, James Isaacs was declared elected Patrick Healy (for supervisor) received 49 votes, for town clerk, Sam T Isaacs 26 votes, Peter Eckert 24 votes, assessor, Patrick McCullough 27 votes, W Donaldson 22 votes; collector, Patrick McCullough 22 votes, E J Southworth 22 votes. After drawing Patrick McCullough was declared elected. For overseer of the poor, D T Bells received 50 votes, S F Wyman 2 votes, for constables, J. R Smith received 48 votes, H B Withrow 46, M Healy 1, justice of the peace, Elias Conner 47 votes, James Isaacs 24, Daniel Riegle 27"

From this it appears that fifty-two ballots were cast, and that the first town meeting was closely contested as to some of the officers At this meeting a tax of $100 was directed to be levied to defray town expenses It was also unanimously voted that the town be divided into four road districts—the northeast quarter of the town to be designated as No 1, the northwest quarter No 2, the southwest quarter No 3, and the southeast quarter No 4

Patrick McCullough was chosen overseer of district one, Jonathan Howell of district two, Patrick Murray of district three, and James Isaacs of district four

It was determined by the voters present that cattle, horses and mules, over one year old, should be allowed to run at large It was also declared that a "rail fence on crotches or spiles four rails high, staked and ridered, or a board (fence) four feet and a half high, with three boards five inches wide, should be a lawful fence " The meeting then adjourned until the first Tuesday in April, 1859

The proceedings of this meeting are given in full, because it was one of great importance to the township, and because it shows how orderly and intelligently the pioneers of this county conducted public affairs, notwithstanding the slurs of Eastern editors about the "wild and woolly West."

The German Methodists held services in this town at the house of Chris Remund as early as 1856 In 1860 they erected a small church, and in 1885 they built the present building in the Remund neighborhood The German M E society in the Saufferer neighborhood was organized in 1858 For many years services were held at the residence of Hon John L. Saufferer and then in the school house until about 1873, when they built a brick veneered church on section 1 In 1885 this building was reconstructed and given a handsome spire.

The Norwegian Lutheran church, on section 19, which accommodates people both in Iosco and Blooming Grove, was built in 1864 The Norwegian Lutherans of that neighborhood held their first church services at the house of Alec Herlugsen, Oct 17, 1858. Rev Laur Larson was the first pastor He was followed successively by Rev B J Muus, Rev Quammen, Rev O A. Mellby of New Richland, Rev Quanbeck, and Rev R P Wasbotten of Waseca, the latter now being in charge.

The first recorded death was that of Mrs Josiah Smith, who died in the fall of 1856 A postoffice was established in the town in 1857, and Mrs William Gibbs was made postmistress. The office was situated on section 5 It afterwards passed into the hands of James R Davidson, and was suspended in 1880

W H H Jackson, one of the very early settlers, is authority for the statement that the first death among the old settlers of the township was that of Henry Howell, a native of England, who was frozen to death in 1858, as elsewhere detailed

William Reinhardt, born in Berlin, Prussia, Feb 10, 1850, came to America in 1855 with his parents and to Blooming Grove in 1857 His father died in 1876 He married Caroline Kruger in 1878 Justus Reinhardt, a brother of William, was born in Illinois, Oct 12, 1857, and came with his parents to Blooming Grove in 1858 He married Miss Helen Fehner in 1883. They are prosperous residents of the town

Francis Brossard, son of Augustus and Agatha Brossard, was born at Lenox, Mass, Nov 18, 1833, and came to Blooming Grove in 1859 with his father's family There were ten children of the Augustus Brossard family Francis Augustus, Edward, Charles Joseph, Julia (Mrs Oliver James), Adele (Mrs Constant Brossard), Rosalie (Mrs O P Smith), Louise (Mrs J. E Jones) and Josephine (Mrs D T Ballard). The Brossards took an active part in the early development of the country The old gentleman and several of the sons resided in St Mary at an early day

IOSCO

This township is one of the favored ones of the great Northwest. It is rich in soil, with an undulating surface, plenty of timber, and ample drainage. Upland, meadow, and groves are so evenly distributed that nearly every farm has its proper proportion of each.

The first settlers in this township were Luke B Osgood, Daniel McDaniels, and John H Wheeler. David Wood followed a few days later, and Buel Welsh made a claim here in 1855, but soon returned to Faribault

This township was organized separate from other territory the 5th day of April, 1858 On that day the board of county commissioners, consisting of Messrs E B Stearns, of Otisco, John Bailey, of St Mary and Luman C Wood, of Woodville, made an order constituting township 108 N of Range 23 W. the town of Iosco, and appointed Messrs. H W Peek, George L Leonard, and David Smith judges of the election which was to be held at the house of Daniel Tripp, in said township

The minutes of the first town meeting read as follows.

FIRST ELECTION OF IOSCO

"At an election held at the house of Daniel Tripp, in the town of Iosco, Waseca county, Minn, on the 11th day of May, A D 1858, the following named persons received the number of votes set to their respective names for the following offices, to wit "

Then followed in detail the names of all the candidates and the number of votes each received N E Strong was elected chairman and David Smith and John G Ward supervisors, Spencer J Willis, clerk, L B. Osgood, town collector, A J. Bell, assessor, B W Gifford, overseer of the poor, A J Walton, constable, L P Kellogg and Silas Ward, justices of the peace The names of E Carpenter, James Babcock, Samuel Hardy, William Rockwell, G L Leonard and H P Chamberlain are recorded as receiving complimentary votes, but nearly the whole vote was cast for the successful candidates Only forty-two votes were cast and the successful candidates received from thirty-nine to forty-one The result of the election is certified to by H W Peck, David Smith, and G L Leonard, judges of election, and attested by N. E Strong and M L Kellogg, clerks. The town was divided into seven road districts and the following road overseers were appointed: A J. Walton, Daniel McDaniels, Silas

Ward, John Otis, Segur Johnson, Charles Billings, and Hugh Healey

There was a large addition to the population of the township in 1856 Early that spring, N. E Strong, George L Leonard, Daniel Tripp, Benjamin W Gifford, and A A Cotten platted a village site on section 20 and called it "Empire" It was surveyed and platted by H W. Peck William Long, father of Seth W, George and Frank Long, built a saw mill at this place Thomas and Daniel Tripp built a hotel It was at this village of Empire that Peter Farrell stabbed and killed Jacob Hagadorn on election day, in October, 1857 After the defeat of Empire in the county seat contest of 1857, the village soon disappeared, and the township reverted to its normal condition as a paradise for farming

JANESVILLE TOWNSHIP

This is the northwest corner township of the county, and boasts of the largest lake in the county—one which abounds in pickerel, bass and croppies It is a very fine body of water in the midst of a fertile country Elsewhere in this work is given a record of the first settlement which occurred in 1855 John Douglas and a man named Hughes were the first settlers and John Davis and Alfred Holstein, Indian traders, came next

The early records of this township were lost years ago—forever lost no doubt

The board of county commissioners, April 5, 1858 set off and organized the township under the name of Okaman, with two polling places The one at Okaman had, for judges of election, Alex. Johnston, C H Bishop and W N Buckhout, and the election was to be held at the house of A. Tuttle The other polling place was at the house of Caesar De Regan, with R Brown, John Cunningham, and De Regan as judges On the 17th of the next May, upon petition filed, the name of the township was changed to Janesville Under the township organization, adopted by the first state legislature, N E Strong was the first chairman of the board of supervisors, and served as a member of the board of county supervisors during the year The next year he was followed by J W La Paul. Mr La Paul, within the year moved to St Mary, and was succeeded by W. W Cowles Both La Paul and Cowles were noted for their talking propensities

The only town records to be found commence with the year 1868 The town meeting of that year was held at the house of Amos Roberts in Okaman village, on the 7th of April Mr Hiram Christman was chosen moderator, the town clerk and town treasurer each made a report, and both reports were adopted From all that appears upon the record book, these reports might have been verbal As to their contents, the record book is altogether silent The town then had ten road districts and the following gentlemen were chosen overseers of highways: R C. Wilkins, A J Patchen, Richard Cahill, Thomas McHugo, John Cahill, J R Wright, Henry Lane, Hiram Fish, William Popham, Nelson Thwing The meeting voted a tax of $315 for town expenses, the sum of $400 for the payment of outstanding soldier bounties, and one per cent upon all taxable property for road expenses The supervisors elected were Silas Waterbury (chairman), William Patchin, and Hiram Fish; W N Buckhout, town clerk, J. H. Ricker, treasurer, A N. Roberts, assessor, C. P Pratt and Hiram Christman justices of the peace C Hover and C Peaslee, constables That year there was paid from the road fund $83 91, and for ordinary expenses $104 60

Caesar De Regan made a claim in 1856 and had surveyed and platted the old village of Janesville The town site subsequently fell into the hands of J W Hosmer and others, but when the present Janesville was platted the old site was gradually abandoned.

The village of Okaman at the head of Lake Elysian was platted in May, 1857 The proprietors were W. P Mathes, B S Hall, S M. Cooley, F E Roberts, and G H Bishop. Here was situated the famous Buckhout flouring mills, which furnished flour to the early settlers as far south as the Iowa state line for years Okaman was one of the prettiest little villages in the state of Minnesota from 1857 to 1864, and was inhabited by an orderly, intelligent, and cultured people who had great hopes that it would grow into a city Alas, for human hopes and expectations! Okaman now exists only in name

The reader is referred to "biographical sketches" for particulars regarding early settlers in this township

VILLAGE OF JANESVILLE

Janesville, or "East Janesville," as it was platted, is one of the substantial and permanent towns of Southern Minnesota It is in the midst of a beautiful and rich farming country, inhabited by an industrious and frugal people, who earn and command prosperity. It was platted in August, 1869, by Surveyor S H Mott for J. W. Sprague, general manager of the W & St P railroad at that time Nine additions have been added since Buildings were constructed as if by magic. James Cummins hauled the first load of lumber for the first building, Baldwin's hotel. J O Chandler, A W. Jennison, F H Miner, D J Dodge & Co, J D Andrews, and others erected buildings that fall Dr Craig was the first physician, and John Bradish, Esq, the first attorney, as he was the first in Waseca county In the winter of 1869-70, several buildings from Old Janesville were moved to the new town, and in the spring of 1870 the new town was full of life and vigor James Cummins, born March 5, 1840, in Kenosha county, Wis, came to Blue Earth county in 1857, lived in Old Janesville for a time, and soon took a hand in the business of the new town Joseph Davison, born in the state of New York, in 1834, came to Byron township in 1862, enlisted in Company D, First Minnesota heavy artillery Oct 20, 1864 served until Sept 27, 1865, returned to Minnesota the same year, and in 1869 went to Janesville and helped to build the town as a contractor and builder. The Banner flouring mill, now owned by Jennison & Co, was built in 1873, by the firm of Stokes, Kimball & Co The Diadem flouring mill was erected in 1877, by Harn, Snyder & Co They became financially involved and the mill passed to Hillyer & Tillotson, then to J S Sutcliffe, and finally, in 1886, it became the property of Jennison Bros The W & St P railroad company erected a grain elevator in 1869, which soon after passed into other hands Among the business houses, that of Byron & Barden is very popular

The first school house was erected in 1871, at a cost of $2 800. Another school building was erected in 1877, and a third in 1885 The latest is a brick building costing $7,000

The Freewill Baptist society built the first church in 1870, at a eost of $3,000

The Episcopalians next built in 1877, at a cost of $2,000 The

Catholics erected their church building in 1876, and expended thereon about $6,000.

The Methodist Episcopal church was built in 1880 It is a brick structure, costing $4,000.

The Lutheran Evangelical church building was erected in 1885 at a cost of $2,500

The town and village together, in 1878, put up a building 45x 100 feet, which is used as a town hall and for public meetings of all kinds It cost about $5,000, and is a credit to the place.

A lodge of A F and A M, No. 124, was organized under dispensation, Aug. 10, 1875 Its present charter was issued Feb. 11, 1877 The dispensation members were R N Sackett, Kelsey Curtis, Darling Welch, and J O Chandler, the officers being. R. O. Craig, W M., E H Gosper, S W.; F H Miner, J W, R M Redfield, S D, J. W Tefft, J D, S C L Moore, S S; C H Younglove, J. S, R Heritage, Tyler The lodge does good work, and is in a prosperous condition.

BIOGRAPHICAL SKETCHES.

CHAPTER LXXIX.

BIOGRAPHICAL SKETCHES—REMINISCENSES OF EARLY DAYS IN THE SETTLEMENT OF THE COUNTY—MISCELLANEOUS MENTION OF PERSONAL MATTERS—THE CLOSE

NEW RICHLAND, BY HON ANTHONY SAMPSON.

Mr Sampson was born in Norway, August 21, 1827, and Mrs. Sampson was born in the same country, October 12, 1825. They left their native land May 15, 1853, and settled in Rock county, Wisconsin, July 10, of that year, where they remained three years Mr Sampson finally concluded to remove to Minnesota He went around among his neighbors and got up a company to go with him The men's names are as follows H H Sunde, K O Rotegard, H T. Hangrud, O. K. Hagen, W Anderson, Kresten Knudson, and E. O Strenge. They were all from Norway originally, but had settled in Rock county, Wisconsin They started from the latter place on the 3d day of May, 1856, and after encountering and overcoming the various obstacles and hindrances incident to an overland trip with ox teams and lumber wagons, reached New Richland on the 10th of June following.

Until the arrival of these people there was not a white settler in the township There were some Winnebago Indians around almost every day, but they never did any harm Mr Sampson says:

"The whole company of us had only twelve yoke of oxen, thirty cows, fifty head of young cattle and about $600 in gold The first thing we did was to rig out two breaking teams and break four acres of ground for each family This we planted mostly to flint corn, but as soon as the corn came up the blackbirds and gophers took it all It was hard times for us the first two years Flour was high in price costing us $11 a barrel, and we had to go seventy-five miles to get it. But we got along any way. We had plenty of milk and made butter and cheese; and we could catch all the fish we needed in the lake and the river at that time

"The company never had any trouble among its members Whenever there happened any differences three or four of us got together and settled it all right, and without any cost, and there is not one of those old settlers has ever had a costly law suit yet

The first white child born in the township was a daughter of O K Hagen in July, 1856 The first death was that of Sam A Samson, August 22, 1861

Each of the eight families bought 160 acres of land for which they paid the government $1.25 per acre

The first school district in the town was organized in 1860 John Larsen was elected clerk, Anthony Sampson, director, and T Tidmanson, treasurer The first school house was erected on a half acre lot given by Mr Sampson from a portion of his farm in 1862

The first church (Lutheran) was organized in 1861. H Halvorsen, Anthony Sampson and H. Taraldson were elected trustees of the society; and the first church building was erected by this society in 1862 It was a log building, 20x26 feet, and 14 feet in height We got a minister from Goodhue county who held services once every two months. There were at that time about twenty families belonging to the society, but now it contains one hundred and thirty families In 1872, we sent a call to Norway for a minister, and obtained Rev O A Mellby. He is our minister yet, and is an honest, able worker in this society. The society bought eighty acres of land and put up buildings for him and his family that cost about $1,800

We now have two good churches that cost about $8,000 There is a good Congregational church in the village, and there are seven good schoolhouses in the township"

Mr Sampson, besides holding numerous town offices, represented this county in the house of representatives in the session of 1877 He was one of our most substantial citizens who, in a modest way did his part toward developing the country and changing it from a wilderness to one of the most productive regions in the West He died May 16, 1899, at his home, honored and respected by all.

CAPTAIN EARL OF FREEDOM.

This gentleman was born August 10, 1832, in Jamestown, Crawford county, Pennsylvania His mother died while he was quite young, and in 1838 he went to live in the family of Mr Samuel Fitch, who resided three miles east of Youngstown, Ohio He was a very worthy man and instilled into the mind of young Earl, both by precept and example, the principles of honesty and uprightness of character Captain Earl lived with this family eleven years

In the spring of 1850, he started West coming as far as Rock Island, Illinois In February 1851, he went north into Jefferson county, Wisconsin, where he worked until November 25, 1855 He then married Miss Mary O. Hubbard, of Hebron, in that county She was born in Troy, N Y, and came West with her parents when she was four years of age.

In September, 1856, they moved to Richland county Wisconsin, where they resided until July 4, 1859, when they started for Minnesota with two yoke of oxen, one wagon, a cow and a calf. They arrived at their new home in the town of Yucatan, Houston county, on the 11th of July. When they had reached their destination they had about $20 in gold left, and were owing $250 on the one hundred and twenty acres they had bought.

Captain Earl says there had been considerable railroad excitement, and the Southern Minnesota had been graded as far as Houston, but the bubble had burst, and the hands were going out when he was moving in. He found a vacant shanty a mile from his land, and took possession of it. He immediately went to work cutting and hewing oak logs for a house, 16x20 feet, which he covered with oak shingles. His nearest neighbor was three miles away, and help to raise the house had to come from three to four miles. He worked out through harvest at $1.50 per day, and did not get his house raised until September, but completed it in November and moved into it. For a year and a half he had to work out for enough to support his family. His land was what is known as grub and openings. He grubbed and broke and fenced and thus opened his farm to cultivation.

In March, 1865, he sold his farm for $1,200 and in April following, in company with J. L. Graham and Arthur Graham, started for Redwood Falls. He furnished the team and they the provisions, and they camped out. Nine miles west of Wilton they came across Darling Welch, who was living upon the Winnebago reservation. He described the beauties of the land and the natural advantages of the situation in his enchanting style, but they had made up their minds to visit Redwood Falls, which they did, spending two weeks looking over that section of country. They found timber rather scarce and the land not yet in market. They were pleased with Waseca county, and returned to Mr. Welch's place. J. L. Graham and Earl each bought 160 acres of land. Captain Earl's farm cost him $960.

The improvements consisted of six acres broken and in crop, forty acres fenced with a two-rail fence, and a log house 12x18 feet. After going back to Houston county, he returned in June and broke up twenty acres—keeping "bach" during the time. He then went to Fillmore county and worked through harvest with his team.

On the 1st of September he started from Houston county with his family and arrived at the new home on the 7th. He had one span of good mules—which he sold that fall for $400—three good cows and six young cattle. Mrs. Earl drove the team on the road while he drove the cattle. He had his hay to cut and stack after his arrival. He hired a man and mower one and a half days, and the rest he cut with a scythe.

In speaking of that fall he says: "The weather, till late in the fall, was very fine, but the first snow storm was a terrible one. It was my first experience with a blizzard, and it came in all its glory. That was the night Billy Adams, the stage driver, was so badly frozen. It was about two miles west of my place where he brought up at a vacant shanty and stayed that fearful night It was one never to be forgotten by the early settlers of Freedom "The next summer," says he, "was very wet, and it was almost impossible to get around It cost one dollar per hundred to get flour from Mankato to our settlement, a distance of twenty miles. We had very good crops, however, that season, and in the fall we were as happy as could have been expected We had a splendid neighborhood, very little sickness, and no reason to complain of our prosperity."

The first office held by him was that of assessor in the town of Forest, Richland county, Wisconsin, in 1859 In Houston county, he was elected chairman of the board of supervisors in 1861 and re-elected in '62, '63 and '64 In that time he paid out over $8,000 for volunteers, and kept the town clear from draft He served as chairman of the board in Freedom in 1866, and was the first commissioner elected from the fifth district in Waseca county He was assessor in Freedom for the years '73-4 and '75 and in the fall of 1875 was elected one of the representatives from this county to the legislature of 1876

After having faithfully served his generation and his country he joined the great majority on the other side

MR EDWIN E VERPLANK, NEW RICHLAND

Mr Edwin E Verplank was born in 1834, two and a half miles from Auburn, N Y His wife, Anna Sophia, was born near Konigsberg, Norway, and is forty-two years of age Mr Verplank came to Minnesota by way of Iowa, in a "prairie schooner," and settled at Faribault, in November, 1855. Settlements were then few and far between, but the country was delightful and fruitful Larger vegetables grew here that year than were ever seen before or heard of since The weather was delightful that fall—Indian summer extending into December Mr Verplank writes

"A young man named Tyler and myself went to Wilton in the spring of 1857, and took claims a little southwest of that village We bought lumber, and with saw, hammer and hatchet we made music, while the gophers stood around on their hind feet whistling a chorus of welcome until we completed our structure"

"Well, if we were not as virtuous as the virgins of the Bible, we were at least as foolish for we had neither oil, lamps nor provisions, and none were to be obtained. We concluded that for two young, unmarried men, with well developed appetites and no visible means of supply the prospects of growing up with the country were not very flattering We finally abandoned our claims and returned to Faribault where we could get plenty of work and enough to eat I remained in Faribault until 1861, when I enlisted in Co G, First Minnesota volunteers'

After his term of service Mr Verplank purchased eighty acres of land where he now resides.

OLE H SUNDE

Ole H. Sunde and others of New Richland, had some rough experience in the early days They had to go to Iowa for food and supplies, taking the round-a-bout way over which they came from Wisconsin They started on bare ground in the fall, the weather being fine, but were caught in a snow storm while out, and were detained three weeks while their families had only a small quantity of corn meal, ground cob and all, which they sifted and ate with milk The anxiety of each of the separated parties as to the fate and welfare of the others was intense None but those who have been placed in similar circumstances can realize the feelings of husband, wife or relatives thus separated

W H H JACKSON

Mr W H H Jackson, of Blooming Grove, being interviewed, said "I call to mind most of the early settlers Michael Johnson, who still lives on the claim he pre-empted, Mr Hatch, father of Mrs H. P. Chamberlain of Iosco, who moved away years ago, the Messrs Remund, most of whom are still with us, Mr Gray and family, J. M. Blivens, Mr Simeon Smith and his son, A C , Jonathan Howell, deceased, and I presume others settled in 1855 Among those who came in 1856, were E R Connor, now of Dakota, George Dean, John Walker, James Walker, Boss Sharp, Wm Donaldson, Patrick Healy, the lamented Capt Lewis McKune who was killed in the battle of Bull Run, Hon J L Saufferer, James Hand, Hon J N Powers and his father, Hon Philo Woodruff, John Gibson and Mr Winthrow

"Thomas Jackson, his three sons, and one daughter came there in May, 1858, from Indiana He bought a farm of Mr Walker, which he afterward sold, and then moved to Morristown where he died years ago

"Caleb B Jackson enlisted in Captain McKune's company of the First Minnesota regiment, served three years, and then enlisted as a veteran in the Second Minnesota cavalry, serving until the close of the war

"Thos B Jackson enlisted and served three years in the Fourth Minnesota, then re-enlisted as a veteran, was wounded in the battle of Altoona, and died from the effect of his injuries soon after

"W H. H Jackson enlisted in the Third Minnesota and served two years and four months He was born in Indiana, 1840, and came to Blooming Grove with his father in 1858 The same year, in the fall, he married Miss Mary Eckert, daughter of Peter Eckert, who came to the same township in 1857 Mr Eckert sold his farm and went to Illinois in 1870, returning to Minnesota in 1877 He died some years ago

"It is claimed that George Connor was the first white child born in the township

"The first schoolhouse was built in 1856. The Baptists organized a church society in 1856, and held services in the schoolhouse"

JAMES CUMMINS.

Mr James Cummins, of Janesville, first inhabited the earth at a place known as the town of Bristol, Kenosha county, Wisconsin, his birthday being March 5, 1840 His wife's name was Hester J Coddington; she was born in Livingston county, New York, on the 18th of February, 1841

"Jim," as he is familiarly called, moved to LeRay, Blue Earth county, in 1857, and to "Old Janesville" in 1862. At this time, he avers, he had neither lands, houses nor cattle He writes

"The first fall after our arrival, having put up our hay, my father, John Cummins, sent me, with Charles and Ed. Bennett, to New Auburn, Iowa, for flour We went with three wagons and six yoke of oxen, and brought back 7,500 pounds of flour, so we did not go hungry that winter Our family of eleven had 2,500 pounds, while the Bennetts had fifty work hands and nearly "all Lord's Creation" to eat from their two loads Ed Bennett's father was putting in a mill dam at Tivoli, that winter.

"The next season, 1858, my father had a job of breaking one hundred acres of prairie for the Winnebago Indians Two brothers and myself took turn-about, each going there for a week We had four yoke of oxen and a self-holding breaking plow. The breaking was done in patches, not over three acres in a place, and we were all the time moving about and camping in different places

"By the way C. A. DeGraff, while excavating for his cellar, dug up the ashes and coals where I camped about four weeks—so you see I was there first During the summer I camped a portion of the time with John Barden, of Wilton, a brother of Thomas Barden John Barden also had a contract for breaking one hundred acres for the Winnebagoes. He was a gentleman in every respect and I heard of his death in the war with much sorrow By the way, I saw a man two years ago by the name of James Dobson, who was in John's company and stood by his side when he was shot. Dobson gave John the same good name he enjoyed while here

"I am of the opinion that Sam Crump was a little rattled, at the old settlers' meeting at Seaman's, when he blushingly accused me of camping with an Indian all summer

"In the fall we started to build a log schoolhouse The body was raised and bark peeled and packed for the roof, but that was as far as we ever got The bark was afterwards used to cover a shop, and the logs rotted down

"That winter my parents hired Miss Hattie Northrup, then of Wilton, now of Morristown, to teach their nine children at home We had a good school Our house was built of logs 16x24 feet, and covered with bark

"During the winter I took a job of cutting five cords of white ash wood. I didn't then know enough about the business to know which way to run when the tree commenced to fall. In fact the trees wouldn't fall if they could help it I chopped all around the tree until it would commence to fall, and then it would be sure to lodge I worked very hard, broke three axes and gave up the job after cutting three and a half cords

"The next spring my brother Horace and I took a job of clearing a road. We were very thirsty, at least I was I tapped a maple, and he a butternut tree My tree didn't seem to furnish much sap, at any rate I kept the trough dry Horace said his tree had plenty of sap and that it was sweeter than maple I tried it and found he was about right, and so kept the trough empty till night During the night I was taken with a fever—had three relapses, each time being worse than the first—and when I finally got around the summer was gone; and I felt all " gone" too.

"I worked here and there and finally commenced work at "Old Janesville," Jan 1, 1862 In June of the same year I was married and have been in sight ever since

"The first religious services held in our neighborhood, in Blue Earth county, were at the house of my uncle, Moses Bennett, father of Ed Bennett, of Waseca, in 1857 In "Old Janesville," religious services were held in private houses until the schoolhouse was built The first church organized in "East Janesville," the present Janesville, was the Free Baptist

'The first child born, that I remember about, was a daughter of J W LaPaul The deaths were a child in the family of James Savage and two daughters of David Jenkins

"The first buildings in Janesville, as I remember, were the houses of P Ratchford and Mary Corcoran.

"Among the oldest settlers of LeRay township, I call to mind Thos Davis, who died in 1860, my father, John Cummins; A P Johnson who went to Wisconsin in 1863, Ed Clocksun, Adna Carpenter, late of Janesville, A Lamer, of "Old Janesville," Henry Lane, who died in 1879, and Captain Dane, who used to preach to us Moses Bennett and Hollis Whitney both died some years ago These were among the men who at the time of the Indian outbreak in 1862, moved to the old town site of Iosco Mr Bennett took a large drove of cattle with him, and a wagon loaded with cheese of his own make with two yoke of oxen attached. They camped in military array for a few days and then returned to their homes

"When I came to old Janesville there were many old settlers, but they were mostly Indians Among the first white settlers were J W Hosmer, N E Strong, John Cunningham, John Davis, John Wind, John Bradish, Richard Dreever, John Put, Wm. Cahill, Thos McHugo, Thos. Bichel, John McCue, James McCue, and Patrick McCue.

'Oh' by the way, I came near forgetting Geo Dreever, and only for the fact that he was here today, telling some of his early doings, I should have forgotten him. George says he once broke into lake Elysian through the ice He stood with one toe on a pond lily root and pawed ice until he wore his finger nails off to the first joint—was in the water about two hours and twenty minutes by the watch Pat Cahill was standing on a piece of rotten ice not more than a rod away and dared not come to help him for fear both would be drowned Richard Dreever and another man, as soon as they could cut a boat loose out of the ice, came to George's relief by sliding the boat along on the ice After getting to George, the man with Richard, instead of at once helping him out, had to stop and ask, 'What in h—l brought you here?' George and Cahill finally got out of it all right.

"George is a live corpse yet, and looks as though he would be here until the Winnebagoes come again He has a good farm and house, and can 'sling' the Indian dialect 'right smart' yet He was here when the Winnebagoes came, I suppose, but he could not talk fast enough to keep them from tying to his horse bridle one of the big toes severed from the body of one of the Sioux Indians murdered by the Winnebagoes, in 1862, to appease the anger of the whites on account of the Sioux massacre on the frontier

"I am giving too much attention to George, so I return to David Coddington, my wife's father He died here in 1878 A H Coddington moved to Kansas in 1884 Jerry Hogan was found dead in his house several years ago. James Hogan lives on the same farm, and Thomas Hogan now lives in Alton. John Hogan, I think, came first in 1855, returned to Kentucky for a time, but now lives on his old farm."

[Mr Cummins wrote the foregoing in 1896—The author]

MR S. A FARRINGTON

Among the early settlers of Waseca county there are few more unassuming or more worthy than the subject of this sketch Mr Farrington was born August 27, 1827, in the county of Kennebec, state of Maine In 1850 he left his native state to seek a home in the West, first stopping in Peoria, Illinois, and afterward in Green Lake county, Wisconsin In 1855 he was married to Miss Mary A Foster, who was born in Cayuga county, New York

May 10, 1857, a company from Green Lake county started for Minnesota in "prairie schooners" The company consisted of S A Farrington and wife, Mr. Farrington's father and mother, his sister, Sarah, a brother, Franklin and his wife, widow Lincoln, afterwards wife of Hon B A Lowell, of Waseca, with her four boys and a girl, Volney Dewitt and wife, and a young blacksmith named Michael Quiggle.

The company had five wagons and nine yoke of oxen, with some cows and other cattle Near LaCrosse they fell in with other emigrants, among them Daniel Styles and wife, and son Elijah and wife, who joined the company and settled in the same neighborhood

Some of the way the company made slow progress There were few bridges in the country and the roads were not graded at all

In many places they were obliged to hitch all the teams to one wagon at a time in order to haul the vehicles through the mudholes or sloughs, with axles dragging on the ground, sometimes pulling out wagon tongues and breaking log-chains One day they made only one mile, camping in sight of the camp-fire of the night before

After many days of weary toil they arrived at their place of settlement, in what is now Otisco, June 14 They soon selected claims and went to work building places to live in Mr S A Farrington built a log house, 14x20, one story high At first they had only an earth floor The cover, or roof, was made of poles, hay and prairie sod Later he obtained a few narrow, poplar boards, at the Clinton mill, by waiting to have them sawed The other houses were all about the same

S A. Farrington took a claim on section 25—his father, brother, Dewitt and M Quiggle on section 26. Daniel and Elijah Styles and Mrs Lincoln took claims near by. As soon as possible after their arrival, they commenced running the breaking plow, using from five to seven pair of oxen to the plow, and breaking some on each claim

The first child born in the settlement was Minnie Farrington, daughter of the subject of this sketch She died at the age of eighteen years.

The seasons of 1858-9 were very wet and the settlers raised but very little grain In the fall of 1858, Phillip Quiggle and family, joined the settlement from Wisconsin As he was a blacksmith, he went to work in his son's shop on the day of his arrival, that night the shop was burned to the ground with all its contents His means being limited, he went to Owatonna to work at his trade On the 1st of January, 1859, he started for home with an ox team in the morning About midnight of that day some one found him and his team in a snow bank near Owatonna. He had traveled all day and at midnight he was found near the place from which he started in the morning, almost frozen

Times were hard then—not such hard times as we have now with granaries full of grain—but genuine hard times, when it was difficult, at times, to get enough to eat, some of the settlers got discouraged and left, and others would have done the same if they had had the means to go with.

On account of the wet summer of 1858 there was not much raised, as not much wheat was sowed and the corn did not ripen that year Those who had money—and they were few—went to Mankato and other points for their supplies.

Of Mr Farrington's company there are none now living in this county His brother, Franklin, resides in Mineapolis, and his sister Sarah, in Dakota Mrs Dewitt died some years ago, and Mr Dewitt is living in Iowa with his second wife Uncle Daniel Styles and wife lie buried in the Otisco cemetery, and Elijah Styles sleeps in a soldier's grave in the South His widow is living with friends in the East

Mr S A Farrington lived on his Otisco farm for twelve years, then sold it and bought another two miles south of Waseca, where he lived fourteen years. He then traded that for a farm on sections fifteen and sixteen, town of Wilton, containing 240 acres, where he resided for a number of years He then sold his farm and moved to Waterville where he resided until his death, which occurred Jan 17, 1905

MR ANDREW NELSON OF BLOOMING GROVE

was born in Sweden, in the year 1829, and came to America in 1854 He first lived in Moline, Illinois, where he remained about a year The tidal wave of emigration was then pushing toward Minnesota, and young Nelson was among the number who came to the state in 1855 He stopped in Red Wing where he found employment After remaining there a little over a year, he came to Blooming Grove and selected a claim where he resided until the time of his death, which occurred April 11, 1901 He first built a log house, and, being a single man, worked out much of the time until he was married in 1861. His first wife's maiden name was Christina Evanson

In 1865, he returned to visit friends in his native land Shortly after his return from Sweden, his first wife died He married again some time afterwards

At the time of his death he was well-to-do, having three hundred and forty acres of land, eighty acres of which was timber. He came to this county empty handed and worked by the day to get his start He cradled grain many a day in the harvest field for a dollar a day Like many another old settler, he hauled wheat to Hastings, camping by the wayside, and sold it for fifty cents a bushel—often spending five or six days in making the trip with one load

THE HONORABLE WILLIAM BRISBANE

"I received a card from you requesting me to give what information I may possess in regard to the early settlement of the county. I may state that the county was partially settled when I came, and no doubt there are old settlers still living better qualified to give you the information you desire than I am, however, if I can contribute anything interesting to your historical department, you are welcome to it I see you ask replies to twelve different questions First, my full name, age, birth place, and that of my wife My name is William Brisbane. I was born in the city of Glasgow. Scotland, December 11, 1811, and have just passed the seventy-fifth milestone in the journey of life My wife's name is Janet Scott She was born in the Parish of Minto, Roxburghshire, Scotland, and is now seventy-six years old I may state that my father was a soldier in the British army, and that my mother and I were sent home a little before the battle of Waterloo. My mother being a native of the town of Hawick, I lived there until I emigrated to America, hence I have always called myself a Hawick man I came to America in the spring of 1839, lived ten years in the state of New York I then lived ten years in Fon du Lac county, Wisconsin, when I came to Minnesota and settled in the town of Wilton in the spring of 1859 The season before had been very wet, and the county was literally a quagmire I recollect that we would some times camp two nights in sight of the same house and have to unload two or three times a day and carry our goods to dry ground It was called a new country I thought it so new that it hadn t had time to dry since the spirit moved upon the face of the waters, but upon examination, I found that the soil was very rich, and by proper cultivation might become well adapted to the raising of either grain or stock, for to keep land in heart, grain and stock must go together I am happy to say that my expectations have been fully realized, in fact, I have found that even our wire grass sloughs, by being properly drained, may become the most profitable land we have I bought one hundred and sixty acres of prairie and nine acres of timber from a Mr. Wattles, who was paying interest at the rate of ten per cent a month to Thomas E Bennett of Winona. I brought with me forty-two head of horned cattle, young and old, with a span of yearling colts The original farm, on the prairie, now consists of two hundred forty-eight acres, with about one hundred fifty acres under cultivation, the remainder in hay and pasture, with twenty acres of timber. There are on the place thirty-eight head of horned cattle and thirteen horses, young and old There is a barn 30x40 feet, with an ell 16x40 feet, with underground stables, two granaries, one 22x30 feet, the other 16x22 feet, a frame house 20x28 feet, with two wings, one 16x20 feet, the other 12x16 feet My wife and I occupy the old frame building The whole is now in possession of our son, W R, with whom we are living and quietly waiting the time when we shall bid farewell to all earthly possessions I may say that my wife and I who have shared the joys and sorrows of life together, have just completed our fifty-fifth year of married life

You then want to know if I hold any offices Yes, lots of 'em I have held so many that if I hadn't been a Scotchman, I should have died from softening of the brain long ago, for I have been school district director, town supervisor, assessor, and I believe the first member Waseca county sent to the state legislature as an independent representative district I am now town clerk, justice of the peace, and president of the anti-horse thief society. It is said the words, "Man, know thyself," were posted up in a heathen temple, but it is of no use for a man to study his own character nowadays The editors will do that for him I had no idea that I possessed such a many-sided character until I became a candidate for legislative honors My friends gave me credit for virtues that I am certain I never possessed, and my enemies ascribed vices to me I never had even dreamed of

Then you want to know all about my lucky hits I have been in regard to lucky hits what Artemus Ward was to railroad accidents. Artemus says he never had a railroad accident, he was always a little too early or a little too late, that is my case exactly I have always been before or behind the lucky hits My wife, looking over my shoulder, whispered softly in my ear, I know of one lucky hit you made" When was that? I said "When you married me," said she, with an air of triumph gleaming in her eyes I freely acknowledge the fact, as I am always willing to give honor to whom honor is due

Then you want to get all the facts within my knowledge regarding the early settlement of my neighborhood That would take a volume, and I have neither time nor ability to write a book; you must be content with a few facts jumbled hastily and incoherently together. I have often wondered why our magazine writers have not seized upon the experiences and hardships undergone by early settlers They might be woven into more thrilling and instructive narratives than the sickly, sentimental novels so destructive to the morals of our youth I find from town records that the first town meeting was held at the house of Joseph Doty (now F. Hollander's) on the 11th day of May, 1858, pursuant to an act to provide for township organization. The meeting was called to order, and Philo C Bailey was appointed chairman, whereupon, the object of the meeting being stated, Buel Welsh was duly elected moderator and Thomas L Paige, clerk On motion of Mr Woodbury, the name of the township was called Wilton Polls were opened, and the following named persons were elected. For supervisors, W W Robinson (chairman), John Brand, A J Woodbury, town clerk, Tarrant Putnam, assessor, L Curtiss, collector, Tarrant Putnam, justices of the peace, J. B Jackson, Philo C Bailey, overseer of poor, A. Miller; constables, P VanDyke, — Stevens

The day that I arrived in Wilton, April 5, 1859, I found that the town meeting had just been adjourned from the Globe hotel to B A Lowell's hall There were some unconverted sinners in the whisky business then Even Pat himself could then, occasionally, turn up his little finger for medical purposes I merely mention these things to show the advance in civilization Uncle Biis was then, as now, a conservative, as most Scotchmen are

I will give two or three extracts from reports made by committees in those early times They are what Squire Green would have called "characteristic" A committee (No 1) was appointed (1859) to take into consideration the amount of tax necessary to defray township expenses It reported that "for the repair and construction of roads and bridges no money is needed above road tax and land road tax, and that a tax not exceeding one hundred fifty dollars is all that would be necessary to defray the expenses of said town the ensuing year, all of which was respectfully submitted by A T Peck, Thomas Barden and Peter VanDyke, committee" A G Sutlief then made a motion that no breachy, horned cattle shall be allowed to run at large. I thought this was a chance for the muleys. Committee No 2 reported "that, first, for the current and incidental expenses of the town, we recommend the raising of one hundred twenty-five dollars; second, that twenty five dollars be raised for the immediate erection of a pound in the town of Wilton third, that for the assistance and support of the poor we recommend the raising of twenty-five dollars, making a total sum of one hundred seventy-five dollars All of which was respectfully submitted by M S Gove, P C Bailey, and George W Watkins, committee" They were so economical that I was surprised that a motion wasn t made to set the poor to herding the cattle and thus save the pound money Another report was made "that the poundmaster shall receive as fees for impounding hogs twelve and one-half cents, letting the same out, twelve and one half cents, and twelve and one-half cents per day for every day said hog is kept in the pound For sheep, the same fees be allowed as for impounding hogs, cattle and oxen The pound master shall receive as fees fifty cents for letting a stallion into the pound, and fifty cents for letting said stallion out, and fifty cents per day for keeping said stallion —S P Child, chairman, attest, Tarrant Putnam, clerk" I may state that the first ballot box used was made by D L Whipple, and cost one dollar. It might have passed for an antediluvian rat trap, and as it is still in existence, it may be eagerly sought after as a curiosity for our county museum, when we get one

Everything in and around Wilton, although it was then the county seat, seemed dull and stagnant Hastings was the nearest market, and there was nothing to stimulate enterprise The only things that broke the monotony of life were law suits, in which J T Eldridge figured conspicuously, for in almost every suit J T appeared either as a witness or one horse counsel and in many cases he appeared as both witness and counsel, that is, he gave outside counsel, and inside evidence So notorious as a witness did he become that I recollect in one case a lawyer in court said "Mr. Eldridge will be sworn" "Of course," said Judge Donaldson, "Mr Eldridge will have to be sworn" His evidence was impeached, but instead of blushing at the exposure, he seemed rather proud of the notoriety the impeachment gave him He was my nearest neighbor, and I often talked to him about the value of a good reputation I really began to believe that he had turned a corner and like Balaam prayed that he might die the death of the righteous, but, as we say in Scotland, what is bred in the bone is hard to eradicate from the flesh.

I had almost forgotten to state that the first bridge built in road district No 2, was built by S P Child and his brother Pat It cost five dollars, a sum in perfect harmony with the economy of the times It was the narrowest bridge I ever saw; so very narrow that a religious enthusiast might have mistaken it for the road to paradise Next year, being overseer of highways, I tore it out, as I considered it dangerous for a Scotchman coming home from Wilton after dark I have an idea that a broad bridge isn't so apt to lead to destruction as a narrow one; so, actuated by a feeling of self preservation, I built a broader one, and the feeling of safety I enjoyed was ample compensation for my trouble.

INDIAN WAR

But Wilton was soon to be aroused from her Rip Van Winkle slumber, with this difference, that instead of waking up after the war, she awoke to find the nation engaged in a hand to hand struggle for existence.

One day the citizens had met to bid good bye to a number of the boys who were starting for the front, some of whom never came back, but offered up their lives a willing sacrifice upon the altar of their country The last wagon was barely out of sight when the stage from the west brought us the terrible news of the Indian massacre The people were so confounded that they couldn't be brought to realize the fact that such a bloody tragedy had been enacted About mid-afternoon, when the excitement had somewhat cooled, it was suddenly kindled again into fever heat, by the appearance of two men in a covered buggy, one a white man, the other an Indian grasping a rifle The white man said they were from the agency and that the Winnebagoes were making very warlike demonstrations, and that they had come to solicit immediate help. Here then, we thought, was war at our very doors, and most all of our young men gone South A meeting was soon held and volunteers called for All seemed chock-full of patriotism, and spoiling for fight It was agreed that the volunteers should secure what arms they could and meet at the Globe hotel, at 8 o'clock that night On my way to Wilton, I called upon Peter Van Dyke who, in the afternoon, seemed to have no other thought but just to kill two at a blow, but a change had come over his dream of military glory, for I found Peter in bed groaning with neuralgia His wife, the better man of the two, shamed him and called him a coward Very few came at the time appointed, and I began to think neuralgia had become epidemical. If memory serves me right, three wagons started about 11 o'clock. The night was pitch dark, with a heavy, drizzling rain falling, and the roads almost impassable We had taken with us all the ammunition Wilton could furnish, not forgetting a little drop of the "craithur," but on such a night the supply was not equal to the demand, and the men began to doze They were suddenly startled into life again by the second wagon running into the one ahead, which had stopped Upon enquiring what the matter was, the teamster said that he had heard an Indian war whoop and refused to go on While deliberating upon the situation, the loud crowing of roosters broke the stillness of the night air

So, after a not very hearty laugh, we started ahead again, and arrived at the Agency as the day began to break, wearied and jaded enough Balcombe, the agent, received us with apparent gratitude, and thanked us for responding so promptly to the call for aid A few bales of Indian blankets were ripped open and spread down as couches for us to lie upon and rest, but our nerves were too much excited by the novelty of our surroundings to get the rest we so much needed, so, getting up and performing our ablutions, we thought we would take a stroll and reconnoitre a little, but here we were met by a difficulty we were hardly prepared for Col Ide and Balcombe objected to our taking our guns with us, as it might excite the Indians, they said I remarked that if the Indians had any hostile intentions they would be more apt to attack unarmed men than if they had arms in their hands The Colonel didn't think that there was any danger Then if there is no danger, I said, why are we here? I saw I had no influence, and finally gave in, leaving my gun in a room of the government store house While sauntering along, a few indians passed us One of them complimented us by calling us G--d d--n whites He could swear in English, anyway. We concluded that things presented rather a warlike aspect, and that we had better go and secure our guns, but to our surprise we found the door of the room in which we had left our guns locked, and nobody could tell who had the key I said I would find a key, grasping a stick of cordwood Just then a man by the name of Dyer came running with the key He said that he had gone out on the prairie for a load of hay and taken the key with him At night we were doomed to another surprise The storekeeper, Jim Hubbell, Col. Ide, and agent Balcombe proposed dividing the men and stationing one party at Hubbell s store and the other part at the government store house. This I strenuously opposed, as there were so few of us, however, I told Balcombe it he would assume the responsibility of command, I would willingly serve under him until troops arrived. He said he would assume no responsibility, though he distributed a few flasks of powder among us Here then we found no one to act as leader, and with no plan of action, so that in case of an attack it would be every man for himself and the devil take the hindmost It looked to me as though we were running with eyes open into a trap, and I began to wish myself well out of it The next day was distribution day, but few Indians were around, they were down in the woods holding a pow-wow. The squaws came for the provisions and they cut a very ludicrous figure as they waddled away with a bag of flour and a chunk of pork strapped on their backs In the afternoon the Indians came from the woods, dressed in all their toggery and war paint A sort of council was held; the Indians formed in a circle with the chiefs and interpreter in the center The chiefs, according to the interpreter, complained of unfair dealing by the agent The scene, with its surroundings, was extremely picturesque While walking around in the evening along with a man by the name of Burgess, we saw two squaws leave a store carrying something between them They kneeled down on the prairie, applying their hands in quick, successive movements to their mouths I felt a curiosity to see what they were doing I found them engaged in the delectable employment of eating sugar They motioned me to kneel and partake with them I did so, but I believe I forgot to ask a blessing, my mind being too much engrossed by the novelty of the scene Then the idea flashed across my mind like greased lightning, wouldn't this be a precious item for Pat Child to hear that Uncle Bris was found out on the prairie after dark eating sugar with a couple of squaws? I began to realize that I might be committing an act of impropriety, and, like St. Paul, I mentally exclaimed oh, wretched man that I am, and, being a virtuous man, I trembled for my reputation So, girding up my loins, I bowed a graceful acknowledgement to my entertainers, rejoined my companion, and I never saw my dusky doxies any more

The Indian scare over, and the country becoming more settled, considerable business was transacted, and Wilton began to show signs of awakening to new life and activity But this dream of future greatness was soon dispelled Time, that great wonder-worker, had been hard at work Waseca was built, and the railroad had arrived It was the old story of the boys and frogs, what was fun for Waseca was death to Wilton She died rather hard, but has gradually melted away and is not now even the shadow of her former self The old settler when he has crossed Wilton bridge always finds a sort of melancholy feeling creeping over him He can hardly realize that this lonely spot was once the scene of active life, and will ask himself, "Is this the place where judges once held court, where juries sat, where criminals were confined, and the business of the county transacted?" and concludes that the past must be all a dream, a mere phantasy of the brain, but a wild, unearthly yell recalls him to consciousness—it is the scream of a locomotive a mile east of Wilton, the demon that murdered her But, upon mature reflection, he concludes that the change is for the better, after all, when he thinks of the long and weary journeys he used to make to Hastings, with wheat at fifty cents a bushel, and Waseca within a few hours drive from home, with the pleasure of sleeping in his own comfortable bed at night, instead of lying down by a camp fire on the open prairie, with the thermometer ten degrees below zero He thinks it is best to be philosophical, accept the inevitable, and be thankful for the change And surely every citizen of the county ought to feel proud of the little gem Waseca, our present county seat There is such an air of calm and dignified superiority about her that captivates every stranger who has the good fortune to visit her Lying as she does between two crystal lakes, she appears like a beautiful bride locked in the arms of her husband I may likewise say of the ladies of Waseca what the Irish beggar said to a Scotch lady who was as remarkable for charity as she was for beauty: "Thank you, ma'am, I see, your honor, that your manners and charity are equal to your beauty"

'Eve's bonny daughters,
Priests blame sorely for our fall,
But still—but still—I like them dearly—
God bless them all!'"

Yours respectfully,
William Brisbane

FIRST WHITE SETTLERS IN IOSCO

(By M. S Green)

It may not be generally known, even by the present people of Iosco, that the first, permanent settlement in that township was made by Luke B Osgood, Daniel McDaniels, and John Wheeler Mr Osgood erected the first shanty, in July, 1855, made of logs and covered with shakes. It had a doorway, but no door, and possessed neither window nor floor.

The family lived in this cabin till fall when a better house was constructed Having camped in the wagon and by the roadside for about three months, the family was glad of even such accommodations

In the early part of winter, Mr Osgood cut two saw logs, put them on his sled and started for Morristown to get them sawed into lumber for a house floor Although he had three pair of oxen attached to his sled, he made slow progress There was considerable snow and it was piled into huge drifts here and there There was no traveled road and he had not proceeded more than a mile when he rolled off one log He then shoveled and traveled until evening, having made a distance of about five miles. Here he camped for the night—camped all night with three yoke of oxen in the open air There was a heavy snow storm during the night and the wind blew a gale The next morning, he concluded to throw off the other log and get along with a ground floor, as they had been doing, and go on to Faribault with his team and bring back some flour After five days spent in shoveling snow, prying up the sled, unloading and reloading he arrived at home with a very small load of flour

The winter of '55-6 was one of the most severe ever known in the state The snow was deep, the thermometer away down to the bulb, and very few ventured from home except when compelled to go to obtain the necessaries of life At one time there was prospect of a famine, and Mr Osgood furnished money while David Smith furnished the pluck, energy and endurance to go to Iowa for a supply of provisions As he was detained a much longer time on the road than was anticipated by the settlers, some of them had to boil their seed wheat and corn Thinking it poor economy to use their seed grain in that way, they concluded to send Jake Conrad, for flour He started for Faribault with an ox team and sled About five miles from home, one of the oxen fell dead Here he camped for the night, and the next morning drove the live ox toward Faribault until he came to a house where he left the ox and proceeded to Faribault on foot He bought one hundred pounds of flour and started with it on his back to return to the settlement After toiling through the snow drifts for a mile or a little more, he concluded that it was too much of a load for even German pluck, so he sold the flour to a settler, returning home to report progress and "ask leave to sit awhile"

In the mean time Mr Smith had returned with his load from Iowa, to the relief and joy of the "Plum Valley" settlement The settlers in this township not only suffered much hardship, but they lost nearly half their cattle during the winter of '55-6, owing to the poorly built, open stables, the intensely cold weather, and, more than all else, the poor hay Owing to the lateness of the season when the settlement was made, much of the hay was not cut till after the first frost

THE FIRE FIEND

In the fall of 1855 Mr Osgood went to the Winnebago Agency to move John Davis to a claim near where the village of Janesville is now situated While Mr Osgood was absent, one of his neighbors, very imprudently, undertook to burn around a stack of hay The fire got away from him and all the hay in the country was in danger of being burned Mrs Osgood, ever watchful of her husband's interests, went out to look after his hay Mr McDaniels had succeeded in arresting the progress of the fire, in part, and went to another part of the farm, telling Mrs Osgood to keep watch of the fire and, if it should get over the trail which they had made for protection, to let him know She had been on the ground but a short time when, to her utter dismay, she discovered that she was entirely surrounded by fire She first endeavored to escape to the woods near by, but soon became entangled in the vines that had clambered over the thick underbrush She turned despairingly in the direction of the fire—it roared and crackled and screamed equal to sheol itself—the flames at one moment rising mountain high, then, driven by the force of the wind, along the ground at railroad speed, it would devour everything in its path, and then rise again in its fury as though to scorch the very heavens Mrs Osgood with rare presence of mind stepped behind a large tree, gathered her clothing closely about her, and awaited the result with Christian heroism and resignation On came the fiery monster, and almost in a moment the flames enveloped her She fell upon her face and lay there until the fire passed over. When she arose she found her clothing on fire Blinded with smoke and smarting from the burns she had received, still she had presence of mind enough to go to a marsh near by, where there was some water, and extinguish the fire in her clothing It was a narrow escape from a most painful death She was so badly burned that it was nearly eight months before she could use one of her hands, and her face was so blistered that the skin all came off She finally recovered, however, without showing many scars

Mr. Osgood sold out many years ago to the Messrs Timlin, and moved East

THE HONORABLE JOHN S ABELL, OF OTISCO

Of the hardy pioneers of this county, Mr Abell ranks as one of the first He was born in Constantia, Oswego county, N Y in 1834 His father, who was one of the early settlers in that portion of New York, and who was one of the owners of a saw mill, a grist-mill, and some manufacturing establishments, during the financial crash of 1837, lost all his property, and died in 1841, when John was only seven years of age The lad then went to live with his grandfather, where he remained until he was ten years of age, when his grandfather died From that time forward John earned his living by working out summers and attending school winters until he was thirteen. He worked at whatever came to hand until he was sixteen years old, when he commenced work on the Erie canal which he followed summers until the fall of 1856

In the fall of '56 he came West, more to visit the country than with any expectation of remaining here He visited his uncle in Winona county,

HON. AND MRS. J. S. ABELL.

arriving there in October, 1856 Austin Abell, his cousin, had already made a claim in Otisco, the September before, in company with H. G. Mosher, who afterwards was superintendent of schools in this county for several years, and is now in California.

About the first of January, 1857, H G Mosher, John S, and Austin Abell, left Winona county bound for Otisco On the first day out, just west of St. Charles, they met a blizzard which forced them to stop with a pioneer settler until the storm abated They reached Judge Canfield's place in Otisco, January 8, 1857. After remaining a short time, they returned to Winona county During the summer of 1857, John worked for R D Fellows of that county, to earn money to pay for eighty acres of land which he bought from his cousin, Austin. In the spring of 1858, he came out with Austin, and the two did breaking for themselves and others After the breaking season was over, they returned to Winona county and ran a threshing machine during the fall The next spring they came out and put in crops, made some other improvements, and returned to Winona county, where John S. was married in August, to Miss Hannah Harshman, who was born in the state of Pennsylvania in 1840

Their wedding tour was something out of the ordinary and a little amusing. Mr Abell bought a yoke of large, four-year-old steers that had never been used He also bought an ox-cart, strong and trusty He put on bows and a cover, making what is known in western phrase, as "a prairie schooner" With the assistance of three or four men he got the steers yoked and hitched to the cart, with Mrs Abell on board, and away they went over the prairie The exciting scenes of the trip would fill a small volume Whenever they met a team the steers would give the whole road and more too, generally making a large circuit before coming back to the road It took them a week to come to Otisco, camping by the way They remained a week at their farm, and then returned as they came, only in a more moderate and orderly way

That fall, Mr Abell made a trip to Stillwater to visit a brother He planned to work on the Mississippi steam boats a while but concluded, after the first half day trial, that he was not put up for a roustabout to be cursed by a half drunken boss, and abruptly cut his acquaintance with that noble functionary, and returned to Wilton on foot

He remembers that on the 5th day of June, 1859, there was a heavy frost which killed the leaves on the trees and cut the corn to the ground Nevertheless the corn came on and there was a good crop

During the winter of '62-3, H G Mosher and the two Abells "bached it" in a dug out 10x14 feet, with a fire place to cook by. It was originally a lime kiln He says it was so cold that winter that the water froze in one side of the bucket while the staves next to the fire were being scorched brown

Austin Abell lived here until 1863, when he enlisted and served in the army till the close of the war In the mean time he sold his other eighty acre lot to John who has since added eighty acres more, making a farm of 240 acres.

Mr and Mrs Abell have been the parents of eight children, seven of whom are living. Sarah, born July 11, 1862; John H, July 3, 1865, Marie, December 7, 1860, Irving O, Jan 3, 1872, Helen L, April 23, 1874, Emma and Jennie, July 13, 1876 John H died Jan 16, 1882

Mr Abell, though differing from a large majority of his townsmen politically, held some town office continually until his last year He served as town clerk of Otisco for twenty years, justice of the peace two terms, a member of the legislature in 1879, and county superintendent of schools from 1890 to 1894 In every station to which he was called he performed his duties with ability and fidelity

DEATH OF MR ABELL.

Since the foregoing was prepared for this history, Mr Abell has passed away About Nov 1, 1904, he suffered a slight stroke of paralysis, which deprived him of the use of one of his arms On the 27th of January he received another severe stroke, after which he remained in an almost helpless condition On the evening of June 30, 1905, he appeared to be as well as usual, but about two o'clock the next morning, Mrs Abell was awakened by a noise at her husband's couch and upon going to him found that he had fallen to the floor Irving Abell hastened to his mother's assistance and placed him back upon his couch, and a few moments afterwards he breathed his last

Mr Abell was a man of much more than ordinary ability He was a reader, a thinker, and a close reasoner He was not only honest in his business dealings but he was honest in his politics He believed in the doctrine of equal rights and privileges for all men—not only as a theory, but as a principle that should be maintained at all hazards and by all means He was a good neighbor and a kind husband and father, and a citizen, of whose record, private and official, Waseca county may well feel proud.

JAMES B HILL, VIVIAN.

The following facts were obtained from the late Mr Hill, in 1887.

The first permanent settlement in the town of Vivian was made in the summer of 1856, by two bachelors, B F Hanes and E. Woodruff The latter died in 1865 Mr Hanes was an educated man and somewhat of a recluse in his habits of life He was honorable and upright and a good citizen He died at his farm in Vivian in 1872 The memory of Mr. Hanes is still held in great respect by all the old settlers

The next settlers were Mr J B Hill, wife and children, Mrs. Hill being the first white woman to settle in the township. Mr Hill took a claim and dated his settlement July 2, 1857. He selected a beautiful farm on the Cobb river, section 31

James B Hill was born at Smithboro, Tioga county, N Y, in 1824 He learned the blacksmith's trade and followed the business for several years. He married Myanda E Stevens, who was a native of Ridgebury, Pa, in 1846 She was born in 1826

They moved to Wisconsin in 1850, and lived in what is now Green Lake county, where they carried on a farm. They were not entirely pleased with that location, and sold their farm, making their way by team to Minnesota, and opened a farm in Vivian as before stated.

Mr Hill came better prepared than the average immigrant of those days to open a farm in a new country. He brought a span of horses, a yoke of oxen, eight or nine cows and some young stock

The season for breaking was nearly closed when he made his claim, so that little of it was done that year.

The year 1858 brought little return to the husbandman for his toil, in Minnesota, and Mr. Hill opened a blacksmith shop in the then thriving village of St. Mary, in 1859, where he carried on the business for a year, and then returned to his farm

Mr. Hill narrowly escaped death in the spring of 1858. As he was going from St Mary to his home, with an ox team, he stopped to chat a moment with Mr. McLin, who then lived at Silver Lake Mr. McLin said that they had discovered large quantities of artichokes, and brought out some and gave them to Mr Hill, saying that they were good food for hogs He advised Mr Hill to plant some, if there were none growing wild on the Cobb Mr Hill put them into his pocket and soon after commenced eating them. He ate quite a quantity and soon became very sick. He must have had spasms, for when he recovered, he found that he had bitten his tongue severely He left his team and lay on the prairie for several hours unconscious

He was found by Nick Kremer and another man who took him up and carried him home Kremer, at first, supposed that he was intoxicated, but Mr Hill, by showing the roots and making signs, for he could not talk, made him understand that he was poisoned. Dr. Gove, of Wilton, was called, under whose treatment he soon recovered. It was soon discovered that the so-called artichokes were what are called wild parsnips

This narrow escape of Mr Hill explained the death of Michael McLin, which occurred a few days before, while he was plowing in the field It was at first supposed that McLin died of heart disease or in a fit, but after Mr. Hill's experience, no one doubted that he was poisoned in the same way It was Dr Gove's opinion, that Mr Hill owed his escape to the fact that he ate a quantity sufficient to cause vomiting and thus threw off the poison

Several Irish-American families settled in the eastern part of Vivian, in 1857, and the first death in the township occurred among these settlers An unexpected and very severe storm occurred early in that fall Mr. Sweeney was at St Mary He was thinly clad—not expecting such severe weather—and, in returning home, got bewildered and lost on the prairie, and was found dead not far from his home He left a widow, who was a sister of the Shanahan brothers

The next death was that of Henry T Daggett, who died of consumption, in July 1858

The first children born were a boy (George) to Mr and Mrs. Montreville Sias, and a child of Mr and Mrs Henry T Daggett George Sias is now a successful merchant in Kansas

Among the early settlers were the Wests, Moore, W. H Harman, Nels Sanderson, and Ole Johnson, who came in about 1858

At an early day, a post-route was established through Vivian, and Mr Hill was appointed postmaster under Buchanan's administration, a position which he held for the accommodation of the neighbors for a good many years He was elected chairman of the board of supervisors, and served as a member of the county board during the supervisor system

The pioneer school house was built in 1859, and a new one was built in 1866 Elder Smith, a pioneer clergyman of Wilton, used to hold services frequently in the school house

The first marriage ceremony was solemnized by Esquire Hill, the parties being an old bachelor named Clark, and Ann Stocker

The settlement in Vivian, as well as many other towns, experienced some demoralization during the Indian outbreak of 1862 They took the women and children to Wilton, the men returning the next day to look after stock and crops There were some losses both of cattle and crops, but nothing serious In a few days the women and children all returned

In February, 1864, Mr Hill enlisted in the Tenth Minnesota infantry and went to the front He was at the battle of Nashville, the siege of Spanish Fort, and was with his regiment in Kentucky Missouri, Mississippi, Tennessee, and other states He was honorably discharged at the close of the war

In 1872, he leased his farm and moved to Minnesota Lake, where he opened a blacksmith shop which he carried on for a time but finally disposed of He served as justice of the peace for several years at the Lake, but of late has devoted his time to the sale of marble work

He has two children Myron V Hill, of Minnesota Lake, who is doing a successful merchandise business there, and Viola S., now Mrs R N Gale, of Minneapolis

Mr Hill has always been a republican in politics and has taken much interest in public affairs

We are glad to know that he and Mrs Hill have a comfortable home, with enough to insure comfort in their declining years Their hospitality was proverbial among the early settlers, and they were liberal minded as well as liberal hearted They belong to that class of citizens who give stability to our form of government, and who make it possible that free institutions may exist without running into anarchy and lawlessness

Shortly after the foregoing was written, Mrs Hill suffered a stroke of paralysis and became a confirmed invalid for the remainder of her life, requiring the constant attendance and attention of Mr Hill

Mr Hill's health no doubt became impaired by his constant attention to Mrs Hill, and he passed to the great beyond at Minnesota Lake, Jan. 11, 1902, honored and respected by all who knew him

SPENCER J WILLIS

Among the young men who came to Minnesota early in 1857, was Mr S J Willis, who afterwards became quite prominent in the politics of the county We can best give an idea of the times and of the conditions of the country at that date by quoting his own words

"I was born in Franklin, Delaware county, N Y, July 28, 1833, and voted for John C Fremont in 1856

In the spring of 1857, I started for Hancock, our nearest depot, on the N. Y & E R'y At this place I flipped a cent to see whether I should go to California or Minnesota—heads Minnesota, tails California—and heads won West I went and stopped awhile in Chicago where I met S P Kellogg with whom, on the 30th day of April 1857, I left for Minnesota Our nearest route was via Galena, Ill, where we took passage on the "Old War Eagle," and I assure you it was one of the most stormy passages in some respects I ever saw Gambling was far above zero, and racing with other steamers was all the go We arrived at Reed's landing about 10 or 11 o'clock in the evening

After great effort we secured lodgings for the night at the American house, I think they called it And in some respects it was American—at any rate it seemed to be the asylum of every nationality on earth Such pandemonium! Such beds! Such rooms! I had never seen the like before

The 'school section' in which I tried to sleep, was filled with men, women and children of many nationalities and ways Most of the beds were made of blankets laid on the bare floor Our grips were our pillows And those sheets! I don't believe they had been washed since they were made, and they bore evidence of having been made long before, and used often

They would almost rise up like a board when one took hold of the end to get into bed The breakfast was substantial but coarse and for such lodging and breakfast we paid $2 50 each

May 4, 1857, we left Reed's landing and started with teams for Red Wing, passing over snow and snowdrifts from one to ten feet deep We were all day in making the trip to Red Wing There were many sleighs and numerous people in our van We remained over night in Red Wing, and in the meantime hired a conveyance to take us to Faribault for which I paid $48

At this point there were much talk and excitement about the Spirit Lake massacre which occurred in Iowa, the previous March, a number of the murdered victims having been former residents of Red Wing The name of Inkpaduta was in every one's mouth

We went by way of Cannon Falls where we had to stop over night We found that the further we got from the Mississippi river the less was the Indian excitement, and the less frightened people were Of course the scare at Red Wing was the cause of the enormous charge of $48 for taking us out into the dangerous (?) vicinity of Faribault

This was the time of the town site speculations I was shown lots in Cannon Falls that were only from three to five hundred dollars apiece, and I was assured over and over that by investing I would soon become rich. There was one log hotel on the town site, and that was all

It was long after dark the second day out from Red Wing before we arrived at Faribault, and here, for the first time since leaving Chicago, we found some of the comforts of civilized life. Mr Kellogg was a fine carpenter and joiner and soon got work enough. My health had been poor, but soon the invigorating climate and roughing it made me tired of loafing, and I told Kellogg that I thought I would go to work at my trade Having known me all my life, he nevertheless wanted to know what my trade was, and I had to confess that I did not know myself But as I sauntered down the street a day or two afterwards, it struck me, upon seeing a saw and hammer exposed in a store window, that I might as well start in as a carpenter, so I purchased a saw and hammer and secured a job as a journeyman carpenter at the same place that Kellogg was at work, for which I received $2 50 per day in gold coin And that was how I became a carpenter

After that week's work, Kellogg and I took the job of building the Tripp hotel, at Empire, later Iosco It was in May that, with packs on our backs and hatchets in our belts,—the latter to fight hostile Indians with—we struck out, via Jewett's Valley, for our new Eldorado, near the shores of Lake Elysian After some miles of journeying on foot we became tired and hungry and seeing a cabin in the distance made for it, hoping to get something to eat The woman said no, but that four miles further on we would find a hotel at the village of Swavesey We finally got there, and such a village! Such a hotel! It was here that we first saw H W Peck and John H Wheeler on their homeward way to Empire.

It was about 5 o'clock p m, when we struck Hotel Swavesey, and midnight when we arrived at Wheeler's place in Iosco The dogs gave us an uproarious and glorious welcome, the kind hostess and her daughters gave us a good lunch and blanketed us down as well as they could for the remainder of the night

In the early morning we took our frontier breakfast I shall never forget it The table top was of rough boards laid upon a couple of rough carpenter's saw-horses. Half barrels, boxes, tubs, etc, served as chairs, and everything was of the primitive order After breakfast, Mr Kellogg and myself went over to the embryo city, consisting of some three hundred and twenty acres of town lots and romantic streets, with only one small, log shanty and the saw-mill, as yet only sun-covered, in the whole city The shanty was used by Hosmer & Gifford as a store I think these gentlemen put up the first frame and board building in the place

Our next business was to make a fortune by securing a claim. Of course there were claims on all sides, but for all that, it was the fashion, in those days, to go claim hunting for a time So I started out, securing an Indian canoe, and crossed Lake Elysian from Long's point, armed and equipped for almost any emergency, and bound to find the best claim on the shores of that beautiful lake. Already there were several settlers in the timber west of the lake, but I thought there still might be some choice claims, hence my journey into the then wilderness.

"I traveled for a long time, that day, and looked the country over pretty thoroughly, but found nothing that really suited me for a claim I returned to Mr. S W Long's place, where I was kindly treated, and from there I got as far back as to N E Strong's ranch, when I was thoroughly tired out There I called for a drink of water and was waited upon by Mr Strong's young wife It was so neat in the little house, and the beds looked so comfortable that I pleaded hard for a night's lodging and finally succeeded I stayed for many a day at the home of these people where everything was so pleasant and agreeable. My search for land continued and I finally located on eighty acres one mile south of the west line of our young city.

I built a log cabin 12x14 feet, and seven feet high in the center It had an open door and window—most claim shanties had. A day and a night, shortly before proving up, I spent with Mr. Moses Emerson, brother of Mrs Strong, on his claim Emerson had an extra board and gave it to me to hang as a door to my house. In the morning I started with the board on my back. I took the trail for my shanty, but, in some way, the trail divided and I got on the wrong side of the divide. I traveled and traveled, yes, traveled, and should have been traveling yet, perhaps, had my strength held out I became tired, awfully tired, and very hungry, but I hung to my board, for it was my board—the only one in southern Minnesota for me, and yet I was bored. I was in the woods, I knew not where, and tired out, so I took the board I could not eat and laid me down upon it to rest I soon slept, and when I awoke it was near night I was confused, yes, lost in the woods. I sat down to think what to do, and, remembering that moss grew heavier on the north side of trees than on any other, and knowing that, by going east, I would strike the Indian trail running from Krassin's to Lake Elysian, I directed my course as nearly due east as possible and struck the trail about seven miles east from my base of operations Following this trail, I came to Jim Chadwick's place where, without over-much persuasion, I was induced to partake of a good, square meal, such as his good wife knew how to get

The next night we had to stay on my farm Emerson and I were to be witnesses, each for the other On that memorable night we spread our blankets in my own home to be This was one of my sick headache nights, and, as I was groaning, praying, scolding, on my pallet of dried grass, almost wishing I was dead, Emerson, in his dry way said 'Willis, you have one thing to be thankful for' Said I, 'For God's sake what is it?' 'Why,' said he, 'you ought to be thankful that you are at your own home while sick?' The thought was so ridiculous, under the circumstances, that I could but laugh most heartily, and it really drove away my headache The next day we did, as all others did, went to Faribault and proved up

I can remember only a few of the early settlers of Empire proper Those I remember are as follows Mr. McArthur, a brother-in-law of N E Strong, with his wife and child, Hosmer, Gifford, Jack Walton and wife from Ohio, Esquire M. S Green and wife from the same state, Mr Hagadorn and wife, and L P Kellogg John H Wheeler and family opened a hotel about this time Mr Ulysses Kellogg came out from the state of New York to help build the Tripp house Soon after, a Mr. and Mrs Francisco came to town, and 'Pap Tripp and wife came soon after Next came Mr A A Cotton, who was made one of the original proprietors of the town site and agent for all Wm Rockwell, from Smithport, Pa, also became a resident of our prospective city

In the winter of 1857 8 was established our first school which was taught by Mr L Kellogg, a brother of Mr L P Kellogg Mr L Kellogg is now employed in the custom house in New York city In the summer of 1857 Iosco, Okaman, and Elysian were rival towns so we, of Iosco, concluded to get up a glorious Fourth of July celebration We had our bills printed at Faribault, wherein we advertised martial music The people of our city thought they could get a drum and fife at Faribault, and appointed a committee to visit the town and report The committee, after making strenuous efforts, were compelled to report that such instruments could not be obtained there What was to be done?

I finally told Mr Strong that if he could saw me some thin boards for a drum barrel I would make a drum He sawed the boards and I put them in 'sweat' all day I then succeeded, after considerable work, in turning one over a nail keg Some one furnished a calf skin which I tanned with ashes and water, and succeeded in having the drum ready for the 'glorious' day Father Ira Willis beat the drum and a man from across the lake, whose name I have forgotten, played the fife It was a great day for Iosco, I assure you Okaman had also advertised a celebration and, not to be outdone by Iosco, had advertised martial music But ours was the only drum in the county, and negotiations were in order So it was determined that Okaman should join with Iosco and we would reciprocate by assisting them And thus we had a double celebration of the Fourth, and all had a grand, enjoyable time

In the winter of 1858-9, I taught the Okaman school, and, for pay took corn, potatoes, oats, or any other commodity the parents saw fit to bring in as pay Notwithstanding the almost universal poverty of all the ploneers, resulting from the financial crash and panic of 1857, the early settlers of Iosco and Okaman were a social, intelligent, and cultured people, and managed to get a great deal of enjoyment out of misery during the early days of the settlement of the county They were brave, courteous, open-hearted, and hospitable "

Mr Willis served as first town clerk of the town of Iosco, in 1858 In the spring of 1859, he went to St Paul and was employed as clerk in a store for a time He then returned to this county and was elected that fall as county auditor—the first auditor in the history of the county—and his salary was fixed at the magnificent sum of $360 per annum. He afterwards served as clerk of the court in this county He was appointed a clerk in the postoffice department at Washington in 1872, afterwards to a clerkship in the military department, which he held until his death which occurred January 3, 1900

"UNCLE BEN GIFFORD."

(By M P Satterlee)

One scarcely knows how far some little specialty in a local paper may reach and interest many readers Myself and others in this extreme north have lived in the bounteous county of Waseca in the earlier days Among the others are three daughters of a Mr. Egan, who lived, I think, at Wilton They are now Mrs. W T Spillane, Mrs J A Duffy, and Mrs J J Doe Mr Daniel Linnihan, section foreman for the N P Ry, also lives here. We have been much interested in your historical sketches of Waseca county, and it has brought many remembrances of old friends and happy days.

In your issue of December 11, I find in the account of the celebration of the Fourth of July, 1856, at Iosco, that Father Ira Willis played the drum and a "man from over the lake," (Elysian) played the fife I think this was "Uncle" Ben Gifford, whom I find mentioned in the same article, in the election of 1858, as overseer of the poor In 1863, when I came into the country, he lived at Elysian He was one of the oddest geniuses I ever knew, and with your permission I would like to pay a slight tribute to "Uncle Ben " There was not a man, woman, or child, horse, dog or cat, in Elysian, but knew and loved "Uncle Ben ' And it must have been for himself alone, for he was poor, unkempt, and unknown His life, till he came among us, was a blank to all As a musician, he was the impressario of the whole country Well do I remember those celebrations of Independence Day Uncle Ben, who resembled the revolutionary heroes in build, countenance, and military bearing, was always fifer and chief musician, and, from morning till night, "Yankee Doodle, Hail Columbia, Haste to the Wedding, and the Girl I Left Behind Me," (the last of which was a favorite of his) filled the people with patriotic fire And, on the side, let me say that the allowance for real good boys on that day, was one bunch of fire-crackers, at twenty-five cents per bunch They were hauled by team over a hundred miles.

Uncle Ben "led the singin'" in all the religious services without regard to sect or belief There was a melodeon at Okaman, which was the only instrument in the country, but he had no such assistance We took up the hymn-books containing words only, and Uncle Ben, snapping his tuning fork, said "la" with a strong nasal intonation, so we had the pitch and the words, and all knew the tune, and you may be assured that it was not long till the air was full of music, not lacking in spirit or erratic rendition The only meeting when Uncle Ben was "not in it" was a Methodist camp meeting at which the horse thieves got after the preachers' horses, probably a visitation of judgment upon the parsons

He was a patriot too, and when the dreadful draft, in the spring of 1865, took several of our respected citizens to the front, he was a great comforter with his homely philosophy, telling us "he knew as how the war weren't going to last long, noways ' etc He lived alone in his shanty, caught fish, trapped muskrats, and did various odd jobs, for subsistence Nor would he leave his own home to die He was taken with fever which developed into pneumonia, and it was two days before he was discovered, having been all that time without food or fire or care, suffering alone He calmly disposed of his insignificant estate, and died peacefully as a child God bless Uncle Ben There may be greater and wiser men from whom I have learned lessons of life, but his simple, honest, sunshiny nature has left its rays with me forever

MR THOMAS McHUGO

was one of the 1856 settlers of Janesville He was born in County Galway Ireland, in 1825, and came to America in 1845, first arriving in New York From there he went to Vermont where he was employed as a farm hand for seven years. In 1852 he came to Wisconsin, where he spent four years In 1856 he moved to Minnesota and located at Janesville, this county, where, by good judgment, economy, and foresight, he succeeded in acquiring a goodly share of this world's goods

He was married in 1866 to Miss Hannah Kelly, a daughter of Michael Kelly, of Faribault He was often known as a benefactor, always willing to assist those who merited assistance He was the architect of his own fortune and the builder of his own home In the storms of life he was always oak and rock, but in sunshine his warm heart opened up with genuine sunshine and showed a frank, open-hearted man He died as he lived, fortified with the sacraments of the holy Catholic church He left a wife, four sons, and four daughters to mourn his loss He died of paralysis Nov 21, 1896, at the age of seventy-one

MR. AND MRS THOMAS BARDEN

Mr and Mrs Thomas Barden are among those who came to this county at an early day, not to speculate in town lots, nor to loan money at six per cent a month, nor to seek to live upon the misfortunes of others, but to get a home for themselves and for those that might in the future

MR. AND MRS. THOMAS BARDEN.

constitute their family, and from the virgin soil of the then territory, by industry and frugality, obtain a living and accumulate a competency for old age Would to God that every citizen of this great republic were as industrious, as moral, as honest, and as upright, then indeed should we be very near that great day when that ancient rule—"Whatsoever ye would not that others should do unto you, do ye even not so unto them"—would become almost universal, and the cost of government be thereby reduced to the minimum

One winter evening, in 1891, Mr Thomas Barden told the following story of his settlement in Waseca county

"My full name is Thomas Barden I was born in the county of Meath, Ireland Mrs Barden's name was Honora Roark, and she was born in the county of Roscommon, Ireland I am now (1891) fifty-eight years of age and my wife fifty-four I landed in New York Aug 12, 1846, and she landed at the same place Nov 3, 1852 We were married in Pittsfield, Mass, Jan 30, 1855, and came to Minnesota in 1857, arriving at the then village of St Mary, in this county, May 27.

We were then blessed with one child, Henry, sixteen months old, one yoke of oxen, one cow, six chickens, a dog, an old wagon, a breaking plow, twenty-five cents cash capital, and a small stock of provisions But we enjoyed good health, and possessed a fair share of pluck, with a determination to build up a home of our own on some of Uncle Sam's lands

Our luck was of the mixed variety—sometimes good and sometimes not so good, but we have always managed to keep the wolf from the door

We had come from Hastings by wagon, and, although the weather was cool and raw, we had to sleep under our wagon at night in order to save money to buy feed for the oxen, and, as I said before, our money was all gone when we reached St Mary, except twenty-five cents Of course we had to stop there We made inquiry for vacant land, and found a vacant eighty on section five, in Wilton township We immediately filed on it, and went to work to break up the sod, to plant corn, potatoes and beans. This work had to be done before we could think of a house, and during that time we lived out of doors, often the rain poured down upon us during the night while in bed, and then everything had to be spread out and dried in the sunshine I tell you it was a sad change for the young wife to move from the heart of Yankeedom, where everything was comfortable to such an out door place as that was—and the half will never be told. It was bad enough to live thus exposed to the elements, but that was not the worst of it We were living on the border of the then Winnebago Indian reservation, and one day, lo and behold! we received a visit from eight or ten Indians, the first Mrs Barden had ever seen They were dressed in breechclouts and feathers, and carried guns and knives She thought her time had come, but it hadn't They looked about awhile and then left There was only one thing that saved me from destruction and that was that Mrs. Barden belonged to the Catholic church, and you know there is no divorce allowed by that She certainly had causes enough for divorce for taking her to such a place, but she 'broke in' all right and soon became a heroic pioneer, having many face to face encounters with the Indians before they were removed in 1863, often staying at the place nights and days alone except for our little boy.

But I was speaking of the house. We had no money, no lumber, no nails, but there was plenty of good timber on the Indian lands, and we did not steal it, of course, but then we took it in broad day without asking their leave We could not very well do otherwise, you know, as we could not talk their language. Nearly all the other settlers went along to keep us company, but they would not steal any Indian timber; O, no! However, I got a good set of logs, and the kind neighbors helped me raise my house, as was the fashion, you remember, and the last money went for a little something to drink, for in those days we thought it not lucky to raise a house without something to moisten the throat

Such is fashion or custom!

Well, the next thing was, what were we to do for a roof? We had neither lumber shingles, nor nails A good old Yankee neighbor told us to cut and peel the bark off from elm trees and lay the bark on some poles for a roof, we were Irish enough ourselves to cut some sods and cover the bark to keep it from warping and also to make the house warm for winter Well, we don't live there now, but I tell you it did us good service for a long time in our days of need

Finally the Indians complained of us for taking timber I think Major Mix was the agent at that time So one day he sent a posse of white men and half-breeds to arrest us and scare us off. I saw them coming as I was going home with a fine load of logs, and they steered straight for me and the oxen the men being well supplied with firearms. Thought I to myself, I am 'gone up' When they got close to me, one of them shouted 'Whoa!' and my oxen stopped. Then one of them asked, 'Where did you get them logs? A thought struck me that I would answer him in the Irish language, as I was pretty good at it So I gave him back correct answers to everything he asked Finally he got mad and swore a big oath saying 'You damned Norwegian, I will soon take you where you will talk English,' and then passed on

That fall, 1857, there was a financial crash, and we really did have hard times, and no mistake Money was scarce Property depreciated In fact there was no money in circulation here We used to swap one thing for another We didn't have money enough to pay letter postage It was no uncommon thing for us about St Mary to ask Warren Smith, then our postmaster, at St Mary, to charge up our letter postage to us Warren was a father to us all in those days. He kept a store in St Mary and proved a good friend to everyone in need during what we called 'Johnny-cake times' None of us had anything to make bread of except corn meal We had no grist mill nearer than Faribault or Okaman and only oxen to make the journey with. So, in the fall, we made a mill of our own by taking a tin pan and punching it full of holes in the bottom with a hammer and a nail, thus making a grater Then each evening we would grate meal enough to do for the next day

My first experience with wheat raising was not very flattering I sowed six bushels of club wheat in the spring The next fall we cleaned a spot near the stack, and when the ground was frozen we went at it with a flail After two or three days we got it threshed We had no fanning mills then, so we waited until the wind blew and then cleaned our immense crop I had just six bushels of very smutty wheat I took it to mill and had it ground When I got home the good wife was overjoyed with the prospects of some good biscuits, but disappointment is the lot of man and, in this case, of woman, for when the biscuits were baked they were as black as the ace of spades, with smut, and we had to fall back on corn cakes and mush

Well the next year the wheat was a great deal better and more to the acre Besides, Christie Hefferon and I hit upon a new way of threshing —we trod out the wheat with oxen

Some people complain that wheat is cheap now, but in 1859-60, we used to haul wheat thirty miles, to Faribault, and sell it for forty cents a bushel, if we hauled it to Hastings—sixty-five miles—we used to get from fifty-five to sixty cents a bushel It took us from five to six days to make the Hastings trip with oxen We were compelled to sleep under our wagons nights, and sometimes it rained or snowed on us. Times may be hard now for the tender-footed,' but they are not what they 'used to was' by several dollars to us in hand paid "

MR ISAAC BALLARD

was born in North Hamptonshire, Eng, eighty-five miles from London, Dec 14, 1834 He came to America in 1857, and stopped in Pennsylvania one summer He came to Minnesota in the fall of 1857, and boarded with Mr Chas Billings, of Iosco, who had been here one year He made a claim adjoining Mr Billings' place Mr Wm. Taylor, his half brother, came about the same time, and settled on a farm in Blooming Grove

Mr Ballard had no property whatever to commence with His first investment was changing work with a Mr. Churchill for a pig, and also with old Uncle Brossard for a calf He was compelled to keep bachelor's hall By working out a little here and a little there he was soon able to buy a pair of three-year-old steers from Enoch Roe, of St. Mary, paying therefor $45 He was obliged to change works to get some breaking done After this he raised a crop of wheat, part of which he traded for a wagon Some of his first crop of wheat he hauled to Wilton, and sold it for twenty-five cents a bushel in store pay. He remembers that the first good bargain he ever made was when he sold two chickens to two Indians for twenty-five cents each. He says he never felt so rich before in his life. The Winnebago Indians were near neighbors and frequent visitors in those days He married Catharine Erwin, Oct 7, 1865 His first investment in land was sixty acres, which he thoroughly improved.

His nearest cash market was Hastings or Redwing After a few years he was enabled to buy one hundred and sixty acres more, and he afterwards added another eighty to his large farm A few years ago he sold a half section of his land, and retained only eighty acres, upon which he now resides

He enlisted in Company C, First Minnesota infantry, as a recruit, and served during a portion of the war

Mr and Mrs Ballard have seven children—Carrie, Arthur, Clifton, Walter Isaac, Marshall, Eugene, and Maud Mr Ballard is one of our best and wealthiest farmers, and has a comfortable home in which to spend his declining years Mrs Ballard is a refined and worthy woman, a sister of Mr D A Erwin, of St Mary

MR WILLIAM M GRAY

Among the Blooming Grove settlers who faced the storms and blizzards and exposures and hardships of 1855, was William M Gray, one of the earliest settlers, who was born in Genesee county, New York He was married in his native state to Miss Lucina Fuller They came West at an early day and settled first in Illinois, then came to Iowa, where they tarried two years, and finally came to Blooming Grove, in the early summer of 1855, where they spent the remainder of their lives The last days of December, 1855, Mr Gray, in company with Simeon Smith, J M Bliven and Daniel Riegle started for West Union, Iowa, to obtain a supply of provisions They found the roads blocked with snow, the weather being intensely cold, and they made slow progress They had horse teams, but even with those they were long on the road Miss Jane Gray, now Mrs. O Powell, came back with her father from Iowa, on that trip Messrs Blivens and Riegle did not return at that time with the others Messrs. Gray and two Mankato men encountered rough weather and bad roads on their return, and between the Vaughn settlement and Owatonna they got caught out and had to remain in a grove or thicket over night They built a fire and managed to keep from perishing, but Mrs Powell frosted her feet and suffered much from the cold They had nothing to eat except flour wet with snow water and baked before the campfire on the end board of the wagon box When Mr Gray got back as far as Mr Hatch's place, he left his daughter and his load and went home on foot to get oxen to haul the load the rest of the way, the horses being nearly tired out The family had eaten the last potatoes the day the father reached home Mr and Mrs W M. Gray reared a family of nine children, one of whom, Melissa, died at the age of twelve years Mr Gray died in 1872, of dropsy, aged sixty-four years. Mrs Gray died some years after, aged seventy

WILLIAM HENRY GRAY

known as Henry was born July 22, 1840, in the state of Illinois He came to Minnesota with his father and participated in all the labor and hardships incident to pioneer life At the age of twenty-one he enlisted in Company F., Fifth Minnesota infantry, and served his country faithfully for over three years. He participated in many battles and was always found at his post On the fifth of June, 1865, he married Miss Rosalia Ketchum, who was born in Ohio, May 24, 1846, and who came to Minnesota with her parents in 1856

This worthy citizen, after years of suffering, passed to the "Great Beyond" Monday morning, Feb 27, 1905 He left surviving him his widow, one son, Fred W, and four daughters, Mrs E R Stevens, Mrs D M Tanner, Mrs W R Ellis, and Miss Isora, to mourn his departure He was an honored and prominent member of Comee lodge, No 25, I O O F, of Waseca, and of McKune Post G A R He owned a farm of one hundred and sixty acres, a mile northwest of Waseca, and left his family in comfortable circumstances.

MR H P CHAMBERLAIN

Some years ago, when the writer was considered a pretty fair republican, he had a chat about "ye olden times," with Mr. Chamberlain, who gave substantially the following account of himself

"I was born in Sparta, Livingston county, New York, April 13, 1833 My parents emigrated from there to Florence, Erie county, Ohio, when I was a year old My father, being the victim of the saloon traffic like thousands of others, made it necessary for me, at the age of nine years, to shift for myself I worked out by the month and day, in Ohio, until I was about twenty years of age when I went to Grand Island, Lake Superior, and worked about a year I was also employed in the Michigan pineries one winter Early in the spring of 1855, I started for Minnesota, coming through from Michigan, accompanied by my brother, Orlando, and arriving at what is now the city of Rochester, Olmsted county, April 13 My personal property consisted of one horse and a small amount of money for expenses After looking the country over, I made a claim south of Rochester, near Root river, put up a small cabin, and eight days afterwards sold my improvements for $200 to a man named Wilson. Then, in company with Messrs Tuttle, Keys, Roberts, and Thomas, I came to LeSueur county, about a mile north of Okaman, and took another claim The next June, 1855, Fred Roberts, George Johnson, Chas Christenson, Eph Davis, Frank and John Conway, came in and settled near by George Johnson was the first proprietor of Okaman village site. I held my claim in LeSueur county until March, 1856, when I sold to Patrick Kelly and removed to Iosco, on section 28. But before I sold out in LeSueur county, late in the fall of 1855, I was employed by George Johnson to take my oxen and sleighs and go with Jim Johnson, the hired man, to Iowa for provisions We started about the 17th of December, with two sleighs and four pair of oxen, with instructions to bring back 8,000 pounds of flour, pork, etc We arrived at Auburn, Iowa, about the first of January, 1856, and while purchasing our loads, there came a heavy snow storm blockading all the roads We bought the pork in West Union, and the flour in Auburn, putting 4,000 pounds on each sleigh We started on the return trip about January 6 It was one of those undertakings which tried a man's pluck and powers of endurance

"In many localities the stopping places were from eighteen to twenty-five miles apart The roads were very little traveled and badly drifted In many places we were compelled to shovel through the drifts, and sometimes had to unload and reload to get through. At two places we stayed at the same house three nights The first night, we left our loads on the prairie, five miles away, in order to get to the house. We went back the next day and brought in the loads, again staying over night The third day we went on five or six miles, and returned to stay the third night The next morning at break of day we were again on the road

"Jim Johnson was a peculiar fellow He was a large muscular man, would swear like a trooper, and was full of brag and bluster, pretending not to believe in any hereafter, and apt to ridicule all religious belief The day we started to cross the large prairie, between the two Cedars, near the Iowa line, the weather was cold and stormy Night came on before we got in sight of any house, the lead cattle were tired out and refused to face the storm, so we were obliged to stay all night without shelter or protection from the cold blasts, and nothing to eat but frozen bread As soon as all hope of getting to a house was lost, Johnson's brag and bluster and profanity turned in the opposite direction, and he commenced to weep like a child, and pray like a lunatic He was so beside himself with fear of perishing, that it was some time before he could be induced to secure his teams or take any precautions against freezing All night, at intervals, he would cry and pray, exhibiting the most abject fear He was considerably frost bitten before we reached the settlement next morning, where we found food and shelter

"The fact is that this state has never seen colder weather than during the winter of 1855-6

"Between Austin and Owatonna we were again caught out all night, but it was not so bad as the night between the Cedars, as we found a grove which afforded some protection From Owatonna we went northwest and reached a house in Blooming Grove The next day we reached Okaman under the sheltering wing of the Big Woods, thankful for a chance to rest a little."

Mr Chamberlain was married to Sarah Hatch, February 22, 1857 She was the daughter of Curtis Hatch, who settled in Blooming Grove in 1855 He was a blind man and died in Moody county, D T, in 1884 Mrs Chamberlain was born in the state of Ohio She resides on the old farm at this writing, (1904) while Mr Chamberlain does business in the city of Waseca

Mr Chamberlain was elected to the office of justice of the peace soon after the organization of the township, and held the office for ten consecutive years by reelection Before the railroads were built into this section, he did his share of marketing grain, at points on the Mississippi river—camping out on the green-carpeted prairie, under the broad canopy of infinite space, with prairie wolves as watch dogs and prairie chickens to sound the reveille

MR ANTHONY GORMAN

This gentleman, for many years justice of the peace in St Mary, was born in the county of Donegal, in the north of Ireland, in 1825. He came to America in 1848, and landed in New York He was employed in Orange county, New York, where he remained some ten months He afterwards went to Duchess county, the same state, where he lived three years He then came west to Aurora, Ill, where he remained thirteen months. He next came to St Mary, Waseca county, where he arrived in the month of June, 1856, and settled on section 28, which has since been his home He had at one time two hundred forty acres of land, but now, has only two hundred, one hundred thirty-five acres of which are cultivated He was elected justice of the peace in 1859 or 1860, and held that office for nine or ten years. He has been chairman of the board of town supervisors, and for some years was town treasurer He brought with him to the county some $400 or $500 in money His first house was made of sod. He afterwards built a small farm house, and some years ago he built his present residence He is a bachelor and rents his land One season during the early years of his settlement he made ten trips to Hastings with wheat He says he distinctly remembers the "Johnny cake and cold water" times when he had to pay twenty-two cents a pound for pork and fifty-five cents per hundred for corn meal, and only got three pounds of sugar for a dollar At this writing (1904) he is hale and hearty for a man of eighty years.

MR ROSCOE A PHILBROOK

About 1895 Mr Philbrook gave the following story of his life

"I was born in the town of Palmyra, Somerset county, Maine, June 16, 1839 My parents came to Wisconsin in the year 1844, and lived first in Jefferson county, afterwards in Marquette county

"In the spring of 1856 we covered two wagons and started for Minnesota We first lived in Olmsted county In the spring of 1857 we again started west, arriving, about the first of June, in the town of Byron, in this county We had four yoke of oxen, two covered wagons, very little money, and no stock Our family numbered six in all, William and Sarah Philbrook, and their four boys

"After locating our claims, the first thing we did was to start the breaking plow, and that summer we turned over ninety-five acres of the prairie sod We planted a few potatoes, some corn, etc We did considerable breaking that season for others at $5 and $6 per acre We lived in our covered wagons five months before we built our house We raised very little the first year, and experienced many hardships the first few years of our settlement I remember that almost every one went barefoot summers, and wore bag pants and other coarse clothing We often paid as high as $6 per hundred for flour, which had to be hauled from Hastings, eighty miles distant. At one time we lived two weeks on potatoes and salt and no bread.

"The first public school was taught in our district in 1863—kept in a vacated house Several terms were taught in this house, but in 1866 we built a school house

"The first death that occurred in the neighborhood was that of the infant daughter of Asa Francis on the 17th of June, 1858

"William Philbrook, my father, died in 1864, and was buried in the Freeborn cemetery, and Sarah Philbrook, his wife, died in June, 1890, aged eighty-three years Lyman and George, the two youngest sons, are both dead Byron lives in California."

"One of the first settlers in Otisco was Zachariah Holbrook, who was born in Courtland county, N Y, in 1820 He went to Chautauqua county N Y, when a young man, and married Mary Jane Bumpus, who was born in Cataraugus county in 1824 They came west as far as Wisconsin, where they lived a few years, and then came to Otisco early in May, 1856, settling near the LeSueur Their first house was built of bark and poles In August, 1858, their oldest son, Marvin, was drowned Mr Holbrook died April, 1887, and was buried in the Wilton cemetery

"David Beavins, Wm Beavins and Isaac Lyng settled in Byron township in June, 1857, where they resided for many years David Beavins now lives near Alma City, this county Mr Lyng died in the service of his country Wm Beavins served as a soldier during the Sioux outbreak under Gen Sibley, and also with the Fifth regiment in the south He died some time ago, and was buried in the Wilton cemetery"

Roscoe was a modest, retiring man and held no office except that of supervisor for one term He was ill for a long time and died some years ago.

MR SAMUEL W FRANKLIN,

one of the early school teachers of the county, a number of years ago wrote the following characteristic letter to the author

"I received a circular from you asking for my biography At least, it amounts to something like a biography to answer your questions Now I have some objections to having my biography published My principal objection is that I have sometimes been very foolish and have done things that I don't like to talk about Besides I have not been a successful man in making and saving money By the way, I have been studying to find something that I can tell of with a feeling of complacency and I can think of only one thing and that is, that I have paid out in Waseca county between four and five thousand dollars in interest money

"Now, I am not sure that this is a matter to feel complacent about It is true that I had only the handling of this money, but then, what more do the successful moneyed men have? Surely, I have been of some use The foxes would not fare well if there were no geese! But I confess that this is not much satisfaction to me

"But now for the autobiography In the autumn of 1845, a youth of twenty-one was slowly plodding his way from the northern part of Pennsylvania to Illinois He was driving a pair of very poor old horses, which required the almost constant use of the whip to keep up a slow motion He does not own the team but is working his passage and camping out. There is nothing striking in his appearance except verdancy Except for this, he is very common place in his appearance You can see nothing very smart or heroic But he is bound for the land of promise and is in dead earnest He is full of wild and extravagant notions, and nothing but a severe discipline in the school of experience can dispel his illusions and make him reasonable He is going to get rich, to make money, but he has no reasonable, well-defined plan of action His first idea is to teach school His education is very limited and he has not the quickness of eye necessary to a teacher But he is full of hope and expectation Difficulties are nothing, and, at last, the sight of Illinois and its prairies, its immense stretch of unoccupied land, so rich, so beautiful of promise for the future, dawns upon his vision Is it to be wondered that he was full of enthusiasm for Illinois, and of contempt for the comparatively rough and poor soil of northern Pennsylvania? An extract from a letter he wrote home at the time of his arrival at the then new town of Dixon, Ill, will illustrate. Speaking of the land he had left, he apostrophizes

"Land of stones and cradle-knolls,
Land of hard-pan and hemlocks,
Land of stumps and broomsticks,
Is there nothing amid all thy pleasant scenes
To call forth one long-drawn sigh of regret
At leaving thy peaceful shores?"

"He engaged a school, the first district school taught in the now city of Dixon, but after a month's trial became satisfied that he had undertaken more than he could do and he gave it up

"This was failure No. 1 Could he have been moderate and reasonable, and engaged in some country school he might, no doubt, have succeeded passably well But he now gave up all thoughts of that kind and hired out to work on a farm It was a time of depression in business Farmers had to draw their wheat one hundred and ten miles to Chicago and sell it for sixty or seventy cents per bushel, pork was $3 per cwt; beef was not much better, butter six to eight cents per pound, eggs three to four cents per dozen, corn fifteen cents per bushel, oats about the same He hired out for $12 per month by the year and worked three years for the same man. There was but little of the country occupied. There was as good land as ever was seen in market at government price, but no buyers

"His next extravagant idea was to keep stock—be a kind of cow-boy.

I don't think the plan was necessarily altogether extravagant, but his plans were very extravagant There was a very good, unoccupied house several miles from inhabitants and in the timber Around and near the house was a beautiful stretch of natural meadow and pasture His plan was to occupy the house entirely alone and keep his stock. It was a kind of hermit plan, very wild and extravagant, and ended very disastrously He found himself alone in the world without means, almost without friends—for his wild notions had alienated those who would have been his friends. But he was not disheartened

Among some poetic effusions which he contributed at this time to a Chicago literary paper, was this:

Though all the powers of fate combine
To blast my prospects, and consign
    My hope unto the dust
My spirit proud will never yield,
Nor shun the fight, nor quit the field,
    But still the future trust

This was failure No 2

"He next went to Dupage county, Ill, and hired to the same man for whom he had formerly worked

"When the time came for winter school, he with some difficulty engaged a school which, they said, was badly run down There would not be more than eight or ten scholars and they would give him $14 per month and board. He asked them if they would agree to give him $20 per month if he would make the school average twenty scholars They agreed that they would He went to work and succeeded in filling the house with scholars He taught three winters in the same district at $20 and board He had now considerable popularity as a teacher, more than his abilities warranted

"He came to New Richland the spring Buchanan was inaugurated, in the month of March He came from Illinois the fall before, and staid at Willow Creek, twelve miles this side of Red Wing, through the winter He kept a hotel there, and O Powell and likely some others in the county were his customers

"He had been looking over the state considerably and was well satisfied with it He found here when he came A G Sutliet, E B Stearns, Z Holbrook, N Lincoln, the Northups, Grovers, Scotts, and Jenkinses Besides, in his neighborhood, there were several town proprietors trying to start a town near the Holbrook place, called Otisco The only wholesale drygoods store ever built in that city is now a part of Wm Ivers barn There was a saw mill and some boards were sawed there A school house was built the next year costing about one hundred dollars Miss Rachel Dodge, who afterwards married Dr Gove, was the first teacher, and Mrs G R Buckman the next The house was used for religious meetings, political and other debates, etc Few of our more costly, modern school houses do as well

'A. G. Sutlief was the only wealthy man in the settlement, and he had some enemies as well as a good many friends At one time a party of his enemies were coming from Wilton in the evening by a very lonely place which had the reputation of being haunted Sutlief managed to occupy the haunted place when they were passing, and acted the ghost to his own satisfaction The fright caused a stampede of the ox-teams, when Sutlief slipped back by a short way, and when they came by in some excitement he asked all about the trouble

"He ought to have told you that he brought with him, when he came, four yoke of oxen, a span of horses, and three cows But he left some debts behind which he had to pay, and he puts that in as a partial excuse for not being rich now"

Mr Franklin was one of our best and most conscientious citizens He owned a good farm in New Richland township, and died Aug 21, 1898, of erysipelas, highly respected by all who knew him

MR THOMAS MALONEY,

of Iosco, was born in Ireland, in 1834. He came to America in 1852, and lived in the state of New York about two years He then went to Pennsylvania where he lived ten years, and then came to Minnesota in 1863, and settled in Iosco He married Miss Catharine Gorman, in 1861, in Pennsylvania She came from Ireland in 1852 They have eight children, four boys and four girls. They have a valuable farm In the first years of his settlement in this county he, like others, hauled his wheat to Hastings, that being our nearest market One year he obtained fifty cents a bushel for his wheat In the year 1871 he lost all his crop by hail. He is one of our most public spirited citizens, and honorable in all matters

MR SAMUEL LAMBERT

Among the pioneers who earned their daily bread by honest toil, few are more entitled to honorable mention than Mr Samuel Lambert, of St Mary In an interview with him in 1897 he said

'I was born in Three Rivers, Canada, May 15, 1836. When nineteen years of age I went to New Hampshire I lived there until 1863 and was married Jan 15, 1863, to Miss Catharine Sullivan She was a native of Waterford, Ireland In March, 1863, we came to Minnesota and stopped in Hastings for a time We opened a boarding house on the railroad then being constructed near Hastings, for one G W. Cummins, a contractor, and ran it some four months Cummins then left without paying anyone, and we lost $450 by the deal. I followed the rascal as far as Crow River, and then lost track of him. I then worked in a stave factory for some time I bought my land in St Mary in 1864, but did not move onto it until 1868. In that year we built a shanty. I remember when the shanty was completed I got of Tom White a dollar's worth of sugar, a sack of flour and a pound of tea, and had only sixty cents in money left. When we got the flour home we found that it was so injured by kerosene oil we could not use it, and I hired a man to take it back, as I had no team of my own then Soon after I got a yoke of cattle of Matt Keeley for which I agreed to pay $130 Our first crop was that of 1868—had twenty acres broken in 1867 I paid for seed wheat $1 25 per bushel to John Baldwin, and raised one hundred eighty bushels We put one hundred bushels into the house and eighty bushels into a crib outside Late in the fall, Tom White, having a grading contract on the W & St P R R. set a prairie fire, which burned the eighty bushels of wheat and nearly burned the house I was absent from home at the time, working for $3 a day in the Faribault stave factory Tom refused to pay for the burned wheat and other damage, and for some years after we had a tough time trying to make a living and pay debts After a while we got along better and have managed to make a living. I now have the old home eighty and we have eighty acres more for the boys"

Mr Lambert died of paralysis April 17, 1899, aged sixty-two years, eleven months and two days

MR. WILLIAM LEE

of Iosco, is one of the prominent pioneers of Waseca county In his notes, furnished by request in 1897, he said

"I was born Oct 10, 1831, on a farm, in county Wexford, Ireland, at a place called Killcotty, midway between the town of Enniscorthy and the village of Oulart The last named places are ten miles apart I emigrated to America and landed in New York on St Patrick's day 1851 I had a cold reception from the elements as it was snowing when I landed from the vessel, and it continued to snow and blow all day I hired to a farmer on Long Island, a few miles from Brooklyn, and worked for him until navigation opened in the rivers and lakes and then I started for Milwaukee, Wis I went to Albany by steamboat, thence to Buffalo by freight train, and by steamboat from Buffalo to Milwaukee. The journey took ten days and the weather was cold for April I lived on the poorest and roughest kind of food and did not see a bed during the whole journey

On the 25th of April, I went to work for a farmer twelve miles from Milwaukee, for eight dollars a month The next June, I went to work on the Prairie du Chien railroad My pay was seventy-five cents a day in script, worth seventy-five cents on the dollar at the bank in cash At that time there were but twenty miles of railroad in all Wisconsin, from Milwaukee to Waukesha

After remaining a little more than a year in the state, I went to Chicago and worked unloading lumber from vessels in the harbor May 4, 1852, I commenced working on the Rock Island railroad, near Ottawa, Ill. That scourge of the human race cholera, broke out among the men, and I shouldered my "turkey" and went to Elgin, Ill, where I worked for the C & G. railroad company and was with the track layers when the track was built into Rockford I was on the first train that ever crossed the railroad bridge at that place, this was the first railroad bridge across Rock river After a time I was fireman on a locomotive that hauled the construction train This was the first train that ran to Beloit, Wis Next I was night watch in the round house at Turner Junction

I went South in the winter 1853-4, to Memphis, worked on a levee in Arkansas, returned to Chicago in the spring and worked in a livery barn for a month, and then worked as a section hand on the Dixon Air Line railway, at Lodi, Ill.

I was united in marriage with Catharine Behan at Freeport, Ill, Aug. 10, 1854 She came from Ireland to America in 1853 We went to the same school in Ireland In the summer of 1855 I ran a stationary engine in a machine shop and foundry, at Rockford, Ill

We came to Minnesota, Hastings, Nov 15, 1855 It was a small place at that time, the population was made up of whites, half-breeds, Indians, and one black man Red Owl's band of Sioux Indians camped near the village all winter

That winter I cut cord wood and scored timbers for a mill that was being built in the Vermillion river, near town

While there I saw a glowing account in the Boston Pilot about the Lake Elysian country, so I came to look for a claim and arrived at Lake Elysian March 26, 1856 I traveled in parts of Waterville, Janesville, Elysian and Iosco I selected the claim I now live on in Iosco

There was a man in company with me named James Hennessy He took the southwest one half of section 6 We left the claims with the intention of not coming back, if we found land that suited us better, not finding any, we returned about the middle of April At that time a young man by the name of James Foard came with us and we worked together building shanties by cutting small logs and carrying them to the building place Neither one of us had a team, and a yoke of oxen at that time would cost about $200.

I had $200 when I came to Minnesota but I bought a lot in Hastings and paid $100 for it which left me short of funds

There was claim jumping in those times, so Mr Hennessy remained to watch the claims and I went to Hastings to bring his wife and mine and our household goods out here.

We got on a steamboat and went to St Paul and thence by steamboat to St. Peter on the Minnesota river The Minnesota river was very crooked and we were three days on the journey

I made every effort in St Peter to hire a team to take us out to the claims but was unsuccessful, and we started to walk the twenty-five miles It was four o'clock in the afternoon when we started and we intended to stop over night at some house on the way, we were told the country was settled for a short distance.

We kept on traveling until we got beyond the settlement, and night coming on we found ourselves in the dense woods Not wishing to go back we traveled on and soon came to a claim shanty It was unoccupied but we stayed there all night I built a fire in one corner and we warmed up, for the nights were cool, being the second week in May, 1856 I found some potatoes in a hole under the floor and we cooked them in the fire and had roast potatoes for supper We had some quilts and the women slept on a bunk in one corner, while I kept fire all night

Next morning we started, on empty stomachs, for our destination Nothing could be seen but large timber

About the middle of the forenoon we began to meet Indians by the hundreds They were all shapes, all sizes, and all ages. We were told there were three hundred of them but there seemed to us to be nearer three thousand After traveling ten or twelve miles we came to a house where Greenland is now. George Jaqua lived there (he now lives in Elysian), it was then long after noon but we got some dinner which we ate with a relish

After dinner we came through in good shape Mr Hennessy met us on the bank of Lake Elysian and there was joy all around

We boarded with a Mr Johnson until our cabins were fixed so we could occupy them We peeled the bark off the elm trees and roofed our cabins with it as there was no lumber nearer than Faribault twenty miles distant

There were five families living in the town when I came to Iosco. There is but one of them here now, Mr David Wood's, on section two"

Mr and Mrs Lee have been the parents of eight children Mary Ann, Catharine Ellen J., John, Maggie, Susan, James and Emma

Mr Lee served as county commissioner from 1871 to 1873 inclusive, and has been elected to various town offices for many successive years. He has also held important positions in his church parish and in his school district. He owns a good farm and is in a position to enjoy the fruits of a well-spent life

MR EBENEZER B STEARNS

This well-known gentleman and early pioneer, in September, 1897 furnished the following brief facts regarding his life and works

He was born in Readsborough, Bennington county, Vermont, Oct, 1, 1812 When he was four years of age, his parents removed from Vermont to near Syracuse, Onondaga county N Y

In that locality he learned the carpenter and joiner trade which he followed for a number of years, at times working as a millwright Fifty years ago he built a mill at Bellville, Canada West

In 1853, he married Miss Emily Garrett, a native of Onondaga county, N Y, and late the same year they came west, living first at Greenbush, Sheboygan county, Wisconsin There he bought eighty acres of land, built a house and barn, and made other improvements. After three years of hard work in Wisconsin, he concluded to try his fortune in Minnesota.

Early in the spring of 1856, in company with Mr Zachariah Holbrook, he visited the new settlement along the LeSueur river in this county After a pretty thorough examination, he concluded to cast his lot in Waseca county

His first arrival was April 7, 1856 He then returned to Wisconsin, settled his matters there, and returned by prairie schooner, arriving on the Le Sueur about the first of August His first introduction was to the claim jumping struggle going on at Wilton He was the innocent cause of the claim changes which took place between Tom Kerr, "Uncle" Fisk, Tarrant Putnam and Col Ide, as related elsewhere in this history in the statement of Thomas J Kerr He soon cut loose from all entangling alliances at Wilton and moved up the river to Otisco, where, on the 5th of August, 1856, he made his claim Here he broke the native sod, built a house and stables, and made large improvements He sold his first claim after a few years, and then obtained the fine farm where he now resides

He was early called upon to take an active part in piloting our new county through the financial disasters and business depressions of 1857 and following years At the October election of 1857, Mr Stearns was elected county commissioner—his associates being Mr John Bailey, (late of Medford, Steele county,) then of St Mary, and Mr L C Wood, of Woodville, who died a soldier of the Union He was re-elected for three successive years, and was one of the ablest and most conscientious officers that ever served the county

After three years of faithful and poorly-paid services for the county, he declined further honors as an officer, and devoted himself wholly to his own affairs He did some building for other parties in an early day, erecting the first frame school house in the Brisbane district Farming, however, was his principal business He now owns a farm of two hundred fifty-two and one-half acres, all improved His family were three boys and three girls The boys, William H., George, and Charles, are all married and living in the vicinity The eldest girl married Frank Weed and died several years ago Mary married M R Baldridge, a clergyman, Cora became the wife of Mr Wm. Root, of Wilton

At this writing (1897) Mr Stearns is almost eighty-five years of age and yet he retains to a remarkable degree his physical and mental vigor He and his wife are general favorites, socially, with old and young

In addition to rearing their own six children, they have had the care and education of two grandchildren left by their daughter, Mrs Weed

Ah, if the world were only filled with such people, what a paradise it would be! Courts and lawyers and constables and a horde of office-holders who now "eat our substance" could be dispensed with and put to work

Since the foregoing was written, Mr Stearns passed peacefully away on the 15th day of May, 1899, honored by the whole community The son, William H, also died Jan 10, 1905.

MR. SIMON HENRY DRUM

contributed the following to the Waseca County Herald, Feb 25, 1898

"I came to Waseca county, May 3, 1859 After visiting with Mr Austin Vinton's family and others in the neighborhood for several weeks, I became a clerk in Dr D S Harsha's drug store in Owatonna, where I remained until August of the same year

My first visit to Clear Lake was in that month, when I accompanied Mr Vinton, who was going after lumber at Forrest's saw mill, which was situated in the hollow just east of where Wm Deverell now lives, near the lake shore This trip will always remain very distinct in my memory We had two yoke of oxen On our arrival, Mr Vinton requested me to unhitch the cattle and let them run in the yoke to "bait", while he went to hunt up Mr Forrest I was decidedly green at that business Whether it was my greenness that he objected to, or a natural viciousness that he possessed, I am unable to say, but certain it is, one of the steers, when I went between them to take them off the wagon-tongue, began to kick and paw and finally ran off leaving me sprawling in a fashion that Mr Vinton seemed to think very amusing, though I failed to see the fun of it But I was only a tender-foot" then However, when he saw that I was unable to rise, he helped me up and apologized for his levity, for he was one of the kindest of men I must have been a sight as I was scratched considerably and my clothes were pretty badly torn, especially my pantaloons But my worst hurt was my left leg, the small bone of which was broken between the knee and the ankle I didn't realize that it was fractured at the time, so it was never properly set

Among the settlers I found here when I came were Austin Vinton, of Woodville, T J Stevens, M T C. Flower, Geo Hatch, Howard Hatch, Anton Schuldt, Wm Schuldt, and C H Wilker, of Meriden Of these, Mr Vinton has gone to his long home, Mr Stevens is living in Massachusetts, Mr Flower is in St Paul, Mr Geo Hatch has a farm in Byron township in this county, but lives in New Richland. Howard Hatch is dead Anton and William Schuldt are still living in green old age on their preemption farms, and are very prosperous. Mr Wilker and wife are living near San Diego, California Their children are respected and well to do. most of them are still living in Meriden. [Mr Wilker died in the spring of 1905 —Ed]

The year '58-9 was what is known as the 'Johnny-cake year' among the old settlers, when the best-to-do had mush and milk for breakfast, Johnny-cake for dinner, mush and milk for supper, with fried mush next morning for breakfast. Lucky the family that had fifty pounds of white flour for the year It was treasured and only used when distinguished guests arrived I well remember one of the matrons censuring a hostess for extravagance in making a pan of biscuits when only her neighbors were present "

MR GEORGE R BUCKMAN

Died, April 17, 1899, at 11 o clock p m , of neuralgia of the heart, George R Buckman, of Waseca, Minnesota, aged sixty-six years, three months and twenty-four days

Mr Buckman was born December 23, 1832, at Crown Point, New York, and in his boyhood days played many a time under the old oak tree to which Gen Putnam was bound by the Indians when taken prisoner during the French and Indian war, prior to the Revolution. The tree was still standing there when he visited the place during the War of the Rebellion.

At the age of twenty he went to New Hampshire and spent somewhat over two years with an uncle in the hardware business Prior to this he had learned the carpenter and joiner trade

In 1855 he came West, arriving at Winona on the 29th of April At that time Winona was a decidedly small village About the 1st of May following, he, in company with another young man, went to Rochester This place then contained only one or two houses, one of which, of course, was an inn There was no bridge across the Zumbro, and the water was high They went down the river some distance and finally waded the stream, putting up at Head s tavern He staid a few days, selecting a claim in the mean time After taking the claim he needed an ax, but not an ax could he purchase in Rochester As Mr Head was going to Winona with a team, Mr. Buckman concluded to return with him.

Shortly after his return, he fell in with a Scotchman, by the name of Brownlee, and the two soon commenced to burn lime. The bluffs just west of the village contained excellent limestone and he and his partner did a thriving business, lime then being worth a dollar a barrel at the kiln After working hard through the summer they both took the ague in the fall. Not being used to that disease, he thought he would surely die They left the shanty by the lime-kiln and went over to town After considerable shaking and taking medicine, he got better and taught the Winona school that winter—the second term taught in the place

The ague still hung about him, and all the next summer he was unable to work much The next October he came as far west as Waseca county, looked the country over pretty thoroughly, and entirely recovered his health. He returned to Winona and settled up his affairs, coming again to this county in January, 1857 His entry this time was in a hard storm or blizzard. He and George Tremper, with a horse team, left Owatonna about noon and did not reach Wilton until 9 o'clock in the evening. The next day he went to St Mary and stayed with a Mr Crossman who had opened a boarding house. Everything in and about St Mary was then new, and the carpenter business offered inducements which Mr Buckman accepted

He taught the St Mary village school during the winter of 1860-1.

In the spring of 1861, as the report of the rebel guns fired on Fort

Sumter reverberated over the continent, G R Buckman was among the first to respond to the call for volunteers, and enlisted in Company G, First Minnesota regiment. His comrades from the village of St Mary were Norman B Barron and Charles C Davis, and though they passed through all the hard-fought battles of three years' service, they came out without a wound. His company when it entered the service was commanded by Capt Lewis McKune, who was shot dead at the first battle of Bull Run

He and his company participated in the siege of Yorktown, the Peninsular campaign, the battles of Antietam, Fredericksburg, Fair Oaks, West Point on York River, Gettysburg, and numerous other battles His company participated in a sharp fight at Bristow station, where Sergeant Niedam captured twenty prisoners in a most daring and reckless manner

At the close of his term of enlistment he was mustered out of the service, May 5, 1864. Shortly after, he opened a country store in St Mary, as modestly as though he had never taken part in the most terrific battles of civilized times

He was nominated for county treasurer in 1865, without solicitation on his part, and elected He held that office for four successive terms, with honor to himself and to the satisfaction of the public

He was married to Miss Isadora A Wood, of Woodville, March 12, 1867. Just prior to the close of his term of office, as treasurer, he opened a real estate and loan office in Waseca, and made that his main business until December, 1880, when he became one of the founders of the Peoples bank, serving the first year as president, and afterwards as cashier until June 29, 1897, when, his health having become somewhat impaired, he resigned the position

The robbery of the Peoples bank by the Guarantee Loan swindlers, of Minneapolis, we doubt not, shortened his life at least ten years It was a terrible blow to a man of his high sense of honor and to one with his sensitive feelings Himself a man of the strictest integrity and of unimpeachable character, he became prostrated by the financial blow dealt by the Guarantee Loan assassins A suspicion that he might be misjudged or misunderstood by former friends and the people generally, disturbed him more than all the hardships and terrors of the battlefield

But his life struggle is o'er A brave, gentle, and noble spirit has been set free from the cares and burdens of this transient and incomprehensible life, to take its flight to that eternal state where, let us hope, the scales of justice are held with equal poise, and where duplicity, deception, double-dealing, and falsehood shall not prevail against honesty, sincerity, and true manhood.

MR. GEORGE W WATKINS

Few men, even in the West, have had more experience and less real manual labor than Geo W Watkins, Sen He was born of wealthy parents, at Hamptonburg, Orange county, N Y, May 27, 1820

One would hardly believe, to look at him, that he is over eighty years of age. But such he declares is his record.

The first twenty-four years of his life were spent on his father's Orange county farm, and then he came west as far as Dupage county, Ill

He spent about six months on horse back, exploring a great deal of country, in Wisconsin, Iowa, and portions of Missouri That was in 1844 when Chicago and St. Louis were frontier villages He rode his horse over two thousand five hundred miles and back to his home in the state of New York A detailed account of his travels and experiences among the pioneer settlers of the west fifty-five years ago, would fill a large volume

Returning to Orange county, N Y, in 1844-5, he remained there until 1850, when he went to California, by way of the isthmus, and at once engaged in mining How well he succeeded in his mining operations he has always kept to himself, simply remarking whenever approached on that subject that he made enough to pay expenses

He returned to his New York home within a year, and remained there until 1853, when he again came as far west as Chicago. He engaged in railroading on the Galena road for some time as a contractor, and finally came to Faribault, in this state, in November, 1855. There he remained for nearly a year and then returned to Chicago where he married Miss Annetta Ward, in 1856 They remained in Chicago about a year, and in the spring of 1857 came to Wilton, then the county seat of this county, where they made their future residence They built a very pleasant home in that village, but his wife did not live many years to enjoy it One son, George, was born to them, and shortly afterwards the mother passed to the Eternal Home in 1860.

A little over a year later he married Miss Anna F Green, of Wilton who bore him one daughter, who is now Mrs Adams and resides with her husband, Prof Adams, in Oregon His second wife died in May, 1895

For many years he was engaged with Hon P C Bailey in the hardware business in Wilton and Waseca He also had an interest in the firm of Dodge & Co, hardware merchants, of Janesville.

He has hosts of friends wherever he has lived who are always glad to greet him.

MR OBADIAH POWELL

was one of our worthiest pioneers The following was taken in the form of an interview in 1897

"Come, Obe," said a Herald reporter, 'give us a little biography, open confession is good for the soul"

"Well, to begin with,' said he, "I commenced life very young, so young, in fact, that I have always had to depend upon my parents to refresh my recollections regarding my first start in my biographical career. According to that recollection, I entered upon the scene of action Feb 1, 1828, in the town of Hartsville, Steuben county, N Y In due time, I worked westward and arrived in the then territory of Minnesota, the last of October, 1855 I settled where I now live, May 9, 1856 It was then called Swavesey precinct, Steele county I found in the southwest corner of what is now Blooming Grove, a small settlement made in the month of June, 1855 There was John M Blivens, now in Missouri, Wm M. Gray, who died about fifteen years ago, Simeon Smith, who also died some thirteen or fourteen years ago, Alfred C Smith, who has the honor of being father to the first child born in the neighborhood, (Lovica, now Mrs H N Carlton, born Oct. 15, 1855), and Ole Knuteson, now of Renville county."

" How about your property qualifications," queried the reporter

"Property! Well, it was immense. It inventoried about as follows An ax, iron wedge, two beetle rings, $90 in cash and my every day clothes, all of which I easily carried in a satchel strapped upon my back. Having neither family nor property, the settlers treated me rather coolly—did not rush around to show me the best claims—and some of them plainly told me they did not want single men to settle among them So, not to crowd them too much, I left, but did not go far, making my claim on sections four and five, in Woodville The part of my claim running down to Clear Lake was fractional, as I learned on going to Winona, the next October so that I got one hundred and forty-four and fifty-nine one-hundredths acres I must say, however, in justice to my neighbors, that when they saw me strip my coat and go to splitting rails in hot weather, in order to get some breaking done, they softened, so to speak, and without exception, treated me very kindly

"Two weeks after my settlement, E K Carlton, now living with his son near me, came with his family to be my neighbor, and I broke bread with them until I was married July 5, 1857 My wife, Mary J, daughter of Wm M Gray, was born in Alleghany county, N Y, March 22, 1837 As she was as poor as myself, we had about an even start, and suffered and enjoyed all the inconveniences incident to poverty and a new country

"In the summer of '56 our settlement was increased in population by the coming of Daniel Riegle, now living in Kittson county; Patrick Murphy, still living here, Joshua R. Smith, now of Greenland, LeSueur county, Josiah Smith when last heard from being in Nebraska, Henry Smith, now of Montana, Sam Smith, now of California; Jacob Oory, now in Kansas; Wm H. Young, deceased, Jos Churchill, who removed to Renville county and died there several years ago; Jacob Myers, who preempted the present site of the city of Waseca, sold it to I C Trowbridge, and soon after removed to California, where he now resides, E G. Wood, Loren C Wood, who died of disease contracted in the army, and some others "

"I think ours was the first school district organized in the county At any rate it was originally No 1 When the township district was adopted, under the law of 1861, we lost the number and now it is No 7 Our first school house was built in the spring of 1857 We had three months school that summer and paid the teacher six dollars per month "

"In June, 1857, Patrick Farrell and his father-in-law, Daniel Eagen, settled in our neighborhood. Mr. and Mrs Eagen died years ago Mr Farrell and wife, Patrick Murphy and wife, W H. Gray, who came with his parents when he was about sixteen years of age, H N Carlton and wife, Uncle E. K Carlton, A. C. Smith and wife, and your humble servant and wife are about all that remain in our neighborhood of the settlers prior to 1860. In the early days we were known as the 'Blivens settlement'

Mr. Powell died April 3, 1901, honored and respected by all

(See Year 1901)

MR SEGURD JOHNSON.

In January, 1897, in a chat with one of the sons of the late Mr. Segurd Johnson, of Iosco, I learned something of the life of that early settler He was born at a place in Norway called Gjoslor Ovre Telemarkan, on the 29th day of May, 1821 It seems that he commenced life as a cattle herder; afterwards learned and worked at the carpenter and joiner trade, and finally became a traveling merchant or peddler, traveling from town to town among the people of his own country. This variety of work and experience qualified him, in his younger days, for the duties of after life in Minnesota He heard much, in his travels, of that great country, North America, and, in the year 1845, made up his mind to make his future home in the United States Before leaving Norway, he married Miss Anna Livorson, who was his faithful and devoted helpmate all through life.

He and his young wife were among the first to emigrate from that part of Norway to this country They took passage on a sailing ship and endured the hardships incident to a long and stormy voyage across the sea, with only the fickle winds as motive power They finally reached their destination, Sun Prairie, in Wisconsin. They were twenty-three weeks on their journey Wisconsin was then a new territory and Mr. Johnson was among the first settlers in that section of country He endured many hardships and privations in Wisconsin His first market place, in the Badger state, was Milwaukee, seventy miles distant from his Sun Prairie home He lived there about eleven years and then, in 1856, sold his possessions and came to Minnesota

It appears that he came to Iosco early in the spring of 1856, and settled on section 11 where he secured three hundred acres of fine land upon which he resided until the time of his death, which occurred Sept 12, 1886. He came to Minnesota with considerable property, and was, to a great extent, exempt from that struggle with poverty which marked the early lives of very many of the first settlers of the county. He participated, however, in all the arduous labors incident to pioneer life, and made many trips to Hastings with ox-team, camping by the way-side with the other early settlers

He helped to organize the Norwegian Lutheran church of Iosco and Blooming Grove, in 1863, and became one of its directors and principal supporters. He helped to build the church edifice with his own hands He also took a leading part in the erection of the school house in his district, No. 10, about the same time Six of his children survive him, three sons and three daughters Anna, John, Taaraand and Gunhild were born in Wisconsin, and Louis and Segurd S, in Minnesota Louis is said to have been the second child born in the township of Iosco.

He brought with him, from Wisconsin, one span of mules, one yoke of oxen, and twenty-four head of other cattle. He also brought with him a new wagon and necessary farm implements, and money enough to pay for his land He was one of our best and most reliable citizens, and was a leading and influential man in his community He exemplified the piety, the patience, the endurance, the industry, the frugality, the honesty, and the sound judgment so characteristic of the successful Scandinavians that came to this country in the early days

MR. HIRAM A. MOSHER

Company F of the Tenth regiment was almost entirely made up of men from Waseca county, and among them was Hiram A. Mosher, who was mustered in August 18, 1862

Hiram was born in the state of Ohio in 1834 and came to Wisconsin with his parents in 1845 They settled in Chester, four miles south of Waupun

Hiram came to Minnesota in 1856 and pre-empted a claim on section one in Otisco He returned to Wisconsin that fall where he remained until 1860, when he married Miss Frances Robbins, and returned to Minnesota settling in Woodville He engaged in farming until August, 1862, when he enlisted in Company F, of the Tenth Minnesota infantry, commanded by Capt George T White, of this county His company was stationed at the Winnebago agency, Blue Earth county, during the winter of 1862-3, did duty at Mankato at the hanging of the Sioux murderers, and "chased the Indians o'er the plains," as mounted infantry, under the command of General Sibley

After the Indian expedition, he went South with his regiment and participated in all its gallant history there He was at the battle of Tupelo, helped to chase Forrest for some days, drove Price out of Missouri, and fought the good fight at Nashville where he lost his left arm and was wounded in the side and abdomen. At the battle his regiment lost some twenty-five killed and seventy-five wounded It was at this battle that Captain George T White gave up his life for his country, shot through the bowels. Privates Theodore Hacker, Hanson Oleson, Chaudler Fleming and J D Ferguson, were killed Lieutenant Isaac Hamlin, sergeants H A Mosher and George H Woodbury, and private Edward Brossard, of this county were wounded, more or less severely Corporal David Snyder was also wounded at the battle of Nashville

After his return from the service, with his armless sleeve he was elected register of deeds in November, 1865, in this county, and reelected for seven consecutive terms—fourteen years. He then gave way for Mr Charles SanGalli, but was again elected to that position in 1883 He died Nov. 13, 1884 very suddenly, of heart disease He was one of God's noblemen in every sense of the word and came about as near perfection as any human being gets.

MR AUGUST MINSKE,

of Iosco, was born in Belgen, Prussia, near the city of Berlin, August 14, 1837 He came with his parents across the ocean and landed at New York, Sept 11, 1855, after a voyage of seven weeks They came on to Dodge county, Wisconsin, where they spent the winter and made preparation to come to Minnesota They started from Dodge county, in March, 1856, with two covered wagons and four pair of oxen The company that came together consisted of John Minske, father of August and F W, and family, Gottfried Kanne, who died in 1886, and his sons, F Kanne, August Kanne, Gottlieb Kanne, and his only daughter, Mrs Wm Marzahn and her husband There were five covered wagons and nine pair of oxen in all

They were little used to the ways of the country or that mode of traveling, and were six weeks on the road, reaching Iosco, the 25th day of May, 1856 The country, as is generally the case in early spring, was wet and the sloughs soft, and some days the company would not make more than two miles At nearly every soft place they had to double teams, and in some places they had to put all the teams to one wagon, often breaking chains and having a rough time generally

Mr Minske says "As soon after our arrival as we could select our claims we commenced breaking with four yoke of oxen and broke about sixty acres—twenty acres on each of our claims. The season was a busy one, breaking and building.

"The next spring we bought seed wheat, Scotch fife, near Morristown, for which we paid $2 a bushel The crop was a light one We got only forty bushels, having harvested it with a cradle and threshed it on the frozen ground with flails This we saved mostly for seed the next year The next year's wheat crop, that of 1858, was almost a total failure Our corn crop that year was middling good, and we had a good crop of vegetables, so we had to fall back on corn for bread

"As we were not well informed then on prairie fires, we came near losing everything that fall by fire"

August Minske was married to Miss Karoline Schultz, February 27, 1860 Mrs Minske was born in Prussia, April 12, 1838, and came to America in the same ship with Minske. They have had twelve children, ten boys and two girls Three of the boys are dead Robert died of croup at the age of two years, six months, Emil was so badly burned in a prairie fire that he died within twelve hours thereafter The third death was that of an infant, twenty days old, on Sept 25, 1879 .

John Minske, the father of August, died in 1862, after a long illness, brought on, no doubt, by hardship and exposure to which he had not been accustomed in earlier days Mr Minske says

"When we first commenced to cut grain I had to cut it with my 'armstrong' reaper, my wife following, raking and binding. Then, after threshing, we had to haul it to Red Wing or Hastings with ox teams and got from forty-five to fifty cents a bushel It took a round week of travel and camping out before we saw home again On one trip, our trusty engines, the oxen, in the night, left for better quarters, and it took nearly all the next day to hunt them up Another time, in the fall, I camped on the yellow prairie, ten miles out from Hastings It was a cold night I wrapped myself in an Indian blanket, lay down under the wagon, and awoke in the night to find myself covered with about three inches of snow, with a keen wind from the northwest. While I was getting ready to bid my landlord and his white feather-bed good-bye, I was surprised to miss my watch, the only time piece we had After a half hour's search I found it in the snowy bed At another time, Wm Priebe, now deceased, and myself made the round trip to Hastings, with ox teams, in three days and nights, but we drove day and night—and the last night I fell asleep in the wagon about midnight and did not awake until I found myself at home the next morning

"On the 9th of March 1865, I enlisted in the First Minnesota battalion, Company C, and proceeded to the front at Petersburg. The next day after my arrival, the company had to fall into line of battle and march upon the enemy My first lesson in war was in a hail storm of bullets from 9 a m, till dark at night, but after three days of hard fighting, Petersburg was ours Then followed days and nights of marching and fighting while following Gen Lee At High Bridge many a soldier saw daylight for the last time till the day of resurrection After Lee's surrender we marched back to Burk's Station, and on this march the men suffered very much for want of provisions, as the army wagons could not be brought along, owing to the swampy roads We were without provisions for nearly three days While in camp there, H P Chamberlain, Wm Allen, Isaac Ballard, and Isaac Billings came to us from Washington, to rejoin the company After camping there for about four weeks, we marched to Washington, thence we were shipped to Louisville, Ky, where I was taken with dysentery and ague and became so weak that I could not care for myself Here our company lost fifteen strong men by disease Shortly after, we started by boat for Fort Snelling After camping a week, near Minnehaha, we received our discharge, and reached home July 26, 1865"

MR GEORGE W SOULE

is one of those, who at an early day, followed Horace Greeley's advice by coming West when a very young man He came with elder brothers and a widowed mother, in 1849, from Coeymans, Albany county N Y, and settled first at Watertown, Wis Coming thence to Minnesota, the family settled just over the county line, in Morristown, arriving at their new home August 10, 1855, when George was only eleven years of age

Mrs Soule, nee Nancy Canfield, daughter of the late Judge Canfield, of this county, was born in the town of Chester, Dodge county, Wis, July 27, 1846, and came with her parents to this county, arriving here, June 9, 1856

George W Soule enlisted in the Third regiment, Minnesota volunteers, Feb. 15, 1864, and served until the close of the war Soon after his discharge, he bought eighty acres of land on section 4, Blooming Grove, where he settled down to farming. He was elected assessor in 1877, to which office he was re-elected for five consecutive years He was then elected county commissioner and served one term.

In reply to inquiry as to pioneer experience, he says

"Hardships were many and lucky hits few. Some of my older brothers were here a year previous to our coming, and had a potato and a buckwheat patch, and a little sod corn They had the body of a log house raised and covered with bark That was a lucky hit as we learned before the next spring, for the winter following was one of Minnesota's coldest

"We had to go to Hastings to get that buckwheat and corn ground We had only the ground for a floor, the first winter, and other comforts in the household line to correspond

"The first school house was on the site now occupied by the Remund school house. In that old log building, I finished my education

Among the earliest settlers were B K. and W R. Soule with their younger brothers Of these the following have died L E Soule, Dec 2, 1859, F. N Soule, Sept 28, 1864, at Pine Bluff, Arkansas, member of Co. H, Third Minnesota volunteers, H. S Soule, June 9, 1880, at Baker City Oregon, (he also was in the service during the war), S G Soule, June 30, 1882, at Morristown; Jane Soule, mother of the Soule boys, July 12, 1877, at the old homestead in Rice county

There is a silent yet glorious eloquence in the fact that a brave mother, away back in 1855, came to this unsettled country with her young sons and endured all the hardships and privations of frontier life that they they might make for themselves free homes and acquire a competency for themselves and their children It requires no small amount of courage, devotion, and heroism for a mother thus to face the dangers of the frontier, and endure the privations incident to early pioneer life

Mr. George Soule, at this writing, 1904, resides in Oregon

MR DANIEL RIEGLE

Among the first settlers of Blooming Grove, the name of Daniel Riegle must not be forgotten. He was born in Erie county, N Y, Oct 23, 1829 His forefathers, away back, came from Germany, and retained their mother tongue, and Daniel can converse fluently in that language He left his native state, when twenty-two years of age, and came West—stopped one month at Chicago, and then went to Stevenson county, Ill, where he remained one year He next moved to Clayton county, Iowa, and thence to Delaware county, the same state, where he ran a saw mill about two years While living at the latter place he married Miss M C Bliven, daughter of J M. Bliven, one of the earliest settlers in Blooming Grove She died in 1870 J M Bliven came here early in the season of 1855, and in the month of December of that year, Bliven having returned to Iowa for supplies, Riegle came up with him and another man, driving ox teams Between Fort Atkinson and Cottrell's grove, in Iowa, they met a blizzard which detained them three days and nights They wandered off the road, got some of the oxen down in a creek, and came near losing one pair They finally found a Bohemian family, who had just moved in that fall The house was small, and contained a family of children, and a sow with a brood of young pigs in one corner There was no room to lie down, but then they had plenty to eat, could keep from freezing, and could sleep some while sitting

After much hard work and many exposures, they reached Blooming Grove—then Swavesey. After looking the ground over, Mr Riegle, accompanied by Wm M Gray and Simeon Smith, returned to Fayette county, Iowa This was during the last days of December Messrs Gray and Smith went to West Union, Iowa, for provisions

Mr Riegle returned with his family in the spring of 1856, and made a claim on section 31 which he afterwards bought of the government, and on which he resided until 1874 The first death in the settlement was in the family of Mr Riegle, being that of his son Mahlon who died in the winter of 1857. Mr Riegle enlisted August 18, 1862, for three years, in Company F, Tenth regiment Minnesota infantry, and served until July, 1865

For his second wife he married Miss Melvina Gray, in 1871 She was born in Illinois, Oct 11, 1847, being a daughter of Wm M Gray Mr. Riegle remained on his farm until 1874, when he sold out He lived for a time in Morristown, then went to Waterville, and from there he moved to Renville county where he bought a farm There he remained until 1883, when he moved to the farm where he now resides, in Kittson county

MR ALFRED C SMITH.

The first claim taken in the town of Woodville was that of Mr Alfred C Smith, who came to the county in 1855 Under date of Jan 10, 1891, he wrote as follows

"In answer to your request I will say that I came to Minnesota and settled in the town of Woodville, June 20, 1855. I came in company with my father, Simeon Smith, and William Gray and John Bliven We all settled in what they called then the Swavesey district Our nearest neighbor, except the Indians, was old Mr Morris, of Morristown, ten miles away

I was born in Chautauqua county, N Y, in 1830 My wife, Armanda C

Smith, was born in Cataraugus county, New York, in 1833 We brought with us, when we came West, one yoke of oxen, a wagon, a cow, a calf, and a five franc piece. My wife and I are the only settlers left in the neighborhood of those who settled here in 1855. Mrs Simeon Smith died in 1871, and Simeon died in 1872 Mr Gray died in 1871, and Mrs Gray died some time afterwards.

The first year we were here we had to go to Iowa for provisions. I remember that I worked for one dollar a day, and paid seven dollars a hundred for flour, four dollars and a half a hundred for corn meal, and twenty-five and thirty-five cents a pound for pork The first school house was built of logs Ours was the first district organized in the county, and we used the building also for religious meetings The first birth in the neighborhood was that of my daughter Lovica, and the first death was that of Mrs Josiah Smith E G Wood, L C Wood, Henry Watkins, Jacob Myers, O Powell, E K Carlton, Patrick Murphy, Joshua Smith, Samuel Smith, Daniel Riegle, Joseph Churchill, Henry Smith, William Dunn, and perhaps others settled here in 1856 Our circumstances were such that we were compelled to go barefoot during the summer. We built our houses of logs with puncheon floors and elm bark for roofing. I remember that I gave an acre of breaking for a pair of boots that had been worn a year. Of course we had to haul our wheat for many years to Hastings, camping by the roadside, and getting from fifty to sixty cents a bushel"

Mr Smith was an industrious, honorable man He died Jan 28, 1902

MR SIMON HENRY DRUM

This early and worthy settler was born April 14, 1840, at Fort Gratiot, Michigan. His wife, Ella A Sutliff, was born May 13, 1850, at New Haven, Conn, and came with her parents to Houston county, Minn, in 1856, coming from there to Waseca county in 1865. Mr. Drum arrived in Owatonna, May 4, 1859, and found employment in the drug store of Dr Harsha, of that place, until the following August He taught school eight successive winters, spending his summers at farm work He was elected clerk of joint school district No 21-35 and held the position for upward of twenty years. He was town assessor in 1881-2, elected justice of the peace in 1883, and re-elected for many successive terms The first school house in his neighborhood was built in Meriden in 1860 The school house in joint district No 21, Steele county, and 35, Waseca county, was built in 1870.

Mr Drum now has two hundred acres in his farm and devotes considerable attention to dairying. He is the father of ten children—four boys and six girls Two of the sons and four of the daughters have been teachers in the county. One son and two daughters attended the State University in 1904-5.

MR JESSE R WEED

will be remembered by early residents of Byron as one of its oldest residents He was born in the town of Angelica, county of Alleghany, state of New York, May 23, 1819. His wife was Miss Clarinda Maxson, born April 9, 1819, in the town of Deruyter, Madison county, New York

Mr. and Mrs. Weed settled in the town of Byron, in this county, October 7, 1860, on sections twenty-seven and thirty-four, where they reside at the present writing, 1896 Mr Weed brought with him two yoke of oxen, a wagon, three cows, two steers, and a calf He has held the office of town clerk, supervisor, justice of the peace, and assessor He has been school district clerk for more than half the time since since the district was organized He is at this writing the oldest school district clerk in the county, being nearly seventy-two years of age

His nearest flouring mill, for years, was at Okaman It often took from three to four days to make the trip to mill At one time, in February, 1862, he was four days going from Okaman to his home, a distance of thirty miles by the road In many places the snow was up to the oxen's necks

The first school house built in that neighborhood was in 1860, on the line between the counties of Freeborn and Waseca The first child born was Maggie Davis, daughter of Jeremy and Keziah Davis. The first death in the neighborhood was an old lady by the name of Hodge, the mother of Mrs. Parvin

MRS ALMIRA WHEELER AND FAMILY

Mrs Wheeler, now residing in the town of Woodville, in January, 1891, gave the following short sketch of her family.

Mr Lewis W Wheeler, her husband's father, was born in the state of New York, in the year 1791, July 6, and lived there until the spring of 1844, when he moved to Janesville, Wisconsin He came next to Faribault, Minn, in 1854, where he lived until 1857, when he moved to the then village of St. Mary. In 1866 he again moved, this time settling in Wilton, where he died in 1867, at the age of seventy-six years and six months.

Mrs Almira Wheeler's late husband, Whitney L Wheeler, son of Lewis W., was born in the state of New York, in the year 1822 In 1846, he was married to Miss Almira Kibby, who was born in the state of New York, April 2, 1821 They resided in their native state until 1856, when they came to Faribault, in this state, where they tarried until the spring of 1857, when they moved to St Mary where Mr. Wheeler carried on a saw mill and worked his farm They remained in St Mary until the fall of 1866, when they settled in Wilton, where the family resided until after Mr Wheeler's death, which occurred Nov 4, 1870 Mrs. Wheeler has three children, two sons and a daughter

Mr Whitney L Wheeler practiced as a veterinary surgeon He was prominent as a very active republican during the days of James Buchanan's administration

After her husband's death, Mrs Wheeler secured a farm in Woodville, where she has since resided. She is not only one of the early settlers of Minnesota, but one of the oldest now living in the county

MR GEORGE DREEVER, OF JANESVILLE.

The following facts were gathered from Mr Dreever in 1892

This gentleman was born in the county of Kildare, Ireland, in 1837, and came to America in 1855, first living in Newark, N J. He soon after came as far west as Illinois and settled in Stevenson county There he remained until the spring of 1857 when he came to Minnesota. Soon after he married Rosanna McQuade, who was also born in the Emerald Isle

Like many another patriotic young man, he enlisted in the Union army, Co F, Tenth Minnesota regiment, volunteer infantry, under Captain White He served until 1864, when he was discharged for disability

He first bought a quarter section of land in Janesville of a Mr. O'Rourke He next bought the Haines farm and afterwards forty acres more of a Mr. McArthy, of Faribault. He was somewhat unfortunate in the purchase of some of his lands The land warrant which had been laid on the McArthy land, turned out to be a forgery and Mr. Dreever was compelled some years afterwards to pay the price of the land to the government to protect the title In regard to the Haines farm, one of the title sharks of the country discovered a flaw in the title, and Mr. Dreever was compelled to pay a large bonus in order to save it

When Mr Dreever came to Minnesota, he took steamboat from Galena, Ill, to Hastings, Minn, and then drove across the country to Janesville with four yoke of oxen, two wagons, and fourteen cows His brother, Richard Dreever, also came in 1857, and settled near him in Iosco Richard died some years ago

George has three children living His son, George F. Dreever, is a graduate of the Watertown, Wis., college, of Notre Dame college, Indiana, and of the medical school of Ann Arbor, Mich.

MR W D ABBOTT

Mr Abbott, now of Winona, one of the prominent and leading lawyers of the state, was born July 13, 1859, at Clinton Falls, Steele county, Minn He is one of nine children born to Mr and Mrs A J. Abbott, who settled at Clinton Falls, in the fall of 1857 Mr and Mrs A J. Abbott were born in New Hampshire—Mr Abbott, May 10, 1829, Mrs Abbott, March 5, 1830

W D Abbott is a graduate of the law department of the Minnesota state university He practiced for a time in Owatonna as a member of the firm of Sawyer. Abbott & Sawyer, in March 1885, he came to Waseca, where he practiced law until November, 1892, when he accepted a position in the law department of the C & N W Ry Co, and is, at this time, 1904, a member of the firm of Brown, Abbott & Somsen, of Winona

Mr Abbott was married Oct 7, 1886, to Miss Mary Lorena Adams, of

Prairieville, Rice county, Minn They have an adopted daughter, Helen D Abbott, but no children have been born to them.

Mr Abbott is still a young man and his prospects for the future are promising indeed He recently came prominently before the public as leading attorney in the defense of Dr Koch, of New Ulm

MR OBADIAH MOSHER

This man was a natural pioneer He was born in June 1797, in Washington county, N. Y His wife was Miss Nancy Allen, of Vermont, who was born Jan 29, 1797 She died at Minneapolis, June 1, 1890, being over ninety-three years of age Obadiah went to Ohio in 1816, at the age of nineteen years, and remained there until 1845, when he removed with his family to Dodge county, Wisconsin In 1859 he and his wife came to Minnesota and lived on section 35, Woodville. He sold out here in 1866, and moved to Plainview, Minn, where he died in 1867, aged seventy years Mr and Mrs Mosher were the parents of eight children, who grew to manhood and womanhood—five sons and three daughters—John, Robert, Asa, Hiram A, L J (Jim), Mrs W S Baker, Mrs J A Canfield, and Mrs Esther Young.

L J, better known as Jim, Mosher, son of Obadiah, came with his parents to this county in 1859. He was one of the first to enlist in the Union army and joined Company G, First Minnesota infantry under the first call in 1861 He participated in many battles and returned home with one leg and one arm crippled Soon after the war he moved to Iowa, and afterwards lived in the state of Kansas.

THE REVEREND W J CLELAND,

who was born Feb 14, 1814, in Butler county Pa., was one of the pioneer clergymen of this section. He was a graduate of one of the Presbyterian colleges of the East, and preached to the people of Delaware county, N Y, until 1863, when he came West and lived temporarily in Owatonna. In 1864, he bought a farm in Otisco, just east of the old village of Wilton, where he resided until the time of his death, which took place August 31, 1876 He was a devout man and preached the gospel wherever he could find a school house, hall, or church to preach in. Mrs Cleland's maiden name was Judith A Wilson She was born in Albany, N Y., in the month of August, 1819

J. W Cleland, son of the foregoing, was born in Delaware county, N Y, and was one of the nine children born to Mr and Mrs W J Cleland His birthday was Sept. 27, 1847 He came West with his family in 1863 He carried on the homestead farm until 1885, when the place was sold and he purchased a small farm on the west shore of Clear lake, near Waseca J W. Cleland and Miss Amanda C Connor, of Blooming Grove, were married Oct 3, 1877. Amanda was born Sept 11, 1852, in the state of Indiana, and came to Waseca county with her parents in 1856. The children of Rev W J Cleland were known as Anna M, Wm T, E E,

Maggie A, John W, D. M, J McKay, and C S. James W was stricken by paralysis while working about a threshing machine He never recovered from the stroke, and died after a very prolonged illness, July 15, 1903

CAPTAIN JACOB W. PIERCE

was born in Cumberland County, N J, Oct. 15, 1833. His wife, Sarah A, was born in Herkimer county, N Y, in 1837 Captain Pierce came West in 1855, tarried in Wisconsin a little over a year, then returned to New Jersey, remaining until 1857 when he came to Freeborn, Freeborn county. Soon after he took a claim on section 35, town of Byron where he now lives. The date of this settlement was May 27, 1857. He worked at the carpenter and joiner trade in Byron, Freeborn, and Wilton for several years, putting up a number of frame buildings for the early settlers He went with James D. Andrews and D. Skinner to Superior, Wisconsin, in the spring of 1861, where they worked until the next summer

He returned in the summer of 1862, and in August enlisted in Company F, Fifth Minnesota infantry. He participated in many battles, being wounded at the second battle of Corinth. He served until September, 1865, when he was mustered out at Fort Snelling with all the honors of war.

He married Sarah Horning, Jan. 1, 1867, and they immediately commenced housekeeping on their farm. They are the parents of five children: Clarence E, born Jan 4, 1868; Albertus M, born March 12, 1869; Vilmer E, born March 20, 1872, Bertrice M, born March 19, 1874, and Claude A, born August 18, 1877

MISS LOVICA SMITH IN THE JAUNARY STORM OF 1873

In the afternoon of Jan 7, 1873, a very mild day, dark clouds gathered in the west, and about 3 o'clock the wind commenced blowing a gale from the northwest, producing a rapid change in the temperature, and at the same time the air became filled with fine snow which was driven with great force into every opening, however small, by the terrific fury of the howling blast The sun was soon hidden from view, and darkness settled upon the earth like a funeral pall, bringing with it intense cold, made doubly severe by the driving, penetrating force of the wind This most terrible storm in the history of the state since its first settlement by white men continued throughout Wednesday, Wednesday night, and until Thursday about midnight. It was one of those intensely furious storms which once in a while visit this high northern latitude. The remembrance of it is retained by the old settlers and constitutes the theme of their conversation upon each succeeding similar occasion. The fierce blasts of the Storm King, on this occasion, deposited snow in vast quantities over the whole Northwest, making a winding sheet for many of the men, women and children that were caught in its icy embrace. No pen can fully describe the terriffic death-chill of the fifty-six hours during which this storm raged.

In the history of Waseca county, printed in 1887, by the Union Publishing company appears the following

"The day opened as a pleasant one, and many people had taken advantage of it to go to town, or to visit neighbors It so happened that Alfred C Smith, then living on section 5, Woodville township, had gone over to the farm where his father had settled, about a mile away, with his team. About the time the storm had got well under way, his daughter Lovica, born in this county and about seventeen years of age, who had been washing clothes, threw a shawl over her head, and taking a little brother with her, went out and up the road looking for her father For part of the way the grove on the west side of the road shut off the gale, and she did not realize that the storm was of any unusual character Coming to the end of the grove the brother ran back, but she pushed on, nothing daunted, thinking that she must soon meet her father But thinly clad, no wrap around her except a light cotton shawl thrown over her head and held together by her naked hands, she soon became aware that she must turn back or perish from the cold, for the wind that swept down upon her was of Arctic severity Retracing her steps, blinded by the whirling, drifting snow, confused by the savage fury of the wind, she took the wrong road where the two crossed and wandered on across the bleak prairie, death staring her in the face. Battling bravely she pushed on, her limbs chilled by the cold, her form growing weak beneath the merciless pelting of the storm, until she reached the grove near the house of Obadiah Powell, where she halted but a moment, when knowing that it was death to stop, she pushed on, and spying a light, made her way to Mr Powell's house So confused was she, so bewildered by the blizzard, and unhinged by the tension upon her nerves, that she did not know for a few moments where she was nor who were the friends she had stumbled upon But soon the genial hospitality of Mrs Powell, the light and warmth of the room restored her, and she was made comfortable until the storm abated."

THE HONORABLE WARREN SMITH

This worthy pioneer was born in Barnstable county, Mass, Nov 15, 1821 His father's name was Amasa Smith Warren grew to manhood in his native county and attended the public schools of the neighborhood until the age of sixteen, when he learned the trade of boat builder. Between boat building and wrecking he employed his time until 1855-6. In the mean time, 1853, he married Miss Susan E Johnson, of Provincetown, Mass They came to Minnesota in 1856 and resided in Faribault Mr. Smith and his brother-in-law, J S Fuller, engaged in the mercantile business at that place In the winter of 1856-7, he came to the then village of St Mary, in this county, purchased the general stock of merchandise of Chamberlain, Bailey & Co, and entered into the mercantile business

HON. WARREN SMITH.

in that village He remained in business in St Mary until 1862, when he was appointed assistant sutler of the Tenth Minnesota infantry, and accompanied the Sibley expedition in pursuit of the Sioux Indians in 1863

Prior to this time he had also become a member of the Wilton firm of J W Johnson & Co, which carried a large stock of general merchandise in the village of Wilton About 1863 he moved his family to Wilton where they resided until 1870 when they came to Waseca

He was elected to the house of representatives and served during the session of 1869. In 1870, upon the retirement of Captain Comee from the office of county auditor, Mr Smith was appointed by the county board to fill out the unexpired term. In 1873, he was elected county treasurer by a majority of over six hundred votes. He was twice re-elected, thus serving as treasurer six years In 1881, when Waseca first became a city, he was elected mayor, and served one year He declined a re-election and the common council, upon his retirement, unanimously adopted the following resolution:

"Whereas, the retirement of our esteemed fellow citizen, the Hon Warren Smith, from the office of mayor of the city of Waseca, presents a suitable opportunity of expressing the esteem in which we hold him, as a faithful and courteous public servant, therefore, be it

Resolved, that the common council of the city of Waseca tender him a vote of thanks for the impartial and faithful performance of his duties as such mayor in having the laws and ordinances of the city duly enforced during his term of office, and for the appointment of competent and faithful persons to the several offices of the city during his said term as mayor"

From that time to the close of his life he steadfastly refused to accept any office, though often urged to do so

His children were Minnie M, Mary L, George W, and Charles A Minnie and George both died soon after reaching womanhood and manhood Miss Mary L and Hon. Charles A., only survivors of the family, reside in the city of Waseca

In religion Mr. Smith was a Universalist, and in all that goes to make up a true Christian life he was pre-eminent In every calling of life, he was scrupulously honest, truthful, kind, charitable He made no loud professions, but his everyday life was a living, practical sermon of good works He was a member of the Masonic organizations, of this county, as high as Knight Templar, and was a true and worthy brother in all the relations of life

He visited the Pacific coast in the winter of 1892-3, where he was taken with influenza, from the effects of which he never recovered His death had been long expected, by both himself and family, and his departure was quiet and peaceful. He expressed, a few days before his demise, his entire readiness for the change, and his desire to depart as soon as possible He was a grand, good man, and a true friend.

MR. NOAH LINCOLN

and family were among the early settlers of the county. Mr Lincoln and his wife were representative pioneers Mr Lincoln was born in the state of New York, June 16, 1822. He came as far west as Michigan when a young man He and Emma S Davis were married Dec 7, 1844 She was born Dec. 19, 1826. They came to Minnesota in 1855 and first took a claim in Fillmore county which they sold the same fall, and in 1856 came to Waseca county and bought the claim of Chris Scott—the place where the Messrs Carmody now reside, in Wilton This farm they sold to Mr John Carmody and then bought a farm on section 1, in Wilton, where they resided until the time of Mr Lincoln's death which occurred March 23, 1875 They had a family of eight children Maria W, born Oct. 13, 1845, died in Rochester, Francis M, born July 4, 1847, died April 7, 1865, in the army at Mound City, Ill; Charles F., born Sept 9, 1849, died recently of consumption, in Oregon, F A, born Dec 11, 1851, died the following August, Elva V, born July 13, 1853, married and resides at Mankato, Louisa T, born Nov 20, 1855, died July 8, 1887, Mina A, born Nov 19, 1855, died March 30, 1862, Ida V., now Mrs H M. Buck, born April 4, 1862 During the winter of 1856-7, times were hard and this family, like the most of their neighbors, had to live on buckwheat flour ground in a coffee mill, and on corn meal made in a mortar with a pestle.

MR JACKSON TURNACLIFF

was among the very young men who came West in 1855 Mr Ferdinand Turnacliff, father of Jackson and Dellevan, was born in the state of New York, Sept 11, 1813 He lived for some years in Jefferson county, N Y, while a young man, but finally moved to the state of Ohio when that state was in "the far West" His wife, Maria, was also a New Yorker, born April 4, 1812 She died Dec 6, 1862 Five children were born to them, Jackson, May 6, 1835 Amelia Ann, deceased, born Jan 2, 1837, Dellevan, born Sept, 30, 1838, Sally M, deceased, born August 27, 1842; Matilda, now Mrs J M Dunn, born March 16, 1848, and Seymour, who was born May 8, 1851, and died Jan 17, 1854. Jackson came from Ohio to Iowa in the fall of 1855 In December 1855, in company with "Doc" Ambrose Kellogg and William Young, the last a Scotchman, he came from Jackson county, Iowa, to Minnesota most of the way on Norwegian snow shoes, arriving at the Suthef farm, in Wilton, on the last day of December, 1855 He took a claim on section 7, Otisco, where he made his future home He returned to Ohio in 1858 and married Miss Lucia E Barber, who was born in Ohio Feb 6, 1839 They were married August 25, 1858, and at once came to their home in Minnesota The Turnacliffs were well supplied with money and experienced few of the real hardships endured by most of the early settlers Nine children were born unto Jackson and Lucia Minnie D, June 6, 1859; Lolah M, Jan. 26, 1861, Elsie L, Oct 26, 1863, Linna M, Dec 6, 1865, deceased, Laura M, Aug

9, 1867, Ferdinand, April 26, 1872; Walter D, May 1, 1876, J B., Sept 5, 1880, Bill, May 1, 1885

Dellevan ("Tip") Turnacliff came to Minnesota with his father and sisters about 1863 and settled with them in Wilton where, at this time, 1904, he still owns an excellent farm. He and Miss Maggie Brisbane were married some years later and now reside in Waseca

MR JOHN DORAN,

one of the really honest men that have lived in Waseca county, was born in Ireland, June 20, 1829 He left his native land for America, Dec. 11, 1851. He landed in New York and worked as a laborer in that state, living the greater part of the time in Erie county where he remained until about 1855 He and Catharine Kohl were married March 16, 1855, and became the parents of fourteen children, nine of whom reached adult years The family came West in 1856, residing for a time in Wisconsin. They came to Minnesota in 1865, and finally settled on section 33, in the town of Wilton John Doran was a man absolutely honest For several years he worked a farm on shares, and so honest was he found to be that the proprietor used to allow him to thresh and divide the grain himself and bring it to market, contrary to all custom He was quite deaf for many years and finally met a tragic death. On the 11th of July 1891, he was thrown in front of his mowing machine and run over, receiving injuries from which he died on the 17th of the same month

MR JAMES A ROOT

was one of the pioneers of the West He was born in Jefferson county, N Y, Feb 26, 1832 While yet a boy his parents removed to Ellicottville, Cattaraugus county, N Y, where his mother died His father's name was Joseph N Root, and he died April 12, 1869 aged sixty-eight years and eight months, being a resident of the town of Byron at the time of his death James A came to Waseca county in 1859, his father and other relatives coming later Miss Hannah Brisbane, daughter of the late Hon William Brisbane, of Wilton, was married to James A Root, Dec 12, 1859 Mrs Root was born in New York state, Delaware county, August 18, 1840. Ten children were born to them. Charles E, Feb 27, 1861, Wm L, Jan. 29, 1863, Joseph S., April 16, 1865, Cora B, Aug. 26, 1867, Hattie M, March 4, 1870; James A, May 22, 1872, Maggie J, May 31, 1873, Freddie, July 2, 1877, Dora E, March 14, 1879, and Marvin L, Oct. 9, 1880. Freddie died August 24, 1877, and Marvin died Feb 22, 1882 Mr and Mrs Root were among the first to plant a forest of trees about the house and barn Their timber lot shows what may be done in the way of providing timber and fuel for the future Mr Root died August 23, 1891

MR REZIN NELSON,

of Wilton, was born in Crawford county, Pa, Dec. 16, 1837 At the age of twelve years he moved with his parents to Wisconsin His father was a lawyer and died in the Badger state In 1857, Rezin visited this county with his brother-in-law, James D. Andrews, but soon returned August 9, 1862, he enlisted in the Thirty-second Wisconsin infantry and served until October, 1863, when he was discharged and came to Wilton where he farmed until Feb. 2, 1865, when he again enlisted, this time in the First Minnesota Heavy Artillery, and went immediately to Chattanooga, Tenn. Here he remained until the close of the war He then returned to Minnesota, and on the 18th of March, 1866, he married Miss Rhoda A Sutlief daughter of Asa G Sutlief, deceased, the first white man to open a farm or settle in Waseca county. Rhoda was born in the town of Herman, Dodge county, Wisconsin, Sept 18, 1848 She came to this county with her father when she was only six years of age and when the whole county was an unbroken wilderness of prairie and woodland Mr and Mrs Nelson are the parents of seven children, born on the following dates Lee B, Dec 31, 1868, Rezin Jr., Feb. 15, 1871, Clarence W April 13, 1873, Mary Jan 22, 1876, Roy, Sept 23, 1878, Volney F, Feb 10, 1881, Nellie D, Aug 20, 1884, and Rex, March 5, 1887. Mary died Feb 22, 1882, and Volney died Feb 5, 1882, two deaths the same month

MR WILLIAM RODDLE,

born June 2, 1822, in "Old England," came to America in 1840 He first stopped in Cayuga county, N Y From there he went to Onondaga county and thence to Tompkins county in the same state From there he came West in 1844, and settled in Kenosha county, Wisconsin In 1849 he married Mrs Mary Green, a widow with three daughters In the fall of 1860, he came to Wilton with his family and purchased a farm near the old village of Wilton His wife bore him three children Wm H, born Dec 28, 1850, Ben F, born April 9, 1854, and Ella, born Jan 12, 1863. Mrs Roddle died in Wilton, June 19, 1876 Miss Ella married Charles E Root, Feb 2, 1883. She became the mother of one son, Oren E, born Feb 4, 1884 Her health was never of the best, and after a prolonged and severe illness, she died some three or four years after the birth of her child

William H. Roddle learned the tinner's trade of P C Bailey, went to Brookings, S. D, some twenty-five years ago, engaged in the hardware business, was finally elected secretary of state of South Dakota, for two terms, and is now practicing law in company with Philo Hall, his half sister's son, who was also a Waseca boy Benjamin F. is also a resident of South Dakota

Dec 17 1879, Mr William Roddle married Miss Emily M Loder who was born in Wisconsin October 26, 1852 Her father, John W Loder, was also an early settler with his family in Wilton. Mr Loder enlisted at the beginning of the Rebellion and died in 1862 while in the army Mr William Roddle died Nov 9, 1889 He was one of our best citizens

MR BUEL WELSH,

was one of the noted men of this county among its early settlers. He was kind and humane at heart, much beyond the average of men He was liberal to a fault. In sickness or want or sorrow, he was always ready and willing to extend a helping hand He was a carpenter and joiner by trade and first lived in Faribault having come hither from Wisconsin in 1854 He made his appearance in Iosco, as a carpenter, in 1855, and settled in the village of Wilton in the fall of 1856 Soon after his settlement in Wilton, work in his line being slack, he commenced to read law and practiced before justices of the peace. He was quite illiterate, but he managed to pick up considerable knowledge of law, and often won his cases against some more pretentious practitioners He had one sad failing—alcoholism—which he could never overcome long at a time On Saturday, April 24, 1886, he died suddenly in a neighbor's wagon while going from Alma City to his boarding place in Freedom township With more favorable environments, he might have been a more useful citizen and enjoyed life to a greater extent. He was a good man at heart

MR. A. J. WOODBURY,

came to Wilton in the fall of 1856 and built the first hotel in that place His sons, George H, and Henry C, assisted in carrying on the hotel business until about 1882, when it was abandoned by them They also carried on a farm in connection with their hotel business The old gentleman was a native of Beverly, Mass., and was born in 1808 The family lived for a time in New Orleans before coming to Wilton A J Woodbury and Elizabeth Stratton were married in 1830, and only two sons were born to them George H, enlisted in company F, Tenth Minnesota infantry, and served for three years. Henry C, a man of much 'cheek" but small brain capacity, made up in self assurance what he lacked in ability, being at one time judge of the municipal court of Waseca Henry finally went to Jamestown, North Dakota, where he died some years ago George was the exact opposite of Henry. He was a man of ability and high character, yet modest and unassuming. After his return from the war, he married Miss Hannah Robbins, then of Otisco, and they now (1904) live in Jamestown, North Dakota.

MR. MICHAEL McGONAGLE, SEN,

was one of the 1856 pioneer settlers in St. Mary where he still owns a valuable farm He was born in Ireland, Sept 10, 1825, and came to America, March 7, 1862 He and Margaret Gill, she being also a native of Ireland, were married Oct 10, 1855, and commenced farm life at once. They experienced many of the hardships and deprivations incident to frontier life, but overcame them all and enjoyed a competence at last The following named children were born to them Michael, Jr, Mary Ann, Kate, Neil, Maggie, Hugh, John, William and Lizzie Mrs McGonagle died some years ago, and Mr. McGonagle, at this writing, 1904, is living with his daughter Lizzie, Mrs Tim Dónovan, in Waseca, enjoying the rest and comfort of a well spent life

CHARLES W AND JANE C JOHNSTON,

were of the pioneers that came to this county in 1857. They located on section 13, St Mary Charles W Johnston was born in Montpelier, Vt, March 9, 1834 Mrs Johnston was born at Chelsea, Vt., Feb. 5, 1833. She is the daughter of Samuel Scribner, a native of Washington county, N H Her mother's name was Louisa Clark. Mr. and Mrs Scribner had five children Charles, who married Emma Horn, Geo F, who married Abbie Chapman, Alzoa, who married S D Osterhout, Mary A, and Jane C Mr and Mrs Johnston were married April 6, 1857 Five children were born to them: Nellie M L, August 7, 1858; Alma S, May 22, 1860, Charles F, April 17, 1863, Willard C, June 29, 1866, and George S, May 28, 1869 Charles F died March 25, and George, March 31, 1873, of scarlet fever and diphtheria Charles W Johnston, the father, died in California, Feb 17, 1899, as elsewhere noted in this book

MESSRS WILLIAM AND JOHN PRIEBE,

brothers, both deceased, came from Prussia and settled in St Mary as early as 1860 Both were single men. Wm Priebe married Miss Augusta Prechel, who came to Minnesota in 1855 with her brother, Gottlieb Prechel They were the parents of five sons and two daughters—all living but one, Gust Priebe, who was accidently killed in 1903, in Renville county, by a passing railroad passenger train

William settled on section 22, town of St Mary John settled on section 10 in the same town, where he and his wife, by very hard work and close economy, saved quite a fortune His wife's maiden name was Caroline Vondrie John died in 1872 Wm Mittelsteadt married his widow about a year later, and she died June 19, 1880 John Priebe left three children August, who owns a large farm in St. Mary, William J, who lives in Waseca and deals in farm machinery, and Amelia, wife of Julius Mittelsteadt August Priebe who owns the old homestead married Molvena Krienke, a native of this county, June 16, 1887 She is the daughter of August and Henrietta Krienke, of St Mary

MR DANIEL T BALLARD,

was born in England, Oct 16, 1839. He is one of three brothers, all of whom settled in Waseca county at an early day They came to America in 1856 Daniel worked his way West and arrived in Waseca county in 1858 He resided first in Iosco He enlisted in Company F, Eighth Minnesota regiment in the fall of 1862, and was discharged the same year for disability at Ft Snelling In 1866, with D A Erwin and others, he made an overland trip to Montana, with ox teams He returned in Nov 1872, and settled in St Mary On the 17th of June, 1873 he married Miss Josephine Brossard, who was also one of the early settlers of the county

Mr. Brossard was a very successful farmer. He sold his farm here some years ago and removed to the state of Washington, where he and his family now reside

THE ERWINS

Mr P. A Erwin was one of the aged men that came to Waseca county at an early period in its history. P A Erwin was born in the Green Mountain State, in 1797, and served his country as a soldier in the War of 1812-15 with Great Britain His wife, Jane Erwin, was born in Ireland She was a sister of Rev James Erwin who was quite a noted Methodist minister in Northern New York about 1833 P A Erwin and his family settled in St Mary about 1863 Mrs Jane Erwin passed to the Great Beyond in September, 1867 Her husband lived to the age of ninety-two, when he, too, joined the silent dead, honored and respected by all who knew him

D. A. Erwin, son of P A, was born in the state of New York, Aug 4, 1839 In September, 1862, he enlisted in Company D, Ninety-eighth New York infantry, and served until May 1863, when he was honorably discharged for disability He remained in the state of New York until 1864, when he came to this county and joined his parents in St Mary In 1866, in company with D T Ballard and others, he made a trip to Montana with ox teams in search of gold After three years of unsatisfactory toil in Montana, he returned to this county where he has since made his home. He married Miss Orrilla Ketchum, daughter of Rev Alvin Ketchum, deceased, Sept 15, 1870. Mrs Erwin is one of the pioneer girls of Minnesota, having come with her parents in 1856 They are the parents of nine children Sidney, born Sept 15, 1871, died Oct 11, 1873, Claude, born March 26, 1873, Stanley, May 1, 1875, Grant, April 26, 1877, Roland, Jan. 27, 1879, Eugene, Jan 17, 1882, Ray, Nov. 29, 1886, Ruth and Ruby (twins,) born Oct 7, 1890 Ruth died March 13, 1900 The Erwins are of Revolutionary stock D A Erwin's grandfather, David, who was born at Castleton, N J, 1758, was four years in the Revolutionary War as a private, in the War of 1812 he was captain of a company and served until the close of the contest with Great Britain His father, P. A, served in the War of 1812, and participated in the battle of Plattsburg, Sept 11, 1814, where the British under General Prevost and Admiral Downie, were defeated by the Americans under Gen Macomb and Admiral McDonough

MR JULIUS PAPKE,

now a retired farmer, was born in Prussia and came to America in 1861 with his family He married Miss Eliza Buscho in Prussia, February 15, 1857 They first lived in Wisconsin, remaining there until 1865, when they located on section 26, St Mary Mr. Papke and wife were good farmers and accumulated a handsome property They have been the parents of eleven children Adolph, Melia, Augusta, Fred, John, Julius Jr, Sarah, Mary, Edward, Lewis and Elia Adolph became a prominent farmer of Blooming Grove he died June 16, 1904 Mr and Mrs Papke are now residents of Waseca.

MR WILLIAM MITTELSTEADT,

born Feb 15, 1848, in Prussia, came directly to Waseca county in 1867 He settled on section 9, and has become one of the wealthy farmers of the county He has been married three times His first wife was Caroline, widow of John Priebe, of St Mary, by whom he had two children She died June 19, 1880 Jan 13, 1881, he married Augusta Fischer, who died March 20, 1884, leaving one child His third wife was Mrs Wilhelmine Leeck He was town treasurer of St Mary for a number of years, and is influential among his neighbors He has also served as town supervisor for three terms

MR. PATRICK FARLEY,

a native of Ireland, was born March 16, 1836, came to America in 1855, tarried a year in Albany, N Y, then moved to Wisconsin where he lived until 1865, when he came to Alton, where he resided until 1887 He then bought a farm of Ed Brossard, in St Mary, where he lived up to the time of his death, which occurred February 2, 1902 He married Miss Mary Ann Hagearty Feb 2, 1870 She was born in Wisconsin in November, 1848 Eight children were born to them Emma May, Thos P, Wm H, Edward, Nellie J, Katie, James and Sarah An account of Mr Farley's sudden death is noted elsewhere

MR S S PHELPS,

was a prominent citizen of this county during his life time He was born in the state of New York, April 5, 1840 He was the son of John and Nancy Phelps and was reared on their farm When Seth S first came West, he lived near Portage, in Wisconsin. He and Miss Elspa Sutherland were married there Oct 13, 1861 In 1865, Mr Phelps visited Waseca county and purchased land where the family residence now stands He then returned to Wisconsin to settle up his business He moved hither with his family in 1866. In 1867 he became a railroad contractor and hauled freight from Waseca to Mankato, St Peter, and New Ulm. He also had the contract for distributing ties along the railroad track as the road bed was completed west from Waseca In 1869 he took a contract to furnish a very large quantity of wood for the W & St. P. railroad company. This business he followed for six or seven years He put up a number of wood sawing machines and kept a boarding car for the accommodation of his workmen His large and convenient farm residence now occupied by his widow, was built by him in 1869, and cost about $10,000

The death of Mr Phelps caused a sensation all along the line of the C. & N W railway in Minnesota On the 11th of March, 1884 he had been in Waseca on business and started to drive home late in the afternoon

As he reached the crossing of the C. & N W railway just west of Waseca, he was struck by an engine and instantly killed, cut off in the prime of life He left surviving him his wife, two daughters, and two sons. The two sons are married and live on the farm, Ellen, Mrs Fitch, resides in Belview, Redwood county, Nancy, Mrs Henderson, now a widow, makes her home on the farm with her mother.

MR MICHAEL GALLAGHER,

born in Marquette county, Wis, Feb 22, 1858, is one of the prominent men of St. Mary He came to Waseca county with his parents, Michael and Maria (Foley) Gallagher, about the first of July, 1863. On the 20th of October, 1886, he married Miss Ellen Lynch, who was born in St. Mary, Jan 16, 1861 Her parents, Mr and Mrs Andrew Lynch, were among the very early settlers of that town Michael Gallagher, Sen, and his wife came to America in 1847, and first lived in the state of New York for seven years, and then moved to Wisconsin The children of Michael, Sen, were six in number Bernard, Rose Ann, John, Michael, Maria, and Celia. The last was burned to death when eleven years old, at the time the family residence was destroyed by fire Mr Gallagher senior, died at the home of his daughter, Mrs Barden, at the advanced age of ninety-four years His death occurred Sept 24, 1903

MR HUGH HEALEY

was one of the prominent early settlers of Iosco, having settled there in 1857 He was a native of County Mayo, Ireland, born in September, 1821. He came to America in 1849, landing in New York, March 31 He lived for some time in Pennsylvania He married Miss Sarah Coleman, Dec 14, 1852, and they reared a family of eleven children

MR CHRISTIAN KOESTER

was born in Alsace, France, July 31, 1832 His father died when his son was eight years of age Christian came to America in 1853 He resided in Pennsylvania, Wisconsin and Michigan, but finally settled in Iosco, in 1864, where he purchased a farm He married his first wife, Miss Catherine Eppingler, in 1858 She died March 9, 1873, leaving five children. March 22, 1874, he was again married, his bride being Anna Rudolph He still resides on the old farm enjoying the fruits of a well spent life

MR JOHN McWAIDE

is another of the early settlers of Iosco He married Miss Ann Lynch, at Lowell, Mass, in 1855, and they came to Iosco in 1856 Mr. McWaide was born in Ireland on Christmas, 1829, and came to America in 1849, accompanied by his sister, Ella They landed in Boston after being on the water seven weeks and three days Mr and Mrs. McWaide have a fine, large farm of 280 acres with a large residence, and are possessed of all the comforts of life Mr McWaide has held many town offices and for several years has been president of the Waseca County Horse-thief Detectives With this society he is very popular Mr and Mrs McWaide have had five children, three of whom are living. Mrs McWaide is the daughter of Mr and Mrs. Patrick Lynch and one of a family of six children Her brother, John Lynch, enlisted in 1861 and served during the war He participated in many battles, and was especially commended for his bravery in the battle of Cedar Creek in the Shenandoah Valley.

THE HONORABLE JOHN MOONAN.

In this connection it is proper to correct a mistake made on page 41 It is there stated that Patrick Moonan settled in Janesville in 1855. It should have read Iosco instead of Janesville

Hon John Moonan was born in the township of Iosco, Feb 9, 1866, the year before the present city of Waseca was founded His parents, who had lived in Iosco since 1855, moved to the village of Janesville about 1870, where they resided until November 22, 1882, when they removed to Waseca, and built what is now known as the Waverly Hotel John is a graduate of the Waseca high school and studied law in the office of Lewis Brownell, Esq, being admitted to the bar March 21, 1887, by Judge Buckham He at once took front rank at the bar of this county, and now has an extensive practice in this and adjoining counties

He was married to Miss Rosemary Breen, of this city, February 12, 1890 Their children number six—three boys and three girls.

Mr Moonan was elected Mayor of Waseca in 1897, and served one term He was elected and served as county attorney two terms—from Jan 1 1899, to Jan 1903 He is now a member of the school board of this city and takes a deep interest in our educational affairs

Mrs Rosemary Breen Moonan is a daughter of the late Nicholas Breen, of this city. She was born in Iosco, in this county, in 1868, and came to Waseca with her parents when she was about four years of age She is a graduate of the Waseca high school, and was for a time a teacher in one of the departments of the same school She is a woman of marked ability and force of character This county can't have too many such women

MR. GEORGE H GOODSPEED

Mr George H Goodspeed of Waseca, son of Henry Goodspeed, a Union veteran of the war of the Rebellion, was born in Barnstable, Mass., March 8, 1858, and came to Minnesota with his parents in 1872 His father died in 1876, leaving a widow, three sons, and two daughters George was the oldest and upon him devolved the duty of carrying on the farm and business pertaining thereto

On the 25th of May, 1880, he was married to Miss Orilla Justina Child, second daughter of Mr and Mrs James E. Child. Orilla was born in Wilton, Dec 15, 1861 Mr and Mrs Goodspeed are the parents of three

HON. JOHN MOONAN.

sons Henry Erwin, dentist, of Waseca, born March 23, 1881; Claude Martin, born July 13, 1883; Frank Bradford, born Jan 25, 1888 Claude is a sheep herder in Montana, and Frank is in the senior class of the Waseca high school at this writing

George H held the office of chairman of the board of supervisors of the town of Woodville prior to his removal to the city of Waseca He was elected sheriff of the county in 1896, and again in 1898 In 1901 he opened up a small farm in the eastern part of Waseca He soon after became foreman of R. P Ward's large farm just west of Waseca, a position he still holds at this writing

THE HONORABLE HENRY GOODSPEED

The subject of this sketch was born in Barnstable, Mass, Nov. 13, 1834, where he grew to manhood He was the first man to enlist in Company E of the Fortieth Regiment of Massachusetts Volunteers under Captain Bearse His health failed him to some extent, but he was admitted to the reserve corps and served until the 28th day of June, 1865, when he was honorably discharged He was elected a member of the Massachusetts legislature, house of representatives, in 1871. In 1872 he came with his family to Minnesota and resided on a farm on the west side of Clear Lake, just northeast of Waseca He was never a very rugged man, and died of consumption October 19, 1876.

He married Miss Temperance H Parker in 1856 She was also a native of Barnstable, Mass, born July 15, 1836. For years prior to her death she suffered from cancer of the breast and side, and finally departed this life at Waseca, Dec 9, 1896, at the age of sixty years, respected and mourned by all who knew her

Mr and Mrs Goodspeed had five children· George H, Allen C, (deceased) Stanton W., Mrs O L Smith, and Mrs. Elmer Herrick Stanton and Mrs Herrick reside at Glendive, Mont. The others are residents of this county

MR. EMIL H PRECHEL.

This gentleman was one of the earliest settlers of St Mary township He was born in the town of Princeton, Wisconsin, April 13, 1855. His father, Mr Gottlieb Prechel, started with an ox team and a covered wagon for Minnesota about the 1st of May following, in company with Martin, John F., and Gottlieb Krassin, Frederick Wobschall and Frederick Prechel, the last known as "Big Fred" Emil came a babe and was reared in St Mary where he has ever since resided. He married Miss Alvina Lawin of the same town Nov. 26, 1880 Mrs Prechel was born in Germany April 27, 1857, and came to America with her parents in 1864 They first lived in Wisconsin, near the city of Oshkosh, where they remained until 1878, when the family came to Minnesota, making their home on a farm near the south line of St Mary township Mr and Mrs Prechel have a large well-improved farm and good buildings. They are the parents of three sons all grown to man's estate

THE HONORABLE GEORGE A. WILSON

Judge Wilson was born Jan. 22, 1856, in the town of Hammond, St Lawrence county, New York. He did not come West to "grow up with the country" for he was fully developed in old St Lawrence county, and must have come because the West at that time needed such a man He moved to Janesville and captured first place in that village without a struggle In 1894 he was a candidate for judge of probate against one of the most popular men in the county and was elected by a safe majority In the campaign of 1904 he had the field all to himself. He married Miss Mary E Wilson of Janesville July 3, 1895. Mrs. Wilson is also a native of St Lawrence county and is prominent in church and W C T U work.

MR EDWARD BENNETT

was one of the early pioneers of Blue Earth county and our city of Waseca He was born August 17, 1839, and moved with his parents near Mankato in 1856 In 1861, he enlisted in company A, Forty-fourth New York infantry and was afterward transferred to the One Hundred and Forty-sixth New York He participated in nearly all of the battles of the Potomac, and was discharged as lieutenant July 26, 1865. He was married August 22, 1865, to Miss Eliza J Brackett, of New Hampshire In 1867 they settled in Waseca and he engaged in the meat market business In 1872 Mr Bennett platted Bennett's Addition to Waseca, which still bears his name He died after a long illness Oct 16, 1898

His widow, his son, Moses E, and daughter, Georgiana, who reside in Waseca, and his daughter, Jennie, now Mrs. Campbell, survive him.

MR J W AUGHENBAUGH

Mr John W Aughenbaugh, a member of the enterprising milling company of Everett, Aughenbaugh & Co, is a native of Ohio, born Dec 25 1846 His parents removed to Vandalia, Illinois, where they tarried about two years They came to Minnesota in 1856 and settled in Freeborn, Freeborn county, where his father engaged in farming When J W Aughenbaugh was only fifteen years of age he enlisted to serve in the navy While in the navy he served on the lower Mississippi and along the Red River under Commodore Porter After three years' service in the navy he enlisted in Company B, First Minnesota and served about two years in Virginia At the close of the war he returned to Minnesota and entered the milling business at Faribault Aug 25, 1865. He remained thus employed for four years, and mastered the millers' trade. He then entered a mill at Redwing, Minn, where he worked at his trade. He afterwards had charge of mills at Warsaw, Waterville and for a time ran a windmill at Freeborn He came from Waterville to Waseca in

J. W. AUGHENBAUGH.

1877 and formed a partnership with Mr William Everett, which continued until about 1888 when E A Everett, son of William, was admitted to the partnership He married Miss Carrie Kocher, of Faribault, Nov 18, 1868, and they are the parents of two daughters, Mrs. Harry Miller, and Mrs. G W. Strong, and of one son, Master Dana. Mr Aughenbaugh stands at the head of the flour milling business and knows all about the manufacturing of flour from A to Z.

MR EDWARD A EVERETT

This gentleman was born in the town of Arena, Wisconsin, February 20, 1867, and sometimes remarks that he is two days older than Washington. His parents came to Waseca the following August and his father, Mr Wm Everett, commenced the erection of the first store building in Waseca Edward is therefore a Waseca pioneer of the old school He played marbles and fished and hunted and attended the village school until he was fifteen years old when he entered the school of schools, a business career with his father in the mercantile and milling business He could shoulder as much wheat, pack as much flour, or shovel as much coal as the best man in the yards By universal consent he soon became general manager of the immense business of the company, and throughout the state he is known as a safe and reliable business man He is also president of the First National Bank of Waseca, having held that position since its organization His mother's maiden name was Amelia S Addison. She was the daughter of Dr Addison, an English physician of note in Wisconsin On the 2nd of September, 1890, Mr E A Everett and Nettie Miller of Waseca, were united in marriage, she being the daughter of Mr and Mrs. R. Miller of Waseca They are the parents of two children, a son, William R., and a daughter, Constance Antoinette In addition to his extensive milling business, both in Waseca and New Richland, he has large interests in Louisana and Texas in connection with the rice lands of those two states

MR GUY W EVERETT,

brother of E A Everett, was born in Waseca, Sept 21, 1876 He attended the public schools of Waseca for some years and then was a student in a school in San Francisco, Cal, during the sojourn of his parents in that city Upon his return from California after the death of his father which occurred June 16, 1892, he took up work in the milling business of Everett, Aughenbaugh & Co. He was salesman on the road for some time and then took charge of the sales department of the business He thoroughly understands his branch of the business, and gives it the most careful attention He married Miss Esther Lewis, daughter of the late B. S. Lewis, of Waseca, June 15, 1898 They are the parents of one child, a daughter named Esther

MR WILLIAM EVERETT

founder of the Eaco mills, of Waseca, was born in New Jersey, near Newton, in the year 1828 There he lived until twenty-two years of age when he came West and lived at Hayworth Wis. He married at the age of twenty-four and in May, 1859, came to Minnesota, with his family, and resided at the south end of Lake Shetek, Murray county There he opened a farm and cultivated it until Aug 20, 1862, when the murderous Sioux Indians commenced the indiscriminate slaughter of men, women and children all along the western frontier On that terrible day the little band of white settlers, consisting of some six families, were surrounded by a band of two hundred Sioux Indians, and the most of them either killed or wounded Mr Everett was shot in one leg and one arm and his wife and two little boys were murdered after having surrendered to the Indians His little daughter, Lilly, was taken captive and afterwards recovered. Mr Everett lost all his property, besides being ill for a long time of his wounds and exposures He remained in the Mankato hospital till the following February when he went to Wisconsin His loss at Lake Shetek was fully $5,000 of which he afterwards recovered of the government only $800 Mr Everett then resided in Arena, Wis, and married Miss Amelia S Addison, daughter of Dr Addison, Oct 29, 1865 In August, 1867, he came to Waseca and erected and opened the first mercantile house in the village of Waseca He continued the sale of merchandise in this city until he commenced the milling business By nature he was a very strong, robust man, but wounds and exposure at the time of the Indian Massacre so undermined his physical strength that he never recovered He went to California for his health and died there June 16, 1892

MR JOHN B SULLIVAN,

cashier of the First National Bank of Waseca, is a native of Newburyport, Mass His parents came to Minnesota in 1863 and lived on a farm in Dakota county, near Farmington, until 1872, when they settled in the town of Bath, Freeborn county John attended the public schools of his neighborhood until about 1883-4 when he attended school at Winona and graduated from the Winona Commercial College In 1885, he went to Kingsbury county, D T, and opened a real estate and loan office at Lake Preston For two winters he returned to Minnesota and taught school In 1888 he bought a half interest in the Merchants Exchange Bank at that place, and in 1893 went into the flour milling business at the same place He continued in the milling business until 1896, when he sold his interest in the mill and accepted the position of cashier of the First National Bank of Lake Benton In 1901 he became interested in the Citizens State Bank, of Arlington, S D, which was afterwards changed to a National Bank About October 1, 1902, he, in connection with others, bought the Citizens State Bank of Waseca and changed it to the present First National Bank of Waseca This institution began business under its new charter Jan 2, 1903 Mr Sullivan has been cashier of this bank since its opening He is familiar with all the details of the banking business, and is very kind and obliging in all business and social affairs He was joined in marriage with Miss Gertrude Utley Anderson, Nov 10, 1892, at De Smet, S D. Mrs Sullivan was born in Fryeburg, Maine, Feb 16, 1875, and settled with her parents in South Dakota at an early day Mrs Sullivan, who was never very rugged, died of heart disease Sept. 3, 1904, leaving two little boys to the care of the father and a maiden aunt.

MR EUGENE A. SMITH.

Among the very early settlers in the village of Wilton came Mr E A Smith, brother of our county surveyor, Orson L Smith. E A was born at Kingsville, Ashtabula county, Ohio, Dec. 26, 1833. He graduated at the Norwich University of Vermont in 1856, and immediately after came to Minnesota and settled in Wilton. He married Miss Sarah Ide, of that place, about 1861 He was an honorable and highly respected man He died of typhoid pneumonia, Sept 19, 1864, at Wilton, leaving a widow and one daughter, Miss Winnie, who is a resident of California at this writing Mr Smith had accumulated quite a property in real estate at the time of his demise

MR ORSON L SMITH,

for twenty-five years county surveyor of Waseca county, was born in the town of Perry, Lake county, Ohio, April 7, 1845 He attended the public schools of his county, and at the age of seventeen, in 1862, enlisted in Company K, Fifty-second Ohio infantry and served for three years At the close of the war, he went to Montana and worked in the mining regions five years He then enlisted in Company E, Second United States cavalry, and served five years under Gen. Crooks, the noted Indian fighter. The most serious fighting in which he participated was at the destruction of the "Crazy Horse" camp, March 17, 1876, near the close of his term of service. He was honorably discharged soon after, and came to Waseca county in December, 1876 In the spring of 1877, he bought the farm on the north shore of Clear Lake where he has ever since resided. He married Miss Ruth Mabel Goodspeed, sister of George H Goodspeed, Nov 28,1878 They are the parents of two daughters, Mrs Herbert Star, and Miss Isadore T. Mr Smith was first elected county surveyor in 1880 and has held that office continuously by re-election ever since He has also acted as city engineer for the city of Waseca for many years

MR JEROME E MADDEN,

insurance agent and real estate dealer, of Waseca, was born in St Louis, Mo, Dec 14, 1854, and is one of the youngest old settlers in Waseca county. His father, Jerome Madden, deceased, came to this county in the summer of 1856, in company with Patrick Kenehan, Terrence Lilly and their families Jerome Madden, Sr, secured a half section of land in the township of Wilton which belongs to his heirs at this writing The family moved to Faribault about 1864, and opened a hotel where the Rice county court house now stands Mr Madden sold out in Faribault about 1868 and came to Waseca and erected what was known as the Madden House Jerome E attended St John's college, near St Cloud, Minn, at a place now known as "Collegeville," for some time, and then went to Prairie du Chien, Wis, where he finished his school studies and graduated from St John's college, at that place, June 24, 1875 Very soon after that he accepted the position of deputy auditor of Waseca county under Mr Cronkhite He held this position until the close of the year 1880 He then went to Faribault where he was deputy auditor of Rice county for two years He next went to Deadwood, S D, where he was employed as bookkeeper in the First National bank until the death of his mother which occurred in Waseca, August 30, 1888 Shortly after her death, he went to Ely, in St Louis county, Minn., where he spent one year as bookkeeper in a store owned and operated by a large mining company, a hundred miles north of Duluth He soon after returned to Waseca, and in 1895 opened a real estate, loan and insurance office He also has a complete set of abstract books and furnishes abstracts in connection with his other business His father died in Waseca, Nov 18, 1895

J E Madden and Miss Edith Bellm, of New Ulm, were united in marriage Feb 9, 1899 Miss Bellm was born July 2, 1872, in New Ulm, of German parents Mr Madden is a stockholder and one of the directors of the First National bank of Waseca, and a first-class business man

HALVOR K. STEARNS,

of New Richland, was born in Nomedal, Norway, Christmas Day 1836 At the age of seventeen he came to America, and lived in Rock county, Wisconsin Here he was married in 1860 to Miss Betsy Sevets who was born in Norway in June, 1840 He came to Waseca county, accompanied by his wife and one child, in 1862, settling on a farm about two miles east of the present village of New Richland He lived on his farm from 1862 to 1880, when he removed to the village of New Richland and opened a general merchandise store He served as county commissioner from January, 1874, to December, 1879, with credit to himself and satisfaction to his constituents He departed this life February 16, 1905

MR GARRETT SHEEHAN,

of St Mary, was born in County Cork Ireland, about the year 1830 He came to this country In 1852, landed at New York and came immediately to Detroit, Mich, where an uncle resided Shortly afterwards, he commenced work in the copper mines on the south shore of Lake Superior where he remained about two years He also worked some time on the Sault Ste Marie canal and afterwards in the Ontonagon, Mich mines He then started for Waseca county and arrived on election day in the fall of 1856, his brother Dennis and Mr James Brown having settled here a short time before Mr Sheehan made a claim on section 20, town of St Mary, where he still resides. He married Miss Ellen Daly in the fall of 1858 She passed to rest October 13, 1903 At this writing, (1905) he has one son and three daughters. His son James, is on the farm with him, as are also two of the daughters. The third daughter, Mrs Wm Wheelock, resides in Waseca Mr Sheehan's experiences in hauling produce to the Hastings market in the early days, and with the Indians would fill much space He was a strong, vigorous man, and few have done more than he in developing the natural resources of the country He has two farms and has a competency for his old age

MRS SUSAN E SMITH

Mrs Susan E. Smith, widow of Hon Warren Smith, deceased, died at the family residence, June 21, 1896, after a lingering illness of some twelve weeks. She was prostrated at first with grippe from which she was unable to recover She was a sister of the well-known merchant, J W Johnson, of Waseca, and was born in Boston, Mass, August 8, 1825 She married Mr Warren Smith, October 9, 1853, and came to Minnesota with him in 1856 They first lived in Faribault, but came to St Mary, in this county, in 1858, where they made their home until 1862, when they removed to Wilton where they resided until the fall of 1870 when they settled in Waseca Mrs Smith was a model wife, mother, neighbor, and citizen. She was thoroughly devoted to the welfare of her family and neighbors, and enjoyed the highest esteem of all who knew her She possessed all the Christian virtues and graces. She left surviving a daughter, Mary L, a son, Hon. Charles A, four sisters, and two brothers

MR HENRY J MEYER

This gentleman was born in Germany, February 12, 1832, and lacked only ten days of being seventy-three years of age at the time of his death He came to Waseca county about the year 1860, and first lived in Wilton He married Miss Justina Krassin, daughter of Gottlieb Krassin, April 1, 1861 They commenced married life on a farm in the south part of Wilton He soon after sold that farm, and then bought and sold several in succession, finally settling in Freedom in the early seventies. October 15, 1873, his left arm was torn off in a threshing machine He still carried on his farming operations, however, until a few years ago when he built a residence in Waseca and turned his farm over to his sons For about two years prior to his death, which occurred Jan 30, 1905, he suffered from bladder trouble He was the father of three children—Mrs S J Krassin, Hon W H Meyer, and Julius Meyer, all of whom, with his wife, survive him. Mr Meyer was an energetic, prompt man in business, thoroughly honorable and upright in his dealings, and a good citizen.

THE REVEREND FATHER HERMON.

This gentleman was one of the early priests of this county and officiated for a long time in the St Mary parish, some thirty years ago. He was an earnest, eloquent worker and did perhaps more than any other one person to promote temperance and total abstinence among his church members The principles of total abstinence, which he inculcated in the hearts of the young men of this county, have been of uncounted value to the people of the parishes where he officiated and to all the people of the county While he sometimes erred, as a rule, he was a worker for the right, and an efficient worker. He died Jan 27, 1905, at St Joseph's hospital in St Paul, of Bright's disease, at the age of sixty-five His funeral was held in the Catholic church of Waseca, Jan 29, 1905, Father Treanor officiating, and his remains were interred in the Janesville cemetery beside those of relatives gone before.

WM. H. STEARNS

This gentleman was the son of Mr and Mrs E B Stearns, early settlers in the town of Otisco He was born in that township in May, 1859 He resided the greater part of his life there, leaving the farm only a short time to buy wheat in this city for Everett, Aughenbaugh & Co He spent a short time in the mercantile business in New Richland and then returned to the farm for awhile before settling in Waseca He taught school for a number of winters while engaged in farming In the spring of 1884 he was united in marriage to Miss Sarah Armitage, who survives him. One daughter, Monna, was born to them After a prolonged and severe illness, he departed this life, Jan 10, 1905 Some six years prior to his death, he underwent an operation for tuberculosis of a bone of one leg The operation cost him the loss of his entire limb. He had not been in robust health since that time, but had been able to keep about and attended to light work until about a year prior to his demise

MR. FRED M PAPKE

This gentleman was born in St Mary, this county, September 17, 1866, Mr and Mrs. Julius Papke, of Waseca, being his parents. He was a prosperous farmer, and one of the largest men, physically, in Waseca county He was a genial, good-hearted citizen, a kind father and husband He owned a good farm on section 36, in Blooming Grove, and was a successful farmer He died June 16, 1904, of pneumonia after a short illness His wife and two children—a son and a daughter—survive him.

MRS JENNIE WEED STEARNS

This lady, wife of Mr George B Stearns, of Otisco, died at her home, June 10, 1904, of Addison's disease of the kidneys from which she had been ailing for some time and for which she underwent an operation at the Mayo hospital in Rochester a few weeks prior to her death Mrs Stearns was a daughter of Mr. and Mrs B F Weed and was born on the home farm in Wilton in 1859, she grew to womanhood in that part of the county and was married at the age of seventeen With the exception of a few years in New Richland, she and her husband made their home in Otisco

Four children were born to them Edwin, who is married and resides in Waseca, being a fireman on the C & N W railway, Charles, Floyd, and Walter, who are yet at home

MR. FREDERICK McKUNE

This gentleman was born in Illinois, February 10, 1854 His father, Capt. Lewis McKune, who was instantly killed at the first battle of Bull Run, came with his family to Minnesota, and settled in Blooming Grove, in 1856 With the exception of a few years at Morristown, Frederick had been a resident of Blooming Grove to the time of his death He married Miss Clarissa C Gore, of Morristown, in 1883, and three children were born to them. Mr McKune was elected county commissioner in 1900, and, although a very modest man, performed his duties with fidelity His death from brain trouble occurred June 14, 1904 He had been sick for some time, but it was not generally known that his illness was of a serious nature

MR NICHOLAS J BREEN KILLED INSTANTLY.

This gentleman, senior member of the firm of N J Breen & Sons, proprietors of the oatmeal mill, was instantly killed at Waseca, June 8, 1904, on the side track of the M & St. L. railroad, at the Wood street crossing, near their mill Freight cars were standing on the crossing, the rear end of the hind car being about half way across the sidewalk crossing As Mr Breen stepped upon the track, in going around the end of the car, the cars were suddenly shoved back The bumper struck him and knocked him down He attempted to get off the track upon his hands and knees when the wheels caught him at the waist and cut him in two—the skin only holding the body together It is said that three cars passed over his body One arm was badly broken as was one of his legs Death must have been almost instantaneous.

Sympathetic citizens rolled the car wheel off the body and put the remains upon a stretcher, whence they were taken to the Comee & Pfaff undertaking rooms.

Mr Breen was born in Dublin, Ireland, January 29, 1830. His parents died when he was twelve years old and he was cared for by an uncle who lived in county Wexford While living there he learned blacksmithing When only nineteen years of age he came to America, first stopping at Binghampton, N Y In the fall of 1849 he came as far west as Milwaukee where he lived two years In 1851 he opened a blacksmith shop at Franklin, Wis, where he lived until 1866 when he came to the town of Iosco where he opened a farm This he carried on until about 1871, when he came to Waseca to live and erected a blacksmith shop on the corner of First and Elm streets. This he sold to the city for a city hall, June 14, 1888, and at once erected the oatmeal mill situated at the side of the M. & St L railroad tracks

He married Miss Rose Anna McAnany, a native of New York city, in 1857, by whom he had seven children Margaret M, John J, Thomas, Francis M, Agnes C, Mrs John Moonan and Alice, all of whom reside in Waseca Mr Breen was one of our most honorable, upright, and reliable citizens All his life he was a Father Matthew total abstinence advocate, a man well read and thoroughly informed, especially in matters pertaining to America and Great Britain He was a prominent, de voted, and consistent member of the Catholic church, and if all men were such as he, there need be no fear of the Hereafter

MRS RUDOLPH BABLER

This good woman died at her home in Merton, Minn, Monday, May 30, at the age of seventy-four years, of cancer of the stomach She was born at Canton Glarus, Switzerland, in 1830 On February 16, 1853, she was married to Rudolph Babler and on February 27, eleven days after their marriage, they started for the United States, reaching Greene county, Wisconsin, May 1, 1853 There they lived eleven years, and then came to Minnesota to the town of Woodville, Waseca county, in 1864 They arrived on May 1 of that year and lived there until 1887, when they moved to Clinton Falls, where they lived until May 1903, when they moved to Merton The deceased was a most estimable woman She was the mother of eight children, six of whom survive her, as follows Mrs A C Sanders, Merton Mrs George Irvine, Woodville, John Babler, Humbird, Wis, Christopher Babler, of Hennepin county Mrs. William Biram, of Idaho, and Rudolph Babler, Jr, of Perham, Minn

Mr Rudolph Babler died June 24, 1905, at Genesee, Idaho, where he was visiting his daughter, Mrs W L Biram He was born in Switzerland Jan 21, 1828 Mr Babler was a good citizen, a kind husband and father, and an obliging neighbor

MR. L. F PETERSON

Mr Peterson was one of the prominent and influential men of Otisco He was born June 25, 1825, in Smoland, Skarstad Socken, Sweden At the age of twenty-eight, in the fall of 1853, he sailed for America, arriving at New York, Oct 20, 1853 He then journeyed to La Fayette, Ind, and entered the employ of a farmer named Murdock where he worked until the spring of 1857 In the month of March, of that year he was united in marriage with Miss Britta Christina Peterson, of Chicago, and they at once came to Minnesota, arriving the same month He settled on section 21, in Otisco where he resided at the time of his death. His first wife died in August, 1862 leaving one daughter, Miss Mary C Peterson

In 1864, Mr Peterson visited his native land, leaving America in May

He remained in Sweden a year, leaving there in June, on his return trip, arriving at New York, July 4, 1865 On the 18th of August following, he was united in marriage to Miss Helena Johnson, of Otisco. Ten children were born to them, of whom only four are now living. He died at his home in Otisco at the advanced age of seventy-three, April 25, 1898 His son, Theodore Peterson, was born in Otisco, Sept 26, 1871 He is an active, influential young man He was appointed deputy county auditor, by Auditor Bailer, in 1901, and still holds the position, giving general satisfaction to all concerned

MR JOHN FRATZKE

This gentleman was one of our Union veterans, and an early settler in the town of Freedom He was a native of Germany, born Oct 25, 1833 At the age of twenty years, he sailed for America on a sail ship, being nine weeks on the sea He landed at New York, Jan 3, 1854, and immediately came west as far as Princeton, Wisconsin. Three years later his parents, five brothers, and one sister, arrived at Princeton from Germany He married Miss Gering in 1859 On the second day of December, 1862, he enlisted as a private in Company A, Sixteenth regiment of Wisconsin Volunteer infantry to serve for three years or during the war He went South with his regiment the same fall At Louisville, Ky, he was wounded twice At Atlanta, Ga., he was in a hot place and received two gun shot wounds one bullet passing through his left thigh and another through his left ankle He was sent to the hospital and remained there five months At one time the rebel firing was so hot that the hospital had to be moved seven times in one day After his recovery, he again took the field, this time at the battle of Gettysburg, which continued three days and nights At the close of the war he marched to Washington and passed the Capitol in grand review He was soon after honorably discharged and returned to his home in Wisconsin In 1866, he and his brother William and their families came with ox teams and covered wagons to the town of Freedom, then a new settlement Two years later his wife died, leaving three small children For three years he lived with his brother William in a log cabin 12x14 feet, with a clay floor Feb 1, 1870, he visited Germany and there married Miss Gussey and returned to America in May, 1871 Three years later, his second wife died leaving a daughter, Hulda, and a son, Gust J, the latter only three weeks old Gust J was cared for and reared by Mrs. Henry Literman In 1875, Mr Fratzke was again married, this time to Miss Mathilda Barbknecht. Mr Fratzke was treasurer of the town of Freedom for seventeen years. In 1894, he moved into the town of Wilton where he died in 1896 at the age of sixty-three years. He was an honorable, upright man, and a true patriot

Two years after John and William came to Minnesota, their father and mother, three brothers, and a sister joined them The father died at the age of seventy-seven years, the mother at the age of sixty-six

Wm Fratzke still resides in Freedom. Carl Fratzke owns a large farm in Freedom, but resides on another farm near Cottonwood Julius died in 1891 at the age of fifty-five years. Gustave, another brother of John, owns a large farm in Freedom, but resides in the village of Janesville and runs a general store Another brother, Herman, is living in Ripon, Wisconsin The only sister of the family married Mr Ernest Miller, who owns a large farm in Freedom, while managing a store in Janesville where he resides with his family John Fratzke had three sons by his first wife Herman, a carpenter, who is married and lives in this county, William, who went to Wisconsin ten years ago, married and lives at Fox Lake, Charles, who left home at the age of fourteen years and has not been heard from since John's daughter Hulda, by his second wife, at the age of twenty-one, married Fred Kelling, and died five years later at Janesville.

Gust J Fratzke, the son by his second wife, married Miss Amy Lang, of Vivian, daughter of Mr Herman Lang, one of the old settlers of that town Gust J ran a threshing machine for some time, and then moved to Janesville, at the same time becoming traveling salesman for a Minneapolis machinery company After being with the company three years, he accepted a position with the J I Case company, of Wisconsin

John Fratzke had three sons by his third wife—Ed, now in Texas; Henry who is married and lives on a farm in Wilton, and Frank W, who enlisted Dec 23, 1901, in the army of the United States and served three years He was a private of Troop H, Sixth regiment of cavalry, and served the most of the time in the Philippine Islands Near the close of his term he was stationed at Fort Meade, South Dakota He enlisted at the age of eighteen years, and was honorably discharged on the 22nd of December, 1904.

MR H. W. REINEKE,

of Blooming Grove, was born in Deerfield, Steele county, Oct. 5, 1866, and is the son of Mr Conrad Reineke, now of Faribault His grandfather, whose name was also Conrad, was born in the Province of Hanover, Germany, and came to America with his family about the year 1853 They were eight weeks on the ocean They first lived in Schonberg, near Chicago In May, 1855, Conrad, Christian, and Henry Reineke, with their parents, started for Minnesota with ox teams and wagons. They arrived in Deerfield about the first of June 1855, where Grandfather Conrad Reineke made a claim Here the family made their home in spite of the hardships incident to pioneer life. Conrad Junior, father of H W was then about twelve years of age, having been born July 19 1843 Grandfather Conrad died in the early sixties Conrad Junior enlisted in Company F, Third Minnesota, in 1863, and served until 1865 Conrad was married soon after his return from the army to Miss Otelia Wilkowski They have ten children Henry W, Anna George, William, Albert, Louis, Hulda, Ernest, Rudolph, and Stella Henry W was married to Miss Winnie

MR. AND MRS. CONRAD REINEKE.

Fehmer Oct 23, 1900 She was born March 25, 1867 They have six children, one boy and five girls. H W has been secretary of the Deerfield creamery association and prominent in all public affairs His brother, Dr George Reineke, lives at New Ulm where he practices medicine William and Albert are well-to-do farmers in Blooming Grove Louis is a farmer in Deerfield Ernest is studying for the ministry in the German M. E. church. Rudolph is attending school in Faribault Fred and Edward Reineke, sons of Christian Reineke, of Deerfield, also reside in Blooming Grove The Messrs Reineke are all well-to-do people and very reliable.

MR ELLING JOHNSON

Mr Johnson was born in Norway Jan 6, 1840, and came to America in 1856, living first in McHenry county, Ill In Dec, 1859, he, with others, went into northern Wisconsin and chopped and cleared the timber from a public highway which was being constructed at public expense From Dec 2, 1859, to March 1, 1860, they camped out in the open air and slept in their working clothes The only protection they had was a covering of evergreen boughs overhead and a bed of the same material with a big campfire in front. In March he went to work in the copper mines at Rockland, Michigan From there he came to Dodge county, Minnesota, and in 1864 enlisted in Company H, Eleventh Minnesota Volunteer infantry He served until June 26, 1865, when he was honorably discharged, and returned to Dodge county, Minn. There he engaged in the lumber business until 1872 when he came to Waseca and took charge of the Winona Lumber company's business in Waseca where he has since resided He married Miss G. Anderson while yet in McHenry county, Ill. Mr and Mrs Johnson are prominent and leading members of the Norwegian Lutheran church.

MR JOHN A KRASSIN

This gentleman is a native of this county He was born in St Mary township, Sept 6, 1856 He followed farming until 1889, when he came to Waseca and went into the machine business with San Galli and Herman Lawin About a year later he sold his interest in the machine business and commenced the buying and selling of cattle and hogs, the business in which he is now engaged He was married to Miss Emma Lawin, then of St. Mary, March 29, 1887 Mrs Krassin was born near Oshkosh, Wisconsin, April 25, 1865, and came to Minnesota with her parents in 1878 Mr and Mrs Krassin are the parents of five children—two boys and three girls Mr. Krassin still owns his farm and other lands, in all about two hundred seventy acres.

MR JEROME MADDEN.

Jerome Madden, who was born in County Galway, Ireland, in 1828, and who came to America in 1848, lived first in Illinois and afterwards in

St Louis, Mo He came to Waseca county with his family and settled in Wilton in 1856. He was the father of four sons and one daughter. Mary, now Mrs Carroll of Waseca, was born in St Louis, Mo, May 3, 1850, Jerome E. was born at the same place Dec 14, 1854, Thomas was born in Lacon, Ill, Jan 18, 1857, Francis was born in St Mary, Minn, Jan 30, 1859, and James was born at the same place July 27, 1862 Thomas Madden is a resident of St. Mary, Frank is at Dedham, Wis, and James is in Minneapolis The mother died August 30, 1888, and Jerome, the father, died Nov 18, 1895 Other facts are given under the title "Jerome E Madden"

MR ROSCOE PERCY WARD

Mr Ward is the well-known cashier of the People's State bank of Waseca, and a son of Hon W G Ward, deceased, who was one of the pioneers of the West and chief engineer in charge of the building of that portion of the C & N W railway, known as the Winona & St Peter branch R P was born in the city of Waseca, Jan 5, 1872 He attended the city schools and graduated from the high school in the class of 1889. He then began the academic course at the State University of Minnesota, but, on the death of his father, which occurred Sept 21, 1892, he was obliged to leave his university studies in order to look after the large business interests of his father's estate He married Miss Daisy M Cole of Minneapolis, Aug 10, 1893, she being about his own age They have one child, Emerson Mr Ward entered upon the duties of bank cashier in July, 1897, and under his administration, the business of the bank has been largely increased In addition to his banking interests, he is largely interested in farming He owns one of the finest farms in the state just west of Waseca He has been alderman from his ward for a number of years and president of the city council for several terms He resigned the office of alderman in the spring of 1905, having served less than half his last term

MR H P NORTON.

Mr. H. P. Norton, who came to Minnesota in July, 1855, is a native of Richford, Tioga county, New York He was born May 26, 1823 His father was a blacksmith H P attended the public school of his town, learned his father's trade, and worked at home until he reached his majority. For two years he worked at his trade as a journeyman In the spring of 1846 he came West, arriving at Woodstock, Ill, about the 1st of June. He remained there for several years, working at his trade, and then went to Chicago where he was employed in the railroad shops until 1856, when he came to Minnesota, arriving at Owatonna in July of that year Here he found employment with "Uncle" Joel Wilson, the pioneer blacksmith, of Owatonna He remained with "Uncle Joel" until fall, when he came to Wilton, then a new town, and opened the first blacksmith shop in that place Those were the days that tried men's

H. P. NORTON.

souls it was work and trust and trust and work, and barter and dicker and dicker and barter Mr Norton's books still show several hundred dollars of "trust" unpaid, but the "trusts" of those days were not like the "trusts' of to-day His brother, C O Norton, also a blacksmith, joined him in 1857, and they carried on the business together for a long time In 1859 H P Norton was appointed and elected to fill out the term of clerk of the district court, made vacant by the removal of Thos L Page This office he held until Jan 1, 1862, when he was succeeded by H P West He was then made postmaster of Wilton for two years, when he was elected register of deeds He served two years as register, and at the same time held the position of agent for the American Express company He was married at Woodstock, Ill, March 2, 1863, to Miss Anna G Kimball, an accomplished lady possessed of some property They have one son, Charles N, who is married and resides in Waseca In 1867, Mr Norton and his wife became part proprietors of the First Addition to Waseca, and were among the very first to make their home in the new town Mr Norton still held the position of agent of the American Express company and opened the office in Waseca in the fall of 1867 In connection with the express business, he opened a real estate office, which he carried on until 1884, when he retired from active business Mr Norton was the first village marshal of Waseca and held various other positions of honor His father's name was Amzi He was a native of Connecticut and was born Feb 12, 1783, and his mother was a native of the same state They were the parents of ten children At this writing—March 1905—Mr Norton is nearly eighty two years of age and is remarkably well preserved. The picture accompanying this sketch, was taken March 13, 1905 Financially he is well fixed, and in every way he is surrounded with all that is agreeable and comfortable.

COLONEL W W ROBINSON

This gentleman settled in Wilton in 1856 He was born at Fair Haven, Vermont, Dec 14, 1819 He graduated from Rutland Academy at the age of nineteen He also took a course at the Norwich Military academy He married Sarah Jane Fisk, daughter of Daniel Fisk, Feb 5, 1842 At the breaking out of the war with Mexico, in 1846, he promptly enlisted and was elected first lieutenant, his commission bearing date June 12 1846 Oct 26, 1846, he was promoted to captain At the close of the Mexican war he returned to Ohio, where he remained until 1851, when he made a trip to Wisconsin on a land speculation In the spring of 1852, he went to California overland, being six months on the way thither He remained in the "Golden State" until the fall of 1855, when he rejoined his family at Sparta, Wisconsin. As before stated, he came to Wilton, in this county, in the fall of 1856, where he resided with his family He practiced law to some extent while in Wilton and was prominent in local affairs. In 1859 he disposed of his property here and returned to Sparta, Wis At the breaking out of the Rebellion he engaged in drilling men for the service, and on the 15th of August, 1861, was commissioned lieutenant colonel of the Seventh Regiment Wisconsin volunteer infantry This regiment, with four others, constituted the famous Iron Brigade He was promoted to colonel of the regiment in February, 1862 He resigned in July, 1864, on account of sickness and the breaking out of a wound received at Gainesville, in 1862 He participated in over thirty battles and skirmishes After a partial recovery of his health he engaged in lumbering at Chippewa Falls, Wis In 1875 he was appointed U. S consul at Madagascar by President Grant and held that position until the fall of 1886, when he resigned and returned to his family At this writing, 1905, Mrs Robinson is living at Seattle, state of Washington, in good health at the age of eighty-six years. Colonel Robinson died April 27, 1903

MR JOSEPH FROMLATH

Joseph Fromlath was born in Stadel Baden, Germany, March 19, 1853. He came to Waseca, Minn, Feb 1, 1871. He obtained employment for three years on the farm that he later bought of Mr S F Repstein The farm is situated on section twenty, town of Otisco, Minn, and was the home of Mr Fromlath's family for many years It was to this farm that, in the year 1876, he brought his bride, Minnie Frank, daughter of Ludwig Frank, of Wilton Here were reared their six children Caroline, born May 4, 1877 George, born July 29, 1879 Anna, born Jan 19, 1881, Edward, born August 16, 1887, Martha, born January 18, 1893, Joseph, Jr, born March 19, 1904

In 1904, Mr Fromlath and family removed to North Dakota Mr and Mrs Fromlath reside in the city of Lisbon, their older children are carrying on a large farm near that place

While a resident of this county Mr. Fromlath held at different times the offices of school director, town supervisor, treasurer of the Otisco Station creamery association, and county commissioner. At the time of his removal to North Dakota, he was one of the directors of the First National bank, of Waseca, and is at this writing a stockholder therein

THE HONORABLE JOHN N POWERS

Hon John Neil Powers was one of the early settlers of this county and a good citizen He was born of Irish parents, at Providence, Rhode Island, September 26, 1836, and with his parents, at an early age, moved to Woodstock, Illinois, where he resided until 1856, when he came to Blooming Grove, in Waseca county, Minnesota In 1861, he enlisted in Company I, Fourth regiment, Minnesota volunteers, serving for three years After being honorably discharged he returned to Waseca county, where he studied law and was admitted to the bar in 1867 Here he practiced law for some time He was married Nov 2, 1868 to Miss Anna Josephine Conners He removed to Morristown soon after, where he practiced law and also edited the first paper published in Morristown during 1876 He also published a paper at Waterville during 1877 He was elected to the legislature as a member of the house of representatives from Rice county in 1866 Mr Powers died March 1, 1901, after having suffered from paralysis for a long time He was survived by a widow, eight children, and two sisters He was a very kind-hearted, good man He was in no sense a money maker—much less a money schemer Coming from the ranks of working men, he was always their friend and champion The world would be better if there were more such men

MRS CHARLES MUNSON

This lady is a daughter of the late James Jones, known as "Jones the joker," and came with her parents to Iosco in May 1856 Mrs Munson was about five years old when her parents settled in Iosco, and has a very distinct recollection of the early days in this county She has a vivid remembrance of the Indians, who made frequent visits to the farm and often camped in the vicinity Her father, who died January 24, 1902, at the age of ninety-two years, was one of the jolliest of all the pioneer settlers of the county.

THE HONORABLE GOTTFRIED BUCHLER

Mr Buchler was born in Baden, Germany, in 1836, the last day of February. His mother died when he was about a year old He came to America with his father when Gottfried was eight years of age They lived in Sheboygan county, Wisconsin, when that section was a wilderness of heavy timber. He helped to clear and cultivate the farm, and married there, carrying on his farm until 1868, when he sold his property there and came to Waseca that fall. He first opened a boot and shoe store, and afterwards added clothing—a business which he continued to the time of his death In 1886 he was elected mayor of this city, and served one term His administration was noted for its strenuous economy in all departments.

As a business man, he was conservative, never a plunger, and he accumulated quite an amount of property

On Christmas morning, 1904, he arose apparently in his usual health, he ate his breakfast, smoked his pipe, and talked with his children as usual About 11 30 a m he went from the kitchen into the dining room and sat down in his arm chair near the table Evidently he took from a plate on the table a piece of candy, and when about to eat it, was suddenly stricken His daughter heard a peculiar gasping and went to his side He gasped a time or two more and was dead without speaking. He had not been feeling very well for some days, a pain in the region of the heart being felt at times But his doctor told him it was only the result of indigestion, and little was thought of it His sudden death on Christmas morning was a painful shock to the community as well as to his immediate family He left surviving, three daughters and two sons—Messrs Louis and Edmund, and Misses Mary, Louise and Josephine, all of age.

SUICIDE OF MATT CHRISTIANSON

The Waseca Herald of April 1, 1904, contained the following

Wednesday morning last, Mr Raymond Doyle, business manager of the Plum Valley creamery, brought the sad news that Matt Christianson, of Vivian, was found upon the floor of his house, beside his bed, with a bullet hole in his head The facts, as we hear them, are substantially as follows

Some time ago Mrs Christianson, fearing that her husband, in his bursts of passion or madness, would kill her, left her home to live with relatives or friends

Christianson and a son thirteen or fourteen years of age, had been keeping house by themselves On Monday the father went to Mankato, to see his wife Returning, he stopped at Minnesota Lake, bought a revolver, and proceeded homeward

In the meantime his son did the chores Monday night and went to stay over night with a neighbor boy Tuesday morning the son, accompanied by the neighbor boy, returned to the Christianson house Upon opening the door, a terrible sight met their astonished gaze There upon the floor, covered with blood and with blood all around him, lay Christianson with a bullet hole in his head apparently unconscious, but still breathing The terrified boys at once alarmed the neighbors, who soon gathered at the house, but no one seemed willing to attempt to do anything for the wounded man until a physician could be obtained from Minnesota Lake

This is the same Christianson who, over a year ago, assaulted his neighbor, Ewald, with a loaded gun and who was himself thoroughly bruised at the time by young Ewald, who defended his father Mr Christianson was arrested at that time, heavily fined, and put under bonds to keep the peace It is generally thought by those acquainted with him that he has been insane for a long time

It also appears that Mrs. Christianson had commenced an action for divorce, on the grounds of cruelty

Our Vivian correspondent writes that the victim shot himself through the mouth, the bullet piercing the brain This is confirmed by Coroner Blanchard who visited the remains on Wednesday, the man having died on Tuesday

Our Vivian correspondent also writes that Christianson, a short time before, attempted to kill his wife with a butcher knife It also appears that Mrs Christianson, since that time, has been living wih a daughter at Mankato.

TRAGIC DEATH OF DR EDWARD DOLAN

Tragic in the extreme was the death by accidental poisoning of Dr Edward Dolan, of Worthington, Jan 8, 1904 Not feeling well Saturday night when leaving the farm house of a patient five miles south of Worthington, he reached for his medicine case, pulled out a bottle and drank a quantity of carbolic acid

He had made a mistake in the darkness, but with great presence of mind, poured several ounces of alcohol down his throat, but his efforts to save himself were vain Doctor Dolan gasped out an order to his driver to hurry at full speed to Worthington, and while the buggy rushed over the road he exerted every effort to save his own life About a mile from town he alighted from the vehicle, intending to keep the vital spark alive by walking He had walked but a few paces when he reeled and fell, racked with convulsions Death ended his sufferings very soon and the driver brought the body into town Doctor Dolan was about thirty-seven years of age and had practiced medicine at Worthington for ten or twelve years He was born in Iosco and many of his relatives live in this vicinity

At the outbreak of the Spanish-American war he left his large practice to serve as captain of Company H, Fifteenth Minnesota volunteers, and continued in the service until his regiment was mustered out He left surviving him his wife and one son two years old

PROFESSOR F. V HUBBARD

This gentleman was superintendent in charge of the schools of Waseca for nine years, having come here from Redwood Falls where he had taught for six years. He was highly esteemed and stood high among the schoolmen of the state He had been one of the vice presidents of the State Teachers' association and an officer of the National Association of Superintendents He was suddenly killed at his home in Red Wing, August 27, 1901 He had been remodeling his house and was directing work with a horse scraper on the lawn. The driver had some trouble with the scraper, and Mr Hubbard, who was in haste to be done, tried to help him. As Mr Hubbard unhooked it, the load of dirt threw the scraper over suddenly and the end of the lever hit him in the back of the head, breaking his neck. He died instantly He was forty-six years old His wife and four sons survived him

He was a graduate of the Whitewater, Wis., Normal school. He was one of the best teachers, if not the best, that ever had charge of the Waseca schools

MR JOHN DALTON

This gentleman was one of the prominent farmers of Iosco, who settled there about the year 1866 He was born in Ireland, coming to this country in 1847, at the age of twenty-three He worked on the Erie canal in the state of New York, and later resided some years in Illinois before coming to Minnesota He accumulated considerable property, having a fine farm and a pleasant home, at the time of his death He died Dec 8, 1899, at the age of seventy-five years

MR AUGUST F GRAPP

Mr August F Grapp, who stands at the head of the Grapp Furniture

& Carpet company, was born July 26, 1841, at Ukermark, Prussia, where he was educated in the public schools and learned the trade of cabinet maker At the age of eighteen, as is the law there, he entered the army and served in all four years—the last year, 1864-5, he saw active service in the war with Denmark As soon as the war was over he came to America, arriving in August, 1866. His parents had preceded him and resided at Fountain City, Wis, where he joined them. He worked at Fountain City a few months, and then came as far west as Owatonna There he worked until the village of Waseca was platted in 1867, when he was one among the very first to buy a lot in the new town and build He had only $75 to begin with, but, nothing daunted, he purchased a lot on time, put up a small building with his own hands and opened a furniture store before the grain crop then standing on the plat had been stacked. The lot he then built upon is the adjoining lot on the north of the one he now occupies From this small beginning has grown the immense business of the present firm On the first of December, 1869, he was wedded to Miss Ottilie L Roesler, who was born Sept, 17, 1852, in Michigan City, Indiana, and came to Waseca county with her parents in 1862, about the time of the Indian massacre in Minnesota Mr and Mrs Grapp are the parents of nine children, eight of whom are living. Wm. L, born Dec 14, 1871, Otto W, born Nov 7, 1873, Albert E, born Sept 6, 1875, Frederick C., born Sept. 27 1877, and died July 19, 1885, Lydia A R, born Feb 14, 1882, John H, born Jan 10, 1885, George L, born Aug 17, 1887, Edward A, born Feb 10, 1889, and Roy E, born Jan 9, 1893. Wm L. Grapp manages the popular store at Janesville, and Otto W is at the head of their business at Redwood Falls Mr A Grapp is one of the solid business men of Waseca, who has succeeded by hard work and attention to business

SUPERINTENDENT H A PANZRAM

Herman A Panzram was born in Olmsted county, Minn, Oct 1, 1877. His mother died when he was a babe, and he was adopted by his father's sister and her husband, Martin Helwig and wife, resident farmers of Freedom He remained in Freedom until 1885, when the family moved to Alton and thence to Janesville in 1888 He graduated from the Janesville high school and attended the State University one year When the Spanish war broke out, he was one of the first of the patriotic young men to enlist in Company K, of this county He spent the summer of 1898 in the service, being stationed most of the time at Chickamauga He was honorably mustered out in the fall For the three and a half years following, he was engaged in school teaching In the fall of 1904, he was elected to the office of county school superintendent, and holds this position at the present writing. He is also publisher of the Waseca County Teacher, and is thoroughly devoted to the cause of education. He was married to Miss Pansy E Jenkins Oct 4, 1905

AUGUST GRAPP.

MR CHAUNCY E PARKER.

This aged pioneer of the West died at the residence of his son, James E Parker, of Waseca, March 23, 1904, of pneumonia, in his eighty-eighth year He was born in the state of New York, in the month of June, 1816 When a young man, he started West and first lived near Ashtabula, Ohio About 1850, he moved to Evanston, Ill, where the family remained until about 1857 when they removed to Marquette county, Wisconsin His wife died about 1858 He remained in Wisconsin until 1885, when he came to Waseca where he resided with his sons He was a well-preserved man and had enjoyed good health nearly all his life up to the time of his last illness He left surviving him three sons and two daughters A H and J E Parker, of Waseca, Orson Parker, of Pomona, Cal, Mrs Bort, of St Paul, and Mrs Hibbard, of Fond du Lac, Wis.

MR C. H BAILER

Charles H Bailer, the present efficient county auditor, was born March 19, 1861, in Schuylkill, Pa, and came to Minnesota, March 17, 1884, first stopping at Mankato but soon after going to Janesville There he entered the store of Mr Cordry as clerk and afterwards as partner He remained in Janesville until the fall of 1900 when he was elected county auditor He has been re-elected twice since, at the last election having no competitor Sept 25, 1888, he married Miss Emma Farnum, of Janesville, who was born in Minnesota May 7, 1866 They are the parents of three daughters and one son Mr Bailer followed farming, when not at school, until he became of age, when he was employed as clerk He graduated from the high school of his town and also from a business college in his native state

HENRY G BLANCHARD, M D

Dr. H G Blanchard, son of Mr Gustof Blanchard, one of the very early settlers of Winona county, was born April 17, 1868, in Winona county, Minn When the doctor's parents first settled in this then territory, the Indians were numerous. The family lived fifteen miles west of Winona, and his father, who was a carpenter by trade, worked in Winona and often made the distance on foot, sometimes carrying family supplies the whole distance on his shoulders Doctor Blanchard attended the public schools of his county, took the academic course at the Grand Forks, N D., university, and graduated from the medical department of the Minnesota university. He practiced medicine and surgery for some time in Hutchinson, afterwards in Minneapolis, and came to Waseca in 1898, where he soon enjoyed an extensive practice On June 25, 1902, he was joined to Miss Catharine Kiesler, of Hutchinson, in holy wedlock He has a fine suite of rooms in the First National Bank building and is supplied with all modern implements and appliances for surgical and other work in the art curative

FRANK B ANDREWS, ATTORNEY

Frank B Andrews, Esq, present county attorney of this county, was first "brought to light" in the town of Wonewoc, Wisconsin, March 30, 1862 His parents removed from Wonewoc, Wis, to Wells, Minn, about 1871 He attended the Wells schools and studied law with his brother Oct 1, 1885, he was joined with Miss Jessie Smout in marriage and commenced life in earnest In 1889, he was admitted to the bar by Judge Severance, at Blue Earth, and the same year moved to New Richland, this county At the election in 1890, he was chosen county attorney and served acceptably one term In 1902 he was again elected county attorney and re-elected in 1904 He is the father of five children Florence, born in December, 1886, Robert, born in September, 1889, died Oct 14, 1905, Clifford, born in October, 1891, Catharine, born in July, 1897, Marian, born in April, 1904 In the performance of his duties as county attorney, he is very conservative, and takes extra precautions against extravagant expenses Socially, he stands at the head of his class

MR WILLIAM HOOVER

This gentleman, who was one of the early settlers in Vivian, was born in Ontario county, New York, April 30, 1824 His parents moved to Bradford county, Pa., while he was yet a small lad He remained there with his parents till Nov 8, 1845, when he married Miss Susan Hill He then engaged in lumbering Mr and Mrs. Hoover are the parents of one daughter, now Mrs A T Wolcott, of Waseca, and one son, who died at the age of seventeen years Mr Hoover was in the Wisconsin lumber work until 1862, when he came to Minnesota to section 27 Vivian, where, in 1864, he owned two hundred acres of farm land He joined the army Dec 17, 1864, enlisting in Company G, Fifth Minnesota infantry He returned from the army in September, 1865, and resumed farming. Mrs Hoover died Jan 8, 1880 In 1885 he sold his farm in Vivian and came to Waseca where he has since resided At this writing he is still hale and hearty although over eighty-one years of age

MR B J CHAPMAN

This gentleman was born in Madison county, New York in 1835, came to Wisconsin in 1856, to Rice county, Minnesota, April 16, 1857 He built a claim shanty, which some one soon appropriated He bought a yoke of oxen and paid down $50 which was all of his available capital In his statement he says

"My aunt, Mrs Chapin, signed a fifty-dollar note with me to pay for the oxen By the way she did not have it to pay. I got a few acres broken that year, and next year sowed it to wheat, but the wheat did not fill, hence I had nothing to harvest I broke more land and sowed all to wheat the next year I got it harvested, threshed and put into a rail pen. Soon after the pen caught fire and the wheat was burned, except a part of it, which was badly smoked After that I had better success

HON. P. C. BAILEY.

Within five years I had my farm of one hundred sixty acres paid for, one hundred twenty acres fenced, seventy acres broken, a comfortable house, etc I then went back to York State but returned in 1863 The following year, 1864, I purchased the E B Stearns old farm in Otisco, and moved there in the spring of 1864. October 15, 1865, I was united in marriage with Miss Samantha Reynolds who was born in Grant county, Indiana, Sept 17, 1846 She came to Minnesota in 1857 with her parents who settled on what is known as the McLain farm"

Mr. Chapman is one of the successful farmers of the county who has made his property, not by sharpness or shrewdness, but by hard work and economy He is the father of two sons and four daughters His oldest son, George, is on a farm in Stevens county The younger, Orange, is attending school in Mankato. His daughters are Mrs Thos Ivers, of Byron, Mrs. Wm. Lust, of Olivia, Minn., Mrs Wm Duncan, of Fairmont, Minn, and Miss Lilian, attending school at Waseca

MR B SIMONS

This gentleman is the popular proprietor of the restaurant on the corner of Second and Wood streets. He was born in Norway, March 11, 1852, came to America with his parents in 1857, and lived for six months in Manitowoc, Wis His parents then moved to Adams county, same state He married Miss Emma Thompson, March 29, 1880, coming to Minnesota in 1882 Miss Thompson was born Dec 29, 1856, near Madison, Wis In the fall of 1882, he opened the Nicollet House in Waseca, which he conducted for four years In the fall of 1886, in company with Fred Byersdorf, he opened a grocery store. In the fall of 1894, he sold his interest to Byersdorf, and traveled a year for a cigar house In the fall of 1895, he commenced the business in which he and his family are now engaged At the last city election he was chosen alderman from the First ward He is the father of three sons and three daughters, Malinda, born in 1881; Anna, in 1883, Jalmar, in 1885, Clarence, in 1887, Bert, in 1891, deceased, and Eva, in 1894 Jalmar is attending the State University

MR JOHN RADLOFF

Mr Radloff, who was born in Germany Oct 7, 1834, came to America in 1854 landing at Buffalo, N Y., where he worked ten years for one lumberman In March, 1860, he married Lena Billiard who was born in the state of New York They are the parents of three sons and three daughters They settled on section 11, Vivian, in 1864, where they have since resided Mr Radloff is one of the oldest threshermen in the state, and has earned a great deal of money, very much of it being spent for machinery, repairs, and interest He is one of the leading men of his township

THE HONORABLE P. C. BAILEY.

Philo C Bailey, born in Onondaga county, N Y., Oct 15, 1828, came to Faribault, Rice county, Minn, in 1856, and to Wilton, this county, in 1857, opening the first hardware store in the county with his brother-in-law, H P West—the firm name being P C Bailey & Co Some time after the death of Mr. West, J H Wightman became a partner, while he was at Wilton At the starting of Waseca, Mr Bailey and Geo W. Watkins, under the firm name of Bailey & Watkins, put in the first hardware store, and Mr Bailey has been connected with the store ever since, either as an active or silent partner For a number of years past he and his firm have handled Standard Oil goods in this county He has also been interested in the hardware business at Janesville with his brother-in-law, D J Dodge Mr Bailey married his first wife, Miss Avis Slocum, sister of Congressman Slocum, of the state of New York, in June, 1857, by whom he had two daughters, Kate and Gertrude Kate married Eugene W Fisk and lives in Helena, Montana Gertrude married Mr Franklin Williams She died in August, 1905, in St Louis, Mo Mr Bailey's first wife died in September, 1865 About two years thereafter, Dec 27, 1867, he married Miss Lurinda Dodge, whose parents were among the very early settlers of the county Mr. and Mrs. Bailey are the parents of a son and a daughter Fred, born Nov 7, 1870, is now married and engaged in the flour milling business, at Mitchell, South Dakota Lena, born Dec 5, 1872, is now Mrs Armitage, of Waterville Mrs Lurinda Bailey was born April 12, 1850, at Owego, in the state of New York, and came to Waseca county with her parents about 1857 Mr Bailey has not only been fortunate in business, but he has held a number of official positions both of honor and trust with credit to himself He held the office of justice of the peace in early days, in Wilton, was elected to the lower branch of the legislature in the fall of 1861, and county treasurer in the fall of 1863 He served as state senator during the sessions of 1877 and 1878. He was also county commissioner during the years 1895-6-7 and took a prominent and very useful part in the construction of the new court house. Mr Bailey is a man who keeps his own counsel, but those who have been closest to him respect him most highly Early in life he became a Master Mason and attained to the degree of Knight Templar He is a man of sound financial judgment, and seldom makes a mistake in business undertakings

MR PATRICK McHUGO

came to Waseca when a boy about five years of age. He was born in Ireland in 1854 His mother died before he was two years old. Soon after his mother's death, his father, Lawrence McHugo, came to America and lived for a time in Janesville township He then made a claim in Iosco, on section 31, in 1863, and permanently settled thereon in Nov 1866, where Patrick now resides Patrick McHugo and Miss Mary Kinney were married in November 1880 Her father was Michael Kinney, one of the very early settlers of Janesville, who died in Jan 1897. Mrs McHugo was born in the town of Janesville in 1858 She is the mother of four sons and three daughters Mr McHugo was an only son and inherited his father's estate which he had helped to create He was democratic candidate in his district for county commissioner in the fall of 1904 and made a strong run against an overwhelming republican majority

THE HONORABLE R L McCORMICK

[From the National Cyclopedia of American Biography]

Robert Laird McCormick, financier, was born on a farm near Lock Haven, Clinton county, Pa., Oct 29, 1847, son of Alexander and Jane Hayes (Laird) McCormick The north of Ireland was the home of his remote ancestors—pious, industrious Protestants of Scotch origin. From that region his great-grandfather, John McCormick, emigrated to Chester county, Pa, in 1750 John McCormick became a private in the Revolutionary army.

Robert Laird McCormick was educated chiefly at Saunder's Institute, Philadelphia, and Tuscarora Academy, Mifflin, Pa, but left school before graduation While he was a school boy, his father served in the Civil War with the Ninth Minnesota regiment, the family having removed to the Northwest At the age of eighteen, Robert began to earn his own living by working as a clerk in the employ of the Philadelphia & Erie Railroad at Lewisburg, Pa In 1868 he moved to Winona, Minn, taking charge of the Laird & Norton Lumber company office In 1874 his health became impaired by the confinement of office work and he removed to Waseca, Minn, where he bought a retail lumber yard This he operated until 1881, at the same time doing the auditing for Laird & Norton, whose lumber yards were scattered through Minnesota and Wisconsin He also established for them new lumber yards, in some of which he retained an interest In 1881, with others, he incorporated the North Wisconsin Lumber company and became its secretary, treasurer, and manager Its mill at Hayward, Wis, had a daily capacity of nearly 500,000 feet of lumber Still adding to his responsibilities, Mr McCormick, in connection with Frederick Weyerhaeuser, established the Sawyer County bank, of which he became president, having in 1882 removed to Hayward In 1893 he became president of the Northern Boom company, at Brainerd, Minn; president of the Mississippi & Rum River Boom company, vice-president of the St Paul Boom company, St Paul, Minn, vice president of the Flambeau Land company, Chippewa, Wis, secretary and treasurer of the Northern Grain company, of Chicago, Ill., with warehouses in Minnesota, Iowa, Nebraska and the Dakotas, treasurer of the New Richmond Mill company, (flour) New Richmond, Wis In 1899 the Weyerhaeuser Timber company was organized and Mr McCormick became its secretary and western manager. This company has acquired all the timber lands belonging to the Northern Pacific Railway company west of the Cascade mountains, including 1,300,000 acres in Washington, and is buying the remainder of the railroad's grants as fast as surveyed

Meanwhile Mr. McCormick has taken an active part in civic and political affairs In 1876 he was elected president of the village council of Waseca, and in 1881, as senator, secured the passage of the bill for the incorporation of the city He was mayor of Waseca, serving until 1880, when he was elected to the state senate, where he served for two sessions For five years he was president of the school board of Hayward, and was president of Ashland academy at Ashland, Wis , also president of the Hayward library association and vice-president of the Wisconsin State Historical society, which he also served in 1901-04 as president. His deep interest in the American Indian led him to agitate for and finally secure through congress the establishment at Hayward of schools for the Chippewa tribe In 1904 Mr McCormick removed to Tacoma, Wash., and in 1905 resigned his offices in the eastern corporations already mentioned, to devote himself to the Weyerhaeuser Timber company s interests in Washington, and the Lumbermen's National bank of Tacoma, of which he is president He is also president of the Washington State Historical society, having been elected in 1905 Mr McCormick is a republican in politics, and in 1900 was a delegate from Wisconsin to the national convention of Philadelphia He is a thirty-two degree Mason, a Mystic Shriner and a Knight Templar, serving as its grand commander in Minnesota for one term, 1881 and 1882, a member also of the Sons of Veterans, of the Washington society of the Sons of the American Revolution, and of the Chicago Chapter of the Society of the War of 1812 He has published a "History of Journalism in Sawyer County, Wisconsin" (18.) and with Prof James G Adams, a "History of the Schools of Sawyer county," (18) Mr McCormick writing the chapters devoted to the Indian schools He is an attendant of the Congregational church

Mr McCormick was married at Tiffin, Ohio, Sept. 10, 1870, to Anna E daughter of Daniel and Minerva (Mills) Goodman They have had three children, William Laird, Robert Allen, and Blanche Amelia The daughter died in infancy

MR GEORGE H. WOOD

Mr Wood is one of the most extensive and prosperous dairymen in the county, his dairy farm being situated just east of Waseca. He was born in Wisconsin, Sept 29, 1849 His father and family settled in Woodville June 11, 1866 George is one of the sons of Ezra H. and Catharine (Gamble) Wood, the former born in Massachusetts May 1, 1814 and the latter in the state of New York, Sept 15, 1820 Ezra died Oct 11, 1885, and George's mother, Sept 29, 1886 George married Miss Jennie Deverell, of Woodville, July 4, 1877 She was a Badger state girl, born Dec 22, 1857 Mr and Mrs Wood are known in the state as high-grade butter makers and first-class dairy managers, their butter always commanding the highest market price They are the parents of six children four sons and two daughters Casper A., born Feb 2 1879, Augusta A Jan 6, 1883, Frank G , Sept. 29, 1885, Effie, Jan 18, 1888 Ezra, March 21, 1892, William, Oct 6, 1893 Casper A and Augusta A are graduates of the agricultural department of the state university. Augusta A. married Mr Louis J. Sheldon, July 6, 1904, and they reside on one of her father's farms. For a number of years Mr Wood has been treasurer of the town of Woodville, which is a very responsible position, as he holds and handles a large amount of money now in the sinking fund to pay off railroad bonds issued years ago In the summer of 1905 he bought a house in Waseca and now occupies it with his family His sons Casper and Frank, manage the farm near town Casper was married to Miss Lottie Snyder, August 16, 1905

MR. PATRICK MURPHY

This energetic, old-time settler of Alton, was born in Ireland and came to America in early life We first learn of him in Milwaukee, Wis, where he was married The family came to Alton in 1865, and settled on the northeast shore of Buffalo Lake. Here he opened a large farm where he continued to reside the remainder of his life His wife died Oct. 12, 1887, and he died March 5, 1894, at an advanced age They were the parents of six sons and two daughters—Rose, now Mrs Thos Lynch, Ellen, John H, Hugh S, Robert, Peter, James C, and Patrick Joseph Hugh S and Robert were twins as were Peter and James C John H was born in Dodge county, Wis., in 1858 His wife was Miss Jennie A. Markham, daughter of Mr Patrick Markham, one of the early and successful farmers of Alton, near Alma City She was born in Ireland Mr John H. Murphy is largely engaged in raising fine stock, especially Angora goats, horses and Short Horn cattle He is one of the wealthy, solid farmers of the county, and a stockholder and director in the Janesville Waseca County bank

MR. TERRENCE LILLY.

Among Waseca county pioneers was Terrence Lilly, who, with his family, settled close to what then was the eastern border of the Winnebago Indian Reservation, in St Mary He was a cooper by trade, and in 1849, taking his family and a few tools, he left his native city of Enniskillen, Ireland, that he and his might enjoy the blessings and privileges of a free country For six years he followed his trade in Cincinnati, Ohio. He then moved westward to Lacon, Ill, and two years later concluded that Minnesota farm life offered peculiar inducements and so, early in the year 1857, he came to this state Living near a populous Indian reservation offers a great field for the imagination of romantic boys It didn't require a curfew ordinance in those days to call the children in at night, and it is recorded that even men in those days kept good hours. Every age and time has its utilities Now, the city parent reminds the young hopeful to look out for the policeman, but in those early days, to secure good order and early hours, a mother had but to speak of Indians The old settler still recalls Indian days and tells the newcomer that men went to bed in those days not knowing whether they would "wake up dead or alive next morning" The trials of the Lilly family were incidental to all early settlers in ante-railroad days, but the head of the family never lost faith in the productive future of the county His first house was a "cotton top" It caught fire one windy day and, although the alarm was promptly sounded and the boys responded with a pail of milk, there was nothing saved A better house succeeded that one, and for this father, as for most men that patiently and willingly toil, better times were ahead Mr. Lilly did not entirely give up his trade, for in early times a man that could make pork and sorghum barrels, and incidentally and occasionally a coffin for the indigent, was in demand However, he came to Minnesota to farm and his success as a farmer was evident from the large farm he left at his death He and his wife thoroughly cast their lot in Waseca county, for they came at an early day and never left the county except to do marketing Both are asleep in the Catholic cemetery near Janesville Mr and Mrs Lilly were reared in Enniskillen, Ireland, Mr Lilly was born in 1808, and Mrs Lilly, whose maiden name was Mary McManus, was born in 1822 The former died May 15, 1891, the latter Jan. 2, 1901 Seven children blessed their home one daughter, Margaret, born March 4, 1863, died June 30, 1894; six sons—Owen, born in 1845; P. A., born in 1848, Thomas, born in 1854, B J, born in 1856, T J, born in 1860, and J F, born in 1865. Terrence J Lilly resides at St Paul with his family and is the efficient and gentlemanly state adjuster of losses for the Continental Insurance company B J. Lilly resides in Waseca and is local insurance agent for the Continental. P. A and Owen are engaged in farming and reside in Alton

THE HONORABLE W E YOUNG

This gentleman, who is now a member of the State Railroad and Warehouse Commission, was one of the early boy settlers in the town of Freedom His father's name is Delos P Young and his mother was Miss Ruth Lockwood. The former was born in Massachusetts, May 11, 1838, and the latter was born Oct. 8, the same year They were married in Wisconsin, May 27, 1858 W E Young was born in Adams county, Wisconsin, Oct 26, 1861 When W E was three years of age, his parents moved into the town of Freedom, to a farm about a mile west of what was then called Peddler's Grove Here the family resided for ten years when the elder Mr Young engaged in mercantile business at Alma City, removing his family to that place W E attended the country school and also served an apprenticeship as tinner He then attended the State Normal school at Mankato, and there graduated in 1881 He then commenced the study of law, reading at Mankato and St Paul and then at the Iowa City State Law school where he graduated in 1884 He practiced law one year in Pope county, then opened a law office in Janesville, Minn, where he practiced two years. In 1887 he moved to Mankato where he has since lived and practiced his profession For six years he was city attorney in Mankato, and for seventeen years he has been a leading attorney in

HON. WM. E. YOUNG.

that place He was admitted to the bar in Waseca county at the age of twenty-one years. He married Miss Nettie Shingler, of Pope county, in 1885 She is a native of Wisconsin and was reared on a farm They are the parents of three children two sons, nearly men grown—Paul, aged nineteen, and Donald, aged sixteen—and one daughter, Alice, aged four years W E Young has long been known as one of the ablest attorneys of the state, and he now occupies a position in which he may become very useful to the people. His father, D. P. Young, after leaving Alma City, carried on a store at Minnesota Lake, then at Rock Rapids, Iowa, and finally, for the last ten years, at Mankato Mr and Mrs D P Young spent the winter of 1904-05 in California Arthur E Young, a brother of Wm E, is a dentist, married and living in Minneapolis The sister of W E and Arthur, born in 1881, is teaching at Little Falls, Minn, at this writing. The Youngs were prominent in social and political circles in this county during their residence here, and are remembered kindly by all the early settlers of the county

MR THOMAS H JOHNSON

Mr Johnson, who is now a leading hardware merchant in Waseca, was born in Iosco, Feb 11, 1864 His father, Albert Johnson, was one of the early settlers, having settled in Iosco in 1856 Thomas H was reared on the farm, but in early manhood developed a liking for machinery He first engaged in putting down tubular wells, and then drifted into farm machinery and especially threshing outfits He married Miss Helen Olson, daughter of Andrew Olson, of Iosco, in March 1884 They have two sons—Alfred, born Feb. 7, 1885, and John, born in 1891—and one daughter, Clara, born in March, 1887 The family moved into Waseca about 1898 Thomas H remained in the machinery and lightning rod business until the spring of 1904 when he accepted the appointment of city marshal of Waseca This position he resigned in February, 1905, when he bought the extensive hardware stock of O. J Johnson & Co, of Waseca He carries an extensive stock of hardware and is a popular dealer

MR C W REDESKE

C W. Redeske is the son of Frederick Redeske, who came to this country from Prussia in 1873 C W. was born in Eshen Rieze, Prussia, Jan 13, 1868. He and his parents reached Chicago in 1873, and came to Waseca county in 1881 They first lived in Wilton In 1883 they moved to Otisco Frederick died Dec. 28, 1898 His wife is still living C W. married Bertha Stolz, of Waseca, Oct 21, 1903 They have one child living Mr. Redeske has three sisters Mrs Gus Stolz, Mrs J T Johnson, and Mrs Thos Curley, all of this county He owns what is known as the John Hilton farm in Otisco

MINGES BROTHERS.

Joseph, Edward, and Charles W Minges are sons of Joseph Minges, who was born in Bavaria, Germany, in 1817 He landed in New York in 1847 where he lived until 1858, when he came with his family to Otisco where he continued to reside until his death on June 21, 1886 He died of paralysis, at the age of sixty-nine years Joseph, Jr, was born in New York city, Feb 9, 1851, Charles W, Feb 14, 1853, and Edward, Nov 28, 1855. Joseph married Emma Brandt, of Iowa, Oct 17, 1889, and they are the parents of three boys and three girls. Charles W married in New York, but is now a widower, his wife and children being dead Charles W. lives at Wilmot, S D Jo. and Ed have a farm of one hundred and sixty acres and a timber lot of six acres They have four sisters: Mrs Wm Luff, of New Richland, Mrs Henry Brandt, of Phillips, Neb, Mrs Gertje, of Wilmot, S D, and Mrs Chris Billings, of Lisbon, N D Ed is a single man and resides with the family of his brother Jo Joseph Minges, the father, was prominent in the political history of the county, during his life time Few were the republican conventions he did not attend and his voice was potent in their management He served the county well and faithfully in the legislative session of 1875

MR W H WHEELER

This gentleman is the son of Whitney L Wheeler, one of the early settlers whose life-sketch is in this history W H was born in St Mary, June 28, 1866 He owns a farm of one hundred sixty acres in Woodville, and is a successful farmer. He was joined to Miss Mary Kief in holy wedlock, April 15, 1890. Miss Kief was born March 18, 1864, in Canada They are the parents of three girls and two boys Mr Wheeler moved from Wilton to Woodville in 1871, his father having died in Wilton, Nov 4, 1870

MR KNUTE JAMESON

Mr Jameson, of Blooming Grove, was born in Norway May 9, 1855, and is therefore about as old as Waseca county His father, Tarrel Jameson, came to Waseca in the fall of 1862 Knute's wife's name was Margaret Hagen, and they have seven children He is one of the industrious and well-to-do farmers of that township

MR STEPHEN J KRASSIN

is a native of Waseca county, born in St Mary, August 14 1859, his father, Martin Krassin, having explored Waseca county in the fall of 1854 and settled here in June 1855 Steve was married to Miss Lizzie Meyers of St Mary, March 15, 1886 She is the daughter of the late Henry Meyers of Waseca, and was born Feb 9, 1861 S J owns land in this county and considerable land in Ward county, North Dakota He is a breeder of good horses and an expert thresherman His wife is a sister of Hon. W H Meyers

MR LEWIS L FRETHAM

Erick Larson Fretham, father of Lewis, a native of Norway, settled in

Waseca county in 1864 Lewis was born in Iosco, Feb 25, 1867, and was the only son. He joined Miss Christina Quitney in the holy bonds of matrimony in 1889 They are the parents of four sons and two daughters Their pleasant home is on section 20, Blooming Grove He has been one of the supervisors of his town for several years, and is prominent in the management of the Palmer creamery as one of its officers

MR JOHN S JOHNSON

at present a county commissioner of this county, and grandson of John Segurdson, was born in Dane county, Wisconsin, Oct 27, 1850 He came to this county in 1855 with his parents, Mr and Mrs Segurd Johnson, a sketch of whose life is given elsewhere in this book John Segurdson, John's grandfather, was one of the 1855 settlers in Iosco He was born in 1794, and died in 1864 The grandmother was born in 1796, and died in January, 1881 John's father, Segurd Johnson, came to America in 1845, and his father and brothers came in 1850 The grandfather settled in Iosco in 1855 John's father did not come until the next year John Segurdson had six sons—Segurd, Thomas, Torgus, Albert, John and Ole—and two daughters—Gonield and Birget One of the daughters became the wife of Jacob Jackson, and the other the wife of Tarrel Anderson, both of them early settlers John S Johnson and Angeler Bagne daughter of S O Bagne, of the town of Iosco, were married Oct 18, 1874 They are the parents of twelve children, six sons and six daughters—no 'race suicide" there John S. Johnson states that Mr Tarrel Anderson, who settled in Iosco in 1855, was the father of four sons and two daughters. Both Mr Anderson and his wife died some years ago Jacob Jackson, who married the other aunt of Mr Johnson, also died some years ago, but Mrs Jackson is still living Segurd Jackson, the merchant at Palmer creamery, is her son and grandson of John Segurdson the first Norwegian settler in Iosco The several branches of this family are numerous in this county, notwithstanding the fact that a number of them are residing elsewhere in the Northwest Tom Johnson, an uncle of John S, was born May 23, 1833 He came to America in 1850 and lived in Dane county, Wis, until 1855, when he came to Waseca county and moved to his present homestead, in Iosco, July 5 His first wife was Mary Olson Kin, who died Jan 16, 1869. His second wife was Miss Mary Evenson He is the father of thirteen children—nine sons and four daughters—all of whom are living except one son. He is one of the very few left of the settlers of 1855.

MR A K. LEE

is one of the substantial farmers of Blooming Grove. He was born in Norway May 16, 1839 He came to America in June 1861, and worked at various places in Wisconsin and Minnesota until 1868 He married in June of this year, while living at Meriden, and in 1869 settled on his present farm in section 7, Blooming Grove, where he owns two hundred ninety-two acres. They have had nine children, seven of whom are living His mother died when he was two years old, and his father died about twenty-four years ago He is an energetic, prosperous farmer

MR JOHN BYRON

The subject of this sketch was born in 1819, in the parish of Kitteely, county of Limerick, Ireland He sailed from Ireland in 1846, and after a long and tedious voyage landed in New York. After a short stay there he went to the state of Virginia where he was a contractor for the construction of Macadam and turnpike roads, there being at that time very few railroads In 1851 his brother William came over from the old home and joined him, and from that time their history runs together The brothers, when they left Virginia, came as far west as Cincinnati, where John met and married Miss Catharine Murray. The marriage ceremony was performed by Father Wood, afterwards Archbishop of Philadelphia. They then started for the far West, spending the winter of 1855 in Lyons, Iowa In May, 1856, they, in company with several other families, and with William Byron, then a single man, started for Minnesota with all their worldly goods in a prairie schooner drawn by oxen There were no roads, only tracks or trails, in those days, and traveling was indeed slow and tiresome They arrived in St Mary about the 18th of June, 1856. Mr Byron selected as his home one hundred and sixty acres in section 21 of St Mary. William Byron and Michael McGonagle, both elsewhere sketched in this volume, settled adjoining him From that time forward, for a number of years, his history is the same as that of the other early pioneers--one of hardship, privation, self-denial, and economy, securing after many years of industry and careful management a competency for his declining years He was a man of excellent habits, large of heart, and always ready to help a neighbor in distress Of a home-loving and retiring nature, he seldom took part in politics outside of township and school district affairs He held school-district and town offices for a number of years He was the father of nine children, five of whom are living. James A, living on a farm near the old homestead in St. Mary is a prominent and successful farmer. John M, well and favorably known as clerk of the district court of this county from Jan 1, 1892, to Jan 1, 1897, is now engaged in the clothing business at Janesville One daughter, Mrs. John Cahill, also resides at Janesville, and two daughters are with their mother in Waseca Mr. Byron retired from active farming some years before his death and spent his last years quietly and peacefully in his Waseca home, where, surrounded by his family, he died April 14, 1900, at the age of eighty-one years. He was buried in the St. Mary Catholic cemetery not far from the spot where he camped on the 18th day of June, 1856 He was an excellent, useful citizen, respected by all who knew him

JOHN BYRON.

MR STEPHEN H PRESTON,

son of Lucius and Rebecca, was born Sept 11, 1842, in the Green Mountain state and reared on a farm. At the age of eighteen years, his heart swelling with pure patriotism, he enlisted in Company G, Fifth Vermont infantry and served through all the campaigns of the army of the Potomac He was honorably discharged Sept 24, 1864, and then re-enlisted in Hancock's First Veteran Reserve Corps serving until Jan. 24, 1866, when he was finally mustered out with all the honors of war The same year he came West to Sheboygan, Wis, and entered a drug store. He remained there a year when he came to Waseca county and lived on a farm in Woodville until about 1872, when he took a soldier's homestead in Lyon county where he and his family spent the winter of 1872-3. They were literally buried by that terrible blizzard known as the "great storm of Jan 7, 1873" The family returned to Waseca the next season, and Mr. Preston engaged in the drug business which he has ever since followed. He was with E P Latham for some time, then in partnership with Mr. Middaugh, then with H. H. Sudduth, since deceased, and now with Anton Stucky He married Miss Emily Durkee, in Sheboygan, Wisconsin, Oct 8, 1866 They have one daughter, Josie, now Mrs. Charles Leuthold, and one son, Lucius F., clerk in Leuthold Bros' clothing store.

MR. THOMAS J. KERR,

one of Scotia's sons, became a resident of St. Mary, Waseca county, in 1856. He was born on a farm near Dumfries, Scotland, March 24, 1826 He came to America and reached Buffalo Dec 31, 1851, where he worked, except when sick of fever, until May of the next year, he then went to Cattaraugus county where Thomas Dunn, father of James M Dunn, his cousin, lived There he worked for four years by the month In 1855 he came as far west as Sparta, Wisconsin, where he worked during the winter, and the next spring came to this county. He made a claim and worked around for others until fall when he returned to York State There, on the 5th of May, 1857, he married Miss Agnes Afleck, who was born in Scotland, Nov 16, 1837 They at once started for Minnesota with a horse team and a prairie schooner, in company with Messrs. Lindsay and Daniels and their families Mr and Mrs Kerr are the parents of two sons and two daughters Robert A, now a prosperous farmer of Bruce, S D, Agnes, now Mrs A H Kinyon, of Bruce, S D, Luverne, now Mrs B G Sutliet, of Wilton, Minn, and Thomas J., Jr, merchant in Waseca Mr and Mrs Kerr moved from their old farm in St Mary to their present cozy home in Waseca, in 1888. Mr Kerr is now in his eightieth year and very rugged and hearty for a man of his age

MR NELS M NELSON

This gentleman is one of our best citizens He is an American by choice He is a native of Smalan, near Jonkoping, Sweden, born Dec 8,

1848 He started for America the first week in May, 1868, in company with thirty young people, all single men except two young families and three young ladies. Nearly all of the company, except himself, had relatives in different parts of America. The party had all been residents of the same neighborhood, or township, in the old home and made a jolly company Among the men were two brothers of Mose Johnson, of Otisco —John Johnson and Gus Johnson—and a third man, John Swanson. These four became close friends and kept together At Chicago they tried to get tickets for Owatonna, then the nearest station to Otisco, but the agent couldn't find Owatonna, and so sold them tickets for Prairie du Chien, telling them they could get tickets from that point They were getting short of money when they got to the last place, and there the baggage master charged them a dollar apiece—$4—for what he called excess baggage. Upon reaching McGregor, they found themselves short of funds The fare was $8 each, and they had only $5 each None of them could speak much English and two of them could not write so it was determined that John Johnson and John Swanson should come on to Owatonna and that Mr Nelson and Gus Johnson should remain at McGregor to await results. The two, who came on, finally found Mose Johnson, of Otisco, through whose means money was forwarded to the two left in McGregor, and in due time they came on Mr Nelson immediately went to work at whatever he could find to do, and in 1876 was able to purchase a farm in Otisco This farm he sold in 1883 and bought another which he still owns, on section 9, town of New Richland. He was elected town supervisor of Otisco in 1877 and 1878, county commissioner in 1879 and re-elected a second term He is now holding second term as court commissioner of this county He married Miss Lottie Johnson, of Otisco, March 9, 1884 She died Jan 8, 1885, leaving an infant daughter, now Mrs C F Johnson, of Waseca His second marriage was in the fall of 1889, to Mrs Lina Newquist, who had two daughters by her first husband There is no issue by the second marriage They own a comfortable home in Waseca, which they have occupied since 1889 They have a comfortable income from their farm and other sources, and are most excellent citizens

MR JOHN M BYRON,

merchant at Janesville, was born in St Mary, Jan 25, 1865, his father, John Byron, having settled in that town in 1856 He received his education in the old log school house, known as the Gallagher school house At the age of sixteen, he entered the Waseca high school, attending the school in the winter and working on the farm in the summer In the winter of 1883, he taught school in the Brisbane district and thereafter taught two winter terms of school in the Sheehan district, St Mary, working on the farm summers In 1890 he was elected clerk of the district court, his term of office beginning Jan. 1, 1892 and expiring Jan 1 1896 He was then appointed by Judge Buckham for one year to fill the vacancy existing under the election law Since 1897 he has been in the clothing business and is senior member of the firm of Byron & Barden, of Janesville In September, 1893, he married Miss Martha Burns, daughter of the late Peter Burns, of Wilton She was born July 4, 1873, in Wilton, and is a graduate of the Waseca high school. They are the parents of four children—two sons and two daughters Mr Byron is the owner of the old homestead in St Mary, where he was born He is a thorough business man, and enjoys the confidence of the people in a marked degree.

MR WILLIAM EDGAR HEATH

This enterprising and progressive farmer, who resides in Freedom, was born in the town of Dryden, Tompkins county, N Y, Dec 13, 1838 Mrs Heath, whose maiden name was Maria Elizabeth Cantine, was born in the town of Caroline, in the same county, Nov 29, 1840 They were married May 21, 1862, and came to Waseca county and settled in Freedom, in the fall of 1866, where they still live He brought with him a pair of good horses, but no other stock Mr. and Mrs Heath have a very fine home, with all the comforts of farm life The first school house in their district was built in 1868 They came to Minnesota more on account of Mrs. Heath's health than from choice, she having throat trouble They started in May, having one son, Jay C, three years of age They came by car to Waupun, Wis, where they remained with an uncle about three months In the meantime Mr Heath and his uncle visited Minnesota, and Mr Heath bought his Freedom farm, near Peddler's Grove, a new town with 'great expectations" The Heaths came to their new home in the fall in a regular prairie schooner, heavily loaded with household goods Mrs Heath writes

"We started from near Waupun, Aug 31, 1866, Saturday, in a thunder storm, expecting to camp out and sleep in our wagon nights Every one was very kind to us along the way and many times we accepted the proffered hospitality instead of camping in our wagon We were eighteen days on the road and it was a really enjoyable trip But soon after getting onto Minnesota soil we got stuck in mudholes a number of times The roads tended to make one sick of the country At one place, near Rochester, Minn, wagon, horses and all were stuck so fast in the mud that we could not get out until aided by four or five ox teams It was Saturday afternoon when we arrived at our abode in Freedom The family then living in it moved out that afternoon and we moved in. When we awoke Sunday morning in that log hut, all open up to the rafters, was it any wonder that we were a little homesick? The hut had two half windows, one-half in each end of the building, and only one door When the letters that awaited us at Peddler's Grove, from the dear, old home land were opened, the gloom was lightened a little Friends there thought we might as well die of disease among friends as to die of home-sickness among strangers. But we didn't die In five years we returned East with our three children Our only daughter, Georgia, was born the first winter we were in Minnesota, and Edgar I was born the fall of our visit to the East, where we remained two years Since then two other sons have blessed our home Our oldest son, Jay C, married Harriet A Willsey, of Janesville, and lives a mile and a half west of us, Georgia married Frank M Smith, son of Hon. L. D. Smith, late of Alton, and they also live near us, Edgar I married Wm M Oldfield's daughter and they live in New York state, Roy L. is still at home, taking care of the farm, and our youngest is one of the class of thirteen who graduated from the Janesville high school in 1905 In our first winter here, Mr Heath and several of the neighbors went off across the prairie (there were no fences then to obstruct) to buy wheat and get some flour They were gone a week but finally came home with flour. Sometimes that winter we had to cook whole wheat for the horses and ourselves as well Often that first winter, I thought perhaps it was wrong that we had brought our boy away from Grandpa's place where apples, pears, peaches, and other fruits were plentiful, with no prospect of ever raising any here But, strange as it seemed then, it is now a fact that we have apples to waste and for cider too, besides other fruit, and to-day, May 16, 1905, the trees are a mass of bloom, a bower of beauty O, what a change for the better since 1866!"

MR A S MALONEY,

is the youngest son of Mr and Mrs John Maloney, and has recently opened a law office in Waseca His father, John Maloney, was born in the county Mayo, Ireland, 1829, he went to England in 1848 where he worked in a manufacturing plant two years, he came to America two years later, to near Scranton, Pa, where he resided until 1857 In 1854, he married Miss Bridget Nilan, at Binghamton, Pa Mrs Maloney was born in county Clare, Ireland, in 1835, and was fourteen years of age when she came to America In 1857 the family came to Iosco where Mr Maloney bought one hundred sixty acres of land. He also bought eighty acres in Blooming Grove He carried on his farm until 1867, when he came to Waseca and went into business—kept for a time a bakery and grocery store and was proprietor of the "Old Minnesota House," a popular resort for farmers His hotel was burned in 1888, after which he built his home on First street where he spent the remainder of his life as a private citizen, passing away Feb 24, 1904 Mrs Maloney, who survives him, was a worthy helpmeet, and encouraged him through all the hardships they endured in early days John Maloney was always a vigorous champion of Ireland, and helped its onward progress whenever and wherever possible. Eleven children were born to them, six of whom are still living Mrs Henry Smith, of Byron, (deceased), Mrs Geo McGrath, of Renville county, Miss Beezie, teacher in the Minneapolis schools, Francis, Vincent and Albinus S, residents of Waseca Albinus S Maloney graduated from the law department of the State University June 1, 1904, and very soon after opened a law office in Waseca At the last two sessions of the legislature, he served as a legislative appointee upon the commendation of Senator Collester.

MR. GEORGE W. COMEE

is one of the pioneers of the city of Waseca, having become a resident there in 1867. He was born June 9, 1838, at Henderson, Jefferson county, N. Y. In 1864 he went to Ashburnham, Mass., where he sojourned three years. In the spring of 1867, he came West, arriving in Waseca at its christening. He erected a building and opened a furniture store, in company with Major Wm. C. Young in the fall of 1867. Capt. Helms succeeded Major Young as partner. In 1873, S. S. Comee took the place of Mr. Helms, and the firm remained Comee Bros. until 1882 when the Waseca Furniture company was organized. After this company wound up its affairs, the firm name became Sawin & Comee. In 1904, Mr. Sawin sold his interest to Geo. W. and some time after Mr. Pfaff bought an interest and the firm name became Comee & Pfaff. Mr. Comee is one of our best citizens. Dec. 26, 1877, he married Mrs. Elizabeth L. Kittredge, widow of Fred Kittredge. She is a native of Ohio and one of the pioneers of this county. She had three daughters by her first husband: Mary Abbie, now Mrs. Kennedy, of Evanston, Ill.; Laura E., now Mrs. Kirkpatrick of Parker's Prairie, Ottertail county, Minn.; and Jessie C., now Mrs. Ed. Rausch, of Winona. Mr. Comee is a worthy member of both the Masonic and Odd Fellow organizations of this city and a member of the Congregational society. So far in life he has been the soul of honor, true and trusty, a man worthy of all confidence.

SENATOR E. B. COLLESTER.

Hon. Eugene B. Collester is a native of Gardner, Mass., born Dec. 20, 1847. He attended the schools of that city, entered Amherst college and graduated therefrom in 1873. Soon after he took up his residence in New London, Conn., where he became principal of Bulkeley high school. This position he held until 1880 when he resigned and came to Waseca where he joined his half brother, Hon. M. D. L. Collester, and entered upon the practice of law. He married Miss Sarah Jane Holande, of Conn., April 6, 1875. They have one daughter, Alice, now Mrs. Meacham, who resides with her parents in Waseca. Mr. Collester has held numerous official positions: mayor of the city of Waseca in 1887; judge of probate from May, 1889, to Dec. 31, 1894, state senator from Jan. 1, 1895 to Dec. 31, 1899, and again in the fall of 1902 he was elected to the senate for four years. Senator Collester has the confidence of the people to a marked degree. He is a member of Comee Lodge I. O. O. F., and also of Tuscan Lodge No. 77, A. F. and A. M., of Waseca. He is also one of the leading lawyers of the county.

MR. BYRON G. SUTLIEF,

son of the first settler in the county, Mr. Asa G. Sutlief, is a native of

Wilton, born on the old homestead, Sept 10, 1858, where he still resides December 18, 1884, he married Miss Luverne Kerr, daughter of Mr and Mrs. T J Kerr She was born in St Mary, this county, Oct 1, 1863 He owns the oldest farm in the county, about two hundred acres, and is extensively engaged in raising, buying, fattening, and selling hogs and cattle. He is wealthy and has an interesting family of children Mr Sutlief is not only a well-to-do farmer, but he is interested in the New Richland bank, the Byron creamery, etc.

MR WILLIAM BYRON

Among the many who have helped to make Waseca county blossom as the rose, Mr Wm Byron, of St Mary, occupies a conspicuous place At the request of the author he gave the following sketch of his life

"I was born and reared in the parish of Kitteely, county of Limerick, Ireland, in May, 1828 My brother John, who was five years older, came to America in 1846 I left Ireland March 12, 1851, and after a stormy voyage of seven weeks landed in New York, April 29 After a week of sight seeing there, I proceeded to Virginia via Philadelphia, Baltimore, city of Washington, Alexandria, Fairfax Court House and Warrenton, to Little Washington, at the foot of the Blue Ridge, where John Byron and Matt O'Brien had a contract of turnpike building from Little Washington to Waterloo, a distance of ten or twelve miles. We finished the turnpike that year, and in May, 1852, started across the Blue Ridge At the top of the Ridge we took stage, crossed the Shenandoah bridge near where General Shields won a victory over the Confederates, passed through New Market and stopped at Staunton After a week in Staunton, we again took stage and went to Christiansburg We remained there two years building turnpike roads In November, 1885, we started West on foot and went eighty miles to Charleston, now the Capital of West Virginia, then a little village of a few small houses and a small hotel We then went down the Kanawha and Ohio rivers to Aurora, near Cincinnati, where I made the acquaintance of my wife that was to be After a short stay there, we took the cars to Chicago I concluded to see the 'far West' before venturing upon matrimony John and his wife remained in Chicago, and I took the cars to Rock Island, crossed the river into Davenport, Iowa and then traveled on foot forty miles to Lyons The snow covered the grass among the bur-oaks, and I thought it the worst country I ever saw—wished I was back in Old Virginia John and family soon came on and we spent the winter in Lyons In the spring, we bought two yoke of oxen, two cows, and two wagons, and on the 16th day of May, 1856, in company with the families of M P Fitzgerald, Michael McGonagle, and L J Fitzgerald, started for Minnesota We came through Freeborn county and for miles had nothing to guide us on the way except the sun and a slight Indian trail After getting into Minnesota, we never saw a house or a human being until we arrived at Peddler's Grove, Waseca county We then went as far west as the Winnebago Agency, then turned and came back

MR. AND MRS. WM. BYRON.

to St Mary and camped on the hill where the St Mary church now stands, June 18, 1856 That night we had a terrible battle with the mosquitoes After resting a little we selected our claims, turned over some of the virgin sod, sowed a little buckwheat, made hay and in the fall built our log cabins No one without the experience can know how we labored and struggled along, and to young people our stories of the past seem incredible. In the fall of 1858, I gave a mortgage on forty acres of my land for $40—all I could raise on it, the rate being 'thirty-six per cent interest from date till due, and sixty per cent from due till paid' I soon saw that I never could make enough off the farm to pay it, so, in Nov 1859, I went down the Mississippi river and was lucky enough to strike a job of 'bossing' on a levee at $60 per month I married Miss Catharine O'Mara, April 12, 1860, at her father's home in Old Geneva, Ind, and at once returned to Minnesota In 1862, during the Indian excitement, we used to gather at the house of John Byron for mutual protection At one time there was a frenzied report that the Winnebago Indians were to 'break out that night' Some ten families hitched up their ox teams, gathered together their valuables and, with the women and children, went into camp on the prairie east of where Mike McGonagle, Jr, now lives. We formed our wagons in a circle, camped inside the circle, placed pickets on guard and camped without a fire Everything was quiet until toward morning when the dogs commenced to bark, and the pickets came running in with the cry—'They're coming! they're coming!' All was in commotion for a while There were only three or four shot guns in camp, but every man was on one knee looking for Indians that never came. At the coming of daylight, we broke camp and all went back home We all felt worn out for want of sleep, and I went to bed in my own cabin I had not been in bed ten minutes before there was a knock on the door. I jumped, seized my gun, and demanded, 'Who is there?' A neighbor, and he too wanted sleep and so we slept a while The week before I had sent my wife to Rochester on account of the Indian scare, and our second child was born at that place a few days after the camping incident

I was elected town clerk in 1858, and held the office three different terms. I was justice of the peace one term, town supervisor three different years, and county commissioner two terms, from 1869 to 1874 We built our first school house in 1861, and our first church in 1862 Rev Father Keller, of Faribault, visited our church three or four times within the first year. The first person buried in the St Mary burial ground was Mr. Morris The next to be consigned to that ground was Michael O'Brien, who was killed by lightning in September, 1858 Ah! but that was the most terrific thunder I ever heard"

MR JOHN REIBOLD

John Reibold, Sr, was born in Hesse Darmstadt, Germany, July 31, 1830 He came to America in 1849 and lived in Fonda, N Y, until 1860, when he came to Minnesota He was at Northfield on the day that Lincoln was elected, and came on to St Mary the next day Oct 1, 1851, he married Miss Mary Baldwin, and to them four children were born Peter, (deceased) born in 1853, Thomas, now of St Mary, July 7, 1855, John, Jr, July 27, 1857, Johanna, July 24, 1861, who married Thomas Burns Mrs Reibold died March 21, 1864 The following July 4, he married Miss Margaret McWaide, sister of Mr John McWaide, of Iosco. She died Jan 28, 1903, at the Rochester asylum For several years he worked, and "worked mighty hard," for $15 a month and boarded himself, and upon so small a pittance he and his family managed to live His wife kept some poultry, and his employer would occasionally make him a present of a little flour. In later years the proprietor of the mill raised his wages to the magnificent sum of $20 a month and one barrel of flour a year, Mr Reibold to board himself. What would young men of to-day think of such a wage?

John Reibold, Jr, was born at Fonda, N Y, July 27, 1857, and came to St Mary with his father in 1860 He learned the blacksmith trade at Mankato, when a lad He then came to Waseca, worked as a journeyman for some years and finally rented the Roland shop then standing on the southwest corner of Wood and Third streets, and opened shop for himself That was twenty-two years ago In 1884 he formed a co-partnership with Theo Brown and they carried on business at what is now known as Reibold's foundry and shops for five years, when Mr Reibold became sole proprietor About nine years ago he bought a half interest in the Crane foundry, and three years later bought the remaining interest of Mr Crane. He is now sole proprietor of a flourishing business. He married Miss Mary McDermott, May 20, 1882 They have one son, Wm J, born July 1, 1884, who is now a stenographer in the employ of the Minneapolis Iron Store Co, dealers in heavy hardware. Thomas Reibold, brother of John, is a prosperous farmer of St. Mary, and has an interesting and intelligent family

HONORABLE D. S CUMMINGS

Dr D S Cummings is now the oldest resident physician in Waseca He is son of Dr. D J Cummings, deceased, one of the pioneer physicians of Hastings, in this state Our Doctor Cummings was born in Otsego county, N Y, Nov 17, 1850. When he was six years of age his parents came to the territory of Minnesota and became residents of Hastings. D S. attended the public schools of Hastings, spent one year at the Shattuck school, Faribault, studied two years at the Cooperstown, N Y, academy, took a course in medicine and surgery at the Ann Arbor, Mich, university, and graduated at the Northwestern Medical college, of Chicago He practiced medicine for a time with his father in Hastings, and then came to Waseca, in 1876. He at once became popular with our people and very soon enjoyed an extensive practice His first public service was that of county superintendent of schools. He held this office for four years, from 1882 to 1886. In 1888 he was elected mayor of the city of Waseca, and again in 1889 and 1890 After an intermission of three years, he was again elected mayor in 1893 He succeeded himself each year until and including 1896. It was during these four years and under his administration that the water and light systems of the city were installed He has been president of the board of education of the city "since the memory of man runneth not to the contrary" He is a man of public spirit and of marked ability and has the happy faculty of often harmonizing conflicting interests

Oct 6, 1897, he was married to Miss Mattie Ward, an accomplished daughter of Hon W G Ward. They are the parents of two boys

For years Dr Cummings has been the local surgeon and physician of both the railroads crossing at Waseca He has also had charge of the construction of the local telephone lines in and about Waseca since the local telephone company was organized His capacity for hard work seems to be almost unlimited, as he employs no stenographer or assistant

MR. NATHANIEL GARLAND

This gentleman was the first sheriff of Waseca county He was appointed by Governor Gorman in the spring of 1857; in June of the same year, at the time of choosing the county seat, he was elected sheriff and held the office for two years. He then went to Iowa and engaged in the sheep business He returned to Wilton in 1864 and engaged in the mercantile business in company with John Forrest, also one of the early settlers of the county About 1868 he sold out in Wilton and opened a meat market in Waseca in company with J. A Claghorn He followed this business until his death, July 26, 1880 Mr Garland was born April 5, 1827, at Kingston, New Hampshire, and came to Waseca county in 1856 He married Miss Ladorna P Dodge Feb 3, 1864, at Wilton Miss Dodge was born in Owego, New York, April 27, 1842, and came to this county with her parents in the spring of 1857 Two sons were born to them Harold N was born in Wilton, June 26, 1867, and died of consumption in California, Feb 26, 1893 Ralph D was born in Wilton, April 19, 1869 He attended our public schools and learned the tinner s trade with his uncle, Hon P C Bailey He afterwards became a partner of Mr Bailey and is now the active member of the popular hardware firm of Bailey & Garland On the 14th day of June 1899, he was united in marriage with Miss Blanche Stewart, who was born in Waseca, Nov 3, 1873 They have one daughter, Helen, now five years of age They live in a very pretty, modest home on Lake avenue Mr Garland was alderman from the Second ward for several years, and declined a re-election in 1905

MR JOSEPH E GREGORY

Joseph is the grandson of Mr Barney Gregory, one of the pioneers who settled in St. Mary in 1855, on the farm now owned by Mr Gus Somers

Joseph is the son of A D Gregory, and was born in the town of Freedom, June 12, 1875 His father died in Roseville, California, Nov 29, 1904 When five years of age, Joseph went with his parents to South Dakota where they remained until 1892, when they returned to Waseca county On July 27, 1899, he married Miss Virgie Anthony, of Blue Earth county. They reside on a farm in the town of Wilton The young man has been compelled to rely upon his own resources since he was old enough to work and it is a credit to him that he has succeeded so well.

MR TIMOTHY DONOVAN

This well-known and popular groceryman, of Waseca, is the eldest son of Cornelius and Mary Donovan, natives of the Emerald isle, who came to this country in early life and lived for a time in Wisconsin The elder Mr Donovan settled in Woodville, this county, in 1868, when Timothy, who was born July 3, 1867, was about a year old The other sons and daughters of the family are John, Daniel, Dennis, Ellen, Hannah, Cornelius, and Mary—the two last are twins Timothy Donovan and Miss Lizzie McGonagle were married Dec. 26, 1893 They have four children living They buried their second son who died in infancy Mr Timothy Donovan learned the carpenter's trade, later he worked as clerk a while in a store, and in 1898 formed a copartnership with O N Jellum and entered the grocery trade. In the fall of 1903, he bought his partner's interest, and his youngest brother, Cornelius, is now with him They are doing a prosperous business Mrs Donovan is a daughter of the well-known, early settler, Mr Michael McGonagle, Sr

MR. LEWIS C PRECHEL

of Woodville, is a son of Gottlieb Prechel, one of the very first settlers of the town of St Mary, and was born in that township, Sept 16, 1864 He was reared on the farm and brought up to hard labor He married Mathilda Bethke, of Woodville, March 19, 1890 He carried on his father's farm in St Mary for two years and then bought a farm on section 4, Otisco, where he has resided since 1892 Mr and Mrs Prechel are the parents of two sons and one daughter They have a pleasant, cozy home, Mrs Prechel being a model housekeeper

MR PATRICK HEALY

was one of the very early settlers of Waseca county, having moved to a farm in Blooming Grove in 1856 He was born in Roscommon county Ireland, March 17, 1817, and came to America in 1836 In early life he was a manufacturer of woolen cloths, and an advocate of "protection for home manufacturers" He married Miss Emma Dearborn, of Windsor county, Vt, in 1843 She was born in 1825, and died in 1887. Mr. Healy carried on his farm in Blooming Grove until the 'seventies when he removed to Waseca and formed a copartnership with A E Dearborn in the mercantile business In 1880 he sold his interest in the Waseca store and retired from active business. He died Sept. 1, 1884, at his Blooming Grove home, respected and honored by every one. During the early days of the county, Mr. Healy was noted as about the only Irish-American republican in it, and in those days it required nerve and backbone to be a republican or "Black Abolitionist," as such men were called in those days. Mr. and Mrs. Healy were the parents of nine children, five of whom are living: Martin J., Mrs. Emma McLoughlin, Mrs. Almira G. Flyn, Mrs. Sarah L. Bird, and Patrick Healy.

MR. ROBERT MOORE.

This quiet, unpretentious, and honorable citizen, was born in Cattaraugus county, N. Y., Dec. 2, 1835. He came to this county in June, 1856, and began to make his home on the northeast quarter of section 8, in Wilton. He married Miss Martha M. Gregory March 3, 1857. Martha M. was one of the daughters of Mr. and Mrs. B. Gregory, who settled in St. Mary in June, 1855. She was born in Coldwater, Mich., May 22, 1838. Mr. and Mrs. Moore were the parents of eight children, five of whom are living. Emma, born Dec. 13, 1857, Mary E., born Sept. 3, 1859, James R., born Jan. 20, 1865, Lucia E., born June 5, 1870, Charles F., born July 28, 1872. Mrs. Moore died Dec. 5, 1875, aged thirty-seven years, six months and thirteen days. Mr. Moore has for years suffered with asthma. He spent the winter of 1902-3 in California. He is in every respect a good citizen. He was one of the high privates in the organization of the republican party, and cast his first presidential vote for the election of Abraham Lincoln and his last for William Jennings Bryan. Mr. Moore now resides on section 13, town of Freedom, and is a well-to-do farmer.

MR. H. F. KOECHEL,

who owns and manages a most complete stock of harnesses, trunks, valises, etc., was born in Marquette county, Wisconsin, Nov. 26, 1866. His father, Daniel Koechel, was born in Germany. He came to Wisconsin prior to the Rebellion, and served one year as a Union soldier in a Wisconsin regiment. The family came to Minnesota in 1881. Mr. and Mrs. H. F. Koechel were married Feb. 18, 1888. Mrs. Koechel's maiden name was Hulda Kanne, and she is a daughter of that well-known pioneer, August F. Kanne, of Waterville. She was born Dec. 19, 1865. The year of their marriage they went to live in Redfield, S. D., where Mr. Koechel carried on the harness business until 1895, when they returned to this county. In November of that year, he opened business in Waseca, and keeps on hand a large stock of goods. He makes a specialty of McConnell's patent-rivet, curled-hair-face horse collars. He is the father of five children—four boys and one girl. At the recent city election, he was elected alderman at large without opposition.

MR. DENNIS McLOUGHLIN,

of the firm of McLaughlin Bros., prominent grocery merchants of Waseca, was born in County Meath, Ireland, Dec 6, 1852. His parents were Dennis and Judith McLoughlin They came to America in 1853, and first lived in Clinton, Oneida county, N Y They came to Minnesota in September, 1862, tarried a short time at Faribault, and settled permanently at Cannon City soon after Young Dennis was reared on the farm, attending the schools of his village until qualified to teach, he then taught winters until 1871, when he accepted a clerkship in a hardware store in Faribault He was engaged as teacher and clerk for a number of years Nov 12, 1877, he married Miss Emma Healy, daughter of Mr. Patrick Healy, one of the worthy pioneers of Blooming Grove Mr. McLoughlin's father died at his home in Cannon City, in the year 1898, at the age of eighty-one years His mother is still living There were twelve children in the family, seven boys and five girls, of whom three girls and three boys have died. Mr. and Mrs D McLoughlin, of Waseca, are the parents of six daughters.

Mr McLoughlin came to Waseca in March, 1878, and bought the interest of Mr A E Dearborn in the mercantile firm of Dearborn & Healy Two years later he bought Mr. Healy's interest and has continued the business here ever since His brother, Thomas, bought a one-third interest in the business in 1884, and is still a member of the firm, although engaged the most of the time as traveling salesman. Dennis served as alderman in the year 1881-2, and again in 1904-5 He served as postmaster most efficiently for eight years, having been appointed by President Cleveland at the beginning of both terms of his administration. Mr McLoughlin is justly popular with all classes of our people

MR SAMUEL LESLIE

June 15, 1894, the following was penned

"Young man and young woman, if you want to learn what a couple of youngish people have done, and consequently, what you may or can do, go visit the farm of Mr. and Mrs. Samuel Leslie, of Otisco Twenty five years ago they located where they are now without any capital except a homestead right, which they applied to eighty acres Since then they have added one hundred twenty acres more There were no trees when they went there in 1869 Now they have a magnificent grove They have also a large, convenient farm house, an excellent hay and cattle barn, a creamery (dairy) that takes the first premiums everywhere. They milk twenty-four cows, have horses, raise cattle for beef, and hogs for pork They have all that people need in life And all these things they have gathered together by twenty-five years of industry, care, and frugality. Young man, there is no reason why you should not do as well"

Mr Leslie was born in Essex county, N Y, Sept 9, 1837, came to Waseca county in 1866, helped survey the village of Waseca in 1867, and lived in Waseca until 1869 He married Mary E Sisson, Sept 23, 1860 Ten children were born to them, seven of whom are living: Jennie M., now Mrs C G Mosher, of Pine county born Dec 6, 1861, Frank

J, born Oct 6, 1863, Herbert J, born Feb 7, 1866, Ralph B, born April 7, 1869, Mark P, born June 6, 1871, and Ella, born July 12, 1875 In the early part of 1867, that wet year, Mr. Leslie shipped flour and other goods in a skiff by way of Crane creek. He is noted as a breeder of fine, pure-blood Holstein cattle, and a manufacturer of high-grade butter.

MR. EDWIN R KRASSIN

is one among the early native-born sons of Waseca county He is the second son of Martin Krassin, deceased, and was born July 27, 1857 He was inured to hard toil from infancy, and after his father's death had charge of the several farms left to the heirs. He is an expert at sinking tubular wells and handling farm machinery He is a single man, owns a good farm in Wilton, and a comfortable home in Waseca

MR JOHN F. KRASSIN,

brother of Edward, was born August 26, 1862 He has been reared a farmer and owns one farm in Wilton and another in St Mary He married Miss Augusta Stolz, Sept 28, 1889 They have four sons, and reside on the old homestead where John's father first lived in St Mary

MR. EMIL W. KRASSIN,

another brother, the youngest of the sons, was born Feb 5, 1865 He has also spent his life on the farm He married Miss Edith Gehring, daughter of Gottfried Gehring, a pioneer settler of Wilton, Dec 4, 1894. She was born in Wilton, Feb 14, 1873 They are the parents of two daughters Emil has a well cultivated farm in St Mary and leads a happy and contented life

MRS JULIA KRASSIN BATHKE,

only daughter of Mr and Mrs Martin Krassin, deceased, was born in St Mary, this county, June 15, 1869. She married a man named Wm Bathke, Dec 5, 1896 They separated the following May and have since been divorced A daughter was born to her in December 1897 and remains with her Mrs Bathke resides in Waseca and keeps house for her brother Edward They have a pleasant home in Broughton's addition to Waseca

MR S S COMEE

This gentleman was born June 11, 1830, in Gardner, Mass. His occupation was that of chair maker Mrs Sarah White Sawin Comee was born July 3, 1836, in Gardner, Mass These two were married May 13, 1855, in Gardner. They moved to Ellisburg, N Y., where their two children were born In 1865, the family came to Vivian in this county where they carried on a farm until 1870, when they moved to Waseca They have resided in this place the greater part of the time since. Mr Comee was engaged for many years in company with his brother, G W Comee, in carrying on a furniture store in this city From 1888 to 1893, Mr Comee was employed in a furniture factory in Minneapolis He then came back to Waseca where he has since carried on a market garden They have two daughters. Myra, wife of Rev Robinson residing at Madison, Wisconsin, and Martha, wife of Judge C E Leslie, of Carrington, N D Judge Leslie was for many years a practicing attorney in this city, and at one time judge of the municipal court of Waseca

NORTH STAR EDITOR

C W Brown, editor of the New Richland paper, is one of the bright, industrious young men of the state He was born Sept 24, 1874, in the town of Kalmar, Olmsted county, Minn His father served in the Tenth Minnesota regiment in the War of the Rebellion • He was an early settler of Dodge county, Minn In February, 1891, C W went to live in Janesville and commenced work in the office of the Argus Here he learned the "art preservative,' and remained until 1898 In the fall of that year he purchased the Eagle Lake News, and published it for two years He then sold the News and purchased a half interest in the Janesville Argus He remained with Mr Henry until June 15, 1903, when he sold his interest in the paper to his partner, and bought the North Star at New Richland He at once moved to that place and has made the Star a successful, local "luminary ' Mr Brown and Miss Gertrude Pressnell were joined in holy wedlock June 17, 1896 Miss Pressnell was born near Eagle Lake, Feb 7, 1878, her parents being early settlers in that locality Mr. and Mrs. Brown are the parents of two boys.

MR JOHN FISK MURPHY

This gentleman is the oldest practical printer in the county, and understands the business thoroughly He is the son of Dr. William and Mrs Sophia (Fisk) Murphy, and was born in Philadelphia, Pa, Jan 7, 1850 His father was born in County Armagh, Ireland, and came to America when three years of age He was a graduate of the Hahnemann college, Philadelphia, and practiced medicine in that city before coming to Minnesota in 1857 The family resided in Wilton where Dr Murphy died, after a long illness, May 14, 1859 In the fall of 1862, John F went to Iowa where he herded and cared for sheep being employed by N Garland, the first sheriff of Waseca county In the fall of 1863, John returned to Wilton and was soon after employed as an apprentice in the office of the Wilton News In January, 1864, he went to live with relatives in Philadelphia and worked for a time in the office of the Daily News of that city, as proof taker and copy holder He returned to Wilton July 15, 1865, and again went to work in the Wilton News office where he remained until 1869 He then went to Davenport, Iowa, worked a while in the Gazette office, went thence to Monona county made a claim, and soon after went to Omaha, Neb, where he worked on the Daily Republican. In 1870 he was foreman of the Pilot, of Blair, Neb, and afterwards returned to Omaha where he again worked at his trade, being for some time employed in a large job office In 1871, he returned to Waseca, and put in a job office He was the first to bring a job printing press to Waseca. He published a small campaign sheet for the Horace Greeley campaigners of Waseca county in 1872 He sold his outfit to W. J Graham who, for a time, published a small paper called the Record John F. remained in Waseca working at his trade until 1877 when he went to Baltimore and took charge of the mechanical department of the Presbyterian Weekly, of that city He returned to Waseca in March, 1879, and again worked on the Radical. He continued with that paper till 1883, when he purchased a half interest in the Waseca County Herald which he still holds. He married Miss Emma J Hiller, Nov 15, 1871, they have one daughter, Martha Inez, born Nov. 7, 1872 Mr Murphy is a Master Mason, and served as worthy master of Tuscan Lodge No 77 in 1903-4

MR. JOHN A HENRY

This gentleman was born in Crawford county, Pa, May 25, 1855, the year that Waseca county was first settled He is the son of Dr J N Henry and Diana (Merchant) Henry When John A was very young his parents went to the state of New York and remained there until 1872, when they came to this state and located near Mankato His father was not only a physician but a Methodist clergyman John N attended the Mankato Normal school three terms, and then read law for a time He finally went with his father to Janesville where the latter was sent as the M E clergyman Soon after moving here John was employed as post-office clerk and assistant in the newspaper office of C E Graham, who was postmaster and also publisher of the Argus at that place In August 1881, Mr Henry purchased the Argus of Mr Graham which he still owns and publishes He was appointed postmaster at Janesville in the fall of 1881, and has held that position, either as postmaster or deputy, ever since, except during a portion of President Cleveland's latter term He is prominent in the councils of the republican party and a strong party man As a local editor, he is active and alert, and no local matter, important or otherwise, escapes him In social matters he is prominent and useful. He was married to Miss Frances J Allyn, daughter of Mr Wm. G. Allyn, one of the very early settlers of the town of Janesville, in 1878 They are the parents of three children J Harold, Miss Ethelyn, and Allyn Harrison, all of whom are living.

MR H S. CLEMENT

Mr. H S Clement, father of Wm A Clement, editor of the Journal-Radical, was born in Cornish, N H., March 19, 1835 He came West to Iowa in 1853, thence to what is now Meriden, Steele county, Minn, in July, 1856 He was the first assessor of that township He came in company with Col Wm. Drum, and Hon F J Stevens, all of whom took claims near what was then known as Meriden He lived on his farm just over the county line until 1868, when he purchased a farm in Woodville where he lived until 1883, when he removed to Waseca and engaged in the sale of farm machinery He continued this business until 1900 He owns a residence and truck farm on North street, Waseca. He married Miss Nellie M. Wilcox Dec 22, 1868 She was born in the state of New York in 1841 and died June 12, 1883 Four sons and two daughters were born to them. Wm A, of Waseca, Arthur R, of Glendive, Mont; Mary, deceased, Lucien O, a physician of Lamberton, Minn, Benjamin, of Waseca, and Miss Emma, at home Mr Clement is a man who does his own thinking and is a staunch prohibitionist

The first winter he passed here was the hardest he ever experienced Messrs Clement, Vinton, and Drum, bought hay of Daniel Riegle, who lived in Blooming Grove Mr Clement says "We drew this hay during the winter of 1856-7 We had three yoke of oxen and two sleds. The snow was very deep and had a sharp crust which cut the cattle's legs so that they refused to go The men had to go ahead of the teams and tramp the snow to make a track for them, and, as a final expedient, the oxen's legs were wrapped in cloths to protect them from the sharp crust In this way it took two days to make a trip. Mr. Riegle could not keep us, so we would, on arriving there, load up and return as far as Joshua Smith's where we would stay over night, and next day make home. In this way twenty tons of hay were hauled in bitterly cold weather We were thinly clad for this climate and suffered intensely from the cold

"The nearest postoffice that winter was Owatonna, twelve miles away We used to take turns going after the mail on foot."

MR WM A CLEMENT,

son of H S Clement, was born Feb 13, 1870 He commenced to learn the printer's trade in the office of the Waterville Advance, owned by Howard Farrington, in 1889 He remained there until 1891 when he journeyed to Albert Lea and worked on the Enterprise until March, 1892 Then he took a "sit" on the Austin, Minn, Daily Register. In June he went to Lake Benton, Minn, where he worked until December when he returned to Waseca and worked on the Waseca Herald from Jan. 1, 1893, to Oct 25, 1894, when he purchased the Annandale, Minn, Post This he sold March 1, 1895, and worked on the Ellendale, S D, Commercial until July 5, 1895 In August of that year he entered the employ of the Owatonna Journal and remained there until December, when he returned to the Waseca Herald Here he remained until the fall of 1896, when he entered the Waseca Journal office as foreman He remained with that office until the first week in April, 1905, when he became sole proprietor of the plant. He married Miss Hilda Ranke Nov 16, 1898. She was born in Politz, Pomerania, Germany, July 28, 1871, and came to America with her parents in 1884 They settled in Beadle county, South Dakota Mr Clement is a very industrious man and popular with all classes

MR. BARNEY BURNS

Mr and Mrs Barney Burns are among the high privates of the army of pioneers that poured into Minnesota in 1856 Barney was born in Monaghan county, Ireland, in 1828, and Mary Duffy, his wife, was born in the same county in 1832 They came to America as far as Ohio about 1850 They were married October 11, 1854, and came to Waseca county in 1856, settling on a claim near the old village of St Mary, where they still reside They have reared a family of eleven children, all living and in good health Their names in the order of birth are as follows George, in business at Burlington, Iowa, Benjamin, R R conductor, Green Bay, Wis , Anna, Mrs Ed Bowe, of this county, Mary, Mrs. Gearin, of Webster, S D , Elizabeth, Mrs John Madden, of Waseca; Thomas, of Minneapolis; Rose, Mrs J A Curran, of Woodville, P H , of Minneapolis; Wm J , of Webster, S D , Catharine, Mrs Robert Collins, of Woodville, and Frank, of Minneapolis There was a happy reunion of all the family Oct 11, 1904, on the occasion of the golden wedding of the aged couple

MR. W. G GALLIEN

This gentleman is one of the popular business men of Waseca He was born in Albany, N Y , Nov 6, 1862 His father died when W G was an infant. Two of his uncles lived near Wilton, at an early day, but soon after settled near Winona on account of nearness to market Mr Gallien came with his mother to Winona, when he was nine years of age He graduated from the Winona high school in 1881, and the same year entered the drug business at St Paul. In 1891, he purchased the drug stock of Mr. Rhode of Waseca and has since continued the business at the corner of Second and Elm streets. He married Miss Jessica B. Parker, daughter of Mr Albert H Parker, of Waseca, June 20 1895 He is a prominent member of the M. E church, and of one or two fraternal societies. He is a very careful and safe druggist and enjoys the confidence of the public to a marked degree Mr. and Mrs Gallien have three children Helene Guernsey, Jeanne La Page, and William Cross

MR AND MRS J L WERDIN

John L Werdin was born March 10, 1830, Henrietta, his wife, was born Sept 25, 1835, both were natives of Prussia They were married Oct 2, 1853, in the Fatherland They came to America in the spring of 1857, arriving at Ripon, Wis., April 3, of that year They remained there a short time, when, with eight other families, they started with ox teams for Minnesota, their destination being Mankato. It was a rainy season which caused them to be two months on the road and to meet with many discouragements on the way. Arriving at Mankato, then a small town, they held a consultation and concluded to return to Wilton, this county Mr Werdin met with a serious accident at Mankato in the breaking of his ox-yoke He had no money with which to purchase a new one and no way of making one Fortunately, Mr. John Sell—now of Waseca—who was one of the party of movers, loaned him sufficient money to purchase a new yoke. Mr Werdin's first location was on eighty acres of land that he bought of Jo Manthey in the town of St Mary and that is now owned by Mr McLoone His first house was built of logs and was twelve by sixteen feet in size For a number of years the Winnebago Indians lived in close proximity, and, while they were peaceable, they were constantly begging food from their white neighbors, thus making the lives of the new settlers a great hardship, for food, at this time, was high priced and scarce During the Indian outbreak of 1862, the white settlers gathered nights at the house of John Priebe, returning to their homes to spend the days Mr Werdin was the first carpenter to settle in that neighborhood and constructed a number of the first frame buildings in that locality. The first frame house he built was for Mr Harding He built several other houses, among them being one for Mr. Fred Stoltz, and others for Gottlieb Kanne, August Kanne, and Christian Seewald In 1859, while he and his family were at Wilton, his house, and all its contents were burned In 1866, he sold his land in St Mary and bought one hundred and sixty acres in section thirty-three, of Iosco, where he resided until his death, which occurred Jan 25, 1875.

The children are Ferdinand W, born Sept 16, 1855, in Prussia, Henry J, born Jan 29, 1858, in St Mary, Minn,, Amelia, now Mrs Weishaar, of Los Angeles, Cal, born March 12, 1862, in St Mary, J L Werdin, Jr, born in Iosco, Minn, Aug 26, 1864, Otelia, now Mrs H O Riebeth, of Minneapolis, born in Iosco, March 23, 1867, Ernest R, born in Iosco, Feb 16, 1869, Herman E P, born in Iosco, Aug 9, 1872 The two latter reside in Los Angeles, California

The grandchildren of Mr and Mrs J. L Werdin now number twenty-six, and the great-grandchildren, three

Mrs Henrietta Werdin, the widowed mother, will be seventy years of age on her next birthday She resides with her daughter in Minneapolis, and is in the enjoyment of good health.

MR FERDINAND W. WERDIN,

who was born Sept 16, 1855, in Prussia, was married in October, 1878, to Miss Anna Roesler, daughter of Mr. and Mrs G Roesler, of Woodville Mr Werdin is a prominent business man in Glenwood, Pope county Minn. He is the father of three sons and three daughters. His eldest daughter Blanche is now Mrs Commings

MR HENRY J WERDIN,

who was born Jan 29, 1858, in St Mary, Minn, was married to Miss Bertha Seewald, daughter of Mr. and Mrs C Seewald, of Iosco, Dec. 10, 1880 Mr Werdin owns a fine farm in Alton near Alma City His family is composed of five sons—Edward Theodore, Benjamin Henry, John B, Henry J, Jr, and Ernest C—and three daughters—Dorothy, (now Mrs. Gottschalk), Laura, and Tillie.

MR HENRY GEHRING

Mr. and Mrs Gottfried Gehring came to this county in 1863—first living in the town of St. Mary and afterwards in Wilton on section 13 where they now reside. Gottfried was for many years chairman of the board of supervisors of Wilton He was always a very successful farmer Mr Henry Gehring, one of his sons, is also a prominent farmer He was born in Marquette county, Wis, Dec 25, 1857, and came to Minnesota with his parents in 1863 He married Miss Augusta Michaelis, daughter of John Michaelis, of New Richland. Augusta was born in Germany, Sept 8, 1866 She came to America with her parents in 1869 They first lived in Marquette county, Wis, and then came to New Richland in this county in June, 1875. Henry and Augusta were married Dec 5, 1885, and have eight children, four sons and four daughters They have a comfortable home and a well improved farm.

MR. JAMES M. HANLEY

Mr. Hanley is one of the rising young men of the West, and is now practicing law at Mandan, N D He was born at Winona, Minn, January 6, 1877, graduated at Kasson, Minn, high school June, 1893; resided in Waseca from June 1893 to January 1903; attended Carleton college in 1894-95, commenced the study of law with Hon Peter McGovern, in Waseca, in June 1895, and was city recorder of Waseca during Mayor Moonan's administration in 1897-8 He was ready to take the bar examination in the spring of 1898, but enlisted in Company K, of the Twelfth Minnesota regiment, and went South He took the state board examination shortly after his regiment was mustered out, at the age of twenty-one, and was admitted to the bar in 1899 He was deputy state oil inspector from January 1899, to June 1900 At the state democratic convention of 1900, he was elected as alternate delegate to the St Louis national convention He was a member of the democratic, First Congressional district central committee and its secretary in 1902 He was secretary of the Waseca county agricultural society from 1900 to 1902, and a member of the Waseca board of health in 1902 He removed to Mandan, N. D, in 1903, and formed the law partnership of Voss & Hanley He married Miss Irma Lewis, of Waseca, March 3, 1903 She was born in Waseca, July 10, 1876, being the daughter of Mr and Mrs B S Lewis, early settlers of Waseca. Her father, in his lifetime, was one of the leading attorneys of Southern Minnesota, and always a prominent and influential citizen of Waseca. Mr and Mrs. Hanley have one child, a son, born April 22, 1905

THE HONORABLE PETER McGOVERN,

the oldest law practitioner in the county, was born in Watertown, Wisconsin, Oct 9, 1845, of Irish parentage He attended the public schools, took an academic course and graduated from the law department of the Wisconsin State University in 1871 He came to Waseca in 1872, and opened a law office In 1873 he was elected county attorney and in 1874 state senator, serving two years in the latter position He was county attorney from 1884 to 1888, from 1892 to 1894, and also from 1896 to 1898 In the fall of 1898 he was again elected to the state senate and served four years. In the fall of 1902 he was democratic candidate for congressman from the First district and made a strong campaign At various times he has been city attorney, and holds that position at the present time He is also one of the board of education of Waseca. In 1883 he married Miss Minnie Gilmore, a native of Canada, they are the parents of five children

MR. WILLIAM GRUNWALD

One of the substantial farmers of St Mary is Mr. Grunwald, who was born in Prussia, April 9, 1866, and came to America in May 1872 He worked in and near Waseca as farm hand and laborer several years. He was married to Miss Dora Prechel, of St Mary, March 22, 1889. Her parents, Mr. and Mrs Gottlieb Prechel, now deceased, settled in St Mary in 1855, and she was born March 22, 1868. Mr Grunwald lived in Waseca until Dec 9, 1891, when he moved to the farm where the family now reside In 1897, he added another eighty acre lot to the farm making in all about two hundred forty acres of very fine land They are the parents of six children Edwin A., born August 27, 1890, Elsie R., born Nov 4, 1892; Lilian F, Feb 20, 1895, John G, May 5, 1898, Henry W, Nov 21, 1900, and Adeline E, Nov 3, 1903.

THE HONORABLE KELSEY CURTIS

This gentleman who was one of the early settlers at Alma City was born in the state of Connecticut Nov 8, 1825 He married Eliza R Sutliffe April 11, 1848 She was also a native of the Nutmeg state and was born in the year 1824 Four boys and four girls were born to them, but only two sons and two daughters are now living Though Mr Curtis followed blacksmithing in younger life, he was engaged in the sale of merchandise while in Alma City. Some years ago, in consequence of failing health, he retired from active business and has since resided in Janesville He represented Waseca county in the house of representatives in the sessions of 1872 and 1876 He served as justice of the peace for many years and has always been popular with the people.

MR ANDERS LIANE

This successful, New Richland farmer was born May 16, 1845, in Uper Sansver, Norway He remained in his native land until April 27, 1870, when he sailed for America, landing in New York the 14th day of the following May He arrived in Dane county, Wis., May 21, and at once entered the employ of a farmer Jan 23, 1874, he united in marriage with Miss Dorothea Brotten, who was born in Norway, May 4 1849, and who came to Dane county, Wis, in May 1873 Both were natives of the same town They came by team to New Richland, arriving June 7, 1875 That year he bought eighty acres of land and opened a farm He now owns three hundred twenty-six acres in section 39, well improved. He is the father of ten living children and two boys who died in infancy He has held the office of town supervisor and is now town and school-district treasurer. The names of his children are as follows: Caroline, now Mrs. Paska, of Ransom county, N D , Oluf, married and on the farm, Christine, now Mrs Christianson, of New Richland, Nels, Sam, Karl, Albert, Daniel, Potter, and Dora, all at home His success in life should be an inspiration to young men everywhere

MR DANIEL DINNEEN,

son of John Dinneen, was born in the town of Byron, Oct 29, 1866 He is now one of the mail carriers from New Richland. His father, John Dinneen, is a native of Ireland, born in June 1828. He came to America in 1850, landing in New York He remained in the East until about 1858 when he came to Waseca county He married Mary Burke in February, 1856, and they have been the parents of five sons and three daughters The elder Mr. Dinneen at first took one hundred sixty acres of land and afterwards bought three hundred twenty acres more, making a large farm Some years ago he retired from active business, and now resides in Waseca

MR OTTO L. LUECK,

now of Augusta, Wisconsin, formerly of this county, was born in Minneapolis, Oct 19, 1876, but was reared in Waseca county. He enlisted in Company D, 16th U S infantry, at Seattle, Wash , March 25, 1898, served in the Philippines with rank of corporal, and was honorably discharged at San Francisco, Cal , Nov. 8, 1900 He married Miss Amy Blodgett April 30, 1902 They have two children Madyline, born June 20, 1903, and Livingston, born Jan 25, 1905 Otto is a grandson of Mr. Rudolph Babler, one of the early settlers of Woodville His mother is now Mrs. George Irvine, of Woodville

MR ORLANDO M SIMONS,

of Janesville, one of the fathers of Waseca county, was born June 12, 1821, at South New Berlin, Chenango county, N Y He married Miss Phoebe Stenson Oct. 30, 1845 She was born April 21, 1824, at Gilbertsville, Oswego county, N Y. About two weeks after their marriage, they moved to Berlin, Erie county, Ohio They came to Minnesota, to the town of Janesville in 1859 They endured many hardships on the journey and arrived November 5. They soon after settled on their claim near Elysian. They were here during the hard times of 1859-60, and at the time of the Indian massacre He was a wagon and carriage maker by trade, but followed farming after he began his residence in Minnesota Mr Simons passed to his final rest June 27, 1905, aged eighty-four years and fifteen days, of heart failure He had been ill about two weeks. His widow, two sons and five daughters survive him. The sons and daughters are T. A Simons, Mrs John Williams, Mrs J Bignall, Mrs C N. Smith, Mrs Clarence Thwing, of Chetek, Wis., P. R. Simons, and Mrs. P Galagan, the last of LeSueur Center

Mr. Simons was always a temperate, honorable, upright man, an affectionate husband, a kind parent, a good citizen, and an accommodating neighbor. It is said of him that he died without an enemy

MR JULIUS GEHRING

This gentleman is to "the Manor born," being a native of Waseca county and the second Christmas boy in the family, having been born Dec 25, 1866—his brother Henry being just nine years of age at the time Amelia Bethke, daughter of August Bethke, of Woodville, deceased, was born in Germany, Feb 8, 1870 She married Julius Gehring May 24, 1894, and has borne him three sons and two daughters They have a pleasant little farm in Wilton, their house being on the old John C Hunter residence block of the old village of Wilton The site belonged to the William Roddle estate at the time of Mr. Roddle's death.

MR PHILIP GEHRING,

son of Gottfried Gehring, of Wilton, was born in the town of St Mary, Jan 12, 1864 He lived on the farm with his parents until 1886, when he came to Waseca and worked as a cabinet maker for some time, afterwards learning the painter's trade. He opened a paint shop and commenced business for himself in 1892 He afterwards formed a copartnership with Mr Klohe in the paint and paper-hanging business. Mr Gehring served as alderman of the first ward of Waseca four years Nov 5, 1892, he married Miss Annie Tetzloff, of Janesville She was born in Germany, March 9, 1873, and came to America in 1880. Her parents first lived in Janesville village and four years later on a farm in Janesville township Mr. and Mrs. Gehring have eight children, three boys and five girls.

MR B J LILLY

This gentleman represents the Old Reliable Continental Fire Insurance company, and is a life-time resident of the county He was born at Lacon, Ill, on Feb 9, 1856 He is a son of Terrence Lilly, deceased, and came to this county with his parents in 1857 He was reared a farmer, and resided on his farm in Alton until 1895 when he came to Waseca and engaged in the insurance business He married Miss Nellie G Sheehan, daughter of Mr Dennis Sheehan, an early settler, Nov 9, 1887 She was born in Detroit, Mich, on January 28, 1863, although her parents' home was in St Mary Mr and Mrs Lilly are the parents of three daughters Anastasia M, born October 11, 1888, Evelin L, born April 24, 1892, Marcella, born Jan 31, 1901.

WASECA FENCE TOOL COMPANY.

MR. EMIL SAHLER,

of Woodville, farmer and inventor, was born in Baraboo, Wis, June 28, 1859 He came to Clinton Falls, Minnesota, with his parents in 1869, and lived there until 1884 Emil Sahler and Miss Minnie Krassin were married June 15, 1882 Minnie is a daughter of the late Christian Krassin, of St Mary, and was born Dec. 6, 1860. They own a farm of two hundred acres, and have growing thereon, fourteen hundred fruit trees, mostly apple and improved plum They have a grove of five acres about the house, consisting of Norway poplars, evergreens, and soft maples Including the orchard, they have about sixteen acres devoted to trees They are also engaged in dairying and general farming Mr Sahler is the inventor of the "Boss Fence Tools." He is also a prominent member of the Minnesota horticultural society, and has invented a number of fruit picking implements Mr and Mrs Sahler are the parents of three children, one son and two daughters, Christian, born Dec 3, 1888, Emma, born Nov 15, 1890, Lizzie, born July 9, 1898 They have one of the largest and finest fruit orchards in the state, and as they are hard workers, they realize a comfortable income

"WASECA FENCE TOOL COMPANY"

This company was organized about the first of March, 1905, by Emil Sahler, the inventor, and Mr Harry P Shafer, with headquarters in Waseca, Minn. Mr Sahler calls his invention the "Boss Fence Tool" This invention of five tools in one is for stretching wire on wire fences, mending wire fences, pulling and driving staples, etc It has been patented and on recent improvements patent has been applied for He has also invented a cow-tail holder whereby the milker, in fly time, can prevent the cow from switching her tail in his face or throwing dirt into the milk Agents for the sale of these simple, yet valuable implements, are operating in many of the western states, and within the first six months of the company business, they disposed of some twenty-five thousand fence tool implements The company give liberal terms to agents In the office picture, Mr Sahler, the inventor, sits next to the door on the left hand side with a hammer and wire-stretcher in his hands, and Mr Shafer, business manager, sits opposite him near the office desk

MR OWEN LILLY,

of Alton, one of its wealthy farmers, was born in Enniskillen, Ireland, in 1844, he came to America with his parents in 1849, and to this county in 1857 In April 1883, he married Miss Johanna Fitzgibbon whose parents were among the very early settlers of the county Mr and Mrs Lilly are the parents of one son and two daughters

PATRICK FARRELL,

of Woodville, is another of the early pioneers Born in 1831, he came to America from West Meath county, Ireland, in 1847, when sixteen years of age. He spent one year in New York, eight years in Indiana, and on the last day of August, 1857, came to Woodville John Forrest and Wm M Green then owned and operated a steam saw mill at the foot of the hill on the road from Waseca to the south shore of Clear Lake This looked like business and Mr. Farrell concluded to make his home here He was married to Miss Julia Egan, June 9, 1857, a few days before starting for Minnesota Ten children were born to them, only four of whom are living Mrs Farrell died some years ago. His son Lewis was born in Woodville, in 1858, and now lives in South Dakota Two daughters reside in Minneapolis, and one daughter, Mrs John Keeley, resides with her husband on the old homestead

MR EDWIN R STEVENS

was born in Washara county, Wis, Oct 29, 1859 He came to Vivian, this county, with his parents, who settled there in October, 1863, the next year after the Indian massacre The family moved to Wilton in 1866, his father carrying on blacksmithing there for some years Edwin went to Lake Benton in 1880, where he made his home until 1895. Nov 30, 1892, he married Miss Lura A. Gray, daughter of the late Wm H. Gray, an early settler of Woodville and an old soldier, now deceased Lura was born in Woodville Nov. 11, 1866. In 1895 Mr. and Mrs Stevens returned to Woodville and lived on a farm, east of Waseca, which they carried on until the spring of 1900, when they moved into Waseca Since Aug 11, 1902, Mr. Stevens has been mail carrier on route No 2 Of Mr Stevens' brothers and sisters, Franklin J resides in Moorhead, Minn ; Olive A., Mrs. B F. Roddle, and Fannie R , Mrs W H Roddle, reside in Brookings, S D , Walter, in Waseca Florence, Mrs Mudgett, at Chattanooga, Tenn , Charles F. enlisted March 24, 1864, and died at Helena, Ark , Sept 1, 1864, of disease contracted in the service

MR CHARLES P SPILLANE.

This active young attorney was born in Faribault county, Minn , March 15, 1873, and was brought to Woodville by his parents, Mr and Mrs Patrick Spillane, in 1875 He was reared on his father s farm, but upon reaching his majority, entered the law office of Hon John Moonan of Waseca, as a student. He went to North Dakota in the spring of 1901 Nov. 27, of the same year, he married Miss Agnes I Moonan, a native of this county, daughter of Mr. Patrick Moonan, who was an early settler. They returned to Waseca in 1903, and went to live in New Richland in the fall of the same year Mr Spillane was admitted to the bar in North Dakota in 1902, and is in active practice at New Richland He is chairman of the democratic county central committee, and holds the office of deputy oil inspector for this county He was a very strong supporter of W J Bryan during the campaigns of 1896 and 1900.

FARM BUILDINGS OF MR. AND MRS. E. SAHLER.

E R. CONNER AND FAMILY

This gentleman and his family were among the early settlers in Blooming Grove Mr Conner was born in Indiana, Feb 17, 1814 His wife, Sarah (Lilly) Conner, was born in West Virginia, Dec. 16, 1824, and died in South Dakota, Jan 3, 1900 They were married in Indiana March 13, 1845 Twelve children, six sons and six daughters, were born to them Three of the daughters died before reaching maturity The family came to Waseca county with ox teams and covered wagons, arriving June 11, 1856, hoping thereby to escape the malaria, which was prevalent in Hoosierdom They were six long, weary weeks in making the toilsome journey Two of the sons enlisted in the Union army John G. enlisted at the age of eighteen years in Company H, Third Minnesota regiment, and died at Pine Bluff, Arkansas. James L enlisted Dec 20, 1861, at the age of sixteen years, and served until July 19, 1865 Mr. and Mrs Conner were noted for their hospitality All the early farm settlers in the south part of this county will remember their many acts of kindness. On one occasion Capt E A Rice (afterwards major) and about twelve of his men were caught in a heavy snow storm when going from Wilton to Ft Snelling, and arrived at the Conner place at night There was also a clergyman and a student from Faribault along. They all asked to remain over night There was but one room in the log house and not a large one at that, but they all gathered in and most of them slept on the floor Mrs Conner gave them supper and was up nearly all night making ready for breakfast The family experienced all the privations and hardships incident to pioneer life. In 1883 Mr Conner sold out and removed to South Dakota with his family, so that the boys might secure farms in that then new country. At this writing, 1905, he is still living in that state

Mrs. J W Cleland, whose maiden name was Amanda C. Conner, is a daughter of E R, and was born in Indiana, Sept 11, 1852 She taught school for several years before she married Mr J. W Cleland, Oct 3, 1877 [A sketch of Mr. Cleland's life is given elsewhere in this work] Mrs Cleland has four sons Edgar J, born May 16, 1884, Spencer B, born Dec 20, 1886 Jay Conner, born Dec 21, 1889, and Ralph E, born July 20, 1893 Her home is pleasantly situated on the west shore of Clear Lake.

MR. JOHN CARMODY, SEN

This man of rugged honesty is a native of Ireland, born in County Kerry, in the year 1821 He came to America with his parents in 1835 and lived on a farm in New York until 1843. That year he came with his parents to Wisconsin, and made his home on a farm in Milwaukee county. He married Miss Mary Purcel in September, 1851, and they continued their residence in Wisconsin until 1867, when they came to Waseca county and bought the Noah Lincoln farm on section 26, in Wilton, where Mr. Carmody still resides. Mrs. Carmody died Feb 11, 1885, mourned by all who knew her Eight children were born to them, two of whom died in infancy John, Jr, is a lawyer and resides at Hillsboro, N D Mary is the wife of Mr John Curran, of Woodville, and was married to him Nov 9, 1876 Margaret married John Murphy, of Byron, May 16, 1882 Thomas, Eliza, and Julia are living at the old home, which is one of the oldest and best farms in the county It was first taken by Chris Scott in February 1855, and contains prairie and timber land and running water

MR JAMES B HAYDEN,

a war veteran, born in Ireland Nov. 30, 1840, son of Peter and Anna Hayden, came to Canada with his parents when he was two years of age, and thence to Wisconsin, where, in 1862, Jan 2, he was mustered into Company H, Seventeenth Wisconsin infantry, in which he served until May 5, 1865 He was in a number of battles, and at Atlanta received a wound in his left wrist, which has largely deprived him of the use of his arm He went to live in Alton in 1865, and was elected clerk of court in the fall of 1871, holding the office for twelve years He was express agent in Waseca for a few years and then received an appointment in one of the departments at Washington where he remained until the year 1904, when he retired from business, his health not being very good. His wife was Miss Goff, of Alton, and they have several children grown to maturity Mr Ed Hayden, of Alton, prominent as an ardent and consistent Populist, and a successful farmer, is James brother He settled in Alton in 1865

MR JENS T DAHLE,

born March 5, 1839, in Norway, came to America in 1858, and to Minnesota soon after, working at whatever he could find to do Jan 22 1862, he enlisted in the second company of Minnesota sharpshooters. He was afterwards transferred to the "Old First Minnesota," participating in all the bloody battles of the Chickahominy, and also the battles of the Wilderness, Spottsylvania, North Anna, Cold Harbor and Deep Bottom He was captured at Ream's Station August 24, 1864, and taken to the rebel prison pens of Libby and Belle Isle, Va, and Salisbury, N C He was finally paroled, reaching the Union lines March 13 1865 He was then in very poor health, and was sent to the parole camp at Annapolis, Md, and from there to St Louis in a box car At St. Louis he obtained a furlough and went to Chicago, where he became very ill and entered the hospital where he remained for some time Getting better to some extent, he came on to St Paul where he received his discharge. He then engaged in the grocery business at Faribault for two years, and then bought the Philo Woodruff farm in Blooming Grove where he has since resided He married Miss Anna Olena Seim whose parents came from Norway They have a very pleasant home.

FATHER SCHUETTE

and his sons were among the early settlers of Blooming Grove The mother died in 1868 and the father in 1883 Edward Schuette was ordained a German Methodist clergyman at the age of twenty Julius E Schuette married Henrietta Saufferer, daughter of Hon John L Saufferer, in 1878 A H, John H, brothers of Julius, and William E, a nephew, all live in the same neighborhood, in Blooming Grove, and all have well improved farms

MR. J. C. JOHNSON,

is a son of Carl Johnson who moved to section 19, Blooming Grove, May 17, 1857. Carl Johnson, the father, was born in Sweden, Sept 22, 1825, and came to America in 1853, landing at New York Oct 22 He came West to Milwaukee, Wis, and from there went to Rockford, Ill, where he worked some two years He next went into the Wisconsin pineries where he remained two years and then came to Minnesota He married Miss Julia Johnson, of Vivian, July 16, 1862 She was born in Norway in February 1825, and came to America in 1853 She came to Vivian with her married sister in 1858. From there she walked all the way to Faribault where she worked until a short time before her marriage. Of such courageous stock come the sons and daughters of Waseca county. John C. and Christina are the only children and they are kindly caring for their father in his declining years They have a very pleasant, comfortable home, and are highly esteemed by their neighbors On May 18, 1896, John C Johnson married Miss Emma Lee, daughter of Aleck Lee, of Blooming Grove They have four sons—the oldest eight and the youngest three years of age

MR JAMES HAND,

born Feb 22, 1835, in the state of Ohio, son of Cornelius Hand, settled in Blooming Grove, in 1856 His grandfather, Cornelius, of New Jersey, was a soldier in the war of 1812-15 James married Lydia A Sprague Aug. 24, 1856. He enlisted in Company E, Minnesota heavy artillery Nov. 15, 1864, and served until Sept. 27, 1865.

MR KEYES SWIFT,

a native of Fond du Lac, Wis, came to Blooming Grove in 1856. He was left fatherless at an early age and thrown upon his own resources He owns a valuable farm and has accumulated a handsome property He was married July 3, and has two children In 1896, he was the Populist candidate for representative of this district

THE REVEREND J. C JAHN,

born in Prussia, July 1, 1839, came to America in 1846 He resided in Baltimore, Md, for a few years and then came to St Paul In 1861, he enlisted in the First Minnesota cavalry, and was in the battles of

Fort Henry, Fort Donaldson, Shiloh, and Granville At the last place he was wounded and made prisoner. He was afterwards paroled, and honorably discharged in July 1863 He was married in 1864, then studied for the ministry and was licensed to preach in 1870. He was pastor of the Blooming Grove M E. church in 1886 He was the father of ten children

MR HENRY BEHNE,

who is now deceased, was born in Germany, near Hanover, April 29, 1839, and came to this country in 1853. He worked in Illinois until 1855, when he came to Minnesota He married Hannah Muller, March 28, 1860, and settled down to farming They had eight children Henry W, Emma, (now Mrs Henry Beck,) George, August, Mary, Ida, Willie, and Lewis.

THE REVEREND HENRY SINGENSTRUE,

born in Oelber, Germany, Nov. 16, 1821, sailed for America in 1852, landing at New Orleans and coming north as far as Cincinnati In 1854 he came to Red Wing, Minn, and bought a claim, remaining two years, when he was appointed missionary of the German M E church, a position which he held for sixteen years He married Salome Bider, a Swiss woman, in 1861 They own a little farm in Blooming Grove Mr Singenstrue was a pioneer in the church work of the state.

MR CHRISTIAN KNAUSS

and family came to Blooming Grove in 1881 The parents came from Alsace, France, about 1846, and settled in Cook county, Ill There were nine children in this family John, Charles, Christian W, Henry, William, Bertha, Carrie (who died in Illinois), Benjamin, and Edward.

MR JOHN L BAHR,

born August 18, 1847, in Saxony, Germany, came to America with his parents in 1853, and resided in Waukesha county, Wis In 1867 his family came to Deerfield, Steele county, where John L remained until 1873 Having married Miss Julia Reineke, March 26, 1872, he began housekeeping on a farm in Deerfield, where he remained with his family four years. They then bought a farm on section 15, Blooming Grove where they now reside with their children They are leading members of the German M E. church.

MR ANDREW J. HENDERSON,

born in Scotland, Aug 15, 1849, bought a farm in Vivian in 1882 and for a number of years was extensively engaged in raising cattle and horses Of the latter, he chose the Clyde breed. He was very successful in the business, and a short time ago retired from his farm to a home in Owatonna

MR HERMAN BALDUAN,

one of the wealthy farmers of Byron and New Richland, born in Germany Jan 10, 1847, settled in Byron in 1877 upon a farm containing two hundred forty acres He married Augustina Dumpka, of Dunbar, Faribault county, April 5, 1878

MR E W FISKE,

born March 8, 1851, in Oneida county, N. Y, came to Waseca in 1872. After following various employments, he engaged in the business of contracting and building He married Miss Kate I Bailey, daughter of Hon. P. C. Bailey, Dec 21, 1880. They now reside in Helena, Montana, with their family of five children

MR JOHN W. JOHNSON

"Bill Johnson," as he is familiarly called, was born in Provincetown, Mass, March 31, 1832 He came West to Faribault in 1856, where he was employed as clerk for his brothers-in-law, Fuller & Smith, until the spring of 1857 when he went to St Mary, and for a time "boomed" that ancient village. In 1858, after the first county seat contest, he moved to Wilton, and opened a store for the sale of merchandise in the firm name of J W Johnson & Co. There he remained ten years, when he came to Waseca and opened a grocery store, a business in which he is still engaged He married Mary A. Marston, of Massachusetts, June 27, 1866 They have two sons, Edward P, married and an express agent at Fort Dodge, Iowa, and William M, single and American express agent at Waseca J W is a local politician whom the office seekers generally consult.

PEOPLES STATE BANK OF WASECA

This bank was organized in December 1880 The stockholders were W G Ward, C H Smith, A F Kelly, G. R Buckman, Mrs W G Ward, E B Collester, M Madden, E M. Broughton, W J Jameson, M A. Green, and C M Star The officers were G R Buckman, president, A F Kelly, vice president; C. H. Smith, cashier, directors—Ward, Buckman, Broughton, Smith and Kelly. It started with a capital of $25,000 The capital was afterwards increased to $50,000, and again reduced to $25,000 The bank is now in a flourishing condition, with the following officers and directors E. C Trowbridge, president, D S Cummings, vice president, R P Ward, cashier, H C Didra, assistant cashier, R P Ward, D S. Cummings, Marion Buckman, E C. Trowbridge, E. W. Ward, and C H Watson, directors

THE HONORABLE M H HELMS,

born Dec 19, 1831, in Cattaraugus county, N Y, came with his parents to Dane county, Wis, in 1845, where he resided until 1861, when he enlisted in Company E, Eighth Wisconsin infantry and was commissioned as second lieutenant He served until Dec 12, 1865, when he was mustered out, and returned to Madison, Wis, where he remained until 1868, when he came to Waseca He married Miss Eleanor M. Dodge, Nov 30, 1870 She died June 30, 1877, leaving two daughters, Vinnie M, now Mrs Rausch, of Grand Forks, N. D., and Jessie R., now the wife of Dr Lynn, of Waseca Mr Helms ably represented this county in the legislative house during the session of 1891

MR. CHRIS HANSEN,

a native of Denmark, born in 1845, came to America in 1869 He arrived at Waseca in 1872 For some years he was engaged in the saloon business, but now carries on a small farm north of Waseca, in Woodville He has a family of bright and intelligent children Aside from the business he followed, he is a good citizen

THE REVEREND FATHER A CHRISTIE,

a native of Vermont, born in 1851, came to Waseca about the first of the year 1878 When he was yet a child, his parents came West as far as Adams county, Wisconsin, where they remained until 1866, when the family came to Austin, Mower county, Minn Mr Christie attended the public schools while a lad, and later attended the college of St Joseph, near St Cloud, Minn He finished his school days at Montreal, Canada He was a power for good works in Waseca, and remained here for a number of years He is now the very able bishop of Alaska He was succeeded by the Rev. Father J J Treanor, under whose management the present splendid church edifice was constructed

MR S S ROLLINS,

a native of New Hampshire, born May 1, 1836, son of Reuben and Lovina Rollins, came to Minnesota in 1855, first living on a farm in Houston county He moved to Freedom in 1866 In 1860 he married Martha M Elmore, who was born Oct 31, 1843 They have been the parents of six children Mr Rollins is an ideal American citizen For years he was clerk of his township and treasurer of his school district He now resides in Janesville, having retired from active business.

THE HONORABLE W G WARD

(By his daughter, Mrs D S Cummings)

William Grosvenor Ward was born December 26, 1827, in Boonville, N Y, the sixth child in a family of twelve

Possessing an inquisitive mind, naturally studious and reflective he readily absorbed all that the high school was able to offer, and at an early age was graduated from the Boonville Academy where he had earned his tuition by tutoring the younger pupils Although excelling in his favorite study,—that of mathematics in all its branches,—much of his time was devoted to perfecting his knowledge of Latin and Greek.

At the age of seventeen, having proved himself a brilliant scholar and already showing those traits of character which made him conspicuous in later years, to the great grief of his mother, who fully realized his natural ability, instead of entering, a sophomore, in Union College, he began the practice of civil engineering,—his first position being that of assistant on the Black River canal

Rapidly rising in the profession for which he was so well equipped, he became in turn chief engineer and road master on the Long Island railroad during the construction of two new branches, and superintendent of car and engine repairs of the entire road with headquarters in the city of Brooklyn

At this time, the year 1852, occurred his marriage to Martha E. Dodge This union was blessed by a family of two children, Clarence T. and Annie L Soon after he became first assistant engineer on the Lake Ontario and Auburn railroad, after which he was given a similar position with the Utica and Black River railroad With visions of better things in the opening up of new country, the year 1856 finds him turning westward to take his place as chief engineer on the Watertown and Madison, (now Milwaukee & St Paul) system, after which came the construction of the Oconomowoc and Columbus railroad

The financial crash of 1857 which involved so disastrously the whole country, put a halt to further projection of railway systems, and Mr Ward began the study of law in Madison, Wisconsin, with the firm of Wood and Blake. He was admitted to the bar and practiced only long enough to try one case when the war broke out, and he was appointed quartermaster in the Thirty fourth Wisconsin For three years after that, he held the appointment of postmaster in Madison In 1865 he was called upon to sustain the loss of his wife who died in Jefferson After taking his motherless children East to place them in the care of relatives, Mr Ward returned West to resume railroading, this time as chief engineer in the construction of the Winona and St Peter railroad This line was completed in 1868. Investing largely in property in and about Waseca, he became one of the early promoters of resident industries In 1867 he was married to Ella C Trowbridge, youngest daughter of the founder of Waseca He built a home to which in time there came four children· Martha E, Roscoe Percy, Florence Trowbridge, and Earl W. Always an ardent politician, Mr Ward spared neither pains nor expense in the support of republican candidates for office, generally taking an active part in the campaign He was twice elected to the legislature as state senator, and was, in 1880, the republican candidate for congress, but, owing to party differences, was not elected

In whatever place we find him, as a youth in studies and athletics; or in maturer years, directing the laying out of many lines of traffic, or presiding with unwonted grace and dignity in the senate chamber, Mr Ward was ever a leader of men His commanding presence attracted the beholder whose attention was held by the eloquence and versatility of a ready talker A constant student all his life, his mind was stored with learning,—science, history, theology, poetry,—the best the great minds had to offer, all were his His last days of suffering were lightened and uplifted by the ennobling sentiments inspired by long hours of companionship with his beloved books. In September, 1892, after a long illness, death brought him relief from pain

The poor had lost a friend to whom they never turned in vain, and, if his enemies did not regret the sharp spur of his active animosity, his hosts of friends do not yet cease to mourn the loss of one who never wearied in deeds of kindness for those who merited his esteem.

MR LUMAN S. WOOD,

was born in St Lawrence county, N Y, in 1836, and came to Woodville in 1857 He was one of the patriots of the "Old First Minnesota' He married Miss Fannie Lansdale in 1867, and in 1872 emigrated to Oregon where he now resides

MR JAMES M DUNN,

was born in Dumfrieshire, Scotland March 3, 1839, and came to America with his parents, Thomas and Isabella Dunn, in 1840 They first lived in Cattaraugus county, N Y, and removed to Lee county, Illinois, in 1856, where the father was killed by a stroke of lightning Sept 16, 1862 The family came to Minnesota in 1866 There were ten of the children, Ann, James M., Isabella (drowned), William, George T, Walter, John, Eliza, Andrew, and Isabella (second) In the spring of 1867. James M. bought eighty acres of land on section 36, Woodville, which was the beginning of what a few years ago, was the noted Oak Hill stock farm He married Miss Matilda Turnacliff, daughter of Ferdinand Turnacliff, July 18, 1868 For many years Mr Dunn was engaged in breeding pure-blood horses and cattle He kept Percheron and French coach horses, and Short Horn cattle The health of himself and wife finally became impaired, and a few years ago he retired from farming and now resides with his family in Waseca They are the parents of six children, four of whom are living

MR N J. LEAVITT,

another prominent cattle raiser and dairyman, born in Vermont Nov 19, 1841, came to this county in 1869, and bought the farm southeast of Clear Lake, in Woodville, now owned by George H Wood He enlisted in Company C, Eighth Vermont regiment Nov 20, 1861, and served until Sept 4, 1863 May 1, 1864, he married Lizzie P. Sterling, of Vermont, who was born Aug. 10, 1845 Mr Leavitt's favorite cattle were pure-blood Holsteins He removed from the county some years ago and resides in Minneapolis

MR. JOHN CURRAN,

of Woodville, a prosperous farmer, born near Milwaukee, Wis, Nov 28, 1847, came to Woodville, in this county, with his father's family, in 1874 He followed the saw mill business some seven years in the northern portion of the state before coming here He finally settled on section 28, town of Woodville. He married Miss Mary Carmody Nov 9, 1876, and they have a model home

MR JAMES CURRAN,

brother of John, learned the carpenter trade, but follows farming. He was born near Milwaukee, September 11, 1857, and came to Minnesota in 1877 Some years since he married Miss Rose Burns, daughter of Mr Barney Burns, of Wilton He has held the office of town supervisor and is one of the prominent men of the township of Woodville

MR. LOREN A GAGE,

of Woodville, section 4, was born in the state of New York, April 11, 1838 As early as 1846, his father moved to Dodge county, Wisconsin, about five miles south of Waupun Loren came to this county over forty years ago His wife was Miss Catharine Collins, a native of Ireland She died March 16, 1902, leaving no children Mr. Gage lives on his little farm by himself and is an honest, upright man

MR THOMAS KENNEDY

is one of the prosperous farmers of Woodville He was born in Ireland, May 28, 1848, the son of Patrick and Mary Kennedy His parents brought him to America the same year, going to St Johns, N B They spent three years there, two years in Vermont and then came West as far as Wisconsin. Oct 11, 1862, Thomas married Miss Rose Reynolds, also a native of Ireland, born Dec 28, 1844 Their children are John, Mary, Rose, Thomas, Bernard, Joseph, William, and Edward

MR. CHARLES LOCKWOOD

was born in Connecticut, Dec. 2, 1824, and settled in Alton in 1865. In his younger days he was a seafaring man, having followed a sailor's life for ten years He married Louisa Merrill Sept 3, 1855 She was born in Erie county, New York, May 9, 1832 They were the parents of four children—one son and three daughters.

MR GEORGE W DUNHAM

was born in Fairfield county, Conn, Nov 24, 1837 He came to the town of Alton, in 1866, and bought a farm on section 23 where he has since resided. He married Mary J Lyon, Sept 23, 1857 She was born in 1836 in Massachusetts. Four sons and two daughters have been born to them

MR. TERRENCE HAMMEL,

who for many years was the assessor of Alton, was born in Ireland in

1845 He is the son of James Hammel, who came to America in 1850 Terrence was married June 2, 1865, to Mary Smith, who was born in Ireland in 1847. They settled in Alton in 1866 They are the parents of ten children—one son and nine daughters.

MR PATRICK MARKHAM

settled near Alma City in 1867, on section 34, in Alton He was a native of Ireland, born Dec 25, 1805 He came to Canada when a young man A sketch of his life and death appears elsewhere in this work

MR M S HOPKINS

and family came to the town of Alton in 1867, and made their home on section 25 Mr. Hopkins died Sept 25, 1871, and Mrs Hopkins passed away June 3, 1882

MR. H M. HOPKINS,

son of M S, was born in Ohio, Nov. 15, 1845. He has followed farming all his life, buying land in Alton in 1866, and carrying on farming until a short time ago when he sold the farm and removed to Minneapolis, where he now resides He is an unmarried man of a somewhat poetical temperament

MR ANDREW HOGAN,

born in Ireland in the year 1835, came to America in 1856, landing in New York, and going thence to Ohio, where he remained until 1858 when he moved to the town of Janesville In 1874 he went to live in Alton on section 3 He was married to Mary Handerhan in 1860, and they are the parents of three sons and three daughters

MR JAMES A VAUGHN,

son of Edward and Mary Vaughn, born in Ireland in 1831, came to the United States in 1838 with his parents, and in 1873 moved to Alton His parents died in Illinois—the mother in 1861, and the father in 1866 James married Catharine O'Lochlin in 1859. She was born in Ireland July 26, 1843, and her parents—Mr and Mrs John O Lochlin, came to this country in 1863 Mr. Vaughn is the father of four sons and four daughters

MR GEORGE HOFELD,

born March 4, 1838, in Germany came to the United States in 1854, and to Freedom in 1868 He remained on the farm in Freedom until 1877, when he sold it and entered the mercantile business in Alma City He is an old school teacher, having taught some thirteen winters in all He has held a number of town offices and is a reliable man He was married to Anna Huff, of Michigan, July 5, 1868, and they have had five children, three sons and two daughters, one of the sons dying in infancy

MR FRANK FIELD,

a native of Illinois, born Nov 1, 1855, came to Freedom June 6, 1864, when only a lad His father is John H, born in 1834, March 19, also a resident of Freedom Frank Field and Martha A Boston were married in 1880 She was born in Wisconsin Feb 23, 1850, and is a capable woman

MR WILLIAM ORCUTT,

now deceased, was born in Ohio, March 17, 1840, and came to Minnesota at an early day He was a poor lad and commenced to earn his living at twelve years of age June 29, 1861, he enlisted in Company C, Second Minnesota volunteer infantry, and served three years He settled in Freedom, in 1866 He married Miss Mary Morrirson, June 1, 1869 She being Louise Connor, by whom he had two daughters—Dora Belle, born April 31, 1876, and Anna Louise, born May 1, 1878

MR F W BROMAGHIN

This gentleman, born in St. Lawrence county, N Y, June 29, 1820, settled in Freedom in 1866 He came a poor man, having with him a feeble old father, a sick wife, eight children and only $19 in money. He had no house of any kind. It was the scarce year in Minnesota with high prices· wheat $2 per bushel, potatoes $1, pork $25 per barrel, and butter from 25 to 50 cents per pound He finally bought a small board shanty for $60 on credit, and managed to pull through and pay for his land in the course of six or eight years He served in the Union army from Feb 27, 1864, to July 27, 1865

THE HONORABLE JOHN WILKINSON,

a native of Wisconsin, born Feb. 28, 1846, bought a farm in section 4, Freedom, in 1866 He married Miss Mary Morrinson, June 1, 1869 She was born August 1, 1851 They now reside in Janesville. Mr. Wilkinson served in the house of representatives during the sessions of 1897 and 1899

MRS MARY (HEALY) HAYDEN

Of this lady, later Mrs Henry Converse, the following is related in the "History of Steele and Waseca counties " "Mrs Converse had an experience in the Indian troubles in 1862. It seems that she and her first husband, Mr Hayden, then lived in Renville county. Hearing that the savages were murdering people within five miles of them, they fled from their house and their neighbors from theirs When they had gone but a short distance, Mr Hayden returned to the house for something or other, and was killed by the red fiends, who had just arrived Mrs Hayden and the neighbors pushed on as rapidly as possible, but they were overtaken by the Indians; the men with them were butchered, the women and children taken prisoners Mrs Hayden leaping from the wagon, with her child in her arms, ran and hid in the woods till night, and then walked to Fort Ridgely, eighteen miles distant, where she found protection" She married Mr Henry Converse in 1863, and lives in Freedom

MR. JOHN E. GEARY,

born in Scotland, July 28, 1840, came with his parents two years later to America and resided in St Lawrence county, N. Y He enlisted in Company A, One Hundred Forty-second N Y. infantry, and served until June 15, 1865. He married Eliza Fields, March 14, 1867, and they settled in Freedom the next November, where they have since resided.

MR SAMUEL HODGKINS,

a veteran soldier and farmer, born in St Lawrence county, N Y, June 15, 1839, son of William and Almira Hodgkins, enlisted May 1, 1861, in Company K, Eighteenth N Y infantry, and served until May 28, 1863 The following August 7, he again enlisted, this time in the heavy artillery, and while in that service received severe injuries. He was mustered out in September 1865, having served over two years in the artillery company. He married Lucretia Ackerman Dec. 28, 1865. He carried on his father's farm until 1870 when he came to Freedom, arriving April 7, 1870, and then bought eighty acres of land for $500. He has since added to it until he has a large farm—half a section or more He is a man of very decided opinions and is prominent in the community where he lives

THE HONORABLE OTTO HANSON,

a prosperous farmer of Otisco, born in Norway, March 16, 1850, came to the United States with his parents in 1867, and settled in Otisco. His mother died in 1869, and his father in October 1885 Otto married Miss Ellen Thompson, of Wisconsin, March 15, 1874. He owns a large farm with fine buildings, cultivated groves and fruit trees. When he came to America he owed $35 for his passage. He first worked three weeks for a farmer for $5 and his board. How many young men would do that today? He worked through haying and harvest for $13 a month. During the winter he worked for $5 a month and board. And thus he labored faithfully for what he could get until to-day he possesses a competency He worked out among farmers by the month until 1873, when he bought an eighty acre farm on section 24, Otisco This he cultivated for three years and then sold it. He then purchased the quarter section where he now resides

Mrs Hanson was born in Hadeland, Norway, Oct. 23, 1851, and came to America with her parents in 1861 They were thirteen weeks and three days on the ocean Seven children, four boys and three girls, all living, have been born to them Martin O, born July 7, 1875, Helma S, Sept 1876, Emill Theodore, May 19, 1879, Minnie, Jan. 16, 1880, Henry O Jan 13, 1885, Selmer, Nov 5, 1887, and Ella C, Jan 28, 1892

Mr. Hanson has the confidence to a marked degree of those who know him He has been school director, town supervisor or chairman of the board for twenty years, president of the Farmers' insurance company for twelve years, and representative in the legislature in 1889. He is one of the trustees of Augsburg Seminary, Minneapolis, and a director of the First National bank of Waseca. Besides his large farm in Otisco, he owns two farms in Western Canada

MR BENJAMIN L BALLARD,

son of the late Daniel Ballard, was born in St. Mary, where he now resides, June 7, 1877 He spent the years 1899, 1900, and 1901 in Montana. With the exception of these years his home has been in St. Mary. He married Christine Johnston Sept 24, 1903 She was born in Scotland, Nov. 3, 1877, and in 1881 came to America with her parents, who settled in Milwaukee, Wis Mr and Mrs Ballard have one son, born Dec. 22, 1904 Mr Ballard is an industrious, frugal farmer

MR. WILLIAM A HENDERSON

This gentleman was born in Menstrie, Clackmannonshire, Scotland, on the 5th day of May, 1838. At the age of thirteen years, he came to this country in company with a maiden aunt, and stopped in Dane county, Wisconsin Two years later his father and the rest of the family followed, and they made their first home in Springdale, Dane county, in 1852 This was Mr Henderson's home until he was twenty-eight years of age At that age, he had saved from his earnings in working in the pinery in the winter, ratting in the spring, breaking grub land in early summer, and running a threshing machine in the fall, the sum of $2,000 The harvest times were given to his father during these years since his majority and so helped relieve the old homestead of debt

In 1867 Mr Henderson located his present home in Minnesota by the purchase of two hundred eighty acres of land in the town of St Mary In this purchase, the $2,000 of savings was invested, and a debt of nearly $5,000 incurred, bearing 7 and 10 per cent interest

In 1868 Mr. Henderson was married to Miss Grace Hunter, who is still living They have five children, four sons and one daughter For the first few years of his farm life in Minnesota, Mr Henderson was a wheat raiser, but in 1878 he determined to change his mode of farming, and made a visit to Scotland to study sheep-husbandry as a preparation for his new pursuit He followed sheep farming for several years, and then changed to diversified farming He has one of the finest farms in the county which he keeps under a high state of cultivation He is also a stockholder and director in the First National bank of Waseca

On May 18, 1905, his team ran away with him, on Second street, Waseca, throwing him out of his buggy at the Grant House and severely injuring him, though no bones were broken He was compelled to remain at the Grant House for nearly four weeks before he could be taken home It was a narrow escape from death.

MRS. MICHAEL BURKE,

of Janesville, is one of the enterprising women that came West at an early day She moved with her family from Ripon, Wisconsin, in 1865, and settled in Janesville where she still resides.

MR. ROBERT MARZAHN

is a native of Iosco, having been born in this county on July 27, 1866. His father, Wm Marzahn, was a native of Germany, and settled in Iosco in 1856, having arrived in America in 1855 The father died June 27, 1893, at the age of seventy-three years Robert married Miss Lydia Miller, of the same town, a daughter of Mr. and Mrs. Michael Miller, Feb 25, 1891. They have one son and two daughters Mason, Esther, and Adeline. Mrs Marzahn's parents, Mr and Mrs Michael Miller, were among the early settlers of Iosco, and reared a family of four sons and five daughters Mr Miller died Aug 2, 1900, and Mrs Miller Nov 14 of the same year Mr. Robert Marzahn's mother is still living at Morristown Robert owns a valuable farm of three hundred twenty acres in sections 1, 2, 10 and 11, in that township, and is one of the prosperous young farmers of the county.

MR WILLIAM CAHILL,

of Janesville, came to this country from Ireland when young He settled on section 35, Janesville, in June, 1858, where he has since resided He married Miss Bridget McCarthy, of Marysburg, Minn , in 1873 Ten children have been born to them, seven of whom are living—four sons and three daughters

MR THOMAS CAHILL,

born in Ireland in the month of November, 1825, came to America in 1847, lived for a time in Kentucky, then came West to Iowa and finally settled in Janesville April 9, 1857, on section 27 Here he secured the ownership of seven hundred ninety-five acres of fine land He married Mary Harney, also a native of Ireland, in March 1855 She was born August 15, 1831 They have been the parents of five children.

MR. ALBERT JAMESON,

a native of Norway, bought a farm on section 19, Blooming Grove in 1893 His wife's maiden name was Mary Olsen, of the same town They have one child, a daughter. Mr. Jameson's father's name was Jens Longlie. He resided in this county a number of years, but moved to Steele county in 1896

MR SEGURD JACKSON,

born in Blooming Grove, July 29, 1863, is a grandson of Segurd Johnson, one of the very early settlers of Iosco His wife's name was Christina Wad, she was also a native of Blooming Grove They have one daughter,

Geda, born Dec. 22, 1899 Mr Jackson owns a farm and is also proprietor of the Palmer Creamery store.

DOCTOR R O CRAIG,

a native of the state of New York, was born in 1834 He studied medicine at Ogdensburg and, in 1855, graduated at the Albany, N Y, Medical college He practiced medicine in that city one year, served as assistant surgeon in the U S. army five years on the Pacific coast, and was appointed surgeon of the Tenth N Y infantry serving until the close of the war He moved to old Janesville to practice as a physician about the year 1866 He served as county superintendent of schools in 1870-71, and for several years as county commissioner In 1874 he entered the drug business with Hon J. O Chandler They are also largely interested in farming operations as farm proprietors He was state senator in 1883 and 1885, and again in 1891 and 1893. He married Miss Lamb, a sister of Hon. M H Lamb, of Alton She died some years ago without issue The doctor is an active member of the society of the G A R, and prominent in all public affairs He has the confidence of the people in a marked degree and is worthy of it

THE HONORABLE J. O CHANDLER

is a native of the state of Maine, born Sept. 21, 1837. He came to Minnesota in 1857 and resided at Pleasant Grove He went to Idaho in 1858, returning in 1859, to make his home in Winona In 1863 he entered the military service as paymaster's clerk and served until 1865, when he returned to Minnesota and was traveling salesman for J D Blake & Co, of Rochester, Minn A year later he opened a store at Janesville He was postmaster of Janesville from 1867 to 1870 In 1873 he disposed of his old line of goods and joined with Dr. R O. Craig in the drug store business He served this county in the legislative house during the session of 1877 He has always been active and prominent in the public affairs of Janesville His first wife died many years ago, and he afterwards married Miss Elizabeth Reid, one of the early school teachers of the county and one of the best and most successful Her father was a Scotchman and one of the early settlers of Freedom, afterwards removing to California

MR. BARNEY McANANY,

of Iosco, born in Milwaukee county, Wis, Jan 9, 1841, came to this county March 21, 1866. Rochester was then the terminus of the railroad, and from there on the stage fare was ten cents a mile Mrs McAnany's maiden name was Ellen Dyson, and she was born in Milwaukee county August 16, 1848. They are the parents of seven children, five sons and two daughters Mr McAnany owns a fine farm and is a prosperous farmer and stock raiser

MR FRANK H MINER.

This gentleman was one of the early settlers of New Richland, and started in as a "granger" He was born in the year 1840, in the state of New York The family came as far west as Wisconsin when Frank was a lad In 1863, they settled upon a farm in New Richland In 1867 Frank moved to Waseca and formed a partnership with A W Jennison in the machinery business. When the W & St P railway was extended to Janesville, they were among the first to open a general stock of merchandise there He remained with Mr Jennison for fourteen years, when Mr S. F Shepherd bought the Jennison interest Mr. Miner was married to Miss Addie Wookey in 1869 He has accumulated a competency and is able to take life easy.

MR CHARLES GUTFLEISCH,

a native of Germany, born in 1856, came to Waseca in 1872, where he worked at tailoring until 1878, when he moved to Janesville and carried on business for himself He suffered from the 1887 fire, but soon after formed a copartnership with R L H Britton They erected a brick building and opened a stock of men's clothing, Mr Gutfleisch having charge of the tailoring department. He is a popular man and served one term as president or chief magistrate of the village

MR ROBERT McDOUGALL,

whose early settlement is elsewhere noted in this book, was born in the Highlands of Scotland March 26, 1820, and came with his parents to America when a small boy They settled near Guelph, Canada, where he endured the hardships incident to making a home in a heavy timbered wilderness. In 1854 he and his brother Hugh came West to Iowa, and in the fall of 1855 to what is now Otisco Here they took land About 1858, Hugh returned to Canada, but Robert packed his "traps" and, with his faithful horse, traveled over prairie and mountain to the gold mines of the western mountains and the Pacific coast In 1861 he returned, stopped for a few weeks in Otisco and then went back to the old home in Canada There he remained until 1866 On the 6th of April of that year, he married Anna McKersie, of Rockwood, Ontario, and they immediately came to their farm in Otisco where he resided until his death, which occurred Jan 15, 1887 Nine children were born to them Catharine L, Nov 7, 1866, now Mrs. Jos S. Root, of Wilton, Anna R , Mrs Frank Erfurth, deceased, born July 22, 1868, Janett C, born March 26, 1870 now Mrs Eugene Turnacliff, of Otisco, Wm. W, born August 12, 1872, Robert B, born June 15, 1874; Margaret G., born May 6, 1876, now Mrs Walter Brisbane, of Stevens county, Bessie C, born March 1, 1878, now Mrs Aldis Brisbane, of Stevens county, Isabelle M, born Nov 4, 1880, now Mrs Walter Johnston, of New Richland, and Hugh P., born April 27, 1882 The sons are all single and live (except Hugh) at or near Malta, Montana Catharine has five children, Anna left surviving two sons and a daughter; Janett C, has two girls, Bessie has two children living, one dying in infancy, Margaret has three children and Isabelle has three Mr Erturth and his children live at Malta, Montana Mrs. McDougall is with her aged parents in Rockwood, Ontario. Hugh McDougall, the elder, resides at Guelph, Canada, and has never visited Minnesota since his early settlement here

MR. JOSEPH S ROOT,

son of James Root, was born in Wilton, April 16, 1865, and was married to Miss Catharine L McDougall Sept 24, 1891. With their five children, four girls and one boy, they reside on the old James Root homestead, one of the best farms in Wilton. James Root, born Feb 26, 1832, in Cattaraugus county, N Y, came to Wilton in 1859, settling on section 34 He married Miss Hannah Brisbane, daughter of Hon. William Brisbane, Dec 12, 1859 They were the parents of eleven children Charles E, Orin E, William L, Joseph S, Cora B, Hattie M, James A, Maggie J, Freddie, deceased, Dora E. and Marvin L., deceased. Joseph was chairman of the town board of Wilton for several terms and has held other offices In 1900 he was democratic candidate for county commissioner in the Fifth district and lacked only eight votes of an election.

MR EDGAR CRONKHITE,

was born Jan 26, 1826, at Glens Falls, N. Y He entered Williams college in 1845 From 1848 to 1852 he traveled extensively in the South, making headquarters in Washington, D. C. He studied law at Buffalo and was admitted to the bar in 1853 He then came West to Neenah, Wis., where he practiced law and was register of deeds one term He came to Rochester, Minn, about 1860 He served as lieutenant in Company L, Second Minnesota cavalry during the Indian war and from Dec 18, 1863, to May 4, 1866 He enlisted as a private and was promoted to second lieutenant Oct 11, 1864. After his discharge, he returned to Rochester where he practiced law to some extent In 1867 he went to live in Alma City on a farm, which he has since made his home In 1870 he was elected county auditor of this county and served ten years by re-election, although a democrat, the county being largely republican He has always been a generous hearted man without show or parade He is a man of education and of much ability and refinement He has lived a single man, and has no relatives in this section of the country Some years ago his eyesight became impaired and of late he has been nearly blind—not able to read at all

MR C N SMITH,

son of J R Smith, was born in Blooming Grove, Jan 25, 1857 He married Miss Mary A Simons, daughter of Orlando Simons, of Janesville, Aug 17, 1878, and they live on their farm in Janesville, a mile and a half southwest of Elysian They have had three children. Bessie C, born Aug 12, 1879, Frank J., born Mar 27, 1888, died Mar 22, 1889; and Dessie A, born Aug. 10, 1893 Joshua R Smith and wife were early settlers, both American born. Joshua was born Jan 26, 1833, Almeda Smith, daughter of Simeon Smith, was born July 5, 1836. They were married at West Union Iowa, in 1854, and went to live in Blooming Grove, on what is now known as the James Bowe place, in June, 1856. They were the parents of six children Agnes, born at West Union, Iowa, Jan 21, 1855, C. N. Smith, born Jan 25, 1857, Clara Smith, Nov 20, 1859, John, Feb 12, 1861, Ida Dec. 30, 1863 The last four were born in Blooming Grove Etta, the youngest, was born in Elysian, LeSueur county Mr Smith served in the Union army at the time of the Rebellion, and after the close of the war, in 1865, sold his farm in Blooming Grove and engaged in the sawmill business at Elysian for two years He then sold the mill and bought an Elysian farm on which he lived until 1891, when he removed to Delano, Cal, with all his children except C N Mrs. Smith died there Oct 20, 1895, and Mr Smith, July 31, 1900

MR GOTTLIEB GRAMS,

born in Germany, Sept 7, 1828, came to America in 1853, and settled on a farm in Janesville township in 1857. October 16, 1855, he married Miss Louisa Wandrie, who was born in 1833 Four children were born to them Charles, Ottila, Eliza, and Pauline

THE REVEREND GEORGE W MORSE

George Warren Morse was born at Williamstown, Vt April 23, 1847. His wife's maiden name was Lizzie J Baker, and she was born in Erie county, Pa., Dec 22, 1847 They were married at Deerfield, Minn, April 5, 1868 They have one son living, Orwin A Morse, who is director of the music department of Stetson University, DeLand, Florida He is married

In June, 1856, Mr Morse, with his parents, moved to Steele county, Territory of Minnesota, in what afterwards became Deerfield township At the age of seventeen, he began teaching school, and continued this work for twelve years His wife was likewise a school teacher, and at one time taught in the McKune district, Waseca county In 1876 Mr Morse purchased the Mantorville Express and engaged in the newspaper business In 1880 he purchased the Waseca Leader At the same time his former foreman, S M Rose, bought the Waseca County Herald, into which the leader was merged Mr Rose died in 1883, and Mr. J F. Murphy bought Mrs Rose's interest in the business In 1885 Mr Morse sold his interest in the business to J E Child and removed to Battle Creek, Mich, his present place of residence to engage in editorial work with the Review and Herald Publishing company Three years later he was sent by that company to Toronto, Ont, to establish and conduct a large book publishing business He remained in this work nine years.

MRS. ANNA CARMODY.

HON JOHN CARMODY

He then accepted an invitation of the International Medical Missionary and Benevolent association to go to Australia to superintend a sanitarium enterprise. He remained in Australia three years and then returned to Battle Creek where he is now pastor of the Seventh-Day Adventist church at that place, with a congregation of about three thousand people

THE HONORABLE JOHN CARMODY

John Carmody, Jr, attorney-at-law, living at Hillsboro, N D, is a man whose public spirit and excellence of character have never been questioned He is a life-long Jeffersonian Democrat and total abstainer.

Mr Carmody was born in Granville, Milwaukee county, Wis, on Jan [illegible], 1854, and moved with his parents to Waseca county, in the spring of 1868, to the old Lincoln place on the banks of the LeSueur river in Wilton township, where his father, brother, and two sisters still reside He received his education in the common and public schools of Waseca and Faribault, teaching school for several years thereafter.

He next studied law in the office of James E Child, and was admitted to the bar in March, 1880 He held the office of municipal judge and city justice of Waseca In August, 1885, he removed to Hillsboro in the territory of Dakota, now North Dakota, entering into partnership in the practice of law with Hon L E Francis, a boyhood friend

On July 12, 1886, he was united in marriage with Miss Anna Madden, eldest daughter of the late Malachi Madden, of Waseca county. Three children have been born to them: Winifred M, now a student at Villa Maria, Montreal, Canada, Irene Frances and George Christie, in attendance at the Hillsboro schools.

Mr Carmody is widely known in fraternal society circles and holds membership in the American Order of United Workmen, Independent Order of Foresters, Knights of Columbus, Brotherhood of American Yeoman, and the Elks

For twenty-five years he has been an enthusiastic fireman, having been a member of the department while in Waseca and also taking an active part in the Fireman's Association of North Dakota He is now president of the state organization He has held the office of city attorney of Hillsboro for fourteen years, has served as mayor of the same city, and as prosecuting attorney of Trail county, North Dakota.

Mrs Carmody was born in Blooming Grove, June 29, 1862 She received her education in her home district, in Professor Carman's select school and Waseca's public schools She taught in the various schools of the county for a number of years

MR MALACHI MADDEN,

lately deceased, was born in Ireland, near the city of Tuam, on Nov 3, 1828 He came to America when but a youth of sixteen years and took up his residence at New Orleans, La From this city he moved to St Louis, Mo, where he lived for twenty years Sept 9, 1861, he was married to Miss Mary Loftus, of the same city, and came North to Waseca county, settling on the old Isaac homestead, in Blooming Grove. There were but few people save Indians in the vicinity at that time, but this young pioneer had most abundant faith in the future of Minnesota Always sober and industrious, he labored faithfully for forty-one years to subdue the wilderness that surrounded his home and saw Waseca county surpass even his fondest dreams of her future greatness.

During the latter years of his life a complication of diseases fastened themselves upon him, against which he fought with indomitable courage, until January 29, 1902, when in his seventy-fourth year, he arose at the call of the Master and journeyed forth into the shadows

Mrs Malachi Madden was born in Galway, Ireland, June 29, 1842 In 1851 her parents came to America and made their home in St. Louis. Mrs. Madden has borne and reared four sons and six daughters. Three daughters are married—Mrs A E Paulson, of Kenmare, Ward county, N. D.; Mrs. John Carmody, of Hillsboro, N D ,and Mrs Richard Maloney, of this county Mrs Madden is a woman of refinement and has performed well her part in life She deserves well of her kindred and neighbors in her declining years

MR MARK POMEROY LESLIE,

now of Wheatland, Wyoming, is the son of Samuel Leslie, of this county, and was born in this county June 6, 1871 He married Miss Laura Jorgenson, of Steele county, in 1898, and they have three children, two sons and a daughter. They moved to Wyoming three years ago where they are engaged in farming

MR OMER H SUTLIEF,

born May 2, 1836, in Warren county, Pa , came to Waseca county in 1856. Dec 11, 1860, he married Mary Holbrook, daughter of Zachariah Holbrook, who settled in Otisco in 1856 They have one son and four daughters Mr Sutlief volunteered in the old First Minnesota regiment in April, 1861, served three years and three months, taking part in twenty-one battles, and having one thumb shot off He owns a farm near New Richland, but lives in the village with his family

MR HARRY A READ,

born in Cleveland, Ohio, in 1846, came to Iowa with his parents in 1856 He enlisted in the Union army in 1863, and served until 1865 He commenced railroading as fireman and engineer in 1869. He has run an engine on the W & St P division of the C & N W railroad for over twenty years, and is one of the oldest engineers on the road

MR H W BLUHM,

son of Henry Bluhm, born in Meriden, Steele county, Sept 20 1856 is a prominent farmer of Vivian His father, who was born in Germany in

MALACHI MADDEN.

MRS. MALACHI MADDEN.

1832, came to America in 1854. He married Margaret Beck, also a native of Germany, in 1855, at Guttenberg, Iowa They settled in Meriden early in the summer of 1856 In 1880 H. W. Bluhm married Mary Remund, daughter of John Remund, an early settler Mary was born Sept 2, 1857, in Blooming Grove. They have one son and two daughters. The son and elder daughter are married, the younger daughter being at home They settled on their present farm in 1880 Mr H W. Bluhm was town clerk for eight years, assessor for several years, took the United States census in 1900, and the state census in 1905. He was county commissioner from 1892 to 1896 His father and mother own a farm in Freedom, are still living and reside with him.

MR PATRICK CAMPION,

son of Malachi Campion, was born in Ireland, in October, 1842, and came to America with his parents in 1849 They landed in New York and proceeded thence to Cleveland, Ohio, where they lived three years They then came as far West as Wisconsin and lived near Watertown In 1858 they came to Minnesota and resided near Winona. Some time after, the family moved to near Rochester, Minn. In 1865, Patrick invested in lands in Waseca county and the next year broke thirty-eight acres. His brother John came at the same time and lives a single life Patrick was married in 1871 to Miss Margaret Mahoney, at Rochester, Minn They are the parents of four sons and three daughters Mr. Campion has seven hundred twenty acres of land all under a high state of cultivation, except forty acres of timber His father died August 31, 1885, and his mother, Aug 11, 1894. He was chairman of the town board for seven years and was a school officer of his district for many years He is one of the wealthiest farmers of the county, and enjoys the confidence of all his neighbors He takes an active interest in public affairs—not as a politician but as an independent citizen desiring the welfare of his country

MR. JAMES McGUIGAN,

residing in Iosco, is the son of the late Christopher McGuigan He was born in Wisconsin, May 13, 1865 His father, Christopher, was born in Londonderry, Ireland, in 1822, and came to America when twenty years of age, arriving in the month of September He landed in New York and soon after went to Pittsburg, Pa, where he remained two years. He then went to St Louis, Mo, where he resided several years We next find him in LaFayette county, Wis, where, in 1855, he married Miss Rose Bradley. She was also a native of Ireland. They settled on the farm in Iosco in 1867 They were the parents of three children, two of whom, James and Susan, are living. Mrs. McGuigan died Nov. 1, 1868, and Christopher died April 10, 1900.

"Christie" McGuigan made his money and property by strenuous labor, sober living and sensible economy. He met with a hard loss in 1888, on account of the defalcation of Charles McKenna, county treasurer He was on the bond of that smooth rascal, and suffered a loss, all told in the way of costs, expenses, attorneys, etc, of close to $4,000 Some of the bondsmen slank out of their share, and Tim Sullivan, of Janesville, and Mr McGuigan, had to bear the heavy part of the loss. James and his sister have a fine estate and they seem to enjoy life They have traveled quite extensively. James has indulged moderately in local politics, not on his own account, but for the benefit of others He was an enthusiastic supporter of W. J Bryan.

MR JOHN T JORDAN,

of St Mary, farmer and dealer in cattle and horses, was born in St Mary June 22, 1862. His father was Martin Jordan, who settled in St Mary as early as 1857 Martin, son of James and Mary Jordan, was born in Ireland Nov 12, 1824, and came to America in 1844, landing at New York. He remained in the New England states until 1846 when he went to the South spending three years at St Louis, Mo, in railroad employ, and some time in Illinois at the same business He followed the building of the railroad from Chicago to Milwaukee and thence to Watertown, Wis He then returned to New York state and in 1852 married Mary Gallagher, who was also born in Ireland Her mother's name was Shanley and she was a relative of Bishop Shanley of North Dakota John's parents then came to Illinois where they remained until they came to Minnesota For a number of years, Martin was yard master in the employ of the Illinois Central railroad, and was a brakeman on one of the first trains run by that road He was well acquainted with young Guiteau, the murderer of President Garfield and with Guiteau's father, who worked for the same railroad company Martin, after a well-spent life, died Jan 8, 1904, respected by all who knew him John T was married to Miss Elizabeth Brady, of St Peter, Oct 12, 1896 She was born Oct 15, 1872 John T has been in the cattle and horse buying and selling business, more or less, for the last ten or twelve years, and is a prosperous farmer.

MR EDGAR C TROWBRIDGE,

son of the late Ira C. Trowbridge, founder of the city of Waseca, was born at Woodstock, Ill, about 1854, and came to Waseca with his parents in August 1866. He is president of the Peoples State bank of Waseca, and an extensive owner and dealer in Waseca real estate He was for many years engaged in the hardware business On May 29, 1901, at Sacramento, he married Miss Stratton, daughter of Judge Stratton, of California She is a native of Santa Barbara, Cal Mr. Trowbridge has been an efficient member of the board of education of Waseca for eleven years

MR JOHN A JOHNSON,

born in Otisco, in this county, July 25, 1861, is the son of Charles and Christine Johnson, early settlers in this county His father, Charles Johnson, was born in Sweden Dec. 11, 1829, and came to America about 1852

B. S. LEWIS, ESQ.

He married Miss Christine Anderson, also a native of Sweden, about 1856, while living in Indiana He remained in that state until 1860, when he came to Otisco with his family and made his home on section 16 Here he purchased one hundred sixty acres of land, which he still owns. Some fifteen years ago Charles became so afflicted with rheumatism that he quit his farm and bought him a home in Waseca where he has since resided with his family John A Johnson married Miss Anna Larson, of Idaho. She was born in Sweden in 1869, and came to America while young They are the parents of six children, two sons and four daughters. He owns one hundred sixty acres of land in section 16, and his residence is surrounded by one of the finest groves in the state He has been town supervisor for a number of terms and is prominent in the public affairs of his town

MR. BENEDICT S LEWIS

This gentleman was born in Courtland county, N Y, Dec 20, 1839. He was of Welsh descent, and his father was a clergyman His parents came West to Columbia county, Wis, in 1851, and he came with them He received his education after leaving the public schools, at Union college, N. Y., and at the State University of Wisconsin in Madison He read law with Gregory & Pinney, of Madison, and was admitted to the bar in 1867 He came to Waseca in 1868, where he practiced law the remainder of his life very successfully. In addition to his local business he was the retained attorney of the M & St L railway company from 1884 until the close of his life. He was united in marriage with Miss Mary Eaton, of Wisconsin, July 7, 1869, and four children were born to them, one son and three daughters—Harlow E, Esther, Irma, and Mary E (deceased). Esther is the wife of Mr Guy W Everett, of the firm of Everett, Aughenbaugh & Co., of Waseca Irma is the wife of James M Hanley, Esq, a prominent attorney of Mandan, N D Harlow E is connected with the milling business of Mapleton, Blue Earth county, Minn., and is doing a prosperous business He married a daughter of Hon M R Everett, a lawyer and banker, and for a number of years a state senator, of Waterville, Minn

Mr B S Lewis died of bronchial consumption May 16, 1891, after many years of suffering Judge Buckham and all the members of the bar of Waseca county attended his funeral in a body Mr Lewis was a very thorough student of law and an able attorney, always true to the interests of his clients. He was public spirited and took an active interest in the welfare of his adopted city

MR. W F ROURK,

born at Beechwood, Ontario, Canada, came to Minnesota with his parents when he was nine years of age. His parents settled on a farm in Watertown, Carver county, which they still own and reside upon W F married Miss Mary Suel, at Credit River, Scott county, Minn, in 1882

She was born at Dayton, Ohio, and came to Minnesota with her parents when she was a babe They settled on a farm in Credit River township In 1882 Mr. Rourk engaged in the construction of cement walks at Minneapolis, and carried on the business in the Twin Cities for eighteen years In 1900, he came to Waseca and established a factory for the manufacture of cement stone especially for sidewalks, crossings, curbs, gutters, hitching posts, etc He also owns a neat residence property in Waseca, although he does a great deal of work in other places. Thus far his work has been highly satisfactory, and cement-stone walks are taking the place of lumber walks His address is Waseca, Minn

THE HONORABLE S P. CHILD.

Simeon Potter Child, son of Zabina and Orrilla (Rice) Child, was born Nov 16, 1835, in Medina county, Ohio His boyhood days were spent in Ohio, St Lawrence county, N Y, and in Wisconsin He lived in the latter state from 1844 to 1855. He came to Waseca county in January and February, as elsewhere detailed in this book At the age of twenty-one years, he claimed and pre-empted a quarter section of land on sections 23 and 24 in Wilton township In 1855, as soon as he was able to walk, after freezing his feet so badly, he entered the employ of the United States as chief cook for the employees of the government at the Winnebago Indian Agency In 1856, he was put in charge of a large number of breaking-team crews engaged in breaking lands for the Winnebagoes. Soon after he commenced improving his own claim On the eighth of August, 1858, he was united in marriage with Miss Clarissa Armenia Northrup, daughter of Caleb Northrup, one of the pioneer settlers of this county She was born in the town of Horner, Steuben county, N Y, Nov 5, 1841, and came to Wisconsin a babe in arms, and to Waseca county with her parents in 1856 With the exception of one winter which S P spent as clerk in a Wilton store, he remained upon his farm until the Sioux Indian massacre in August 1862. Upon receiving news of the Indian outbreak, he at once tendered his services to the government, and was formally mustered in as a corporal of Company B, First regiment of Minnesota mounted rangers, Oct 17, 1862. Hon Horace Austin, afterwards governor of our state, was captain of the company His company went into winter quarters at St Peter, after having performed patrol duty on the frontier from the time of enlistment Mr. Child was detailed for hospital duty at St. Peter during a portion of the winter, but was with the company at the hanging of the Sioux at Mankato, Dec 26, 1862. Nothing other than the execution of the Indians transpired during the winter worthy of note He kept a diary while following the Indians of which extracts are here given, as follows

"Tuesday, June 16, 1863—Left Camp Pope, marched about seven miles and camped on the bank of the Minnesota river, called it Camp Crooks.

"Wednesday, June 17 Infantry marched about thirteen miles and camped at Wood Lake We called it Camp Miller. On Thursday, June 18, we made only seven miles and camped at Camp Baker, on the Minnesota river where there is plenty of good water and grass for stock.

"Friday, June 19—Lay in camp all day Weather cold and threatened rain

"Saturday, June 20.—Moved above Camp Release, making about fifteen miles Weather very cold, a little rain. The camp is on the river We call it McPhail.

"Sunday, June 21—Remained in camp Weather continues cold

"Monday, June 22—Broke camp early, made about fifteen miles, crossed the Lac Qui Parle river and camped near a small lake Weather warm and ground very dry.

"Tuesday, June 23—Traveled fifteen miles. The ground is so dry the grass is all dead or has not grown any this season There are no lakes of clear water in this section—only nasty frog ponds There is occasionally a spring, but, as a rule, water is very scarce and of poor quality Camped by a little lake—called it Camp Averill

"Wednesday, June 24—Broke camp at 5 a m, crossed the Yellow Earth river Earth completely parched, and almost all the lakes dry No timber along the river near which we camped.

"Thursday, June 25—Made ten or twelve miles. Country more hilly, uplands bare, some grass in marshes Stone on the surface Camped at a beautiful lake two miles west of Big Stone lake. Named the camp 'Jamison'

"Friday, June 26—Traveled about ten miles Ruble's company killed a buffalo to-day. Five buffaloes were seen on left flank Camped on the Minnesota river.

"Saturday, June 27—Remained in camp—also over Sunday. Plenty of good water by digging ten or twelve feet, and plenty of grass.

"Monday, June 29—Major Buel, with two companies of Rangers, while reconnoitering, found signs of Indians to the southwest

"Tuesday, June 30—A portion of our command was dispatched for Fort Abercrombie for supplies under command of Lieutenant-Colonel Averill Here a mule driver broke his leg Moved about ten miles and camped at a small lake July 1.—Made about twelve miles more Lakes more numerous; water clearer, no timber..... July 2—Scouts saw signs of Indians but no redskins Traveled about ten miles. Vegetation all dead except around margin of lakes. Camped at Skunk lake—water shallow—plenty of fish . July 3—Made about fifteen miles Weather hot, ground stony; grasshoppers in great numbers, water very poor, grass scarce.. .July 4—Marched about twelve miles Grasshoppers very thick, no grass except in sloughs; camped on the Cheyenne river This has a little timber along its banks July 5—A detachment of twenty-five mounted men was sent to Fort Abercrombie, a distance of forty miles Land in this section is of the poorest kind, very little grass and no water. There are elks and buffaloes here Two buffaloes were killed to-day. We arrived at Fort Abercrombie that evening where we stayed over the 6th and into the 7th until the mail arrived from the east On the evening of the 7th we started on our return to the Cheyenne and camped at Rice river Here Latowell got lost. I took Fay and started back to hunt for him, got back to the fort about 2 o'clock next morning On the 8th and 9th we returned to camp on the Cheyenne.. July 10—Remained in camp, on the 11th we moved up the river twelve miles where we found plenty of hay and wood and springs of good water July 12—Sunday, remained in camp all day Found fresh signs of Indians in vicinity . July 13—Moved ten miles and camped between two small lakes Found plenty of grass, but no wood, and no water except lake water Fresh buffalo tracks numerous July 14—Traveled about fifteen miles Camped on bank of river Plenty of wood and water Weather cold and windy . July 15—Marched about ten miles Found many small lakes, grass better Camped near a good sized lake; water very poor—too much alkali July 16—Made about ten miles, crossing the Cheyenne at Fisk's ford Here Colonel McPhail killed an elk Camped on a muddy lake Grasshoppers not so thick and grass better Ground rolling and stony July 17—Made another move of about ten miles over a broken country with many small lakes, ponds, and marshes, most of them nearly dry now To-day the boys killed an elk, and two half-breed Indians came into camp Camped on the shore of a pond, plenty of grass, but very poor water—no wood July 18—The expedition moved about nine miles and camped on the shore of a beautiful lake Here a man of Company L was accidentally shot by a lieutenant of Company G Remained in camp over Sunday.. July 20—We made a long march, some eighteen miles, over a broken and stony country Water poor—has a brackish taste Weather cold for time of year and no wood. In the evening another man was accidentally shot and wounded Here several half-breed Indians reported war-like Sioux on the James river ..July 21—Made only about ten miles and camped at a lake where there is a little timber July 22—The expedition made about twenty miles and went into camp near a large grove of timber Grass rather poor, water not very good. Here an Indian came into camp .. July 23—Marched about fourteen miles over a broken, stony rolling country with some lakes Camped near a long, narrow lake, had good grass and water, but no wood. Found spring water strongly impregnated with sulphur .July 24—Was an exciting day Got an early start and made about ten miles when we came within sight of a large body of Indians camped about four miles from our army We went into camp about 1 o'clock to await results The train was brought into corral by a shallow lake under the shadow of a high hill, called Big Mound The Indians appeared in large numbers on this mound and in larger numbers still at the west of it They asked to have a personal conference with General Sibley, but he, having been warned of treachery, declined Doctor Welser, surgeon of the mounted rangers, however, ventured to go among the Indians, many of whom he knew personally, and returned to the Sibley camp saying that they only wanted peace He was permitted, at his own request, to return to the top of Big Mound, with two or three other rangers, and was almost immediately shot and killed. His companions escaped by fast riding and the poor marksmanship of the murderous Indians General Sibley immediately ordered the Minnesota mounted rangers to attack the Indians. They did so, followed by companies of the Sixth and Tenth infantry regiments The ground was so rough and steep that the rangers had to dismount and fight their way up the hill on foot, driving the Indians before them A terrific thunder storm occurred during this battle, and John Murphy, of Waseca County, was killed by lightning within a few yards of me. One section of the battery was brought into action and did most effective service The Indians had a dread of artillery and soon began to retreat. The battery and the mounted rangers followed them closely until the artillery horses tired out and could go no further The rangers continued the pursuit, following the Indians closely for about fifteen miles The Indians were completely routed and demoralized. They threw away everything that would impede their retreat Several Indians were killed and many wounded The horses were tired and the pursuit ceased about sundown. Besides Murphy, who was killed by lightning, a man named Stark was killed by being shot in the abdomen Lieutenant Freeman, while hunting in the morning, had been waylaid and killed, and his body badly mutilated Wm Hazlep, was shot in the shoulder, and Andy Moore was shot in the thigh and bowels A sergeant of Company L received a wound in one leg We had no ambulance, and carried our dead and wounded in buffalo robes for some distance, and finally loaded them into an ammunition wagon We traveled all night in returning to camp"

Captain Wilson, in his account of the expedition, says the mistake of the campaign occurred at the close of the battle that day Lieutenant Beaver brought an order to Colonel McPhail to "return" to camp General Sibley said his order was to "go into camp"

As Lieutenant Beaver soon after died, the mistake or blunder rests with him No doubt the mistake was made either by Beaver or McPhail, for General Sibley had started the infantry out in the morning to support the rangers before the latter reached the camp The cavalry should have camped upon or near the battle field and awaited the arrival of the infantry The Indian squaws and children were close by. They could not have escaped if they had been pursued the next day But, on account of the blunder, they got two days the start

On the 26th of July, at Dead Buffalo lake, the Indians made a dash for some men and mules that were out gathering hay The mounted rangers at once went to the rescue and charged upon the Indians It was a smoky day, and the horses of whites and Indians made such a dust that it was often difficult to distinguish friend from foe The fight lasted for half an hour when the Indians made a hasty retreat. The savages were led by Grey Eagle, who fought bravely but was soon killed. The Indians left several of their number dead on the field

The last battle was at Stony Lake. As the train was moving along on the morning of July 28, the Indians appeared in great numbers mostly mounted warriors, and attacked with great boldness. They made frequent charges but were easily repulsed The artillery was too much for them, and they soon abandoned the field and made haste to cross the Missouri river"

This terminated the campaign and the troops soon after commenced the homeward march

Mr Child was mustered out November 9, 1863 He returned to his farm for a few days and then went into the quartermaster's department and went South with the Federal army He was placed in charge of the Little Rock & Memphis railroad, where he encountered more dangers than when in the ranks He was engaged in the transportation of men and supplies and in keeping the road in repair He returned home in the spring of 1864, with his health much impaired. He remained ill for nearly two years, but finally got better, sold his property in Waseca County, and removed to Blue Earth City, where he engaged in private banking, real estate and collections He also opened a brick yard and manufactured brick for a number of years

He served in the state legislature as a member of the house from Faribault county in the years 1872, 1873, and 1877, and as a member of the senate in 1874 and 1875 He was appointed assistant postmaster to the United States senate in 1875, and held the position until June 29, 1878, when he was appointed postoffice inspector. He held this position continuously until June 30, 1886, when he resigned He was requested by Postmaster-General Vilas to serve in the Department of Justice to aid in the prosecution of the star-route thieves and he remained in that capacity until January 14, 1887. The latter years of his service as inspector were largely devoted to the work of detecting and bringing to trial the star-route rascals, and in that work he traversed large portions of New Mexico, Texas, Kansas, Nebraska, Indian Territory, and California In New Mexico he drove one pair of horses over one thousand miles in searching for witnesses and looking up evidence

In 1887 he came home and gave attention to his private affairs, remaining until July 27, 1889, when he was again appointed postoffice inspector This time he held the position until April, 1893, when he resigned to accept the agency of the American Surety company of New York, with headquarters at St Paul This position he held for ten years, resigning November 30, 1903 While holding this position he had supervision of portions of Wisconsin, Iowa, all of Minnesota and all of the two Dakotas.

Since that time he has devoted his attention to the management of his large farm, five miles east of Shakopee, known as the Barden farm. Mr and Mrs. S. P. Child have been the parents of six children, four of whom are living Ruth, now Mrs Forrester, of St Paul, Eugenia, Mrs John McLoughlin, of Blue Earth, Edith, Mrs. Andrew Bottleson, of Blue Earth; and Hugh Child, mail route agent between St. Paul and Omaha

MRS. EMMA A (MOORE) REIBELING

was born in Wilton, December 13, 1857 She married Theodore J. Reibeling July 5, 1880. Theodore was born in the town of St. Mary, April 1, 1859, and died March 18, 1903 Mrs. Reibeling is a daughter of Mr Robert Moore, one of the early settlers of Wilton Nine children were born to Mr. and Mrs Reibeling, six of whom are living: Robert T, born April 27, 1881, Wm. H, born November 30, 1884; Elmer S, born April 6, 1887; Martha I, born September 9, 1890, Theo J, born March 22, 1896, and Leland R, born April 21, 1898 Mrs. Reibeling, with the aid of her children, is bravely carrying on her farm in St Mary and making a comfortable living.

MR. HENRY KROEGER,

of Iosco, was born in Schleswick-Holstein, Germany, February 28, 1832. His wife, Anna (Sommers) was born in the same country August 22, 1842. They came to America in the early spring of 1866, and settled in Iosco, May 8, 1866 They have been the parents of eight children, four of whom are living John, Henry W, Herman O. and Louise

HENRY W KROEGER

Henry resides in Wilton on a farm of one hundred and sixty acres. He was born in Iosco, February 7, 1870 October 30, 1895, he was married to Miss Ida Manthey, of Iosco, who was born October 30, 1869. They are the parents of two girls Henry W is one of the prosperous farmers of his township

THE REVEREND ALVIN KETCHUM.

This gentleman, a Baptist minister, came from Ohio to Rice county, Minnesota, in 1856. He moved to Blooming Grove in 1857, on the "Bliven's Hill," near where John Diedrich now lives He afterwards moved to Morristown where he died in 1863. While living in Blooming Grove, Rev Ketchum and Joshua Smith carried on a shop, the first in the county, for the manufacture of chairs, bedsteads, stools, spinning wheels, woodenware, etc They had a turning lathe run by foot power Rev Ketchum preached in what is known as the Bowe school house up to the time of his death in 1863. His wife died some years before he passed away They left surviving them, Rosalia, now Mrs. W H. Gray; Orrilla, now Mrs D A. Erwin; Charles F, then a young lad, Alvin, since deceased; Wm. K., now a resident of Wisconsin, and Luman, now dead Charles was about a year old when his parents came to Minnesota, and he knows a good deal of the hardships of pioneer life. He is married to Alice Luceba Smith, daughter of the late A C Smith They now live within forty rods of where Mrs Ketchum was born

MR THOMAS McHUGO

This gentleman was among the honest, sturdy farmers that settled in Janesville in 1856 He was born in County Galway, Ireland, in 1825, and came to America in 1845, landing in New York He went thence to the state of Vermont where he worked on a farm seven years In 1852 he came West, stopping in Wisconsin four years, and then coming to the town of Janesville, where he made a fine home, and where he lived until his death, which occurred November 26, 1896, of paralysis He married Miss Hannah Kelly, of Faribault, in 1866, who survived him.

THE HONORABLE JOHN L SAUFFERER

Hon John L Saufferer, one of the 1856 settlers, is a native of Wurtemberg, Germany, and was born January 20, 1821 At the age of twenty-four years, he came to America, landing in New York, from here he made his way to Lawrence county, Ohio, where he found steady employment as a farm laborer, thus fitting himself for the calling in which he has been so successful He then went to Clay county, Ill, and purchased a farm of his own At the age of thirty-one, needing a housekeeper, he returned to his native land, married Miss Henrietta Miller, and again sailed for the "land of the free" where they arrived safely without any incident of note After some five years, he sold his Illinois farm and came to Blooming Grove They are the parents of twelve children, ten of whom are living He was elected a member of the lower house of the legislature in 1872, where he served with fidelity to his constituents He is one of the wealthiest men in the township, and, in politics, is a Populist or free-coinage advocate He has always been popular with the people of his town, having held some town office nearly every year since the town was organized He is at this writing in his eighty-fifth year and remarkably well preserved

The following named children were born to them George, born October 25, 1852, deceased; Henrietta, born November 14, 1853, Charles John, born March 19, 1855, Maria Anna, born January 26, 1857, Caroline, born April 9, 1859, Matilda W., born December 1, 1860, deceased, Henry, born October 12, 1862, Amelia J, born September 19, 1864, Lydia, born October 23, 1866, John G, born February 25, 1869; Benjamin, born January 6, 1874, and Louis, born June 27, 1876

MR FRANK ERFURTH

This gentleman was born at Madison, Wisconsin, April 13, 1863 He came to Minnesota in 1884, and married Miss Annie R McDougall, January 1, 1886 She was born in Otisco, Minn, July 22, 1868. They resided

MR. AND MRS. FRANK ERFURTH.

in this county until 1898, when they emigrated to Malta, Montana, where Mr Erfurth still resides Mrs Erfurth while here on a visit in 1902, was taken ill of typhoid fever and died October 25, 1902 Three children were born to them Mary A, February 10, 1887, Robert F, February 25, 1888, and Ronald E, April 19, 1890 Mr Erfurth carried on a sheep ranch for a number of years, but is now engaged in the grocery and confectionery business He was at one time elected sheriff in the county where he now lives, but declined to serve. His children are with him in his Montana home

MR SAMUEL DODGE

was among the early settlers of this county, having moved near Wilton in 1856 His family came the next year He was born in the state of New York about 1823 He married Myra Azuba Dix, who was born in Pennsylvania about the year 1827. They were the parents of eleven children five of whom are living: Hon D J Dodge, of Janesville, Mrs P. C Bailey and Mrs. N Garland of Waseca, and Mrs Myers and Mrs Draper of California. Mr. Dodge started from this county to Missouri, but died before reaching his destination There has always been some suspicion that he was murdered on the road, although no official investigation was ever made.

MR SETH W LONG,

one of the most popular sheriffs Waseca county ever had, was born in the state of New York, June 29, 1821 He married Sarah Broughton December 6, 1842 She was a native of England, born June 23, 1821, and died at Janesville, March 8, 1876, of congestion of the lungs Nine children were born to them—three sons and six daughters—four of whom are now living Mr and Mrs Long resided upon a farm on the east shore of Lake Elysian, afterwards kept a hotel at Okaman, and in 1863 moved to Wilton where they kept hotel Mr Long was elected sheriff in 1868 and held the office for ten consecutive years He was not a money-getter, but he was an honest man and a good neighbor

MR. GEORGE WILFRED STRONG

is a son of Nathan E. Strong, one of the very early settlers of Waseca county, who now resides in California The maiden name of G W Strong's mother was Sarah Ide She was one of the 1855 settlers of Minnesota G W is one of the 'Wilton group" of four boys, and was born in Wilton May 31, 1867 His parents came to Waseca soon after and remained here until about 1885 when they removed to Pomona, California, where they still reside George W returned to Waseca in 1897, and entered the mill of Everett, Aughenbaugh & Co He and Miss Jennie Aughenbaugh were united in marriage February 8, 1898. They are the parents of one son, Harry. Mr. Strong is still in the milling business as miller He is also president of the Water and Light commission of Waseca and is well qualified for the position

MR. JOSEPH CLAYTON

This gentleman is one of the pioneers of Woodville, having come to the romantic shores of Gaiter lake in April, 1857 He was born in England, July 24, 1830, and came to America in 1852 His father Matthew, came over to America in 1851, and they made their home at North Lee, Mass., where Joseph engaged in the manufacture of woolen cloth He afterwards resided at Uxbridge

In 1856 there came to the New England residents glowing accounts of Minnesota as a very paradise, and Joseph and his father decided to come West and get land. They left their Massachusetts home April 7, 1857, in company with ten others. Three days after they started, a number of the company got homesick and returned The others came on and reached Lake Pepin, which was still closed by ice There they were compelled to transfer from Reeds Landing to Red Wing by stage At Red Wing they met posters issued from the Pioneer office calling for volunteers to fight the Ink-pa-du-tah band of Sioux Indians that had murdered over forty people near Spirit Lake and carried four women into captivity—Mrs. Marble, Mrs. Noble, Mrs. Thatcher and Miss Gardner. Of these, Mrs Thatcher and Mrs Noble were killed and Mrs Marble and Miss Gardner were afterwards released. This report of Indian fighting was too much for all the company except the Messrs Clayton, and all save them returned to Massachusetts The Messrs. Clayton came on and took a half section of land, less that portion of Gaiter lake included in the half section They arrived here the latter part of April. They did some early breaking and planted corn, potatoes, etc The elder Mr Clayton returned in the fall, leaving Joseph to bachelor housekeeping and pioneer life Joseph knew little or nothing of farm life or farm work. Everything went awry. The oxen that he bought would run away on slight provocation and he was obliged to lead them with ropes. He had never done any chopping timber or felling trees, and when he went to "hooking" government timber with the other fellows, on the island, the "Yankees" had some sport at his expense His trees wouldn't fall where they ought, and when he came to loading his first load of logs, he lost all patience After finally getting the logs on he went only a short distance when his sled broke down, and he was compelled to leave his load It was only by the most persistent perseverance that he accomplished his farm work The winter of 1857-8 was a very cold one—nobody knows how cold. Along about the first of March, Mr. Clayton greased his shoes and put them under the stove to dry when he went to bed The next morning he found them burned to a crisp He had no other shoes and was obliged to go without for a time When at work out doors he used to draw his pantaloons down over his feet and tie them over his toes with a cord. On one occasion, in March, 1858, he had nothing but potatoes to eat.

They soured in his stomach, so he and his neighbor, McKinstry, took some seed corn to one of their neighbors and ground it in a coffee mill thereby enabling them to indulge in corn bread made of water, salt and meal But soon after, two of his cows commenced to give milk, his hens produced some eggs, and he lived off the fat of the land

In the fall of 1858, having enjoyed batching alone for over a year, he concluded to return to the land of steady habits There he again engaged in the manufacture of woolen goods. He was superintendent of woolen mills at Lowell, Mass, for eleven years He then took a trip to Europe, visiting his old home in England He came to Minnesota again in 1875, spent a short time here and then went to Rhode Island where he accepted the position of superintendent of the Carolina mills, owned by Roland Hazzard, a very wealthy man whose wife was an Indian woman He remained there until 1877. He then spent some six months in Laconia, N. H, and three months in Philadelphia, working at his trade In 1878 he returned to his land in Woodville and began improvements on it C. I Woodbury, a nephew of Mr Clayton's second wife, came out with him They cleared and broke a quantity of land ready for a crop for the ensuing year and erected a large farm house and other farm buildings Soon after, Mr and Mrs C. I Woodbury were married and moved to the farm here Mr. Clayton then accepted the position of superintendent in the Lawrence, Mass., woolen mills where he remained until 1881, when he came West to Jacksonville, Ill, and took charge of the Jacksonville woolen mills. He was in charge of these mills until 1886, when he bought an interest in a large grocery store with his son-in-law, Mr Wm A Jenkinson. They soon after changed it into a wholesale establishment and are now running it as such

Mr Clayton married Miss Urania Taft, his first wife, March 31, 1857, by whom he had two daughters—Mrs Susan Woodbury of Waseca, and Mrs Ellen Jenkinson, of Jacksonville, Ill His first wife died in May, 1865

He married his second wife, Miss Harriet Ann Chase, at Pelham, N H January 1, 1872, by whom he also has two daughters, Annie Urania and Maud, both of whom are at home

John Taft, who works his Woodville farm, is a nephew of his first wife.

For a number of years Mr Clayton has spent his summers in Minnesota and occasionally rehearses the experiences of his first two seasons on his farm in Woodville. He tells a story of a kingbird that lived during the winter and spring in an old treetop that he had hauled up in front of his cabin The kingbird, as is well known, is a great fighter, and Mr. Clayton took great satisfaction in watching his pet pitch into the hawks that hovered around watching for chickens

Mr. C I Woodbury, who married Susan Clayton, is a nephew of Mr Mr. Clayton's second wife Mr and Mrs Woodbury have purchased one hundred acres of the original half section, and Mr Clayton has added to it fifty-two acres.

MR. AUSTIN VINTON AND SONS

Austin Vinton, whose life, public services and death are noted elsewhere, was born in 1816. He settled in Woodville, September 29, 1856 He had two sons. Wilfred Vinton was born in Ellington, N Y, December 11, 1843 He married Ada M Beebee in 1874. She was born at Mt Vernon, Ohio, in 1849, and died in 1892 One son was born to them, Herbert W, in 1879 Wilfred enlisted in Company F, First Battalion, Minnesota Volunteers, March 22, 1865, and was mustered out July 14, following

W H Vinton was born at Ellington, N Y, in 1847 He married Emma Garver in 1872 She was born in Billingsville, Ohio, in 1845 They have one daughter, Julia, born in 1874

Both the Vinton 'boys" are now residents of Owatonna, W H. being engaged in the drug business

MR CHARLES N NORTON

of the 'Wilton group of four," was born in the village of Wilton, November 2, 1865 He is the only son of Mr. H P. Norton, who built and operated the first blacksmith shop in Wilton The family came to Waseca in 1868 Charles was reared in Waseca and educated in our public schools Upon leaving school he entered the service of the American Express company and continued therein for twenty years The last twelve years of this service he was traveling auditor in Western Minnesota and South Dakota, with headquarters at Mankato, Minn, and Huron, S D He married Miss Mattie Simpson, of Mankato, March 28, 1894 She was born in December, 1871 They have been the parents of two children, the older of which died some years ago. Mr Norton has retired from the express business entirely, and devotes his attention to the management of the large estate belonging to his father and himself

THE HONORABLE CHARLES A SMITH

This gentleman was born in Wilton, June 12, 1866, and came to Waseca with his parents in the fall of 1870 He received his education in the public schools of Waseca, and finished with a business course at Minneapolis He worked for some time in the Waseca coffin factory, but had to abandon it on account of his health. He worked off and on at the printer's trade in the Radical office for several years prior to his father's death Since then he has been engaged in the management of his own and his sister's estate He held the office of mayor of Waseca for six consecutive terms from 1898 to 1904 inclusive He was deputy county treasurer from 1889 to 1901 under Dieudonne, and for six months under Krassin He is one of the four boys that were born in Wilton and are now living in Waseca

MR. WALTER S. BROWN,

manager of the extensive dry goods, grocery and boot and shoe store of H. A Brown & Son, of Waseca, is a native Minnesotan He was born at Rochester, Minn., May 10, 1870, and received his education in the public schools of that city His father, H A. Brown, was one of the very early settlers at Rochester, Minn, having invested in property there in 1855, and settled there permanently in 1856. H A Brown built the second frame building erected in that town, and engaged in the mercantile business Walter, upon leaving school, entered the mercantile business. In 1889 he married Miss Maud A. Toogood, of Rochester, who died at Waseca in 1896, leaving three children

Walter came to Waseca in 1891, and with his brother, R W Brown, commenced business under the firm name of H. A. Brown & Sons They erected the large, double store where they have since done business. Some years ago R W. withdrew from the firm and since then Walter has managed the business Walter married his second wife, Miss Mary Kurkowski, of Waseca, in 1900. Her parents were among the early settlers of the city of Waseca and highly respected The name of the present firm is H A Brown & Son, it enjoys a lucrative trade.

MRS VIOLA PATCH

This lady and her husband were residents of this county for a number of years, but now reside at Motley, Minn The parents of Mrs Patch—Mr and Mrs Orrin Pease—came to this county in 1862 Mrs. Patch writes that Mr Pease was born in Ohio, May 1, 1813, and from there moved to Illinois at an early day Her mother, whose maiden name was Mary J. Turner, was born in Cayuga county, N Y, Nov 9, 1829 Mary J Turner first married Oscar F Eaton, with whom she lived in Chicago until his death. Soon after his death, she removed to DeKalb county, Ill, where she met and married Mr. Pease in 1859 In 1862 Mr and Mrs Pease moved to this county by horse team and lived in St Mary, not far from Wilton Mrs Pease had at that time two children, Wm Eaton, now a resident of Woodville, and Mrs Patch, who was born in Illinois Aug 27, 1860 Soon after their arrival here, Mr Pease's horses were stolen, but subsequently he recovered them. At the time of the Indian outbreak, in 1862, the family went to Faribault, but shortly afterwards returned to this county About 1865, they settled on a farm on the township line between Otisco and Woodville, where Mr Pease died Feb. 10, 1894, and where Mrs Pease died Feb 20, 1903

There was one little incident in their lives worthy of note It was while all the country was flooded with water in the early part of 1867 Mr and Mrs. Pease made a trip from their farm to Wilton, having Viola with them. When they arrived on the east side of the Le Sueur river they found the bottom lands covered with water and water running over the road, but they made an attempt to cross. When well out into the water, the oxen went with the current a short distance and finally the wagon struck a snag, and there was danger that the family and the oxen would be drowned A number of men, among them Buel Welsh, who saw the accident, went to the relief of the persons in peril and finally saved them and the oxen from drowning Mr Pease was unable to get his wagon out until the waters subsided some weeks later.

Mr. Patch is of New England parentage, and came to Waseca county about 1880 Mr and Mrs. Patch removed to Morrison county about 1884

CAPTAIN R MILLER.

This gentleman was born in Burg, near Trarbach, on the Mosel, Rhine Province of Prussia, July 17, 1843 His parents came to America in 1848 and made their home in Fond du Lac county, Wis, where they resided until the breaking out of the Rebellion. R. Miller was one of the first of our patriotic young men to enlist for the defense of the Union. He joined the First Michigan Volunteer cavalry June 15, 1861, and served until Sept 13, 1865, when he was mustered out. He was a member of Company E, and served in the Army of the Potomac under Generals Banks, Geary, Pope, McClellan, Burnside, Hooker, Meade, and Grant, and under Corps Commander P H Sheridan, Brigadier Commander Custer, Division Commander Kilpatrick.

He was wounded in the cavalry fight at Buckland Mills, Va, Oct 19, 1863, and was taken prisoner at Trevillion Station, Va, June 11, 1864 He was paroled Feb. 24, 1865, and mustered out of the service in September, 1865

After the Rebellion he opened a retail store at Lomira, Dodge county, Wisconsin, and continued the business until 1872, when he came to Waseca, arriving in February Here he engaged in the sale of general merchandise, and followed the business for twenty-seven years. He was the efficient cashier of the Citizens State Bank of Waseca from the time of the death of Mr Swenson, in 1898, to the close of the year 1902

Mr Miller and Miss Julia A Snider were united in marriage Feb 26, 1867 Mrs Miller is a native of West Virginia, born in 1848 Her parents and grandparents were born in Virginia, and at the time of Mrs Miller's marriage her parents resided at Grafton Captain and Mrs. Miller are the parents of eight children, three sons and five daughters Of the daughters, two are married—Mrs E A Everett and Mrs E W Ward John Miller, the eldest son, has charge of the New Richland flouring mill. The second son, Harry, is an active partner in the Lakeville flouring mills at Lakeville, Minn Hugo, the youngest son, is with his father in Louisiana

Since the first of the year 1903 Captain Miller has had charge of the business of the Sabine Canal Company, with headquarters at Vinton,

R. MILLER.

La. This company furnishes water for the irrigation of thousands of acres of rice lands and receives its income from a share of the rice crop produced James Quirk and E A. Everett are largely interested in the enterprise

Captain Miller aided in organizing Company K of the Minnesota National Guards and served as captain and drill master of the company for some time.

MR EDWARD CASTOR,

son of Mr. Jacob Castor, was born at New Ulm, Sept, 26, 1857 His father was born in Germany, Oct 6, 1831, and settled in New Ulm in 1856. At the time of the Indian massacre, in 1862, his father was mistaken for an Indian and killed by his friends. It was at the second battle of New Ulm, August 23, in the evening Jacob had been fighting Indians all day Towards night, while the rain was falling, he took a basket of bread from his bakery, and, throwing a blanket over his shoulders, started to carry the provisions to some people whose houses had been burned and who had no provisions of their own It was just twilight, the rain was falling, and some of the armed men in a building with port holes mistook him for an Indian and fired upon him while he was trying to make himself known to them. He was wounded and fell, but arose and was about to enter his own house when he was again shot He died the next morning of his wounds It was indeed a sad death In 1867, Edward's mother married Conrad Zeller, since deceased Mrs. Zeller and one daughter still reside in New Ulm

Edward came to Waseca in the fall of 1875 Having learned the trade of jeweler, he was employed by John F Preston, of Waseca, for whom he worked two and one-half years In 1878 Mr Castor opened a jewelry establishment of his own He married Miss Rose M Wollschlaeger, Jan 2, 1882 She is a daughter of Mr. August Wollschlaeger, and was born Feb 20, 1861 Mr and Mrs. Castor have three sons and one daughter Robert J, who is in the jewelry business with his father, was born Oct 12, 1882, Florence C, was born July 9, 1884, Arthur E J. was born Aug 26, 1888; and Harry A., Feb 26, 1895 Mr Edward Castor is an expert workman and a reliable business man He keeps a good stock of jewelry and musical instruments.

MR MICHAEL SHEERAN,

of St Mary, one of the prominent men of that township, was born in Ireland in the year 1840 He came to America in 1860, and to Waseca county in 1862, after having lived in Michigan about two years. He made an extensive tour of Minnesota and returned that fall by way of Ashland, on Lake Superior, to Michigan He worked in the copper mines of Michigan until 1865 when he again came to Minnesota This time he bought land on the Winnebago reservation, section 18, St. Mary, paying therefor $2.60 per acre He later worked for some time in Faribault Feb 19, 1867, he married Miss Mary Dardis, of Blooming Grove, daughter of Mr John Dardis of that township. She is also a native of Ireland and was born in 1843, coming to America in 1859 with her parents and settling in Blooming Grove in 1866 Mr and Mrs Sheeran have four sons and five daughters living, one daughter having died Mr Sheeran and his sons have taken up a large tract of land in North Dakota to which they have already secured title He is still living on the old farm where he settled in 1867.

THE REVEREND O A MELLBY

Pastor O A Mellby was born in the parish of Hurdale near Christiania, Norway, Jan 9, 1843 He worked on his father's farm and attended the parish school until his eighteenth year, when he entered a Latin school in Christiania. After having finished the college course, he went to the Royal University, where he graduated as bachelor of theology in 1872 Already having as a student received a call as pastor of Le Sueur river and northern Waseca congregations in this county, he was ordained in the cathedral as a minister of the gospel by Rt Rev J. L Arup, archbishop of Christiania, in October, in November of the same year he started for America Arriving at New Richland in December, he found everything in a primitive state,—a small log church and no parsonage He had to live with a farmer in a very small house the first winter, which was a very severe one. For many years he served seven congregations in Waseca, Steele and Blue Earth counties He had to be on the road much of the time and experienced many hardships. Three pastors are now working in the same field His present charge consists of Le Sueur river, New Richland and Berlin churches The progress of these churches is marked by magnificent church buildings, supplied with fine bells and pipe organs and a very convenient and commodious parsonage for the free use of the pastor In 1867 he was married to Miss Sigrid Grunot of Christiania They have had eight children, of whom five are living Carl August, doctor of philosophy and professor at St Olaf college, Northfield, Agnes Theodora, preceptress at the same institution; Oscar Fredrich, M D, of Warren, Minn, Marie Elizabeth, music teacher at home, and Gisle Bernhard, photographer, of Waseca, Minn

MR HARVEY S. SMITH

Both the father and grandfather of this gentleman settled in this county in 1855, and Harvey was born in Woodville, March 7 1859, his father being Alfred C Smith, deceased He attended his district school, is a graduate of the Waseca high school and of the Mankato State Normal school He taught in the public schools of the state twelve years He commenced carrying the United States mail on route No. 3, from Waseca, July 20, 1903, and is still so employed He owns his grandfather's old farm in Blooming Grove, and one of his brothers is carrying it on The buildings—house and barn—are among the oldest in the county The frame barn was built as early as 1858, and the frame house as early as 1863. The frames of both are made of heavy timbers put together by mortise and tenon and fastened together with wooden pins The buildings on the farm, though aged, are well preserved, and Harvey is justly proud of the old homestead with its historic surroundings.

Harvey held the office of justice of the peace for several years and is now school district clerk. He married Miss Eugenia Owens, of Mankato, August 28, 1900 She was born in Steuben county, N Y, March 5, 1872, and came to Minnesota with her parents in 1897 Mr and Mrs Smith have one son a year and a half old Mr Smith's father and mother were the parents of fourteen children, ten of whom are living, namely Mary, Lovica, Harvey S, Willis, Luceba, Nellie, Jennie, Clara, Celia, and Jasper

DOCTOR FRED A SWARTWOOD

Dr F A Swartwood is a native of Minnesota, born at Cannon City, Rice county, Minn., Dec 8, 1860 His father, Hon. Henry A. Swartwood, is a native of Pennsylvania, but came to Minnesota in 1857, settling at Cannon City Dr. Swartwood attended the public schools of his district, took a four-year elective course at Carleton College and graduated from the medical college at Ann Arbor, Mich, in 1886 He and Miss Ida M. Poe were joined in marriage Nov 20, 1886 They moved to the city of Waseca the same fall, where they have since resided Mrs Swartwood was born in Rice county in 1863 They have two children one daughter, Madeline, and one son, Harold The doctor has had an extensive practice since his first year and has been interested meanwhile in other business enterprises. He was the first president of the Waseca Savings and Loan Association, is president of the Waseca telephone company, is a stockholder of the W. J Armstrong wholesale company of Waseca, owns a farm of seven hundred and twenty acres in Kandiyohi county, was for one term a member of the Waseca board of education, served as president of the Waseca Commercial Club in 1903, and took an active part in securing the paving of Second street. He has been postmaster of Waseca since the first year of President McKinley's administration For many years he has been very active in party politics, and has often furnished "inspiration" for the local papers of his party He is temperate in his habits and capable of performing an immense amount of labor

MR. JOHN J ISKER

This gentleman was born in Buffalo county, Wisconsin, Dec 30, 1878 His father, Rev Herman E. Isker, was born in Holstein, Germany, Aug

6, 1847, and came to America about the year 1865. His mother was born in Saxony, Germany, Sept. 22, 1852, and came to America when about seven years of age John's parents were married in Buffalo county, Wis, in 1872, and came to Minnesota about 1881. The father, being a clergyman of the German Evangelical church, has moved from place to place since From 1886 to 1900 the family resided at Mankato, and John J attended the Mankato high school from which he graduated in 1899 After graduating he taught school in Cottonwood county three winters. The family came to Waseca in 1900, and soon after John commenced the study of law with ex-Mayor Moonan, of Waseca He took the state examination and was admitted to the bar in September, 1903. He at once commenced the practice of his chosen profession in Waseca He was appointed city clerk of Waseca in the spring of 1904, and elected to the same office in the spring of 1905.

MR SERENAS HOWARD FARRINGTON

Editor Farrington, of the Waterville Advance, was born Oct. 31, 1859, in Otisco, Waseca county, Minn He was reared on a farm, but learned the printer's trade on attaining his majority He has been editor and publisher of the Advance for twenty years. He married Miss Nellie Berner, at St Charles, Minn, Oct 15, 1884 She was born at Manchester, Wis, Feb. 25, 1862 They have living one son, William S, and two daughters, Mary Helen and Minnie Etta One daughter, Myrtle, died in infancy. Mr. Farrington was school director at the age of twenty-one, in Waseca county Since residing in Waterville he has been village recorder four years, member of the school board six years and for three years president thereof, was appointed postmaster Jan 19, 1899, and served five years He is a member of the Waterville lodge I O of O F, of the K. P lodge, being past C C, of the Sakatah Masonic lodge No 32, now serving as its Master, and is King of Royal Arch Chapter No 56 Mr Farrington owns the only paper published in the village and is doing a good business, and serving well the village of his choice.

MR. JOHN FAIRLEY.

This gentleman hails from Scotland, being a native of Lanarkshire He came to America in 1862, and lived near Janesville, Rock county, Wisconsin He spent five years in that state and then came to Wilton, in this county, in the spring of 1867 He was accompanied by his brother, Hugh, and settled on what was known as the Baker claim, in section number 15 He served as clerk of school district No 91 for twenty years He married Miss Bessie Henderson, April 1, 1869. She is also a native of Scotland, having been born in Sterlingshire.

They have two sons and four daughters A few years ago they retired from their farm and have since lived in Owatonna where their children may enjoy the advantages of Pillsbury Academy Their son Andrew carries on the Wilton farm and is also town clerk of Wilton.

JAMES ERWIN CHILD

The family name of Child, or Childs, as some write it, is English without any doubt History agrees with tradition in that respect Josiah Child, born in 1630, was for many years at the head of the East India Company Charles II made him a baronet and his son became Earl of Tylney, but with him the peerage expired and the name sank to the common level Since then every Child has been called upon to "paddle his own canoe"

According to the family record as handed down from father to son, Elijah Child stands at the head of this branch of the Child family in America He, in company with two brothers, came from Old England to New England in Colonial days, some years prior to the American Revolution It is said that he married a Welsh woman, but the writer has never been able to get her father's name Elijah first settled in Connecticut on the banks of the river of that name and engaged in the flour or grist-mill business He afterwards moved to Sharon, Windsor county, Vermont, where he again engaged in the milling business on White river Elijah served for a time in the Continental army, but was obliged to return home on account of illness. Shortly after the War of the Revolution, he lost nearly everything by a flood, his mill dam giving way, and he and his family were reduced to moderate circumstances in his declining years Elijah's children, seven in number, were all boys Stephen, David, Abner, Artemas, Daniel, Simeon, and Elias. Daniel, J E Child's progenitor, was born Nov 10, 1777, in the state of Vermont There he grew to manhood and was bred a miller When twenty years of age he married Rebecca Howe, who was seventeen She was born April 13, 1780, of Irish parents Daniel followed his trade as miller at Royalton, Vt, until about 1824, when he moved to the town of DeKalb, St Lawrence county, N Y Here he bought a small farm which he carried on until his death, which occurred in 1849, his age being seventy-two years. Daniel and Rebecca had eight children whom they named as follows Delani, Avery, Hannah, Zabina, Clarinda, Martha, Simeon and Eliza

Zabina, father of James E, was born Nov 22, 1808, in Vermont, and at the age of fourteen years was apprenticed to learn the carpenter and joiner trade At the age of twenty, having one year more to serve, he bought his time of "Boss" Dustin, and went to St Lawrence county, N. Y, where he worked as contractor and builder He married Miss Orrilla Rice (originally Roice), of Jefferson county, N Y, Feb 14, 1833, and they settled in the town of DeKalb Orrilla was a native of Jefferson county and was born March 2, 1810, being one of the younger children of Eneas Rice by his second wife, whose maiden name was Sarah Parmenter.

Both Eneas and Sarah were natives of Connecticut Eneas was of Scotch parentage and Sarah of English stock Rice was a Revolutionary soldier and was present at the surrender of Burgoyne's army at Saratoga, Oct 17, 1777 He was the father of nineteen children and died at the age of seventy-five years Grandfather Parmenter was also a soldier of the Revolution

Zabina and Orrilla were the parents of seven children James Erwin, born in Jefferson county, N Y, Dec 19, 1833; Simeon Potter, born in Medina, Ohio, Nov. 16, 1835, Sarah Minerva, born in Ohio, Aug 23, 1837, Reuben Parmenter, born in DeKalb, N. Y, Aug 10, 1840, Julia Maria, born in DeKalb, N Y, Oct 26, 1842, Stephen Rice, born in Trenton, Dodge county, Wis., July 2, 1848, and John Benton, born near Appleton, Wis, Aug 14, 1854 John B died in his native town Nov 21, 1861 Zabina moved with his family in 1834 from his New York home to Medina, Ohio, by horse team Ohio was then a new country There was a severe drouth and extremely hard times about 1836-7, and the family returned to DeKalb, N Y, in the fall of 1837 They remained there on a farm until 1844 when they again moved to Ohio—this time to the town of Perry, Lake county The next spring, leaving his family in Perry, the father pushed on to Wisconsin, where he worked during the season and sent for his family in the fall The mother and children, late in the fall, took boat at Fairport and after a stormy passage landed in Sheboygan, the last days of November, 1844 The father had already selecteda claim, in Dodge county, Wis, five miles south of Waupun, and in January, 1845, moved his family thither He remained in Dodge county—a part of the time in the town of Herman—until 1853, when he removed with his family to Ontagamie county, near Appleton, Wis.

James E taught school in Herman, Dodge county, in the winters of 1851-2, 1852-3 and 1853-4 In October, 1854, he made a trip into the Oconto pineries where he worked on the river and in camp until Dec 19, when he returned to Dodge county and there made arrangements for a winter trip to Minnesota, as elsewhere related in this work He married Miss Justina Krassin April 19, 1856 She is the youngest daughter of Gottlieb and Elizabeth (Gadske) Krassin, deceased, and was born near Posen, Prussia, March 3, 1834 She came to America with her married sister, Mrs. Gottlieb Prechel, in August, 1853 Her parents and brothers followed soon after Her family owned a small farm in Posen, but concluded to sell it and come to a country where they could get more land for less money.

Nine children have been born to James and Justina, three of whom died in infancy The living are Capt Walter Child, of Superior, Wis, Stephen M, of Jackson county, Minn ; George E, of Kenmare, North Dakota, Annie E, now Mrs Frank A Wood, Orrilla Justina, now Mrs. George H. Goodspeed, and Dora M, now Mrs Mark D Ashley, of Jackson, Minn.

James E carried on his farm in South Wilton from 1855 to 1863 when he entered upon the practice of law in Wilton. In the fall of 1863, he commenced newspaper work, and with the exception of about four years spent on a farm in Jackson county, from 1881 to 1885, has made newspaper work his principal business. He was chairman of town supervisors, school district clerk, county attorney, member of the legislature in 1861, and justice of the peace while on his farm in Wilton He was deputy United States marshal in 1863-4, and had charge of the draft in several towns of the county. After that he served as county attorney, judge of probate, superintendent of schools, municipal judge of Waseca from 1890 to 1892, member of the state senate in 1872, member of the house of representatives in 1874, and again in 1883. The latest work of his life thus far is the production of this history—labor more pleasant than profitable He has served as president of the Waseca charter commission since its appointment and organization in 1902

MR FRED W. MAHLER,

senior member of the hardware firm of Mahler and Habein, of Waseca, was born in Neinburg, Province of Hanover, July 27, 1857 He landed at New York May 6, 1874, and arrived at Meriden on the 11th of the same month. For seven years he worked as a farm hand in Steele and Waseca counties He then purchased what was known as the old Parmelee place in Woodville He married Miss Sophia Beese, of Deerfield, March 11, 1881 She was born in Waukesha county, Wis, Jan 6, 1861, and came to Minnesota with her parents when she was five or six years of age Mr and Mrs Mahler at once made their home on their farm, which they improved and cultivated until March, 1898, when Mr Mahler bought the half interest of Mr. W H Roesler in the hardware business of Goodman and Roesler. In 1900 he bought Mr. Goodman's interest also, and carried on the business alone until 1903, when Mr William Habein bought a half interest The firm name is now Mahler and Habein. They do an extensive business. Mr and Mrs Mahler are the parents of seven children, two sons and five daughters The elder son, George E, was born August 1, 1884, and is now clerk in the store Mr Mahler was town assessor of Woodville for three years and is a member of the charter commission of Waseca

HARLOW S LEWIS

Mr Lewis, a Waseca boy, son of the late B S Lewis, Esq, was born July 10, 1872 Upon reaching manhood he engaged in the milling business and has followed that business ever since with the exception of two years when he was engaged in the banking business at Madison Lake, Minn. While at Madison Lake he was mayor from January, 1898, to July, 1898, the only public office he has ever accepted He married Miss Grace L Everett of Waterville, Oct 12, 1898 She was born in Waterville, Minn, Dec 19, 1874 They have two sons one born April 4, 1901, the other

May 15, 1904. In 1903, Mr Lewis bought an interest in the Mapleton mill, and since April of that year, has been general manager of the business of the Mapleton Milling Company. Recently the capital stock of the company was increased to $100,000, and Mr Lewis was chosen president and general manager. He is a young man of marked business ability

THE TIMLIN GROUP.

This group, published in this work, is the only one of five generations of which the author has a record Mrs. Patrick Burke, Mrs. Michael Haley, Mrs John Timlin, Mr. F. J Timlin and Master A. Donald Flaig, constitute the group. The first three came from Pennsylvania to Minnesota in 1858 and have since resided in Iosco. John Timlin, with his parents, brothers and sisters, came to Minnesota from Wisconsin in 1868, and settled in Iosco F J Timlin was born and reared in Iosco, and A Donald Flaig, grandson of Mr. and Mrs. John Timlin, was born in Seattle, state of Washington.

HERBERT CLEVELAND HOTALING,

editor and proprietor of the Blue Earth County Enterprise, was born at Mankato, Minn, Aug 5, 1865. He received his education in the public schools of Mankato and at the Mankato state normal. At the age of sixteen years, he entered the employ of the late John C Wise, publisher of the Review at Mankato, as "printer's devil" At the age of twenty, he performed his first journalistic work in the publication of the "Third District Messenger," a monthly paper devoted to temperance. Always an active temperance worker, he joined the Prohibition party, and at the age of 23 years, attended the state convention and had the honor of being chosen its secretary. As a journeyman printer he worked in the following offices for a time, the Janesville Argus, the North Star, at New Richland, and the Waseca County Herald He also edited and managed the North Star at Lake Mills, Ia, for a short time. In 1888, he founded the Mapleton Enterprise, one of the successful county papers of the state. June 26, 1889, he married Miss Janie L Mann, an educated and accomplished lady of Brownton, McLeod county, Minn Mr Hotaling is at present clerk of the Mapleton board of education, president of the public library association, a director of the Mapleton bank, of the Mapleton Milling Co, of the Mankato Citizens Telephone Co, president of the Euclid Avenue Land Co, of Seattle, Wash, and was for a long time village recorder of Mapleton He attributes his success in life to the fact that he has never used intoxicants or tobacco and has attended strictly to the work he found to do

PROF V. G. PICKETT,

now at the head of the Waseca public schools, was born on a farm near Albert Lea, Minn, June 20, 1874 His parents, located there in 1860

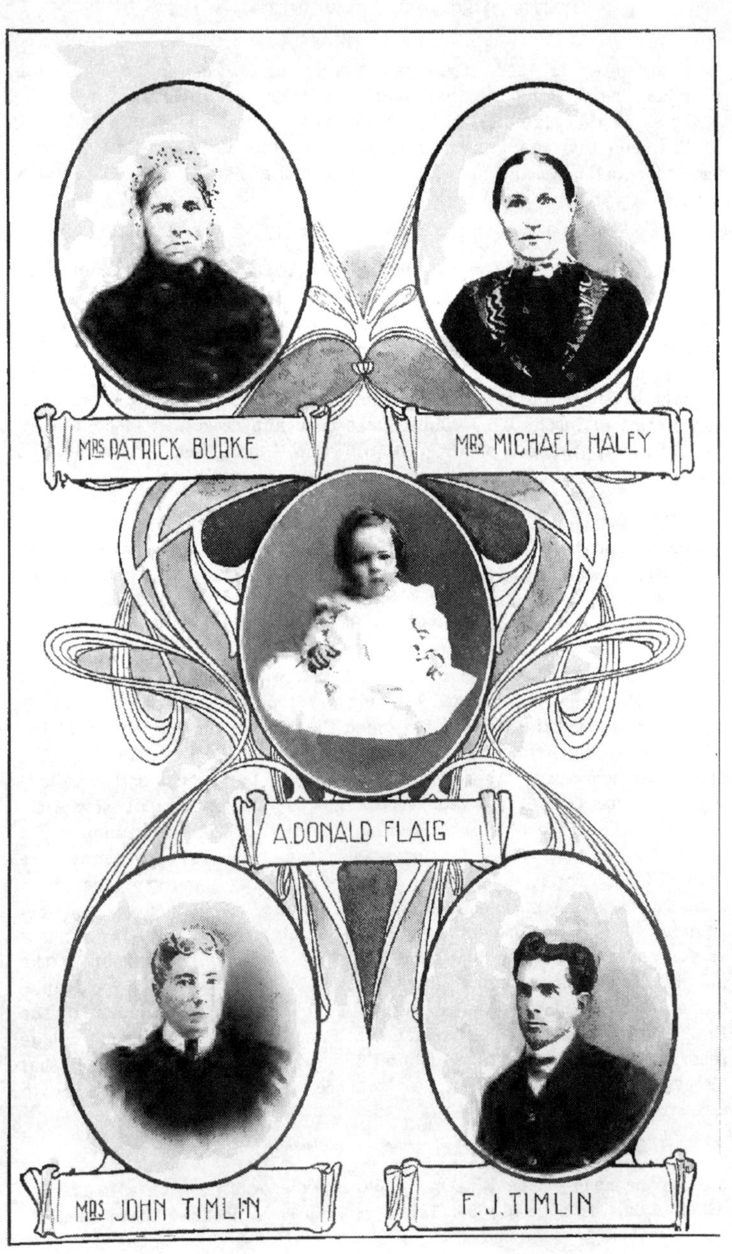
Mrs PATRICK BURKE
Mrs MICHAEL HALEY
A.DONALD FLAIG
Mrs JOHN TIMLIN
F. J. TIMLIN

HON. I. C. TROWBRIDGE.

He attended country school at first, graduated from the Albert Lea high school, took a course at the state university and graduated therefrom in 1896 He commenced teaching as principal of the Stewartville, Minn, schools, taught one year at Long Prairie and six years at Janesville He took charge of the Waseca schools in September, 1904. He married Miss Zada McMillen of Albert Lea, in 1898 She died at Janesville in 1903 without issue. Professor Pickett has traveled in America quite extensively Last year he visited many of the Southern states, Northern Mexico and also Western Canada During his vacation in 1905 he traveled in Eastern Canada and through many of the Eastern states, spending considerable time in the large cities He is enthusiastic in his work as an educator and seems to be very successful in his chosen vocation

HON IRA C TROWBRIDGE

The most prominent figure in the early history of Waseca was Mr Ira C Trowbridge, who, according to his own statement, was born in Lyle, Broom county, in the state of New York, March 16, 1823 He was the son of Henry and Betsey (Lockwood) Trowbridge, they being among the early settlers of that section. He learned the tanner's trade with his father, and remained in his native state until he was of age. About that time he came west as far as Chicago, and engaged as clerk in a boot and shoe store. There he remained until the spring of 1846, when he located in Woodstock, Ill, and opened a boot and shoe store of his own. In the early fall of 1846 he returned to Lyle, and was married to Miss Judith Church, who was born Sept. 28, 1826

He did an extensive business both as a merchant and real estate dealer in Woodstock; but after a time, as we are informed, he met with some reverses of fortune, and in 1866, made a trip to this county and secured an option on the farm of Mr Meyers, the present city of Waseca He came here with his family early in 1867 He labored unceasingly for everything that he thought would build up Waseca and promote his own interests

To say that he was sometimes mistaken as to methods is no more than to say that he was human. That he met with fair business success is evident from the large property interests which he left to his family at the time of his death, which occurred Oct 3, 1893

He was a man of nerve and iron will and allowed no man to thwart his plans without suffering for his temerity sooner or later Many of his plans were wise and many of his public acts were highly praiseworthy

As soon as the cars arrived in 1867, Mr Trowbridge obtained lumber and erected a large temporary hotel for the convenience of the incoming throngs that were to build Waseca In this enterprise, Mrs. Trowbridge will be remembered with a kindly feeling by the many who found her a kind and obliging hostess, although suffering from ill health

In the early days of Waseca, Mr Trowbridge was ably assisted by Hon W. G Ward and J. H Jenkins, Esq, the former being chief civil engineer of the W & St P railroad, and the latter his first assistant, both of whom became sons-in-law of Mr and Mrs Trowbridge, the first year of the city's growth.

He died suddenly of heart failure Oct 3, 1893

[This sketch of Mr Trowbridge was mislaid by the author, and that is why it does not appear in its appropriate place among biographical sketches.]

MR. CHARLES LEUTHOLD,

resident manager of the extensive clothing store of Leuthold Brothers, of Waseca, was born in Kasson, Minn, August 16, 1868 His life business has been that of merchant clothier He is one of five brothers, all of whom are engaged in the same line of business The Leuthold Brothers now own fourteen clothing stores, located in different towns, and their joint custom is sought for by all wholesale dealers and manufacturers. Their joint purchases constitute a valuable asset in their business. Mr. Charles Leuthold married Miss Josie E Preston, daughter of S H. Preston of Waseca, Nov. 30, 1894 They have a very fine home in the eastern part of Waseca, and are the parents of three daughters and one son. In 1887, Charles carried on a store in Winnebago City, and in 1888 came to Waseca with his stock of goods. He has never sought or held any office but accepted a membership on the charter commission of Waseca and has been an able and efficient member of that body

DR M. M DAVIDSON

Matthew McDougall Davidson was born in Breckville, Canada, Dec 19, 1857, and came to Waseca July 23, 1884 He attended school in his native town and took a dental course in Milwaukee, Wis. He has practiced dentistry constantly since he became a resident of this county His father, Alexander Davidson, was born in Coldingham, Scotland, June 3, 1822 His mother, Ellen McDougall, was a native of Moffit, Scotland, born May 13, 1825. She died some two years ago. His father is still living Dr Davidson married Miss Minnie Howard, of Tomah, Wis, Sept. 17, 1890 They have had two children a daughter that died in infancy, and a son, Howard McDougall, born August 15, 1897 They are members of the M. E church and prominent in the social life of Waseca

JOHN M WOLLSCHLAEGER,

register of deeds, was born Sept 19, 1858, at Lichtenau, Germany, and came to America with his parents in 1871, locating in Waseca the same year. The next year while playing on a horsepower with other boys, he had one foot injured so severely that he has been crippled for life. He was a faithful student at our public schools and learned harness making of his father In the spring of 1890 he was elected city assessor of Waseca, and in the fall of 1890 he was nominated by the Democratic party for register of deeds and elected by a large majority He has been elected at each subsequent election by large majorities At the last election his majority was 672, while the majority against his party averaged 625 Mr Wollschlaeger married Miss Louisa Ida Neidt, of Waseca, April 18, 1900. She died of cholera morbus July 17, 1901, without issue He is very correct as a copyist and keeps his records in fine shape.

A. LINCOLN,

of Morley, Michigan, who was born in that state Oct. 10, 1853, came to Minnesota in the fall of 1875, arriving in this county October 17 He resided in Waseca county until July 4, 1883, when he married Miss Matilda Hollander, of Wilton, and settled in Mankato where they resided until 1897, when they moved to Morley, Mich, where they bought a farm upon which they now reside Mrs Lincoln was born in Indiana in 1856, and came to Wilton with her parents about 1860. She is a daughter of the late Florian Hollander.

WILLIAM H TAYLOR,

one of the early settlers in Blooming Grove, was born in England, Feb. 12, 1845, and came to America with his parents when eighteen months old The family first settled in New Orleans where they remained until 1850 when they moved to Missouri Soon after they located in Illinois and in 1857 came to Waseca county when the father bought a farm in Blooming Grove. William H, upon attaining his majority, bought a farm in Byron Soon after he married Miss Emma E Barnes, whose parents were among the early settlers in Wilton township Mrs Taylor is a native of Nunda, McHenry county, Ill, and was born Nov 8, 1849 They spent several years farming in this county and then sold their farm here and moved to a sheep ranch near Saco, Montana, where they have met with good fortune and are meeting with marked financial success in sheep farming They reared a family of children some of whom are married

GOVERNOR JOHN A JOHNSON

There was an uprising of the people in 1904—not an organized, permanent movement, but an intuitive, spontaneous protest against machine politics The gold and corporation combines that manipulated the so-called Democratic national convention drove many Democrats from the polls and others to the support of the Republican candidates. The lumber barons and boodlers of the Republican party of Minnesota controlled the state convention and the masses repudiated them by going to the support of Hon. John A Johnson, of St Peter Democrats in Wisconsin supported Republican LaFollette, Republicans in Missouri voted for Democratic Folk, and Republicans in Massachusetts elected Democratic Douglas All over the country there was an unorganized, independent movement in repudiation of the party slavery which for years had held the masses enthralled to combined greed and dishonesty The people of Minnesota made no mistake Governor John A Johnson is a native son of Minnesota, born in the midst of poverty in pioneer days By the efforts of his brave, noble mother and his own exertions, he arose from the depressing surroundings of his infancy and made for himself a bright home, with a fairly lucrative business With every surrounding influence to induce him to join the dominant party of the state, he remained loyal to the honest sentiments of his own brain and conscience and attained local prominence in a community where his chosen party was in a hopeless minority The people recognized his honesty, his ability, his devotion to fundamental principles, and more than all else, they expressed their condemnation of the timber and other thieves of the state To American boys the life of John A. Johnson is an object lesson Born one of the poorest of the poor, deprived from infancy of a father's protection and care, he arose to the highest official position in the state What he has done another American boy may do. And the spirit of the American people in conferring honors upon men like Abraham Lincoln and John A Johnson is admirable and commendable and speaks volumes for our nation notwithstanding the demoralizing influence of "graft" which works from everlasting to everlasting in all countries and among all peoples All honor to John A Johnson and to the independent Republicans who thus rebuked their unworthy leaders May Governor Johnson forever remain worthy of the confidence of the American people

MISCELLANEOUS MENTION

Christian Melchior, of St Mary, is one of those who made early settlement in this county He came from Germany and landed in New York Soon after he came to this county where he worked as a farm hand two or three years when he married Caroline Arndt, who came to Waseca county in 1855 with Mrs Krassin They at once settled on a farm in section thirty where Mr Melchior now owns a farm of 235 acres. They are the parents of two daughters, one of whom, with her husband, Mr Oswald Baer, resides on the farm and keeps house for the family The other daughter, Mrs C Dobberstein, resides in Waseca Mrs Melchior was very unfortunate She became ill some time after her marriage and finally became blind and insane and has for years been an inmate of the Rochester asylum

John Sell, a native of Germany, arrived in Waseca county in 1857, first working as a farm hand and afterwards purchasing a quarter section of Indian Reservation land on section 31, in St Mary, which he still owns. He married Miss Amelia Arndt, who came to Waseca county with her sister, Mrs Martin Krassin, in 1855 They remained on their farm until a few years ago when they rented it to their son, Rudolph, who still carries it on, and they moved to Waseca where they have a nice home in Broughton s addition

Edward Schmitt is one of the early settlers of Otisco and settled on sections 17 and 20 about the year 1857 His worthy wife died many years ago and his only child is the wife of Mr. Rudolph Jacoby Mr and Mrs. Rudolph Jacoby, their sons, and Mr Schmitt, live on the old homestead adjoining the village plat of Otisco

Dr. Fred W. Prail, dentist, is a native of Waseca county He is married, has no children, and is the second oldest dentist in Waseca He is the only son of Sam Proechel, the well known blacksmith of Wilton, for a number of years, and later of Waseca

Mr. O. S. Bagne, on section 12, town of Iosco, settled in this county in 1856, as a boy. He is prominently connected with the Palmer creamery.

Carl, Frank and J F. Bauman, residents of Otisco, settled in this county in 1871-2 They are of German birth

C J. Bluhm, proprietor of the Waseca Marble Works, settled in this county in 1859.

The Bowe brothers, John, T R, E J, and J D, settled in Blooming Grove in 1866-7

Nels O Breck and Ole O Breck, located in Blooming Grove in 1864, and are prosperous farmers.

C J Brush, of Blooming Grove, located there in 1868, with his parents who were German born

The Collins brothers, Thomas, Frank and Robert, settled in Woodville with their parents in 1868.

Charles Clement, of Waseca, settled in Waseca county in 1866 He is a farmer and has reared a large family of girls

J T Crow settled in the town of Janesville in 1864, and Nathaniel settled there in 1867

The Dardis brothers, Michael, Andrew and Thomas, located in Blooming Grove in 1857

The Davidson brothers, of Freedom, John D, and William, came to this county in 1864.

John Diedrich, of Blooming Grove, came to this county as early as 1870

Carl Dobberstein, a very extensive Byron farmer, located there in 1874

The Albert Domy family settled in Woodville as early as 1858

The Hagen brothers, of Blooming Grove, Ole T. and Sivert, located in the county in 1865.

George Irvine, now manager of the Farmers Elevator at Waseca, located in Woodville in 1886 Mrs Irvine, his wife, came to the county with her parents in 1862

Julius Sell settled in St. Mary at an early day and married Miss Julia Krassin He was thrown from a sleigh while driving home in the winter of 1886-7 and killed His wife died a short time after, leaving three daughters, Emma, Edith and Lizzie. Emma married Henry Kuk, Edith married John Kuk and Lizzie married Herman Hillman The three families now reside near Redwood Falls, Minn

Mr Ed Hayden, an old resident of Alton, is one of the prominent farmers of the county. He was an active member of the Farmers Alliance, and a strong advocate of the Peoples party movement He has a farm of 160 acres on section 13

Hon Hial D Baldwin was one of the early settlers of the county. He located at Empire (Iosco) about the year 1858, and opened a law office He was elected chairman of the board of supervisors of Iosco in 1859 and was ex-officio a member of the county board In the fall of 1859 he was elected county attorney, and was re-elected for two terms more, serving until Jan 1, 1864 He was defeated for judge of probate in 1864 by seven votes, and as a candidate for representative in 1866 he was defeated by Hon Wm Brisbane by five votes. He located in Wilton with his family in 1860 and remained there until 1868 when he settled in Waseca. When East Janesville was platted in 1869 he built the first hotel there He soon after sold it to "Uncle" Frank Johnson and removed to Redwood Falls where he now resides His life has been a checkered one financially, ranging from extreme poverty to affluence. His liberality and generosity have been proverbial His love of speculation has been his besetting error As elsewhere related he was one of the first to open a bank in Waseca and one of the first to fail in business. At Redwood Falls he has been successful He served a term as judge of the district court and has accumulated quite a property He and his family are successfully engaged in the banking business at that place

Hon S M Owen, editor of the Farm, Stock and Home, though not a resident of Waseca county, is so well and so honorably known by his writings to our people, that his name is worthy of mention in this connection Though not an office seeker or an office holder, his influence for good government in this state is wide spread His honesty, sincerity and wide range of information on all subjects make him and his journal great factors in the educational uplifting of the people His labors in behalf of agricultural residents of Minnesota entitle him to high standing in the affections of all our people.

George Tallon is one of the substantial men of Waseca He is a native of Ireland, and in early life became a seafaring man In that capacity he visited very many portions of the world Early in the history of this state he located in Winona where he engaged in wheat buying He located with his family in Waseca more than a quarter of a century ago and has been employed as a grain buyer ever since he located here For over twenty years he was prominent as one of the school directors of this city Mr and Mrs Tallon are intelligent and highly respected residents of Waseca, and prominent and influential members of the Catholic church

Mrs Eliza Sutlief, widow of the late Asa G Sutlief, departed this life at 11 o'clock Sunday forenoon, Sept 10, 1905, at the age of seventy-nine years In February, 1904, she fell and broke her hip bone She remained almost helpless from this accident till death came to her relief

As this volume, already much larger than the author at first anticipated, draws to a close, the writer cannot resist the desire to mention the merits of Hon Frank A Day, of Martin county, who recently brought honor to Minnesota by ably representing its governor at the launching of the war ship Minnesota, at Newport News, April 8, 1905 On that occasion he made a splendid address of which the following are short excerpts He opened by saying

"The first object which meets the eye of the visitor in the doorway of Minnesota's state historical library is the steering-wheel of the old United States frigate Minnesota, launched on the Potomac just fifty years ago That was three years before Minnesota was admitted into the Union as a state The territorial delegate, Henry M. Rice, who had persuaded congress to give the name Minnesota to one of the six new frigates then being constructed, carried water all the way from the Minnesota river with which to give the new vessel a proper baptism."

Continuing he further said "The engines and boilers and small screw propeller, considered somewhat of an innovation in those days, constituted one-fourth of the vessel's entire cost Not content to rely upon steam for power, the vessel spread 2,400 feet of sail, and by the combined aid of steam and sail was able to attain a speed of twelve knots an hour On the day of its launching it was pronounced by the leading Washington newspapers as a very leviathan upon the waters, its displacement was just one-fifth that of the vessel we have launched today Its armament was the heaviest of any battleship of any nation up to that time, its guns showed a tonnage just one-sixth that of the batteries which the new Minnesota is to carry * * *

"The old Minnesota had a history which the new Minnesota may well emulate Its first commander was the famous Dupont, commander of the East India squadron It bore the first tidings of American civilization to China and Japan, and was known as the greatest war vessel that had yet visited the Eastern world When the Civil war broke out in 1861, the Minnesota became the flagship of the Atlantic squadron under command of Flag Officer Stringham. On May 13 it was anchored down your harbor here at Fortress Monroe On May 14 it participated in the capture of three schooners. Inside of ninety days it took part in the capture of ten vessels, one of which, the Savannah, bearing a commission from Jeff Davis, was the first war vessel captured from the Confederate forces

"On August 26, 1861, from your harbor here out through Hampton Roads the old flagship Minnesota led the Atlantic squadron, bearing the troops and artillery of Gen Ben Butler, south of Hatteras and Clark In that two days' bombardment the Minnesota stood on the inside firing line at the head of the squadron, and its heavy main battery, consisting of two 10-inch guns and fourteen 8-inch guns, was the prime factor in compelling those forts to raise the flag of surrender—the first Confederate forts to surrender to Union arms * * *

"But the greatest engagement in which the old frigate Minnesota took part—indeed, the greatest naval battle of the Civil war, if not the most epochal naval engagement in the world's history—you yourselves witnessed here in your own harbor on May 8 and 9, 1862 On the 8th you saw the famous ironclad Virginia, formerly known as the Union frigate Merrimac, emerge from Norfolk, across the bay, and, steaming directly into the fire of the Union batteries, attack the Cumberland and Congress off your shore, and you saw the Minnesota hasten to the rescue of the doomed vessels

"You know, also, why it was that on the morning of the 9th the fate of the Minnesota was not that of the Cumberland You saw the ancient cheese box on a raft,' the little historic Monitor, product of that patriotic genius, Capt John Ericsson, steam to the rescue of the Union flagship Minnesota and go out to meet the ponderous Virginia, five times her size, and you witnessed the greatest naval duel of ancient or modern times—that which sealed the fate of the Confederate cause on the sea and changed the naval armaments of the world

"'The new battleship Minnesota which you launched into Hampton Roads to-day could easily meet and vanquish single handed the combined Union and Confederate squadrons of 1862 What more significant testimony to the industrial, commercial, maritime and political transformation of America in the brief period of forty years' * * *

"From the battleship Minnesota of 1855 to the battleship Minnesota of 1905 is a far cry. It marks an era in the history of the state, nation and world In shipbuilding, it marks the transition from the age of wood to the age of steel In Minnesota, the half-century records the growth from a frontier territory of 20,000 souls to a great commonwealth of 2,000,000 people"

Hon Frank A Day was born in Wisconsin, 1855, settled at Fairmont, Minn, in 1874, and entered upon newspaper business, was elected to the house of representatives, in 1878, to the senate in 1886, 1890 1894, delegate to republican national convention in 1892, was a bimetallist and supported W J Bryan in 1896, is married and has four children, and is at this writing private secretary to Governor John A Johnson, and chairman of the state democratic central committee

THE CLOSE

It is said that all things must have an end and certain it is that all history writing must come to a stop somewhere, and hence the close of this last life-work of the author In going over the printed pages, as I have been compelled to do, many matters of some interest are found to have been omitted for want of space Soon after the work of typesetting commenced it became evident that I had prepared more "copy" than could be crowded into six hundred pages, and the work of copy pruning and condensation commenced, and, like the poor woman whom the Angel of Death called upon to designate which one of her twelve should be taken, it was difficult to choose which items should go into oblivion Suffice it to say that no effort has been spared to make the work as complete and perfect as possible with the means at command. Some people, it has been learned, fail to appreciate the value of a correct history of their county, and therefore neglected to furnish facts peculiarly within their own knowledge It is not for me to say how well or how imperfectly the work of writing the history has been done The book must speak for itself A sincere effort on my part has been made to make it a truthful and impartial history In looking back over the history of this grand county one can but feel pride and satisfaction at the great progress made and the high standing it has attained The first settlers found an inland wilderness, without habitation, without navigable waters or railroads, and surrounded by savages What a change! Many, very many, of the old and honored pioneers have passed away, and it is not egotistical to say that there may remain no record save this history that they ever lived and labored here to help make this county what it is. Let it be remembered that it was in our day—the fifty years covered by this record— that the greatest battles were fought for the preservation of self-government and the perpetuity of civil and religious liberty, and it will be for those who follow us to perpetuate the great heritage of the revolutionary fathers The revelations of the last fifty years are as miraculous as any recorded in biblical history. Electricity, now the greatest force known to man, has wrought wonders in the last fifty years, and is destined in the near future to revolutionize the industrial and commercial activities of the world To the unknown people who shall come after us and who, in their great advancement in the methods of government, the sciences, the arts, inventions, discoveries, in the mastery of the powers of nature, in virtuous and happy living, may look back upon us, perhaps, as a rude, ignorant, semi-barbarous people, we bid a genial, kindly welcome to our "happy hunting grounds"—to a county that for fifty years has never suffered a total loss of crops.

"And now, dear friends, farewell for many a day,
If e'er we meet again, I cannot say
Together have we traveled o'er long years,
And mingled sometimes smiles, sometimes tears,

Now droops my weary hand and swells my heart,
I fear, good friends, we may forever part,
O'erlook my many faults, and say of me,
'He hath meant well that writ this history'"

JAMES E CHILD

DIRECTORY.

DIRECTORY.

CITY OF WASECA

Atwood, E M
Anderson, Charles
Anderson, Olaf
Anderson, Anton
Anderson, Andrew J.
Anderson, Andrew
Adams, H J
Asmundson, Ole
Atkinson, R E.
Abraham, Wm.
Andrews F B
Armstrong, W J
Anderson, Richard
Aughenbaugh, J W.
Anderson, Magnus
Brown, Hugh
Bennett, E M.
Blowers, James
Blanchard, H. G., M. D
Beck, Anna
Bennett, G T.
Bullard, L A
Bartelt, Robert
Bruhaker, G E
Bane, J O
Blatchley, A.
Blaeser, Henry
Buckman, W A.
Belding, E E
Billiard, Paul
Brisbane, W. R
Brisbane, Arthur
Brisbane, Clarence
Buck, H M
Breen, Tom
Breen, John
Brauhen, Louis
Bailey, P C
Bluhm, C J.
Breen, Francis
Bartelt, Albert
Bythen, Aug
Byron, Miss B
Buchler, L. T
Buchler, Ed
Bishman, Clara E.
Buckman, I A.
Barden, Thos.
Boucher, John
Brown, Walter
Bailer, C H.
Beauleau, Rev C. H.
Bergeson, Nick
Blair, S H
Bivens, C.
Clayton, P A
Clayton, Fred
Conway, Ed
Cunningham, G B
Chapman, H. H
Cunningham, James
Clement, W A.
Crough, Wm.
Colwell, R P
Carroll, W F
Crimmins, Patrick
Castor, Ed
Clement, Chas
Cobb, A G
Callahan, John C
Conkwright, W T
Chamberlain, H P.
Coyle, J B
Coleman, J J
Cummings, D S, M. D
Courtney, John
Colligan, Ed
Collins, Frank
Chamberlain, W A., M D
Comee, S S.
Child, James E
Collester, E. B.
Cleary, William
Cawley, Jos
Colwell, R P
Crandall, Martin
Cashman, T A
Castor, Robert
Degnan, John
Dolan, James L
Deverell, Ralph
Dalton, Robert
Davidson, M M
Derth, C. G.
Donovan, Tim
Donovan, Dan
Davis, T J
Devine, D D
Dean, Mat
Day, F T
Dunn, J H
Deverell, Wm
Drysdale, E C.
Davis, H V
Dahl, D O.
Dobberstein, Chas.
Durigan Patrick
Didra, H C
Degner, John
Dunn, Roy
Dye, J B
Dean, Matt
Dinneen, John

English, Ed
Erickson, John
Everett, E A
Everett, Guy W
Engstrom, Charles
Fitzgerald, Thos
Faes, Robert
Foster, A S
Fuller, A. S
Fahmer, Henry
Ford, Pat
Fitzpatrick, James
Freemore, A. E.
Gasink, Albert
Gottschalk, P. E.
Guyer, Anthony
Gutfleisch, John
Gallien, W G
Grapp, A
Gallagher, P F.
Gallagher, B M.
Grunwald, August
Gutfleisch, Henry
Gunderson, Iver
Grunwald, Martin
Gunn, E S ,
Gormley, Terry
Greener, Oscar
Grant, M. C.
Geist, Henry
Garrett, F W
Gatzman, Mike
Garland, R D
Goodsell, E E
Gehring, Phil
Gallagher, John H
Goodspeed, E. C
Goatz, John E.
Garlick, D E
Gongoll, Rev. J.
Goodspeed, Leslie
Grant, Charles
Garrett, L
Gillis, W H
Garland, Ralph
Gasink, Albert
Glines, Tom
Gratz, John
Hemmingway, G L
Hayes, Mike
Hayden, J B
Hawkes, C. M.
Hallgren, A
Hutchinson, E. A
Holtgren, A
Hanson, Andrew
Herbst, W L
Herter, E. O.
Habein, Wm
Hagen, Andrew
Helms, M. H.
Hartson, C
Habein, Henry
Herbst, Adolph
Hartson, A. H.
Henkle, H
Hagerty, Thos.
Hartson, C L
Hartson, H C
Hemmingway, M.
Johnson, Frank
Johnson, John
Johnson, C J
Johnson, Bank
Johnson, C
Jackson, Andrew
Johnson, Elling
Jenkins, Augusta
Jenson, A. F
Johnson, Nels
Johnson, T H
Johnson, C F
Johnson, Charles
James, G L
Johnson, J W
Kempin, Henry
Krassin, John A
Kawfelt, Geo
Korbitz, G C
Keeley, James
Keeley, John
Kerr, Thos J, Sr
Kerr, Thos. J Jr
Krassin, Gust
Krassin, G J
Kelley, P J
Kennedy, Patrick
Keeley, M B
Krassin, E R
Kinn, Andrew
Kenehan, P H
Kempin, Wm
Keefe, D O
Kletschke, Emil
Kronrei, Emil
Knutson, Martha
Kakuschke, Fred
Koechel Daniel
Koechel, H F
Keil, L E
Klohe, Otto
Kramer, Martin
Knutson, G E.
Kaible, August
Lortis, W C
Leuthold, Charles
Long, Emil
Leeland, A
Lynn, J. F., M. D
Lohren, A J
Lynch, Thos
Larson, L J
Lindell, P. G
Lang, Thomas
Lawin, Fred
Lawin, Siegfried
Linnehan, Tim
Lossman, Simon
Lawson, O J.
Lawson, Guy
Lilly, Barney J.
Lochte, Rev Fred
Lewis, Mrs B S
Lynch, A
Magner, B
Martin, Zack
Madden, J E
Miller, R T.
Murphy, Henry
Maguire, John
Mahler, F W
Moore, J A
Murphy J F
Moore, F A
Meyer, W F.
Murphy, John D
Merrill, S
Madden, John
Moen, G
Marquardt, Emil
Madden, Pat
Monroe, H. C
Murphy, J C
Minske, August
Mellor, A J.
Moonan, John
Murphy, James H
Miller, Frank
Meyer, Robert
Mix, L E
McLoughlin, D
Miller, R
Messerknecht, Chas
Menke, Ernest
Moonan, M F.
Main, N
Mitchel, J K
Massowick, Anton

Maloney, W F.
Maloney, Barney
Maloney, Vinz
McCarty, Pat
McLoone, John
McLoone, Mike
McWaide, F J.
McLin, J M
McCarty, T. F.
McMahon, Frank
McDonnough, Mike
McLoughlin, T F.
McCleary, O. L
McDermott, John
McGovern, Peter
McCarty, Joe
McLin, John
McCall, G.
McLoone, Charles
McDonald, Anthony
Madden, Patrick
Madden, Will
Minske, Paul
Mahoney, D
Nerbovig, H H
Nissen, Nis
Nelson, Alfred
Nelson, Geo. E
Norton, H. P.
Norton, C N.
Nelson, N M
Nelson, Eiler
Nelson, Nels
Neidt, Albert
Nelson, Henry C.
Nelson, Andrew
Olson, O C
O'Brien, Peter
Olson, Abraham
Olson, John
Odekirk, Ed
Peterson, Axel
Peterson, Theo
Perrin, D E.
Priebe, W. J
Price, Thomas
Prail, F W.
Preston, L. F.
Popple, A
Parker, James E.
Proxel, Frank
Poster, John
Pierce, Daniel
Proxel, Ludvig
Pancerewski, B C.
Proechel, C.
Preston, S H
Papke, Julius
Peterson, C A
Parker, A. H
Pfaff, Rev. Daniel
Pfaff, L W.
Place, J H
Phillips, Frank
Phillips, Louis
Pickett, V. G
Plowman, Louis
Quinn, Thomas
Roesler, R F
Ryan, M W.
Rothke, Wm
Ranney, E C.
Ringer, H
Reynolds, Henry
Remund, F J
Roedecker, Chris
Rudy, Christian
Reigel, Charles
Reibold, John
Rogers, H U.
Ryan, T R
Rourk, W F
Records, T. F
Roth, F W
Reinschmidt, Wm
Roesler, R J.
Rhode, John
Ryan, Hugh
Riley, John
Reinschmidt, Ernest
Reinschmidt, Wm.
Robbins, Geo. L.
Swenson, D A.
Santo, August
Shaver, C H.
Sterling, L. W
Sandretzky, E C.
Smith, Frank
Smith, E. H.
Schank, W F
Swift, W. A.
Skocdopole, F. J.
Smith, F M.
Smith, Mary
Smith, C A
Sell, John
Shortell, G
Schultz, A. J.
Schlicht, Chas.
Snyder, A M.
Schaacht, Wm F.
Swartwood, F A, M.D
Stucky, A
Stevens, E. R
Shaw, D J
Smith, Geo. A.
Scott, W E
Smith, C P.
Seastrand, H D.
Simons, B
Stoltz, Louisa
Sutter, S C
Sullivan, J B
Sotebeer, Ernest
Sotebeer, Olaf
Smith, Mike
Seismer, Charles
Strong, G W
Severson, Martin
Snyder, Frank
Simpke, Wm
Santo, Aug
Snyder, A. L
Sweet, Al
Senske, Geo
Treanor, Rev. J J.
Tisdale, J E
Turnacliff, D
Turnacliff, Cleve
Tallon, George
Turnacliff, J
Taylor, John
Turnacliff, F. J
Torkelson, Nels
Thompson, Nathan
Thompson, Wm
Trowbridge, E C
Thoreson, Andrew
Teis, And
Ungerman, J. B
Ross, Ed
Ross, E. A.
VonSein, Geo
VonSein, Ed
Vondrashek, C
Wollschlaeger, J. M.
Wollschlaeger, A
Weckwerth, Ed
Wood, L G
Wobschall, W C
Woskie, F T
Whipple, R. F
Wollcott, A T.
Witte, W F
Weckwerth, H
Walter, L
Weyrauch, C
Wobschall, Aug

Wright, C A.
Wert, Lindsay
Wallroff, H H
Wert, A
Wolf, W R
Wolter, L H
Walter, A. O
Wheelock, Wm
Wobschall, G E
Werner, Michael
Wasbotten, Rev. John

Wobschall, J F.
Watson, C H
Ward, R P
Wightman, G R
Webber, E C
Winters, H V
Wyman, G N.
Wilson, G A
Wamsley, J H
Weller, Michael
Wyman, S F

Wolf, Ernest
Webb, George
Westerfield, A.
Wolterm, O
Wood, Frank A.
Wobschall, Ernest
Wright, Will
Young, J D
Young, D L

VILLAGE OF NEW RICHLAND

Anderson, S T.
Anderson, H A
Adams, F J
Adams, D E
Bruzek, W
Batchelder, E J., M D
Berg, S A
Byersdorf, A
Brown, C. W.
Christensen, E E
Christianson, C. A
Crain, Andrew
Christensen, C E
Drake, F D
Dinneen, Daniel
Ferguson, A.
Gilbertson, J O
Gilbertson, C. O.
Gorgen, Gile
Gardson, M. O.
Gorgen, J H
Hunt, J. F.
Huseby, G
Hanson, Torger
Heckes, Fred
Holgrimson, Ole
Harrington, Fred
Harrison, A J.

Hagen, H O
Haugen, M H.
Johnson, Nels
Johnston, Archie
Johnson, C B
Jaehning, Henry
Jeddeloh, H E
Johnson, F W
Kreuger, John
Kingsley, F T
Kreuzer, John
Kelleher John
Laudert, Martin
Laudert, F W
Lange, C G
Lofty, M P
Lynch, J C
Lutze, Theo
Luff, Phillip
Michaelis, L. E
McGannon, T J
Michaelis, Wm
Martinson, A O.
Morgan, John
Newgard, A J
Newgard, C A
Peterson, L P.
Reynold, J A

Rogstad, Moren
Rodegard, K O
Ryan, Michael
Ryan, Pat
Ritchie, A
Spillane, Charles W.
Schindler, Max
Swift, John
Sunde, O O.
Scott, Samuel
Samuelson, Martin
Sybelrud, A C
Sunde, P. O.
Sievert, Ed
Steinhaus, W
Schwenke, E M
Tyrholm, J A
Tyrholm, N O.
Thompson, Ole
Vilsmeyer, H E
Wickman, N H
Wagner, C A
Witcher, C A
Wagner, F J
Wightman, J H
Wightman, Samuel
Wightman E R
Zenk, R A

VILLAGE OF JANESVILLE

Abraham, Albert
Anderson, Jens
Ash, John
Arnold, Fred
Ash, Richard
Ayers, H D.
Ayers, P C.
Amberg, Joe
Bratz, John
Boeke, W C
Barden, John

Bengtson, Fred
Borland, W E
Banker, A A
Beske, John
Byron, J M
Berndt, August
Benson, B.
Banker, Z
Chandler, J O.
Coughlin, Will
Converse, C

Cahill, Will
Coughlin, Ed
Cook, Geo
Crystal, Rob
Cummins, Jas
Cordry, J E.
Craig R O
Cahill, W R.
Clark H A
Cahill, Richard
Canfield, M

Crippen, Sam
Comstock, H. A
Cameron, H D.
Curtiss, K.
Carpenter, D. D
Burke, Will
Dane, Salma
Dunham, Oliver
Dieudonne, Emil
Devereaux, Ruth
Dunham, Charles
Davidson, Mond
Dunham, C H.
Dane, B B
Dalton Mary H.
Dooley, John
Day, Mary J.
Don, Fred
Donder, August
Davis, A B
Dodge, O J
Dalton, Chris
Davidson, J L.
Eustice, Thos.
Eustice, J D.
Empey, P K
Fratzke, Gust
Fetzloff, Otto
Finley Bros
Fratzke, Fred
Finlev, Joseph
Fischer, Dorotha
Goodrich, Joe
Graham, Anton
Gordon, J. W.
Grapp, W L.
Gayer, Ed
Gayer, Christ
Glunn, D
Gutfleisch, Chas
Gottschalk, Aug
Harrington, M E
Hennesey, J E
Holmichel, L.
Hagen, F L
Hellebo, A S.
Henry, J A
Janke, John
Jennison, A. W.
Jennison, J W.
Joyce, James
Kruger, A. F
Krause, Fred
Krause, Ayers
Keeley, M W.
Kee, James V.
Knopf, Wm.
Krimheuer, W E
Krimheuer, Frank
King, James
Ketzback, J F
Kreuger, Christ
Kelfing, Christ
Lau, W F
Laase, John
Lang, Theo
Lynch, John
Lange, Herman
Lang, August
Lang, Emil
Moonan, Thomas
Miner, H I
Manthy, Chas
Miner, F H
McGinness, John
Miller, Ernest
Montgomery, S G
McCracken, James
McCullough, J. P.
Norton, W H.
Nyquist, M
O'Grady, A J
O'Toole, Martin
Paddock, Ed
Price, A L
Priem, Frank
Peschl, John
Quast, August
Quade, F H
Rahmel, L
Rickerman, Chas
Rogers, L D
Roberts, P C
Strassen, Henry
Strunk, Will
Stevens, S M.
Shepherd, Frank
Santo, Will
Stewart, C R.
Slider, H C.
Secor, Alta E.
Santo, Gust
Smith, Henry
Stewart, Burt
Schaffer, C H
Schraeder, Aug
Sackett, A D
Singer, Anton
Sacharias, F
Severson, S E
Springer, R B
Scheerschmidt, Aug
Scheerschmidt, Albert
Schmidt, H
Stewart, L J
Taylor, M J, M D
Ulrich, Julius
Volz, F B

TOWN OF NEW RICHLAND

Name	Address
Anderson, Albert	New Richland
Anderson, Olaus	. Hartland
Burtness, O H.	New Richland
Brix, Gust....	R. 6, New Richland
Brechtel, A .	New Richland
Breilein, Fred	R. 4, New Richland
Bomengen, Ole O	R 1, New Richland
Berg, M. A .	. New Richland
Bjorklund, J. A	R. 4, New Richland
Bettner, Fred, Jr,	.New Richland
Bettner, Fred	New Richland
Bakke, Ole .	.R 1, New Richland
Balduan, Herman,	R 3, N. Richland
Belling John	R. 4, New Richland
Betz, Herman	R 6, New Richland
Berg, Edward A	. Hartland
Burtness, O H	R 6, New Richland
Burtness, Olaf	R 6, New Richland
Berg, A. N...	R. 1, New Richland
Christensen, Chris	New Richland
Christensen, Andrew E.	R. 6, New Richland

Name	Address
Crandall, G W.	Hartland
Christiason, Mathias	R 1, New Richland
Christensen, Nels	R 1, N Richland
Discher, J H	R 4, New Richland
Engen, Ingeborg	R 6, New Richland
Echternach, Jacob	New Richland
Echternach, W F	R. 4, N. Richland
Finseth, K A.	R 1, New Richland
Finseth, T K	New Richland
Foslein, Andrew	New Richland
Foelz, Adolph	New Richland
Franklin, A	R 4, New Richland
Hanson, H J	R 6, New Richland
Haugan, H H	New Richland
Hendrickson, T	R. 1, New Richland
Hendrickson, H	New Richland
Hagen, K.....	R. 6, New Richland
Halverson, M O	New Richland
Hendrickson, Carl O..	.R 1, New Richland
Hendrickson, C. F..	New Richland
Heckes, L	.R 5, New Richland
Heckes, W E	R 5, New Richland
Heckes, Herman	R 5, New Richland
Hoelz, A P	New Richland
Herbst, Paul	R 6, New Richland
Herbst, Joe	R 6, New Richland
Hagen, Martin K	R. 6, N Richland
Hammar, Chas.	R 6, New Richland
Hast, Carl	New Richland
Hendrickson, Ole	R 6, N Richland
Hendrickson, Ole C	R 6, N Richland
Holen, Andrew	R 6, New Richland
Hagen, Knute C	..New Richland
Halverson, Ole K	R 6, New Richland
Hagen, K O	R. 6. New Richland
Hagen, Ole C.	R. 4, New Richland
Halverson, Ole....	New Richland
Johnson, A W	New Richland
Johnson, C A..	R 6, New Richland
Johnson, James	New Richland
Johnson, Edward E.....	Ellendale
Johnson, John A	R 6, N Richland
Johnson, Alfred M	R I N Richland
Johnson, A D	R 6, New Richland
Johnson, Ernest R,	R 4, N Richland
Kreuger, Albert ..	New Richland
Klessig, Louis	New Richland
Kroeger, John	New Richland
Kittleson, Carl	R 1, New Richland
Knutson, Knute	R 6, New Richland
Kopstad, Peter	R 1, New Richland
Kopstad, John	R. 1, New Richland
Kin, C J	R 6, New Richland

Name	Address
Liane, Sam.	New Richland
Liane, Olaf	New Richland
Liane, A O	New Richland
Liane, Amund	R 6, New Richland
Lund, Mrs T	New Richland
Lund, Alfred	New Richland
Larson, Knute.	New Richland
Langlie, Segar	New Richland
Loken, Jens J	..New Richland
Lindberg, C O	New Richland
Lee, Thomas	R 6, New Richland
Loken, Martin J	R. 6, New Richland
Loken, A. J	R 1, New Richland
Larson, Nels	R 6, New Richland
Lange, William	New Richland
Midgarden, O N	R 4, New Richland
Mathies, Albert	New Richland
Michaelis, John	R 2, N Richland
Mathwig, G B	R 1 New Richland
Mellby, Rev O A	R 6, N Richland
Nelson, Charles P	R 4, N Richland
Nelson, Gotfried	R. 4, New Richland
Newman, Gust	New Richland
Newman, Wm	New Richland
Nelson, Aug C	R 6, New Richland
Nelson, Andrew	R 4, New Richland
Nelson, Walfred	..New Richland
Nelson, A W	R 4, New Richland
Olsen, Fred	R. 4, New Richland
Olsen, Charles.	R 4, New Richland
Peterson, Victor	R 4, New Richland
Peterson, Alfred O	New Richland
Peterson, F O..	New Richland
Paulson, Peter	New Richland
Peterson, Levi	New Richland
Pofahl, Albert	New Richland
Peterson, C A.	New Richland
Peterson, John S	R 4 New Richland
Quarna, P O	New Richland
Ruth, S	New Richland
Rotegard, Andrew	New Richland
Rukke, Ole K	R 1, New Richland
Rugroden, Mathias	New Richland
Randall, Miles	R 4 New Richland
Rasmussen, James	New Richland
Samuelson, Anna	New Richland
Swenson, Andrew P	New Richland
Sampson, A A	R 1, New Richland
Sunde, S O	New Richland
Sunde, Ole H	New Richland
Sunde, Jonas O.	New Richland
Shurson, S O	R. 1, New Richland
Sommerstad, T K	New Richland
Swenke, Henry	New Richland
Schlosser, B H.	New Richland

Name	Address	Name	Address
Siverson, Knute....	. Hartland	Thoreson, Hans H ,R 6,N	Richland
Strenge, Henry E, R 6,N	Richland	Verplank, W E	New Richland
Swift, M J . R 4,	New Richland	Verplank, Edwin	New Richland
Schwartzkop, C. R 4,	New Richland	Verplank, Albert	New Richland
Swenson, A. A R 4,	New Richland	Verplank, E E ...	New Richland
Swift, R O R 4,	New Richland	Wilson, J M	New Richland
Sybelrud, C C. R 1,	New Richland	Weckwerth, Stephen, ... R 5,	New Richland
Stearns, H K R 1,	New Richland	Weed, Adelbert, R.4,	New Richland
Sybilrud, E. E , R 6,	New Richland	Whiting, A L	New Richland
Sunde, Paul H .	New Richland	Wilson, Calista J	New Richland
Strand, John R 1,	New Richland	Wagner, C A	New Richland
Swenson, John A , R 4,N	Richland	Wagner, Christopher	New Richland
Strenge, Even O .	New Richland		
Thompson, O N .	New Richland		

TOWN OF BYRON

Name	Address	Name	Address
Anderson, Peter .	New Richland	Ivers, Thomas ...	New Richland
Adams, Joseph.	New Richland	Johnson, Erick	New Richland
Betchwars, W J.	New Richland	Johnson, Frank.	New Richland
Brix, Adolph .	New Richland	Johnstone, Archie	New Richland
Bumgardner, Mat...	New Richland	Johnstone, Walter	New Richland
Bumgardner, Wm .	New Richland	Kreuger, Frank	New Richland
Bumgardner, M ...	New Richland	Kreuger, William	New Richland
Bumgardner, John,	New Richland	Korman, Fred	New Richland
Breilein, P D .	New Richland	Korman, John	New Richland
Berg, Nels. .	New Richland	Ladd, W J	New Richland
Brisbane, John Y	New Richland	Loranson, Ernest	New Richland
Buck, I D .	New Richland	Lee, James E	New Richland
Briese, Rudolph....	New Richland	Luft, W J .	New Richland
Cummings, Wm	New Richland	Linnihan, J J .	New Richland
Concannon, L W...	New Richland	Linnihan, Henry..	New Richland
Concannon, Lary.	New Richland	Linnihan, T W ..	New Richland
Casper, P H	New Richland	Linnihan, John ..	New Richland
Christianson, Hans	New Richland	Linnihan, M. H.	New Richland
Collins, Martin .	New Richland	Linnihan, J W .	New Richland
Dobberstein, C	New Richland	Linnihan, T F	New Richland
Dinneen, Nick	New Richland	Linnihan, Daniel	New Richland
Dinneen, John W ,	New Richland	Linnihan, M. J. .	New Richland
Fischer, A D	New Richland	Michaelis, Henry	New Richland
Geary, M F	New Richland	McGrath, C .	New Richland
Grau, Albert .	New Richland	Munch, Chris .	New Richland
Gabloff, Wm.	New Richland	Munch, John	New Richland
Greenwood, Grant	New Richland	McDonnough, Ed .	New Richland
Greenwood, Herman	New Richland	Murphy, John.	New Richland
Greenwood, Osmer	New Richland	Moore, John	New Richland
Heffernon, M	New Richland	Moen, John	New Richland
Hausauer, Henry	New Richland	McArdle, John .	New Richland
Hatch, Dwight .	New Richland	McGovern, Chris	New Richland
Hanson, Chris	New Richland	Matson, Albert	New Richland
Haas, John	New Richland	McGannon, Michael	New Richland
Horn, W J. ..	New Richland	Neary, Ira .	New Richland
Haas, Julius	New Richland	Paul, Julius . ..	New Richland

Name	Address
Peters, W D	New Richland
Pick, Herman	New Richland
Patschke, Martin	New Richland
Partridge, P S	New Richland
Partridge, U G	New Richland
Partridge, Z M	New Richland
Partridge, Wm	New Richland
Pierce, C A	New Richland
Pierce, A. M.	New Richland
Pierce, Clarence	New Richland
Pierce, J W	New Richland
Reb, John	New Richland
Ryan, Tom	New Richland
Ryan, Patrick	New Richland
Rice, Albert	New Richland
Root, C E	New Richland
Seaton, A J	New Richland
Shannahan, John	New Richland
Stenson, John	New Richland
Schwenke, Robert	New Richland
Turner, E. W	New Richland
Van Seius, Geo	New Richland
Volz, Joe	New Richland
Weed, C S	New Richland
Westerlund, John	New Richland
Westerlund, Nels	New Richland
Winnegar, Wm	New Richland
Winnegar, Frank	New Richland
Winnegar, W F	New Richland
Whiting, Frank	New Richland
Weise, Frank	New Richland
Yerks, August	New Richland
Yopka, August	New Richland
Zahalka, Joe	New Richland

TOWN OF VIVIAN

Name	Address
Abrahamson, A	Minnesota Lake
Allis, Amos	Minnesota Lake
Brandt, Ernest	Minnesota Lake
Beck, Henry	Wells
Brandt, Wm	Minnesota Lake
Buschow, John	R 2, New Richland
Brandt, Herman	Minnesota Lake
Buschow, Albert E	New Richland
Beyer, Wm. Jr.	Minnesota Lake
Bohm, Chas	R 3, New Richland
Bartelt, Wm	R. 3 New Richland
Bluhm, F A	R 5, New Richland
Bluhm, H. W.	R. 3, New Richland
Bluhm, J H	R 3, New Richland
Baker, Perry	R. 3, New Richland
Bluhm, Aug	R 5, New Richland
Buttner, Wm.	R. 3, New Richland
Bleck, Henry	R 1, Minn. Lake
Bleck, Aug.	R. 1, Minn Lake
Barges, Christ	R 1, Minn Lake
Beyer, C. W.	R. 1, Minn Lake
Burmeister, Mrs Wm	R. 1, Minn Lake
Burmeister, Aug. E	R. 1, Minn Lake
Burmeister, Aug	R 3, New Richland
Brecht, F P	R 1, New Richland
Cook, Herman	R 5, New Richland
Cook, Chas.	R 5, New Richland
Christianson, Olaf	R. 3, New Richland
Degner Wm A	R 1, Minn Lake
Deneffe, Joe	R 1, Minn Lake
Degner, Wm M	R 1, Minn Lake
Degner, Wm. C	R 1, Minn Lake
Eichorst, F W	R 5, New Richland
Eichorst, Herman	R 5, N Richland
Engel, Wm	R 5, New Richland
Eichorst, Chas	R 5, New Richland
Ewald, Wm Jr	R 5, New Richland
Ewald, William	R 5, New Richland
Erickson, Knute	R 1, Minn Lake
Ewert, William	R 1, Minn Lake
Ewert, Bruno	R 1, Minn Lake
Fennert, Albert	R 3, New Richland
Fennert, August	R 3 N Richland
Fauchald, Anton	R 1, Minn. Lake
Fahlbush, Adolph	Minnesota Lake
Fletchenheuer, Herman	R 1, Minesota Lake
Fritsche, Albert	R 3, New Richland
Fritsche, Chas	R 3, New Richland
Foesch, Caroline	R 1, Minn Lake
Foesch, August	R 1, Minn Lake
Fratzke, Herman	R 3 N Richland
Fry, Samuel	R 4, Wells
Groskreutz, August	R 4, Wells
Groskreutz, Herman	R 1, Minn Lake
Groskreutz, Gotleap	R 1, Minn Lake
Groskreutz, Otto	R 3, N Richland
Gentz, Henry	Minnesota Lake
Gebauer Gustav	Wells
Gadient, G L	R 3, N. Richland

Name	Address
Gadient, Joe,	R. 3, New Richland
Gadient, Joseph,	R 3, New Richland
Hamburg, Cryas	Minnesota Lake
Habick, Wm	R 1, Minnesota Lake
Hinz, Herman,	R 1, Minn Lake
Hoechst, Wm.,	R. 1, Minn Lake
Jeddeloh, John,	R.3, New Richland
Jeddeloh, J B,	R 3,New Richland
Krause, Henry,	R 3, New Richland
Kaiser, Mrs C .	R 4, Wells
Kunz, Math,	R 5 New Richland
Klender, Robert,	R 1, Minn Lake
Klender, Frank,	R 1, Minn Lake
Klender, Carl,	R 1, Minn Lake
Kamrath, Albert,	R. 1, Minn. Lake
Linnihan, D J,	R 5, New Richland
Lewer, Wm.	R 3, New Richland
Leifermann, F G,	R 1, Minn Lake
Lechner, Wm,	R 3, New Richland
McArdle, James	R. 3, New Richland
Miller, Wm A	R 4, Wells
Miller, F A	R. 4, Wells
Miller, Wm F	R 4, Wells
Mickelson, Thomas,	R 3,N Richland
McGuinnes, Wm,	R 5, N Richland
Miller, Wm C,	R 1, Minn Lake
Miller, H L, .	R 4, Wells
Muller, Wm...... ..	Minn Lake
Neitzel, Herman,	R 1, Minn Lake
Neitzel, Wm .	R 4, Wells
O'Brien, Thomas,	R 5, N Richland
O'Brien, Wm	R 5, New Richland
Pick, Ernest	R. 3, New Richland
Pofahl, Wm F F,	R 3, Minn Lake
Puetz, C J	R. 3, Minn Lake
Putz, Herman	Minn Lake
Putz, Joseph,	R 1, Minnesota Lake
Pieper, Chas	R 1, Minnesota Lake
Pieper, Wm,	R. 1, Minnesota Lake
Pick, John,	R 3, New Richland
Pieper, Herman,	R 3,Minn Lake
Ryan, John,	R 3, New Richland
Radke, Wm	R 3, Minn Lake
Roesler, A F . .	R 4, Wells
Ryan, Michael,	R 5 New Richland
Ryan, Patrick,	R 1, New Richland
Radloff, Ed,	R. 1, New Richland
Radke, Carl	R 1, New Richland
Radloff, John	R 1, New Richland
Rusch, Herman,	R 5, New Richland
Radloff, Fred .	R 3, New Richland
Schultz, Otto, ...	R 1, Minn Lake
Sumnicht, Fred,	R 3, Minn Lake
Schultz, C. E....	R. 4, Minn. Lake
Schultz, A C	R 4, Minn Lake
Stiernagle, Fred,	R 4,N Richland
Schroder, August,	R 3, N Richland
Syring, Otto,	R 5, New Richland
Schwarz, Wm	R 1, New Richland
Schultz, Herman,	R. 4, Minn Lake
Tolzmann, Wm	Minn Lake
Tolzmann, Herman,	R 1,Minn. Lake
Tolzmann, Walter,	R.4,Minn Lake
Tolzmann, Otto,	R 5,Minn Lake
Thompson, Edward,	R 3, N Richla'd
Venm, Thos	R 3, New Richland
Vocks, Julius	R 3, New Richland
Vogelsang, Wm	R 2, New Richland
Wuest, Henry	R 3, New Richland
Wuest, Ed	R 3, New Richland
Wobschall, Reinhart, .	R 4, Wells
Weise, Carl,	R 3, New Richland
Weise, Ed	R 4, Wells

TOWN OF OTISCO

Name	Address
Abell, Irving .	R 2, Waseca
Amley, Ole	Ellendale
Anderson, Albert.	R 2, Waseca
Anderson, Wallfred	Waseca
Anderson, Alfred ..	Waseca
Anderson, L M	Otisco
Anderson, E O . .	New Richland
Anderson, John	Otisco
Bredshall, John, . .	R 2, Waseca
Blowers, John ...	R 2, Waseca
Branwald, T H	R 2, Waseca
Branwald, T. O.. ..	R 2, Waseca
Branwald, Guro	Waseca
Branwald, L. H	R 2, Waseca
Bahr, Otto .	Waseca
Bauman, Ernest	R 7, Waseca
Brunken, Fred	Waseca
Bauman, Arnold	R 7,Waseca
Bauman, Otto .	Otisco
Bigham, C W.	Otisco
Bauman, Carl	Otisco
Bishman, Adolph..	R 7, Waseca
Bishman, Ben P	Otisco
Bishman, Alfred ...	R 7, Waseca
Bishman, Henry, .	R 7, Waseca
Bauman, John F.	R 7, Waseca

Name	Address
Chapman, O E,	R 4, New Richland
Chapman, B J.,	R. 4, New Richland
Carlson, Emil F	R. 2, Waseca
Carlson, Gustav	Waseca
Esping, John H......	R. 2, Waseca
Eaton, W F	R 2, Waseca
Erickson, Charles	Lemond
Eklund, Peter	R 2, Waseca
Elton, O M	R 4, Waseca
Elton, O M	R 4, Waseca
Fette, Wm H.	Lemond
Fette, Conrad	R 2, Waseca
Fette, Wm J.	Waseca
Geese, Andrew	R 2, Waseca
Grasshoff, Chas	R 2, Waseca
Houg, L G,	R 1, New Richland
Hanson, C N.	New Richland
Hanson, Olaf T	R.4, New Richland
Haugan, H K	R 4, New Richland
Hanson, Knute	New Richland
Hedquist, Andreas	Otisco
Hultgren, John,	R 4, New Richland
Helms, Deidrich	R 2, Waseca
Halland, Timand,	R 4, N Richland
Halland, Ole	New Richland
Helle, Peter O,	R.4, N Richland
Hanson, John L,	R 4, N Richland
Hanson, Otto,	R 2, Waseca
Henkenseifken, Fred,	R 2, Waseca
Hokanson, Carl	Otisco
Holtz, E H	R 7, Waseca
Hause, Henry	R 6, Waseca
Harguth, John	Waseca
Irwin, James	R 2, Waseca
Johnson, Edward L,	R 4,N Richl'd
Johnson, John F.	Otisco
Johnson, August	New Richland
Johnson, Moses	Otisco
Johnson, O R	Otisco
Johnson, E W	R 2, Waseca
Johnson, C A.	R 2, Waseca
Johnson, Alfred C	Otisco
Johnson, Alfred	New Richland
Johnson, Hedda	Otisco
Johnson, Otto C,	Otisco
Johnson, E V	R 2, Waseca
Johnson, John A	R 2 Waseca
Jacoby, R	Otisco
Kroll, Emil	R 2, Waseca
Kugath, Wm	Waseca
Kugath, Fred	Waseca
Koerner, Aug	R 2, Waseca
Kampen, C A	Otisco
Kreuger, Gust	Waseca
Lindberg, C	R 2, Waseca

Name	Address
Larson, Gustav	Otisco
Larson, Johnny	R 2, Waseca
Larson, John L	Otisco
Larson, C A	R 2, Waseca
Larson, Alfred J	Otisco
Leslie, Sam	R 2, Waseca
Leslie, Ralph	R 2, Waseca
Leslie, John	R 2, Waseca
Larson, Charles O	Otisco
Lewer, Fred	R 4, New Richland
Mattison, Mathias	R 2, Waseca
Monson, Erick	New Richland
Monson, Trond O	R 1, NewRichland
Munson, L R	R 1, Ellendale
Minges, Joseph	R 2, Waseca
Minges, Edward	R 2, Waseca
Monson, Edwin	Otisco
Neugebauer, J B	R 4, New Richland
Nelson, Charles	Otisco
Nelson, Alfred G	Otisco
Nelson, Aug P	R 4, New Richland
Nelson, E C	Otisco
Orman, A. J	R 4, New Richland
Olson, Andrew B	R 4, New Richland
Palm, Victor P	R 2, Waseca
Peterson, Otto	New Richland
Peterson, Theo	Waseca
Peterson Ole C	R. 2, Waseca
Priebe, Theo	R 2, Waseca
Priebe, Henry	R 2, Waseca
Pommerening, Theo	R 7, Waseca
Peterson, Aug. J	Otisco
Palm, Gust	R 2, Waseca
Peterson, E. A	R 4, New Richland
Peterson, David	R 2, Waseca
Prechel, L C	R 2, Waseca
Peterson, Alfred	New Richland
Palm, Albert	R 2, Waseca
Peterson, P J	Otisco
Poplow, Fred.	Otisco
Priebe, Herman	R 2, Waseca
Porath, Fred.	R 1, Waseca
Priebe, Edward	R 2, Waseca
Radtke, Richard	Meriden
Roeglin, Robert	R 7, Waseca
Rudolph, Carl	Otisco
Roslund, John	R 4 New Richland
Rudolph, John A	Otisco
Runnerstrom, G R	Otisco
Redeske, C W	R 2, Waseca
Rudolph, Gotfried	Otisco
Rick, F	R 2, Waseca

Name	Address	Name	Address
Swenson, John E.... .	Lemond	Thamert, J E .. .	Otisco
Swenson, Peter ...	R 2, Waseca	Tollefson, Gustav	R 1, Ellendale
Schultz, Adolph... ..	R. 2, Waseca	Tolin, John A	R 2, Waseca
Swenson, Aaron . . .	Otisco	Turnacliff, Eugene..	R 1, Waseca
Swenson, August.. . .	Otisco	Wik, O N . .	New Richland
Swenson, C. O............	Otisco	Wetterbom, Otto .	R 2, Waseca
Sotebeer, B	R 2, Waseca	Wetterbom, C J	R 2, Waseca
Stearns, G B	Otisco	Weed, E S ..	New Richland
Swenson, A K . .	Otisco	Wood, R B .	New Richland
Swenson, Carl ..	R 2, Waseca	Wallstrom, J A	New Richland
Smith, H W .	New Richland	Youngberg, Carl O. .. .	R 4, New Richland
Schultz, John.	R 4, New Richland	Youngberg, John	R 4, New Richland
Swenson, Charlie	Otisco		
Sommers, J. P. .	R 2, Waseca		
Spoonberg, A. F	Otisco		

TOWN OF WILTON

Name	Address	Name	Address
Atwood, George	R 7, Waseca	Frederick, George .	Waseca
Arndt, Arnold.......	R. 1, Waseca	Fairley, Andrew	R 1, Waseca
Allen, M. H. C .	Otisco	Foels, Adolph.	R 5, New Richland
Allen, H B	Otisco	Frank, A A .	R 4, New Richland
Below, Paul.	R 2, Waseca	Gabert, Wm ...	R 7, Waseca
Briese, Herman . .	Otisco	Gearin, John...	R F D, Waseca
Bartz, Fred .	R 1, Waseca	Gregory, Joe .	R 1, Waseca
Bartz, Richard . .	R 1, Waseca	Gehlof, Max. . .	Waseca
Burns, James ..	R 1, Waseca	Grunwald, R .	R 1, Waseca
Bathke, Albert	R. 7, Waseca	Gehring, G .	R 7, Waseca
Brisbane, Walter	Otisco	Gehring, Mike	R 7, Waseca
Bird, Eugene .	R 1, Waseca	Gehring, Ed	R 7, Waseca
Bartels, Fred	R 1, Waseca	Gehring, Henry	R 7, Waseca
Burns, Geo ..	R 1, Waseca	Gehring, Julius .	R 7, Waseca
Burns, Martin. .	R 1, Waseca	Hollander, Amos.	R 1, Waseca
Byrne, Owen .. .	R 1, Waseca	Hope, Pat	R 7, Waseca
Barden, Henry .	Waseca	Holtz, Emilie. . .	R 7, Waseca
Bird, Isaac . .	R 1, Waseca	Henkenseifken, Aug	Waseca
Bird, Abraham ...	R 1, Waseca	Hoelz, A P.	R 4, New Richland
Bartz, Gotlieb	Waseca	Jacobs, N . .	R 7, Waseca
Borchert, Ernest .	Waseca	Kroeger, Henry	R 7, Waseca
Byron, Thomas .. .	Waseca	Kugath, Fred .	Waseca
Burns, Barney ...	R 1, Waseca	Kelleher, John . .	R 7, Waseca
Conway, Richard . .	R. 1, Waseca	Klug, Peter	R 1, Waseca
Courtney, James.	R 1, Waseca	Krewatt, Otto..	Waseca
Curley, Tom .	R 1, Waseca	Krause, Paul .	R 1, Waseca
Connor, Mrs Alice...	R 1, Waseca	Krause, Charles	R 7, Waseca
Carmody, Tom.	R 4, New Richland	Kroeger, Hans	R 5, New Richland
Doran, Geo	New Richland	Krause, Frank .	R 1, Waseca
Englehardt, Aug .	R 1, Waseca	Koechel, August .	Otisco
Ewest, Ferdinand ..	Waseca	Klinger, Frank .	R 7, Waseca
Ewest, Herman	Waseca	Koechel, Silas .	R 7, Waseca
Fox, Peter . .	R 1, Waseca	Krumrie, Emil ..	Waseca
Fox, M	R 1, Waseca	Lang, Mike .	R 1, Waseca
Foels, Wm. .	R 5, New Richland	Lipke, C ..	Waseca

Name	Address
Lipke, K	Waseca
Lechner, William	Otisco
Lenz, Gotlieb	R. 7, Waseca
McLin, Pete	R. 7, Waseca
McLin, Mike	R 7, Waseca
McLin, Andrew	R 7, Waseca
Madden, Joe	R 7, Waseca
Miller, Henry	R 1, Waseca
McDonough, Pat, Jr	R 5, New Richland
Metzler, Theo	R 1, Waseca
Metzler, Henry	R 1, Waseca
Mulkentine, John	R 5, New Richland
Mann, Michael	R 1, Waseca
Morig, Carl	New Richland
Munch, Wm	R 5, New Richland
McDonough, James	R 5, New Richland
McGannon, Mike	R. 1, Waseca
Matthews, Geo	R 5, New Richland
Matthews, M.	R. 5, New Richland
Nelson, R	R 5, New Richland
O'Brien, John	R. 1, Waseca
O'Brien, Will	R 7, Waseca
O'Brien, Mike	R 7, Waseca
Poplow, William	R 1, Waseca
Poplow, Herman	R 7, Waseca
Price, August	R 4, New Richland
Pugh, John	New Richland
Raetz, Wm	R 5, New Richland
Roesler, Emil	R 1, Waseca
Riley, R R	R 1, Waseca
Roesler, Ferdinand	R 1, Waseca
Ruehl, Carl	R 1, Waseca
Reick, Fred	R 7, Waseca
Randall, Alfred	R. 5, New Richland
Reitsfort, Geo	R 7, Waseca
Ramming, Albert	R 7, Waseca
Root, W L	R 4, New Richland
Root, Joseph	R 5, New Richland
Roesler, A A	R 1, Waseca
Schultz, Charley	R 1, Waseca
Schlaack, Gustav	R 7, Waseca
Schlaack, Wm	R 5, New Richland
Schlaack, Herman	R 5, New Richland
Sutlief, Delancy	R 5, New Richland
Sutlief, Austin	New Richland
Sutlief, B G	R 4, New Richland
Scott, Chas.	R 4, New Richland
Schultz, Chas.	R. 4, New Richland
Schauer, Wm	R F D, Waseca
Schauer, Herman	R 1, Waseca
Stageman, Carl	R 1, Waseca
Suemnick, Herman	R 7, Waseca
Sheeran, Martin	R 5, New Richland
Turnacliffe, Walter	Otisco
Turnacliffe, Ralph	Otisco
Tetzloff, Wm	R 5, New Richland
VanLoh, Wm	R 1, New Richland
VanLoh, Fred	R 7, New Richland
Weckwerth, Albert	Otisco
Weller, John	R 7, Waseca
Wierzbiscke, Otto	R. 7, Waseca
Wussow, Wm	Waseca
Weckwerth, Emil	R. 7, Waseca
Zell, Charles	Waseca

TOWN OF FREEDOM

Name	Address
Armstrong, B D	R 1, Waseca
Amberg, M A	Alma City
Amberg, M P	Alma City
Adams, Joe	R 5, New Richland
Adams, T W	R 5, New Richland
Boetcher, Charley	R. 4, Janesville
Boetcher, Herman	R 1, Minn Lake
Bentson, Andrew	Cream
Bathke, Robert	Waseca
Born, Gust	R 2, Janesville
Bromaghin, M J	R 3, Janesville
Bromaghin, W C	R 3, Janesville
Barsch, Ernest	R 2, Janesville
Brandenberg, H	R. 4 Janesville
Bluhm, Henry	R 5, New Richland
Blaisdell, G L	R 3, Janesville
Brown, Wm	Alma City
Behrnes, Wm	R 5, New Richland
Bronson, G W	Alma City
Convey, Pat	R 2, Janesville
Coffin, Ed	R 3, Janesville
Courtney Hugh	R 2, Janesville
Courtney, Frank	R 2 Janesville
Cronkhite, Edgar	Alma City
Connor, Simon	R 1, Waseca
Corry, Dr J P	Alma City
Dixon, Thomas	Cream
Davidson, J D	R. 2, Mapleton
Davidson, Wm	R 4 Janesville
Dittberner, H C	R 4, Janesville
Doyle Raymond,	R 5, N Richland
Davidson, R E	R. 2, Mapleton

Name	Address
Elmore, J H	...Alma City
Ewert, Wm	R 5, New Richland
Eustice, Chris	R. 5, New Richland
Engel, Wm	R 5, New Richland
Field, Rob	R. 4, Janesville
Fratzke, Carl	..Alma City
Ford, Edward	R 5, New Richland
Fox, Joseph.......	R 1, Waseca
Fesselt, C	Alma City
Fratzke, Julius .	R 4, Janesville
Fratzke, H F	R 4, Janesville
Fratzke, Wm . .	Alma City
Flemming, Michael	.R 7, Waseca
Gerdts, Adolph	R 2, Janesville
Geary, Geo E	.R. 3, Janesville
Geary, J E	R 3, Janesville
Geary, A. J	R 3, Janesville
Gehloff, Herman	R 2, Janesville
Garlich, S O	.R 3, Janesville
Gunsolus, Fred........	Alma City
Gottschalk, Edward	R 2, Janesville
Griffith, Wm M	R 4, Janesville
Gerdts, Borthof	R 2, Janesville
Graham, B W	R 3, Janesville
Grawander Wm G	..Alma City
Grawander, Herman C	Alma City
Graham, A W	R 3, Janesville
Hydorn, S	. R 2, Mapleton
Hass, M	. R 1, Waseca
Heath, J. C	R 4, Janesville
Heath, W. E.....	R 2, Janesville
Heath, R L.	R 2, Janesville
Hodges, Geo F	Cream
Hofeld, Geo	Alma City
Hofeld, H C	Alma City
Holmes, John	R 5, New Richland
Hickey, John F.,	R 5, New Richland
Hawkins, Pat	R 5, New Richland
Hodgkins, D H,	R 5, N Richland
Hodgkins, Sam, Jr	New Richland
Hoverson, Theo	Alma City
Janike, Fred	R 1, Minn Lake
Jacobs, Nick .	Alma City
Kaiser, Ferdinand	R 2, Janesville
Kaiser, Anton .	R. 2, Janesville
Kaiser, Martin	R 2, Janesville
Klempe, Gust	R 2, Janesville
Koplen, F C ..	R 4, Janesville
Kelling, Edward	R 2, Janesville
Kelling, Ernest	.R. 2, Janesville
Kelling, Wm	R 4, Janesville
Koplen, Wm	R 2, Janesville
Kroiling, Martin .	Alma City
Koplen, Wm	R 2, Janesville
Krause, Wm	R 1, Minn Lake
Kopischke, Gustav	R 2, Janesville
Kopischke, A F	R 2, Janesville
Krueger, E	R 4, Janesville
Knutson, K A	R 1, Minn Lake
Krause, Fred . .	Alma City
Kleeman, Louis	R 2, Janesville
Lassell, B .	R 4, Janesville
Lynch, Mat. ..	.R 2, Janesville
Lau, Gustav . .	R 4, Janesville
Lyksett, Ole .	R 2, Mapleton
Linkesh, Joe	R 5, New Richland
Linnihan, Michael . .	.R. 5, New Richland
Larraboo, B F	Alma City
Lienke, Wm. . .	R 4, Janesville
Moore, James R	R 2, Janesville
Moore, C F .	R 2, Janesville
Moore, R B ..	.R. 2, Janesville
Manthey, John	R 2, Janesville
Manthe, F. W ...	R 2, Mapleton
Manthey, Carl	R 4, Janesville
Manthey, F .	R 2, Mapleton
Miller, Carl	R 2, Janesville
Miller, E H	R 2, Janesville
Miller, H	R. 4, Janesville
Myers, J H .	R 1, Waseca
Mackey, M	R. 5, New Richland
Maurer, Christ...	R. 2, Janesville
Marquardt, Gustav	R 2, Janesville
Marquardt, Carl	R 4, Janesville
McCracken, R C	R. 1, Minn Lake
Miller, Aug	R 4, Janesville
Norman, Matt	R 1, Minn Lake
O'Brien, Ed	R. 5, New Richland
Prechel, J A .	R 1, Waseca
Possen, Fred	R. 2, Janesville
Priem, A J	Janesville
Priem, Herman	R 2, Janesville
Petrie, W J.. .	R. 3, Janesville
Remmington F F	Cream
Roekor, Charles	R. 2, Janesville
Rollins, H C	R 3, Janesville
Schroeder, C F	R 1, Waseca
Schroeder, Wm .	Alma City
Smith, F M	R 2, Janesville
Stindt, Carl.	R 4, Janesville
Schonrock, Gustav.	R 4, Janesville
Sandsmark, Thomas	Janesville
Sheeran, Ed	R 2, Janesville
Sheeran, M J	R. 5, New Richland
Schultz, Fred .	Alma City
Schultz, A C	R 4, Janesville
Schultz, H W .	R 3, Janesville
Seaman, E B	R 4, Janesville
Schrieber, L	R 3, Janesville

Name	Address	Name	Address
Tesch, Carl ..	R 5, New Richland	Woltgram, H . .	.Alma City
Vogler, Gust	. R. 2, Janesville	Witts, W G	...R 4, Janesville
Vandawaker, Mrs D	.......R 3, Janesville	Witts, S N .	. R 4, Janesville
Werth, Fred	R 4, Janesville	Waknitz, Thos	... .. Alma City
		Wagner, J P .	...Alma City

TOWN OF WOODVILLE

Name	Address	Name	Address
Abbe, Fred .	R 2, Waseca	Frahm, Dick .	. Waseca
Abbe, Wm	Waseca	Fell, Charley .	Waseca
Abraham, John	R. 2, Waseca	Gray, Fred .	Waseca
Anderson, Martin	Waseca	Glines, Thomas . .	. Waseca
Born, Wm .	Waseca	Gage, L A	Waseca
Beede, Gerhard	Waseca	Gerts, E H .	. Waseca
Block, Fred . ..	Waseca	Goodspeed, Geo H.....	Waseca
Brown, Elizabeth..	Waseca	Hanson, Chris ..	Waseca
Bivens, David .	..Waseca	Hawkes, Allen	Waseca
Bartelt, Wm	Waseca	Harshman, Vinton .	Waseca
Bathel, Wm	. Waseca	Honhouse, G . .	Waseca
Bethke, L	Waseca	Irvine, Geo . ..	Waseca
Broughton, T T	Waseca	Johnson, Ed	Waseca
Brandt, Wm	Waseca	Jorks, Theo	Waseca
Buker, Wm	Waseca	Jackson, Andrew	Meriden
Buker, John	R 2, Waseca	Kuss, Paul	Waseca
Buker, H F .	. R 2, Waseca	Kreutz, Wm .	Waseca
Buker, Henry.......	R 2, Waseca	Kennedy, Wm	Waseca
Born, Walter .	Waseca	Kennedy, Thos	Waseca
Coats, Wm	... Waseca	Keeley, John .	Waseca
Cleland, Mrs A C	Waseca	Ketchum, C F. ..	Waseca
Collins, Robert	Waseca	Kanthack, Herman	.Waseca
Collins, Thomas	Waseca	Kanthack Fred	Waseca
Curran, James	Waseca	Kinney, D A .	Waseca
Curran, John .	Waseca	Kugath, Carl .	Waseca
Curran, Arthur	Waseca	Lueck, Chas.	Waseca
Curran, John B	Waseca	Lueck, Herman .	Waseca
Cortis, H	... .Waseca	Landers, Morris	Waseca
Cook, Chas	.Waseca	Lee, Henry . .	Waseca
Davis, Orin .	....Waseca	Lewer, H F	Waseca
Donovan, John .	.Waseca	Noeske, Albert	Waseca
Donovan, Dennis	Waseca	Naporra, Adolph	Waseca
Dierks, H .. .	Waseca	Olson, Tarron .	Waseca
Domy, Frank	Meriden	Oswaldson, Anton	Waseca
Domy, Albert	Waseca	Oswaldson, Halvor	Waseca
Debair, James W.......	Waseca	Olson, Castin	Waseca
Damn, F	Waseca	Olson, Fritz	Waseca
Domy, Chas	Waseca	Priebe, Lewis	Waseca
Draheim, Aug .	Waseca	Prechel Fred	Waseca
Draheim, Julius .	Waseca	Powell, R B	Waseca
Drum, Harry	.Waseca	Powell, Mary J	Waseca
Drum, S H	Waseca	Powell, Hiram	Waseca
Erno, Andrew .	Waseca	Rockney John	Waseca
Fette, H C	Waseca	Roesler, F W	Waseca
Fette, Wm ...	Waseca	Roesler, L J	Waseca

Name	Address	Name	Address
Ruedy, Valentine	Waseca	Taylor, C. B	Waseca
Ruedy, F	Waseca	Taft, John	Waseca
Ruedy, John	Waseca	Thompson, William	Waseca
Rieck, H	Waseca	Wood, Alfred	Waseca
Ross, August	Waseca	Wood, Geo H	Waseca
Scholer, Caroline	Waseca	Woodbury, C L	Waseca
Sander, Christ	Waseca	Webber, C L	Waseca
Suemnick, August	Waseca	Weber, H	Waseca
Sell, H	Waseca	Wendt, Adolph	Waseca
Scholljegerdes, Geo	Waseca	Wickman, Carl	Waseca
Schendel, Wm	Waseca	Willock, H W	Waseca
Schmidt, Fred	Waseca	Ward, C D	Waseca
Spillane, D	Waseca	Ward, Arthur	Waseca
Spillane, W	Waseca	Wheelock, L C	Waseca
Spillane, F M	Waseca	Wheelan, W. H	Waseca
Sahler, Emil	Waseca	Wheeler, A	Waseca
Spies, Wm	Waseca	Wilken, D	Waseca
Smith, O L	Waseca	Zimmerman, Chris	Waseca
Schippel, Herman	Waseca	Zimmerman, John	Waseca
Schuck, Aug.	Waseca	Zimmerman, David	Waseca

TOWN OF ST MARY

Name	Address	Name	Address
Andriole, Wm	Janesville	Fischer, C	Janesville
Born, August	Janesville	Fischer, Herman	Waseca
Bisson, Alex	Waseca	Flynn, Michael	Waseca
Baer, Oswald	R 6, Waseca	Frank, William	Waseca
Bartels, Wm	Waseca	Geraghty, Thos	Waseca
Ballard, Isaac	Waseca	Grunwald, William	Waseca
Bowe, Mary E	Waseca	Gallagher, Michael	Waseca
Byron, Wm	Waseca	Gorman Anthony	Waseca
Barden, Richard	Waseca	Geese, Hugo	Waseca
Byron, James	Waseca	Gilhart, Robert	Waseca
Baldwin, Tim	Waseca	Gorman, James	Waseca
Baldwin, Tom	Waseca	Holmes, Michael	Waseca
Baldwin, Mary	Waseca	Henderson, William	Waseca
Burke, Michael	Waseca	Henderson, Joe	Waseca
Conway, John	Waseca	Henderson, John	Waseca
Conway, Mrs Thos	Waseca	Johnston, William	Waseca
Conway, Frank Jr	Waseca	Johnston, Mrs Jane	Waseca
Conway, Frank Sr	Janesville	Krassin, Steve	Waseca
Conway, J W.	Waseca	Krassin, John F	Waseca
Conway, J H	Waseca	Krinke, H D	Waseca
Conners, Frank	Janesville	King John	Waseca
Culliton, James	Waseca	King, Fred	Waseca
Culliton, Thos	Waseca	Kahnke, George	Waseca
Conway, Richard	Waseca	Keeley, Mrs 'Mike	Waseca
Dimmer, Gust	Waseca	Keeley, John Sr	Waseca
Erwin, D A	Waseca	Kahnke, Frank	Waseca
Foley, James	Waseca	Keeley, James C	Waseca
Farley, Mrs Patrick	Waseca	Krassin, Emil	Waseca
Fritz, Theo	Waseca	Lannon, James	Waseca
Foley, Thos	Waseca	Lynch, Marguerite	Waseca

Name	Address	Name	Address
Lechner, Adolph	.. Waseca	Oestreich, Mrs. H........	Waseca
Lambert, Samuel	Janesville	Paulson, Mrs Hans	Waseca
Lambert, Michael.. ...	Janesville	Pofahl, Herman....	Waseca
Lannon, John, Sr	. Waseca	Priebe, John .	.Waseca
Lannon, John, Jr.........	Waseca	Papke, Julius .. .	Waseca
Lannon, Richard . .	Waseca	Phelps, Joseph	Waseca
Leick, Deidrick	Waseca	Prechel, Emil ..	Waseca
Matz, Joseph . .	Waseca	Priebe, Stephen . .	Waseca
Mittelsteadt, Wm	Waseca	Papke, John . .	Waseca
Murphy, John .	Waseca	Phelps, Geo... .	Waseca
Matz, I . .	Waseca	Priebe, August	Waseca
Minske, H C . .	Waseca	Roseneau, Henry...... ...	Waseca
Mittelsteadt, Gust .	Waseca	Reibold, Thos	Waseca
McBride, Matt . .	Janesville	Ryan, Thomas	Waseca
McGonagle, Mike	Waseca	Reibeling, Mrs Theo.	Waseca
McLoone, Anthony .	Waseca	Sheehan, James . .	Waseca
Millerlile, Herman	Janesville	Sheeran, Michael . .	Janesville
Madden, Thos .	Waseca	Sheehan, Dennis . .	Waseca
Magner, John	Waseca	Stoltz, Henry . .	Waseca
Myers, Wm . .	Waseca	Schroeder, Gust	Waseca
Miller, Fred	Waseca	Sheehan, Garrett, Jr .	Waseca
McDonough, Mrs John	Waseca	Sheehan, Garrett, Sr	Waseca
Mulcahy, Henry .	Waseca	Sommers, Gust, Jr	Waseca
Moylan, Mrs Ed .	Waseca	Sommers, Gust, Sr .	Waseca
Manthey, Wm	Waseca	Wobschall, Robert	Waseca
Matz, Andrew	Waseca	Wolter, Wm A ...	Waseca
Norton, James, Sr	Waseca	Wobschall, E .	Waseca
Norton, James, Jr	Waseca	Wagner, H A .	Waseca
Norton, Daniel	Waseca	Weckwerth, Godfrey .	Waseca
Norton, Richard	Waseca	Wobschall, Ben .	Waseca

TOWN OF ALTON

Name	Address	Name	Address
Brown, Thomas	Alma City	Cassidy, Wm	Janesville
Brooks, Lewis. .R. 3,	Janesville	Correy, J P	Alma City
Britton, R H L R 2,	Janesville	Campion, Wm R 6,	Waseca
Baker, Geo A....R. 3,	Janesville	Clausen, J W	Alma City
Burke, Rosetta R 2,	Janesville	Campion, James R 6,	Waseca
Burke, W. E . R. 2,	Janesville	Dimmel, William R 5,	Janesville
Borne Julius	Alma City	Dimmel, Emil R 3,	Janesville
Bevins, Edward	Janesville	Dollman, Wm	Alma City
Bush, C A	Alma City	Eustice, James R 2,	Janesville
Bush, W J . .	Alma City	Ewert, Herman R 6,	Janesville
Bevins, W	Alma City	Ewert, Charles R 6,	Janesville
Burns, John	Janesville	Fanning, Charles	Janesville
Born, Reinhold	Alma City	Foley, Patrick R. 6,	Janesville
Bradlow, Otto..	Alma City	Foley, John . R 6,	Janesville
Crump, C W	Alma City	Foley, Thomas R 6,	Janesville
Campion, John . R 6,	Waseca	Flemming, August R 3,	Janesville
Cahill, T J	Janesville	Gallagher, John H	Janesville
Cody, Owen ...	Janesville	Gates, H E ..	Janesville
Campion, Patrick R 6	Waseca	Griffith, Edward H	Alma City
Cody, James B R 6,	Waseca	Gallagher Anna M ..	Janesville

Name	Address
Gallagher, Martin, Jr	R 2, Janesville
Gahler, Herman	Alma City
Gallagher, Owen	R 2, Janesville
Glynn, John	R 6, Janesville
Guse, Ludvig	R 2, Janesville
Gunn, Alexander	Janesville
Gleason, John	Alma City
Graminske, M	Alma City
Glynn, Wm	R 6, Janesville
Gahler, Otto	R 4, Janesville
Gallagher, Martin L	R. 2, Janesville
Gerdts, Emil	R 2, Janesville
Gates, Emerson	Alma City
Gallagher, Jas	R 2, Janesville
Gerdts, Emil	R 2, Janesville
Gotschalk, A C L	R 4, Janesville
Hinto, Sarah A	R 2, Janesville
Heatherman, James	Janesville
Hammel, J E	R 3, Janesville
Hogan, Andrew	Janesville
Heatherman, Michael	Janesville
Hammel, Terrence	R 3, Janesville
Hayden, Edward	Janesville
Hogan, Thomas	R 6, Janesville
Jennison, J W.	Janesville
Joyce, Martin	Janesville
Keso, Emma	Janesville
Kelling, W. H	Janesville
Kopischke, Aug.	R 4, Janesville
Krahn, August	R 2, Janesville
Kopischke, Henry	R 3, Janesville
Kreinke, Julius	Janesville
Kreinke, Herman	R 2, Janesville
Kreinke, Aug	Janesville
Kreinke, Gustav	R. 2, Janesville
Kopischke, Ferdinand	Janesville
Kraske, Wm	Janesville
Kaiser, Theo	R 2, Janesville
Kukuk, John	R 3, Janesville
Lau, Ludvig	Alma City
Lachelt, Julius	Alma City
Lachelt, Reinhart	Alma City
Lilly, Owen	R 6, Janesville
Lau, Richard	R 4, Janesville
Lilly, P A	R 6, Janesville
Lau, Fred	R 4, Janesville
Lundquist, Ole.	R 3, Janesville
Larkin, Michael	R 6, Janesville
Lau, August	Janesville
Land, Andrew	Janesville
Lamphere, Lyman	R 3, Janesville
Lau, Julius C	Alma City
Markham, J A	Alma City

Name	Address
McFarland, D D	Alma City
Morris, S W	R 2, Janesville
Meyer, Henry	R 2, Janesville
Morton, F E	Janesville
Marshman, Robert	R 3, Janesville
McWhorten, C E	Janesville
Myer, August A	Janesville
Morrill, James L	R 3, Janesville
Murphy, John H	R F D, Janesville
McDonough, Thomas	R 3, Janesville
McBride, Terrence	R. 6, Janesville
Mulcahy, Patrick	Janesville
Morrill, F M	R 3, Janesville
McBride, James	R 6, Janesville
Morrill, Frank D	R 3, Janesville
O'Harra, J J	Janesville
Proechel, Wm	R 2, Janesville
Priem, Wm	R 4, Janesville
Paddock, E L	Janesville
Pogle, Herman	R 2, Janesville
Priem, J C	R. 3, Janesville
Peters, Charles	R. 3, Janesville
Priem, Christian	R 2, Janesville
Porker, Theo	R 5, Janesville
Quadde, Charles	R 2, Janesville
Quadde, John	Alma City
Quadde, Herman	Alma City
Quadde, William	Alma City
Roecker, Robert	Alma City
Ryan, Michael	R 4, Janesville
Rux, Daniel	R 4, Janesville
Resenberg, Aug	R. 2, Janesville
Ryan, Thomas	R 4, Janesville
Rudolph, Wm	R 2, Janesville
Rosethal, Chas	R 3, Janesville
Risto, Adolph	R 3, Janesville
Rutz, Wm	R 2, Janesville
Reycraft, Joe	R 6, Janesville
Sievert, Geo	R 2, Janesville
Schunke, Paul	R 2, Janesville
Santo, Edward	R 3, Janesville
Scheerschmidt, C F	R 2, Janesville
Schmitz, Nicholas	R 4, Janesville
Stankey, Albert	R 5, Janesville
Smitz, Peter	Alma City
Seaman, F D	R 3, Janesville
Schnepf, Frank	R 3, Janesville
Schroeder, Henry	R 3, Janesville
Smith, C H	Alma City
Tew, W E	Alma City
Tannar, M. T	R 2, Janesville
Trahms, W F	R 4, Janesville
Trahms, Julius	R 2, Janesville

Name	Address	Name	Address
Tanner, Geo M	Janesville	Vaughn, James	R 2, Janesville
Underwood, J. D.	Alma City	Vaughn, Martin L.	R. 2, Janesville
Vaughn, J J	R 2, Janesville	Werdin, H L.	Janesville
Vaughn, Dennis	R. 2, Janesville	Werdin, E. J.	R. 4, Janesville
Vaughn, J L	Janesville	Waggoner, John	Alma City
Vaughn, Edward	R 2, Janesville	Witts, Nelson	Alma City

TOWN OF BLOOMING GROVE

Name	Address	Name	Address
Alland, Mrs T K	Waseca	Hand, George	R 3, Waseca
Bosshart, John	R. 1, Morristown	Hanzbeck, F	R 3, Waseca
Brusch, Charles	R 4, Waseca	Hackett, Pierce	R. 4, Waseca
Beisner, Edward	R. 3, Waseca	Healy, Frank,	R 4, Waseca
Bowe, Thos	Waseca	Hagen, O T.	R. 3, Waseca
Blaeser, John	Waseca	Hagen, Sievert	R. 3, Waseca
Bahr, G E	R. 3, Waseca	Iverson, Iver	Waseca
Bahr, J. L.	R. 3, Waseca	Janke, Minnie	Waseca
Breck, Ole	R 4, Waseca	Johnson, Alfred H	Waterville
Broughton, Thos.	R. 3, Waseca	Jameson, Knute	R 3, Waseca
Breck, Nels	R 3, Waseca	Johnson, Thos.	R 5, Waseca
Boucher, G. L.	R. 4, Waseca	Jackson, Segar	R 5, Waseca
Bagne, N S	R 3, Waseca	Jackson, John	R. 5, Waseca
Bonnin, Albert	R. 1, Morristown	Jameson, Albert	R 5, Waseca
Beisner, Henry	R 3, Waseca	Johnson, John E	R 3, Waseca
Bird, Albert	R 3, Waseca	James, George	R 4, Waseca
Bowe, J K	R 5, Waseca	Jellum, Ole N	R 3, Waseca
Behne, A J	R 3, Waseca	Jellum, M	R 3, Waseca
Behne, Geo C	R 3 Waseca	Johnson, John	R 3, Waseca
Bonnin, W H	R 3, Waseca	Kanne, R H	R 3, Waseca
Curran, J B	R 3, Waseca	Kanne, G E	R 3, Waseca
Curran, A J.	R 3, Waseca	Krienke, F W	R 4 Deerfield
Cawley, Thos F	R F D, Waseca	Karsten, Henry	R 4, Waseca
Cawley, John	R 3, Waseca	Knutson, Sam,	R 5, Waseca
Carlson, Bernhart	Waseca	Keene, O A	R 5, Waseca
Dahle, J T	R 3, Waseca	Kanne, F	R 3, Waseca
Dardis, Thomas	R 3, Waseca	King, Wm R	R. 4, Waseca
Deiderich, John	Waseca	Knauss, J C	R. 3, Waseca
Evenson, Edward	R 3, Waseca	Knauss, C W	R 3, Waseca
Engebritson, E O	R 3, Waseca	Knauss, Ben	R 1, Morristown
Eichorst, G.	R 3, Waseca	Knauss, C J	R. 1, Morristown
Fingerson, W. K	R 3, Waseca	Kahlscheuer, John	R. 3, Waseca
Fell, Wm.	R 3, Waseca	Kalek, O H	Waseca
Fait, Vincent	R 4, Waseca	Larson, Martin	Waterville
Flatz, Fred	R 1, Morristown	Lorenz, F	R 4, Waseca
Fietham, L L.	R 3, Waseca	Lee, A K	R. 3, Waseca
Geisler, F C	R 3, Waseca	Lorenz, Carl	R 4, Waseca
Garity, Thos	R. 4, Waseca	Leverson, John	Waseca
Geisler, Fred	R 3, Waseca	Larson, Joseph M	Waseca
Garske, Lorenz	R. 4, Waseca	Martinson, Ole	Waseca
Hackett, Anna	R 4, Waseca	McGuire, Thos	R. 4, Waseca
Hecht, J C.	R 3, Waseca	McGuire, Martin	R 4, Waseca
Halverson, Hans	R. 5, Waseca	McGuire, Frank	R. 4, Waseca
Hand, Steven	R 3, Waseca	Madden, Geo.	R 4, Waseca

Name	Address	Name	Address
McGuire, Mrs Mary	R 4, Waseca	Reineke, H. W	R 4, Waseca
McGuire, James .	R 3, Waseca	Remund, G H	R. 3, Waseca
McGuire, John E	R F D Waseca	Remund, Edward B	R 2, Waseca
Moore, John . .	R. 3, Waseca	Sutter, Charles	R 3, Waseca
Marti, Fred	R 3, Waseca	Sutter, Albert.	. R. 3, Waseca
Moe, Claus	R 3, Waseca	Schuette, A H.	R 3, Waseca
McKune, Fred	R 1, Morristown	Schuette, J F.. ..	R. 3, Waseca
Matz, Joseph .	Waseca	Saufferer, C. J.	R 1, Morristown
Mahler, Adolph	R. 3, Waseca	Seljeskog, Louis	R. 3, Waseca
Nordmeier, Wm ..	R. 3, Waseca	Schlossein, Herman	Waterville
Nordmeier, Ed	R. 3, Waseca	Seljeskog, Martin .	Waterville
Nelson, Peter	Waterville	Saufferer, Henry .	R 1, Morristown
Nelson, W O. .	R 3, Waseca	Saufferer, Louis	R 3, Morristown
Oleson, Nels	R 3, Waseca	Saufferer, George	R 1, Morristown
Papke, Fred . .	R 4, Waseca	Saufferer, J L .	R 1, Morristown
Papke, Adolph. . .	R 4, Waseca	Schuette, Wm. E .	R 3, Waseca
Paveck, Wm H	R 4, Waseca	Sampson, Albert . ..	R. 3, Waseca
Polsfuss, L	R. 3, Waseca	Sampson, Edward ..	R 3, Waseca
Petrich, J. G .	Waseca	Swift, Kyes . .	R 3, Waseca
Remund, Albert .	R 3, Waseca	Swift, Clarence	Waseca
Remund, Sam A .	R 3, Waseca	Sutter, Christ .	R 3, Waseca
Reinke, Edward ..	R 3, Waseca	Smith, H S	R. 3, Waseca
Reineke, F C .. .	R 4, Waseca	Tyrell, Edward	R 4, Waterville
Reinhart, J .	R 4, Waseca	Tanner, C J .	.... Waseca
Reinhart, Wm. .	R 4, Waseca	Tanner, E A	. Waseca
Remund, Wm A. .	R 3, Waseca	Wendt, Charles B	.... Waseca
Reinhart, Louis H. .	R 3, Waseca	Wilcowske, Julius	R 3, Waseca
Reinhart, Arthur .	R 4, Waseca	Whelan, George .	R 5, Waseca
Reineke, Albert	Morristown	Whelan, J P .	R 5, Waseca
Reineke, W D	Morristown	Wad, F. C	R 3, Waseca

TOWN OF IOSCO

Name	Address	Name	Address
Alland, Hans	R 5, Waseca	Donate, Anton	Elysian
Ballard, Chandler	R 5, Waseca	Fischer, August ...	R 5, Waseca
Ballard, Benj.	R 5, Waseca	Flitter, Lewis	R 6, Janesville
Bagne, O S . .	R. 3, Waseca	Fell, David .	R 5, Waseca
Bathke, A F	Janesville	Fell, Emil.. . .	R 6, Janesville
Bathke, Herman	R 1, Janesville	Fell, Henry	R 6, Janesville
Barbknecht, Wm. .	R. 6, Janesville	Fell, Lewis	R 6, Janesville
Broadbent, Tobias	R 4, Waterville	Guse, Ludvig	R 1, Janesville
Crippen, Wm	Janesville	Guse, John	R. 1, Janesville
Carlson, Martin ...	R. 5, Waseca	Gerdts, Otto ..	R 6, Janesville
Chamberlain, Edward	Janesville	Grubish, Peter	Waterville
Dreever, Geo	Janesville	Halverson, Con ...	R. 5, Waseca
Dawald, Frank	Waterville	Huriska, Anton	Waterville
Devine, John, ...	Elysian	Haley, Mark	R 1, Janesville
Devine, Dan ..	R 4, Waterville	Haley, A H.	Elysian
Devine, Thomas	Elysian	Hayes, Joseph	Janesville
Dusbabeck, Henry ..	Waterville	Hayes, Richard ..	R 1, Janesville
Dolan, Frances	Waterville	Huble, Joseph	R. 1, Janesville
Dahl, Ole	R. 4, Waterville	Hoffman, E. H. ..	R 1, Janesville

Name	Address
Jameson, Thomas	Waseca
Jackson, S.	R 5, Waseca
Johnson, Ole	Waseca
Johnson, John S	R. 4, Waterville
Johnson, S S . .	R 5, Waseca
Johnson, E S	R 5, Waseca
Jones, Geo . .	R 5, Waseca
Jones, Frank	R 5, Waseca
Kinn, Ben.	R F D Waseca
Kinn, John G	R 5, Waseca
Kroeger, Anna ...	R 6, Janesville
Kroeger, John	R 6, Janesville
Kroeger, Herman O.,	R 6, Janesville
Kane, James .	Waseca
Kane, John . .	R. 4, Waterville
Knish, Wenzel	R 4, Waterville
Kaiser, Herman	R. F D, Janesville
Kaiser, George	R 1, Janesville
Kahnke, John	R 5, Waseca
Kahnke, John L .	R 5, Waseca
Kahnke, Theo .	. Waseca
Koester, William	R 6, Janesville
Koester, Christian	R 6, Janesville
Kanna, Gottlieb .	R 4, Waterville
Kuhn, August .	R 1, Janesville
Koentopp, August	R 6, Janesville
Lee, James	Elysian
Lee, William . . .	Elysian
Larson, Hans . .	R 5, Waseca
Larson, David	R 5, Waseca
Larson, Nels	R 5, Waseca
Loftus, S A	Waseca
Miller, Henry	R 4, Waterville
Miller, C P	R 4, Waterville
Miller, Joseph	R. 4, Waterville
Miller, Martin	R 4, Waterville
Miller, M J .	R 5 Waseca
Marvahan, Robert .	Waterville
Mulcahy, Con ...	Waterville
Morgan, J C	R 4, Waterville
Marzahn, Robt....	R. 4, Waterville
Manthey, Herman	R 6, Janesville
Manthey, Ed. . .	R 6, Janesville
Manthey, Charley	R 6, Janesville
Myer, Martin	R. 4, Waterville
Murray, Geo	R 1, Janesville
Murray, Hugh	Janesville
Minske, Lewis	R 5, Waseca
Minske, Ed	R. 6, Janesville
Mankey, John .	R 6 Janesville
McBride, Patrick	R 1, Janesville
McHugo, Patrick ...	R 5, Waseca
McGuire, Henry .	R 5, Waseca
McAneny, Ambrose	R 5, Waseca
McAneny, Barney	R. 5, Waseca
Mittelsteadt, Julius	R 6, Janesville
Mariska, F F .	Waterville
McShane, Thomas	R 5, Waseca
Murphy, Frank	Elysian
Maloney, Richard	R 5, Waseca
Maloney, Thos. .	R 5, Waseca
McGuigan, James	R 5, Waseca
Monson, Charlie	R 4, Waterville
McWaide, John W	R 5, Waseca
Olson, Nels .	Waterville
Olson, Andrew .	Waseca
Osmundson, Ole	. Waterville
Oestreich, Wm. .	R 5, Waseca
Prail, Ernest	R 6, Janesville
Plath, Ed	R 5, Waseca
Plath, Herman .	Waseca
Pfeifer, John.....	R 4, Waterville
Pfeifer Joseph .	R 4, Waterville
Herlugson, Aslag. .	Waseca
Roeske, Mrs Wm	R 4, Waterville
Roach, Wm	Waterville
Ristau, John	R F D Janesville
Ristau, Herman	R 1, Janesville
Ristau, J R .	R 6, Janesville
Roesler, Sam	R 1, Janesville
Rudolph, Fred	Janesville
Schwenke, Gust	R 4 Waterville
Schwartz, Vinz .	Waterville
Slattery, John	R 5, Waseca
Slattery, Albert	R 5, Waseca
Slattery, Andrew.	R 1, Janesville
Slattery, James ..	R 1, Janesville
Stangler, Frank .	R 1, Janesville
Schmidt, Adolph.	Waterville
Stussy, Fred	R 1, Janesville
Seewald, Henry	R 6, Janesville
Springler, Geo	R 6, Janesville
Schatzke, Ernest .	R 6, Janesville
Stiller, F. G	R 4. Waterville
Sheldon, M A	Waterville
Spletstosser, Fred,	R 4 Waterville
Stevens, F A	R 5, Waseca
Seewald, Herman . .	R 4, Waseca
Sill, Geo.	R 6 Janesville
Timlin, James	R 1, Janesville
Timlin, John,..	R. 1, Janesville
Trahms, W E	R 5, Waseca
Thorson, Erick . .	R 3, Waseca
Thorson, Thor .	R F D Waseca
Wendland, Henry ..	R 1, Janesville
Wendland F A	R 5, Janesville
Wood, David.. ...	Waterville
Wood, R V	Waterville
Wolter, Albert ..	R. 1, Janesville
Wesley, Emil	R. 1, Waterville

Name	Address	Name	Address
Witt, Robert	Waseca	Zanke, William	Janesville
Yanke, Otto	R. 1, Janesville	Zell, Ed	Waseca
Zanke, August	Waterville		

TOWN OF JANESVILLE

Name	Address	Name	Address
Abraham, August	Janesville	Hogan, J M	Janesville
Ash, Joseph	Janesville	Haskell, Waldow	Madison Lake
Ayers, P G	Janesville	Hollmichel, Wm	Elysian
Ash, John	Janesville	McHugo, F J	Janesville
Abraham, G J	Smith Mill	Hogan, Pat	Janesville
Adams, S R	Greenland	Higgins, Geo E	Madison Lake
Burnett, Wm	Janesville	Huginnin, Holland	Janesville
Born, C F.	Janesville	Hollmichel, J. W	Janesville
Blaesing, Othea	Smith Mill	Jewison, J H	Janesville
Brox, John	Janesville	Jewison, Wm	Janesville
Burke, Mrs Wm	Janesville	Jewison, Chris	Janesville
Barbnecht, Fred	Janesville	Kotz, Rudolph	Smith Mill
Cahill, R	Janesville	Koabneck, Wm	Madison Lake
Carpenter, James	Elysian	Kukuk, Edw	Janesville
Crow, J F	Smith Mill	Knopf, Gus J	Janesville
Crow, Nathaniel	Smith Mill	Knopf, Wm Jr	Janesville
Cummings, Chas	Smith Mill	Keyes, Frank	Janesville
Chadwick, C G	Elysian	Kaupun, Joseph	Janesville
Clark, J F.	Elysian	Lane, A L	Smith Mill
Campbell, Henry	Smith Mill	McNeil, Donald	Elysian
Chew, John	Smith Mill	Marquardt, F G.	Janesville
Cahill, Pat	Janesville	Miller, O A.	Janesville
Cahill, M. J.	Janesville	McGinness, Abraham	Janesville
Crandall, Geo W.	Madison Lake	Mulcahy, John	Janesville
Cahill, John	Janesville	Mohr, Mark	Smith Mill
Cahill, W. R.	Janesville	Miller, August	Janesville
Cahill, T E	Janesville	Mohr, Henry.	Janesville
Cahill, Walter,	Janesville	Manke, Wm	Janesville
Cunningham, John	Janesville	Mittelsteadt, Adolph	Janesville
Costello, John	Janesville	Miller, Joseph	Janesville
Chase, B	Janesville	Nicholson, Thos	Janesville
Eustice, John	Janesville	Nesbitt, James	Smith Mill
Ewert, R	Janesville	Novotny, John	Madison Lake
Flitter, Wm	Janesville	Newendorf, Wm	Elysian
Frank, Gust	Janesville	Orcutt, Hiram	Smith Mill
Felska, August	Janesville	Orcutt, Ernest	Smith Mill
Grams, Charles	Janesville	Penn, Gust	Smith Mill
Gultz, E J	Janesville	Paupert, Margaret	Smith Mill
Gordon, J Monroe	Janesville	Pelleberg, Herman	Janesville
Gehrke, F	Janesville	Popham, John	Greenland
Grams, Gust	Janesville	Peska, Michael	Smith Mill
Grams, Christ	Smith Mill	Popham, Wm	Madison Lake
Gehloff, Herman	Elysian	Pfeifer, Julius	Janesville
Galagan, J. F	Elysian	Pfeifer, Ignas	Elysian
Garlick, Edward	Janesville	Quadde, August	Janesville
Haskell, A. W.	Elysian	Quast, Herman	Smith Mill
Hogan, J. F	Janesville	Rimmer, R	Greenland

Name	Address
Randall, M B	Smith Mill
Ryan, M J	Smith Mill
Roeske, Fred	Janesville
Roeske, Chas	Janesville
Schnoor, Joseph	Janesville
Schramske, Anton, Jr	Janesville
Stangler, Lewis	Elysian
Shepherd, Geo	Smith Mill
Simons, H C	Elysian
Schramske, Michael	Janesville
Smith, C N	Elysian
Simons, Orlando	Elysian
Simons, P R	Elysian
Schumaker, Wm	Janesville
Sullivan, Tim	Janesville
Sullivan, J J	Janesville
Sibert, G W	Madison Lake
Savage, Joseph	Janesville
Schramel, Eberhart	Smith Mill
Sanasac, J E	Janesville
Seifert, Peter	Elysian
Spoor, A	Elysian
Savage, Thos	Janesville
Sexton, Wm	Janesville
Seha, Chris	Elysian
Stangler, Edward	Elysian
Suhs, Joseph	Elysian
Sexton, Martin	Elysian
Sexton, John	Janesville
Schramske, Anton	Janesville
Tetzloff, August	Janesville
Tetzloff, Julius	Janesville
Teitz, Henry	Smith Mill
Thwing, Nelson	Elysian
Thrall, M. A	Smith Mill
Voegel, Albert	Janesville
Williams, John	Greenland
Willis, Edward	Smith Mill
White, Pat	Janesville
Wilson, A P	Janesville
Zimpke, Adolph	Smith Mill
Zell, Michael	Janesville
Zimbrich, Frank	Janesville

INDEX.

INDEX TO PORTRAITS.

CPSIA information can be obtained
at www.ICGtesting.com
Printed in the USA
BVHW041213290120
570833BV00004B/118

9 781296 761509